020277
WM 260 Coo

ADDICTION
RECOVERY
TOOLS

For Krista

ADDICTION
RECOVERY
TOOLS

A
Practical
Handbook

Robert Holman Coombs, Editor

Sage Publications
International Educational and Professional Publisher
Thousand Oaks ▪ London ▪ New Delhi

For information:

Sage Publications, Inc.
2455 Teller Road
Thousand Oaks,
California 91320
E-mail: order@sagepub.com

Sage Publications Ltd.
6 Bonhill Street
London EC2A 4PU
United Kingdom

Sage Publications India Pvt. Ltd.
M-32 Market
Greater Kailash I
New Delhi 110 048 India

Printed in the United States of America

Library of Congress Cataloging-in-Publication Data

Main entry under title:

Addiction recovery tools: A practical handbook / edited by Robert Holman Coombs.
    p. cm.
Includes bibliographical references and index.
  ISBN 0-7619-2066-8 (cloth: acid-free paper)
  ISBN 0-7619-2067-6 (pbk.: acid-free paper)
  1. Substance abuse—Prevention. 2. Substance abuse—Treatment.
3. Addicts—Rehabilitation. I. Coombs, Robert H.
  HV4998 .A33 2001
  362.29'18—dc21
                                     2001001624

02 03 04 05 06 07 10 9 8 7 6 5 4 3 2 1

Acquiring Editor:	Margaret H. Seawell
Editorial Assistants:	Alicia Carter and Kathryn Journey
Production Editor:	Claudia A. Hoffman
Typesetter/Designer:	Janelle LeMaster
Cover Designer:	Sandy Ng

Contents

PART III: COGNITIVE-BEHAVIORAL TOOLS

PART IV: PSYCHOSOCIAL TOOLS

PART V: HOLISTIC TOOLS

PART VI: USING RECOVERY TOOLS IN VARIOUS SETTINGS AND PROGRAMS

Acknowledgments

I thank Carla Cronkhite Vera and Carol Jean Coombs for their superb efforts in helping bring this book to publication. Carla networked with each author, provided helpful assistance with revisions, and performed a myriad of tasks with efficiency and good cheer. Carol Jean helped revise manuscripts and provided ongoing support and encouragement. Working together as a team has been an enjoyable experience.

From Sage Publications, I am grateful to Rolf Janke, Alicia Carter, Claudia Hoffman, and Elizabeth Magnus for improving the manuscript and seeing it through to completion.

Preface

What works?

No clinical clients are more difficult to successfully treat than those who are chemically dependent or well along the path to addiction. Motivating drug abusers to acknowledge their problem and seek treatment is the first challenge. And once into therapy, they often leave prematurely—"split"—and frequently relapse. Despite their best intentions, and the efforts of their therapists, they typically gravitate back to the same pathological predicaments.

Narrow competing treatment ideologies also impede successful therapeutic outcomes. Although an impressive array of techniques have proven effective, few addiction specialists are comprehensively trained in them, aware of their variety and usefulness, or open to using them. Worse yet, some doctrinaire clinicians argue against any approach that does not fit within the frameworks taught during their professional training—or, if they were addicted, in their own treatment.

Acupuncture, for example, a successful 5,000-year-old practice, can't possibly be of any use, some think, because Western medicine's limited scientific model cannot explain it. Spirituality enhancement, another example, is rejected and even assailed by some because it does not fit their intellectual paradigms, whereas others who credit spirituality for their recovery sometimes vilify those who ignore it.

Politicians and government bureaucrats complicate matters further by imposing draconian drug control policies on the American public, policies that misunderstand the nature of drug problems, are ineffective in their outcomes, and create additional hardships for users, addicts, families, and communities. Amazingly, one out of 147 American citizens is now jailed, most for drug-related offenses. These public funds could be used for, among other useful causes, drug prevention and treatment services. New York City, for example, reportedly spends $8,000 per child yearly in its public schools but $93,000 a year per child in a juvenile detention center in South Bronx (Huffington, 2000).

Though not an exhaustive review of addiction recovery tools, this book provides a comprehensive overview of the best known therapeutic methods to help addicts and others afflicted with drug problems pull out of their self-defeating lifestyles. Part 1, "Motivational Tools," discusses three powerful tools to motivate chemically dependent individuals to seek and accept help: motivational interventions, motivational interviewing, and computer-based interventions.

Part 2, "Medical-Pharmacological Tools," addresses some tools that have a long history of success in clinical practice: detoxification, pharmacological agents, disease orientation training, and drug screening. A number of effective tools developed by behavioral psychologists, presented in Part 3, "Cognitive-Behavioral Tools," focus on recovery contracts, contingency management, cue exposure treatment, and affect- regulation coping-skills training. More traditional psychological tools, reviewed in Part 4, "Psychosocial Tools," include lifestyle planning and monitoring, individual therapy, group therapy, peer support, and family treatment.

Part 5, "Holistic Tools," discusses tools that traditionally have been considered beyond the boundaries of Western medicine: nutritional counseling, meditation, spirituality enhancement, and acupuncture. Finally, Part 6, "Utilizing Recovery Tools in Various Settings and Programs," provides techniques and insights relevant to all these tools: a chapter on harm reduction that explores ways to minimize the impact of drug pathologies while moving the user closer to recovery and a final chapter about selecting appropriate recovery tools for individual clients who vary in circumstances and personality needs.

Each recovery tool discussed in this book, described by a knowledgeable and experienced addictionologist, will help your drug-abusing clients. Your therapeutic results will improve as you incorporate a wider variety of effective therapeutic tools into your treatment armamentarium. The main questions are "Which recovery tools will work best with each of my addicted clients?" and "How can I effectively incorporate these tools into my practice to better serve them?"

⊞ REFERENCE

Huffington, A. (2000, June 25). Little ones overlooked amid the prosperity. *Los Angeles Times*, p. M5.

PART

I

MOTIVATIONAL TOOLS

1

Motivational Intervention

The Only Failure Is the Failure to Act

Edward Storti

wenty-five years ago, a distraught father asked me to perform an intervention on his 25-year-old daughter. I had no idea what to do or how to respond. He began crying and said, "Ed, if you don't come over to the house and try to convince her to seek help, she will die." At the time, books, research, and the Internet were not available to instruct me *how* to intervene. I simply had to learn by trial and error, which intensified the pressure of failing or "doing it wrong." Ultimately, I drove over to their home and knocked on the door. When she opened it, I said, "Hello, my name is Ed Storti, and your dad has asked me to come over and talk to you." We talked for a couple of hours, and she agreed to go to treatment that night. I was shocked, stunned, and elated. Currently, she is happily married with two children, and, incidentally, she ran in the 1999 Los Angeles Marathon.

That first case led to more than 3,000 motivational interventions all over the world, including patients who had suffered from alcoholism, drug addiction, eating disorders, gambling, and sexual addictions. I have learned from every single one of them, and consequently I am proud to give you, the reader, the formulas that I have created from my experiences to spare you the laborious task of reinventing the wheel.

THE BASICS OF MOTIVATIONAL INTERVENTION

I believe that motivational intervention is a process of offering the gift of life to the recipient. It is to honor and persuade, not force, the individual to accept the solution that is of-

---

BOX 1.1   **The Only Failure Is a Failure to Act**

No one knows more about the value of doing a caring intervention, regardless of its outcome, than the family I recently worked with in San Diego, California. We had just entered the third hour of the intervention for Bill, and everyone looked exhausted. Bill had agreed to seek help but only if he could enter in 2 weeks. Although it was not the optimal answer, Bill was adamant about entering in 2 weeks, and the group ultimately accepted his decision. The intervention ended with love, hugs, relief, and encouragement.

One week later, and, incidentally, 1 week before entering treatment, Bill drank himself into a stupor. At approximately 2:30 a.m., he jaywalked across a major thoroughfare and was hit by a taxicab. He was killed instantly.

When I received the news, I immediately called the family in San Diego. Although shocked and overwhelmed with grief, all the participants of the intervention were deeply grateful that they had been given the opportunity to be there for Bill and to honor and demonstrate their love for him before he passed away. "I am so appreciative and thankful that we had the chance to express our care and love for him last week," Bill's mom told me. "I cannot imagine the guilt and regret I would have had to live with if we had decided not to intervene." Indeed, the only true failure in this case would have been the failure to intervene with Bill.

---

fered to him or her. Unlike traditional intervention, the motivational intervention is not threat or consequence based (some styles of intervention are confrontational or are legal, medical, or employer leveraged). Rather, it is an unconditional presentation of love, care, and kindness appealing to the heart and emotions of the patient. Ultimately, the group's goal is to present with dignity and to know that they all gave their energy, time, and commitment in an attempt to save a loved one's life. I believe that achieving this goal creates the ability to release emotionally and allows the individuals of the group to move on with their lives to the best of their ability.

Motivational intervention allows a group of people to alter the inevitable outcome of the disease of addiction. Contrary to traditional opinion, a motivational intervention can be performed *before* a patient's situation has become bad enough that he or she has reached a pain threshold (i.e., has "bottomed out"). Curiously, most professionals believe that "there is nothing you can do until the person hits rock bottom." However, the disease of addiction is medically classified as just that: a disease. All medically classified diseases are describable, predictable, and progressive. Moreover, addiction is chronic, acute, and terminal. Why, then, is it currently believed that one must wait for remission of an addictive disease because the patient has not suffered enough or has not "bottomed out"? The procedure with every other known medical disease is take measures to stop the disease and pain. Why should the disease of addiction be any different? I believe that a motivational intervention can stabilize the patient so that he or she does not have to suffer through the next crisis or tragedy, which could ultimately be death —the inevitable "bottom."

▦ THE PROCESS OF MOTIVATIONAL INTERVENTION

As a direct result of working in the field of addictive diseases for over 25 years, I developed a motivational intervention model that I call the Storti model. There are five steps to this motivational procedure: the inquiry, the assessment, the preparation, the intervention, and the follow-up/case management.

The Inquiry

The inquiry is the initial interaction with the contact person, which usually occurs over the telephone. The inquiry consists of gathering information such as the patient's name, age, city of residence, addiction, and possible diagnosis. Details that I commonly acquire from the contact person include the patient's propensity for violence and/or threats; whether others are, or have been, concerned about the patient's behavior; and any prior treatment or recovery programs that the patient has gone through. I also believe that the inquiry should be used to determine the family's financial resources. A family's financial budget is essential in deciding between appropriate treatment centers, which, incidentally, vary significantly in price range.

The inquiry will also resolve the dilemma of whether the particular case warrants an intervention. Invariably I discover, through the inquiry, that particular cases do not justify an intervention but should be referred to other professionals such as marriage and family therapists, licensed social workers, psychologists, medical doctors, and even attorneys. It is also extremely important, and at times extremely difficult, to get a sense of the person calling to inquire about help. I assess whether this person is someone I can work with or whether his or her expectations are unrealistic. Through the years, I have worked with families that flat out wanted a SWAT team to go in and physically make the person get help, and I have worked with other families who simply expected me alone to perform a miracle. I use the inquiry either to dispose of these unreasonable expectations or to simply refer the case elsewhere. The inquiry is an efficient tool because it allows you to minimize spending valuable time and energy on cases that you will not take or that you will ultimately refer to others.

An inquiry should not be too in depth or involved. Usually, where I truly evaluate and get an in-depth reading of the patient is the assessment. Although I try to give hope and encouragement throughout the inquiry, it is important to keep it limited to fact finding and the basics. Thus, an inquiry usually will not take longer than 20 to 30 minutes.

Assessment

An assessment serves many purposes. Generally, the nucleus of the group is gathered, either by telephone conference call or during an in-person meeting. (Regarding conference calls, usually a comfortable number is around two to five people. A couple of years ago, I participated in a conference call assessment with 11 people. I have found that it is too chaotic to have too many people on the phone at once.) Some of the topics that are discussed during the assessment include dissecting and profiling the addiction of the patient; evaluating the feasibility of the intervention; introducing the group to the inherent risk factors of intervening; modifying and designing the intervention model for that particular family; and explaining the intervention process so that all participants comprehend the ends and means of the procedure. I find that the assessment can also be commonly used to determine the personal characteristics of the patient —the positives (e.g., she is sensitive, kind, loving) and the negatives (e.g., he likes to intimidate and is verbally abusive). I also evaluate complex issues such as physical and psychological health. Personality and health are both immensely important to evaluate during the assessment because by the end of the assessment you must have a firm determination of a primary and secondary diagnosis. That is to say, it must be determined by the end of the assessment exactly what addictive disease and/or complications the patient is suffering from.

Goals

The assessment is an opportune time to speak to the family about the goals of the intervention. I outline, as a significant ingredient of my model, a list of both short-term and long-term goals, and I explain and discuss them during the assessment. Short-term goals that I discuss usually include

- *Availability of the patient.* Simply put, you cannot intervene unless the patient is present and somewhat coherent.
- *Persuading the patient to sit down.* It has been my experience that most do sit down due to the shock of encountering the group of family, friends, and loved ones.
- *Having the patient listen to the best of his or her ability.* If the patient listens, the interventionist can create a rhythm and a pacing of the energy within the group.

Long-term goals that are normally mentioned include the following:

- Obviously, first, the patient accepts the gift of treatment.
- The patient gets serious when he or she is in treatment.
- The patient stays in treatment for the full time.
- The patient accepts aftercare recommendations from the treatment center; this will give the patient the opportunity to use the tools learned in treatment.
- Friends and family members stay unified so as not to block the patient's recovery by overprotecting and pampering him or her or falling back into the "same old patterns." (The immediate family can achieve this by getting help for themselves through self-help groups or therapists.)

Elements of Success

During the assessment, I also explain the fundamentals for success of a motivational intervention to the group. I believe that there are three primary elements of success: surprise, presence of people, and the actual presentation. In what I call "the 30-50-20 rule," they contribute 30%, 50%, and 20% of the success of the intervention, respectively.

Surprise. The surprise contributes 30% to the success of the intervention. Because the patient is unaware of the pending presentation, it has a stunning effect on the patient and is the anesthetic needed to perform the intervention. Most interventions are in the home, which is optimal because this is normally a comfortable setting for everyone involved, including, most importantly, the patient. In the home, everyone can concentrate on the more important goals of the presentation rather than on their surroundings. It should be noted, though, that an intervention does not have to be performed in the home. Indeed, I have performed interventions everywhere from offices to yachts to airports to parks. However, it has been my experience that the home always proves to be the most comfortable.

Presence of Participants. The presence of participants accounts for about 50% of the intervention's success. (Interestingly, we now have an aggregate of 80% success and we have not yet spoken a word.) A very effective method that I use for determining the people to be involved is to ask the family, "If your loved one died tomorrow, who would be the pall bearers, the eulogist, and the people you would call first?" A typical group size to work with for a motivational intervention is approximately 8 to 15 participants. However, this does not represent a minimum or a maximum by any means. I have intervened with as few as 2 participants and as many as 32.

Interestingly, I have discovered it is more powerful to have outsiders involved than insiders. That is, outsiders—friends, neighbors, and people the patient has not seen for a few years—hold more weight and power than immediate family members. I believe this is because patients do not want to embarrass themselves in front of outsiders, whereas they have grown comfortable arguing and battling with the immediate family. Consequently, I have a 40/60 rule on choosing the participants. Forty percent should have knowledge of the problem. That is, they have seen it, they know about it, or in some other way they have a direct connection with it. Sixty percent could be present as mere motivators. They are there in support of the patient and the family. Their presence conveys the message "I care." Additionally, if participants cannot be present during the intervention, I usually ask them to give me a letter that I can read to the patient or an audiotape to play or even that they be on standby near a telephone so that they may convey their message to the patient. Letters, tapes, and telephone standbys have proven to be unbelievably powerful if used at the appropriate time in the intervention.

When choosing who will participate in the intervention, it is important to remember that the group should be composed of the people the family wants as opposed to the people that the patient would want. Logically, there are many people the patient would not choose due to his or her negative feelings toward friends, family, and colleagues, or possibly due to increasing self-isolation. When family and friends tell me that the patient "does not like" or "will not listen to" a potential participant, I tell them that it does not matter if *the patient* likes or dislikes the person. All that matters is that the person is willing to enter the room with the group and contribute his or her presence in the name of the unified goal.

Presentation. The actual presentation accounts for 20% of the success of the intervention. (It should be noted that the presentation is repeatedly discussed throughout the assessment, preparation, and intervention.) Ironically, the words themselves during the actual presentation account for only 20% of the success of the intervention (the specifics of the presentation will be discussed in depth later).

Risk Factors

It is paramount in the assessment to discuss risk factors with the nucleus of the group. It must be explained that an intervention's success, though probable, is certainly not guaranteed. An intervention is an inherently tense situation that may lead to major disappointment. I have found that discussing the following risk factors is an adequate way to fully disclose some of the potentials of the intervention:

- *Timing*: Does the patient need an intervention, or should other alternatives be discussed?
- *Capability*: Is the family physically and mentally able to go through an intervention (as it can be extremely exhausting)?
- *Disappointment*: Can the family handle the disappointment if the patient does not accept treatment?
- *Bolting*: Most people do not bolt, but is it a risk that the patient may abruptly leave the room?
- *Vindictiveness*: Does the patient have the capability to be cold, methodical, threatening? Will divorce result? Will he or she fire employees if they participate in the intervention?
- *Change*: Is the family willing to change, win, lose, or draw?

Preparation

By definition, preparation is the preintervention planning session. It is the last meeting to shore up all particulars, incidentals, and issues. However, there is a popular misconception that the preparation should be a "rehearsal." The preparation is not a rehearsal because this would imply that you were preparing what you were going to say. I tell people when I am preparing a case that an intervention is to be from the heart, it is to be spontaneous. This ensures that the intervention does not mutate into a mere rehearsed play with participants simply repeating memorized lines.

Usually the preparation is where I first meet the majority of the participants. Here I attempt to gain their confidence and prove that I have the ability to lead the group through the intervention the next day. I present three major points to the group during the preparation.

Motivation

I have found that many people who participate in an intervention are fearful and skeptical about the intervention. Basically, they are looking for any reason not to go in and present. Thus, during the preparation, I attempt to counter the fear and skepticism with motivation and stress the urgency of the intervention. *I always stress positive, inspirational energy and remind the group that the only failure is the failure to act.* Ultimately, by being together and united at this level, the group has already won.

Intervention Presentation

I have personally found that an excellent method of defusing the fears of a group is to discuss the actual presentation (the specifics of which will be discussed in depth later). Discussing the presentation illustrates to the group that the intervention is not intended to be confrontational but rather is gift oriented. It is to express how much the group loves and respects the individual and to show that they want to support that person throughout the day and beyond.

Particulars

Another major discussion during the preparation involves something I have called the "particulars." Particulars can include anything and everything from getting a drink

> ### BOX 1.2 The 1-Minute Preparation
>
> It has been my experience that the moment before the patient is expected to walk in, many people, due to fear, stress, and/or anxiety, become nervous and, in a panic, tell me they have "forgotten what to say" or "have nothing to say." Thus, I have developed a "1-Minute Preparation" designed to keep a person focused on simplicity rather than on overintellectualizing the message being conveyed. The "1-Minute Preparation" allows me to quickly remind participants to
>
> 1. Be themselves
> 2. Speak from their heart
> 3. Stay with the theme of treatment acceptance *today*
> 4. Stay unified

of water during the intervention to where we will meet before the intervention to the strategic aspects of where each person should sit during the intervention. The particulars that I usually cover include but by no means are limited to

- *Time*: We determine what time the intervention will begin. (It seems simple, but you would be surprised how many people mess this one up.)
- *Premeeting area*: We determine a place where we will meet before meeting the patient (e.g., hotel room, office). I always premeet 30 minutes before.
- *Walk in*: This is the attitude that must be conveyed when we walk in or when the patient walks in. There must be a feeling radiating from the participants that they want to be there—not frowns or scared looks.
- *Home*: The phone is turned off or down, and any possible distractions are identified and ironed out.
- *Sitting arrangement*: I always assign two people to sit next to the patient, one on each side.
- *Defusers*: I always preassign two or three people who are not intimidated by the patient to retrieve and talk with the patient if the patient walks out. This must be done before the intervention; otherwise, everybody will be looking at each other when the patient gets up and bolts.
- *Introductions*: Making the initial introductions, I set the tone of the intervention. When I am ready, I call on the different participants.
- *Fragmentation*: A patient may request to talk to a particular participant alone. During the preparation, I tell all participants that it is best to respond, "We are here as a group, and anything you say to me should be said to us all." Also, it is important that by not fragmenting the group you are showing the patient that he or she is not in charge of the intervention.
- *Audio/letters*: I make sure that the letters/audios are given to me so that I can edit them before the intervention.
- *Dispensing with the "Yeah, buts"*: I attempt to dispense with any possible excuses the patient will offer in an attempt to refuse treatment (i.e., "Yeah, but I can't go because of my house payment/my cat/my car payment"). Before we go in to intervene, all potential excuses have been thought out and the raised problems

---

BOX 1.3 | **Preparation Checklist**

Always remember this checklist when dealing with the particulars during the preparation:

1. *Patient availability*: You can't intervene without him/her.
2. *Group presence*: You must have people to go in to intervene.
3. *Solution*: You must have a model of treatment to offer the patient.
4. *"Yeah, buts"*: These must be answered and solved.
5. *Escort*: A few people must be prepared to escort the patient.
6. *Guarantor of the account*: If insurance denies, someone must guarantee that the money is there.

---

solved. That is, someone has already agreed to take care of and assume these responsibilities while this patient is in treatment.

- *Packing*: I also like to prepare two people to volunteer to help the patient pack when treatment is accepted. I usually ask two or three people so that the patient is never alone with one person.
- *Escorting*: I also predetermine who will escort the person to the treatment center (perhaps it will be an escort group) and who will fly with him or her.
- *Delayed reaction*: The day after the intervention, participants are drained and exhausted. Some have actually commented that they suffer flulike symptoms. I prepare participants by informing them beforehand that this is most likely fatigue and usually will pass in 24 to 48 hours.

Intervention

The intervention is the actual presentation to the patient. It is the moment that a hand-picked group of caring loved ones, accompanied by myself, walk in and present to the individual. *The primary goal is always to appeal to the patient's heart, not his or her head, and for him or her to accept the solution that we present immediately upon the completion of the intervention.* I believe that the intention of the intervention should be to "unstick" the patient when he or she is stuck in life, no matter what the addiction is.

Through performing thousands of interventions, I have broken down the process into three potential phases: the "heart-to-heart" approach, specific examples, and future concerns. Rarely does an intervention get past the first stage, but when it does, the interventionist and the group had better be prepared and committed to their goal, because they may be in for a long and tedious journey. Incidentally, a typical intervention lasts approximately 45 minutes. However, I tell the group during the preparation to be prepared to stay focused for anywhere between 2 to 3 hours during the intervention.

Heart-to-Heart Phase

The heart-to-heart phase is where 90% of my cases stay. I rarely ever enter the other two phases of the intervention. This phase demonstrates: "*We* know you have a problem, *you* know you have a problem, we have a solution, but before you get the solution,

---

BOX 1.4 **Accepting Treatment for Others or Oneself?**

It is perfectly acceptable for patients to receive the gift of treatment not for themselves but rather for the people in the room that day. It really does not matter *why* they go in; it only matters that they accept the help. In my personal experience, a majority of people, when asked if they want to go into treatment to receive help for themselves, will say "no." However, once they are in treatment, normally desire, motivation, and rigorous honesty surface, and a transformation occurs that allows them to receive help for themselves rather than others. *Thus, how you get the patient into treatment or why the patient enters the center is, for the most part, inconsequential.*

Ramone was surrounded by his friends and soccer teammates. He stated that he would not go into treatment for himself because it was his life and he would live it however he pleased. However, at one point Ramone stated that he would accept treatment out of respect for his teammates. One teammate remarked, "No, Ramone—you must get help for you, not us. You must go into treatment for you, or else it won't work." I knew what the next response was going to be. Ramone looked at his friend and said, "Then I am not going." I interrupted, sensing that Ramone's pride and ego were at stake, and stated, "We are asking you to be a hero to this group. Walk in, fulfill the treatment schedule, and when you leave, it will be your choice to either accept the tools they have given or continue to do what you are doing. By doing that, you will honor us by accepting this gift, and we will respect you for being a hero to all of us." Ramone immediately rose to his feet and remarked, "Let's go!"

---

we want to honor you and express our care and love for you." This phase encompasses the emotional appeal aimed at the heart. The heart-to-heart phase is extremely powerful, for it creates a humbling experience not only for the patient but also for the family and friends. This humbling creates in the patient a vulnerability to listen with his or her heart.

Early in my career, I would normally tell people simply to speak from their heart during this phase. However, I discovered that although people could speak from their heart in front of me, when the moment of truth came in front of the patient, sometimes they would freeze up and forget what to say. Thus, I created a formula to help them concentrate on three major points. Again, in no way do I encourage scripted or memorized statements. This formula is merely a road map for people that will help them to touch on the major points of this phase. The three points are:

1. *I am here today because*: At this point, I will call on the individual, and he or she will inform the patient of the reason he or she is there.

2. *I remember when*: This point includes the individual's fond memories of the past and good experiences with the patient during better times.

3. *I am concerned with*: This point includes the individual's general concerns.

An example of a statement that includes all three points of the formula may look something like this:

I am here today because I am your brother and I love you. (*I am here today because*). Hey, do you remember the time that we were skiing up on Mammoth Mountain and you talked me into coming down a tough and scary run when I didn't want to? I remember that you told me to follow the path and I would be all right, and you were correct. I never forgot that. Now I want you to come down that scary run with me. (*I remember when*). I am scared we won't ever be able to go back up to Mammoth again if you continue this lifestyle. I trusted you that day, and now I am asking you to trust me and take this leap of faith. (*I am concerned with*).

This approach is usually accepted by patients in a dignified way. After I call on particular individuals to speak, I will interweave the solution and introduce that ingredient into the conversation. At some point, I will ask for acceptance of the offered solution. Normally, the solution that I present is accepted, and I will briefly wrap up any other issues that need to be addressed. This phase will generally last for about 40 minutes to an hour.

Specific Concerns Phase

Usually this phase is only entered into when a patient has heard everything that has been said and simply continues to say, "Thanks, but no thanks." Usually, the spectrum of excuses will vary from "Why do I have to go now?" to "I am not going" to "I am going to quit on my own." It has been my experience that this phase is a natural progression, and I can always sense it by the frustration of the group. This stage does not occur at a certain time or by some certain cue; rather, an interventionist should be able to *feel* when this phase has begun.

Normally, when I feel that we have progressed into this phase, I will present to the patient the desperation of the group. I usually tell the patient that we want to show him or her the pattern or "X ray" of behavior that the group has been concerned about. This "X ray" can include examples from 10 years ago to the present. Generally, I will ask anyone in the group if he or she can be more specific with our concerns about this behavior. Particular members of the group will share specific, individual examples of their concerns. An example might be:

Ray, you mean everything to me. A few weeks ago, we went out to dinner, and you began insulting and embarrassing the waitress. It was extremely humiliating for her, you, and everyone else at the table. The worst part about it is that this happens so often that everyone has grown to expect it. This is why you need to get help.

I will sometimes bring in specific concerns as needed. Although many individuals in the group may have specific concerns, sometimes they do not all need to be verbalized. A patient's threshold for listening to the specific concerns may be extremely low due to volatility or pride. Sometimes, when I feel that the flow is beginning to get negative, rather than beating a dead horse by offering more specific concerns, I will make the adjustment to begin to shift our emphasis back toward the solution and the need to accept it, or I will begin to end the intervention with dignity.

Future Concern Phase

Before entering this stage, it is imperative to recognize something I deem the "Rule of Expectations." *This rule states that interventionists must always exceed the family's expectations of what they said they were going to deliver in the assessment and preparation.* This is achieved by exhausting all channels of communication with the patient and ensuring that the intervention is not prematurely ended. Because of this rule, I would rather have a group member say to me, "I am happy we ended because I am exhausted and there was nothing left to say" than "I feel we stopped too early and could have gone a bit longer."

Sometimes when you enter the third and final phase, someone can say something that absolutely strikes a chord with the patient or sparks the energy of the group. Consequently, the intervention can return to one of the first two phases. I describe this phenomenon by what I call the "Rule of Energy": The interventionist is only as good as the continued energy of the group.

Sometimes you have said everything you can, and the person has dug him- or herself in with "no." This is the final stage of the intervention. The goal of this phase is to end with dignity and respect. I always remind the group before entering the intervention that, despite what happens during the presentation, we will walk in with open hearts, and we will also walk out with open hearts. Generally, in ending the intervention, the group will make one last statement with the theme of "We have given everything we can, we hope you will reconsider, we hope you will get treatment, and we love you." The epitome of a wonderful ending when a patient chose not to enter treatment was stated by a daughter to her father who refused to get help. She said,

> I am disappointed you are not going to get help today. I will always love you. I am thrilled I was here today to give you this moment because something positive has happened for me today. That is, I am relieved from the bondage of what more could I have done. Starting today, it is your choice and not mine. It is your life, and all I can do is hope you make the right decision.

In the third phase of an intervention, I debrief the group. Usually, someone stays with the patient, and I discuss the positives of the session and offer further support for the immediate family members. I also advise the family and friends concerning what they need to do for themselves. I always request that everyone remain patient and unified so that if the patient calls any one individual that person stays unified and committed to the group's goals and beliefs.

Follow-Up/Case Management

Once a patient agrees to get help, I immediately call the predetermined treatment center to inform them of the estimated time of arrival, the disposition of the patient, the escort team that will arrive with the patient, and any other relevant particulars about the case (e.g., flight arrangements, pickups at the airport gate). Furthermore, during the next 72 hours, I will contact the case manager at the treatment center and inform him or her of the information I have gathered to help troubleshoot the case. I will also call the family and keep them updated of the patient's prognosis.

Many times the treatment center will need more information about the patient, or the family will want to know how the patient is holding up for the first few nights. Consequently, I act as a liaison between the treatment center and the family, usually for about a week or until the patient gets comfortable and the family can begin to contact the case manager directly. However, in numerous instances I have remained the "middleman" for the entire stay of certain patients.

> ### BOX 1.5 The Surgery
>
> I remember how a long time ago during an intervention a participant, who happened to be a surgeon, commented that an intervention could be analogized to a surgery.
>
> - *Incision*: The incision of the intervention is a sincere, genuine, kind introduction. It is a "clean" opening to the presentation.
> - *Exploration and Probing*: This is the intervention presentation itself. I bring the participants in during the appropriate phases and gain agreement to the solution. However, this is not done the exact same way for every intervention. The means by which we gain acceptance are variable and must be implemented as we explore and find different roadblocks.
> - *Suture*: This is the closing of the presentation. Its purpose is to gain a commitment from the patient, to create a brief ending for the participants, and to activate the escort team taking the patient to the treatment center.

Incidentally, a major part of the time that goes into an intervention is during the follow-up. Inevitably, after the dust settles from the intervention, crises *will* develop, and, as an inherent part of intervening, an interventionist must be there to help.

⊞ PRACTICAL ISSUES

Throughout my career as an interventionist, I have noted a few important and essential issues that must be thoroughly considered before an intervention takes place. They include "red flags" (indications for rejecting a case) and legal issues.

Red Flags

Several red flags are discussed below, but in no way is this a complete list. Moreover, there is a little bit of all of these red flags in *every* patient. It is only when one of these red flags is extremely dominant or prevalent that I will begin to look into these warning signs further and consider refusal of the case.

Violence

Because my primary and most fundamental concern of the intervention is safety for the participants and myself, within the inquiry or assessment I always inquire about the patient's capacity for violence. If I detect, through comments from the group, that the patient has the propensity for violence, a red flag may be established for possibly not going forward. Normally, after questioning the family, I learn that violence is only likely to occur when the patient has been using drugs or drinking. Usually this is a judgment call, and and when in doubt I will continue to evaluate until I feel comfortable progressing with the case. Incidentally, this is why it is optimal to intervene earlier in the day or at a time when the patient is least likely to be toxic. Sometimes I will take a case that I normally would refuse due to the potential violent behavior of the patient because of the participation of certain people in the intervention. Although a person may have the capacity to be violent, there are certain people that the patient would never act that way in front of (e.g., grandmother, boss, mentor). Sometimes, because of the propensity of violence, an intervention is simply not an option. It is essential to determine this during the inquiry and no later than the assessment.

Possible Threatening/Vindictive Response

A person known to be threatening (i.e., to be an intimidator, to threaten divorce, to threaten people over the phone) or vindictive also creates a red flag. This does not mean that the intervention cannot be performed; it simply means you must be aware of it. I usually inquire as to the level of this behavior so I can determine if it may be too hostile to risk intervention. Ultimately, if a person is highly threatening and vindictive, I will not intervene due to the repercussions of the process (I am especially sensitive to these repercussions when a spouse is fearful of domestic violence).

No Documentation

To intervene without the proper amount of documentation is disastrous. The most common situation is that a spouse or girlfriend/boyfriend sees the addictive behavior behind closed doors but the rest of the group does not see such behavior and is unaware of it. Then it becomes that person's word against the patient's word. Ultimately, this transforms the problem into a marriage issue. The group needs evidence and knowledge of specific situations. For instance, without documentation of the addiction, a patient may turn to anyone in the group and say, "Well, have you seen me act this way?" If certain people in the group cannot document the behavior by being specific, then the intervention will implode. Ultimately, if at least 40% of the group cannot prove the addictive behavior or disorder with specific examples, they have no power to convince the person to get help. However, many times I do not use even a fraction of the documentation of a patient's addiction because most patients will agree that they have a problem. Sometimes, a certain person's presence alone, due to what he or she has witnessed or been part of, validates the issue of addiction. But it is necessary to have the capability to use the documentation to put this issue to rest.

Psychiatric Disorders

In my experience, when a patient is suffering from tremendous depression, schizophrenia, psychosis, or any other psychiatric disorder, the motivational intervention is not usually appropriate. In these cases, the patient simply does not have the faculties or capacity to hear the message, and I refer the case to a psychological evaluation team or psychiatric hospital.

Legal Issues

The topic of legal issues, with regard to intervention, could fill volumes. My goal here is to simply offer a cursory outline of the major points of concern:

- *Disclosure in Assessment.* I typically disclose all risks—likely, potential, and even unlikely—during the assessment. If potential risks arise during the development stage of a particular case, I will immediately call the family and disclose the problem. *A good rule of thumb is always to be overinclusive with disclosure of potential risks.*

- *Disclosure in Writing.* When I begin a case, each client receives a packet of information that includes a written list of general risks. Each packet recipient is instructed to read the information and ask me any questions pertaining to it.

- *Preauthorization Agreement.* Before I will accept any case, each client must sign an agreement indicating that he or she has read all the information on the potential risks of intervening and that each risk was verbally discussed with me.

- *Release of Liability.* This form indicates that I am not responsible in any way, shape, or form for any result, direct or indirect, of the intervention. The release further states that I can end, stop, or abort the intervention any time at my own discretion.

⊞ SUMMARY

My goal in writing this chapter is to describe a procedure that saves lives, and it can validate the styles or methods that you use in your own interventions. Perhaps you can take some of my suggestions to enhance your own intervention method or model. As you read this chapter, I hope you recognized that tremendous workmanship goes into an intervention and that the interventionist is not a mere spectator, but rather the attorney, the surgeon, and the pilot of the procedure.

A few years ago, I read a newspaper article regarding leadership and workmanship in the workplace. The following passage accurately summarizes the leadership skills needed by the motivational interventionist:

> When speaking of the responsibility, discipline, and leadership it takes to succeed at work, I will never forget what my grandmother once said to me. She said being a leader is like carrying the baton in a parade because "You can't look away for a moment, or you will lead those 200 drummers astray. You can't get bored, or you'll miss the beat. You have to watch where you are marching, or you will humiliate yourself. The baton carries a lot of responsibilities, and the man holding it has to lead."

I offer all of my colleagues who choose to carry the baton of intervening my fondest regards and best of luck.

⊞ SUGGESTED READINGS

Johnson, V. E. (1978). *I'll quit tomorrow.* New York: Harper & Row.

Storti, E. A. (1988). *Crisis intervention: Acting against addiction.* New York: Crown.

Storti, E. A. (1995). *Heart to heart: The honorable approach to motivational intervention.* New York: Carlton.

2

Motivational Interviewing

Dancing, Not Wrestling

David B. Rosengren
Christopher C. Wagner

Listen, doc. This stuff is killing me. I'll do anything.
Well, have you thought about [_____]?
I can't do that.

Have you had this conversation? The venue shifts, the actors change, and the lines are altered, but the scene plays out the same way. So how are we to understand this behavior? And, more important, what are we to do with it?

UNDERSTANDING THE PROBLEM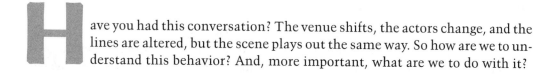

Multiple models in the research world compete to explain the acquisition and maintenance of addictions, but fundamental to most models is recognition that a motivational challenge must be addressed for effective treatment. We use Prochaska and colleagues' transtheoretical model (TTM; Prochaska, DiClemente, & Norcross, 1992), and specifically their hypothesized stages of change (SOC), to help us understand this challenge (see p. 387 for a diagram of this model).

At its most basic, TTM sees the behavior illustrated above as ambivalence. TTM theorists regard it as a normal and predictable part of an intentional change process. Moreover, they think it can be changed.

AUTHORS' NOTE: We wish to thank all the other MINT members who have contributed generously to the ideas presented in this chapter and especially to Chris Dunn, PhD, for his creativity and vision in creating workable models for training others.

The SOC model provides insight into the process of change, as well as the role of ambivalence within that process. It also teaches us to focus on smaller shifts in behavior. For example, if someone has not considered that change in his or her alcohol use may be necessary, it is premature to set a goal of immediate cessation (or even reduction). A more reasonable and achievable goal is consideration of whether the alcohol use warrants the person's attention. If the person decides that the way he or she uses alcohol may be a barrier to achieving goals, accomplishing dreams, or living by his or her values, then the next step is to explore the role of alcohol use in his or her life and weigh the costs and benefits of drinking alcohol. The therapist's role is to help the person explore the various roles that alcohol plays in the person's life. This includes the ways in which the person likes and dislikes his or her alcohol use and the future possibilities that come with a decision to either continue or quit alcohol use. Should the person decide that the possibilities for a future without alcohol appear better than the possibilities for a future with alcohol, it is the therapist's job to help shore up the commitment of the person to change his or her drinking.

Once the commitment is made to do something different, to live differently, the work of change has only just begun. It is still important to identify mechanisms for change and explore the various supports and barriers that will foster or hinder success. Finally, even while someone is actively engaged in a change process, the story may not end with a simple "happily ever after." Making the change can be difficult. The person may experience strong undercurrents of feeling that fight against a change, even after he or she has made a firm commitment to change. The person may find that drinking has positive attributes not considered originally, such as reduction of anxiety, social priming, and relaxation. *Ambivalence still arises even after a decision is made, and it is useful to continue to reaffirm commitment to change.*

This leads us directly to our second question: What are we to do with this behavior? We suggest that you consider motivational interviewing (MI) as one option.

⊞ WHAT IS MI?

Motivational interviewing is a person-centered, directive intervention designed to resolve ambivalence about change (Miller & Rollnick, 1991). This method relies heavily on person-centered counseling skills. However, MI evolved beyond Carl Rogers's original ideas to use these counseling skills in a directive manner. The therapist actively moves clients toward self-examination and increased awareness of those aspects of their existence and behavior that may be problematic, as well as those aspects that signify unrecognized strengths and possibilities. Through this process, clients begin articulating how various behaviors are at odds with fundamental values, beliefs about themselves, and basic life goals. This internal discrepancy creates the motivation, which then fuels the change effort.

Although therapists operating under the MI framework are not confrontational, in another sense MI is a confrontive approach. It brings clients face to face with difficult realities in an environment where it is safe to be vulnerable around another person and honest with oneself about reality. MI forsakes an interpersonal form of confrontation and instead encourages the confrontation to occur internally or *intrapersonally*. Supporting rather than confronting a person seems not to eliminate the momentum toward exploring the problematic behavior; instead, it creates an environment in which the person can more honestly, deeply, and quickly recognize (or confront) the negative aspects of the problem behavior on his or her own. Thus, clients may feel uncomfortable, but it is their own behavior that is creating their discomfort, not the therapist's. As Bill Miller is fond of saying, "Confrontation is the goal of MI, not the method." Therein lies a critical difference from some other approaches.

Research to date suggests that MI can be successful in helping clients change addictive behaviors, as well as increasing participation in other aspects of treatment (see Bien, Miller, & Tonigan, 1993), but the specifics of why and how MI works remain unknown. However, researchers (e.g., Bien et al., 1993; Miller & Heather, 1998) do have some preliminary ideas, perhaps the most important being that clients often have resources within themselves to successfully initiate change. This is not a new concept, but it suggests our job in initiating change: to help clients identify and recognize their strengths and skills. We help clients make a commitment to change and then use what they already know and can do. The client, in conjunction with the therapist, will identify the targets of change. Change efforts then flow from this negotiated and collaborative process and are internally rather than externally driven.

GUIDING PRINCIPLES OF MI ⊞

Five principles guide the therapist in this process. Chris Dunn (1996) created the acronym GRACE to reflect these principles and the spirit of how this work is done. We briefly consider each of these principles.

G stands for *Gap*, the space between where a client is and where he or she would like to be. Clients have varying degrees of awareness of the gap. Some of our recent work suggests that recognition that one's behavior is discrepant from one's core values may be a critical element in providing impetus for change. Creating or enhancing awareness of a gap can be done through an exploration of core values, a review of normative feedback that places a client's behavior in the context of a larger group, or consideration of where he or she stands now in relationship to past dreams and future goals. This gap is an internal one. The therapist does not create it but rather notes and draws attention to it. We help the client recognize its presence and then step back, allowing him or her to infer what it means.

R stands for *Rolling with Resistance*. We avoid meeting client resistance head on. Pushing against resistance appears to increase it (Miller & Sovereign, 1989; Patterson & Forgatch, 1985), and there is evidence that increasing resistance, even in a single session, can have long-term effects on client outcomes. Client resistance comes in many forms: arguing, denying, interrupting, withdrawing, changing the subject, and even leaving the room. Resistance can also take the form of inauthentic agreeing, in which clients say the things they believe the therapist wants to hear without believing those things themselves. Resistance comes from many sources: feeling overwhelmed and vulnerable, being required to talk to someone about a "problem behavior" when you have bills to pay and must miss work to comply with the demand, being angry that people have imposed upon your freedom and are telling you what to do, being annoyed that there was nowhere to park the car, sitting across from a therapist who seems to have all the answers before listening to your thoughts about problems, and so on. The point is, *although resistance to change or to participate in counseling may come from a desire to continue engaging in problematic behaviors, this is only one of many possibilities.*

Therapists may attempt to harness the energy inherent in resistance by diverting it into directions that clients had not considered. Steve Rollnick illustrated this principle nicely in a video where his client states, "My grandfather smoked a pack a day until he was 92." Steve responds, "So it would take quite a lot for you to think about stopping." The client's focus is shifted—sometimes ever so slightly—in a new direction, providing the "juice" for considering his or her circumstance differently.

A stands for *Argue not*, a close cousin to rolling with resistance. The client tells us—sometimes directly but more often indirectly—if what we are doing is helpful. If we find ourselves arguing with our clients, even in subtle ways, that is a signal to shift our tactics. We want to avoid the situation where our clients are arguing for why they do not need to change. Bem's self-perception theory (Bem, 1995) provides a theoretical backdrop for why this focus on change and nonchange talk is important. Self-perception theory, at its most basic, indicates that in situations where we are unsure of what we believe (i.e., ambivalent), we come to learn our beliefs by hearing ourselves talk. If we place clients in a circumstance where they are telling us why they don't need to change, then it is predictable that they will come to believe this—at least in the short term. Conversely, if we can engage them in a discussion where they make the arguments for a change, it is much more likely they will embrace this side of the ambivalence.

C stands for *Can do*, helping clients recognize they have the skills to make successful changes. This is not a Pollyannaish view. Clients do have serious problems, barriers, and impediments to change, as well as self-esteem that has suffered as a result of difficult life problems. But clients' ability to perform specific behaviors on their own behalf is often well within their skill level. With this attitude, one can avoid the "low self-esteem trap." Clients do not have to feel good about themselves globally to believe they can make it to an AA meeting at 3rd and Cherry at 7 p.m. tonight. These small successes can be used to build a new sense of optimism and of self.

E, the final principle, stands for *Express Empathy*, the heart of MI. We try to create a safe environment in which the client can go about the difficult business of exploring change. Reflective listening, the key to this work, is the way this is most directly expressed.

Beyond listening, you will need to understand. Empathy is not simply saying at intervals, "Oh, that must be difficult." An internal indicator that understanding has been developed, that empathy has been achieved, may be when you can say to yourself, "Yes, that all makes perfect sense." If you are scratching your head and saying, "I don't get why he . . . ," then this is not the time to give advice about changing. Instead, it is time to learn more about the person you are trying to help. Expressing empathy requires understanding the person and his or her situation. Developing understanding requires not only intense listening but also the mental effort necessary to put yourself in a client's shoes.

BOX 2.2	**Microskills of MI: OARS**

Miller and Rollnick (1991) refer to these skills as opening strategies. However, we think it is more useful to think of them as strategies that undergird the MI process and can be used at any time with a client. As we tell our trainees, "When in doubt, use your OARS."

O—Open-ended questions
A—Affirmations
R—Reflective listening
S—Summaries

GRACE is the spirit that guides the MI process. We believe it is far more critical to the practice of MI to work in a GRACE-full manner than to employ specific MI techniques. However, we recognize that specific techniques translate into skills, so we turn our attention in that direction.

MI TOOLS ⊞

Microskills

To begin a motivational interview, you will need some tools to help you through a session. Fortunately, these tools are probably already in your toolbox. Once again, we borrow a useful acronym from Chris Dunn (1996)—*OARS*, which stands for *Open-ended questions, Affirmations, Reflective listening,* and *Summaries.* The acronym is a nice metaphor. OARS give us power to move, but they are not an outboard motor. We don't zip from one place to another, yet with sustained effort OARS can take us a long way.

Open-ended questions are therapist queries that clients cannot answer with a "yes," "no," or "three times in the last week" response. Many therapists begin sessions with an open-ended question: "What brings you here today?" or "Tell me about what's been happening since we last met." An open-ended question allows the client to create the impetus for forward movement. Although close-ended questions have their place—indeed, they are necessary and quite valuable at times—the open-ended question creates a forward momentum, which we use in helping the client explore change: "So what makes you feel that it might be time for a change?"

Affirmations are statements of recognition about client strengths. We agree with DiClemente's (1991) statement that many people who come for our assistance are unsuccessful self-changers. That is, they tried to alter their behavior and it didn't work. As a result, clients come to us demoralized or at least suspicious of the assertion that change is possible. As therapists, we can help clients feel that change is possible and that they are capable of implementing that change. One method of doing this is to point out client strengths, particularly in areas where they observe only failure. We often explore prior attempts at change. For example, "So you stayed sober for a week after treatment. How did you stay sober for that week?" We also use resistance as a source for affirmations. For example, "You didn't want to come today, but you did it anyway. So that tells me that if you decide something is important, you are willing to put up with a lot to accomplish it."

Affirmations can be wonderful rapport builders. For clients suffering from addictions, recognition of their strengths can be a rare commodity. However, they must be congruent and genuine. If the client thinks you are insincere, then rapport can be damaged rather than built.

Reflective listening is the key to this work. This is not just "uh-huhs" and "ahas." It is actively feeding back to clients your understanding of what they are trying to convey. If you are doing this well, and you miss the mark in your response, the rapport will not be damaged. The client will simply correct you and move forward.

The best motivational advice we can give you is to listen carefully to your clients. They will tell you what has worked and what hasn't, what moved them forward and what shifted them backward. Whenever you are in doubt about what to do, listen. But remember that this is a directive approach. Unlike traditional client-centered therapists, you will actively guide the client toward certain materials. You will focus on their change talk and provide less attention to nonchange talk: for example, "You are not quite sure you are ready to make a change, but you are quite aware that your alcohol use has caused concerns in your relationships and affected your work and that your doctor is worried about your health."

Vary your level of reflection. Keeping reflections at the surface level may lead to a feeling that the interaction is moving in circles. Reflections of affect can be powerful motivators, especially reflections of those feelings that are unstated but likely to be present. For example, "Your children aren't living with you anymore; that seems to have left you both sad and angry." If you are right, the emotional intensity of the session deepens. If you are wrong, or if the client is unready to deal with this material, the client corrects you and the conversation moves forward.

The goal in MI is to create forward momentum and then to harness that momentum to create change. Reflective listening keeps that momentum going. This is why Miller and Rollnick (1991) recommend a ratio of three reflections for every question asked. Questions tend to cause a shift in momentum and can stop it entirely. Although at times you will want to create a shift or stop momentum, most times you will want to keep it flowing.

Reflective listening is hard to do well on a consistent basis. Typically, this is the piece of MI training that participants are the least interested in practicing, yet it usually requires the most work. They keep waiting for the "magic" of MI to be revealed and are often chagrined and sometimes dismayed to discover they already "know it." Our bottom line—*if you are going to do MI, you have to listen well.*

Finally, there are *summaries,* a specialized form of reflective listening. Summaries are an effective way to pull together the information you heard, communicate your interest in the client, build rapport, call attention to salient and motivational elements of the discussion, and shift focus or direction. Personal preference will determine how often you do these, but we recommend doing them relatively frequently, as too much information from the client can be unwieldy for the therapist to digest and reflect. Also, if the interaction is moving in an unproductive or problematic direction (e.g., reinforcing nonchange talk, encountering resistance), use the summary to shift the focus of the intervention.

The structure of the summary is straightforward. It begins with an announcement that you are about to summarize, a listing of selected elements, an invitation to correct anything missed, and then usually an open-ended question. If ambivalence was evident in the interaction that preceded the summary, include it in the summary. Here's an example:

I'd like to stop and summarize what we've just talked about. You're not sure that you want to be here today, and you really only came because your partner insisted on it. At the same time, you've had some nagging thoughts of your own about what's been happening, including how much you've been using recently, the change in your physical health, and your missed work. Did I miss anything? I'm wondering what you make of all those things.

The goal is not to acquire ammunition and then turn it on the client in a defense-leveling manner but to reflect what the client has said from a motivational viewpoint. Encourage the client to supply the meaning. Watch that your wisdom and experience don't keep you from listening to your client's understanding of the problem. This understanding will guide the client's efforts to change or maintain the status quo.

Use OARS to elicit change talk, or self-motivational statements, that help the person move forward. Change talk involves statements or affective communications indicating that the client may be considering the possibility of change. Miller and Rollnick (1991) organized this talk into four categories: problem recognition, concern about the problem, commitment to change, and belief that change is possible. Essentially, any statement oriented toward the present or future, either in the thinking (cognitive) or the feeling (emotional) realm, may represent change talk. Here are some examples of each:

- "I think that using may be causing problems" (present-cognitive).
- "I'm kind of worried that things may be getting out of hand" (present-emotional).
- "I'm definitely going to do something about that" (future-cognitive).
- "You know, I'm starting to feel like this just might work out" (future-emotional).

In practice, differentiating between these types of change talk is arbitrary; the point is that these client responses indicate openness to the possibility of change and that the therapist should respond by reinforcing these tentative steps.

Macroskills: Strategies

Although OARS will help you move around within a MI session, larger and more strategic skills may help you organize the work and create the direction for the movement. Each of these strategies is designed to elicit change talk and is most typically used early in the change process.

The first strategy, "Good and Less Good Things," a decisional balance exercise, explores the "good things," and the "less good (or not so good) things" about a particular behavior pattern. Steve Rollnick and colleagues (Rollnick, Heather, & Bell, 1992) developed this unusual phrasing for a particular purpose: They wanted to avoid labeling a behavior as a problem when the client was not using that language. Failure to do this may lead to arguments with clients where they state adamantly the behavior is not a problem. Conversely, clients are often willing to acknowledge that there are less good things about a behavior.

The technique also provides the therapist an opportunity to explore what "positives" may be sustaining a behavior. This is often a very fruitful inquiry and typically quite surprising to clients. They are often confronted with why they need to change a behav-

---

BOX 2.3 **Macroskills of MI: Strategic Interventions**

It can be helpful to have techniques that guide the MI effort and provide general matching to a client's stage of change. Four techniques are suggested here:

1. Good and Less Good Things
2. Looking Forward/Looking Back
3. Personalized Feedback Report
4. Importance and Confidence

The Personalized Feedback Report tends to be most helpful for people in the stages of precontemplation and contemplation. Good and Less Good Things and Looking Forward/Looking Back work well with those who are contemplative. Importance and Confidence can be used with people in preparation, as well as the other two stages. But this categorization scheme is not set in stone. For example, Good and Less Good Things can work well with those who are precontemplative. On our research projects, we use these techniques as a menu of options. The therapist selects the intervention that he or she thinks might be most beneficial on the basis of what the client presents.

---

ior but are only rarely asked what benefits they are receiving. This often serves to reduce resistance and allows inquiry into the less good things to be more acceptable to the client.

We start this technique with a prefacing comment and then follow with a question about the good things. We follow up until all the good things have been exhausted. We summarize and then ask about the less good things. These are then explored in more detail. Requests are made for examples of less good behavior. For example, "You said that your use affected your children. Tell me about a time that happened." Once this area is fully explored, we summarize, emphasize any change talk that emerged, and then ask the client what his or her take on this material might be. The most important part of this strategy is to avoid labeling things as a problem.

"Looking Forward" and "Looking Back" are techniques that can be used together or separately. The goal is for the client to gain some perspective on his or her immediate circumstances and to observe either how things have changed or how things might be with and without changes in his or her current behavior. The Looking Back technique can be spurred by a client comment such as "I used to have it all" or "I wasn't always this way." This is a natural segue for a therapist comment and question: "So things have really changed. Tell me a little bit about what life was like back then." Then the therapist uses OARS to keep momentum going and to elicit how the problem behavior fit into this circumstance and/or how it changed over time. The goal is to identify the "gap" discussed earlier.

Looking Forward has a similar focus. Clients envision two futures. In the first, they continue on the same path without any changes and are asked where they might be 5 or 10 years from now. The second future is the future as it might look if—and the emphasis is on if—they decided to make a change in their behavior. The therapist's job is not to argue one position or another but just to elicit the information and then ask the client to comment on these imaginings.

Another strategy involves feedback to clients about their behavior. This can be formalized, as in the Drinker's Check-Up discussed below, or informal, based on information elicited during the course of the intervention. Normative feedback can include information about levels of use, consequences of use, or comparison to others. Standardized instruments such as the Addiction Severity Index (ASI; McLellan et al., 1992), the Alcohol Use Disorders Identification Test (AUDIT; Babor, De La Fuente, Saunders, & Grant, 1989) or the Drinker Inventory of Consequences (DrInC) or Inventory of Drug Use Consequences (InDUC)(Miller, Tonigan, & Longabaugh, 1995) provide ready resources for this type of feedback. The comparison can be to others or within oneself on scales. For example, a therapist could use the DrInC scales to convey where the client acknowledges experiencing problems and where he or she seems to be doing fine. An informal feedback opportunity that arises frequently is tolerance. Clients often point to their ability to "hold" alcohol as a sign that there is not a problem. This statement allows the therapist to offer information about how tolerance operates, including the potential detrimental effects of circumventing this early-warning system. The most important point: The therapist is simply a conduit for information. The client has the job of ascribing meaning. An example of informal feedback might go like this:

> Mary, would it be okay if I offered you a little information based on what we've talked about so far? Correct me if I'm wrong about anything. To begin, it sounds like you've noticed an escalating pattern in your alcohol use. This is a source of some concern to you, both because of your parents' history of substance misuse and because you've begun to drop away from your old friends. You're spending a lot more time recovering from the use, and the financial drain has begun to create some issues with your husband. You've also noticed it's less fun now and you're using more just to feel okay. Finally, you are concerned about your relationship with your kids. You swore that you were going to be a better mom to your kids than your mom was to you, but now you're not so sure how you've done with that. I'm wondering what you make of all this.

Another strategy is called "Importance and Confidence" (Rollnick, Mason, & Butler, 1999). This strategy essentially explores clients' impressions of how important is to make a change and how confident they are that they can succeed in changing. The therapist explores clients' impressions of what makes the change important, how this change fits in with other aspects of their life, and what events may occur to make this change seem more important than it currently does. Confidence is explored in a similar way, but with the question stated in a hypothetical form (i.e., *"If* you decided to make a change, how confident would you be . . . ?"). The therapist may guide clients to review past change attempts and determine how the therapist and significant others could help them succeed in making a change. Rollnick et al. (1999) suggested using simple scaling questions: for example, "On a scale of 0 to 10, how important is to you now to make a change in your alcohol use?" "What led you to choose X instead of Y? What might increase your rating a point or two?" Other useful strategies may be found in the references given at the end of this chapter.

Applications

Therapists use MI in a variety of forms. Previous applications include using MI for a single session, as an integrated part of therapy practice, or more recently, as a form of group therapy. Each of these forms is discussed briefly.

The most common form of MI treatment in the research literature is what could be called the Drinker's Check-Up. Clients complete some type of assessment protocol, and then a staff person reviews the assessment results with the client. For alcohol use, the assessment information often includes information about substance use patterns (including quantity, frequency, and peak blood alcohol), consequences of use, physical effects of use, cognitive effects of use (e.g., neuropsychological tests), family history, general life functioning, and other psychological issues. Goals and values can also be an important component of feedback. The assessment information is presented in an objective manner. The therapist does not argue if the client disagrees with content but may offer additional information if appropriate. For example, a frequent comment from clients when seeing their level of use compared to others is "But all my friends drink like I do." The therapist might respond,

> So it seems like this might be wrong. I wonder if you might be interested in some more information about that. One of the things that research suggests is that as time goes by, people tend to spend more time with people who drink like they do and less time with people who don't. Have you noticed that in your life? So it may very well be that your friends drink as much or more than you do and they may not reflect how most people drink. What do you think about that?

Our guess is that most therapists simply integrate an MI-style into their work without adding a formal testing/feedback component. One of the advantages of an MI approach is that it can be used with a variety of other larger treatment philosophies. For example, the approach does not demand that therapists view addictive behavior or other problems according to one particular theoretical model. For example, around the issue of attending AA, a therapist might offer this:

> May I offer you some information? Most of my clients find it's really helpful to attend AA early in recovery, and I usually recommend doing 90 meetings in 90 days. They find this helps them to stay focused on what's important and to get the support they need. What do you think of that?

Alternatively, the therapist can use a decisional balance or "Good Things/Less Good Things" strategy to explore a client's feelings about attending 12-step meetings. Whatever the motivational issue, and whatever theoretical lens the therapist uses for viewing the issue, a person-centered, ambivalence-exploring approach to the discussion can lower resistance and foster change.

Finally, there is increasing interest in using MI within group situations. An important difficulty to be addressed in offering MI in a group format is how to adapt a person-centered approach, in which therapist responses and interventions build upon client interests and motivations, to a group containing several individuals with divergent interests or levels of readiness. A variety of options are possible in reaching this goal. The group may be offered in a psychoeducational format, guiding clients with similar issues or struggles through a particular motivational topic, such as considering the good things and less good things about using. Alternatively, psychotherapeutic groups may bring together clients with diverse issues, strategically using interpersonal processes within the group to achieve different therapeutic goals for various participants. The needs of the clinical site may dictate whether groups are time limited or open-ended, have open or closed membership, and are offered as the sole intervention, as part of a larger array of clinical services, or as part of continuing care or aftercare. Each of these variations on group format will meet different needs, have different goals, and require different techniques and strategies from group facilitators (Ingersoll, Wagner, & Gharib, 2000).

MI principles are compatible with Yalom's approach to group work (e.g., instillation of hope, universality, imparting of information). The practitioner continues to use group skills already within his or her repertoire, and MI serves as a method for conceptualizing the intervention process and intervening with resistant behavior. For example, a group therapist might use a Looking Back technique to elicit discussion about how life was before the problem existed: for example, "What was life like for all of you, before drinking began to create difficulties?" The therapist would continue to use OARS and reinforce change talk. The therapist would also tie together group member issues, particularly when clients might have similar problems but differ in their readiness to change: for example, "Laura, Richard's situation sounds a lot like yours when you first started coming to group. I wonder if you might share some of the struggles that you had as you thought about making some changes."

The therapist can also use a form of group feedback. For example, in Seattle we are using a group-based MI approach in an attempt to prevent a first DUI among high-risk drivers. This study uses participants' driving records, along with normative information about Washington State drivers, to help at-risk drivers begin sorting through their driving behavior. The participant receives a copy of his or her driving record. The interventionist explains the record and then provides information related to infraction rates and types. Costs and consequences are discussed. Information about individuals' driving habits and attitudes is solicited, as well as information about behaviors that might influence driving. The therapist uses group principles, in addition to MI strategies, to create awareness of a potential problem and elicit decision making around this issue.

Evaluation: So How Am I Doing?

Certainly, practitioners may measure their work by evaluating long-term or short-term client change—measuring (or at least recording verbal reports of) changes in substance use behavior, substance-abuse-related lifestyle issues (e.g., more stable employment, fewer relationship or legal difficulties), or changes in client attitudes or interpersonal behavior (e.g., greater readiness to change, less argumentation). Tracking these changes within and across clients can be very useful in determining the effectiveness of your work. Asking select clients to provide you feedback in the form of rating their perceptions of your interpersonal behavior or their reactions to you can help you determine the extent to which you are observing the spirit of MI. Videotaping sessions and using formal MI rating forms to evaluate your adherence to the method is another possibility.

However, there is a more direct way to determine if what you are doing now with this particular client is useful—Observe your clients. If during the session they are frequently arguing, disagreeing, or withdrawing, then what you are doing is not working. Their behavior is a signal to shift methods. You may convince them of the folly of their ways, but change is unlikely to be sustained. If clients agree to do something between sessions and then fail to do it, this does not necessarily mean there is a problem. It may simply be ambivalence. However, if it happens consistently, then you may be arguing for change and the client may be simply acquiescing. It is time to listen to your client. Finally, if your clients don't return for sessions, it may be a sign that they are giving up on you rather than the problem behavior. You may have pressed too hard for a change the client was not ready to make. Our advice: Pay attention to your clients; they tell you one way or another how you are doing.

◫ WHERE, WHEN, AND WITH WHOM DOES MI WORK BEST AND LEAST WELL?

MI appears to have applications across a broad range of problem behaviors. Research is clearest in the area of addictive behaviors, and there is still much to learn. MI appears to work well as both a front-end adjunct and a stand-alone treatment with mildly to moderately addicted individuals (Burke, Arkowitz, & Dunn, in press). Even with severely addicted individuals, Project MATCH (Matching Alcoholism Treatments to Client Heterogeneity) has shown that a four-session form of MI can have results comparable to those of longer 12-step facilitation and cognitive-behavioral treatments (Project MATCH Research Group, 1997). MI has also been used to reduce HIV risk behaviors (Baker, Heather, Wodak, Dixon, & Holt, 1993; Baker, Kochan, Dixon, Heather, & Wodak, 1994), smoking (Butler et al., 1999; Colby et al., 1998), ER-related visits (Gentilello et al., 1999; Monti, Colby, Barnett, Spirito, & Rohsenow, 1999), eating disorders (Smith, Heckemeyer, Kratt, & Mason, 1997; Treasure et al., 1999), and so on. MI has been used with adults and adolescents; we are unaware of any MI research with children. There have been studies using MI with severely disordered psychiatric patients (Swanson, Pantalon, & Cohen, 1999; Zeidonis & Trudeau, 1997). MI is typically used in brief applications (one to four sessions), though clearly many of our trainees have woven this method into the fabric of their ongoing and everyday work.

Our anecdotal experience is that MI also appears to be helpful in getting practitioners to shift models and methods for working with clients. MI allows therapists to view "challenging" behaviors in a different light and provides methods for dealing with these behaviors without therapists' either having to admit that there is a problem in their present methods or having to drop their current philosophical system. However, research literature in this area is only beginning to appear. Miller is currently conducting an investigation of MI training methods that includes assessment of practitioner qualities and treatment philosophy, as well as the training method used. Rubel, Sobell, and Miller (2000) recently reported on the apparent effectiveness of a 2-day training workshop in changing practitioner knowledge and skills.

Although MI has been applied across a range of problems, settings, and training backgrounds, colleagues and trainees often ask about cultural sensitivity and MI. The basis of MI is careful understanding of a client within his or her circumstances. It does not assume knowledge of the client's life situation, the forces that shaped him or her, the issues that keep them caught in ambivalence, or the correct path to change. Thus, at its most basic, MI works within the client's cultural frame of reference, not the therapist's. Perhaps this is why MI has enjoyed such worldwide popularity and interest. More than half of the members of the Motivational Interviewing Network of Trainers (MINT) are from outside the United States, and many are from areas where English is not the primary language spoken. They train in their native tongues and cultures, though translation of principles is often necessary. The application of MI across cultures is nicely illustrated in the work of our colleague Dr. Angelica Thevos. Thevos and Quick (2000) trained local volunteers to use MI methods to improve water-handling practices in Zambia and noted significant improvement in water contamination rates and reports of diarrheal ailments.

POTENTIAL PITFALLS AND PROBLEMS ⊞

MI is not the Holy Grail of substance abuse treatment, despite our obvious enthusiasm for the method. It appears effective, but there are limits to its utility. It may be most effective with clients whose substance-related problems are of light to moderate severity. Clients do differ in their level of "inherent resistance," and MI will not magically reduce the resistance of some recalcitrant clients. Although it has been used with severely impaired psychiatric clients, it may not work well with psychotic patients because of the reliance on open-ended questions and reflective listening. More closed-ended questions and focused inquiry may be needed there. However, even within those constraints, we believe that MI-consistent methods can be used.

MI simply will not fit every therapist style. Moving from a confrontational style to a supportive style is a formidable task for some therapists. Some believe that the disease of addiction, with its much-noted features of denial and resistance, can be challenged successfully only through high-intensity interventions that point the way for clients to enter into and succeed in recovery. Given the battle that often ensues when a therapist approaches clients in this manner, it makes sense that these therapists feel the disease must be overcome through strength and force. Backing off from this battle can seem unethical: The therapist feels that he or she enabled the disease through inaction.

We applaud this concern for clients' welfare and again note that confrontation is a goal of MI but not its method. MI proponents believe that client resistance can be influenced, up or down, by the therapist. The goal is to have clients examine problem areas in their lives without feeling the need to defend their behavior against unwanted advice or judgment. Research suggests that high levels of therapist confrontation lead to greater resistance, which in turn leads to greater client drinking (Miller, Benefield, & Tonigan, 1993). In addition, therapists who fight the urge to confront may benefit by feeling more connected to their clients, feeling refreshed rather than drained after sessions, and seeing a positive transition in clients' attitudes, even before clients consider behavior change.

Other therapists believe that clients are unable to make good decisions because of substance-produced impairment or that they may need more teaching or guidance than the MI approach provides. Even in these cases, we suggest that aspects of MI may be useful, such as Rollnick's "Elicit-Provide-Elicit" model of information exchange (Rollnick et al., 1999). Using this strategy, the therapist first elicits the client's level of interest in a particular topic, then provides the information that the therapist believes will benefit the client, then follows up by eliciting the client's reaction to the information. This approach seems to promote client receptivity to information and advice and allows the therapist the opportunity to gauge whether the client ever heard the information.

Some trainees indicate that they think that within MI we support whatever the client wants. This is true in a way but not entirely. Although the therapist may not actively oppose the client's desires, disagree with the client's choices, or debate with the client about specific plans, the therapist is active and states opinions. But how the therapist does this is critical. The therapist must recognize that, in the end, the client—not the therapist—will decide what to do about a behavior (even in the face of court mandates) and that the client must be responsible for enacting any change that occurs. Feedback and advice are offered, but in the context of acknowledging the client's right to choose and the many potential paths to a lasting solution. Therefore, therapists ask permission before offering advice or providing information. If the client refuses, then there is little benefit in going forward with the advice, and there is potential harm if resistance is engendered. In the end, our clients, like us, want many things, some of which are congruent with one another and some of which oppose one another. In the MI view, there is little use in adamantly opposing a particular client desire, decision, or plan because of the danger of increasing the client's resistance to change. Instead, it seems to be relatively simple and effective to shift focus to supporting another desire, decision, or plan of the client that *is* likely to lead the client to a happier, healthier, and more productive life. In this way, we use the client's energy to approach change, rather than fighting the client's energy to resist change.

Finally, there will be times when little seems to be accomplished in a MI session. In these instances, the therapist may feel disheartened and may feel internal pressure to push more, provide greater direction, or assign the client to a more intensive level of care. At the end of this session, the therapist needs to be particularly attentive to ending the session on good terms. Then, even if no change occurs, we leave the door open for possible future changes—either with us or with someone else. Responding with frustration may lead to greater client resistance, which in turn will reduce the likelihood of future efforts toward change. We do not know whether it will be today, tomorrow, next year, or never that the client will begin to see things differently or find the internal resources to begin the change process. How you choose to interpret the slow periods between changes may influence what lies ahead for the client.

MI is not an all-or-nothing approach. Many MI writings are sources of good clinical suggestions for approaching clients in a way that does not engender resistance or argumentation, whatever the theoretical model of the therapist. In the end, clients engage in discussions, not with theories or models, but with practicing therapists. Those therapists take a variety of theoretical viewpoints and clinical tools and use their own skill and artistry to create an environment that assists people who are hurting and struggling to make their lives better. The spirit and techniques of MI can be helpful in this endeavor but are not likely to be helpful if a therapist does not believe in them. Perhaps you might ask yourself, "Do I want to dance?"

⊞ PRACTICAL AIDS

To begin, consider the assessment tools already in use at your workplace. These tools could be used to implement a feedback component. This component could be an additional session or could be integrated into a treatment planning session. Assessment tools could include your standard intake interview, typical information about substance use patterns, consequences, medical issues family history, and other life issues. Queries about client goals can be added informally, through questionnaires or card sorts, but typically provide useful information.

Formal assessments can also be added. Although commercial instruments can be used, this is not a necessity. Project MATCH has developed several instruments that are available in the public domain and that include normative information. *Enhancing Motivation for Change in Substance Abuse Treatment* (Center for Substance Abuse Treatment [CSAT], 1999) contains several of these instruments, as well as ordering information.

If you decide to provide feedback, you may want to consider the use of charts. Programs like Microsoft Access can be used to write scoring and chart-making routines. A template can be created and copied and blanks filled in with individual client data.

Charts provide a communication mechanism, so design them with simplicity and ease of understanding in mind. Complicated charts lose clients. TIP 35 provides examples from Project MATCH.

A change plan form can be quite helpful with clients ready to do this type of work. To avoid a premature focus on action plans, we call these forms "The Next 90 Days." This form can then be used to record any number of actions, including simply thinking more about an issue. This form typically includes just a few simple questions or statements (e.g., "Things I want to consider more"; "Things I intend to do"; "People who can help me"), which the therapist and client fill in together.

ADDITIONAL TRAINING/READING RESOURCES ⊞

Several key books and articles provide more information about MI. Our "References" and "Additional Suggested Readings" sections below point you to these. One useful resource for keeping up with ongoing developments related to MI is the MI Web site (www.motivationalinterview.org). This site will link you to background information and seminal articles on MI, a comprehensive bibliography and selected article abstracts, other Web sites with information on MI, information on training and online training, contact information for MI trainers from the international MINT, and the MINUET, a newsletter published by MINT three times annually.

REFERENCES ⊞

Babor, T. F., De La Fuente, J. R., Saunders, J., & Grant, M. (1989). *AUDIT: The Alcohol Use Disorders Identification Test. Guidelines for use in primary health care.* Geneva, Switzerland: World Health Organization.

Baker, A., Heather, N., Wodak, A., Dixon, J., & Holt, P. (1993). Evaluation of a cognitive-behavioural intervention for HIV prevention among injecting drug users. *AIDS, 7,* 247-256.

Baker, A., Kochan, N., Dixon, J., Heather, N., & Wodak, A. (1994). Controlled evaluation of a brief intervention for HIV prevention among injecting drug users not in treatment. *AIDS Care, 6,* 559-570.

Bem, D. (1995). Self-perception theory. In L. Berkowitz (Ed.), *Advances in experimental and social psychology* (Vol. 6). New York: Academic Press.

Bien, T. H., Miller, W. R., & Tonigan, J. S. (1993). Brief interventions for alcohol problems: A review. *Addiction, 88,* 315-335.

Burke, B. L., Arkowitz, H., & Dunn, C. (In press). The effectiveness of motivational interviewing and its adaptations: What we know so far. In W. R. Miller & S. Rollnick (Eds.), *Motivational interviewing: Preparing people to change* (2nd ed.). New York: Guilford.

Butler, C. C., Rollnick, S., Cohen, D., Russell, I., Bachmann, M., & Stott, N. (1999). Motivational consulting versus brief advice for smokers in general practice: A randomised trial. *British Journal of General Practice, 49,* 611-616.

Center for Substance Abuse Treatment. (1999). *Enhancing motivation for change in substance abuse treatment* (Treatment Improvement Protocol [TIP] 35, DHHS Pub. No. SMA 99-3354). Washington, DC: Government Printing Office.

Colby, S. M., Monti, P. M., Barnett, N. P., Rohsenow, D. J., Weissman, K., Spirito, A., Woolard, R. H., & Lewander, W. J. (1998). Brief motivational interviewing in a hospital setting for adolescent smoking: A preliminary study. *Journal of Consulting and Clinical Psychology, 66,* 574-578.

DiClemente, C. C. (1991). Motivational interviewing and the stages of change. In W. R. Miller & S. Rollnick (Eds.), *Motivational interviewing: Preparing people to change addictive behavior* (pp. 191-202). New York: Guilford.

Dunn, C. (1996). Packaging. *Motivational Interviewing Newsletter for Trainers, 3,* 5.

Gentilello, L. M., Rivara, F. P., Donovan, D. M., Jurkovich, G. J., Daranciang, E., Dunn, C. W., Villaveces, A., Copass, M., & Ries, R. (1999). Alcohol interventions in a trauma center as a means of reducing the risk of injury recurrence. *Annals of Surgery, 230,* 473-483.

Ingersoll, K. S., Wagner, C. C., & Gharib, S. (2000). *Motivational groups for community substance abuse programs.* Richmond, VA: Center for Substance Abuse Treatment.

McLellan, A. T., Kushner, H., Metzger, D., Peters, R., Smith, I., Grissom, G., Pettinati, H., & Argeriou, M. (1992). The fifth edition of the Addiction Severity Index. *Journal of Substance Abuse Treatment, 9,* 199-213.

Miller, W. R., Benefield, R. G., & Tonigan, J. S. (1993). Enhancing motivation for change in problem drinking: A controlled comparison of two therapist styles. *Journal of Consulting and Clinical Psychology, 61,* 455-461.

Miller, W. R., & Heather, N. (1998). *Treating addictive behaviors.* New York: Plenum.

Miller, W. R., & Rollnick, S. (Eds.). (1991). *Motivational interviewing: Preparing people to change addictive behavior.* New York: Guilford.

Miller, W. R., & Sovereign, R. G. (1989). The check-up: A model for early intervention in addictive behaviors. In T. Loberg, W. R. Miller, P. E. Nathan, & G. A. Marlatt (Eds.), *Addictive behaviors: Prevention and early intervention* (pp. 219-213). Amsterdam: Swets & Zeitlinger.

Miller, W. R., Tonigan, J. S., & Longabaugh, R. (1995). *The Drinker Inventory of Consequences (DrInC).* Rockville, MD: U.S. Department of Health and Human Services.

Monti, P. M., Colby, S. M., Barnett, N. P., Spirito, A., & Rohsenow, D. J. (1999). Brief intervention for harm reduction with alcohol-positive older adolescents in a hospital emergency department. *Journal of Consulting and Clinical Psychology, 67,* 989-994.

Patterson, G. A., & Forgatch, M. S. (1985). Therapist behavior as a determinant for client noncompliance: A paradox for the behavior modifier. *Journal of Consulting and Clinical Psychology, 53,* 846-851.

Prochaska, J. O., DiClemente, C. C., & Norcross, J. (1992). In search of how people change: Applications to the addictive behaviors. *American Psychologist, 47,* 1102-1114.

Project MATCH Research Group. (1997). Matching alcoholism treatments to client heterogeneity: Project MATCH posttreatment drinking outcomes. *Journal of Studies on Alcohol, 58,* 7-29.

Rollnick, S., Heather, N., & Bell, A. (1992). Negotiating behaviour change in medical settings: The development of brief motivational interviewing. *Journal of Mental Health, 1,* 25-37.

Rollnick, S., Mason, P., & Butler, C. (1999). *Health behavior change: A guide for practitioners.* Edinburgh: Churchill Livingstone.

Rubel, E., Sobell, L., & Miller, W. R. (2000). Do continuing education workshops improve participants' skills? Effects of a motivational interviewing workshop on substance abuse counselors' skills and knowledge. *Behavior Therapist, 23,* 73-77, 90.

Smith, D. E., Heckemeyer, C. M., Kratt, P. P., & Mason, D. A. (1997). Motivational interviewing to improve adherence to a behavioral weight-control program for older obese women with NIDDM: A pilot study. *Diabetes Care, 20*(1), 53-54.

Swanson, A. J., Pantalon, M. V., & Cohen, K. R. (1999). Motivational interviewing and treatment adherence among psychiatric and dually-diagnosed patients. *Journal of Nervous and Mental Disease, 187,* 630-635.

Thevos, A., & Quick, R. (2000). *Motivational interviewing enhances the adoption of safe water handling practices in Zambia, Africa.* Unpublished study.

Treasure, J. L., Katzman, M., Schmidt, U., Troop, N., Todd, G., & de Silva, P. (1999). Engagement and outcome in the treatment of bulimia nervosa: First phase of a sequential design comparing motivation enhancement therapy and cognitive behavioural therapy. *Behaviour Research and Therapy, 37,* 405-418.

Zeidonis, D. M., & Trudeau, K. (1997). Motivation to quit using substances among individuals with schizophrenia: Implications for a motivation-based treatment model. *Schizophrenia Bulletin, 23,* 229-238.

ADDITIONAL SUGGESTED READINGS ⊞

Daley, D. C., & Zuckoff, A. (1999). *Improving treatment compliance: Counseling and systems strategies for substance abuse and dual disorders.* Center City, MN: Hazelden.

Miller, W. R., & Sanchez, V. C. (1994). Motivating young adults for treatment and lifestyle change. In G. Howard (Ed.), *Issues in alcohol use and misuse by young adults* (pp. 55-82). Notre Dame, IN: University of Notre Dame Press.

Miller, W. R., Zweben, A., DiClemente, C. C., & Rychtarik, R. G. (1992). *Motivational enhancement therapy manual: A clinical research guide for therapists treating individuals with alcohol abuse and dependence* (DHHS Pub. No. ADM 92-1894). Washington, DC: National Institute on Alcohol Abuse and Alcoholism.

Project MATCH Research Group. (1993). Project MATCH: Rationale and methods for a multisite clinical trial matching patients to alcoholism treatment. *Alcoholism: Clinical and Experimental Research, 17,* 1130-1145.

Project MATCH Research Group. (1999). Comments on Project MATCH: Matching alcohol treatments to client heterogeneity. *Addiction, 94,* 31-69.

3

Computer-Assisted Interventions

Mouse as Cotherapist

Christopher P. Rice

Today, computers are used to deliver a wide range of information. As a tool for spreading information, computers have the potential of offering not only all of the essential qualities of books but also real-time links to supplementary topics. This latter capacity puts information delivery over the computer on a level that books cannot achieve. To envision this potential, imagine sitting at a computer terminal, logging onto the World Wide Web, going to a search engine, and writing in a query. After a short time, the response to the query appears on the screen in the form of a listing of sites where you can obtain the information you are seeking. You go to one of the sites, where you obtain information about the topic of your query. However, in most cases the site will also have suggestions for additional sites that you might also visit to obtain additional information on your topic or, most important for the point here, information on topics related to your original query.

There is an important benefit in the capacity of the computer to take input from an individual terminal, retrieve information that is available to any other station linked to the Web, and deliver it back to the terminal making the query. This capacity provides the ability to focus information. Suppose you type the words "drinking alcohol." In reading the list of sites retrieved by the computer, you are likely to find sites that span a range of aspects of drinking alcohol, from drinking games, to the types of spirits available in many countries of the world, to information on the health-related consequences of drinking alcohol. You obtain, as in the earlier illustration, a broad range of responses to your query, any one of which could provide you with additional sources of related information. This type of query is primitive in the sense that it provides a generalized response to a specific query. This type of response may be adequate if you are interested in getting a general response, but to answer a more specific question you will need to go through a process of evaluating each site to determine how well that information fits your specific needs.

To refine the level of specificity of a computer link, several iterations of dialogue may be required. The user supplies information that is then used to reshape the parameters of the query toward the desired specificity. From the perspective of the computer system, the success of this iterative process is bounded by the level of detail available to the linked sites searched in the query. The computer can retrieve any set of data. Whether that retrieval satisfies your query depends on whether the information is available to it and how you have shaped the search. Two important points emerge: First, the capacity exists; second, the capacity can be shaped. Currently available computer-based information systems are very flexible, and it is possible, actually quite easy, to provide individually tailored information to every user of the system.

▓ COMPUTERIZED PREVENTION PROGRAMS

The capacity to provide such individually tailored information is not trivial because it means that a universal prevention program is possible. One of the implementation barriers to mounting prevention programs directed at reduction of alcohol use is coverage. Most prevention programs have been directed at a target group in the population rather than at the population as a whole. This is because the expense, time, and effort required to deliver a prevention program to large numbers of people have been much greater than the anticipated results of the program. The cost-offset ratio has not been favorable. Cost-offset ratios improve for targeted groups, particularly if the intervention itself is efficient. But when program delivery becomes more cost-, time-, and energy-efficient, its expansion to an entire population becomes more feasible.

For example, until recently, delivering any of the currently available prevention programs to the entire nation's population of college students would not have been feasible economically or logistically—despite the mounting evidence that the harm related to misuse of alcohol by college students is a national concern (Wechsler, Davenport, Dowdall, Moeykens, & Castillo, 1994; Wechsler, Dowdall, Maener, Gledhill-Hoyt, & Lee, 1998; Wechsler, Fulop, Padilla, Lee, & Patrick, 1997). But recent developments in two areas have combined synergistically to produce sufficient reason for undertaking a universal prevention program in this population subgroup. The first is the development of computer-based student accounts; the second is the development of brief intervention for the treatment of alcohol abuse and alcoholism.

If current trends continue, college and university administrations will be providing all students high-speed connections to the campus computing systems. This trend facilitates the administrative functions of application, registration, billing, and grading. Students are required to access their computer accounts at least once each semester, and this necessary access makes the campus computing system an excellent vehicle for the delivery of a prevention package. With college students, it is for the first time possible to reach the entire population with an effective intervention.

This newly available avenue is important because it introduces a highly complex and sophisticated tool into the array of methods that addictionologists can use to respond to the growing need to reduce the harm attributable to a complex and sophisticated sociocultural behavior: use of alcohol. A computer-based prevention delivery is com-

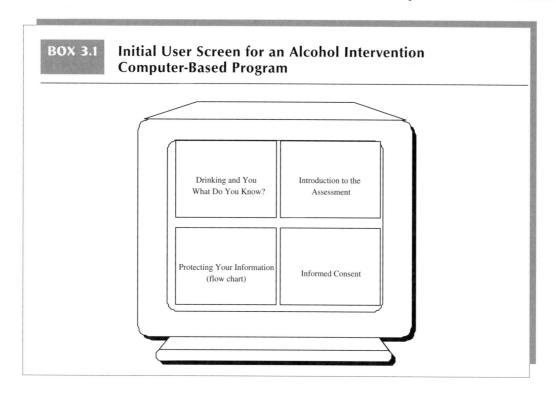

BOX 3.1 **Initial User Screen for an Alcohol Intervention Computer-Based Program**

plex because it must respond to the realities that not all college students use alcohol and not all college student alcohol use results in harm. What this means is that the system must offer the flexibility to tailor the intervention package to the type of involvement each student has with alcohol. A computer-based system does just that. Campus computing systems have, as an inherent property of the system, the ability to allow individual end users to tailor their own use patterns. Consequently, the system can respond to each individual user in a unique way that is shaped by that particular user and no other.

A system of this type that I am currently developing ("Your Profile of Drinking") uses a series of screens to query information from a client. The system then takes the client information and, using a series of algorithms, categorizes the client according to a typology that ranges from "nondrinker" to "hazardous drinker." Box 3.1 provides a schematic representation of the initial user screen. It contains four elements:

1. "Drinking and You: What Do You Know?" invites users to test their knowledge about their alcohol use and learn more.

2. "Introduction to the Assessment" describes the program's assessment of alcohol use, perceptions of alcohol expectations, perceptions of normative consumption patterns, and alcohol-related negative consequences.

3. "Protecting Your Information" tells users how the confidentiality of their data will be protected.

4. "Informed Consent" enables users to give their informed consent when this is required for gathering of data for research activities.

The system then matches the client's information to national norms for alcohol consumption. Additional risk categories are also considered (e.g., other drug use, family his-

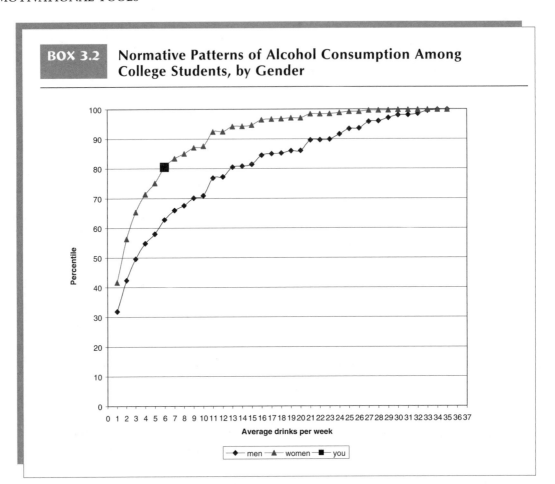

BOX 3.2 **Normative Patterns of Alcohol Consumption Among College Students, by Gender**

tory of alcohol-related problems, current negative consequences) and compared to normative data. Once these internal comparisons are made, the client is presented with a series of screens that present objective assessment of drinking behavior. In the case of the nondrinker, encouragement for choosing an alcohol-free lifestyle is presented instead.

Acquiring client-based information and presenting objective feedback on the consequences of alcohol use are basic elements of brief intervention models of intervention with alcohol users. In general, brief interventions are based on the principles of motivational psychology. Theoretically, these interventions rely on the creation of a discrepancy between the client's current alcohol use, his or her current expectancies about the consequences of alcohol use, and objective data about drinking levels and alcohol-related consequences. Concurrently, the client is presented with a motivational statement designed to reinforce a sense of self-efficacy for changing risky alcohol consumption patterns.

Box 3.2 provides a graphical example of how an individual's comparison to normative drinking patterns might look. In this screen a female student's average number of drinks per week is compared to college students nationally. As the graph indicates, a woman student who has only five drinks per week (less than a drink per day) consumes more alcohol on average than 80% of collegiate women nationally.

The same type of comparison can be made to the general female population, as illustrated in Box 3.3. This screen shows that a woman who has five drinks per week is consuming more alcohol on average than 86% of the general female population. This shift

BOX 3.3 **Normative Patterns of Alcohol Consumption in the General Population, by Gender**

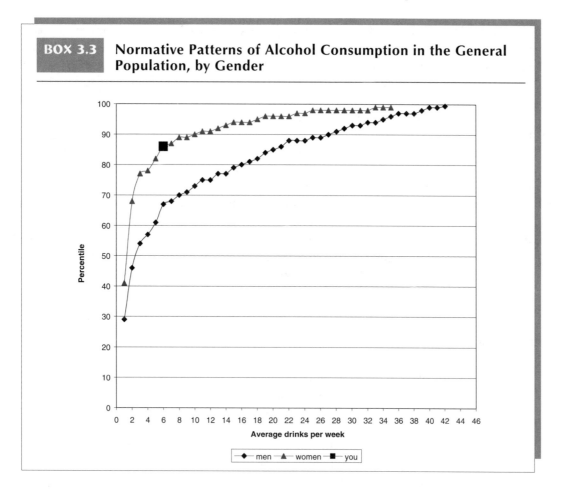

in the position of the student in relation to the normative pattern illustrates the general tendency of college students to drink more than the general population.

OVERCOMING DENIAL AND MOTIVATING CHANGE ▦

One of the fundamental principles of motivational enhancement is use of personalized objective feedback about the circumstances and consequences of alcohol use. Where individuals have been involved in abuse of substances, their lives are generally affected in a negative way across a range of biopsychosocial functioning. Often the person does not recognize or fully acknowledge the link between the substance use and multiple life-functioning problems. The purpose of providing feedback across a range of life-functioning dimensions is to personalize the consequences in such a way as to provoke and then enhance the client's motivation to change his or her relationship to alcohol.

Substance use is such a serious health problem in part because many people who use alcohol do not think of themselves as dependent, or even as abusers. People generally see themselves as normal, moderate users. Although some realize that alcohol use has negative consequences now and then, alcohol use is also the source of enjoyment for them, and they are uncertain that there is a need to make a change. Substance use can seem quite normal if they have friends who use just as much or even more. The principle involved then is to assess with sound, objective measurement instruments across a range of domains of the client's life functioning. The information obtained from the assessment assists you in getting the client to be open to input about substance use and helps the client recognize and acknowledge real or potential problems related to his or her substance use. The assessment provides a foundation upon which you can build an approach designed to elicit from your client expressions of a need, desire, or willingness to change.

To be included in the assessment battery, instruments must have normative data. The information obtained from your client is used to show where he or she falls in relation to these normative standards. The comparison allows you to give the client a different, more objective view of his or her substance use and related consequences. When you present this type of information, the client makes social comparisons and recognizes a discrepancy between his or her own expectancies and the behavior that most other people exhibit regarding alcohol use. Such discrepancy is a key component in motivationally based interventions and can act to stimulate your client's motivation to change.

⊞ ASSESSMENT RESOURCES

As you know from experience, the client intake assessment batteries normally employed in social services differ from agency to agency. You would do well to devote some time to a review and evaluation of the client intake assessments you will be using. In developing the prototype assessment battery for use with college students, I drew on the experience of the assessment feedback procedures developed for Project MATCH (Matching Alcoholism Treatments to Client Heterogeneity; Miller, Zweben, DiClemente, & Rychtarik, 1992). You will find in that monograph a framework for selecting assessment instruments. The monograph presents a similar framework for constructing a personalized feedback report (PFR) that you can tailor to suit the assessments you select.

An example from my own work illustrates this. A small substance abuse treatment agency agreed to participate in a pilot project to develop an assessment and feedback protocol for use with clients seeking treatment for alcohol problems. The agency's client base presented a wide range of involvement with alcohol, and people sought treatment for nonclinical as well as diagnosable levels of alcohol use. Most of the agency's intake assessment battery, although sound, lacked normative information. Fortunately, the agency did use the Addiction Severity Index (ASI; McLellan, Luborsky, Woody, & O'Brien, 1980). It was sufficient to provide a norm-referenced supplement (see Appleby, Van Dyson, Altman, & Luchins, 1997) for normative information on many of the composite indices. If you encounter an agency that does not yet employ psychometrically sound assessment instruments, a good place to begin the process of instrument selection is the reference work by Allen and Columbus (1995).

The PFR is a document that summarizes the information obtained from the assessment battery. It is discussed with and given to the client at the beginning of the feedback session. The PFR presented in Appendix 3.1 is usable as is or can be taken as an example for use with other applications of these techniques. This particular form of the PFR is designed to be used in conjunction with the ASI. The ASI composite score ranges are norms against which the client's own ASI composite score is compared. Composite scores are obtained in accordance with protocols established for the ASI.

Along with the PFR, clients receive a document, "Understanding Your Personal Feedback Report (UYPFR)," to take home with them to read. This document presents a narrative explanation of the information contained in the PFR and helps clients understand the implications of their scores on the assessment instruments. The UYPFR is reproduced as Appendix 3.2.

For clients whose substance use is predominantly alcohol, an additional handout is available: *Alcohol and You,* a pamphlet developed by William R. Miller. This pamphlet, which is in Miller et al. (1992), suggests factors that clients might want to consider when thinking about their use of alcohol.

Text documents of this nature have the advantage of being usable as computer files. When a computer-based delivery system is used for the brief intervention, you can link a text file that contains a completed PFR and an accompanying individualized UYPFR to the feedback presented to the client over the computer screen. The user can then download the file to his or her personal workstation and save the results of the assessment and feedback intervention for future reference.

THE COLLEGE DRINKING PREVENTION STUDY ⊞

The College Drinking Prevention Study (CDPS), which I developed, illustrates these principles. The CDPS collects data through a series of interactive Web pages. Students are made aware of these pages by a pop-up window announcing the availability of a set of drinking assessment screens. They are asked to respond to the assessments through a series of Web-based forms. As they proceed through the forms, the raw data are submitted to a database for future statistical analysis and are analyzed in real time to route feedback only to those students who have been randomized to the feedback intervention group.

The design and implementation of the computer screens, Web pages, and the underlying databases use current industry standards for data collection and security. Emphasis is placed on ensuring the integrity and privacy of the data that are collected. Although students need to authenticate into the system and thereby allow the random assignment to group condition, the list of student identifications (IDs) and assigned study numbers resides on a separate system from the data. Once the data are imported for analysis, they are anonymous and are identified only by the encrypted study IDs. University officials do not have access to this server or the files contained in it. The opening screen informs students about confidentiality procedures. Additionally, the initial screen that students see activates a "pop up" box containing the following message: "You are about to view pages over a secure connection. Any information you exchange with this site cannot be viewed by anyone else on the Web." All commonly used Web browser and e-mail programs have a mechanism for alerting users that they have a secure connection that will be activated by this screen and all subsequent screens. To make sure that the connection is secure, the project employs Secure Sockets Layer (SSL) or similar software. This is the industry standard for encrypting personal information and is the same software that Web-based companies such as Amazon.com use to protect customer information such as credit card numbers, names, and addresses so that it cannot be read as the information travels over the Internet. The programming to develop the type of data-capturing system proposed for the computer-assisted protocol (CAP) is well known.

⊞ COMPUTER-BASED FEEDBACK

There are many applications of computer-based feedback of alcohol-related information. Some of the most commonly available of these applications are programs that calculate blood-alcohol concentration (BAC) from data provided by the user. Users typically input their body weight, the number of drinks they plan to have, and the amount of time they estimate that it will take them to consume that number of drinks. The computer program then calculates the BAC that they are likely to reach. Unlike a Breathalyzer, which is designed to provide a BAC estimate based on a chemical analysis of the amount of ethanol present in the breath that the user exhales into the instrument, computer-based BAC readings depend on an algorithm to arrive at an estimate of the user's BAC. Most algorithms currently in use provide slightly biased results for anyone other than the average-sized young male adult, so adjustments must be made for age, gender, and ethnicity. Their estimates, though slightly less accurate than the current or after-the-fact BACs provided by a Breathalyzer, nonetheless serve as a predictive guide to the level of blood alcohol that users are likely to reach when they consume beverage alcohol as they described to the program. Thus, the estimates offer users the opportunity to adjust their drinking behavior before experiencing any of the negative consequences that might occur as the result of a BAC that reached levels of intoxication. Remember that in most states the "drinking under the influence" BAC is 0.08. Using these simple BAC calculators can help users shape their pattern of alcohol use so that their chances of experiencing negative consequences are reduced.

More sophisticated alcohol-related computer-based information systems are also available. These systems are more often employed as tools for assisting people who have experienced some difficulties as a result of alcohol and whose alcohol use has negatively affected some aspects of their life. One recent example is the Behavioral Self-Control Program for Windows (BSCPWIN). This program is designed to be used in conjunction with a therapist's assistance over eight 1-hour sessions delivered in a 10-week period. The therapist-assisted portion offers you an opportunity to introduce your client to drink-refusal skills, evaluation of triggers to overdrinking, problem solving to deal with those triggers, functional analysis of his or her drinking, and relapse prevention strategies. Results of a clinical trial of the BSCPWIN program showed a reduction in the average number of drinks per week in the groups exposed to the intervention, from an average of 35.2 drinks per week before the intervention to 14.5 drinks per week at 12 months postexposure. A significant reduction in the number of drinks on a day of drinking was also observed (Hester & Delaney, 1997). Results from a clinical trial of the BASICS program (Dimeff, Baer, Kivlahan, & Marlatt, 1999), an application of a computer-assisted brief intervention with heavy-drinking college students at the University of Washington, provide similar evidence that computer-based interventions reduce the average amount of drinking (Marlatt et al., 1998).

There is also research evidence that supports *bibliotherapy* (self-directed interventions based on reading materials), intervention without the assistance of a therapist. Small clinical trials with alcohol abusers (Harris & Miller, 1990) and individuals seeking treatment for depression (Schmidt & Miller, 1983) showed that a self-directed group did as well as the therapist-directed group and that both groups did better than waiting-list controls. In general, bibliotherapy often shows more benefit than no treatment across a range of behavior problems (Gould & Clum, 1993).

Results from clinical trials such as these are particularly promising because they demonstrate the feasibility of employing computer-based monitoring programs with

BOX 3.4	**Percentage of Full-Time College Students Drinking in Specified Time Periods, by Gender**		
Time Period	*Men*	*Women*	*Total*
One or more drinks in lifetime	88.5	89.2	88.5
One or more drinks in past year	83.9	85.0	84.5
One or more drinks in past 30 days	72.9	65.0	68.1
Daily use in past 30 days	5.8	2.7	3.9
Five or more drinks in a row in past 2 weeks	51.5	30.9	38.9

prevention applications. That is, if minimal interventions are effective without therapist involvement across a range of behaviors, including problem drinking, there is reason to anticipate that computer-based intervention should also be effective at reducing heavy drinking episodes among light to moderate drinkers.

MINIMIZING POTENTIAL PROBLEMS ⊞

Although computer-based interventions have demonstrated efficacy with identified problem drinkers, not much is known about how well the approach will work with drinkers who do not see their alcohol consumption as presenting a problem. However, for some subgroups in the population, any drinking is potentially problematic. High school and college students and women who are pregnant are examples of this at-risk-by-definition category.

Pregnant women are high risk because of the potential effects of alcohol on fetal development. With pregnant women, building motivation to change their drinking behavior rests on using maternal instinct to education them about the health risks to their unborn child.

Developing motivation in the student groups is somewhat more complex. Most high-school-age students have already experimented with alcohol and perceive its use as an adult-related behavior that should be acquired as a natural process of becoming an adult. The following data from the Monitoring the Future Study illustrate the high prevalence of drinking among high school students. The prevalence data presented in Box 3.4 are taken from the 1998 survey results (Johnston, O'Malley, & Bachman, 1999).

It is clear that the vast majority of college students (88.5%) have used alcohol at some point in their lives. The data indicate little difference between the lifetime and annual prevalence (88.5% versus 84.5%). It appears reasonable to speculate that most students who drink do so on at least an annual basis. Roughly 20% of women and 11% of men drink at least yearly but less than monthly. Johnston and colleagues (Johnston, O'Malley, & Bachman, 1998, 1999) reported trend data indicating that these differences show only slight fluctuations over the last 5 years of assessment. What has caught the attention of a number of researchers from both cross-sectional and longitudinal surveys (Engs, Diebold, & Hanson, 1997; Leichliter, Meilman, Presley, & Cashin, 1998; Wechsler et al., 1994; Wechsler, Davenport, Dowdall, & Grossman, 1997; Wechsler, Dowdall, Davenport, & Castillo, 1995; Wechsler, Dowdall, Maener, Gledhill-Hoyt, &

Lee, 1998; Wechsler, Fulop, Padilla, Lee, & Patrick, 1997) is the relatively high prevalence of students who report "binge" drinking (five drinks in a row).

From a prevention perspective, a number of considerations emerge from these data. First, it is clear that most college students are exposed to the risks associated with alcohol use. Second, although only a few expose themselves to these risks on a daily basis (3.9%), a clear majority face risk on at least a monthly basis (68.1%). Finally, a large minority (38.9%) of college students expose themselves to the higher risks associated with "binge" drinking. Because most students have used alcohol, prevention efforts should emphasize secondary rather than primary prevention approaches. It seems that among the population subgroup of college students there is reason to be concerned about not only the potential legal problem of underage drinking but also the risks for the sizable minority of students who drink heavily on a periodic basis.

Computer-based interventions might be particularly effective with this population subgroup because of their high computer literacy, but applications of the technology would need to overcome the perception that periodic heavy drinking is a "normal" activity among this age group. Motivation to use the computer-based interventions as an aid to behavior change needs to successfully counter ambivalence over changing a behavior that appears to be widespread.

Building motivation to change and reinforcing any attempts to alter the target behavior are key to the application of any intervention you attempt to make. Fortunately, there are methods, such as the suggestions that follow, that can be used to enhance the motivation both to use the computer-based intervention itself and to take steps to change drinking-related behavior.

- Computer-based interventions can present screens on which you develop target drinking goals. Using a BAC calculator, it is possible to develop a plan for the number of drinks and over what time period these can be consumed to maintain a blood alcohol concentration that is less than a given level, ideally 0.08. These target behaviors can be printed in a size that will fit in a wallet or purse and carried on the person for reference. Drinking goals can be tailored for anticipated conditions so that the person has control in any given social situation he or she might encounter.

- The computer screen presentations can be constructed in a user-friendly way. Simple point-and-click navigation through the screen enables use by even novice computer users.

- The computer-based intervention can present objective feedback to your clients that provides the opportunity to reflect on the effect that drinking has had on their lives. This learning experience can in itself provide motivation to change.

- In presenting feedback, the computer program can explicitly emphasize that the responsibility for change is theirs. Clear messages reinforcing self-responsibility for change have been shown to positively affect reduction in drinking behaviors with problem drinkers (Edwards & Orford, 1977; Heather, Whitton, & Robinson, 1986; Miller, Gribskov, & Mortell, 1981).

- Clear advice to change drinking patterns that result in undesirable consequences can also be given by a computer-based intervention program. For instance, advice to reduce hazardous drinking levels can result in significant change in drinking behavior (Kristenson, Ohlin, Hulten-Nosslin, Trell, & Hood, 1983). With a computer-based intervention program, you can easily identify individual drinking levels that fall within the range of consumption that typifies hazardous drinking. When feedback is given, a brief statement of advice to change can be included as part of the message.

- Providing a menu of change options and suggestions enhances the perception of personal choice and control over behavior change. Persistence at behavior change when options are freely chosen is greater than persistence when behavior change is directed or prescribed (Miller, 1985). Suggestions for change in the form of menus can be programmed into a computer-based intervention.

- When given feedback or direct advice to change a behavior such as drinking, the client is more likely to change if the feedback is presented in an empathetic rather than confrontational style. Feedback can be presented in an empathetic manner (Miller, 1983; Miller & Sovereign, 1989). Computer-based intervention feedback can also be written in an empathic style, improving the likelihood of acceptance by the user.

- Computer-based interventions can also present information so that self-efficacy for change is encouraged. For instance, part of the intervention could be a screen that prompts the client to list other situations in which he or she has successfully changed behaviors. These self-identified successes can be then employed as reinforcing statements for the feedback screens.

HOW TO IMPLEMENT THIS TOOL ⊞

Computer-based psychotherapy has a long history dating to the 1960s (Colby, 1995). The rationale for using computers for psychotherapy rests on the argument that behavior change can be viewed as an education in self-understanding (Colby, 1986). In fact, brief interventions, those treatments used in the substance abuse field that have the best foundation for efficacy (McCrady, 2000), rest on the assumption that the agent of change is the client and not the therapist. In any implementation of computer-based interventions for changing substance use behavior, the tools work because the agent of change is the user, not the computer per se. Once this is understood, it becomes clear that the success of computer-based interventions hinges on the content of the material presented and the manner in which it is presented.

Developing a computer-assisted intervention program requires consideration of the content of the intervention. A basic principle is to include an assessment of the target behavior. In the case of drinking, you want to provide the client with a screen that elicits an honest description of current alcohol use. How much and how often is alcohol used? In addition to these questions, you should also determine how long the drinking pattern has existed. In the process of presenting the screen on the computer that will collect this information, it is a good rule of thumb to also include clear statements to remind clients that the information on their drinking will help them better understand their relationship to alcohol. For instance, the screen that collects the drinking data can be introduced with a short statement that explains the purpose of collecting detailed drinking, the importance of providing honest responses, and the reminder that the information will help clients improve their understanding of their own drinking. In fact, it is probably a very good idea to remind users that you are not collecting the data for your own purposes and that any information they do provide is used for the sole purpose of self-instruction.

People are often curious about behaviors that hold the potential of risk. But in satisfying this curiosity it is often less threatening to have the assurance of anonymity. A computer-based program can easily promise just this type of environment for people to explore in depth a behavior that they might feel ambivalence over changing. People may more readily seek to understand their own involvement if that exploration can be done privately, at least until they can arrive at their own informed assessment of how their involvement fits their own expectations. You can easily reinforce the fact that they are in total control of the information as the data are gathered.

As a rule of thumb, the data that you collect should have a specific purpose. It ought to be transparent that information the user provides is directly connected to enhancing self-understanding. Likewise, it is important to include statements that reinforce the concept of the user as change agent. Users should be frequently reminded that the purpose of the program is to benefit them.

▦ USEFUL PRACTICAL AIDS

In Appendixes 3.1 and 3.2, you will find examples of forms that are used to provide the feedback gathered during a drinking assessment. These can be used with clients who seek treatment. Treatment is only one of the applications for computer-based intervention programs, as these types of programs can also be useful in prevention. In this section, some of the principles and considerations given to selecting an assessment battery and some additional examples are provided.

Patterns of drinking can be collected in a simple quantity-frequency grid. Exhibit 3.1 shows a calendar-based grid that can be used as a computer screen to capture drinking behavior in week-long periods of time. This presentation follows the methods used for drinking assessment instruments that have demonstrated reliability and validity, such as Timeline Followback (Sobell & Sobell, 1992) and Form 90 (Miller, 1996).

Assessment Domains

Alcohol use can have wide-ranging effects on life functioning, biologically, psychologically, and socially. There are numerous ways to assess this functioning. The best rule to follow is to balance comprehensiveness with feasibility in the sense of time it takes to complete the assessment battery. A good guide is to keep the total assessment time to 20 minutes or less. A good framework is provided by Miller and Rollnick, (1991), who suggested covering eight domains of functioning in a comprehensive assessment. You can follow their guidance or shape the assessment presented to better suit the needs of your situation.

Research has shown the importance of students' expectancies in their decisions to use alcohol. The Alcohol Expectancy Index in Box 3.2, from a survey of college students (Core Institute Alcohol and Drug Survey Long Form; Core Institute, 1998), provides an example of an expectancy measure that could be used in addition to a profile of weekly drinking and norm reference charts like the ones presented in Exhibit 3.1 and Boxes 3.1 and 3.2.

The Short Inventory of Problems (SIP), a short version of the Drinker Inventory of Consequences (DrInC; Miller, Tonigan, & Longabaugh, 1995) (see Exhibit 3.2) measures the negative consequences that respondents associate with their drinking. These

EXHIBIT 3.1. Profile of Weekly Drinking

Your weight in pounds: _____   Your height in inches: _____

A. Drinking Pattern Chart

1. If you drank in the 30-day period prior to today, you can fill out the following chart. Providing this information will help you to better understand how and when you drink. You will also be able to learn the approximate blood alcohol content that results from your style of drinking. This information will be used later as part of the overall feedback presented to you at the end of the session. The more accurate you are in providing the requested information, the more you will be able to learn from the feedback report. Take your time and provide your best recollection of the information requested.

2. Beginning with yesterday, record the type of beverage that you drank. You can refer to the chart below, as we have simplified the beverage selection to include the most common types of beverage alcohol. If you drink mixed drinks, you should record those as liquor and give the ounces as the number of shots of alcohol in that drink. For ounces, use the following: one can or bottle of beer—12 oz.; one glass of wine—5 oz.; one shot of liquor—1.25 oz. For example, if you drank two bottles of beer on Saturday afternoon, you would put the letter "b" in the beverage cell and "24" in the cell for ounces, as illustrated in the grid below. If in addition you had a glass of wine in the evening on Saturday, you would place a "w" in the beverage cell and a "5" in the ounces cell for that time period, as illustrated. Note that the program will calculate the total number of drinks in a standardized unit called Standard Ethanol Content (SEC). By describing drinks in their ethanol equivalence, we are able to combine the various types of drinks together. You can easily recognize the advantage of using this unit because it is the total amount of alcohol consumed that is important.

Time period: date start _____   date end _____

Time	Sunday bev.	oz.	Monday bev.	oz.	Tuesday bev.	oz.	Wednesday bev.	oz.	Thursday bev.	oz.	Friday bev.	oz.	Saturday bev.	oz.
Morning														
Afternoon													b	24
Evening													w	5
Total SEC														3.16

Beverage symbols:

b	12-oz. bottled or canned beer, any brand
w	bottled wine with cork
wc	wine cooler
fw	fortified wine (screw top)
l	one shot of 80 proof liquor
ll	one shot of 100 proof liquor
md	mixed drink, one shot of liquor (l)
md2	mixed drink, one shot of liquor (ll)

(continued)

EXHIBIT 3.1. Continued

B. Weekly SEC Summary

Remember that SECs are a standard unit of measure of alcohol content. The following summary measures will be helpful when you compare your drinking with that of drinking that is typical in the general population.

a. **TOTAL SECs per week** -

b. **Total days of drinking reported** -

c. **Average SECs per day of drinking** -

BOX 3.5   **Alcohol Expectancies Index**

Do You Believe That Alcohol Has the Following Effects? (Mark One for Each Line)	Yes	No
Breaks the ice		
Enhances social activity		
Makes it easier to deal with stress		
Facilitates a connection with peers		
Gives people something to talk about		
Facilitates male bonding		
Allows people to have more fun		
Gives people something to do		
Makes food taste better		
Makes women sexier		
Makes men sexier		
Makes me sexier		
Facilitates sexual opportunities		

consequences are typical, and the availability of normative data for the SIP makes it an attractive choice for use with computer-based brief interventions, where it is important for respondents to be able to make comparisons between the types of problems they may have encountered related to their drinking and the problems typically encountered by others. A more detailed description of the SIP is available from Miller, Tonigan, and Longabaugh (1995).

EXHIBIT 3.2. Short Inventory of Problems

INSTRUCTIONS: Here are a number of events that drinkers sometimes experience.

Read each one carefully and circle the number that indicates whether this has EVER happened to you (0 = No, 1 = Yes). If an item does not apply to you, circle 0.

Has this EVER happened to you? Circle one answer for each item.	*No*	*Yes*
1. I have been unhappy because of my drinking.	0	1
2. Because of my drinking, I have not eaten properly.	0	1
3. I have failed to do what is expected of me because of my drinking.	0	1
4. I have felt guilty or ashamed because of my drinking.	0	1
5. I have taken foolish risks when I have been drinking.	0	1
6. When drinking, I have done impulsive things that I regretted later.	0	1
7. My physical health has been harmed by my drinking.	0	1
8. I have had money problems because of my drinking.	0	1
9. My physical appearance has been harmed by my drinking.	0	1
10. My family has been hurt by my drinking.	0	1
11. A friendship or close relationship has been damaged by my drinking.	0	1
12. My drinking has gotten in the way of my growth as a person.	0	1
13. My drinking has damaged my social life, popularity, or reputation.	0	1
14. I have spent too much or lost a lot of money because of my drinking.	0	1
15. I have had an accident while drinking or intoxicated.	0	1

CONCLUSION ⊞

As the use of personal computers becomes more common in our culture, programs for a greater and greater variety of uses have become available. Computers are efficient at sorting through enormous amounts of information very quickly. This capacity is beneficial in many different applications. Computer software allows the data-handling capacity of computers to be selective and directive of the information. In other words, it is easy to develop software that acquires information that can then be modified. By subjecting the acquired information to a series of logic conditions, making comparisons to other associated information, and returning the results, one can influence the user's behavior. The key to achieving behavior change using computer-assisted intervention is to use approaches that have a sound foundation of scientific evidence. Influencing behavior in the manner intended is not an innate capacity of the computer per se. Change in drinking behavior, for instance, results because the information provided by the user, the comparisons made by the computer, and the results presented to the user are elements of protocols subjected to the methods of social science. In a sense, using the computer is simply a means of uniformly delivering this form of intervention to a large number of people in a way that makes it possible in terms of both cost and coverage.

⊞ REFERENCES

Allen, J. P., & Columbus, M. (1995). *Assessing alcohol problems: A guide for clinicians and researchers* (NIH Pub. No. 95-3745). Rockville, MD: U.S. Department of Health and Human Services.

Appleby, L., Van Dyson, J. D., Altman, E., & Luchins, D. J. (1997). Assessing substance use in multiproblem patients: Reliability and validity of the Addiction Severity Index in a mental hospital population. *Journal of Nervous and Mental Health Disorders, 185,* 159-165.

Colby, K. M. (1986). Ethics of computer-assisted psychotherapy. *Psychiatric Annals, 16,* 414-415.

Colby, K. M. (1995). A computer program using cognitive therapy to treat depressed patients. *Psychiatric Services, 46,* 1223-1225.

Core Institute. (1998). Core Institute Alcohol and Drug Survey–Long Form. *edu~coreinst*

Dimeff, L. A., Baer, J. S., Kivlahan, D. R., & Marlatt, G. A. (1999). *Brief alcohol screening and intervention for college students: A harm reduction approach.* New York: Guilford.

Edwards, G., & Orford, J. (1977). A plain treatment for alcoholism: *Proceedings of the Royal Society of Medicine, 70,* 344-348.

Engs, R. C., Diebold, B. A., & Hanson, D. J. (1997). The drinking patterns and problems of a national sample of college students. *Journal of Alcohol and Drug Education, 41*(3), 13-33.

Gould, R. A., & Clum, G. A. (1993). A meta-analysis of self-help treatment approaches. *Clinical Psychology Review, 13,* 169-186.

Harris, K. B., & Miller, W. R. (1990). Behavioral self-control training for problem drinkers: Components of efficacy. *Psychology of Addictive Behaviors, 4,* 82-90.

Heather, N., Whitton, B., & Robinson, I. (1986). Evaluation of a self-help manual for media-recruited problem drinkers: Six-month follow-up results. *British Journal of Clinical Psychology, 25,* 19-34.

Hester, R. K., & Delaney, H. D. (1997). Behavioral Self-Control Program for Windows: Results of a controlled clinical trial. *Journal of Consulting and Clinical Psychology, 65,* 686-693.

Johnston, L. D., O'Malley, P. M., & Bachman, J. G. (1998). *National survey results on drug use from the Monitoring the Future Study, 1975-1997: Vol. 2. College students and young adults* (NIH Pub. No. 98-4346). Washington, DC: Government Printing Office.

Johnston, L. D., O'Malley, P. M., & Bachman, J. G. (1999). *National survey results on drug use from the Monitoring the Future Study, 1975-1998: Vol. 2. College students and young adults* (NIH Pub. No. 99-4661). Washington, DC: Government Printing Office.

Kristenson, H., Ohlin, H., Hulten-Nosslin, M. B., Trell, E., & Hood, B. (1983). Identification and intervention of heavy drinking in middle-aged men: Results and follow-up of 24-60 months of long-term study with randomized controls. *Alcoholism: Clinical and Experimental Research, 7,* 203-209.

Leichliter, J. S., Meilman, P. W., Presley, C. A., & Cashin, J. R. (1998). Alcohol use and related consequences among students with varying levels of involvement in college athletics. *Journal of American College Health, 46,* 257-262.

Marlatt, G. A., Baer, J. S., Kivlahan, D. R., Dimeff, L. A., Larimer, M. E., Quigley, L. A., Somers, J. M., & Williams, E. (1998). Screening and brief intervention for high-risk college student drinkers: Results from a 2-year follow-up assessment. *Journal of Consulting and Clinical Psychology, 66,* 604-619.

McCrady, B. S. (2000). Alcohol use disorders and the Division 12 Task Force of the American Psychological Association. *Psychology of Addictive Behaviors, 14,* 267-276.

McLellan, T., Luborsky, L., Woody, G., & O'Brien, C. (1980). An improved diagnostic evaluation instrument for substance abuse patients: The Addiction Severity Index. *Journal of Mental and Nervous Disease, 168,* 25-33.

Miller, W. R. (1983). Motivational interviewing with problem drinkers. *Behavioral Psychotherapy, 1*, 147-172.

Miller, W. R. (1985). Motivation for treatment: A review with special emphasis on alcoholism. *Psychological Bulletin, 98*, 84-107.

Miller, W. R. (1996). *Form 90: A structured assessment interview for drinking and related behaviors* (NIH Pub. No. 96-4004). Rockville, MD: NIAAA.

Miller, W. R., Gribskov, C. J., & Mortell, R. L. (1981). Evidence for a self control manual for problem drinkers with and without therapist contact. *International Journal of the Addictions, 16*, 1247-1254.

Miller, W. R., & Rollnick, S. (Eds.). (1991). *Motivational interviewing: Preparing people to change addictive behavior.* New York: Guilford.

Miller, W. R., & Sovereign, R. G. (1989). The check-up: A model for early intervention in addictive behaviors. In T. Löberg, W. R. Miller, P. E. Nathan, & G. A. Marlatt (Eds.), *Addictive behaviors: Prevention and early intervention* (pp. 219-231). Amsterdam: Swets & Zeitlinger.

Miller, W. R., Tonigan, J. S., & Longabaugh, R. (1995). *The Drinker Inventory of Consequences (DrInC): An instrument for assessing adverse consequences of alcohol abuse.* Rockville, MD: National Institute on Alcohol Abuse and Alcoholism.

Miller, W. R., Zweben, A., DiClemente, C. C., & Rychtarik, R. G. (1992). *Motivational enhancement therapy manual: A clinical research guide for therapists treating individuals with alcohol abuse and dependence* (NIH Pub. No. 94-3723). Rockville, MD: National Institute on Alcohol Abuse and Alcoholism.

Schmidt, M. M., & Miller, W. R. (1983). Amount of therapist contact and outcome in a multidimensional depression treatment program. *Acta Psychiatrica Scandinavica, 67*, 319-332.

Sobell, L. C., & Sobell, M. B. (1992). Timeline Followback: A technique for assessing self-reported alcohol consumption. In R. Z. Litten & J. P. Allen (Eds.), *Measuring alcohol consumption: Psychosocial and biochemical methods* (pp. 41-72). Totowa, NJ: Humana.

Wechsler, H., Davenport, A. E., Dowdall, G. W., & Grossman, S. J. (1997). Binge drinking, tobacco, and illicit drug use and involvement in college athletics: A survey of students at 140 American colleges. *Journal of American College Health, 45*, 195-200.

Wechsler, H., Davenport, A., Dowdall, G., Moeykens, B., & Castillo, S. (1994). Health and behavioral consequences of binge drinking in college. A national survey of students at 140 campuses. *Journal of American Medical Association, 272*, 1672-1678.

Wechsler, H., Dowdall, G. W., Davenport, A., & Castillo, S. (1995). Correlates of college student binge drinking. *American Journal of Public Health, 85*, 921-926.

Wechsler, H., Dowdall, G. W., Maener, G., Gledhill-Hoyt, J., & Lee, H. (1998). Changes in binge drinking and related problems among American college students between 1993 and 1997. Results of the Harvard School of Public Health College Alcohol Study. *Journal of American College Health, 47*, 57-68.

Wechsler, H., Fulop, M., Padilla, A., Lee, H., & Patrick, K. (1997). Binge drinking among college students: A comparison of California with other states. *Journal of American College Health, 45*, 273-279.

ADDITIONAL SUGGESTED READINGS ⊞

Brener, N. D., McMahon, P. M., Warren, C. W., & Douglas, K. A. (1999). Forced sexual intercourse and associated health-risk behaviors among female college students in the United States. *Journal of Consulting and Clinical Psychology, 67*, 252-259.

Cashin, J. R., Presley, C. A., & Meilman, P. W. (1998). Alcohol use in the Greek system: Follow the leader? *Journal of Studies on Alcohol, 59,* 63-70.

Douglas, K. A., Collins, J. L., Warren, C., Kann, L., Gold, R., Clayton, S., Ross, J. G., & Kolbe, L. J. (1997). Results from the 1995 national college health risk behavior survey. *College Health, 46,* 55-66.

Johnston, L. D., O'Malley, P. M., & Bachman, J. G. (1996). *National survey results on drug use: Vol. 2. College students and young adults, 1979-1994.* Rockville, MD: National Institute on Drug Abuse.

Johnston, L. D., O'Malley, P. M., & Bachman, J. G. (1997). *National survey results on drug use from the Monitoring the Future Study, 1975-1995: Vol. 2. College students and young adults* (NIH Pub. No. 98-4140). Washington, DC: Government Printing Office.

Miller, W. R., & Del Boca, F. K. (1994). Measurement of drinking behavior using the Form 90 family of instruments. *Journal of Studies on Alcohol, 12*(Suppl.), 112-118.

Miller, W. R., & Marlatt, G. A. (1984). *The comprehensive drinker profile,* Odessa, FL: Psychological Assessment Resources.

Prochaska, J., Norcross, I., & DiClemente, C. (1994) *Changing for good.* New York: Avon.

Washton, A. M. (1995). *Psychotherapy and substance abuse.* New York: Guilford.

Wechsler, H., Dowdall, G. W., Davenport, A., & Rimm, E. B. (1995). A gender-specific measure of binge drinking among college students. *American Journal of Public Health, 85,* 982-985.

▦ WEB SITES OFFERING INFORMATION ON ALCOHOL USE

www.motivationalinterview.org

This is an interesting and informative Web site designed and maintained by William Miller. It contains a newsletter and many articles specifically on the topic of motivational interviewing. It is designed for professionals working in the field.

www.talkingcure.com

This site, designed and maintained by Scott Miller and associates at the Institute for Therapeutic Change, is both informative and humorous. It contains summaries of research findings related to substance abuse treatment, with a special emphasis on the brief therapies and the change processes.

habitsmart.com/tipping.htm

An interactive site that clients could use on their own. It guides individuals through a decisional balance activity to help them weigh the pros and cons of their drinking behavior. It contains a comprehensive list of questions designed to elicit information and raise discrepancies related to drinking and other addictive behaviors.

Appendix 3.1

Personal Feedback Report

Name: _____   Date:_____

1. YOUR DRINKING _____

Number of standard "drinks" per week: _____ drinks
Your drinking relative to American adults (same sex):   _____ percentile

2. LEVEL OF INTOXICATION _____

Estimated blood alcohol concentration (BAC) peaks:
In a typical week: _____ mg %
On a heavier day of drinking: _____ mg %

3. RISK FACTORS _____

Tolerance level:
____ Low (0-60) ____ Medium (61-120) ____ High (121-180) ____ Very high (181+)

Other drug risk:
____ Low   ____ Medium   ____ High

Family risk: _____
Low: 0-1   Medium: 2-3   High: 4-6   Very high: 7+

Age at onset: _____ years

Under 25: Higher risk   25-39: Medium risk   40+: Lower risk

Medical Composite

	Low Risk	Medium Risk	High Risk
Alcohol Abusers			
Male	< 0.255	0.255-0.582	> 0.582
Female	< 0.120	0.120-0.356	> 0.356
Opiate Abusers			
Male	< 0.220	0.220-0.550	> 0.550
Female	< 0.313	0.313-0.667	> 0.667
Cocaine Abusers			
Male	< 0.267	0.267-0.600	> 0.600
Female	< 0.186	0.186-0.481	> 0.481
Multiple Abusers			
Male	< 0.226	0.226-0.414	> 0.414
Female	< 0.138	0.138-0.432	> 0.432

AUTHOR'S NOTE: The Personal Feedback Report composite indices and normative data are derived from two sources: McLellan, Luborsky, Woody, and O'Brien (1980) and Appleby, Van Dyson, Altman, and Luchins (1997). The Personal Feedback Report is based on material found in Miller, Zweben, DiClemente, and Rychtarik (1992).

Employment Composite

	Low Risk	Medium Risk	High Risk
Alcohol Abusers			
Male	< 0.702	0.702-0.971	> 0.971
Female	< 0.392	0.392-0.677	> 0.677
Opiate Abusers			
Male	< 0.820	0.820-0.900	> 0.900
Female	< 0.803	0.803-0.900	> 0.900
Cocaine Abusers			
Male	< 0.697	0.697-0.900	> 0.900
Female	< 0.483	0.483-0.700	> 0.700
Multiple Abusers			
Male	< 0.608	0.608-0.900	> 0.900
Female	< 0.448	0.448-0.700	> 0.700

Legal Composite

	Low Risk	Medium Risk	High Risk
Alcohol Abusers			
Male	< 0.074	0.074-0.248	> 0.248
Female	< 0.050	0.050-0.184	> 0.184
Opiate Abusers			
Male	< 0.152	0.152-0.352	> 0.352
Female	< 0.103	0.103-0.317	> 0.317
Cocaine Abusers			
Male	< 0.089	0.089-0.235	> 0.235
Female	< 0.041	0.041-0.167	> 0.167
Multiple Abusers			
Male	< 0.046	0.046-0.145	> 0.145
Female	< 0.074	0.074-0.127	> 0.127

Psychiatric Composite

	Low Risk	Medium Risk	High Risk
Alcohol Abusers			
Male	< 0.236	0.236-0.448	> 0.448
Female	< 0.242	0.242-0.464	> 0.464
Opiate Abusers			
Male	< 0.155	0.155-0.368	> 0.368
Female	< 0.379	0.379-0.575	> 0.575
Cocaine Abusers			
Male	< 0.245	0.245-0.468	> 0.468
Female	< 0.258	0.258-0.471	> 0.471
Multiple Abusers			
Male	< 0.243	0.243-0.460	> 0.460
Female	< 0.225	0.225-0.442	> 0.442

Alcohol Composite

	Low Risk	Medium Risk	High Risk
Alcohol Abusers			
Male	< 0.643	0.643-0.869	> 0.869
Female	< 0.631	0.631-0.808	> 0.808
Opiate Abusers			
Male	< 0.266	0.266-0.521	> 0.521
Female	< 0.098	0.98-0.272	> 0.272
Cocaine Abusers			
Male	< 0.257	0.257-0.520	> 0.520
Female	< 0.241	0.241-0.563	> 0.563
Multiple Abusers			
Male	< 0.289	0.289-0.458	> 0.458
Female	< 0.308	0.308-0.595	> 0.595

Drug Composite

	Low Risk	Medium Risk	High Risk
Alcohol Abusers			
Male	< 0.031	0.031-0.098	> 0.098
Female	< 0.023	0.023-0.084	> 0.084
Opiate Abusers			
Male	< 0.265	0.265-0.396	> 0.396
Female	< 0.314	0.314-0.461	> 0.461
Cocaine Abusers			
Male	< 0.245	0.245-0.327	> 0.327
Female	< 0.256	0.256-0.320	> 0.320
Multiple Abusers			
Male	< 0.284	0.284-0.495	> 0.495
Female	< 0.155	0.155-0.258	> 0.258

4. BLOOD TEST _____

GGTP (GGT): _____   Normal range: 0-30: Low normal   31-50: High normal

51+: Elevated/abnormal

Appendix 3.2

Understanding Your Personal Feedback Report

⚏ YOUR DRINKING

Typical Drinking Level

This section gives you the number of drinks that you reported having in a typical drinking week. These drinks are given as a standard drink: that is, a drink that contains the same amount of ethanol regardless of the beverage consumed. The chart below gives a breakdown for comparison purposes.

A standard drink is equal to

12 ounces of beer
5 ounces of wine
1.25 ounces of 80 proof liquor
1 ounce of 100 proof liquor

The first number in this section of the report tells you how many of these standard drinks you consume per week of typical drinking (if you have not been drinking recently this refers to your typical pattern before you stopped).

Drinking Relative to American Adults (Same Sex)

The second number in this first section is a percentile. A percentile gives you an idea of how your drinking compares with the drinking of adults in the American population. The number tells you what percentage of men (or women if you are a woman) drink less than your own typical number of drinks. For example, a number of 70 indicates that your drinking is higher than that of 70% of Americans of your gender. Expressed in another way, 30% of men (or women, as the case may be) drink as much or more than you do in a week.

How much is too much? It depends on several factors. Current research indicates that people who average three or more standard drinks per day have a much higher risk of health and social problems. However, some people increase their risk of health or social consequences by having only one or two drinks per day. Pregnant women, for example, are advised not to consume *any* alcohol. Certain health conditions (liver disease) make even moderate drinking unsafe. For some people, even one or two drinks leads to intoxication.

The total number of drinks in a typical week tells only part of the story. It is not healthy, for example, to have 10 drinks per week by having them all on Saturday night. Neither is it safe to have even a few drinks and then drive. This raises the important question of *level of intoxication.*

AUTHOR'S NOTE: This explanation of the Personal Feedback Report is based on material found in Miller, Zweben, DiClemente, and Rychtarik (1992).

LEVEL OF INTOXICATION ⊞

You can also look at your past drinking by asking what level of intoxication you have been reaching. Blood alcohol concentration (BAC) is an important indication of the extent to which alcohol is affecting your body and behavior. BAC is an estimate of the amount of alcohol that is circulating in your bloodstream. The two figures shown are calculated estimates of your highest BAC during a typical week and your highest BAC during one of your heavier days of drinking.

It's important to note that there is no known "safe" level of intoxication when driving or engaging in other potentially hazardous activities (e.g., hunting, boating, or swimming). Crucial abilities such as eye-hand coordination can decrease at blood levels as low as 40 to 60 mg %. Often drivers do not typically realize that their coordination is impaired. The only "safe" BAC when driving is zero. The following charts indicate the BAC by the number of drinks for men and women of a given weight and gender.

Blood Alcohol Concentration Produced by Number of Drinks, for Men, by Body Weight

	Approximate Blood Alcohol Percentage								
	Body Weight in Pounds								
Drinks	100	120	140	160	180	200	220	240	
0	.00	.00	.00	.00	.00	.00	.00	.00	Only Safe Driving Limit
1	.04	.03	.03	.02	.02	.02	.02	.02	Impairment Begins
2	.08	.06	.05	.05	.04	.04	.03	.03	Driving Skills Significantly Affected
3	.11	.09	.08	.07	.06	.06	.05	.05	Possible Criminal Penalties
4	.15	.12	.11	.09	.08	.08	.07	.06	
5	.19	.16	.13	.12	.11	.09	.09	.08	
6	.23	.19	.16	.14	.13	.11	.10	.09	
7	.26	.22	.19	.16	.15	.13	.12	.11	Legally Intoxicated Criminal Penalties
8	.30	.25	.21	.19	.17	.15	.14	.13	
9	.34	.28	.24	.21	.19	.17	.15	.14	
10	.38	.31	.27	.23	.21	.19	.17	.16	

SOURCE: Data supplied by the Pennsylvania Liquor Control Board, ol.vt.edu/Student/bac/bacChart.htm.
NOTE: Subtract .01% for each 40 minutes of drinking. One drink is 1.25 ounces of 80 proof liquor, 12 ounces of beer, or 5 ounces of table wine.

Blood Alcohol Concentration Produced by Number of Drinks, for Women, by Body Weight

	Approximate Blood Alcohol Percentage									
	Body Weight in Pounds									
Drinks	90	100	120	140	160	180	200	220	240	
0	.00	.00	.00	.00	.00	.00	.00	.00	.00	Only Safe Driving Limit
1	.05	.05	.04	.03	.03	.03	.02	.02	.02	Impairment Begins
2	.10	.09	.08	.07	.06	.05	.05	.04	.04	Driving Skills Significantly Affected Possible Criminal Penalties
3	.15	.14	.11	.10	.09	.08	.07	.06	.06	
4	.20	.18	.15	.13	.11	.10	.09	.08	.08	
5	.25	.23	.19	.16	.14	.13	.11	.10	.09	
6	.30	.27	.23	.19	.17	.15	.14	.12	.11	Legally Intoxicated Criminal Penalties
7	.35	.32	.27	.23	.20	.18	.16	.14	.13	
8	.40	.36	.30	.26	.23	.20	.18	.17	.15	
9	.45	.41	.34	.29	.26	.23	.20	.19	.17	
10	.51	.45	.38	.32	.28	.25	.23	.21	.19	

SOURCE: Data supplied by the Pennsylvania Liquor Control Board, ol.vt.edu/Student/bac/bacChart.htm.
NOTE: Subtract .01% for each 40 minutes of drinking. One drink is 1.25 ounces of 80 proof liquor, 12 ounces of beer, or 5 ounces of table wine.

▦ RISK FACTORS

Research indicates that some people have a much higher risk of alcohol and other drug problems. "High risk" does not mean that you will have with certainty serious problems with alcohol and other drugs. "Low risk" does not mean that you will not experience such problems. However, "high-risk" people have a *greater chance* of developing serious problems than do "low-risk" people.

Tolerance

Tolerance for alcohol may be a serious risk factor for related problems. A person with a high tolerance reaches high BAC levels but has no built-in warning that this is happening, which can damage the brain and other organs of the body. Tolerance is not a protection against being harmed by drinking; to the contrary, it makes damage more likely because of the false confidence it encourages. Like people who have no sense of pain, people with high tolerance can injure themselves without realizing it.

Many people believe that tolerance ("holding your liquor") means that a person gets rid of alcohol at a faster rate than others. Although people do differ in how quickly their bodies can clear alcohol, tolerance has more to do with actually being at a high BAC and not feeling it.

Other Drug Use

The effects of different drugs can multiply when they are taken together, with dangerous results. A tolerance to one drug can increase tolerance to another, and it is common for multiple drug users to become addicted to several drugs. Decreased use of the drug may simply result in the increased use of another. Use of other drugs, then, increases your risk for serious problems. Based on the drug use that you reported during your assessment interview, your risk in this regard was judged to be low, medium, or high.

Family Risk

People who have a family history of alcohol or other drug problems among their blood relatives clearly are at higher risk themselves. The exact reason for this higher risk is unknown, but it appears that the risk is inherited to an important extent. People may inherit a higher tolerance for alcohol or a body that is particularly sensitive to alcohol in certain ways. In any event, a family history of alcohol problems increases personal risk.

Age at Onset

Research indicates that the younger a person is when drinking problems start, the greater the person's risk for developing serious consequences and dependence. Although serious problems can occur at any time in life, a younger beginning does represent a significant risk factor.

Medical Composite

Alcohol and other drug use is associated with a number of medical conditions (e.g., gastrointestinal disorders, fatty liver, hypertension, diabetes, HIV/AIDS, and hepatitis, to name a few). Use of alcohol and other drugs is also associated with more frequent use of health services. The risks to health from alcohol and other drug use have been well documented by research. The numbers in this section of the report indicate a level of risk to your health for the type of substance you typically use. Based on medical information you provided during your interview, your risk level is compared to that of other people who are of the same gender, use the same substance as you, and were also seeking treatment.

Employment Composite

Use of alcohol and other drugs increases the risk of employment difficulties. The risk level found in this section indicates your risk of problems in the workplace. You should understand that the risk level does not indicate that your alcohol or other drug use caused employment difficulty. It does mean that use of alcohol and other drugs can increase the probability that difficulties at the workplace can occur. A risk level is calculated from responses you gave during the assessment. This level is compared to the average risk of others who have characteristics similar to you.

Legal Status

Use of alcohol, which is a legal substance, and other drugs, which may be illegal, can increase the risk of having problems with the criminal justice system. This number indicates the level of problem risk you are experiencing, based on your responses to questions on the assessment. Your score is compared to that of others like you who are also seeking treatment.

Psychiatric Status

Your mental health, how you feel about yourself and others, is affected by your use of alcohol and other drugs. Sometimes alcohol and other drugs are used to help people feel better. Usually, this slight relief is very temporary, but it can contribute to a cycle of substance use that eventually exacerbates (increases) negative feelings. This section indicates your level of mental health discomfort relative to that of others like you who are seeking treatment.

PART

MEDICAL-PHARMACEUTICAL TOOLS

4

Detoxification

Opening the Window of Opportunity to Recovery

David E. Smith
Richard B. Seymour

DETOXIFICATION AS THE FIRST STEP IN ADDICTION TREATMENT

In the treatment of addiction, detoxification is literally the removing of toxic materials —the drug or drugs—from the patient's system. In the case of addiction to substances that do not produce physical dependency, time is the most important factor, and actual detoxification may be a matter of hours or days during which the body works to excrete, cast off, or metabolize substances into harmless by-products. Whatever bodily processes are needed to eliminate the substance or substances as a threat are employed. In such cases, psychosocial treatment may be the prime form of treatment.

When there is physical dependence, medical interventions may be needed to counter withdrawal symptoms and make full detoxification possible. The tools of detoxification include a pharmacopoeia of medications that work to ease withdrawal symptoms and help the patient's system regain a healthy balance.

These medications are not a magic bullet but are ancillary to psychosocial treatment and counseling, which are at the core of addiction treatment. Detoxification is not just a physical process any more than addiction is just a physical disease. The disease has been described as a "three-headed dragon," of which only one head is physical dependence. The other two are spiritual and psychological dependence. If detoxification is to succeed, if the patient is to progress from active addiction to active recovery, both spiritual and psychological aspects of dependency have to be dealt with as well (Seymour & Smith, 1987).

BOX 4.1   Detoxification Medications

Detoxification medications can include the drug agonists methadone and LAAM; the agonist/antagonists buprenorphine (for tapering from opioids) and long-acting benzodiazepines and phenobarbital (for tapering from alcohol and sedative-hypnotic drugs); and a host of non-narcotic medications for withdrawal symptom relief.

▦ THE ROLE OF PHYSICAL DEPENDENCY IN ADDICTION

Addiction Is a Disease That May Include Physical Dependency

Within the field of addiction medicine, addiction is seen as a disease in and of itself, characterized by compulsive use of a substance, loss of control over that use, and continued use despite adverse consequences. The disease is progressive and can be fatal if not treated. Addiction is incurable in that the addict, by definition, cannot return to controlled use.

The disease can, however, be brought into remission through abstinence from all psychoactive substances and adherence to a program of supported recovery. The first step in achieving remission is detoxification from the addicting sub- stance or substances.

As you can see, the definition of *addiction* employed here is a behavioral definition that looks to the user rather than the substance used. An earlier paradigm looked to the properties of the drug and its physical effects to define *addiction* as synonymous with *physical dependency.* That definition worked as long as the drugs involved were opioids or alcohol or other sedative-hypnotic substances, all of which produce progressive tolerance—the need for more and more of the drug to achieve desired results—and clear symptoms of withdrawal when use is abruptly discontinued.

BOX 4.2   Pickles

In the recovering community, it is said that a cucumber can remain a cucumber but that once it becomes a pickle it cannot return to being a cucumber.

BOX 4.3   Definitions

Physical Dependence = Withdrawal Symptoms + Increasing Tolerance

Addiction = Compulsion + Loss of Control + Continued Use Despite Adverse Consequences

---

The recognition of addiction syndromes involving such drugs as cocaine, methamphetamine, and a variety of hallucinogens, none of which were seen to have either clearly defined withdrawal symptoms or progressive development of tolerance, created the necessity for a new paradigm. Opioids and sedative-hypnotics including alcohol generally fit into a maintenance use pattern in which the addict uses on a regular daily basis, in part to ward off symptoms of withdrawal. Conversely, the stimulants, such as cocaine and methamphetamine, and the hallucinogens lose their effects rapidly as they exhaust the user's supply of certain neurotransmitters. Use of all these drugs tends to be episodic or in a binge pattern rather than steady and progressive. There are forms of withdrawal and tolerance development, but they are not as clear-cut as with the opioids and sedative drugs.

Detoxification Is the Beginning Point of Treatment

No matter what drug is primary or even secondary for the addict, some form of detoxification is the line of demarcation between active addiction and treatment aimed at abstinence and recovery. The tools of detoxification, including symptomatic medications, systemic rebuilders, anticraving agents, and, primarily, psychosocial treatment, are selectively appropriate for everyone who suffers from addictive disease. Implementation of detoxification procedures should be initiated as soon as the patient is medically ready and not in immanent danger or in a medical situation that could be exacerbated by the initiation of detoxification.

Situations in Which Physical Dependency Does Not Lead to Addiction

Detoxification is not always a part of addiction treatment. In the current paradigm of addictive disease, addiction can be seen as more than physical dependency, and physical dependency is not always indicative of addiction. There are, in fact, situations in which physical dependency is not a component and does not lead to addiction. An example can be seen in the use of opioid drugs for the management of postoperative pain. Ten patients are given potent opioids for a period following operations. All 10 develop some physical dependence and need to be tapered off their pain medication to avoid potential withdrawal symptoms. Nine of the patients greet the termination of their medication with relief. They were thankful to have the medication in that it helped control their postoperative pain, but the feelings engendered were not particularly pleasant. They didn't like feeling doped up and were relieved when they no longer needed the medication. The tenth responded to the medication as fulfilling a previously unfulfilled need: "This is what I've been looking for all my life, the answer to all my problems." That tenth person is in danger of addiction. Although in such a case it could be said that the origin of the addiction was iatrogenic, or medically initiated, it could also be seen that the individual had a high vulnerability to addiction and that the postoperative opioid exposure merely triggered what amounted to a genetic time bomb. That individual may turn to the street for drugs or may exaggerate pain reports to secure pain medication prescriptions.

THE ATTRIBUTES OF PHYSICAL DEPENDENCY ⊞

The Nature and Development of Tolerance

Tolerance is the need for more and more of a drug to achieve desired effects. Some addiction-prone individuals seem to have a naturally high tolerance for their drug of choice. It is said that Dr. Bob, one of the cofounders of Alcoholics Anonymous, started out with a legendary capacity for alcohol. He viewed his ability to drink great quantities at first as a blessing and later as a curse (Alcoholics Anonymous, 1980). A naturally occurring high tolerance for alcohol, usually found in conjunction with a family history of alcoholism, can be seen as an indicator for high vulnerability to addictive disease.

Generally, tolerance increases with the abuse of alcohol or other drugs. The mechanism of tolerance is not clearly understood and is thought to be the result of a variety of factors. These may include an increased ability of the user's system to rapidly metabolize frequently abused drugs, a decrease in brain receptor sensitivity, or changes in brain neurotransmitter chemistry. Tolerance may also be behavioral. The inexperienced drunk may get up and stagger around, whereas the experienced drunk knows better than to get up in the first place.

Tolerance and Fatality

Besides the level of tolerance, there is also a level for each individual at which a drug may produce a potentially fatal overdose. With opioid drugs, the potentially fatal level goes up along with the level of tolerance. The greatest danger for the opioid addict can come with a post-treatment relapse. With abstinence, the tolerance level drops, but so does the fatality level. A relapsing addict is apt to take a dose at the level he or she was using just before treatment, a level that is now well above the overdose point.

With sedative-hypnotic drugs, the potentially fatal overdose level remains roughly the same, while the level of tolerance continues to rise. Consequently, as the sedative-hypnotic addict increases dosages to overcome tolerance, he or she becomes increasingly in danger of a fatal overdose. Two things are of particular concern with sedative hypnotic users: cross-tolerance and a synergistic effect. Cross-tolerance means that tolerance that is developed for alcohol or any other sedative hypnotic drug will also exist for any other drug in this category, whether it has ever been ingested by the user or not. The synergistic effect is a result of the uneven metabolization of different drugs. Say, for example, the user drinks alcohol and then takes barbiturates or benzodiazepines. The liver may concentrate on metabolizing the alcohol while allowing the barbiturate or benzodiazepine to accumulate full strength to a fatal level in the brain (Inaba & Cohen, 2000).

The Development of Withdrawal Syndromes

As a rule of thumb, the symptoms of withdrawal from a drug are usually the opposite of the desired effects from use. For example, opioid use may be characterized by cessation of pain, feelings of euphoria, and general constipation. Withdrawal symptoms may include onset of pain, feelings of dysphoria, and loose bowel. The dynamic of withdrawal can be visualized as being like a pendulum that has been pulled as far as it will go in one direction and is then released. It will naturally swing equally far in the other direction before achieving a balance.

Opioid withdrawal can be painful and uncomfortable, but it is not fatal in and of itself. Without some mediation of symptoms, however, "cold turkey" withdrawal—so called because the patient develops piloerection or goose bumps—can be sufficiently dire as to drive the person right back into using.

On the other hand, sedative-hypnotic withdrawal can be fatal in and of itself. One of the primary actions of these drugs is antispasmodic, and untreated withdrawal can result in potentially fatal grand mal seizures.

DETOXIFICATION AS THE INITIATION AND TREATMENT OF WITHDRAWAL ⊞

Generally, the first step in treating chronic abuse is detoxification. This means eliminating the drug from the body and mediating the symptoms of withdrawal: that is, mediating the inevitable adjustments that the body must make to reestablish its balance once the drug is removed.

As was said above, most withdrawal symptoms are the opposite of the drug's desired effects and as such represent symptoms that can range from things the patient would rather avoid all the way to potentially fatal effects, such as seizures. Again, imagine that the pendulum that has been pulled way out of center. When that pendulum is released, it will swing a compensatory distance or more in the other direction, perhaps banging and maybe damaging the walls of the clock before reaching equilibrium. Basically, that is what happens in withdrawal: The body compensates by overreacting to every nuance that was suppressed by the drug. Physical detoxification is only part of early treatment. There is also dealing with mental withdrawal.

For a long time, it was believed that only opioids and sedative-hypnotic drugs (including alcohol) produced withdrawal symptomatology. Today it is clear that all psychoactive drugs abused on a chronic basis will produce withdrawal syndromes. In the following section, we discuss those syndromes and some basic detoxification tools and treatment protocols.

MEDICAL DETOXIFICATION FROM SEDATIVE-HYPNOTIC DRUGS ⊞

The bad news is that sedative-hypnotic withdrawal, including that from alcohol addiction, can be life threatening. Sedative-hypnotic withdrawal symptoms are generally divided into major and minor categories. Minor withdrawal symptoms consist of anxiety, insomnia, tremor, and nightmares. A major withdrawal syndrome includes all the symptoms of minor withdrawal and may also include grand mal seizures, psychosis, hyperpyrexia, and death. Untreated, the high-dose sedative-hypnotic withdrawal syndrome peaks in intensity as blood levels of the sedative drop, and the patient's signs and symptoms subside over a few days.

Symptoms attributed to sedative-hypnotic withdrawal include anxiety; tension; agitation; restlessness; irritability; tremor; nausea; insomnia; panic attacks; impairment of memory and concentration; perceptual alterations, including hyperaculsis or hypersensitivity to touch and pain, paresthesias, and visual hallucinations; feelings of unreality; psychosis; tachycardia; and increased blood pressure. Unfortunately, withdrawal has no pathognomonic signs or symptoms, and such a broad range of nonspecific symptoms could be produced by a number of illnesses, including agitated depression, generalized anxiety disorder, panic disorder, partial complex seizures, and schizophrenic disorders.

Patient Evaluation

In that many individuals develop a sedative-hypnotic addiction at least in part iatrogenically, having been prescribed drugs in this category, it is particularly important

---

BOX 4.4 **Evaluation and Assessment for Sedative-Hypnotic Addiction**

1. *Determine why the patient or referral source is seeking evaluation of sedative-hypnotic use and/or discontinuation.* Determine the indication(s) for the patient's drug use. A discussion with the referring physician should be standard practice. Discussion with any other referring person(s) or close family members often is helpful. Seek evidence to answer the question of whether the patient's use is improving the quality of his or her life or causing significant disability and/or exacerbating the original condition.
2. *Take a sedative-hypnotic use history,* including, at a minimum, the dose, duration of use, and substance(s) used, as well as the patient's clinical response to sedative-hypnotic use currently and over time. The history should include any attempts at abstinence, symptoms experienced with changing the dose, and reasons for increasing or decreasing the dose. The history also should include behavioral responses to sedative-hypnotic use and any adverse or toxic side effects. For long-term users, a determination of the current pharmacological and clinical efficacy should be sought.
3. *Elicit a detailed accounting of other psychoactive drug use* (including medical and nonmedical and prescribed and over-the-counter drugs), as well as current use of alcohol and prior sequelae of use. The history also should include abstinence attempts and/or prior periods of abstinence, in addition to prior withdrawal experiences.
4. *Take a psychiatric history,* including current and past psychiatric diagnoses, hospitalizations, suicide attempts, treatments, psychotherapy, and therapists (names and locations).
5. *Take a family history* of substance use, psychiatric, and medical disorders.
6. *Take a current and past medical history of the patient,* including illnesses, trauma, surgery, medications, allergies, and history of loss of consciousness, seizure(s), or seizure disorder.
7. *Take a psychosocial history,* including current social status and support system.
8. *Perform a physical and mental status examination.*
9. *Conduct a laboratory urine drug screen* for substances of abuse. An alcohol Breathalyzer (if available) often is helpful in providing evidence of substance use that was not provided in the history. Depending on the patient's profile, an EKG, HIV testing, TB testing, a blood chemistry panel, liver enzymes, a CBC, and/or pregnancy testing may be indicated.
10. *Complete an individualized assessment,* taking into account all aspects of the patient's presentation and history and, in particular, focusing on factors that would significantly influence the presence, severity, and time course of withdrawal.
11. *Arrive at a differential diagnosis,* including a comprehensive listing of considered and/or possible diagnoses. This greatly aids and guides clinical management decisions as the patient's symptoms diminish, emerge, or change in character during and after drug cessation.
12. *Determine the appropriate setting for detoxification.*
13. *Determine the most efficacious detoxification method.* In addition to proven clinical and pharmacological efficacy, the method selected should be one that the physician and clinical staff in the detoxification setting are comfortable with and experienced in administering.
14. *Obtain the patient's informed consent.*
15. *Initiate detoxification.* Ongoing physician involvement is central to appropriate management of detoxification. After the patient assessment, development of the treatment plan, and obtaining patient consent, the individualized discontinuation program should be initiated. The physician closely monitors and flexibly manages (adjusting as necessary) the dosing or detoxification strategy to provide the safest, most comfortable, and most efficacious course of detoxification. To achieve optimal results, the physician and patient will need to establish a close working relationship.

---

to sort out the nuances of use and abuse. Box 4.4 shows steps suggested by Eickelberg and Mayo-Smith (1998) for the evaluation and assessment of patients suspected of sedative-hypnotic addiction.

Etiology of Withdrawal Symptoms

The validity of a low-dose withdrawal syndrome has been controversial. Many people who have taken benzodiazepines in therapeutic doses for months to years can abruptly discontinue the drug without developing symptoms. Others, taking similar amounts of a benzodiazepine, develop a physical dependence on the drug and cannot tolerate the symptoms that develop when the drug is stopped or the dosage reduced. Moreover, some physicians believe the symptoms that emerge during the immediate withdrawal period can be explained solely by the return of the symptoms for which the drug was being taken, whereas other physicians propose that at least some of the symptoms are a true withdrawal reaction. At least four possible etiologies could explain the symptoms that begin when benzodiazepines are stopped: symptom reemergence, symptom emergence, symptom overinterpretation, and symptom generation.

1. *Symptom Reemergence.* According to the symptom reemergence etiology, the patient's symptoms of anxiety, insomnia, or muscle tension abate during benzodiazepine treatment, and the patient forgets how severe they were. Because discomfort in the present seems more real than that experienced in the past, present symptoms may be perceived as more severe when, in fact, they are equal in severity to those experienced before treatment.

2. *Symptom Emergence.* If the patient's initial symptoms were secondary to a progressive disease, they may have been masked during benzodiazepine therapy. If this is the case, the symptoms that reemerge will be more intense when the drug is stopped, but the intensity will result from the disease's progression.

3. *Symptom Overinterpretation.* Most individuals experience occasional anxiety, variations in sleep pattern, and musculoskeletal discomfort and accept these symptoms as reasonable consequences of everyday stresses, overexertion, or minor viral infections. Patients who are stopping sedative drugs often expect withdrawal symptoms to develop and may assume that any symptoms occurring during the withdrawal period are caused by drug withdrawal and require medical attention. A study of the frequency with which symptoms attributed to minor barbiturate or low-dose benzodiazepine withdrawal actually occurred reported that many of the same nonspecific symptoms were common among untreated, healthy persons who did not use drugs.

4. *Symptom Generation.* According to the final possible etiology, signs or symptoms may develop as a result of receptor site alterations caused by exposure to sedative-hypnotic drugs.

Receptor-Site Mediation in Dependence and Withdrawal

Assigning causality to symptoms that emerge after discontinuing a drug is subject to uncertainty, especially when a patient is evaluated after dependence is already established. The time course of symptom resolution is the primary differentiating feature between symptoms generated by withdrawal and symptom reemergence, emergence, or overinterpretation. Withdrawal symptoms subside with continued abstinence, whereas symptoms associated with other etiologies persist.

Such short-acting benzodiazepines as oxazepam, alprazolam, and triazolam have an accelerated time course for the sedative-hypnotic type of withdrawal syndrome, and the peak intensity of withdrawal occurs within 2 to 4 days. The fluctuation of symptom intensity of the low-dose withdrawal syndrome illustrates the waxing and waning of symptoms that often occurs without apparent psychological cause. This waxing and waning is an important marker distinguishing low-dose withdrawal symptoms from symptom reemergence.

Chronic use, dosage, concurrent drug use, and individual susceptibility all interact in the development of low-dose physical dependence. Moreover, the short-acting benzodiazepines are no less likely to produce physical dependence if taken on a daily basis than are the long-acting benzodiazepines; and once pharmacological dependence develops, the sedative-hypnotic-type withdrawal syndrome produced by short-acting benzodiazepines would be expected to be more intense because of the more rapid drop in tissue levels of these drugs.

Benzodiazepine Receptor Sites

Since the reports of finding specific benzodiazepine-binding sites, the character of the benzodiazepine receptor site has been the subject of intense research. These receptor sites, localized in synaptic contact regions in the cerebral cortex, cerebellum, and hippocampus, are associated with gamma-aminobutyric acid (GABA) receptor sites and affect their affinity for binding to a specific site; they also modify the cell membrane's permeability to chloride ions. We have hypothesized that low-dose benzodiazepine withdrawal is receptor-site mediated. A receptor-site mediated withdrawal syndrome could plausibly explain why benzodiazepine withdrawal symptoms take more time to resolve than nonbenzodiazepine sedative-hypnotic withdrawal symptoms.

Low-Dose Benzodiazepine Dependence Syndrome

The low-dose benzodiazepine dependence syndrome is not well understood or well characterized. The dose-response relationship is not established, and the development of dependence appears to be idiosyncratic. Risk factors include a family or personal history of alcoholism, daily alcohol use, or concomitant use of other sedatives.

Because the time course and spectrum of signs and symptoms of the low-dose withdrawal syndrome are different from those of the sedative-hypnotic-type withdrawal syndrome, the two probably have different mechanisms. Thus, the low-dose benzodiazepine withdrawal syndrome should be considered, not a "minor" sedative-hypnotic withdrawal syndrome, but a different syndrome. The benzodiazepine syndrome is not completely suppressed by phenobarbital administration; symptoms are rapidly reversed by benzodiazepine doses below those that would be expected to be effective; symptom resolution takes much longer with the low-dose withdrawal syndrome than with typical sedative-hypnotic withdrawal (i.e., symptoms usually take 6 months to a year to completely subside); and symptoms are most intense during withdrawal of the last few milligrams of the benzodiazepine.

Sedative-Hypnotic Detoxification

There are three accepted protocols for sedative-hypnotic detoxification, including detoxification from benzodiazepines. These are reduction of the amount of benzodiazepine taken; substitution of a longer-acting benzodiazepine; or substitution of pheno-barbital. Protocol selection depends on the severity of the benzodiazepine or other sedative-hypnotic dependence, the involvement of other drugs of dependence, and the clinical setting in which the detoxification program takes place.

Even though we have devoted considerable space to the special considerations regarding benzodiazepines, the actual detoxification is relatively straightforward. Given the variables, benzodiazepine withdrawal is no more controversial than alcohol withdrawal. As with alcohol detoxification, a minority of benzodiazepine users experience medically significant withdrawal. Because detoxification for that minority in both cases may involve life-threatening seizures, care must be taken in all withdrawal situations, and, when needed, vital signs should be monitored during threshold periods of inpatient detoxification.

Special considerations arise when the suspected dependency is in that grey area surrounding treatment with pharmaceutical sedative-hypnotics. Because benzodiazepines currently represent the primary group of psychoactive medications used in such instances, we will continue to refer to them in this text. When a patient develops benzodiazepine dependence during treatment of anxiety, the physician must decide whether the patient should undergo detoxification. Abrupt cessation of long-term benzodiazepine use can produce severe and even life-threatening withdrawal symptoms.

The graded reduction of benzodiazepine protocol is used primarily in medical settings for therapeutic-dose dependence. A long-acting benzodiazepine (such as chlordiazepoxide) can be substituted to detoxify patients with primary benzodiazepine dependence but is mainly used to treat patients with alcohol/benzodiazepine combination dependencies, using a fixed-dosage reduction schedule. Substitution of phenobarbital or another long-acting sedative-hypnotic can also be used to detoxify patients with primary benzodiazepine/polydrug dependence: for example, cocaine/benzodiazepine/alcohol combinations. This protocol, which also follows a fixed-dosage detoxification schedule, has the broadest use for all sedative-hypnotic drug dependencies and is widely used in drug detoxification programs. It is particularly valuable for treating high-dose benzodiazepine, barbiturate, alcohol, or other sedative dependence.

If the theory about two benzodiazepine withdrawal syndromes, high-dose dependence of the barbiturate type and low-dose dependence, is correct, drug withdrawal strategies must be tailored to three possible dependence situations. After daily use of therapeutic doses of benzodiazepines for more than 6 months, only a low-dose withdrawal syndrome should be expected. After high-dose use—doses greater than the recommended therapeutic doses for more than 1 month but less than 6 months, or for an average of 3 months—a classic sedative-hypnotic withdrawal syndrome should be anticipated. Finally, after daily high doses for more than 6 months, both a sedative-hypnotic withdrawal syndrome and a low-dose withdrawal syndrome should be anticipated.

To treat a low-dose dependence benzodiazepine-withdrawal syndrome, gradual reduction of the benzodiazepine is pharmacologically rational because seizures, hyperpyrexia, and other life-threatening medical complications are not expected. A stepwise reduction of the drug by the smallest unit dose each week is recommended for patients who are pharmacologically dependent but still in control of their medication use. Patients who have lost the ability to control drug use are likely to escalate the dosage again as symptoms emerge, and they require hospitalization.

During withdrawal, psychometric assessment is useful for establishing trends in the multiple, shifting symptoms. A computer can be used to administer a symptom checklist, with the patient sitting at a terminal and entering responses. This interactive method has proved to be more efficient than interviews for tracking symptom changes.

Propanolol has been found to reduce symptom intensity (Tyrer, Rutherford, & Hugett, 1981), and the drug is begun at a dosage of 20 mg every 6 hours, starting on the fifth day of withdrawal. This schedule is continued for 2 weeks and then stopped. After withdrawal is completed, propranolol is used as needed to control tachycardia, increased blood pressure, and anxiety. Continuous propranolol therapy for more than 2 weeks is not recommended, as propranolol itself may result in symptom rebound when discontinued after prolonged therapy.

Sedative-Hypnotic Detoxification With a Phenobarbital Taper

To treat sedative-hypnotic withdrawal, we prefer a phenobarbital substitution technique. At the Haight-Ashbury Free Clinics, no patients have had withdrawal seizures when phenobarbital was used, whereas two patients have had seizures during gradual benzodiazepine reduction. We believe that when treating a patient for drug dependence, it is best not to administer the drug of dependence during treatment.

An estimate of the patient's daily alcohol or other sedative-hypnotic use during the month before treatment is used to compute the detoxification starting dose of phenobarbital, converting the drug of dependency amount to the phenobarbital withdrawal equivalence dosage. The computed phenobarbital equivalence dosage is given in three or four doses daily. If other sedative-hypnotic drugs, including alcohol, are used, the amount of phenobarbital computed according to the conversion rate for the other sedative-hypnotic is added to the amount computed for the benzodiazepine. Regardless of the total computed amount, however, the maximum phenobarbital dosage is 500 mg per day. After 2 days of phenobarbital stabilization, the patient's daily dosage is decreased by 30 mg each day (Box 4.5).

Before receiving each dose of phenobarbital, the patient is checked for sustained horizontal nystagmus, slurred speech, and ataxia. If sustained nystagmus is present, the scheduled dose of phenobarbital is withheld. If all three signs are present, the next two doses of phenobarbital are withheld, and the daily dosage of phenobarbital for the following day is halved.

The taper process is continued until the patient is drug free. This period of detoxification provides a window of opportunity to initiate psychosocial treatment, including drug counseling, education on the nature of addiction and dependency, anticraving strategies, and other aspects of treatment, as well as the development of a long-term treatment and recovery protocol.

▦ MEDICAL DETOXIFICATION FROM OPIOID DRUGS

The good news is that opioid withdrawal is not life threatening. It can be accomplished on either an inpatient or an outpatient basis. With short-term chronic-use patients, it can even be accomplished within a nonmedical treatment setting.

Craving is a key component in withdrawal, and the severity of withdrawal symptoms has a direct effect on the intensity of craving. In general, the withdrawal symptoms are

---

BOX 4.5	**Daily Dosages (mg) Equivalent to 30 mg of Phenobarbital**

Amobarbital	100
Butabarbital	60
Pentobarbital	100
Secobarbital	100
Chloral hydrate	500
Ethchlorvynol (Placidyl)	350
Glutethimide (Doriden)	350
Meprobamate (Equanil)	400
Methaqualone	300
Methyprylon (Noludar)	100
Chlordiazepoxide (Librium)	100
Clorazepate (Tranxene)	50
Diazepam (Valium)	50
Flurazepam (Dalmane)	30
Oxazepam (Serax)	100

the opposite of the opioid effects. They can include restlessness, irritability, insomnia, marked pupillary dilation, rhinorrhea, cutaneous and mucocutaneous lacrimation and piloerection, yawning, sneezing, nausea, vomiting, and diarrhea.

The duration of withdrawal depends on the drug of use. Meperidine abstinence syndrome may peak within 8 to 12 hours and continue for 4 to 5 days, whereas heroin symptoms peak at about 36 to 74 hours and may last 7 to 14 days. According to Schuckit (1989) and a variety of others, including ourselves, there may be a protracted abstinence syndrome characterized by mild abnormalities in vital signs and continued craving, but this has not been clearly defined.

Treatment of opioid withdrawal ranges from a nonmedical, social model through symptomatic medication to methadone and levo-alpha-acetomethadol (LAAM) maintenance. The decision of which protocol to follow depends on a number of factors and calls for a thorough assessment of health and environmental conditions, including the presence of comorbid medical and psychiatric problems, availability of social support (such as presence of responsible family members who can provide monitoring and transportation), and polydrug abuse. Supportive measures include providing a safe environment, adequate nutrition, and a program of reassuring, supportive, and effective treatment.

Medical Intervention

In some cases, detoxification does not seem to work, at least for the time being. The strategy in such cases is to defray withdrawal by shifting the patient from his or her drug of choice onto a long-acting opioid agonist, such as methadone or LAAM, that can be clinically administered and controlled. Agonists are drugs that have some similar effects to the drugs of choice but are controllable and will keep withdrawal symptoms at bay. These agonists will at least provide some stability to the patient's life by providing a means of avoiding withdrawal and decreasing craving and by occupying the opioid receptor sites so that use of illicit or other opioids will have no further effect. The patient can be maintained on methadone or LAAM until such time as detoxification becomes a feasible option.

Next in line is methadone detoxification. Here, methadone is substituted for the opioid of choice and then withdrawn over time. Withdrawal is managed with initial doses of 15 to 20 mg of methadone per day to control withdrawal symptoms for 2 or 3 days, then reduced by 10% to 15% per day, adjusted on the basis of symptom control and clinical findings. These are averages. Actual amounts and percentages depend on the amount of drug the patient has been using.

Clonidine, an alpha-2 agonist originally used in the treatment of hypertension, is now used extensively in managing opioid withdrawal. Clonidine not only decreases withdrawal symptoms but also seems to alleviate opioid craving. Usually administered for 10 to 14 days, and at a variety of dosages ranging from 0.2 mg orally every 4 hours up to a total daily dose of 1.2 mg, clonidine can then be tapered at a rate of approximately 0.2 mg per day, depending on symptoms. One needs to watch for hypotension during administration. A benzodiazepine such as oxazepam may be helpful for insomnia and muscle cramps.

Clonidine is also used in combination with the long-acting opioid antagonist naltrexone in a form of rapid detoxification, developed to shorten the period of acute withdrawal to a period of around 5 days. Antagonists work by occupying the opioid receptor sites so that no opioid can do so, while producing no psychoactive effects of their own. It is the absence of psychoactive effects that primarily differentiates antagonists from agonists.

Several forms of ultrarapid detoxification (URD) have been developed. In URD, the patient is placed under heavy sedation or general anesthesia, then given oral naltrexone or intravenous naloxone. The patient experiences acute withdrawal while in a sedated or unconscious state. It has been argued that such protocols do not allow a window of opportunity to treat psychological withdrawal during the course of detoxification, increasing the potential for relapse into active opioid addiction.

A promising course of detoxification employs buprenorphine, an agonist-antagonist with qualities similar to both methadone and naltrexone. Buprenorphine can be given once a day to block withdrawal symptoms and can act as a transitional agent between opioids and naltrexone. An ultra-long-acting injectable form of naltrexone is also in development that could be used for opioid addicts in long-term recovery.

Varieties and combinations of these detoxification protocols include symptomatic medication in differing combinations. At the Haight-Ashbury Free Clinics, non-narcotic symptomatic medication is used in tandem with clonidine in one of several outpatient opioid detoxification protocols.

It should be kept in mind that physical detoxification is only part of the first step in treatment. The period of detoxification provides a window of opportunity to initiate the shift from active addiction to active recovery and should never be seen as an end in itself. The goal is to blend detoxification into ongoing drug treatment.

STIMULANT WITHDRAWAL ⊞

Stimulant withdrawal may be characterized by a variety of nonspecific aches and pains, tremors, chills, and involuntary motor movements, none of which should require specific medical treatment. Myocardial ischemia, with coronary vasospasm as a possible contributing factor, may occur during the first week of withdrawal. In general, the stimulant withdrawal syndrome results from the depletion of neurotransmitters, especially dopamine, and may be treated with the dopamine agonists bromocriptine and amantadine. The best treatment regimen is supportive treatment and allowing the patient to sleep and eat as needed. Severe depression may occur and can be treated with antidepressants. Anhedonia, the inability to feel pleasure, may also appear. During the later stages of withdrawal, as the exhausted neurotransmitters are replenished, intense craving may occur, particularly in cocaine addicts, and these patients may need to be hospitalized to be kept from relapse. The time of withdrawal is, again, a window of opportunity to work on avoiding cues for stimulant use and developing a sense of long-term abstinence and sobriety.

WITHDRAWAL FROM TOBACCO ⊞

Nicotine is so far the only stimulant for which a taper withdrawal and detoxification has been developed. It is also the only stimulant, with the exception of chocolate, that lends itself to maintenance abuse. It has been characterized as probably the most addictive substance available and is said to be responsible for over 400,000 deaths a year in the United States alone.

In the past, social reinforcement was a major factor in continued use. As one of the few drugs that our culture had given itself permission to use, cigarette smoking was virtually ubiquitous. Restaurants, bars, concerts, political rallies, and other public gatherings had their aura of tobacco smoke, and that was often unavoidable. In the last two decades, a surge of public health efforts and the recognition of the deleterious effects of secondhand smoke have created a social consciousness of tobacco that has resulted in smoking bans on airplanes and in restaurants, public buildings, and increasingly private homes. As a consequence, tobacco is avoidable. The greatest danger today seems to be from the stealth attacks that the tobacco industry continues to mount with the purpose of luring the young into smoking—attacks whose existence the industry vociferously denies.

Taper strategies using such products as nicotine patches and gums are the most used tools for tobacco withdrawal. However, these products should be used *only* within a comprehensive tobacco detoxification program that includes counseling and medical supervision.

WITHDRAWAL FROM MARIJUANA ⊞

Marijuana withdrawal is characterized by irritability, restlessness, anorexia, insomnia, diaphoresis, nausea, diarrhea, muscle twitches and flulike symptoms, and mild increases in heart rate, blood pressure, and body temperature. If a syndrome does develop,

---

BOX 4.6 **Marijuana Use**

Recovering marijuana users have remarked on the subtlety of the drug and its long-lasting effects on their lives. Several have stated that it was not until 2 or 3 years into abstinence and recovery that they became aware of the full extent of marijuana's disabling effects.

---

it usually manifests within 24 hours of cessation, peaks within 2 to 4 days, and is over within 1 to 2 weeks. In general, the withdrawal is considered mild and rarely requires medical treatment or hospitalization. The greatest danger is relapse into severe psychological dependence. If severe insomnia develops, the serotonergic antidepressant trazodone has been helpful.

☷ WITHDRAWAL FROM HALLUCINOGENS

Use of such hallucinogens as LSD tends to be intermittent. This may be because the very rapid development of tolerance to these drugs precludes sufficiently chronic use to form the basis of a withdrawal syndrome when use is discontinued. Consequently, there is no role for medication in treating hallucinogen withdrawal. There is, however, the potential for long-term psychological damage from these drugs, including a posthallucinogen perceptual disorder and, with MDMA, the release of suppressed psychological materials (Seymour & Smith, 1993). For these and other concerns, treatment can and should proceed directly to behavioral therapies.

Treatment for hybridized hallucinogens that include stimulant elements, such as MDMA and MDA, may call for a combination of counseling and stimulant treatment.

☷ PHENCYCLIDINE AND KETAMINE WITHDRAWAL

The main thing to remember with phencyclidine (PCP) and ketamine withdrawal is that these drugs remain in the body for a long time. In the early years of experience with PCP, the drug was thought to cause permanent brain damage. That assumption was only corrected as extreme cases "came back" over time. As was seen with hallucinogens, PCP experience can trigger long-lasting psychiatric sequelae, ranging from prolonged states of anxiety or depression to mild to pronounced psychotic states. These states can be dealt with in psychosocial treatment and need to be medicated only in extreme cases. Treatment of prolonged psychosis essentially follows guidelines for treating chronic functional psychosis. Flashback phenomena may be experienced up to a year after last use, but the effects are brief, and resulting anxiety can usually be alleviated by supportive reassurance.

BOX 4.7 **PCP Intoxication**

The enduring delusional aspect of long-term PCP intoxication can make detoxification difficult. In one instance, the user had become convinced that he was a Jesus-like avatar of God. To make matters even more difficult, he had convinced a number of disciples of this identity, all of whom were using PCP regularly as a "sacrament." Finally, a counselor challenged the subject to test his divinity by stopping use of PCP for a time and seeing if he still felt holy. After a period of abstinence, the subject entered treatment after admonishing his followers to stop using and saying, "I seem to have made a great mistake."

WITHDRAWAL FROM MULTIPLE DRUGS ⊞

Multiple Sedative-Hypnotics

Individuals withdrawing from several sedative-hypnotic drugs, often including alcohol, are best managed by substituting one long-acting sedative-hypnotic and following a taper procedure such as described earlier in the section "Medical Detoxification From Sedative-Hypnotic Drugs."

Sedative-Hypnotics and Opioids or Stimulants

As a general rule, it is best to treat the sedative-hypnotic withdrawal first. Sedative-hypnotic withdrawal represents the most medically risky and difficult process. When the other drug is one or more opioids, the opioid may be stabilized with oral methadone or codeine while the sedative-hypnotic is tapered, with opioid detoxification beginning once the sedative-hypnotic substitute is completely withdrawn. Clonidine has been suggested as an adjunct to this process in that it alleviates withdrawal symptoms for both drug groups.

MEDICAL MANAGEMENT OF ⊞ DUAL-DIAGNOSIS PATIENTS

The medical management of persons with a dual diagnosis of drug addiction and psychiatric disorders requiring medication poses both conceptual and clinical problems. Although psychoactive medications are helpful when properly used, patients with a personal or family history of substance abuse have a high risk for compulsively using all psychoactive drugs, and these drugs should not be prescribed for them. The question is, What is the appropriate medical response to a person who has addictive disease, or a genetic predisposition to addictive disease, but who is otherwise a good candidate for psychoactive medications? Clearly, physicians must use different prescribing standards for patients with addictive disease and for the general population.

It is in the best interest of patients with both addictive disease and psychiatric problems to first seek nonpsychoactive therapy alternatives, such as nonpsychoactive drugs, acupuncture, exercise, biofeedback, and other stress reduction techniques for the alcoholic patient with anxiety. When the severity of the psychiatric problem limits the person's ability to function, and if the use of nonpsychoactive drug alternatives fails, then psychoactive drugs may need to be administered. Unfortunately, these patients will probably then develop compulsivity for the medications, lose control over them, and continue using them despite adverse consequences. The physician must exercise the utmost caution in prescribing for these individuals. The fundamentals of good prescribing practices can be thought of as the "six D's": diagnosis, dosage, duration, discontinuation, dependence, and documentation.

Physicians make good-faith diagnoses of patients' problems. For an acute problem, such as a brief episode of pain or anxiety, it is within the accepted standard of care to treat that problem on the basis of a tentative diagnosis. As an acute problem lingers and becomes chronic, a firm diagnosis must be made. Because anxiety, insomnia, and pain are invisible disorders, physicians must take the time to find the etiology of the problem.

Once the diagnosis has been made, and a treatment plan outlined, the physician can select the drug that is clinically indicated for the specific problem, prescribing the appropriate drug dosage for the diagnosis and tailoring the medication schedule to the patient. The treatment goal is to neither undermedicate nor overmedicate, and as symptom severity increases and decreases, the medication should likewise be increased and decreased.

The duration of drug treatment should be planned with the patient, and medication should not be provided in an open-ended fashion. Also, periodic evaluations should be conducted to determine whether the medication should be discontinued: Are there problems with the drug? Has the planned duration of use expired? Has the crisis or problem that prompted use of the drug diminished or disappeared? Has the patient learned alternative ways of dealing with the original problem?

During treatment, the patient should be carefully monitored for developing dependence and toxicity problems. Physicians have a legal and ethical duty to warn the patient about both the side effects of the medications and the potential for developing dependence—which, for a person with addictive disease, can trigger an episode of compulsively taking prescribed and other drugs.

Finally, it is critical to carefully document the patient's initial complaints, eventual diagnosis, course of treatment, and all prescriptions and consultations. Consultations with experts in allied fields can be useful to the primary care physician. Addiction specialists can be consulted for cases of addiction and dependence, much as one would consult a pain specialist or a psychiatrist. These consultations, and decisions based on them, should also be documented in the patient's file (Smith & Seymour, 2001).

⊞ CONCLUSION: TREATMENT AS THE BRIDGE BETWEEN ACTIVE ADDICTION AND ACTIVE RECOVERY

A primary component of addictive disease is denial on the part of the addict that there is a problem. This is not lying, although manipulation and subterfuge such as hiding bottles or paraphernalia and swearing that one has not been drinking or using may be part of the addict's behavior. The disease strikes at a primitive level of the brain such that addicts are rendered incapable of recognizing the disease and are unable to connect their actions with their consequences. As a result, unless the denial is broken in a process of intervention, patients usually come into treatment with a lot of resistance. Often, at least at the Haight-Ashbury Free Clinics, users claim that they could actually quit at any time but that they don't really want to quit. What they want is to decrease a habit that, well, may have gotten a little out of hand. It's costing too much, or it's interfering with work, or the family is starting to complain.

Recovery involves a long process that starts with detoxification, and the initiation of treatment presents a window of opportunity to begin the process of education and renewal. Addiction is a chronic disease, and the occurrence of relapses is a recognized factor in the process. It can be very discouraging to the clinical staff when they have put tremendous effort into the treatment of a patient, only to see him or her reentering treatment all too soon and starting the process over again. It is good at such times to remember that every incident of treatment helps to plant the seeds of recovery. They may not take the first, second, fourth, or seventh time, but it is important that the process continues.

At the Haight-Ashbury Free Clinics, before the nature of the disease was as clearly understood, there used to be a rule that a client could return to treatment a maximum of three times. After that, it was judged that the clinics' modalities were not working for the client, and efforts were made to find another treatment center for them. Today, the nature of relapse is better understood, and efforts are continued to detoxify when necessary and to continue to treat and plant the seeds of recovery.

REFERENCES ⊞

Alcoholics Anonymous. (1980). *Dr. Bob and the Good Oldtimers: A biography, with recollections of early A.A. in the Midwest.* New York: Author.

Eickelberg, S. J., & Mayo-Smith, M. F. (1998). Management of sedative-hypnotic intoxication and withdrawal. In A. W. Graham, T. K. Schultz, & B. B. Wilford (Eds.), *Principles of addiction medicine* (2nd ed.). Chevy Chase, MD: American Society of Addiction Medicine.

Inaba, D. S., & Cohen, W. E. (2000). *Uppers, downers, all arounders* (4th ed.). Ashland, OR: CNS.

Schuckit, M. A. (1989) . *Drug and alcohol abuse: A clinical guide to diagnosis and treatment* (3rd ed.). New York: Plenum.

Seymour, R. B., & Smith, D. E. (1987). *Drugfree: A unique, positive approach to staying off alcohol and other drugs.* New York: Facts on File.

Seymour, R. B., & Smith, D. E. (1993). *The psychedelic resurgence: Treatment, support, and recovery options.* Center City, MN: Hazelden.

Smith, D. E., & Seymour, R. B. (In press). *Clinician's guide to substance abuse.* New York: McGraw-Hill.

Tyrer, P., Rutherford, D., & Hugett, T. (1981). Benzodiazepine withdrawal symptoms and propanolol. *Lancet, 1,* 520-522.

5

Medications

One Tool in the Toolbox

Douglas Ziedonis
Jonathan Krejci

There is an old saying to the effect that if your only tool is a hammer, the whole world will appear to be a nail. Recovery from addiction is a complex project that requires the use of a variety of tools. Although psychosocial treatments may be the more critical tools with which the foundation of addiction treatment is constructed, medications are becoming an increasingly important tool in the recovery process. Substance-related uses of medication include detoxification, managing protracted withdrawal symptoms and cravings, treating co-occurring psychiatric disorders, and harm reduction (e.g., methadone maintenance), where the emphasis is on reducing drug-related harm and engaging individuals in treatment. Other uses of medications include the comprehensive management of co-occurring medical problems (pneumonia, HIV, diabetes), including acute and chronic pain.

In recent years, the medication options available to you, the clinician, during the early phases of recovery are expanding for opiate, nicotine, and alcohol addiction, and many others have been developed for treating co-occurring mental illnesses. As with other scientific advances, there are risks and benefits to medications and specific issues to consider when you prescribe medications to your clients. When used appropriately, medications can help support recovery, but inappropriate use can result in misuse or dependence.

This chapter reviews how medications can be important tools for recovery. We emphasize throughout that they are but one tool among many and that treatment should include psychosocial alternatives as well. As with all tools, medications must be used wisely, and there are important issues to consider, including potential misuse, the meaning to your client of taking a pill during addiction recovery, and the relative safety of various medications. Psychosocial strategies to enhance medication compliance are important, including education, monitoring, Motivational Enhancement Therapy, and use of external supports (family, work, legal, etc.).

This is an exciting time to work in the field of addictions. The field is where the mental health field was 25 years ago with regard to integration of divergent treatment approaches. Providers in the mental health community often had strong positive or negative opinions about the use of medications, but few had given serious thought to judiciously blending medications with traditional treatment approaches. Today, blending medications and therapy in the treatment of mental illness is the norm. Similarly, controversy exists today in the addiction field about the proper role of medications, if any, in treating substance abuse clients. We discuss some of these concerns and controversies toward the end of this chapter.

You can play an important role in using medications in addiction treatment. Develop a realistic sense of how medications can be helpful at various stages of recovery, and be able to educate your clients about the pros and cons of using these medications. Working together with physicians, you can play a vital role in helping monitor changes in target symptoms, addressing appropriate use and compliance, and assessing side effects.

In the following pages, we consider in more detail some of the benefits and potential pitfalls of the use of medications in addiction treatment. First, we discuss their use at different stages of recovery, as well as with clients with co-occurring psychiatric disorders. Second, we present a crash course in the basics of psychopharmacology and the biology of the addicted brain. Third, we present specific medications and their applications, side effects, and potential, if any, for abuse. Finally, we detail the psychology of prescribing and taking medications and ways to motivate your clients to manage their medications responsibly.

⊞ WHEN TO CONSIDER MEDICATIONS

Deciding when to use a medication can be complex and depends on several factors. These include the stage of recovery, the severity and clarity of a coexisting psychiatric disorder, the client's motivation to change, and client and clinician preference. We discuss below one framework for thinking about stages of recovery and the proper role of medications in each. We also briefly discuss a concept that transcends the dimension of time but that often becomes apparent only after having worked with a client for a while: the treatment of co-occurring psychiatric disorders. There are several periods during recovery when medications might be useful, including detoxification (the first week or two of recovery) and protracted abstinence (the first 3 to 12 months). Medications may also be useful in the presence of co-occurring disorder or in the service of harm reduction.

Intoxication and Detoxification

When used in excess, all substances can cause intoxication. In cases of dramatic excess or sustained use, intoxication can produce medical or psychiatric symptoms requiring immediate medical attention. This is the case with cocaine and other stimulants, which can cause paranoia and other symptoms of psychosis. Similarly, extreme doses of marijuana and hallucinogenic drugs can cause anxiety or panic reactions in vulnerable users. Fortunately, in most instances medications can have a dramatic

---

BOX 5.1 **Specific Substances and Common Medications for Detoxification**

Substance	Medication
Nicotine	Nicotine replacement treatments
	Bupropion
Opiates	Methadone
	Buprenorphine
	Clonidine/benzodiazepines
	Clonidine/naltrexone/benzodiazepines
Alcohol	Benzodiazapines
	Barbiturates
Cocaine	None
Marijuana	None

---

positive effect on such symptoms. In these cases, medications are used only to treat the presenting symptoms and are discontinued when the period of acute intoxication has ended.

Acute detoxification comprises the first 1 to 2 weeks of abstinence, when clients are most likely to experience discomfort or even medical crises as a result of withdrawal. Each substance of abuse has a common withdrawal syndrome, each of which can have different symptoms and levels of severity, depending on the amount of substance use and other clinical characteristics of the individual. Although nonpharmacological detoxification is an option for some healthy individuals who are only mildly dependent, all clients should be evaluated for the appropriateness of medications during detoxification. A careful assessment for detoxification includes a medical evaluation, vital signs, and withdrawal symptom monitoring. This is true especially with alcohol, sedatives, heroin, opioids, and nicotine, where withdrawal symptoms, even when not medically dangerous, can provoke enough discomfort to lead clients to drop out of treatment (e.g., Rounsaville, 1995). Later, we discuss specific medications that have been shown to be effective in detoxification from these substances (Box 5.1). Detoxification can be conducted safely in either an inpatient or an outpatient setting, depending on medical and psychosocial factors (Barber & O'Brien, 1999).

Detoxification often requires the use of *agonists*: medications that mimic the substance on which the client is physically dependent (see Chapter 4 and the section "Basic Pharmacology" later in this chapter). Two primary examples of this use of medications in addiction treatment are the *benzodiazepines* and *methadone*. Use of agonist-type medications for relatively short periods is entirely appropriate and does not result in physical tolerance.

Benzodiazepines are a class of psychiatric medications that include Valium, Librium, Xanax, and Klonopin. Classified as *anxiolytics*, they are prescribed in mental health settings for anxiety disorders. Because their effects are similar to those of alcohol, they are a double-edged tool. The benzodiazepines have high abuse potential and can induce physiological dependence if used for an extended period (Brady, Myrick, & Malcolm, 1999). For these reasons, they should be used with extreme caution with substance abuse clients who are in nonmethadone maintenance treatment programs. However, these medications are also extremely effective in managing symptoms of

BOX 5.2	**Medications for Protracted Withdrawal Phase**
Substance	*Medication*
Nicotine	Nicotine replacement therapies: patch, spray, gum, and inhaler[a] Bupropion,[a] nortriptyline
Opiates	Naltrexone[a] (Trexan)
Alcohol	Naltrexone[a] (Revia) Disulfiram (Antabuse)[a] Acamprosate
Cocaine or marijuana	None are FDA approved; some clinicians use desipramine, amantadine, or Antabuse

a. FDA approved.

withdrawal and can be vital in preventing the onset of delirium tremens among severely dependent alcoholics (Barber & O'Brien, 1999).

Methadone is an opioid agonist that can be used in heroin detoxification. It provides significant opiate blockade with minimal euphoric or sedative effects. Alternative detoxification strategies are available, including clonidine (an antihypertensive medication), a benzodiazepine, or buprenorphine. Buprenorphine, a partial opiate agonist with high receptor affinity, appears very promising as a detoxification agent, with initial studies indicating that it is both safe and well tolerated (Bickel & Amass, 1995). A study currently underway in our laboratory is investigating the comparative effectiveness of buprenorphine and clonidine for opiate detoxification.

Protracted Withdrawal/Cravings

Depending on the substance, for up to 12 months after the acute phase of withdrawal some clients may experience some symptoms of protracted withdrawal, covering a wide range in terms of intensity and duration. Symptoms you may notice include difficulty sleeping, irritability, mood instability, anxiety, depression, restlessness, problems with concentration, general malaise, and cravings (Jaffe, Knapp, & Ciraulo, 1997). Medications used during this phase may be specific to the substance of abuse or may target more generally the dependence syndrome. Medications for protracted abstinence are typically used for 3 to 12 months, with the duration depending on several clinical factors. These include severity of symptoms, progress in recovery, and leverage from external sources such as the client's employer, family, and the legal system. Medications in this category typically are specifically chosen for their inability to cause physical dependence (Box 5.2).

Medications can work in different ways to reduce protracted abstinence. For example, naltrexone was initially developed to treat opioid dependence. Naltrexone blocks the opiate receptor and prevents the client from feeling the effects of heroin (Tucker & Ritter, 2000). It has also been found to help reduce cravings in alcohol-dependent clients through the interaction of the opioid system and the dopamine reward pathway (see our discussion below).

Using these medications will require philosophical open-mindedness on your part. Some agencies and programs will not use medications in this category on principle. Their objections generally stem from the common misconception that any medication can produce dependence or euphoria. Interestingly, there seems to be less resistance to their use with clients of higher socioeconomic status, and some of these medications are routinely used to help professionals in the first year of recovery. It is common practice in many settings for nurses, physicians, and dentists dependent on opioids to be prescribed naltrexone (Rounsaville, 1995). This appears to be based on the assumption that professional groups can apply pressure on the client to be compliant. Although this is true, other sources of pressure, including social, legal, and family systems, can be equally powerful forms of external motivation for street addicts. We question the legitimacy of the assumption that only the threat of losing one's professional career can induce compliance and wonder whether it instead reflects stigma or a historically determined difference in treatment program cultures.

In reviewing treatment options with a client, the use of a medication should be presented as an option rather than a mandate. An initially reluctant client who relapses may choose to add a medication and/or increase the intensity of the psychosocial treatment. It is also important to consider the psychology of medications and the subjective meaning to the client of taking a drug to recover from addiction. We always inquire into the hopes, fears, and expectations that clients harbor about medications. We also find the following phrases and metaphors useful in our discussions with clients:

- *Medications are not magic bullets* and are only one tool in the toolbox. Clients are accustomed to addressing complex problems with simple answers and to viewing pills as the ideal solution to a variety of problems. It is vital that the prescribing professional emphasize the importance of individual effort and multiple forms of treatment in recovery.

- *Recovery takes time.* Clients typically have little ability or willingness to delay gratification and tend to "want what they want when they want it." Without considerable support and education, they are prone to lose patience with medications that may take 3 weeks or more to have an effect.

- *Your bazooka versus my peashooter.* Clients often want the best of both worlds: the emotional stability or symptomatic relief provided by a medication *and* the euphoria found in illicit drugs. It is important to realize that the positive effects of a medication can be easily overwhelmed by simultaneously misuse of other substances.

- *The orthopedic cast analogy.* For clients committed to abstinence, the idea of reliance upon a medication may seem distasteful or even frightening. We find it useful to draw an analogy between the harm caused by addiction and a broken limb: Both require outside support and protection while healing occurs from within.

Like any other technological advance, medications can be misused. Some of your clients may "play physician" and change dosages and even medications on their own. Sometimes they will double their dosage on a "bad day" and skip their medications on a "good" day. They may have multiple physicians, each of whom is unaware of the others, or use multiple pharmacies, including Internet pharmacies and mail order. We consider these instances of relapse to addiction that must be addressed in treatment. Sometimes we are fooled in the short term by more clever clients, some of whom may be nurses, physicians, or just knowledgeable junior psychopharmacologists with their *Physician Desk Reference* (*PDR*) and stash of multiple medications. As a rule of thumb, anything your clients do with their medication in secrecy—without physician, clinician, or family member input—is a clue to misuse.

Co-Occurring Disorders

Co-occurring psychiatric disorders are common among individuals seeking substance abuse treatment, and substance use disorders are very common among individuals seeking psychiatric treatment. Studies suggest that between 25% and 75% of clients in substance abuse settings have a current or past non-substance-use psychiatric disorder. The most common types of psychiatric disorders you will see are depression, anxiety, and personality disorders. Anxiety disorders include social phobia, panic, posttraumatic stress, and generalized anxiety disorder. Eating and impulse control problems/disorders are also not uncommon.

The use of medications in promoting dual recovery for co-occurring addiction and mental illness can be crucial but is also extremely complex and not without controversy. Chronic use of drugs and alcohol can lead to depression, anxiety, and even psychotic symptoms such as hallucinations and paranoia. When these symptoms are truly substance-induced, they will typically disappear within the first month of treatment without any specialized interventions (Beeder & Millman, 1997). As a result, many in the substance abuse treatment community have assumed in good faith that high-quality addiction counseling will treat both the addiction and any related psychiatric problems. Although this is often the case, research increasingly is demonstrating that a significant percentage of those presenting for substance abuse treatment also have more enduring, recurrent, and serious psychiatric symptoms (Regier et al., 1990). It can be difficult to distinguish between transient, substance-related symptoms and psychiatric symptoms in need of more intensive treatment.

We find it useful to create a time line that graphically depicts the course of both the client's substance abuse and his or her emotional problems. Significant periods of abstinence, as well as periods of emotional instability, should be noted. Also important is information obtained from prior treatment records and stable family members. Indicators of an underlying psychiatric disorder to look for include

- Significant psychiatric symptoms prior to the onset of substance abuse
- Significant psychiatric symptoms during prolonged periods of abstinence (3 months or more)
- A history of multiple, brief psychiatric hospitalizations during which the psychiatric symptoms resolved quickly

We adopt a harm reduction philosophy that suggests that, in the absence of any strong contraindications, it is generally advisable to choose the treatment that the client finds most acceptable. In a psychiatric setting, clients are likely to have less motivation to comply with abstinence-based substance abuse treatment. In such cases, it may be advisable to begin a nonsedating medication with low abuse potential that does not interact with the primary substance of abuse. There is little danger to such a strategy, and refusing treatment will usually lead to unnecessary power struggles, damaged rapport, treatment dropout, and client demoralization. Similarly, in an addiction treatment setting,

---

BOX 5.3	**Medications Commonly Used to Treat Psychiatric Disorders in Addiction Treatment Settings**

Disorder	*Lower Abuse Potential*	*Higher Abuse Potential*
Generalized anxiety disorder	Buspirone (Buspar), SSRIs,[a] nefazadone	Benzodiazepine
Panic disorder	SSRIs[a]	Benzodiazepine
Posttraumatic stress disorder	SSRIs[a]	Benzodiazepine
Phobias	SSRIs[a]	Benzodiazepine
Attention deficit disorder	Bupropion, desipramine	Amphetamines
Depression disorders	Antidepressants (SSRIs,[a] nefazadone, bupropion, etc.)	MAO inhibitors
Psychotic disorders	Typical and atypical antipsychotics	Side effect medication such as anticholinergic medications

a. SSRIs: Prozac, Paxil, Zoloft, Celexa.

---

clients are likely to have greater awareness and motivation to address their substance abuse problem. Complaints of sleep disruption are common, and if you suspect an underlying depression, a more sedating antidepressant may serve to treat both problems simultaneously.

In psychiatric settings, clients may be less motivated to address their substance abuse, and it is often advisable to begin treatment with a medication to treat their psychiatric problem. It is generally advisable to use nonsedating medications and to avoid medications that interact with the primary substance of abuse (e.g., MAO inhibitors and cocaine). Many physicians refuse to treat psychiatric problems with medications unless the client is simultaneously willing to address his or her substance abuse. Although this approach may be effective in some instances, we recommend a more flexible approach. The potential for harm is minimal with a nonsedating medication with low abuse potential, and the probability of treatment engagement is greatly enhanced. Furthermore, it is always possible to renegotiate the treatment contract or to consider a referral if the client is not improving in 6 months.

Addiction treatment settings are likely to include more patients at higher motivational levels who endorse the goal of complete abstinence. In higher levels of care (e.g., partial hospitalization and intensive outpatient programs), a more aggressive treatment approach is advisable, especially in response to agitated depression or severe insomnia. In these cases, we suggest considering either a more sedating antidepressant (e.g., nefazadone or mirtazapine) because successfully treating these complaints will maximize the probability of achieving sustained abstinence (Box 5.3).

Harm Reduction/Maintenance/Agonist Substitution

Maintenance medications may be prescribed at any time during treatment but often are continued for 1 year or more. Maintenance medications typically have effects that are similar to, but less intense than, the effects of the substance of abuse and that consequently produce less behavioral disruption while minimizing the harm associated

BOX 5.4	Harm Reduction/Maintenance Medications
Substance	*Medication*
Nicotine	Nicotine replacement treatment
Opiates/Heroin	MethadoneLAAMBuprenorphine
Alcohol	Benzodiazepines
Cocaine	Methylphenidate

with more typical ways of administering the drug. As discussed below, nicotine replacement medications enable smokers to obtain maintenance doses of nicotine without the harmful tars and gases found in cigarette smoke (Sweanor, 2000). Similarly, methadone acts on the same sites in the brain as heroin but without producing the euphoria or clouding of judgment. Also, as a legal drug, methadone helps the addict to extricate him- or herself from the street life (Lowinson et al., 1997) (Box 5.4).

☷ THE RIGHT TOOL FOR THE RIGHT JOB: MATCHING MEDICATIONS WITH SUBSTANCES OF ABUSE

Basic Psychopharmacology

The understanding of the brain is the final frontier of medical science. Neuroscientists have developed an understanding of the neurobiology of addiction at a microscopic level far greater than that achieved through standard imaging techniques. Our understanding of neurobiology has gone beyond the level of neurotransmitters and brain receptors, although these two concepts continue to drive our approach to treatment and our classification schemes. Through various complex mechanisms, all psychoactive drugs, legal and illegal, affect thoughts, feelings, and behaviors eventually at the level of *neurotransmitters*, the chemical messengers that enable brain cells, or *neurons*, to communicate. Neurotransmitters exist in many different sizes and shapes, and relatively small differences in structure can profoundly alter their effect. Much as a key fits only one lock, each neurotransmitter has a unique chemical profile that is compatible only with its unique *receptor* type on the receiving cell. Neuroscientists have identified over 50 different neurotransmitters, many of which have several different subtypes. With up to 100 billion neurons in the brain, each of which may have up to 10,000 connections with other neurons, it becomes obvious that the brain is a structure of fantastic complexity. To further complicate matters, drugs can affect neurotransmitters differently depending on where in the brain the neurons are located. A single drug can also affect more than one neurotransmitter simultaneously. Thus, it is difficult to make simple statements about the effects of drug use on the brain. We refer you to a clear and comprehensive primer on the neurobiology of addiction by Roberts and Koob (1997).

Drugs can affect neurotransmission in a variety of ways. Specifically, drugs can

- Increase or decrease the production of a neurotransmitter.
- Block the effect of a neurotransmitter by occupying its receptor site. Such drugs are known as *antagonists.*
- Mimic the effect of a neurotransmitter by occupying its receptor site. These drugs are known as *agonists* and *partial agonists.*
- Increase or decrease the length of time that a neurotransmitter spends in the *synapse,* or space between the transmitting cell and the receptor site.

In addition, scientists have begun to identify the neurotransmitters most relevant to psychoactive drugs. A few of these are

- *Norepinephrine*—Plays a key role in arousal and mood. Stimulants, such as cocaine and amphetamines, tend to accentuate the effects of norepinephrine.
- *Serotonin*—Implicated in sleep, depression, pain sensitivity, aggression, and suicidality. Impulsivity has been linked with low levels of serotonin. Alcohol and the hallucinogens may affect behavior largely through serotonin.
- *GABA (Gamma-Aminobutyric Acid)*—Tends to produce relaxation and behavioral inhibition. Alcohol and the benzodiazepines (Valium, Xanax) both affect GABA.
- *Dopamine*—Associated with pleasure, reward, and goal-directed behavior.

Dopamine has generated particular interest, as it is believed to be critical to *brain reward* mechanisms. Research has revealed that virtually all drugs of abuse, including nicotine, increase the production of dopamine in structures in the center of the brain called the *nucleus accumbens* and the *ventral tegmentum* (Gardner, 1997). This is a particularly exciting finding given the wide range of chemical structures and receptor sites; it suggests that these regions of the brain act as a final common pathway for the rewarding properties of drug abuse. As we discuss later, this can have profound implications for the development of medications designed to reduce cravings for substances.

Medications for Treating Substance Abuse

Medications, like drugs of abuse, alter neurotransmission through many known and unknown mechanisms. Though not an exhaustive list, the following discussion highlights some specific medications you may consider in treating substance dependence.

Alcohol

Disulfiram (Antabuse) interferes with the body's ability to metabolize acetaldehyde, a by-product of the metabolism of alcohol, with the result that drinking results in nausea, extreme flushing, and decreased blood pressure. This reaction is experienced as extremely unpleasant and can serve as an effective deterrent to drinking. Unfortunately, Antabuse must be taken daily, and its effects disappear within days of its discontinuation, so its effectiveness is dependent on the client's remaining consistently compliant with treatment. Nonetheless, with appropriate motivation, which can be enhanced by including a significant other in treatment, Antabuse can be an effective "safety valve" for the chronically relapsing alcoholic (Allen & Litten, 1992).

Naltrexone (Revia) is Food and Drug Administration (FDA) approved in the treatment of both heroin/opioid dependence and alcohol dependence. It acts by blocking the action of opiate receptors, which affect other neurotransmitters and neurons. Naltrexone was originally developed as a treatment for dependence on heroin and other opiates (Rounsaville, 1995). Because research demonstrated that alcohol also stimulates opiate receptors, researchers became interested in its effects as an anticraving medication. Several studies have demonstrated that naltrexone can be effective in reducing the frequency and intensity of relapses, as well as the pleasure obtained from drinking. Like Antabuse, naltrexone requires compliance with a daily dosing schedule. However, unlike Antabuse, it has few to no side effects or potential medical complications (Swift, 1999).

Nalmefene is similar to naltrexone in that it blocks opiate receptors. It has been shown to be safer than naltrexone and also effective in preventing relapse (Garbutt, West, Carey, Lohr, & Crews, 1999; Mason, Salvato, Williams, Ritvo, & Cutler, 1999).

Acamprosate is already used in Europe and is currently being evaluated in research studies in the United States. Acamprosate appears to work by blocking glutamate, a neurotransmitter that may contribute to alcohol's effects (Johnson & Ait-Daoud, 1999). One large-scale study involving more than 3,000 alcoholics found that twice as many clients remained abstinent after being treated with acamprosate than with placebo (Swift, 1999).

Cocaine and Marijuana

At present, no medications are FDA approved specifically for the treatment of cocaine or marijuana abuse and dependence. Furthermore, because cocaine and marijuana withdrawal symptoms are not as acute or dangerous as those associated with alcohol or the opiates, medications are rarely required to manage the detoxification period. Despite considerable research and some promising initial findings (e.g., Ziedonis & Kosten, 1991), no medications have yet demonstrated unequivocal effectiveness in cocaine treatment (Barber & O'Brien, 1999). Medications may be very helpful in the treatment of co-occurring mental illness and either cocaine or marijuana dependence.

Our understanding of the neurobiology of cocaine addiction has focused on the depletion of dopamine with chronic cocaine usage. The serotonin system and other neurotransmitters are affected, but most medications studied by researchers have been selected because of their impact on the dopamine system. For example, bromocriptine and amantadine are dopamine agonists and are used in treating parkinsonism, which also results in a dopamine depletion state. These medications have not consistently been shown to be effective in studies, but amantadine is used by some addiction-ologists. Another approach has been to use antidepressants that block dopamine reuptake from the gap between neurons, which in principle would serve to increase dopamine between the neurons. Desipramine was one such antidepressant that exhibited some initial promise but no consistent proven efficacy. However, there is some evidence that antidepressant medications may help to reduce both depressive symptoms and cocaine use among depressed cocaine abusers (Carroll et al., 1994).

Another category of medications tested has been mood stabilizers such as *carbemazepine (Tegretol), valproic acid, neurontin,* and *lithium*. Even amphetamines such as *methylphenidate (Ritalin)* have been evaluated. Amphetamines can be used in the treatment of attention deficit disorder and narcolepsy, a rare but serious sleep disorder. Initial enthusiasm was based on the belief that, by analogy with methadone in the treatment of opiate addiction, Ritalin would prove to be a longer lasting agonist maintenance medication with a lower potential for abuse. Some studies suggested that methylphenidate reduces cocaine cravings, but as a stimulant with high abuse potential it has little usefulness in treating cocaine users (Barber & O'Brien, 1999).

Opiates

Some of the most effective and promising medication approaches are those developed for treating dependence on heroin and other opiates. At present, four treatment alternatives exist: methadone, LAAM, buprenorphine, and naltrexone.

Methadone. The first drug dependence maintenance medication, methadone has been in use in this country for over 30 years. As an opiate agonist, methadone stimulates the same receptor sites as heroin, but it has a longer duration and a far less intense euphoria. As a result, it acts to both attenuate cravings and to reduce the reward potential of other opiates. Methadone produces a profound physical dependence but little euphoria and thus is associated with minimal abuse and behavioral disruption. Methadone has been the source of enormous controversy. Traditional substance abuse workers often have been resistant to methadone, characterizing its use as the substitution of one addiction for another. Others have pointed to the disruptive effect of a dosing schedule that necessitates daily trips to clinics that are often located in impoverished and drug-infested neighborhoods. Nonetheless, research has conclusively demonstrated methadone to be arguably the most effective drug addiction treatment strategy in existence (Herman & Appel, 1993). Study after study has shown that clients maintained on methadone commit fewer crimes, abuse fewer substances, and contract fewer infectious diseases than those who receive no treatment, and that adequate dose is strongly related to treatment retention and outcome (Herman & Appel, 1993). In addition, methadone has a lower dropout rate than most other forms of drug treatment, thus allowing the benefits of treatment to reach more clients. Although we respect the concerns of those who adhere to a strict abstinence model, we urge you to keep an open mind with regard to this highly effective treatment alternative.

Levo-Alpha-Acetomethadol (LAAM; ORLAAM). Approved for use by the FDA in 1993, LAAM, like methadone, is another long-acting opiate agonist. However, because of its longer duration of action, LAAM treatment requires only three dosing visits per week rather than the six or seven needed with methadone. Also, because of its slow onset and more sustained action, a milder, more consistent drug effect is produced. Unfortunately, the treatment community has been slow to embrace LAAM, and only 1% to 2% of opiate-maintained clients receive this medication (Rawson, Hasson, Huber, McCann, & Ling, 1998).

Buprenorphine (Temgesic, Subutex). Unlike LAAM and methadone, buprenorphine is a long-acting opiate *partial agonist*. As such, it occupies receptor sites fully and quickly but reaches maximal effectiveness quite quickly. As a result, it reduces cravings and blocks euphoria almost completely, while having little potential for abuse or overdose. Because of its long duration of action, clinic visits may be required no more than two times per week. Buprenorphine is currently in the final stages of the FDA approval process (Bickel & Amass, 1995).

Naltrexone. As noted previously, naltrexone is an opiate antagonist originally developed for treatment of opiate dependence. Naltrexone is a relatively safe medication, but many physicians have not been trained to use it in treating heroin addiction. Without integrating psychosocial strategies to enhance compliance, a major drawback to naltrexone is an extremely high treatment dropout rate. Currently, studies are evaluating a long-lasting form of naltrexone that is effective for up to 1 month. Unlike methadone, LAAM, and buprenorphine, maintenance on naltrexone requires the client to be opiate-free for at least 7 to 14 days in order to avoid precipitating withdrawal symptoms. For all these reasons, naltrexone is not widely used in opiate treatment and may be most effective for those with relatively high levels of functioning and motivation (Rounsaville, 1995).

Nicotine

Medications are very important in the treatment of nicotine dependence. There are many options, including four types of nicotine replacement medications and a non-nicotine pill (buproprion). Unfortunately, the substance abuse treatment community has been slow to recognize the implications of the overlap between nicotine dependence and other forms of substance abuse, and only recently has it begun to give consideration to simultaneous treatment of smoking and other addictions (Hurt, Eberman, Slade, & Karan, 1993). There has even been a reluctance to emphasize the importance of addressing tobacco dependence later in recovery from alcohol or other drug dependence. Tobacco dependence is the primary cause of death among substance abusers who are otherwise doing well in recovery. In addition, ongoing tobacco dependence predicts greater problem severity and poorer treatment response for alcohol or other drug dependence (Roll, Higgins, Budney, Bickel, & Badger, 1996; Stuyt, 1997). We strongly encourage you to become more aware of the dangers of smoking, to help your clients learn about treatment options and the importance of addressing tobacco use, and to learn about the variety of psychosocial and medication treatment options for nicotine dependence.

Only about 3% of smokers who try to quit on their own will be successful each year. With a brief motivational and educational intervention, the success rate increases to about 10%. The use of either medications or behavioral therapy will double that success rate to about 20%, and the integration of both medications and intensive psychosocial treatment will increase the success rate to about 35% to 40% per year. In contrast to other chemical addictions, most clients will prefer to use just medications in the treatment of nicotine dependence. Although medications are an important tool to address the physical acute and protracted withdrawal symptoms, behavioral therapies are also critically important and underused tools.

Research has demonstrated that the vast majority of harm associated with cigarettes is attributable to the byproducts of smoking rather than to the effects of nicotine (Slade, 1999). Consequently, by analogy with methadone and other agonists, medications have been developed to deliver steady doses of nicotine directly into the bloodstream. Each has been shown to approximately double the probability of a successful quit attempt (Fiore et al., 2000). For a more thorough summary of medication treatments for nicotine dependence, see the various nicotine treatment guidelines published (Ziedonis, Wyatt, & George, 1998).

There are four routes of nicotine administration:

1. *Patch*—The nicotine transdermal patch allows for steady absorption of nicotine through the skin. However, its onset is slow, and nicotine blood levels associated

with smoking are rarely reached. The patch is available in a variety of doses, and higher doses are likely to be more effective with heavily dependent smokers. Side effects include skin irritation at the patch site and minor sleep disruption, but these tend to be minor and transient. Both prescription and over-the-counter versions are available.

2. *Gum*—Nicotine polacrilex gum was the first nicotine replacement therapy. Due to its short duration of action, it effectively replicates the effects of smoked nicotine and must be used approximately hourly. For these reasons, it is quite effective in reducing nicotine cravings but is inconvenient to administer. Side effects include irritation in the mouth, throat, and stomach; nausea; and indigestion.

3. *Spray*—The nicotine nasal spray is available by prescription only. Like nicotine gum, it has a quick onset and effectively replicates the psychoactive effects of smoked nicotine. Side effects include nose and throat irritation, although these are usually transient.

4. *Inhaler*—With this device, nicotine is delivered through a mouthpiece soaked with nicotine. Considerable effort is required to maintain tolerable blood levels, and maximal blood levels are generally lower than those obtained through nicotine gum and spray. Like the nicotine spray, the inhaler is available by prescription only.

In addition to nicotine replacement, there is a non-nicotine pill medication that is now FDA approved. Originally marketed as an antidepressant medication under the name Wellbutrin, *buproprion (Zyban)* has more recently become the only FDA-approved non-nicotine replacement medication for nicotine dependence. Although its mechanism of action is unclear, it has repeatedly been to shown to be effective in increasing quit rates. Possible side effects include dry mouth, insomnia, nausea, and skin rash. As an antidepressant medication, it is available only by prescription, but it has no potential for abuse or dependence. Zyban may be particularly recommended for smokers with a history of depression. Recent studies suggest that nortriptyline may also be an effective non-nicotine medication (Ziedonis et al., 1998).

Tools of the Future: Agents to Intercept and Destroy Substances in the Body

New medication development research supported by the National Institute on Drug Abuse to target cocaine addiction has become increasingly futuristic. Researchers are developing antibodies that would act to neutralize substances by breaking them down in the bloodstream or otherwise rendering them unable to enter the brain. Though currently based on animal studies, preliminary evidence suggests that these treatments may soon be feasible in humans as well. In addition, they could offer several advantages over currently available medications, as they do not require a complete understanding of how or where the abused drug acts in the brain and thus would be effective against drugs that affect several neurotransmitters simultaneously.

These medications can be divided into three categories: peripheral blockers, naturally occurring enzymes, and antibodies. *Peripheral blockers* are similar to enzymes and antibodies of the immune system. One peripheral blocker approach would bind drugs like cocaine or nicotine to antibodies, thus creating a drug-antibody complex too large to pass through blood vessels into the brain. This would trap the drug until it could be eliminated from the body through normal metabolism. A second approach would increase the rate at which *naturally occurring enzymes* break down drug molecules into inactive by-products. A third strategy would use *antibodies* that both bind to and break down drugs. This research program is generating considerable excitement in the scientific community. However, it should be remembered that it is still in its infancy and that the possibility exists that addicts would be able to overwhelm the action of these peripheral blockades simply by taking more of the drug. For a summary of this exciting new line of research, see National Institute on Drug Abuse (2000).

Alternative Medicine

Motivated both by curiosity and by dissatisfaction with traditional models of health care, Americans are turning in growing numbers to alternative forms of treatment. Touted as natural alternatives to harsh, synthetic, mass-produced chemicals, a variety of herbs, vitamins, and amino acids are available for the treatment of a wide range of ailments. Among those frequently cited as effective in the treatment of addictions are vitamins B and C, potassium, milk thistle, ginkgo biloba, ginseng, valerian root, and kava (Ross, 1998). With the recent establishment of the Office of Alternative Medicine, it is possible that some of these will turn out to be valuable adjuncts to addiction treatment, but none have yet been shown to be effective.

In the meantime, we urge caution. First, very few of these substances have been subjected to scientific study, and often the evidence for their effectiveness lies entirely in anecdotes or ancient traditional beliefs. Such evidence, though suggestive, is far from compelling, as the history of medicine is rife with examples of ineffective or dangerous treatments that were fervently endorsed by their advocates. Second, natural alternatives are not subjected to FDA regulation, and little is known about potential harmful effects. It should be remembered that the majority of poisons occur in nature and that many mass-produced medications are simply pure derivatives of naturally occurring substances. Third, because of the absence of FDA oversight, there is no guarantee that these products contain the ingredients or the quantities listed on the label. In fact, studies with St. John's wort and other natural remedies have found that fewer than half of the products offered contained the active ingredients in the concentrations claimed by the manufacturers.

⊞ INTEGRATING MEDICATIONS INTO TREATMENT: OBSTACLES AND STRATEGIES

Obstacles to Integration

Both reasonable and unjustified concerns have led some counselors and clients attending 12-step programs to oppose including medications in the recovery toolbox. Twelve-step programs have emphasized the importance of correcting personality defects, mending damaged relationships, and cultivating a spiritual life. Traditionally, the counselor's role has been to help clients to make amends to those they have harmed, to develop a personal program of recovery that will begin to address underlying problems with emotional instability and personality, and to develop faith, humility, and a personal relationship with a higher power. Toward that end, most treatment programs have emphasized the importance of abstinence from all mood-altering substances. Emphasizing the futility of attempting controlled use of drugs and alcohol, therapists and 12-step members have exhorted the newcomer to be extremely vigilant regarding the use of medications with any effects on mood, thought, and behavior.

As a result, some treatment providers and 12-step "old-timers" alike have been reluctant to work with clients maintained on psychiatric medications. Many programs require detoxification from all potentially mood-altering chemicals before beginning substance abuse treatment, and more than one vulnerable addict in early recovery has been driven from 12-step programs by the well-meaning "old-timer" who sees the newcomer's reliance on a psychiatric medication as just more evidence for the insidious nature of addiction.

However, 12-step principles often differ substantially from the beliefs of individuals attending meetings. In fact, Alcoholics Anonymous (AA) literature explicitly endorses the use of psychiatric medications where appropriate. *The AA Member: Medications and Other Drugs* (Alcoholics Anonymous, 1984) is an invaluable guide written by a group of physician AA members that supports the appropriate use of medications during recovery. We recommend that you read and distribute it to your clients. It states,

> Because of the difficulties that many alcoholics have with drugs, some members have taken the position that no one in AA should take any medication. While this position has undoubtedly prevented relapse for some, it has meant disaster for others. . . . It becomes clear that just as it is wrong to enable or support any alcoholic to become readdicted to any drug, it's equally wrong to deprive any alcoholic of medication which can alleviate or control other disabling physical and/or emotional problems.

It seems that the use of medications in substance abuse treatment is not contradicted by 12-step principles. It is also true that, with the logarithmic increase in knowledge in genetics, pharmacology, and molecular biology, our understanding of a variety of disorders is being radically transformed. Most treatment researchers now understand addiction as a complex disorder that is caused and affected by biological, psychological, social, and spiritual factors, and they recognize that treatment may address each of these factors through a variety of approaches, including counseling and medications.

First, a veritable explosion of studies in the areas of pharmacology and neuroscience has begun to identify the biological and genetic underpinnings of addictive behaviors. With each passing day, the enzymes, neurotransmitters, and chromosomes implicated in addictive disorders are being pinpointed with startling accuracy. Substances of abuse can change the functioning and structure of brain cells and even the DNA of cells (Nestler, 1997). Our understanding of how the brain is affected and changed by chronic and acute substance usage is improving, aided by techniques that graphically demonstrate differences in the brain functioning on MRI and PET scans between chronic users and nonusers. Similarly, although excessive use of drugs and alcohol may stem in part from character defects and disturbed relationships, these increasingly are believed to be partially rooted in neurological and biological structures (McGue, 1997). Second, clinical research is demonstrating very high rates of drug and alcohol abuse among those seeking treatment for psychiatric disorders and high rates of psychiatric disorders among those seeking treatment for addictions (Regier et al., 1990). At the same time, safe and effective medications are being developed for the treatment of these disorders and increasingly are being incorporated into standard mental health treatment. Third, research has identified medications specific to addiction treatment that are safe and effective and, in many instances, have little to no potential for abuse or dependence.

For these reasons, we believe that humane and thoughtful treatment of addictive behaviors requires a willingness to integrate the judicious use of medications into a comprehensive treatment plan. We advocate a biopsychosocial-spiritual model that acknowledges the multifaceted nature of addiction and behavior change and emphasizes flexibility in treating a variety of symptoms through several different modalities. We also believe strongly that for some clients, encountering a clinician who is knowledgeable and open-minded about the proper role of medications in addictions treatment can mean the difference between recovery and relapse.

No tool can fix everything. We acknowledge that medication treatment, like any intervention, is imperfect. Sometimes the dosage is too low or too high, or there is a problem with compliance and treatment adherence. Other impediments to treatment include establishing an incorrect diagnosis, selecting the wrong medication, and overlooking medical, psychiatric, or substance abuse comorbidity. Some medications have a high potential for abuse and should be used with extreme caution. We also acknowledge that some addicts, deprived of the sensations they so desperately crave, will resort to manipulations and chicanery to obtain legitimate drugs under false pretenses. We simply seek to strike a middle ground between rigidity and naïveté and to maintain an open mind toward the judicious use of medications in conjunction with psychosocial treatments.

Strategies for Integration

You have a crucial role to play in the integration of medications into substance abuse treatment. For many clients, you are the first person with whom they will discuss their thoughts, feelings, and concerns about medications. We suggest the following guidelines for navigating this topic with clients.

For clients considering taking a medication,

- DO keep an open mind about medications.
- DO listen to the client's hopes and expectations about using a medication.
- DO listen to the client's fears and misconceptions about a medication.
- DON'T try to answer medical questions unless you are absolutely certain of the answers. Offer to refer to or consult with a medical professional.

For clients already taking a medication,

- DO ask about medication use and compliance at every visit. Ask in a genuinely curious and nonjudgmental manner. Discuss any obstacles to full compliance.
- DO ask about mixed feeling about taking medication. These can be related to side effects, to concerns about not being truly abstinent, or to difficulties in accepting the need for a medication (especially with psychiatric medications).
- DO be sensitive to criticism the client may receive in 12-step groups.
- DO maintain communication with the prescribing psychiatrist.
- DON'T take at face value clients' reports that the medication "isn't working." Make sure to ask in detail whether they are using their medication exactly as prescribed.

REFERENCES ▦

Alcoholics Anonymous. (1984). *The AA member: Medications and other drugs.* New York: Author.

Allen, J. P., & Litten, R. Z. (1992). Techniques to enhance compliance with disulfiram. *Alcoholism: Clinical and Experimental Research, 16,* 1035-1041.

Barber, W. S., & O'Brien, C. P. (1999). Pharmacotherapies. In B. S. McCrady & E. E. Epstein (Eds.), *Addictions: A comprehensive guidebook.* New York: Oxford University Press.

Beeder, A. B., & Millman, R. B. (1997). Patients with psychopathology. In J. H. Lowinson, P. Ruiz, R. B. Millman, & J. G. Langrod (Eds.), *Substance abuse: A comprehensive textbook* (3rd ed.). Baltimore: Williams & Wilkins.

Bickel, W. K., & Amass, L. (1995). Buprenorphine treatment of opioid dependence: A review. *Experimental and Clinical Psychopharmacology, 3,* 477-489.

Brady, K. T., Myrick, H., & Malcolm, R. (1999). Sedative-hypnotic and anxiolytic agents. In B. S. McCrady & E. E. Epstein (Eds.), *Addictions: A comprehensive guidebook.* New York: Oxford University Press.

Carroll, K. M., Rounsaville, B. J., Gordon, L. T., Nich, C., Jatlow, P. M., Bisighini, R. M., & Gawin, F. H. (1994). Psychotherapy and pharmacotherapy for ambulatory cocaine abusers. *Archives of General Psychiatry, 51,* 177-187.

Fiore, M. C., Bailey, W. C., Cohen, S. J., et al. (2000). *Treating tobacco use and dependence* (Clinical Practice Guideline). Rockville, MD: U.S. Department of Health and Human Services, Public Health Service.

Garbutt, J. C., West, S., Carey, T. S., Lohr, K. N., & Crews, F. T. (1999). Pharmacological treatment of alcohol dependence: A review of the evidence. *Journal of the American Medical Association, 281,* 1318-1325.

Gardner, E. L. (1997). Brain reward mechanisms. In J. H. Lowinson, P. Ruiz, R. B. Millman, & J. G. Langrod (Eds.), *Substance abuse: A comprehensive textbook* (3rd ed.). Baltimore: Williams & Wilkins.

Herman, J., & Appel, P. (1993). Historical perspectives and public health issues. In Center for Substance Abuse Treatment, *State methadone treatment guidelines.* Rockville, MD: Substance Abuse and Mental Health Services Administration.

Hurt, R. D., Eberman, K. M., Slade, J., & Karan, L. (1993). Treating nicotine addiction in patients with other addictive disorders. In C. T. Orleans & J. Slade (Eds.), *Nicotine addiction: Principles and management.* New York: Oxford University Press.

Jaffe, J. H., Knapp, C. M., & Ciraulo, D. A. (1997). Opiates: Clinical aspects. In J. H. Lowinson, P. Ruiz, R. B. Millman, & J. G. Langrod (Eds.), *Substance abuse: A comprehensive textbook* (3rd ed.). Baltimore: Williams & Wilkins.

Johnson, B. A., & Ait-Daoud, N. (1999). Medications to treat alcoholism. *Alcohol Research and Health, 23,* 99-106.

Lowinson, J. H., Payte, J. T., Salsitz, E., Joseph, H., Marion, I. J., & Dole, V. P. (1997). Methadone maintenance. In J. H. Lowinson, P. Ruiz, R. B. Millman, & J. G. Langrod (Eds.), *Substance abuse: A comprehensive textbook* (3rd ed.). Baltimore: Williams & Wilkins.

Mason, B. J., Salvato, F. R., Williams, L. D., Ritvo, E. C., & Cutler, R. B. (1999). A double-blind, placebo-controlled study of oral nalmefene for alcohol dependence. *Archives of General Psychiatry, 56,* 719-724.

McGue, M. (1997). A behavioral-genetic perspective on children of alcoholics. *Alcohol Health and Research World, 21,* 211-217.

National Institute on Drug Abuse. (2000). Bloodborne medications could intercept drugs before they reach the brain. *NIDA Notes, 14*(2), 8-10.

Nestler, E. J. (1997). Molecular mechanisms of opiate and cocaine addiction. *Current Opinion in Neurobiology, 7,* 713-719.

Rawson, R. A., Hasson, A. L., Huber, A. M., McCann, M. J., & Ling, W. (1998). A 3-year progress report on the implementation of LAAM in the United States. *Addiction, 93,* 533-540.

Regier, D. A., Farmer, M. E., Rae, D. S., Locke, B. Z., Keith, S. J., Judd, L. L., & Goodwin, F. K. (1990). Comorbidity of mental disorders with alcohol and other drug abuse: Results from the Epidemiologic Catchment Area (ECA) Study. *Journal of the American Medical Association, 264,* 2511-2518.

Roberts, A. J., & Koob, G. F. (1997). The neurobiology of addiction. *Alcohol Health and Research, 21,* 101-106.

Roll, J. M., Higgins, S. T., Budney, A. J., Bickel, W. K., & Badger, G. J. (1996). A comparison of cocaine-dependent cigarette smokers and non-smokers on demographic, drug use and other characteristics. *Drug and Alcohol Dependence, 40,* 195-201.

Ross, J. (1998). Alternative treatments for addictions and eating disorders. *Humanistic Psychologist, 25,* 162-181.

Rounsaville, B. J. (1995). Can psychotherapy rescue naltrexone treatment of opioid addiction? In L. S. Onken & J. D. Blaine (Eds.), *Integrating behavioral therapies with medications in the treatment of drug dependence* (NIDA Research Monograph Series, No. 150, NIH Pub. No. 95-3899). Rockville, MD: National Institute on Drug Abuse.

Slade, J. (1999). Nicotine. In B. S. McCrady & E. E. Epstein (Eds.), *Addictions: A comprehensive guidebook.* New York: Oxford University Press.

Stuyt, E. B. (1997). Recovery rates after treatment for alcohol/drug dependence: Tobacco users vs. non-tobacco users. *American Journal on Addictions, 6,* 159-167.

Sweanor, D. (2000). Regulatory imbalance between medicinal and non-medicinal nicotine. *Addiction, 95*(Suppl.), S25-S28.

Swift, R. M. (1999). Medications and alcohol craving. *Alcohol Research and Health, 23,* 207-213.

Tucker, T. K., & Ritter, A. J. (2000). Naltrexone in the treatment of heroin dependence: A literature review. *Drug and Alcohol Review, 19,* 73-82.

Ziedonis, D. M., & Kosten, T. R. (1991). Pharmacotherapy improves treatment outcome in depressed cocaine addicts. *Journal of Psychoactive Drugs, 23,* 417-425.

Ziedonis, D. M., Wyatt, S. A., & George, T. P. (1998). Current issues in nicotine dependence. In E. F. McCance-Katz & T. R. Kosten (Eds.), *New treatments for chemical addictions.* Washington, DC: American Psychiatric Press.

6

Disease Orientation
Taking Away Blame and Shame

Norman S. Miller

David, a 35-year-old man, while drinking and using drugs, tried to kill himself by cutting his wrists with razor blades and overdosing with sedatives. Depressed and hopeless, he saw himself as a terrible person undeserving of life and unwilling to continue living as an alcohol and drug user. When he substituted narcotic medications for alcohol, he became even more depressed and ultimately took a lethal overdose. Doctors saved his life by maintaining him on a respirator until the lethal narcotic medications cleared his body.

At that point, David did something different; he began attending meetings of Alcoholics Anonymous (AA). To his relief, he discovered that AA participants regard addiction a disease, not a moral problem or character deficiency.

Motivated to treat his disease, he continued attending AA meetings and incorporated its 12-step principles into his daily living. After 20 years of sobriety (continuous abstinence from alcohol and other drugs), he believes that his disease is only dormant and that picking up a drink or addictive drug could reactivate it and return him to his former, pre-AA miserable state. He believes that his continued abstinence from alcohol and drugs is critical to staying alive.

CONTRASTING THERAPEUTIC APPROACHES

The various therapeutic approaches to alcohol and drug abuse consider it to be due to (a) a moral problem, (b) a character disorder, (c) a depressive disorder, (d) a lack of social skills, or (e) a disease state. Let's review the initial interview that you as therapist might conduct for each approach and then discuss David's possible outcomes for each.

Therapist A tells David that he suffers from a self-inflicted moral problem and that he just needs to get right with himself and understand what he is doing to himself. David does not need medical or psychological treatment; he simply needs to pull himself up by his "bootstraps" and exert his willpower to control his drinking, either by moderating it or by just staying away from it.

Therapist B tells David that he suffers from a character disorder and needs long-term psychoanalysis to understand how his early childhood influences his reactions to life. He is encouraged to change his personality by digging deeply into his unconscious mind (below the surface of what he can remember) to understand his basic motivations. Ultimately, he will be able to take alcohol and other psychoactive drugs because the underlying problems will no longer cause him the psychic pain supposedly relieved by these substances.

Therapist C tells David that he suffers from underlying anxiety and depression that cause him to drink and use drugs and that he needs antidepressant medications. Also, he will probably need psychotherapy to understand why he drinks and what feelings he is trying to cover up or relieve with alcohol and other drugs. Once his anxiety and depression are treated, he will either not need to drink or be able to moderate his drinking because his mood will no longer need fixing.

Therapist D tells David that he has low self-esteem, lacks social skills, and needs psychological help to learn how to relate better to people. If he corrects these deficits, he can control his drinking by staying away from people, places, and things that he associates with alcohol and drugs.

Therapist E tells David that he suffers from a disease and needs treatment to stop drinking and using drugs. His treatment will have physical, psychological, and spiritual elements. Anxious and depressed *because* of his drinking, he needs to abstain from alcohol and other drugs to feel better.

⊞ OUTCOMES BASED ON THESE CLINICAL INTERVENTIONS

Therapist A: David listens attentively to the judgmental interpretation about his self-inflicted addictive behavior. On one level, he agrees with the therapist, for he knows he has committed immoral acts, and he blames himself for being a bad person. He also agrees that he needs more willpower over his use of alcohol and drugs. Again and again he tries to exert his will, but to no avail. He relapses to alcohol and drugs, reinforcing his self-view of being morally at fault. In desperation, he puts his rifle in his mouth and blows out the back of his brain.

Therapist B: David understands that he has a character problem. He readily admits that he is irresponsible, self-centered, and immature. His family and friends cannot rely on him; he misses appointments, birthdays, and other important family and personal occasions. Following his DUI (driving under the influence) arrest, he spends a lonely and depressing night in jail with thoughts of ending it all. Fortunately, he does not follow through but instead undergoes a year of psychodynamic therapy talking about his childhood, his emotionally distant, domineering father, and his overprotective, demanding mother. His therapist helps him recall vivid memories of past disappointments and conflicts. During these weekly sessions, David continues to drink, and his pattern of drinking does not change. He also continues Valium use intermittently for anxiety (often a symptom of alcohol withdrawal). Eventually, in desperation, he cuts his wrists with a razor blade, requiring stitches and inpatient hospitalization.

Therapist C: David ponders the concept that anxiety and depression might cause him to drink, but he has reservations about that idea because he often feels best when not drinking. However, when sober, he is bothered by feelings of boredom and impending doom. So he sees a psychiatrist who convinces him that he is self-medicating his anxiety and depression with alcohol and drugs and suggests using prescription medications instead so he will no longer need to drink and use drugs. He takes the doctor's antidepressant for a few months, discontinuing his drinking or other psychoactive drugs, but he eventually relapses to alcohol and becomes depressed again, despite continuing use of antidepressants. After taking an overdose of antidepressants combined with alcohol, he requires hospitalization in an intensive care unit.

Therapist D: David couldn't agree more about his lack of social skills, for he frequently says things he regrets and often has blackouts. When intoxicated, he slurs his speech, stumbles when walking, offends people he cares about, and spends hours talking about irrelevant topics with complete strangers, many of them also under the influence of drugs. The therapist gives him six sessions of social skills training, including learning to manage social situations without alcohol. The therapist also provides relapse-prevention training to teach David to stay away from people, places, and things that tempt him to drink and trains him in controlled drinking techniques. As hard as he tries, David still gravitates to where alcohol is served and overshoots the mark in how much and often he drinks. The therapist doesn't mention that abstainers experience the fewest adverse consequences. Eventually he relapses, slurs his words, makes offensive remarks, and forgets most of what he learned. During one bout of intoxication, he is severely injured in a barroom altercation with a stranger whom he challenged to a fight.

Therapist E: David is greatly relieved to learn he has a disease that overrides his will, not a moral problem or personality deficiency. Fortunately, he intuitively comprehends that his drinking and its consequences are caused by forces greater than himself. He learns that although he is biologically vulnerable to addiction, he is responsible for treating his disease, just like a diabetic or someone with high blood pressure. He also can identify with addicts like him whose disease has led to similar problems. He develops empathy with them and relies on them for support by attending group therapy and regular meetings of Alcoholics Anonymous. Gradually, he develops a commitment to abstain from alcohol and drugs, for by drinking or using again he will run the risk of activating the disease and the compulsion to drink and use other drugs.

OFFERING HOPE   ⊞

When clients come to you for help with a drug problem, they, like David, usually are full of shame or blame themselves for having a self-inflicted moral problem. By adopting a disease-orientation approach, you, as a therapist, help them overcome self-loathing. By persuading them that their alcohol and drug use is not caused by a moral deficiency but by biological, psychological, and spiritual forces beyond their control, you offer them hope. Viewing themselves as moral misfits interferes with clinical progress, is counterproductive, and can be lethal to some individuals. Motivating clients to accept their problem as a disease will help them overcome self-blame and shame and establish a long-term commitment to recovery.

Disease-orientation therapy communicates these concepts to the addicted client:

- You have a disease.
- You are not to blame.

- You can get better and be healed.
- You can help yourself.
- You are responsible.

Think about it. If you went to a therapist or doctor and were told that to get over your drinking you would need to overhaul your moral compass or increase your willpower, what would you do? You'd probably feel guilty and shameful; you might even want to destroy yourself. Would you seize the opportunity to do something to stop your drinking or drug use? Probably not. But what if you were told that you had a sickness, not unlike other diseases; that you had to take charge of its care if you were going to get better; and that recovery was possible only with your participation? Would you agree to take steps to treat your problem? Probably yes. But you may ask, is it that simple?

⊞ WHAT IS A DISEASE?

Most dictionaries define *disease* as "a condition of the living animal or plant body or one of its parts that impairs the performance of a vital function" or as "any deviation from or interruption of the normal structure or function of any part, organ, or system (or combination thereof) of the body that is manifested by a characteristic set of symptoms and signs, and whose etiology, pathology and prognosis may be known or unknown." Addiction fits that definition quite easily. But you say, what about free will, or the control people should have over their appetites and drives? How can we relieve them of that obligation? How easily our judgmental attitudes toward addiction can interfere with objective thinking!

A possible source of our moral dilemma is that alcohol and drugs produce a feeling of well-being, gratification, and pleasure. They stimulate portions of the brain that are responsible for hedonistic regulation. If that is so, we must control the degree and amount of pleasure, as a moral obligation, to avoid appearing out of control. We must use our conscience to control our appetites. Otherwise, we are not adult or responsible for our conduct. Again, we find ourselves in a moral dilemma.

The loss of control over drinking is the *sine qua non*, or cardinal manifestation, of addictive disease. The addict uses alcohol and drugs compulsively despite adverse consequences. Without seeing or accepting loss of control over drinking, addicts rationalize their abnormal use (Box 6.1).

Scientists have examined whether alcoholics can drink normally after developing the loss of control over alcohol. One study (Vaillant, 1983) looked at alcoholics over a prolonged period of time and found that fewer than 1% of the alcoholics drank nonaddictively over their lifetime.

Even controlled drinking studies (Vaillant, 1983) have found that alcoholics with the least adverse consequences from alcohol and drug use are the ones who have had the highest number of abstinent days. In addition, when the alcoholics who underwent controlled drinking behavior modification were followed up over years, many turned out to be dead from out-of-control drinking. *The lesson to be learned is that once the loss of control is present, it remains for a lifetime and cannot be modified by psychological means or medications.*

At AA, addicts must accept their loss of control over alcohol and other drugs. The first step is "We admitted we were powerless over alcohol—that our lives had become

> ### BOX 6.1 Addiction as a Physical, Mental, and Spiritual Disease
>
> | | |
> |---|---|
> | Denial | I do not have a disease. |
> | Minimization | I do not drink that much. |
> | Rationalization | I drink less than somebody else I know. |
> | Projection | I drink because of something else. |
> | Spirituality | I don't care. |
> | Physical | I am not that sick. |
> | Psychological | A drink will make me feel better. |

unmanageable." The word *powerlessness* is the same as *loss of control,* and the word *unmanageable* means " having adverse consequences."

Clearly, clinical experience shows that addicts are much more likely to accept their loss of control over alcohol and other drugs if they believe that they have a disease. Self-defenses are lessened if addicts' already intense self-condemnation is not reinforced with judgmental messages that they are to blame for their self-inflicted condition and should feel shame about their failure to control their drinking.

COMPARISON OF ADDICTION TO OTHER DISEASES ⊞

Interestingly, the term *victim,* as in *victim of disease,* implies a loss of control over the disease process. Addictive disease fits this definition rather easily. Tell your clients to compare cancer, coronary artery disease, or hypertension to addiction, and they will see striking similarities. Cancer is really uncontrolled growth of cells, to the extent that the tumors overtake the body. Several cancers, such as cervical cancer or tumors of the colon, can be detected early enough to prevent their growth and spread. However, the patient must take responsibility in seeking medical evaluation and treatment before the spread of cancer cells. Similarly, the individual with an addictive illness must seek evaluation and treatment to prevent the adverse consequences of out-of-control alcohol and drug use.

Coronary artery disease and hypertension are genetic diseases that require the efforts and cooperation of the affected individual to avoid serious health consequences such as heart attacks, strokes, and death. Individuals must take an active role in adjusting diet, exercising, and taking medications to treat their conditions. However, if they fail in following their treatment plans, they risk complications of their diseases, as does the alcoholic or drug addict who does not follow treatment recommendations (Box 6.2).

HISTORY OF THE DISEASE CONCEPT ⊞

Hippocrates, the father of Western medicine, postulated that diseases were caused by an imbalance of the natural elements in the human body. As recently as the 19th century, diseases such as syphilis and mental illnesses were attributed to moral degeneration.

BOX 6.2   **Comparison of Addiction to Other Diseases**

Coronary Artery Disease	Cancer	Alcohol and Drug Addiction
Genetic/familial	Genetic/familial	Genetic/familial
Modified by diet, exercise	Prevented or modified by early detection	Prevented or modified by early detection
Treated with medications and behavior modification	Treated with medications and behavior modification	Treated with medications and behavior modification
Victims of heart attacks not at fault	Victims of cancer not at fault	Victims of addictions at fault
Disease not caused by individual	Disease not caused by individual	Self-inflicted disease
Many causes (not known)	Many causes (not known)	Many causes (not known)
Recovery possible	Recovery possible	Recovery possible
Out-of-control cholesterol/blood lipid	Out-of-control cell growth	Out-of-control alcohol and drug use
Fatal; relapsing shortens life span	Fatal; relapsing shortens life span	Fatal; relapsing shortens life span
Treatment effective	Treatment effective	Treatment effective

However, in the late 18th century, Dr. Benjamin Rush, founder of the American Psychiatric Association, identified alcoholism as a disease and advocated total abstinence as the only effective cure.

In 1956, the American Medical Association (AMA) published a statement saying, "Alcoholism must be regarded as within the purview of medical practice." At the Council on Mental Health, the AMA's Committee on Alcoholism and the profession in general came to recognize that alcoholism was an illness and should receive the attention of physicians.

Dr. William Silkworth, an early pioneer in the disease concept, treated AA founder Bill Wilson at Towns Hospital in New York. He postulated that alcoholics, because of a physical allergy to alcohol, had a compulsion to drink. Dr. Harry Tiebolt, who worked closely with AA members during this era, emphasized the importance of defense mechanisms in the disease of alcoholism, namely denial, minimization, and rationalization. And Dr. Elvin Jellinek concluded that a majority of the evidence favored the view that alcoholism was a disease like other drug addictions.

⊞ COURT DECISIONS ON ALCOHOLISM AS A DISEASE

The California Supreme Court held that drug addiction is a status, not a crime, when it ruled that the California law making drug addiction a crime was unconstitutional (Miller, 2000). Moreover, the court distinguished treatment and punishment as two differing goals in drug addiction. Similarly, the U.S. Supreme Court ruled that public drunkenness was a crime but that being an alcoholic was not.

In one case, a Maryland court held that

there is no evidence on the record legally sufficient for the jury to find that the chronic alcoholism of the insured is the result of his conscious purpose or design. On the contrary the testimony tends to show that he had vainly exercised his will to restrain and control his desire. The *result* of his disease is a weakness of will and of character that caused him to yield to liquor. The drinking in the first stages was voluntary but there was not testimony that the drinker was then aware of the latent danger in his habit. . . . The result of the indulgence of an appetite *does not necessarily determine that the result was self-inflicted.* Because the actor does not apprehend or is ignorant of the danger of his act, he may not be held to have voluntarily inflicted upon himself the consequences.

Courts on the local level, particularly trial courts, regularly take into consideration the involuntary nature of addiction. Although the courts do not excuse addicts of the consequences of their addiction, they do allow treatment of the underlying cause of the crime, namely alcoholism and drug addiction, and mitigation of the charges and sentencing. The courts view the acceptance of addiction treatment and a commitment to abstinence as retribution and rehabilitation by the offender. As many as one third of those who enter addiction treatment and AA do so through the legal process. Studies (Miller & Sheppard, 2000) actually show that coerced treatment is as effective as voluntary treatment and is in some ways better because individuals who are mandated to treatment are often less severely affected by the addictive disease than those who wait to "volunteer" to get help. In reality, most individuals experience some degree of coercion before arriving at your office, often just short of frank legal consequences.

BIOLOGY OF ADDICTION ⊞

The best predictor, and a key way to show your client the depth of his or her problem, is to determine family history of alcoholism or drug addiction. Someone who has a family history of alcoholism is at higher risk to develop alcoholism than someone who does not. The genetic transmission of alcoholism is probably polygenetic, or carried by many genes, and is influenced by environment. Specifically, those who have more genes to develop alcoholism are more likely to develop a drinking problem with exposure to alcohol.

Inheritance is a very important finding to support the concept of alcoholism and drug addiction as a disease. Jellinek (1960) observed that alcoholism runs in families and that someone who is alcoholic is more likely to have alcoholic family members. In these studies, environmental influences cannot be separated from the genetic influences because alcoholic parents raise alcoholics. However, studies of adoptees who were alcoholics and raised apart from their alcoholic parents separated environment from genes (Goodwin, 1985). The biological parents of the alcoholic adoptees were more often alcoholic than the nonalcoholic adoptees, despite not living with the adoptees; thus, these studies isolated the effects of genes on the transmission of alcoholism.

Studies of twins (Goodwin, 1985) also show that alcoholism and drug addiction are transmitted by genetic contributions. When alcoholism in identical twins (twins sharing the same gene material) was compared to alcoholism in nonidentical twins (twins sharing half of the same gene material), the identical twins were more often found with alcoholism than the nonidentical twins. About 70% of the pairs of identical twins had alcoholism compared to 30% of the pairs of nonidentical twins, meaning that a greater number of shared genes (100% vs. 50%) increased the chances of having alcoholism transmitted in identical twins. The identical and nonidentical twins were raised together in the same environment. Children at high risk to develop alcoholism were more likely to have certain characteristics in common with alcoholics, such as a similar tolerance to the effects of alcohol. Children of nonalcoholics more often lacked these characteristics.

We have a reasonably good idea where addiction occurs in the brain. The brain centers for addiction appear to be in areas where the conscious mind is not ordinarily served; addiction is basically a disorder of the unconscious mind. Interestingly, the same centers responsible for appetite, mood, and sexual drive are involved in both drug and alcohol addiction.

The brain area responsible for the addictive drive, the mesolimbic pathway, begins in nerve cells in the midbrain (upper portion of the brainstem) and projects fibers to the nucleus accumbens in the limbic forebrain. The neurotransmitter (chemical that transmits electrical impulses from one nerve cell to another) responsible for transmission in the mesolimbic pathway is dopamine. Stimulation of the dopamine nerve cells will produce euphoria.

Cocaine causes an increase in dopamine in the synapse between nerves (space between the nerve endings releasing dopamine and the cell bodies of nerve cells containing receptors for dopamine). Consequently, the increases in dopamine may be responsible for the reinforcing effects of cocaine. Cocaine may produce some of its reinforcing effects by enhancing dopamine effects at the nerve cell. Alcohol, marijuana, and other drugs also act on dopamine to produce similar reinforcing effects. In this way, dopamine may play a role in the addictive drive by reinforcing self-administration of alcohol and other drugs in addictive patterns (e.g., preoccupation with acquiring the substance, continued use despite adverse consequences, and relapse over time).

The dopamine nerve cells contain receptors for opiates (morphinelike drugs). Heroin and narcotic medications can act on these receptors. Dopamine links many of the addicting drugs to one common pathway, namely the mesolimbic pathway. Though dopamine remains the central focus, addicting drugs, including alcohol, find their way to dopamine via different routes and actions.

▦ MEDICATIONS

The use of medications can persuade your clients that addiction is a disease. They will be more likely to believe this if their addiction responds to medications. There are medications you can prescribe for alcoholism and drug addiction (see Chapter 5). Naltrexone, for example, may affect the amount of alcohol people drink by reducing intake. Although naltrexone does not lead to greater abstinence in drinkers, it does appear to reduce the amount of alcohol drunk in a particular period (i.e., fewer drinks). Disulfiram (Antabuse) may reduce alcohol intake in selected drinkers by setting up an anticipation of an adverse reaction if alcohol is ingested while taking it. Disulfiram inhibits an enzyme that breaks down alcohol so that a noxious chemical builds up to cause a reaction similar to a hangover that is sometimes severe. As long as people take the medications, they are liable to have a bad reaction if they drink alcohol. However, they can resume drinking within days if they stop taking the medication, although the risk of an adverse reaction may persist for a week or so. Occasionally, the reaction can be severe enough to cause medical complications and even death. Only alcoholics engaged in behavioral treatments and motivated for abstinence should be considered for this medication.

Benzodiazepines, such as Valium and Librium, are used for treating withdrawal from a variety of drugs, including alcohol. Benzodiazepines share cross-tolerance and dependence with alcohol and sedate withdrawal effects from other drugs, such as cocaine and opiates. Benzodiazepines can sufficiently suppress the signs and symptoms of withdrawal from alcohol and other drugs to produce a medically safe and psychologically tolerable withdrawal. Because they reduce severity of withdrawal symptoms, these medications are important in increasing compliance with psychosocial treatments. Medications reduce the irritability of withdrawal from alcohol and drugs. The dropout rates from alcohol and drug abstinence are higher if withdrawal is not adequately treated. The probability of successful transition to a drug-free state is significantly enhanced with adequate treatment of drug withdrawal.

BEHAVIORS OF ADDICTION ⬚

Addictive disease is characterized by a preoccupation with acquiring alcohol and other drugs, compulsive use, and periodic relapse. Drug-seeking addicts secure their supply of alcohol and other mood-altering drugs at any cost. Their compulsive use is obvious to those who witness the accruing adverse consequences of their out-of-control use. Addicts rationalize their use by claiming that the consequences actually cause their compulsive use when out-of-control drug use actually creates the adverse consequences. Experience teaches that fixing the consequences will not alleviate the addiction.

Consequences of compulsive alcohol and other drug use affect all aspects of addicts' lives. Loss of control over substances eventually creates conflicts with others, sometimes subtly through oversensitivity to criticism, loss of confidence, forgetfulness, and insensitivity to others. More pronounced changes include mood liability, irritability, and loss of concern for others. Addicts typically become progressively more defensive, accusatory, argumentative, and suspicious. Addicts become wary of the motives of others, developing feelings of self-persecution and paranoid thoughts.

More overt clinical syndromes develop over time, including depression, anxiety, hallucinations, delusions, and personality disturbances. Developing an attitude that others are to blame for their drinking, addicts rarely accept their own responsibility for the consequences of their actions. Recovery begins when addicts can show responsibility for their actions by accepting that they have a disease and becoming willing to treat their disease. Addicts can understand the disease concept: Treat a disease to avoid adverse consequences.

DEFENSE MECHANISMS ⬚

The full experience of drug use and its impact is only fractionally acknowledged by the addict. Defense mechanisms, largely unconscious beliefs, support the addictive drive to use alcohol and drugs. They help addicts keep from their consciousness the extent and impact of their own suffering and effect on others. They minimize conscious awareness of problems resulting from their drug use.

Your treatment aim should direct clients to confront their denial, minimization, rationalization, and projections, which can be of almost delusional proportions. Evidence of the consequences that result from their alcohol and drug use is the most effective means of breaking through this denial. Also, educating them on the disease process is much more effective in combating defenses than judgmental attitudes and distracting attributions to causes other than addiction (Box 6.3).

> **BOX 6.3** **Treating Addictive Disease**
>
> - Accept addictive disease concept.
> - Reserve moral judgment.
> - Don't blame compulsive drug use on other causes.
> - Instill hope for recovery.
> - Show compassion.
> - Understand how a disease affects behaviors.
> - Compare to other medical and psychiatric diseases.
> - Offer effective treatment.
> - Hold the addict responsible.

As you know, treatment works for many addicts. Recovery from the disease of alcohol and drug addiction is possible and even probable with adequate treatment. By and large, science and practical experience show us that abstinence is really the best way to stem out-of-control drug and alcohol use. For the vast majority of those who manifest compulsive alcohol and drug use, controlled drinking and drug use do not work. Generally, abstinence-based programs are very beneficial. Outcome studies (Miller, Ninonuevo, Hoffman, & Astrachan, 1999) show positive results for a wide variety of individuals and drugs, including alcohol. If your clients complete a standard abstinence-based program, they can expect about a 65% chance of staying abstinent for 1 year if they attend AA after being discharged from the treatment program. Expect an 80% chance of being abstinent for 1 year if they attend an outpatient or inpatient treatment program *and* AA.

Usually, abstinence-based treatment programs focus on addiction as a disease and abstinence as a requirement. The structured treatment programs include group and individual therapies and define drug addiction and alcoholism as diseases that require active and consistent participation by your client. In a typical program, attendance at 12-step meetings (including AA) is strongly recommended and incorporated into the treatment program. However, addiction treatment is distinct from AA and, unlike AA, is delivered by professional staff (see Chapter 15).

Curiously, a paradox may be both the greatest obstacle and the best route to accepting addiction as a disease. On one hand, a disease is something someone has no control over; on the other hand, one is responsible for its treatment. We accept with little difficulty that someone with cancer is suffering from uncontrolled growth of cancer cells or that someone with hypertension has uncontrolled high blood pressure. We accept cancer and hypertension as diseases, despite knowing that these conditions and their consequences are in part preventable. We do not say the complications are self-inflicted even when sufferers are not taking adequate steps to prevent or treat their illness. Is it not true that victims of cancer may prevent the spread of cancer and even obtain an early cure if they seek evaluation for precancerous or localized cancer conditions? We know that treatments at that stage can prevent the spread of or cure the cancer.

Similarly, for hypertension, control of diet and loss of weight can correct some elevations of blood pressure, and taking of medications can often correct it completely. Although individuals may not be responsible for onset of the hypertension, they can alter its course and avoid complications by taking responsibility for its treatment. However, in the cases of cancer and hypertension, if they do not take steps to prevent or treat their diseases, do we blame them? Do we say they do not suffer from a disease? Do we say their conditions are self-inflicted? No, no, no.

If alcoholics or drug addicts show loss of control over their use and cannot or will not accept treatment for their diseases, do we blame them? Do we say they do not suffer from a disease? Do we say their conditions are self-inflicted? Yes, yes, yes. But should we? The answer is: If we want them to seek treatment for their addiction and to recover from it, we should hold them responsible for consequences of their disease if they do not accept treatment for it. We need to acknowledge that the consequences are from the addictive disease and not rationalize with them that other factors cause their alcohol and drug use. We acknowledge their disease and offer them effective treatment. The decision and consequences are ultimately theirs.

SUGGESTED READINGS ⊞

Goodwin, D. W. (1985). Alcoholism and genetics. *Archives in General Psychiatry, 42,* 171-174.

Jellinek, E. M. (1960). *The disease concept of alcoholism.* New Haven, CT: College and University Press.

Miller, N. S. (1991). Drug and alcohol addiction as a disease. In N. S. Miller (Ed.), *Comprehensive handbook of drug and alcohol addiction* (pp. 295-310). New York: Marcel Dekker.

Miller, N. S. (2000). Addictions and the law. *Psychiatric Annals, 30*(9), pp. 609-619.

Miller, N. S., Ninonuevo, F., Hoffman, N. G., & Astrachan, B. M. (1999). Prediction of treatment outcomes: Lifetime depression versus the continuum of care. *American Journal on Addiction, 8,* 243-253.

Miller, N. S., & Sheppard, L. M. (2000). Addiction treatment and continuing care in forensic population. *Psychiatric Annals, 30,* 589-596.

Miller, N. S., & Toft, D. (1990). *The disease concept of alcoholism and other drug addiction.* Center City, MN: Hazelden.

Vaillant, G. E. (1983). *The natural history of alcoholism: Causes, patterns and path to recovery.* Cambridge, MA: Harvard University Press.

7

Drug Testing

A Review of Drug Tests in Clinical Settings

Tom Mieczkowski

D rug testing is using specialized instruments and chemical techniques to ascertain the presence of a drug or a drug metabolite in a biological specimen collected from an individual. From this information, a person such a caseworker, medical review officer, or corrections officer evaluates the drug-using status of the person undergoing assessment. The specimen type is often referred to as a *test matrix*. The most common matrices are urine and blood, but hair, sweat, and saliva are becoming more popular as testing matrices. An important practical aspect of drug screening is the necessity of maintaining the *chain of custody* of the specimen because the specimen is typically collected in one location and sent to another place for testing. The assurance that the specimen matches the correct person is very important. Drug testing may also include *performance-based drug testing*. Although performance-based testing is not commonplace in clinical or criminal justice applications, it is worth examining briefly.

PERFORMANCE-BASED TESTING

Performance-based testing makes no attempt to identify the presence of a chemical toxin in the person's body. Instead, it examines a person's response to various physical challenges and stimuli to see if his or her response to these challenges falls within a defined normal range. The underlying assumption of this approach is that a psychoactive drug will affect a person's capacity to perform particular tasks or actions within a normal range of performance. A person failing to perform at this predetermined level can be considered *intoxicated* or *physically impaired*. The field sobriety test often used by police officers in traffic stops (e.g., walking a straight line, standing on one leg, reciting the alphabet backward) is a simple example of a performance-based test. Variability in human performance is a possible function of many potential factors:

- The quality and quantity of sleep
- Illness
- Medications
- Alcohol
- Other psychoactive drugs
- Some combination of these factors

Performance tests have several desirable features. Primarily, they do not require a specimen, they are noninvasive, and they have no chain-of-custody burden. They are also immediate; there is no lag time between the test and the results. Often, the actual test is largely self-administered. For example, a person may simply look into an instrument and follow simple instructions, such as tracking the pattern of a point of light moving in a dark field. These tests can detect impairment of the individual's cognitive (decision-making) and motor skills. Based on performance, they directly evaluate *impairment*. Because they do not rely on bioassays, they cannot be used to establish drug use in a person. However, performance-based analysis can be useful as a prescreen to identify persons who might merit further examination, including a bioassay or series of bioassays. Performance-based testing also distinguishes impairment from intoxication. Impairment is the measurable cognitive and motor effects from the intoxicant. Strictly speaking, intoxication means the presence of an intoxicating substance (e.g., a psychoactive drug) in sufficient concentration to be detected in a particular specimen. However, intoxication may not necessarily mean impairment, for extremely small concentrations of drugs may have no measurable effect on an individual's ability to function.

⊞ TOXICOLOGICAL DRUG TESTING

What Is Drug Screening?

Drug screening refers to chemical identification of the presence of a drug in a specimen. In addition to looking for the drug (often referred to as the *parent drug*), the drug test may also seek to identify a drug metabolite or even several drug metabolites.

What Do You Test? What Are Test Matrices?

Selection of a particular specimen type is usually based on a series of practical considerations. For example, to determine the blood alcohol concentration of a person operating a car, a breath analysis actually tests the exhaled breath and its associated water vapor to evaluate the plasma alcohol concentration. This test is popular because the exhaled breath is convenient to collect and noninvasive. Collecting blood with a hypodermic needle, in contrast, is invasive. Other considerations are possible infection, ease of transportation and storage, and specimen stability. The commonly used test specimens (or *matrices,* as they are sometimes called) when testing for psychoactive drugs include blood, urine, sweat, saliva, and hair.

Why Use Difference Matrices?

The selection of a specimen (matrix) automatically imposes a *time window* associated with that specimen. From the time drugs are ingested until they are excreted, they are involved in a dynamic process of change. Different specimens reflect different stages of this dynamic process. In the simplest example, consider a person smoking crack cocaine.

Crack cocaine, delivered to the surface of the lungs, quickly moves in large concentrations into blood plasma. Indeed, the rapidity of absorption through the alveoli is very near to intravenous injection. Thus, a blood sample harvested just a few minutes after a person smokes crack will have cocaine present in it. It will take 20 to 30 minutes for appreciable amounts of cocaine or cocaine metabolite to appear in the urine. And after cocaine is no longer in the circulating plasma, it will still be present in the urine stored in the bladder. Thus, blood and urine have different time windows. The longest time window (or the one that "looks back" the longest) is hair analysis. Although it will take 3 to 5 days for cocaine to appear in the hair of a cocaine user, the cocaine appears "locked" into the hair virtually permanently. Unless the hair is removed or dissolved, the cocaine will be detectable even months after the ingestion of the drug. The same is true for the matrix of fingernails and toenails.

Consequently, a major factor in selecting a particular specimen or matrix to use for analysis is the time window of detection. Another major factor to consider is the extent to which you wish to have a quantitative assessment of drugs detected in the analysis. "The more exposure to a drug, the greater the concentration in the body" is a general pharmacological principle. But this is not such a simple principle in practice. For example, it is not accurate to presume that a person with a higher concentration of a drug in his or her urine has used more of that drug than a person with a lower concentration. The excretion curves may have started at different times (i.e., the two individuals did not consume their drugs at the same start time), and there is considerable biovariability in the rates of excretion between individuals, as well as changes in the excretion efficiencies of the body as it ages. So although under theoretically ideal conditions it may be possible to compare two individuals and assess their relative drug use based on urinalysis, as a practical matter this is not done. With hair analysis, and possibly sweat patch analysis, where one measures the cumulative effect of taking drugs over a long period of time, it is possible to make a relative assessment of intensity of drug use but only in a rough categorical manner as, for example, "high," "medium," or "low." The hair (or sweat patch) will be sequestering drugs over several weeks or months, and this "dampens down" the dynamic change problems associated with urinalysis. However, even under these circumstances you should make any interpretation cautiously, and it is probably best to use your client as your "control." Compare multiple tests of the same person over a long time frame to evaluate the relative abundance of drugs in the specimen. For example, if you are using hair analysis in a drug rehabilitation program (which requires drug abstinence), you should expect to see a diminishing concentration of drugs in the subject's hair as he or she undergoes progressive testing over a long time frame.

What Are the Advantages and Limitations of Different Matrices?

Fluid-based specimens (blood, urine, and sweat) are most effective for measuring quite recent drug use. Hair and nail shavings, clippings, or scrapings are very good for long-term assessment. Sweat patches, worn on the skin like an adhesive bandage, are also effective for relatively long-term drug use detection because they act like cumulative dose meters. The hair specimen is collected by clipping the hair at the scalp, not by "pulling out" the hair. Finger or toenail specimens are collected by conventional clipping of the nail, as one would do in any trimming of the nails, or by making very small shavings or scrapings from the surface of the nail.

Advantages and limitations of any particular specimen, beyond the time window issue, are generally practical. The most important is *invasiveness*, intrusion into or invasion of the person, whether the procedure is *biologically* invasive (e.g., drawing blood with a hypodermic needle) or *psychologically* invasive (e.g., collection of a urine specimen or of a hair specimen). A test that uses a specimen collected by the least intrusive or invasive method is preferred, provided that all other needs are met by the specimen's analysis parameters. Other practical matters in considering selection of a specimen type are the convenience or ease of handling, storing, or transporting the specimen and the degree to which the specimen may constitute a biohazard as a disease vector.

▦ SCREENING TECHNOLOGIES

Immunoassays

The most frequently used technology in contemporary drug screening is *immunoassay technology,* the chemistry of the antigen/antibody interaction. By creating and harvesting a series of immunoreagents specific for drugs of abuse, one can create relatively sensitive and specific "detectors" of these substances. Furthermore, this technology lends itself to rapid detection and is readily automated for efficient and low-cost sample processing.

Assay detection is based upon the specific and sensitive interaction between an antibody and an antigen and the competition of the drug (antigen) for the antibody. In Box 7.1, imagine that the top specimen is from a person who has consumed no drug and therefore has no drug in his or her urine, whereas the bottom container represents a urine sample from a person who has very recently taken an illegal drug. To both of these containers we add a small amount of the same drug, only the one we add has a special label or "flag" attached to it (in this case, a marker that generates radioactivity). When we add the antibody for this drug to the mixture, the drug (antigen) and antibody react to form a complex—a large molecule with properties different from those of either of the separate compounds. It forms an insoluble compound and comes out of solution as a precipitate. We can by centrifugation remove the precipitate and be left with the remaining fluid (the *supernatant*). When we measure the supernatant for radioactivity, we will find that the amount of radioactivity is not equal between the two containers, even though we added equal amounts of radiolabeled drug. In the case of the person who took drugs, the material already in his or her urine "competed" with the additional labeled drug for the antibody. It "displaced" some of what we added, and therefore more of what we added stayed in solution. Thus, this person had more radioactivity in his or her supernatant than the drug-free person. Because the amount of displaced radioactivity is

A simple schematic representation of immunoassay technology. In this case, it demonstrates radioimmunoassay. Other forms of this technology use nonradioactive reagents.

proportional to the amount of nonlabeled drug present in the specimen, we can calculate a concentration value for the specimen. There are a number of variations on this basic approach, mostly in the selection of the appropriate "tag" to use with the antibody. For example, it is possible to use a molecular tag that is based upon the relative degree of light polarization that an antigen/antibody complex exhibits compared to the uncoupled antibody. One consideration on a practical level is whether a laboratory wants to handle a radioactive reagent.

In practice, virtually all urinalyses for drugs of abuse use immunoassay technology, and most of them use a qualitative test format. A particular value or *threshold* (also called a *cutoff value* [COV]) is selected, and a reagent sensitive at that threshold is used in the test procedure. The results are reported as "positive" or "negative" (we discuss the various issues associated with selecting a COV a little later). This use of an immunoassay is usually referred to as a *screening test,* and in most applications any specimen that proves to be positive by the screening test will undergo a second test, based on a different technology, called a *confirmatory test.* The rationales for this practice are as follows. First, a positive test may have serious consequences attached to it and should be redone to raise the level of confidence that the first result was not a mistake. Second, under some circumstances the immunoassay test lacks precise specificity. This problem is referred to as *cross-reactivity:* The immunoreagent may react with a number of compounds similar to the target compound. The confirmatory test will specifically identify the precise compound identified by the immunoassay. For example, suppose a client in a treatment program with a history of heroin abuse tests urine-positive for "opiates" by an enzyme-multiplied immunoassay. When questioned, the client states that he or she had a dental procedure and took a prescription opiate, hydrocodone. The immunoassay cannot distinguish between the two substances. A subsequent confirmatory test (normally gas *chromatography/mass spectrometry,* which we will discuss in a bit) will identify the specific opiate and either confirm or fail to confirm the client's explanation.

BOX 7.2   Schematic of a GC column. Through the selective adsorption of molecules to the column, a GC column separates molecular materials.

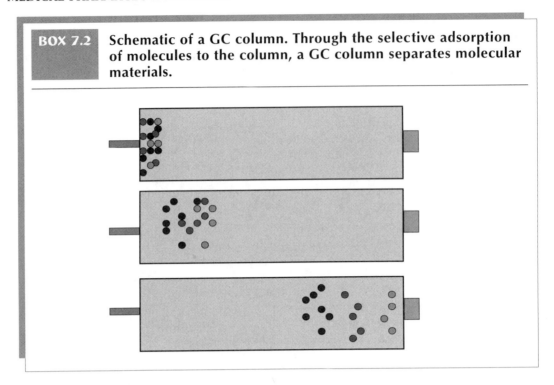

Gas Chromatography/Mass Spectrometry

Chromatography is an analytical technique used for the chemical separation of mixtures and substances (Box 7.2). The technique works on the principle of selective adsorption (not to be confused with absorption), a type of adhesion. In *gas chromatography (GC)*, the material to be analyzed is injected into a coated column. The type of column and the particulars of the analysis depend on the properties of the material being analyzed. Generally, the relative separating or *partitioning* of the gas is dependent on its solubility in the liquid that coats the column. On the basis of a principle known as Henry's Law, gases dissolved together in a liquid will independently reach their own equilibrium. GC uses a moving and a stationary phase. The moving phase is the gas or vapor, and the stationary phase is a solvent applied on the inside of the instrument's column (hence, it is called a *coated column*). The material to be analyzed is injected into this column and travels through the column pushed along by the flow of a *carrier gas* in a process called *elution*. As a solution percolates through the column, its individual components migrate at different rates of speed, and a sensor graphs them as they separate into a characteristic shape, called a *chromatogram*. The chromatogram is a "signature" used to identify particular compounds with high precision.

In addition to the signal that is converted into a chromatogram, the eluted materials coming out of the GC column can be *ionized* (given an electrical charge) and accelerated through a magnetic field and detected as they strike a collector. Because the ions will have different mass/charge ratios, they will travel specific distances, and data on a number of these ions will form characteristic spectra that identify a specific material.

In a *mass spectrometer (MS)*, an electron beam ionizes a sample of gas, and the ions are accelerated toward a magnet, which separates the ions according to their mass. The detector is connected to a computer or other electronic device to process the data and produce a spectral image (Box 7.3). Linking GC data and MS data makes the GC/MS

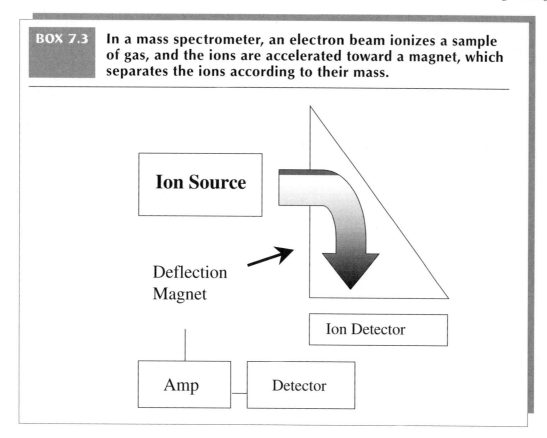

BOX 7.3 In a mass spectrometer, an electron beam ionizes a sample of gas, and the ions are accelerated toward a magnet, which separates the ions according to their mass.

technology the "gold standard" in specificity. GC/MS can identify with exact precision the chemical being assayed and can rule out the possibility that a cross-reacting compound is responsible for a positive immunoassay test.

Why Do Both a Drug Screen and a Confirmatory Test?

Screens usually have acceptable levels of precision and reliability. They are relatively inexpensive and generally are done by methods that lend themselves to high volumes of testing. Many tests can be done very quickly on a large number of discrete specimens. Screens using immunoassay technology (the most common type of screen) may have a problem with cross-reactivity; thus, the confirmatory test—which uses a separate technology—can rule out cross-reactivity. It also ensures the accuracy of the results and increases confidence in the assay interpretation.

What If the Screen and Confirmatory Test Do Not Agree?

As a general rule, the confirmatory test is considered the definitive test. Bear in mind that negative screening tests are not confirmed. Thus, in clinical practice, you would not face the situation of having a negative screening test and a positive confirmatory test.

If the Screening Test Is Reliable, Why Would a Disagreement Between Tests Happen?

There are a number of possible reasons for a disagreement. One is, of course, a mistake in some clerical aspect of the custody or identification of the specimen: For example, a sample is mislabeled, or a value is entered incorrectly into a computer. A second reason could be the improper execution of the test. For example, if the proper protocol is not followed, the specimen may be contaminated in the laboratory, either by a standard or by improper transfer of analyte from one specimen to another. Third, it is possible for a screening assay to give a false positive because of cross-reactivity.

In Clinical Practice, What Are the Consequences of This Two-Test Practice?

Persons involved in drug-testing programs need to be aware of the benefits and costs of the screening/confirmation approach. Obviously, a two-test approach is more expensive than a single test. Confirmatory tests are generally more expensive than screen tests. Thus, in contemplating costs, it is important to be able to estimate the percentage of positive screening assays you are likely to have to confirm. This is, of course, directly proportional to the number of clients whom you expect to fail the screen. This can vary radically depending on the type of population the drug-screening program is targeting.

Another factor to consider is the time element. Screening technologies are rapid, and the turnaround time is very short. In fact, many programs use virtually instantaneous "on-site" testing kits. For example, the client provides a urine specimen, the technician pipettes a small volume of urine to a test plate, and in a matter of minutes the technician reads the results. On the other hand, confirmation tests are slow, and typically require a relatively long time before a clinical report is available. In some applications, the need for rapid information is critical, and the timeliness of drug test information affects the counselor/client relationship.

Programs that use different specimen types (e.g., saliva, sweat, urine, blood, hair) are generally looking at specimens that may not have comparable time frames and should be interpreted appropriately. Some comparisons can be used to link consecutive periods (e.g., plasma, urine, hair), whereas others are looking at parallel time frames (e.g., urine and sweat). The use of multiple specimens provides more comprehensive information on the drug activities of a person and programs. Depending on your needs and budgets, you should probably contemplate having a multispecimen approach to monitoring.

▦ RATIONALES FOR DRUG TESTING

There are a number of reasons why drug testing is performed. Of course, in the simplest and most direct sense, it is done to ascertain if drugs are present in the specimen being tested. But the *meaning* of the presence of a drug in the tested specimen requires *interpretation.* For example, the test may be interpreted as an indication that the person has been exposed to the drug, may have inadvertently ingested the drug, or may have willfully used the drug. Each of these descriptive statements implies important differences and can mean very different responses to a positive drug screen.

Consider the result of the drug screen in context. The test may be done to ascertain if the person has responded truthfully to a question about his or her drug use or to determine if he or she impaired by the drug and consequently unsuited to engage in certain activities. Generally, employee testing is directed at these two areas. Does the person conform to the employer's policy to abstain from drug use as a condition of employment? Also, the employer is concerned with drug-induced impairment. The employer may be liable for injury or damage that employees cause if they operate equipment, for example, while impaired. An employer needs to exercise "due diligence" in detecting drug and alcohol abuse among employees, especially in safety-sensitive positions.

Another application of testing is in the criminal justice system, especially for offenders released into the community after conviction for a crime. While offenders are in a probationary status, they are likely to be subject to some type of drug testing regimen, usually random. It is a typical condition of probation after a criminal conviction to refrain from any illegal activities, including drug use.

WHAT CAN BE LEARNED FROM DRUG SCREENS ▦

A drug screen is a chemical assay indicating the presence or absence of a particular chemical compound or family of compounds in a specimen. The screen may also show the presence of the drug metabolite. An assay in the real world inevitably involves *interpretation*.

A very important aspect of test interpretation is the issue of the particular COVs or *thresholds* that are used. How much of a particular chemical must be present in a specimen for the test to detect it? This is an issue of test *sensitivity*. All chemical assays have a lower limit referred to as the *limit of detection* or *LOD*. In clinical applications, a value greater than this, the COV, is selected. Thus, in clinical settings, a person may be classified as "drug negative" even though he or she has some drug in the urine, hair, or whatever specimen the program is using because the amount in the specimen is higher than the LOD but lower than the COV. A "forensic positive" is based on the LOD, and an "evidentiary positive" is based on the COV. Thus, a person may be a "forensic positive" but an "evidentiary negative." A curious outcome, indeed. Shifting the COV threshold modifies the number of "drug-positive" persons in a target group or population. Lowering the COV will tend to increase the number of positive clients; raising it will decrease that number.

Why are COVs selected that are greater than the LOD? Primarily to be conservative in assay interpretation. Bear in mind that a person may ingest small amounts of a drug inadvertently by contact with contaminated materials, such as foodstuffs and dishware. Also, persons may inhale drugs as particulate matter such as dust or smoke that result from the use of the drug in their environment. So cutoffs are used to try to control for this effect. Controversy arises, however, in trying to determine exactly where the COV should be set and trying to determine the amount of contamination a person can reasonably expect to find in "innocent" (i.e., nonwillful) drug ingestion. This is not an easy problem to resolve. COVs for urinalysis have been modified several times by governmental agencies, sometimes quite dramatically.

COVs are evaluated by the potential of producing what are commonly called "false positives" and "false negatives." A "false" result can occur if the assay procedure is done incorrectly due to the incompetence or carelessness of the laboratory that conducts the test. For example, the inadvertent contamination of a "true" negative specimen by sloppy handling can result in a "false" result. Mislabeling or other procedural error can also lead to a "true positive" being called a negative. Control for this type of "false" result depends on quality control and assurance actions taken by the laboratory and regulatory and licensing agencies.

However, if we assume that the laboratory has not made an error in the processing of the specimen, we still have a remaining issue. These "true" and "false" terms have different meanings depending on whether *forensic* or *evidentiary* criteria are used in assessing the assay outcome. A false negative, in this sense, is one that can be considered a forensic positive (assay value above LOD) but an evidentiary negative (assay value below COV). If the LOD and COV are the same, this problem disappears. A false positive is possible if the interpreter of the assay used a COV that was below the LOD. Thus, if the COV is always at or above the LOD, and the test is done correctly from a procedural point of view, you can eliminate "false positive" outcomes.

⊞ COMPLICATIONS

Client Denial of a Positive Test Result

One of the more difficult clinical situations is the denial of drug use by a client in the face of a positive drug test. Generally, this is not a frequent occurrence in most treatment and criminal justice programs. Most clients in these circumstances will admit to drug use when they are confronted with confirmed positive results. Repudiation or denial of a positive result is more likely to arise in employee testing, with a client maintaining that the positive result is "impossible" because he or she has never used or taken the drug in question or has never used any drugs.

Test Error: Can the Test Just Be Wrong?

Of course, it is possible for the test to be wrong, for it is always possible that an operational error occurred. To minimize mistakes, use a certified laboratory that has professional standards of quality assurance and quality control and is both inspected and evaluated by participation in some type of "challenge" program. It is also possible, and something especially worth considering when using a new laboratory, for you to send "known" negative and positive samples blindly to the laboratory to enhance confidence in their performance. However, recognize that people with positive test results will periodically deny drug use and that no readily identifiable or compelling evidence will allow an absolute determination of the truth of the denial. In such cases, the most pragmatic course is to repeat the test (which is a problem for fast-excretion matrices such as urine) even though the time frame is violated and the results are not actually comparable. Also, if a urine, blood, or sweat matrix was used, hair analysis may prove a good alternative because it will permit a longer retrospective period to be evaluated. This illustrates the difficulties inherent in putting great emphasis on the outcome of a single drug test. Programs are generally better served by looking for patterns of positive outcomes in a series of tests. They are even better served by using more than one test specimen and relying on the outcome of several different indicators, such as urine, hair, and sweat.

Interpretation Error: Can the Test Be Misinterpreted?

The interpretation aspect of drug testing is often overlooked, for we tend to think of the drug-testing process as mechanical. But remember, a drug test must be "interpreted"—a meaning must be assigned to the result. The test tells you that a drug or drug metabolite is present in the matrix examined, but it does not tell how this drug got there. Interpretation involves assigning some meaning to the test in terms of its implications. Sometimes the interpretation seems relatively easy, sometimes it is not.

Typically, the interpretation of a drug test is that the person has consumed the detected drug. And you normally assume that he or she has done so willfully and knowingly. Thus, he or she is a "drug user" or "drug abuser" or "violator," or some such status is assigned to him or her. However, think back to the discussion of COVs and remember that a test may show traces of a drug but in a concentration below the COV that we selected. The person is "negative" (what we called evidentiary negative) but has drug above LOD in his or her sample (what we called forensic positive). This has several important implications.

One of the most important is that the percentage of persons who are positive or negative can be manipulated by moving the threshold. Although the lower limit of the COV is fixed at LOD, the upper limit can be any value. And over time, these values have been manipulated. Let me give an example. In the early uses of immunoassay urinalysis testing, there was great concern that because marijuana was generally consumed by smoking, persons exposed to second-hand marijuana smoke would be classified as "marijuana users," a clear misinterpretation. So the threshold for marijuana was set rather high. However, after a period of time, many persons using urinalysis testing reported frequent cases in which persons who admitted to marijuana use "passed": That is, they were getting a "negative" urinalysis outcome even though they readily admitted smoking marijuana, often quite consistently. An examination showed that marijuana was present in the urine but below the COV. Eventually, the recommended COV was lowered (it is now about one third the value originally proposed) until a consensus was reached that the value was low enough to detect "real users" but still high enough to rule out marijuana inhalation from environmental smoke.

Thus, the development and application of COVs are designed to deal with some of the problems of test interpretation and the assignment of meaning to the test result. COVs are higher than LODs in most cases to help distinguish passive contamination, inadvertent ingestion, and contamination from environmental sources.

Under What Conditions Can Testing Be Beneficial to the Client?

The use of drug tests has always been controversial, especially when consequences (almost always negative) are associated with a positive drug test result. In the criminal justice context, it may mean a violation of a condition of release. In drug treatment programs, it may result in sanctions or prolonging the course of treatment. In employment contexts, it may result in sanctions or even the loss of employment. Furthermore, because the drug test shows the results of past behavior, it is seen as an invasion of privacy, and its relevance to performance and behavior is often questioned, especially when drug tests are done on a basis other than "for cause."

We must recognize and acknowledge these concerns and criticisms, and it is unlikely that they will be readily or easily resolved. Undoubtedly, drug testing will remain controversial and be subject to criticism. And certainly critics of drug testing will point out the negative and harmful consequences that can result from drug-testing activities. However, there are also some positive aspects of drug testing that are worthy of mention. Drug tests, especially for those involved in drug treatment programs, can enhance the motivation to remain drug abstinent. Because the certainty of detection is relatively high in a properly conducted drug-screening regimen, persons undergoing treatment who may be tempted to use drugs can be deterred to some degree by the knowledge that they will be identified by a drug test. It is common for persons in programs to admit that if they "knew they could get away with it" they would be much more likely to relapse into drug use. Drug testing does not allow the person to maintain a subterfuge of undergoing treatment while continuing to use drugs. A related benefit often reported in treatment programs is that clients can use the fact that they are undergoing drug testing to resist peer pressure to relapse to drug use.

⊞ WHAT DOES THE FUTURE HOLD?

This question can be considered on two levels: drug testing's social and legal future and its technical future.

On a social and legal level, it appears that drug testing will continue to be a feature of contemporary life. The courts have generally been permissive in allowing employers and agencies to use drug testing, provided certain safeguards and conditions are met. Perhaps more controversial and less certain is the degree to which drug testing will expand into new areas, such as the testing of students in schools and persons receiving government benefits, as some politicians have advocated. It is worth noting that courts have generally upheld the right of schools to drug-test students involved in extracurricular activities, such as sports. It remains to be seen whether both political and legal support will be sufficient to tolerate more testing. Undoubtedly, testing already being done, especially in criminal justice and drug treatment programs, is likely to be a permanent social fixture.

Several technical trends will affect the nature of drug testing and its applications. The technology of testing will become increasingly miniaturized, specialized, and rapid. Also, sensitivity and specificity of tests will probably be enhanced. Monitoring of drug-involved persons, such as those serving criminal sentences on probation or community release, may also become more comprehensive. For example, it may be possible to link a sensing mechanism (on the skin) that detects drugs as they are excreted in sweat to other information systems, such as positioning technology and a time line. Thus, a sensor system may be able to identify a drug, when it was taken, and where it was taken. The degree to which resources are devoted to the development of these capabilities will depend on the political climate and whether strong sentiment emerges to enhance monitoring or whether reluctance emerges that views such monitoring as an infringement on personal liberty.

⊞ SUGGESTED READINGS

Baer, J., & Booher, J. (1994) . The patch: A new alternative to drug testing in the criminal justice system. *Federal Probation, 58*(2), 29-33.

Harrison, L., & Hughes, A. (1997). *The validity of self-reported drug use: Improving accuracy of survey estimates* (NIDA Research Monograph No. 167). Washington, DC: U.S. Department of Health and Human Services.

Leccese, A. (1991). *Drugs and society: Behavioral medicines and abusable drugs.* Saddle River, NJ: Prentice Hall.

Mieczkowski, T. (1990) . The accuracy of self-reported drug use: An evaluation and analysis of new data. In R. Weisheit (Ed.), *Drugs, crime, and the criminal justice system.* Cincinnati, OH: Anderson.

Mieczkowski, T., Barzelay, D., Gropper, B., & Wish, E. (1991). Concordance of three measures of cocaine use in an arrestee population: Hair, urine and self-report. *Journal of Psychoactive Drugs, 23,* 241-249.

Mieczkowski, T., Mumm, R., & Connick, H. (1995). The use of hair analysis in a pretrial diversion program in New Orleans. *International Journal of Offender Therapy and Comparative Criminology, 39,* 222-241.

Perrine, D. (1996). *The chemistry of mind-altering drugs: History, pharmacology, and cultural context.* Washington, DC: American Chemical Society.

Spiehler, V. (1995). Immunological methods for drugs in hair. In R. de Zeeuw, I. Hosani, & S. Al Munthiri (Eds.), *Proceedings of the 1995 International Conference on Hair Analysis in Forensic Toxicology* (pp. 261-272). Abu Dhabi, United Arab Emirates: Ministry of the Interior.

COGNITIVE-BEHAVIORAL TOOLS

8

Recovery Contracts
Seven Key Elements

G. Douglas Talbott
Linda R. Crosby

Behavioral contracts are used in a variety of settings to effect positive behavioral changes. Recovery contracts, an essential component of any treatment modality, are effectively used in intensive outpatient, primary inpatient, and continuing care settings. Acute care hospitals, psychiatric facilities, correctional institutions, methadone programs, chemical dependency treatment facilities, and many other settings currently use some level of behavioral contracting to reinforce positive desired behaviors.

Contracts with chemically dependent patients are the core of primary treatment and continuing care. A recent study looked at 100 recovering physicians who signed a continuing care contract that included witnessed urine screens, assignment to a primary care physician, attendance at five 12-step meetings and one Caduceus meeting (physician-specific support group) per week, participation in individual and family therapy, and engagement in a spiritual program, a physical fitness program, and a leisure activity program. One fifth (22%) of these participants relapsed, a much lower rate than national averages for recovery programs. Those who relapsed had stopped attending 12-step meetings and denied that their condition elevated their stress, increased their isolation, and impaired their judgment (Gallegos et al., 1992).

It is important to note the difference between a "slip" and a relapse. Box 8.1 helps differentiate these two terms.

The chemically dependent patient requires psychological, physiological, and spiritual frameworks to guide him or her through the recovery process. Contracts are an essential part of this external structure. As a primary disease, chemical dependency is not an issue of "self-will"; patients are unable to change their negative emotional/using be-

BOX 8.1	**Slip Versus Relapse**

Slip	*Relapse*
Promptly/freely admits to "slip"	Withdraws, disappears, and disappoints
Seeks help from treating physician/monitor within 24 hours of "slip"	Is dishonest, lies
Continues in recovery program/contract	Refuses help
Has had no more than one previous "slip"	Has had multiple relapses
Takes White Chip at AA (given for less than 24 hours of sobriety)	Stops going to meetings, stops contacting sponsor, or goes to meetings intoxicated
Sponsor and/or main significant other are informed of "slip" and support continued recovery	Family, friends, and support systems are abandoned
No severe adverse family, professional, legal, or social consequences	Severe and adverse life consequences
Agrees to new stringent recovery contract	Breaks recovery contract

haviors without focused comprehensive treatment strategies to direct, support, and encourage each phase of treatment.

The contract for chemically dependent patients focuses on abstinence from mood-altering substances—including psychoactive drugs, over-the-counter medications, and herbal preparations—and learning positive coping skills. Early in recovery, contracts provide external direction to the patient who has relied upon chemicals to cope with life. As the patient progresses in recovery, the contract becomes secondary to the positive rewards of experiencing recovery with peer support from 12-step meetings, continuing care groups, and individual or family therapy. Identified factors noted in Table 8.2 have predictive value in maintaining successful recovery (Talbott, 1995). It may be helpful to use Box 8.2 in preparing your recovery contracts and assessing your patient's recovery.

We recently asked 672 recovering health professionals about their recovery activities. The respondents had a recovery span from 0 months to 5 years. (You can find the responses to key questions about identified recovery activities and the results on the Talbott Recovery Campus Web site, www.talbottcampus.com.)

Contracting serves several purposes for the chemically dependent patient. It clearly identifies factors that are a risk to relapse, requires a personal commitment, provides a concrete expectation about positive behaviors necessary to maintain sobriety and eventual recovery, and serves as a tool in breaking through denial.

For the chemically dependent patient, we advise you to *view contract noncompliance in the context of "diagnosis" rather than punishment.* The positive/negative motivational outcomes are a double-edged sword. If patients violate the contract by having a positive urine, blood, or Breathalyzer test reported to the counselor (monitor), they usually perceive this as a negative experience and often feel that they have failed the counselor's or program's expectations. In fact, you might feel that your patient's positive body fluid testing report is a failure on your part. Remember that counseling the chemically dependent patient is a challenging task: All progress, including "slips" and

---

| BOX 8.2 | **Guidelines for Preparing Recovery Contract** |

Assessment Category	*Helpful Notes*
Number of 12-step meetings (AA/NA, SAA, CA)	Early recovery: 3-5 per week Professional support groups once a week, not as substitute for 12-step recovery programs
Relationship with sponsor	Identify sponsor for 12-step/professional group, if applicable; minimum contact 3 times a week
Random body fluid testing	3 times per month initially, then decrease; have outside lab collect observed specimens
Monitoring of emotional traps: anger, guilt, anxiety, insomnia, pain, etc.	Assess emotional/behavioral status as it contributes to or blocks quality recovery
Monitoring of compulsive behaviors	Discuss cross-addictions, gambling, spending, eating disorders, sexual compulsivity
Evaluation of therapy/treatment and medications	Specify monthly reports to the counselor from treatment providers and all health care providers Must submit any medications for approval
Assessment of family relationships	Schedule conjoint meeting with spouse/significant others (children, parents, or others) to discuss contracts and progress
Assessment of physical health status	Routine physical exam every 3 months, with reports to monitor and counselor
Participation in leisure activities	List all activities that the patient defines as leisure (e.g., tennis, golf, hiking, water sports, camping) and specify how often
Monitoring of compliance	Specify times, dates, and expected reports
Weekly physical exercise	Specify what the patient defines as exercise and when and how often
Work-related stresses	Changes in job responsibilities, work environment, licensure, restrictions
Financial status	Assess financial stress or improvement
Additional training/continuing education	Does patient need retraining or other occupational education?
Legal/licensure status	Legal issues that affect the patient's recovery Concerns/actions regarding patient's occupational license

relapse, is diagnostic and presents therapeutic opportunity. Measuring progress is a stimulus to constantly reevaluate, reframe, and redesign the patient's treatment plan. Use the framework of the contract to assess key behavioral elements necessary for long-term successful recovery.

The recovery contract also establishes a formal tool for evaluating patients' support systems and how effectively patients are learning to use them. With appropriate release-of-information forms signed, the significant other/spouse, parents, children, the personal physician, the professional monitor (physicians, nurses, dentists, pharmacists, attorneys), the peer assistance program, and you can be freely contacted to offer feedback about your patient's progress. Using the contract as a baseline, you can validate their participation in self-help programs, professional support groups, and contacts with their primary care physicians. For some patients, you will need to include specific details in the contract such as practice/workplace restrictions (e.g., health professionals), prescribing restrictions (health professionals), and driving restrictions (DWI/DUI patients). Each desired outcome or behavior listed in the contract needs a "checks and balances" system to gather data regarding the patient's investment in the contract and ultimately in his or her recovery program. *Emphasize that the goal of the contract is to provide a step-by-step specific recovery plan that the patient will eventually internalize as valuable to his or her recovery.*

▦ BEHAVIORAL ADDICTIONS

Successful treatment of behavioral addictions such as sexual disorders, gambling, eating disorders, and compulsivity disorders includes behavioral contracting as a primary component. For sexual dysfunction, including sexual misconduct violations, use behavioral modification and contracting during the treatment and continuing care process. At this time, there is no objective body fluid testing available to monitor sexual compulsivity and compliance with treatment, so behavioral contracting is the central tool for working with these patients. In dually diagnosed patients (those who are chemically dependent and have sexual dysfunctions), contracting may include objective laboratory testing along with conforming to desired/expected behaviors. In most cases, these patients must agree to abstain from all mood-altering chemicals to avoid sexual relapse.

Behavioral contracts can be highly specific and measurable: In fact, the more specific the better. A male physician remanded to treatment due to sexual improprieties with a female patient, for example, may have a contract with the following specific behavioral guidelines:

- Will have a nurse present during all patient interchanges
- Will have video cameras installed in all examination rooms and office monitored by office manager
- May not see patients after hours or on weekends
- Will have partner write out all prescription orders for scheduled medications
- Will abstain from use of alcohol/other drugs, including over-the-counter medications

The contract becomes the blueprint, with everyone involved—you, the counselor, the spouse, family, work family, partners, and peers.

▦ SEVEN KEY ELEMENTS OF RECOVERY CONTRACTS

The best recovery plan involves seven essential elements: presenting the contract, releases of information, the consequences, primary support systems, time frames, contract review, and slip/relapse clause.

Presenting the Contract

Remember that a contract is not a legal document but a personal commitment by the patient and his or her significant others.

Presentation of the contract is a significant event for your patients. Schedule a specific time with them, and have the family and others attend, anticipating their ques-

---

> **BOX 8.3   Seven Key Elements of Recovery Contracts**
>
> 1. Presenting the Contract
> 2. Releases of Information
> 3. The Consequences
> 4. Primary Support Systems
> 5. Time Frames
> 6. Contract Review
> 7. Slip/Relapse Clause

tions and concerns. Too often, therapists regard the recovery contract as an addendum to ongoing treatment and quickly hand it to a patient to sign with little or no explanation. If patients perceive this as simply "paper compliance," they will not view the contract as a significant recovery guide. Having a third party (family member, the attending physician, clinical director, family therapist, etc.) participate in the contract presentation conveys the significance of the contract and also deters misinterpretation of contract expectations.

Plan the continuing care contract when the patient first enters treatment. The old adage "Timing is everything" applies here. Include the patient, family, and referral source in shaping the contract so that by the completion of treatment the contract is fully developed. Before discharge, present the contract in its entirety to the patient, the family, and the referral source if available. Talking about the contract during treatment prepares your patients for the actual written document. During counseling, group sessions, family sessions, or inpatient treatment, constantly reframe the principles of recovery and reinforce the positive behaviors necessary to move from the sobriety of the treatment phase to the recovery process. By then, your patient will be familiar with all expectations and will not be confused or surprised to see these in writing the day you present the contract.

As treatment providers, we have seen contracts mailed to patients in treatment facilities from state peer assistance programs. This is clearly not the ideal. The presentation of the contract by mail or third party defuses its importance and opens the door to misinterpretation and misrepresentation. Unfortunately, sending contracts long distance to be initiated by a third party is a common practice in some state programs where large geographic distance precludes personal meetings with the patient/participant. One solution is to appoint a patient monitor (a designated individual, usually in the same profession as the patient) as the program representative and have the monitor meet with the patient to explain each detail of the contract. Many of the peer assistance programs sponsored by professional organizations use recovery monitors. Health care professions of medicine, nursing, pharmacy, dentistry, and other professional groups, including attorneys, judges, pilots, counselors, and social workers, have formal programs to assist their members in need. See the references at the end of this chapter for listings of these groups.

For example, when a nurse from Arkansas was discovered diverting hospital drugs, she was reported to the nursing board and referred to a chemical dependency treatment center in Mississippi. The Arkansas nursing board requires that nurses identified as chemically dependent be enrolled and monitored in the Arkansas State Nurses Peer Assistance Program and requires a signed agreement. Sending this agreement to the nurse's counselor for the nurse to sign is not the ideal presentation of this contract because the nurse has no opportunity to personally engage with the program representative to ask questions. This contract would most effectively be presented face to face when the nurse returned to Arkansas after her discharge from treatment. Remember that contracting is one person "engaging" another person in an agreement, and this is nearly impossible if the two parties do not have a personal meeting.

The same principle holds true for having another staff member present your patient's recovery contract. Third-party contracts, no matter how well intentioned, are not adequate substitutes for the counselor-patient contract meeting. Third-party contracts often result in the same old "he said, she said" discussions and may be as reliable as "third-hand information." Recovery contracting is an interpersonal experience, and we know that about 80% of that experience is communicated nonverbally.

The patient's and the counselor/program representative's signatures on the contract provide powerful documentation. For example, a dentist patient signed a contract stipulating that he could not prescribe Schedule II drugs for 1 year. Six months later, a practice monitor (his peer monitor) reviewed the dentist's prescription log and found that the dentist had broken the contract by prescribing a Schedule II drug for a patient— in fact, several patients. When the program director and the monitor contacted the dentist, he adamantly argued that "he wasn't restricted from prescribing." A copy of the contract with his signature was shown to the dentist. "It looks like my signature," he admitted. "I guess I didn't read this very well."

During face-to-face negotiation of the contract, the counselor's attitude is very important. A hostile or demeaning tone conveys negative feelings to the patient, who may perceive the contract not as a helpful tool but perhaps as even punitive. If you have had recent crises to deal with before meeting with this patient, reschedule the contract meeting rather than attempting to "get it done." Because patients in early recovery lack a strong sense of ego boundaries, they can easily absorb stress from you as their counselor and internalize negative feelings to their detriment.

Present the contract to patients in a private setting, and give them your undivided attention and the opportunity to discuss each component of the agreement before discussing it with their spouse/significant other and other pertinent sources of support. Consider the patient's contract appointment as you would a private counseling session (i.e., turn off the phone and beeper and close the door to prevent intrusions and you will convey the importance of this event and minimize the patient's distractions).

Be prepared. Patients often ask questions about what you may regard as "minutiae," a precursor to negotiating a change in the agreement. There lies the crux of the rationale for the recovery agreement: If your patients could manage their addiction on their own, there would be no need for the contract. Depending on where patients are in the treatment process, their attempts to control and manipulate specific criteria in the contract will vary, but always anticipate some level of negotiating. When you schedule adequate time, patients feel that they are heard by you, and the contract will not have a "because I said so" aspect. The ideal contract presentation leaves both you and your patient feeling that you have entered into a mutual agreement.

Patients who have no questions about the contract at the time of presentation may go home and then not understand something you thought was very clear. This is the common "doctor's office syndrome": You are told something stressful by the doctor, but after you leave the office, you have no recall about what he or she said after you heard the bad news. So *assume that patients will not always comprehend the full impact of the agreement during the first meeting,* and be prepared to answer questions days or weeks after the contract is initiated. This is another reason why periodic contract review and reframing is necessary, as we discuss later.

Release of Information

Monitoring recovery progress by contracting is subjective because even the most stringent body fluid monitoring can be misleading. Significant persons in the patients' personal and professional life play an important role in monitoring their recovery. Contracts requiring self-reports throughout the recovery process may offer some insight into your patients' perceptions, but collateral information is essential to objectively track your patients' progress. Whether for chemical dependency or behavioral addiction, the recovery contract includes desired behaviors that are, for the most part, observable by others. Attendance at meetings or other specified therapy sessions can be documented by other attendees or facilitators, as can workplace behaviors and contractual restrictions. Invite the persons who will play a critical role in helping support your patients in their recovery contract to participate. Get multiple releases from multiple people to reduce the risk of enabling; there may be negative reports from someone who may have a conflict with the patient after signing the releases. Check with your agency about the release-of-information forms as to proper signatures and time frame for which the release is valid. Also be sure to have each one witnessed by someone other than the patient.

With your patient, identify the individuals to include for collateral information before completing the contract. Specific release-of-information forms must be signed for each person being invited to participate in the process of providing support and documentation of progress in recovery. If there is no release signed by your patient for a specific person, you may not contact or receive information from this person. The legal protections for patients treated for chemical dependency at both state and federal levels afford privacy and confidentiality and must always guide you through treatment and continuing care. Contact your clinical director or risk management department for more information on releases.

The Consequences

Encouraging positive behavioral change involves clinical staff's use of *leverage,* a mechanism to motivate compliance by linking behavior to a perceived negative consequence or an intrinsic positive reward or non-negative consequence. When leverage is required, it conveys clearly that the desired behavior was not achieved. Think about leverage in motivating patients to comply with the recovery criteria: If they do not, what will happen? Will anything happen? The effective contract contains specific achievable behavioral elements such as "Will attend professional support groups the first and third Tuesdays of each month and will submit meeting attendance form by the 20th of each month," "Will attend monthly counseling with Jane Smith," or "Will provide monthly meeting reports to John Doe (my monitor) by the 10th of each month." Make each behavior specific, and state consequences of noncompliance clearly. There are several levels of leverage for each patient—family, employer, profession, and legal. Choose leverage unique to that particular patient and his or her current situation.

A general clause regarding patient noncompliance in the typical recovery contract states, "Failure to comply with *any* of the above recommendations/agreement guidelines may be perceived as a relapse and comprehensive assessment requested. Noncompliance may also result in unsatisfactory discharge from the program, and information may be forwarded to the appropriate licensing board" (if this is an advocacy or state required program).

Tell the patient clearly the consequences of noncompliance. Many are in treatment due to some precipitating event caused by their alcohol/other drug use and did not voluntarily wake up one morning and say, "I think I'll admit myself to a rehab program today." Someone, either family, friend, coworker, partner, judge, employee assistance counselor, or employer, facilitated the admission through some level of intervention. How the patient came to treatment may determine the consequence of noncompliance. For example, if the patient came to treatment because of the spouse's threat to leave if the patient did not get treatment, the spousal threat of divorce can be used as leverage to get the patient to comply with treatment. Similarly, if the patient was court ordered to treatment, the consequence will be a hearing and perhaps criminal charges; if he or she was sent by an employer, the consequence may be job loss; if he or she was sent by a partner or peers, the consequences may be loss of partnership/practice and subsequent reports to state licensing bodies. In other words, whoever has a vested interest in the patient's recovery becomes the intrinsic leverage for compliance. Acknowledge each of the several levels of leverage (consequences) in the recovery contract.

Primary Support Systems

The recovery contract is interdependent with the patient's primary support systems. Whether the patient is diagnosed with chemical dependency or some form of behavioral addiction, the treatment process must, whenever possible, incorporate the spouse/significant other, children, siblings, partners, administrators, and office staff. Because professionals have two families—their personal family and their "work" family—do not discount the significance of the latter in preparing and drafting recovery contacts.

Remember that because chemical dependency is a family illness, family members are directly affected by the patient's addiction, just as the patient is affected by the family's reaction. As such, family participation in both treatment and continuing care is crucial to the patient's recovery. Address family participation in the recovery contract with the patient early in the treatment process and subsequently during family sessions or counseling. Attempting to generate recovery contracts without family participation is likely to be disastrous for both the patient and the family. When family members are not included in specific aspects of the contract, the family can become more and more resentful about how the patient's "recovery program" is taking time away from family time and activity. Present the recovery contract to the significant others during the presentation to the patient. If the continuing care contract has been addressed with the patient and the family during primary treatment, there should be no surprises for the patient or the family.

Everyone in the patient's significant interpersonal world, with the patient's permission, or by the patient's disclosure, should understand the purpose of the contract and be willing to participate. Identify those who will be a positive support to the patient, as well as those who will be hostile or attempt to sabotage the patient's recovery. Knowing friends and foes up front will help you plan the appropriate strategy if some of these individuals try to interfere. When admission intake information is obtained from the spouse/significant other, employer, and other appropriate parties, you will have a sense of those who will be effective allies in creating the recovery contract.

Referral sources, a valuable resource for the counselor, are key to the patient's primary treatment and provide ongoing support. Contact these referral sources to collaborate in drafting the recovery contract. Likewise, if a specific recovery program (i.e., a peer assistance program) requires a contract, consider the primary counselor a vital participant in drafting the patient's participation.

Early recovery demands total immersion with people who have the tools of recovery in 12-step programs, individual counseling, support groups, and other required activities. This can fill up a schedule. Family members, during their own treatment, need to gain the insight necessary to manage their own recovery issues while offering support (not admonishment) to their loved one.

Monitoring compliance with the recovery contract is essentially dependent upon a cadre of individuals, including those who collect the random urines and Breathalyzer data. Outline in the contract who, what, when, and where regarding meeting attendance, changes in work schedules, work environment, social contacts (if appropriate), and so forth.

Time Frame

Starting the recovery contract with short time frames offers your clients the opportunity to believe they can succeed. A plan of action for a short interval is usually perceived as manageable. Once patients have completed each interval, extend the recovery contract for another designated period. These periodic forced reviews provide a formal opportunity for your clients to receive positive reinforcement and a sense of accomplishment and also provide a clinical opportunity for appropriate mini-interventions if patients need redirection. For example, some program contracts reevaluate patients at the end of each year. For others, periodic evaluation takes place quarterly or every 6 months. The standard of care at this time is a 5-year contract divided into stages or intervals. The reason for the 5-year contract is simple—recent studies indicate a significant drop in relapse after 5 years in recovery. Negotiating a contract for each year gives you and your clients a short-term goal and opportunity to reevaluate the contract, as we discuss in the next section.

It is imperative when you draft your clients' contracts to specify a time frame for each activity—how many times in one week they must attend 12-step meetings, contact their sponsor, attend individual or other counseling, and so forth. Clearly define every activity, and, when appropriate, indicate dates, hours, days, and so on. State exactly "no more than 30 hours work per week," for example, instead of "reduce the amount of hours worked per week." If the contract requires submission of attendance forms or reports, avoid vagueness (e.g., "Reports are to be submitted each month"), and be specific (e.g., "Reports must be received in John Smith's office by the 10th of each month"). Seemingly simple tasks like sending in reports late, or not at all, indicate that the patient may well be noncompliant in other areas of the contract.

Contract Review

Periodically review the contract. As patients progress, the environment in which they live and work may change, necessitating the need for revisions in the recovery contract. Evaluate deaths, divorce separations, hiring/firing of office staff, and the impact on the patient's initial contract at least every 6 months. Again, we highlight the importance of obtaining the release-of-information forms from the patient. During contract review, it is vital to obtain information from collateral sources in the patient's life (e.g., spouse, employer, peer monitor, or others). Often, patients may be the last to tell you that something has changed, as they may not see this as pertinent to their recovery contract. Similarly, some patients are reluctant to disclose information that they perceive as jeopardizing their recovery contract and recovery status.

For example, one physician with 2 years' sobriety, following a relapse 2 years earlier, was under contract with a state peer assistance program by order of the Board of Medical Examiners. His contract required attendance at 12-step groups, body fluid monitoring, a physician-specific support group for recovery (12-step group for physicians only), couples counseling with his wife, restricted prescribing, and other practice-specific criteria. The physician's wife, his main support and advocate, provided such powerful testimony during his formal hearing that his license was reinstated.

One week after Christmas, while sitting at the dinner table, his wife suffered a massive cerebral hemorrhage and died within 4 hours. Devastated with grief, the physician withdrew from his groups and failed to notify the program and his monitors of his wife's death. The local physician, his practice monitor, should have been checking his monthly reports and other required documentation. But when he heard of the physician's wife's death, he let his paperwork "slide." The addicted physician had a few drinks shortly after his wife's death, thinking it would help his grief, and then fully relapsed on alcohol within 2 months. His monitor, who was cutting him some "slack" during this difficult time, did not report the relapse. But the relapse was identified through body fluid testing and reported to the program and to the medical board. The physician's license was revoked, and he was admitted to inpatient chemical dependency treatment.

If a periodic review had been held with the physician about his contract, the crisis and need for support would have been identified and mobilized. The recovery plan would probably have included grief counseling, increased daily contact and support from peers, increased urine screens, and psychiatric assessment.

As you prepare for contract review, *always include feedback from the significant persons* included in the patient's release-of-information forms. Be sure to initiate these forms during the treatment phase and initiate new releases during the recovery phase as you identify sponsors and monitors.

For patients in early recovery, a contract review offers a unique opportunity to provide positive feedback and encouragement about their progress. Scheduling a periodic review (e.g., at 6 or 12 months) designates this as time for introspection and self-evaluation. During the review, address each behavioral item to the patient as an open-ended question: "Tell me about any medications you have taken the last 6 months . . . about any illnesses or surgery you have had the last 6 months . . . about any cravings you have had the last 6 months. Tell me about any "slips" you have had the last 6 months." Asking such questions in a nonjudgmental tone opens the door for your patients to respond truthfully, even if they fear a consequence. This is an ideal teaching opportunity to help your patient to understand cravings, "slips," and relapse. Encouraging the patient to immediately self-report any "slip" reduces the risk that a "slip" will become a relapse and that relapse will present risk to the patient and others.

When necessary and appropriate, modify the recovery contract by changing the intensity of body fluid testing, for example, or the frequency of meetings or other behavioral criteria. You may also need to change names of significant persons and add releases of information.

Contract review is also an opportunity to intervene when patients do not comply. If you suspect that patients are noncompliant, you may invite their monitor, spouse, or other significant person to the meeting to discuss the data you have received. Early interventions are critical to getting them back on track. When patients are resistant to interventions, and deterioration is significant, use whatever leverage you have at your disposal (e.g., the patient's job status, professional license, marriage).

When primary intervention with your patients indicates that they are resistant to compliance, you might ask them to submit to a comprehensive evaluation. This formal evaluation (which takes several days) offers them a professional examination and testing by psychiatrists, addiction medicine specialists, psychologists, family therapists who interview family members, and assessment team staff who gather additional information from appropriate sources. At the completion of the evaluation, the patient will be presented with the assessment findings and recommendations, and reports will be submitted to the referral source with the patient's permission.

"Slip"/Relapse Clauses

Although many treatment professionals do not differentiate between "slip" and relapse, we feel there is a significant difference relevant for recovery outcome. "Slip"/relapse education is a critical component of the primary treatment so that patients understand the early warning signs and any emotional changes that precede a return to chemical use.

FOUR CLINICAL SCENARIOS ⊞

Nurse Contract With Peer Assistance Program

M.W., a 37-year-old female nurse employed at a 400-bed community hospital, was suspected of diverting drugs from the Cardiac Telemetry Unit where she had worked the evening shift for the past 6 years. Irritable and often complaining of being tired, she was easily angered by patients' demands. The staff attributed these changes to her rigorous schedule (she attended classes until 2 p.m., working toward a master's degree, then worked in the hospital from 3 to 11 p.m.). Over several months, numerous patients complained about her performance, which was highly unusual. After the evening charge nurse discussed her concerns with the head nurse, they met with M.W. to discuss their concerns. M.W. assured them that she was just tired from a heavy class load and that things would improve in a few weeks once exams were over. Over the next month, things did improve; there were no more patient complaints, and her mood seemed remarkably improved. But some peers noticed that she seemed "spacey" during her shift.

Six weeks after the first meeting with M.W., the charge nurse found a syringe of morphine sulfate taped inside the toilet paper dispenser in the staff restroom. She immediately called the supervisor, documented the incident, and had narcotic records checked. Although all the morphine doses had been appropriately signed out and the remaining count correct, several morphine dosages were recorded as "wasted" due to patient refusal, and M.W. had signed for these.

A clear pattern emerged: M.W. was on duty each time there was such an occurrence, and her name was signed to the "wastage" for the morphine signed out of the narcotic box. Several patients had complained that their pain was not relieved on those shifts that M.W. worked.

The director of nursing contacted the state nurses' peer assistance program (PAP) director. The PAP director came to the hospital the next day, reviewed all records, and met with the head nurse, charge nurse, director of nursing, and human resource manager to prepare a meeting with M.W.

At this meeting, M.W. admitted to using the morphine. The director of the PAP offered M.W. several choices of evaluation/treatment programs as well as forensic hair sample analysis, which she declined. M.W. was admitted the same day for assessment.

During her treatment phase, M.W. began to work with her counselor and director of nursing on preparing for her discharge and return to work. It was stipulated that M.W. was to have no access to mood-altering drugs during early recovery and that she could not work more than 32 hours per week. Access to drugs is a primary relapse risk factor for many health care professionals, and M.W. could not return to her former position, which required administration of narcotics. M.W.'s primary focus had to be her recovery, and the counselor discussed the treatment team's recommendations for M.W. with the PAP representative and the director of nursing.

The PAP representative and counselor were in contact with the director of nursing while M.W. was in treatment. There was a consensus that M.W. could return to her unit but as the "telemetry nurse" observing and assessing patient monitors for heart rates and rhythms. She would also be allowed to function as charge nurse, but without access to the narcotic box. M.W.'s counselor, director of nursing, and PAP representative met with M.W. to discuss these continuing care contract guidelines from both her employer and the PAP representative. M.W. knew from prior meetings with her counselor that the primary criterion of the recovery contract was that she remain abstinent from all mood-altering drugs. As a nurse, she would also have specific behavioral criteria in her contract: obtaining a 12-step sponsor, attending 12-step meetings, undergoing random urine analysis through the PAP, attending weekly nurses' support group meetings, submitting monthly reports to the PAP, and complying with PAP and hospital guidelines. Work-related issues in M.W.'s contract included a workplace monitor on evening shift, no night shifts or shift rotation, a peer monitor assigned from the PAP, and no more than 3 university class hours per week. She was also requested to identify a primary care physician who specialized in addiction medicine and to either visit or call the physician once per month and before any dental/medical procedures requiring medication. Every aspect of M.W.'s contract was specific, including names, addresses, phone numbers, times per month, and dates.

Following the presentation of the contract with her counselor, director of nursing, and PAP representative, M.W. signed the contract, understanding that it was for a period of 5 years and that it would be evaluated every 6 months. If M.W. was noncompliant with the terms of the contract, the PAP could report her to the state board of nursing for disciplinary action, and the hospital could terminate her as an employee.

Anesthesiologist's Contract With Hospital Employer

Dr. L., an anesthesiologist, was a member of a 13-person anesthesia group employed by a large medical/surgical hospital. He was trained in anesthesia and had had an excellent academic and work performance record throughout his training.

But at age 41, Dr. L., in a way that was completely contrary to his previous behavior, became increasingly difficult to work with. He became angry and hostile, and at the slightest provocation he berated the nurses. Over the next 17 months, his outbursts of verbal violence and insulting and threatening tirades escalated. Following an argument with a colleague, he shoved the doctor into a locker, and an official complaint was filed with the chief of staff. Dr. L. was mandated for a 96-hour assessment. It revealed that he was suffering from a major depressive disorder characterized by anger as a primary symptom. Prescribed an antidepressant, Dr. L. was put on a recovery contract. It stipulated that he would

- Not address any hospital employee or any other individual with whom he was professionally or personally involved in a voice or a tone that was hostile, angry, or derogatory
- Not make any gestures or actions that could be interpreted as threatening or violent
- Seek individual or group counseling on his anger and threatening manner
- Be monitored for inappropriate behaviors and report weekly to his monitor; his monitor would receive reports from his counselor
- Be suspended from practice and not practice until further notice if the contract was violated

He signed the contract and was monitored by the hospital and primary counselor for a 5-year period. He has since successfully completed his recovery contract.

Physician Contract With a Group Practice

Dr. M., a 29-year-old single male family practitioner, joined a multispecialty group. With excellent training and with high recommendations from his residency training, he integrated smoothly into the busy schedule of his new practice group. But at the start of his second year, the administrative director and the head nurse expressed concern about Dr. M's flirtatious behavior toward the younger nurses in the clinic, to whom he had made inappropriate sexual comments and other unwanted sexual advances.

The executive committee asked Dr. M. to obtain a 3-day professional evaluation. The ensuing report from the assessment center suggested that Dr. M. be given the following behavioral contract criteria in the monitoring contract. Dr. M. would

- Receive weekly sexual counseling with Dr. A.G., with reports of progress sent to the chief of executive committee of the practice
- Attend SAA (Sexual Addiction Anonymous) meetings three times a week
- Refrain from any verbal or behavioral flirtations toward any female on the clinic premises
- Have a staff member in attendance during all patient examinations

- Abstain from use of all mood-altering substances, including over-the-counter preparations (mood-altering substances may precipitate inappropriate sexual behaviors)
- Identify a member of the clinical staff to liaison with the executive committee of the clinic to report on the program and progress of his treatment

Dentist Contract With Licensing Board

T.D. was a 48-year-old married male dentist in private practice in a suburban area. T.D. had a partner; an office staff of eight, including dental assistants, hygienists, and receptionist; and an office manager.

A patient called the state dental board to file a compliant about T.D., saying she smelled "alcohol on his breath." Although a patient of T.D.'s for 3 years, she was concerned. A board investigator questioned T.D.'s partner about T.D's possible alcohol use. The partner, also concerned, had noticed changes in T.D.'s behavior. He was coming in to work late, keeping patients waiting sometimes an hour or more, and returning late from lunch almost every day. The partner reluctantly admitted that he had also smelled alcohol on T.D.'s breath on several occasions. When requesting a printout from a popular drug warehouse used by dentists, the investigator found that T.D. had ordered a large supply of Valium for office use. The investigator met with T.D. and his partner about the printout. As general dentists, they had no reason to use diazepam (a tranquilizer) for patients; moreover, they could not produce the Valium (bottles of which should have been locked in the drug cabinet). When the office manager had received an order of Valium and hd asked T.D. about it, T.D. had stated, "It was an error, and I will return it." Because all orders (10 orders in 4 months) for the drugs were under T.D.'s name, he finally admitted he had taken the drug home because he was "having trouble sleeping."

When the investigator brought these findings to the dental board, T.D. was remanded by the board to comprehensive assessment at a treatment facility specializing in health care professionals. His license was suspended until he complied with all recommendations of the assessment. The assessment indicated a primary diagnosis of alcohol dependence. He had been self-medicating with Valium to minimize the effects of withdrawal during the day.

T.D. completed a comprehensive treatment program, and his continuing care contract included specific practice restrictions:

- Loss of DEA privileges for a minimum of 2 years (his partner would do all prescribing for controlled substances)
- No access to mood-altering drugs (keys to the drug cabinet would be kept by his partner only)
- No medications, including over the counter, unless prescribed by his primary care physician
- Attendance at four AA meetings per week and signed documentation of attendance
- Individual counseling weekly with reports monthly to the board regarding his progress
- Random urine monitoring and Breathalyzer testing by the state board lab program

- No treating patients after hours or on weekends unless another staff member was present
- Keeping a log of all prescriptions written and submitting it by the 30th of each month to the state board
- Identifying a member of the practice staff to liaison with the executive committee of the clinic to report on his treatment progress

OVERT CONTRACT SABOTAGE ▦

Be aware of four ways that patients sabotage their recovery contracts.

Patient Claims Contract Was an Act of Coercion and Refutes Contract

When patients will not sign the contract, there is essentially no accountability; this, of course, challenges the counselor. Patients usually ask if you are going to call the licensing board, the airline, or the corporation to notify them of refusal to cooperate. Although treatment providers must uphold confidentiality laws and may not use this type of reporting as leverage to move the patient into engaging in the contract, remember that *someone* always has a vested interest in the patient's treatment and recovery. The individuals responsible for the patient getting to treatment, those who hold significant power, can be utilized to report noncompliance to the appropriate source. This "lever" will get the patient's attention and undermine the coercion argument.

Despite your best planning, some patients will react to one item of the contract, complaining that the contract is too restrictive. At this point, discuss each item again to ascertain the disputed item. Once it is identified, have all parties—including the program or employer who referred the patient, the family, and another counselor—discuss the contract with the patient again. Use a calm, reassuring explanation to convince the patient that this is in his or her best interest and has no harmful intent. A recovering peer can be helpful at these meetings—a program representative (i.e., recovering dentist, nurse, physician, executive, homemaker, student, pilot, etc.) who successfully completed a recovery contract and is now free of restrictions. Of course, you need the patient's permission, but most often he or she will agree simply out of curiosity. The key is utilizing someone the patient will identify with.

Patient Claims That Because He Was Still in a State of Detoxification When He Signed the Contract, It Is Invalid

Competency is an issue for patients soon after admission in any treatment facility. If contracts are generated and presented when the patient is in an acute stage of detoxification, legal issues should be considered. Although you begin working on the contract from the day of admission, do not present the contract to the patient until the last stages of treatment, when the patient is fully detoxed and ready for discharge. *Never* offer the contract while the patient is actively detoxing.

Patient Introduces Lawyers Into the Contract Obligations and Files Legalistic Claims

Some patients threaten to call an attorney. Usually these patients have been remanded to treatment by the courts, licensing boards, or another powerful authority. In other words, they would not under other circumstances voluntarily enter into treatment. In these situations, we recommend that you gain appropriate releases and contact the patient's attorney yourself. Previously having only one source of information (your client's), the attorney will be better able to form an accurate assessment. When appropriate, you may invite the attorney to attend the recovery contract conference, particularly if the patient has pending legal charges. Attorneys can serve as unconditional advocates for their client's best interests and can be an invaluable resource to the recovery contract team.

Patient Follows Some Component of the Contract But, With Passive/Aggressive Behavior, Destroys the Contract's Intent

Few, if any, chemically dependent patients respond with enthusiasm to their recovery contract. Herein lies the difference between recovery and compliance: Patients shaky in recovery, who harbor feelings of resentment and anger, often do just enough to get by but not enough to be considered compliant. This is the difference between "working a recovery program" and merely complying, doing what one "has to do."

Some patients project their anger in passive-aggressive ways toward the program or the counselor who monitors their recovery contract. Sending in reports late is the most common way to irritate even the most competent contract monitor. Other examples include sending in illegible, handwritten, scribbled notes for self-reports; blaming late delivery on the post office; sending torn and wrinkled meeting attendance sheets; constantly reporting every month that "everything's fine;" on checklist inventories for self-evaluation, always checking the highest score every month; sending most *but not all* the documentation requested; sending reports without postage (one of our personal favorites); and constantly complaining about the program or staff. Another favorite is patients' claim that they never received written notice of noncompliance and that you are sending their mail to the wrong address.

These behaviors convey a clear message to the counselor that this patient needs attention. A formal meeting with the patient, significant others, program representative, and counselor offers the unaware patient an opportunity to discuss feelings and for the counselor to again articulate the purpose and importance of the contract, as well as the consequences of noncompliance. It may be appropriate to add stipulations for individual counseling or group sessions for this patient to help him or her identify and resolve issues blocking his or her recovery.

▦ WEAKNESSES IN MONITORING PROGRAM DESIGN

Some patients may be in programs sponsored by their professions or occupations. The primary goal of these programs is to provide early identification of chemical dependency, intervention, treatment referrals, and monitoring. But some of these programs have internal dysfunction that may interfere in your patient's progress. Three of these weaknesses are discussed below.

No One Person From the Program Monitors the Contract; the Program Keeps Switching Individuals and Responsibilities

This is clear danger for the patient and the program, especially when patients are assigned to rotating counselors, thereby disrupting the "therapeutic relationship." With different monitors subjectively interpreting the patient's compliance, the personal aspect of this engagement is lost. One of us (L.C.) had this experience when running a state-level program. New counselors were assigned to the program, and there was some case overlap and shared caseloads. Patients began negotiating and manipulating in passive-aggressive ways. When counselors bond with certain patients, they dilute treatment effectiveness, especially if those patients are given privileges that others are denied. A team approach works best in avoiding such problems with chemically dependent patients. If you are a solo practitioner, it is advisable to recruit a consultant colleague to assist you with case reviews and recommendations. From a legal perspective, we recommend that you take on a part-time consultant, volunteer or paid, to avoid accusations by patients who feel that the director is unjustly handling their case.

Explain and discuss with the patients in advance, when possible, any changes in monitors, counselors, or other significant parties to provide a smooth transition. Trust is a difficult if not elusive concept for recovering patients, and you have the responsibility of nurturing the patients' development of trust with appropriate therapeutic measures.

Superiors in the Professional Program Do Not Agree With or Abide by the Contract and Override the Monitors

As treatment is both person dependent and person centered, and as different counselors' interpretation of a guiding principle or recovery issue may vary, the team approach is critical to providing patients with appropriate direction. Programs dilute their leverage with patients when one person says one thing and another person says the opposite or changes the patient's contract. It is crucial that all parties involved in the patient's care and monitoring develop a consensus and formulate a clear, non-negotiable plan for the patient. Splitting can occur in the treatment facility, the professional assistance program, the patient's family, or the continuing care facility, and if it is not stopped early on, it is an obstacle to the patient's recovery.

Politics Prevent Consequences of Any Enforcement of the Contract

There is always potential risk of a contract with "no teeth." If there is not appropriate monitoring with appropriate consequence and follow-ups, patients may regard the contract as meaningless. If no consequences are given, there is less likelihood the patients will comply with the behaviors requested in the contract. Even in cases of contract non-compliance, some programs are reluctant to report these individuals to licensing boards or other appropriate parties. These evasive actions may stem from the program staff's reluctance to be viewed as "ineffective" by the licensing boards or authorities or the fear of reducing possible referrals to the program if the word gets out that they are "turning people over to the board." When this happens, some noncompliant patients, essentially left to their own, make little progress. As months of noncompliance continue, resistance escalates, and in some cases relapse ensues. *If there will be no follow-through on the stipulations, there is no point in developing a contract.*

▦ CONCLUSION

The recovery contract is the cornerstone of treatment and recovery. When well crafted, it serves as a short-term life plan that can reduce everyday distractors and stresses for the patient so that he or she may focus on activities that reinforce recovery. For the counselor, the recovery contract is the therapeutic tool for the patient's continuing therapy and growth in recovery.

▦ REFERENCES

Gallegos, K. V., Lubin, B., Bowers, C., Blevins, J. W., Talbott, G. D., & Wilson, P. O. (1992). Relapse and recovery: Five to ten year follow-up study of chemically dependent physicians. The Georgia experience: Division of Data and Statistics, Caduceus Foundation, Atlanta, GA. *Maryland Medical Journal, 41,* 315-319.

Talbott, G. D. (1995). Reducing relapse in health providers and professionals. *Psychiatric Annals, 25,* 669-672.

▦ ADDITIONAL SUGGESTED READINGS

Angres, D., Talbott, G. D., & Angres, K. B. (1999) *Healing the healer: The addicted physician.* Madison, CT: Psychosocial Press.

Coombs, R. H. (1997). *Drug-impaired professionals.* Cambridge, MA: Harvard University Press.

Crosby, L., & Bissell, L. (1989). *To care enough: Intervention with chemically dependent colleagues.* Center City, MN: Hazelden.

Crosby, L. R. (1993). *Peer assistance for counselors.* Arlington, VA: National Association of Alcoholism and Other Drug Counselors.

Talbott, G. D., Angres, D., & Gallegos, K. V. (1997). Physicians and other health professionals. In J. H. Lowinson (Ed.), *Substance abuse: A comprehensive textbook* (3rd ed.). Baltimore: Williams & Wilkins.

Talbott, G. D., & Gallegos, K. V. (1998). Impairment and recovery in physicians and other health professionals. In A. W. Graham & T. K. Shultz (Eds.), *Principles of addiction medicine* (2nd ed.). Chevy Chase, MD: American Society of Addiction Medicine.

Talbott, G. D., & Porter, T. (2000, March). *Study of recovery activity of 672 health professionals.* Paper presented at the American Medical Association Conference on Physician Health, Seabrook Island.

PROFESSIONAL ASSISTANCE PROGRAM CONTACTS ⊞

Attorneys/Judges

The American Bar Association maintains a comprehensive director of Lawyers Assistance
Programs throughout the country.

Contact **org/cpr/colap/assistance.html** or contact Donna Spilis: phone (312) 988-5359; e-mail
spilisd@staff.abanet.org

Counselors

State programs for counselors are not as widespread as those for health professionals, but for more
information, contact the National Association of Drug and Alcohol and Addiction Counselors
(NAADAC) at **www.naadac.org** or call (800) 548-0497.

Dentists/Oral Surgeons

Contact Linda Kittelson, MS, RN, CADC, at the American Dental Association for a directory of
state dental peer assistance programs. E-mail **kittelson@ada.org**; phone (312) 440-2622.

Physicians

Contact the Federation of Physician Health Programs, Linda Breshnahan at Massachusetts Physician Health Program for a listing of programs throughout the country.

International Doctors in AA (IDAA) has a compiled list of 12-step meetings state by state. Contact
Dr. Richard McKinley at IDAA, P.O. Box 199, Augusta, MO 63332, or call (314) 482-4548.

Nurses

Contact your state board of nursing for listings of advocacy programs for nurses or the Web site
alternativeprograms.org for listings of advocacy programs for health professional groups. Or
contact Barbara McGill, MSN, RN, Secretary, at (504) 838-5429 for the program in your state.

Nurse Anesthetists

The American Association of Nurse Anesthetists has a directory of peer advocates in each state.
Contact **www.aana.org** for a listing. Or contact Diana Quinlan at **peerassist@aol.com**

Pharmacists

The Pharmacist Recovery Program is available in most states. Contact the American Pharmaceutical Association in Washington, DC, for a listing, or check the Web site
www.aphanet.org/development/prnprograms.html.

Pilots

The Airline Pilots Association Aeromedical office in Colorado has listing for all major airline employee assistance programs. Contact Don Hudson, MD, at (303) 341-4435. The smaller airlines also have programs, and Dr. Hudson may be of assistance in identifying the contact person.

Airline pilots also have a 12-step group called "Birds of a Feather." There is a quarterly publication called *Bird Word* that lists all the meetings in United States and Europe. Check the Web site **www.boaf.org**

Psychologists

Contact the American Psychological Association, Department of Professional Development, Mr. Chris McLaughlin, (202) 336-5865, for a referral to the state-level Advisory Committee on Colleague Assistance.

Social Workers

Some states have programs for social workers called Social Workers Helping Social Workers. Contact your state Association of Social Workers.

9

Contingency Management

Using Science to Motivate Change

Alan J. Budney
Stacey C. Sigmon
Stephen T. Higgins

ontingency management (CM) interventions can effectively motivate and facilitate change in the most challenging substance abuse treatment populations. The CM approach to treatment is based on extensive basic science and
clinical research evidence demonstrating that drug use and abuse are heavily
influenced by learning and conditioning and are quite sensitive to systematically applied environmental consequences (Griffiths, Bigelow, & Henningfield, 1980; Higgins,
1997; Stitzer & Higgins, 1995). A recent resurgence of clinical trials examining the efficacy of CM across multiple types of drug dependence and clinical populations provides
compelling empirical support for the efficacy of this treatment approach (Higgins &
Silverman, 1999). You, like most substance abuse therapists, may not know much
about CM approaches because they have been implemented primarily in research settings. This chapter provides you with a basic understanding of the CM approach to substance dependence treatment and how you might integrate it into a treatment clinic
environment. We hope to stimulate your interest enough to encourage further reading
and training in this innovative and efficacious treatment approach.

AUTHORS' NOTE: Preparation of this chapter was supported in part by National Institute on Drug Abuse
Grants DA12157, DA09378 and DA07242.

⊞ CONCEPTUALIZATION

Within the CM conceptual framework, drug use is considered a case of operant behavior that is maintained, in part, by the pharmacological actions of the drug in conjunction with social and other nonpharmacological reinforcement derived from the drug-abusing lifestyle (Higgins & Katz, 1998). An important feature of this conceptual model of drug abuse is that it facilitates a direct connection between clinical practice and the scientific disciplines of behavior analysis and behavioral pharmacology. Those disciplines include an extensive research literature demonstrating principles and procedures that can be applied to modify behavior of all kinds, including drug abuse. A major strength of conceptualizing drug use and abuse as operant behavior is that, as such, it is amenable to change via the same processes and principles as other types of human operant behavior, irrespective of its etiology. Within this framework, treatment is designed to assist in reorganizing the physical and social environments of the user. The goal is to systematically weaken the influence of reinforcement derived from drug use and the related lifestyle and to increase the frequency and magnitude of reinforcement derived from healthier alternative activities, especially those that are incompatible with continued drug use.

The CM approach capitalizes on knowledge that drug seeking and drug use can be directly modified by manipulating the relevant environmental contingencies. Typically, CM interventions are used to engender therapeutic change within a comprehensive treatment program in a substance abuse treatment clinic. CM programs arrange the therapeutic environment so that (a) target therapeutic behaviors (e.g., drug abstinence, counseling attendance, medication compliance) are carefully monitored, and (b) reinforcing or punishing events (e.g., tangible rewards, suspension of employment) occur when the target behavior is or is not demonstrated.

⊞ BASIC PRINCIPLES OF CM

CM interventions almost always involve the use of positive reinforcement, negative reinforcement, positive punishment, or negative punishment contingencies to motivate increases and decreases in the frequency of a therapeutically desirable or undesirable behavior. You must first master these basic principles if you expect to develop and implement an effective CM intervention. *Positive reinforcement* involves delivery of a desired consequence (e.g., vouchers/tokens exchangeable for retail items) contingent on the individual's meeting a therapeutic goal (e.g., negative urinalysis test results, attendance at a counseling session). *Negative reinforcement* involves removing an aversive or confining circumstance (e.g., intensity of criminal justice supervision) contingent on meeting a therapeutic goal. *Positive punishment* involves delivery of a punishing consequence (e.g., professional reprimand) contingent on evidence of undesirable behavior (e.g., positive urinalysis test result). *Negative punishment* involves removal of a positive circumstance or condition (e.g., reduction in the monetary value of vouchers that could be earned or removal of a preferred schedule of medication dosing) contingent on evidence of the occurrence of an undesirable behavior (e.g., missing a counseling session).

Both reinforcement and punishment contingencies can be effective tools in substance abuse treatment programs, but you and your clients are likely to prefer the former over the latter. You should always exercise great caution when using a punishment contingency by itself, as these can increase treatment dropout, an outcome you want to avoid in substance abuse treatment. This is less of an issue in some circumstances (e.g., court-mandated treatment) and can probably be offset by inclusion of reinforcement contingencies. You will find that a very clear benefit of reinforcement contingencies is that they can increase retention, which is why our most recent CM applications primarily use positive reinforcement principles (Higgins & Budney, 1997).

EFFICACY ▦

Controlled clinical studies have shown that CM interventions can enhance therapeutic outcomes across a wide range of substance abuse treatment populations. For example, in 1989 we developed a CM program for cocaine-dependent outpatients and have now treated more than 300 clients across a series of controlled clinical trials (Higgins et al., 1993, 1994; Higgins, Wong, Badger, Ogden, & Dantona, 2000). This work demonstrated that an abstinence-based incentive program effectively increases cocaine abstinence during and following treatment for cocaine dependence. In our CM program, clients provide urine specimens on a thrice-weekly schedule, and monetary-based incentives (i.e., vouchers) are earned for each cocaine-negative urine specimen submitted. Voucher spending is used to support treatment goals. That is, vouchers are exchangeable for retail goods or services in the community, and purchases are approved only if therapists deem them to be in concert with treatment goals. This incentive program serves two clinical functions. First, the monetary-based incentives provide additional motivation by directly reinforcing abstinence when it occurs. Second, incentive earnings are used to promote healthy activities that support the development of a non-drug-using lifestyle. Of note, we have shown that the efficacy of our CM program for cocaine dependence extends at least 15 months posttreatment: that is, well after the incentive program ends (Higgins, Badger, & Budney, 2000; Higgins, Wong, et al., 2000). As with other treatments, relapse does occur, but the rate of relapse in our CM program appears to be no greater than that observed in the other treatments we have studied.

Similar incentive programs effectively increase cocaine abstinence in methadone-maintained, opiate-dependent clients (Silverman et al., 1996), inner-city crack abusers (Kirby, Marlowe, Festinger, Lamb, & Platt, 1998), pregnant cocaine abusers (Elk, 1999), and homeless, dually diagnosed cocaine abusers (Milby et al., 2000). We also demonstrated that incentive programs increase marijuana abstinence during treatment for marijuana dependence (Budney, Higgins, Radonovich, & Novy, 2000) and opiate abstinence during treatment for opiate dependence (Bickel, Amass, Higgins, Badger, & Esch, 1997). Others have shown that these type of CM programs can improve retention and abstinence rates during treatment for alcohol dependence (Petry, Martin, Cooney, & Kranzler, 2000) and can decrease cigarette use during treatment for opiate dependence (Shoptaw et al., submitted for publication).

CM interventions have also proven effective in the methadone clinic, where the majority of heroin-dependent clients are treated (Stitzer & Higgins, 1995). The methadone clinic structure provides a number of potential reinforcers and punishments that you can use in CM interventions to enhance treatment outcomes in this difficult clinical population (Kidorf & Stitzer, 1999). Methadone is an oral, long-acting opioid substitution medication that effectively reduces heroin and other illicit opioid use and related withdrawal symptomatology. Methadone therapy typically is administered through clinics that provide daily doses of methadone and various types of adjunct counseling. Although methadone treatment effectively reduces illicit opiate use and other antisocial behavior, it does not directly address the full range of problems that most clients bring to treatment.

Usually, methadone maintenance clients are required to attend the clinic daily to ingest their medication under nursing supervision. This is done to protect against diversion of the medication. CM interventions typically use either the methadone take-home privilege or methadone dose alterations to increase desirable therapeutic behavior. The methadone take-home privilege involves providing an extra daily dose of methadone to patients for ingestion on the following day so that they do not need to attend the clinic on that day. Having to attend the clinic daily can be burdensome, sometimes interfering with vocational or family responsibilities. This makes the take-home privilege desirable to patients. If they simply elect to skip coming to the clinic for a day and do not take a daily dose of methadone, they are likely to experience adverse opiate withdrawal symptoms and are at increased risk for using heroin or other illicit opiates. Take-home doses are not provided to all patients because they have the potential for abuse through either the patient's ingestion of the take-home dose before the scheduled dosing time or, as was noted above, the patient's diversion of the medication for sale. Thus, the take-home privilege offers a convenient and valued incentive for use in CM programs and is one of the most potent positive reinforcers available within the context of routine clinic operation (Stitzer & Bigelow, 1978). Contingent take-home procedures can effectively reduce opiate and other illicit drug use, compliance with clinic regulations, pursuit of vocational training, and payment of clinic fees (Kidorf & Stitzer, 1999). The methadone take-home procedure exemplifies how treatment providers can creatively use CM strategies within existing clinic settings to positively influence treatment participation and outcomes.

You can also use the dose of methadone provided to opiate-dependent clients as a positive reinforcer within a CM program. Higher doses of methadone are desirable to some clients because they provide more complete reduction of withdrawal symptoms and cause the client to feel and function better, whereas lower doses are less effective at eliminating withdrawal symptoms or illicit use of heroin. As with take-home privilege interventions, multiple studies have demonstrated that the contingent use of methadone dose increases or decreases can effectively reduce opiate and other illicit drug use, increase counseling attendance, prompt gainful employment, and increase participation of significant others in the counseling process (Kidorf & Stitzer, 1999).

⊞ UNDERUTILIZATION

Despite the abundance of empirical support for the efficacy of CM interventions in the treatment of substance dependence problems, most community substance abuse clinics do not use CM. Most substance abuse therapists have not been trained in the use of CM and are unaware of its potential to enhance treatment outcomes. One explanation for this situation is that the theoretical underpinnings of CM are construed by some as contradictory to the disease model perspective of alcoholism, which has been the model generally embraced by the substance abuse treatment community. Moreover, verbal therapies are well established as the primary modality of treatment for substance abuse problems. The manipulation of environmental factors or treatment program structure (i.e., the typical mode of CM implementation) may seem outside the accepted treatment paradigm to program directors and therapists. Implementation of CM interventions may also appear more difficult and costly than office-based verbal therapies. We believe that each of these factors contributing to the underutilization of CM in the substance abuse field can be remedied. Hopefully, as additional information on the principles and efficacy of CM is disseminated and the cost efficacy is better established, more substance abuse treatment programs will include CM interventions.

EFFECTIVE CM PROGRAMMING ⊞

Whether the contingencies employed in the clinic setting involve reinforcement, punishment, or both, you will find that the frequency and temporal interval used to deliver the consequence, the magnitude of the consequence, the choice of the target behavior, and the method for monitoring the target behavior will influence the efficacy of the intervention. To effectively develop and implement CM interventions, you must be familiar with how these factors affect behavior change. You can find instructional overviews on the application of behavior-analytic principles in a number of sources (Miller, 1984; Sulzer-Azaroff & Meyer, 1991), and more specific examples of CM interventions for substance dependence disorders were recently published in a journal article (Petry, 2000) and a text on this topic (Higgins & Silverman, 1999). Here we offer you an abbreviated summary of these principles and examples of their application in a substance abuse treatment setting.

Temporal Proximity and Frequency of Reinforcment or Punishment

The efficacy of the contingency will generally increase as the temporal delay between the occurrence of the target behavior and delivery of the scheduled consequence decreases. Reinforcement or punishment should be applied as close in time to the detection of the target behavior as possible. For example, all else being equal, a clinic that provides positive reinforcement for cocaine abstinence 5 minutes after a client submits a cocaine-negative urine specimen would generate greater rates of cocaine abstinence than a clinic that waits 4 days after the submission of the specimen before reinforcement is delivered. In our abstinence-based voucher treatment program for cocaine dependence, on-site urine testing allows treatment staff to provide almost immediate reinforcement (i.e., vouchers) each time a client provides evidence of cocaine abstinence (cocaine-negative urinalysis test).

Similarly, schedules involving more frequent reinforcement (e.g., three times per week) are preferable to less frequent schedules (once per week) in establishing an initial target behavior like drug abstinence or regular attendance at counseling sessions. A more frequent schedule allows additional opportunities to reinforce and thereby strengthen the target behavior. For example, if you want to generate higher rates of initial attendance at a group counseling session, you should consider providing pizza and soft drinks to attendees at each weekly session rather than waiting until they attend sessions for a full month. Our CM program for cocaine dependence includes thrice-weekly urinalysis testing, providing an opportunity to reinforce cocaine abstinence frequently during the first 12 weeks of treatment. Once a target behavior (e.g., abstinence or counseling attendance) is established, a less frequent schedule of reinforcement may be used for maintenance purposes.

Magnitude

Second, the *magnitude of the reinforcing or punishing consequence provided* is important. For example, if a patient's goal is drug abstinence, as indicated by a drug-negative urine test, the scheduled delivery of a voucher worth $10.00 for each negative specimen is more likely to motivate drug cessation than a voucher worth $2.50. In general, choice of what magnitude of reinforcement to use requires careful consideration of the severity of the behavior targeted for change and the difficulty patients experience trying to change such behavior. *An effective reinforcer must compete with the reinforcement derived from the behavior targeted for change.* Given the resilience of substance use habits typically developed over many years, and especially when treating individuals who use relatively large quantities of drug, strong reinforcers are likely to be necessary. In our cocaine and marijuana CM programs, the value of the vouchers earned escalates with each consecutive drug-negative specimen, and when an unexcused absence from a scheduled urinalysis or a drug-positive test occurs, the value of the vouchers resets to the initial lower level. This schedule promotes continuous periods of abstinence by increasing the amount of reinforcement earned in direct relation to the number of consecutive drug-negative specimens submitted and by resetting the value of the vouchers back to low amounts of reinforcement if drug use occurs.

Creative use of relatively low-magnitude reinforcers can also be successful in modifying a wide variety of target behaviors among drug abusers, especially when used in combination with other treatment interventions. For example, Petry et al. (2000) implemented a CM program in which alcohol-dependent clients earned the chance to win a prize for each negative breath sample they submitted and for each of three preset therapeutic activities that they completed during the week and that were verified. The prizes ranged in value from $1 to $100. Each time clients earned a chance to win a prize, they drew a slip from a fishbowl that had a 75% chance of being a winner. The slips indicated whether you had won a small, medium, or large prize. The number of small prize-winning slips in the bowl was greater than medium prize slips, which was greater than the large prize slips. This innovative application of positive reinforcement principles effectively increased treatment retention and alcohol abstinence in clients enrolled in intensive outpatient treatment without delivering a monetary reinforcer each time the client completed the target behavior.

Selection of Reinforcers

The *choice of reinforcers or punishers* used in a CM program is critical to its success. Here the treatment program must recognize that individuals vary greatly in terms of the type of goods and services that will serve as reinforcers. A specific reinforcer (e.g., pizza or movie theater passes) that functions as an effective reinforcer for one client may not be reinforcing for another. Our abstinence-based voucher program that allows clients to choose from as wide a selection of items as possible was created with this principle in mind. That is, clients can choose any appropriate item or service available in the community, and clinic staff make the purchase.

Other reinforcers that have been used in CM programs include cash, on-site retail items, specific prizes, desirable clinic privileges, employment or housing opportunities, or refunds on treatment service fees. Each of these has its strengths and drawbacks. For example, providing cash would most likely be highly reinforcing for most clients, but cash also serves as a trigger for drug use for many clients. Having retail items available at the clinic would allow for immediate delivery of the reinforcer, but the diversity of items would have to be somewhat limited. In general, CM programs should always consider providing a diverse set of items that are desirable to a wide range of clientele.

Therapeutic Targets

CM programs must also give careful thought to the *selection of the therapeutic target behavior*. Most of the CM literature has focused on drug abstinence. More specifically, the most successful CM programs have targeted a specific drug rather than abstinence from all drugs. Although this may seem controversial given that many clients are multiple drug users, the strategy of targeting the primary drug has merit and some empirical support (Budney, Higgins, Delaney, Kent, & Bickel, 1991; Piotrowski et al., 1999; Silverman et al., 1998). The few studies targeting the simultaneous abstinence from all drugs of abuse (i.e., studies that provided vouchers only if urine specimens indicated abstinence from all drugs) have found that the majority of their patients were unable to achieve even one drug-free urine specimen and thus never received reinforcement (Downey, Helmus, & Schuster, 2000; Iguchi, Belding, Morral, Lamb, & Husband, 1997). Either the target goal, complete drug abstinence, was too difficult for the patients to achieve, or the reinforcer was not of sufficient magnitude to motivate them to abstain from all drug use. Whatever the reason for the failure, this highlights the importance of designing CM programs that provide ample opportunities to reinforce the target behavior. By definition, reinforcement interventions cannot be effective without an opportunity to reinforce the target behavior. Abstinence from all drugs of abuse is a very difficult goal for many polydrug abusers. Voucher-based programs for this difficult treatment population may need to consider using sequential strategies that require progressively more difficult abstinence goals, providing higher-magnitude reinforcers for more difficult goals, or enlisting adjunct treatment strategies such as medication, short-term hospitalization, or more intensive counseling. We believe that effective strategies for managing polydrug abuse are more likely to result from thoughtful, focused efforts than sweeping goals of achieving simultaneous abstinence from all psychoactive drug use.

CM programs can increase the achievement of therapeutic behaviors other than drug abstinence, such as medication compliance, counseling attendance, or completion of lifestyle change activities. When choosing target behaviors other than drug abstinence, you should recognize that successful completion of these goals may not result in drug abstinence. That is, you may improve treatment attendance by providing vouchers contingent on coming to sessions, but drug use may not change. On the basis of the cumulative data from the literature, the first choice of a target behavior for CM programs for drug abuse should be drug use. If this is not possible or if you would like to add another target to your program, you should probably select specific, individualized treatment goal targets that have a high probability for successful completion by the client rather

---

BOX 9.1   CM Programming

- *Reinforcement Delivery*
  - Provide reinforcement with as little delay as possible.
  - Use a frequent schedule to establish initial behavior (drug abstinence).

- *Magnitude*
  - The higher the value of the reinforcer, the more it will motivate behavior change.
  - Lower-value reinforcers can motivate behavior when delivered on variable schedules.

- *Choice of Reinforcers*
  - Individuals vary greatly regarding what goods and services will serve as reinforcers.
  - If possible, provide a diverse choice of reinforcers desirable to a wide range of clients.

- *Therapeutic Targets*
  - Choose a target behavior with a high probability for successful completion.
  - CM interventions cannot be effective without an opportunity to reinforce the target behavior.
  - Make your first choice drug abstinence.
  - When selecting other target behaviors, choose individualized treatment goal targets.

- *Monitoring*
  - Objective monitoring is necessary for fair and effective implementation.
  - Self-reports are not adequate.

---

than simply attendance at treatment sessions. Last, always keep in mind that you must verify completion of whatever therapeutic target is selected.

Monitoring

When implementing CM interventions, you must employ an effective *monitoring system* such that reinforcement or punishment can be applied systematically. Precise information on the occurrence of the therapeutic target response is necessary to implement a successful intervention. With drug abusers, this is usually whether they have used drugs recently and involves some form of biochemical verification of drug abstinence. Urinalysis testing is the most common verification procedure in CM treatments for drug abuse. Such objective monitoring is necessary for fair and effective implementation of CM programs. Again, when you choose other behavioral targets, such as medication compliance, attending counseling sessions, increasing social activities, and completion of skills-training homework, you must have a method to objectively verify whether the target behavior occurred. Reliance on client self-reports of whether drug use occurred or whether the client completed a therapeutic task would not be adequate for these purposes.

⊞ EFFECTIVE IMPLEMENTATION

Successful implementation of a CM intervention depends on the clinical staff's enthusiastic acceptance of the program and careful implementation of the CM protocol. Clinic staff must develop the skills necessary to promote the CM program, facilitate its ongoing operation, and effectively integrate it with other treatment components. Below, we discuss common tasks for the CM clinician and highlight some typical problems that may arise. We use examples from our abstinence-based incentive programs to illustrate how the clinician can handle these important therapeutic tasks.

Rationale and Contracting

Your first challenge involves presenting the rationale and description of the CM program in a manner that will maximize its acceptability and efficacy. Most clients who enroll in treatment expect to receive counseling that simply involves talking about their problems. If they also expect to receive medication (e.g., methadone), they probably do not expect, for example, that specific requirements will be attached to their dose or dosing schedule. CM programs require that the clients follow certain rules or complete specific tasks to obtain desirable consequences or avoid undesirable consequences. As you well know, many substance abuse clients do not have exemplary histories of following rules and responding to requests from authority figures. Therefore, the therapist must present a description of the treatment process in a manner that fosters understanding, interest, and compliance. Getting off to a good start—that is, having the client on board with the program—will promote a good outcome.

In most CM programs, clients and staff sign a contract before initiating the intervention. The contract used in our incentive programs for cocaine and marijuana dependence establishes an explicit agreement to abstain from cocaine or marijuana use and to participate in a regular schedule of urinalysis testing associated with an abstinence-based voucher program (see Appendix 9.1 for a copy of the Abstinence Contract). The client-therapist interaction regarding this contract serves to ensure that the client fully understands the urine monitoring schedule and voucher program, especially the precise requirements for earning vouchers.

Urinalysis Monitoring

Urinalysis monitoring is used as an objective marker of progress in achieving the goal of drug abstinence. Clients and therapists must clearly understand the rationale for using a structured urine-monitoring program. Many therapists do not have experience with such a monitoring program and may be hesitant about its need and how it may affect the client's willingness to participate. Urine testing is a hallmark of most CM substance abuse interventions; hence, everyone involved must embrace it as a crucial element of the treatment process. Below, we provide sample dialogue for introducing the client to the urine-monitoring program that we use with our incentive intervention:

> I'd like to go over our abstinence contract, which reviews some important parts of treatment as well as the details of the urine-monitoring and voucher program. This contract represents

BOX 9.2	Urinalysis Monitoring Contracts

- Help decrease many forms of drug use, including cocaine, opioid, and marijuana use

- Keep the focus of treatment on the primary problem, drug use

- Provide opportunities to catch the client being good (not using drugs)

- Provide opportunities for incentives, praise, and other positive support for drug abstinence

- Help the therapist detect and work on relapse triggers

- Reduce the client's tendency to hide use because of embarrassment, pride, etc.

- Provide opportunities to regain credibility with friends and relatives

- Provide reassurance to those around the client that he or she is continuing to do well

an agreement between you and the clinic to help you maintain abstinence from cocaine. You will provide urine samples three times per week on a Monday, Wednesday, and Friday schedule during the first 12 weeks of treatment. During the second half of treatment, you will provide urine samples twice per week on a Monday and Thursday schedule. Throughout treatment, a clinic staff member of your same sex will observe the urination. The reason behind this clinic policy is that urinalysis testing is an integral component of our treatment program. Our on-site testing procedures permit us to carefully monitor your progress toward cocaine abstinence and help us design effective treatment plans each week. We realize that this is sometimes awkward at first, but we try to be sensitive to your comfort level while at the same time maintaining the integrity and credibility of the monitoring program.

Research on urinalysis monitoring programs like this one has clearly shown that they help decrease many forms of drug use, including cocaine, opioid, and marijuana use. Our urinalysis monitoring will help us stay focused on the primary problem that brought you into treatment—that is, your drug use. You should realize that we use this program not to catch you being bad but rather to catch you being good (i.e., not using cocaine). In this way, we, as well as others in your life, can reinforce desired behavior. We can provide incentives, praise, and other forms of positive support when you don't use drugs. Most likely, most people in your life get on your case or give you a lot of grief any time you use cocaine, but rarely does anyone pat you on the back or praise you for not using. Our program tries to turn this around so that we and others in your life clearly let you know that not using cocaine is a behavior to be recognized, praised, and rewarded.

In addition, urinalysis monitoring will assist us in helping you learn more about the relationship between cocaine and other drug abuse and certain consequences. If you use cocaine during treatment, the urinalysis test will provide us with that information and an opportunity to work on ways to help you get back on track and prevent further use from occurring. Many times, patients do not want to share the fact that they used cocaine because of embarrassment, pride, or some other reason; however, such information is important for helping you learn more about how to meet your goal of stopping cocaine use.

Many times, drug abusers have lost credibility with friends, relatives, and other persons in their lives by the time they arrive in treatment. Urinalysis monitoring can provide a way to prove that you are doing well. This may be important because once you start doing well, any bad days you have (irritable, tired, depressed mood), may be perceived by others as an indication of relapse. Urinalysis monitoring can provide reassurance to those around you that you are continuing to do well even when you, like anyone else, have a day when you do not feel sociable and your behavior is not so pleasant.

Voucher Program

After discussing the urine-monitoring program, you must provide a similarly thorough description of the voucher incentive program. Like structured urine monitoring, abstinence-based voucher programs are something that most therapists and clients have little or no experience with. Both may find the concept and rationale of directly "rewarding" abstinence foreign and perplexing. In our experience, once they fully understand the premise of the voucher program, as well as the nuts and bolts of its administration, clinicians and clients alike readily embrace these interventions and find them most helpful in facilitating progress and change toward a drug-free lifestyle. You must use your clinical skills and knowledge base to make sure that clients fully understand all aspects of the voucher schedule: that is, how and how much they can earn, as well as the rationale for its use for drug abuse problems. For example, our experimental studies demonstrate that the escalating nature of our schedule and the reset procedure (see below) can greatly influence the amount of continuous drug abstinence that a client is likely to achieve. Therefore, you want to be certain that your client knows the details of how the program works. Rudimentary understanding such as "I will earn vouchers if I'm clean" is not sufficient for the optimal use of a voucher-based incentive program. Below, we provide some dialogue that you might use when presenting a voucher program to clients:

Research has clearly demonstrated that incentive programs such as the one we offer here can effectively increase retention in treatment and drug abstinence. I'd like to spend some time describing this program to you as well as discussing the reasons behind why we think this program works. The purpose of this incentive system is to give you a positive reward for staying in treatment and achieving your goal of not using cocaine. It is also a way to increase your motivation to work hard on this goal and support you as you work toward making some of the lifestyle changes important for increasing your life satisfaction and maintaining cocaine abstinence.

The voucher system itself is designed to help you maintain periods of continuous cocaine abstinence. The points increase each time you provide a cocaine-free urine specimen. For example, the first clean urine specimen you provide is worth $2.50 in points, the second $3.75, and for each week with three consecutive cocaine-free samples, you will receive bonus points worth $10.00. Thus, if you were clean for 6 consecutive weeks, one clean sample during Week 7 would be worth $25.00. If you stay clean every week for your first 12 weeks in treatment and provide all urine specimens as scheduled, you will have $997.50 worth of points that can be spent.

On the other hand, if you provide a urine sample that tests positive for recent cocaine use, the following things will happen. For each cocaine-positive sample collected, you will receive no voucher points. In addition, in this system, one cocaine use during the middle of treatment can cost you quite a few dollars. For example, if you are clean for 8 weeks and then you use cocaine during Week 9, instead of getting $32.50 for the next clean sample, you get only $2.50. And instead of the next clean sample being worth $33.75, it will be worth only $3.75.

You can see that the system is designed to help you stay clean for long continuous periods. However, because we recognize that cocaine use during treatment may occur, there is also a procedure to encourage you to stop using if you do slip. If, following a slip, you provide five clean samples in a row, the value of the vouchers returns to the level you would have achieved before the slip.

The vouchers you earn can be used in whatever way you and I agree would support the lifestyle changes that we discuss in our counseling sessions. They can be used to pay for things like taking a person who does not use drugs to the movies or dinner, but not to a bar or party. The points can be used to take classes or get training in some area that you would like to pursue as a career or hobby. The points can be used to pay to develop regular hobbies or activities like fees for joining a gym or the YMCA or dues for a photography or hiking club. They can also be used for family activities like taking a child for swimming lessons, to a state park, or to an amusement park. In other words, anything that you think will help you remain cocaine abstinent can be considered.

You won't receive cash directly, but all you do is decide with me what items you'd like to spend your vouchers on, and the staff will make the purchase and have whatever you select waiting here for you. One important point, we do retain veto power over all purchases. That is, we must feel that purchases are in concert with your treatment goals of increasing cocaine-free, healthy activities. Items that are not appropriate include cigarettes, alcohol, or gift certificates to places that are primarily bars, or things that don't really help you make healthy lifestyle changes, like televisions or VCRs. You and I will be working together to come up with all the possible healthy ways you'd like to spend your vouchers.

After describing the voucher program, you may want to provide additional information concerning the rationale for using this novel type of program for drug abuse problems:

You might ask, Why do we go through so much trouble to design and implement this voucher program? Well, we and others find that many cocaine-dependent individuals arrive in treatment with their lives in disarray. Many clients find it most difficult to achieve even 1 or 2 weeks of abstinence. Their motivation to quit is high when they first come in following a binge, but many times such motivation dissipates quickly as the cocaine crash lessens and their energy returns. Moreover, many times when cocaine abusers do stop using, initially the experience is not as positive as they might have imagined. They may have to face up to overdue bills, angry partners or bosses, feelings of depression or anxiety, and many other consequences of their cocaine abuse. Typically, few natural rewards occur in the early days of abstinence. Most likely, not many people are looking to pat you on the back or to help with the problems associated with your cocaine abuse. Most are probably still mad at you for abusing cocaine in the first place.

Our voucher-based incentive program provides positive reinforcement for cocaine abstinence even in its most early stages. We think it is important that you receive positive reinforcement for achieving a most difficult task, cocaine abstinence. The vouchers are one way of doing that. At the same time, if possible, we will try to help you arrange your life such that positive reinforcement for abstinence and other positive changes is obtained from other sources. We hope that the opportunity to earn vouchers and be provided with a reward increases and maintains your motivation to stay clean. Further, we hope that the way you spend your vouchers will provide some alternative sources of fun and pleasure other than drug use. Voucher spending can also help support lifestyle changes that might help you maintain abstinence from cocaine and perhaps cope better with some of the consequences that are a fallout of your cocaine abuse.

We believe and now have proof that voucher programs like what I just described can effectively promote drug abstinence and foster positive changes that can assist clients achieve a stable drug-free lifestyle. We think most substance abuse programs could benefit from adding an incentive program to their treatment services.

Common Questions

We often encounter a few common questions from clients when explaining the voucher program. Below we offer some examples of how you can respond to these concerns.

Client: I'm not sure I can make these appointments 3 days a week. My hours at work aren't always that predictable, and some days I end up working straight through two shifts. I guess that means I'll just have to lose vouchers on those days—I just can't help it.

Therapist: Not necessarily. We are always more than happy to help you get to the clinic if you have transportation problems or to collect a sample at a place convenient to you if you can't make it in. We can also meet you here at the clinic earlier or later than our typical clinic hours for a sample if you need it. Basically, as long as you inform me when you have a schedule conflict, we can work something out. So there is almost never a reason for you to have a "no-show." We believe that having a steady job is very important to your long-term success; thus, we will work with you so that you can be successful with both your job and your treatment.

This example highlights how the client immediately identifies a potential reason for not participating in the treatment. The clinician response demonstrates the importance of how, in this situation, the treatment program can provide flexibility regarding the exact time and place the sample is collected but not compromise the validity of the collection process. Substance abusers many times perceive roadblocks to treatment and quickly abandon their efforts and drop out. CM programs must remain very aware of this behavior, particularly because many CM interventions require clients to perform more effortful or at least scheduled behavior than is typically necessary when they engage in their drug-using lifestyle. Removing treatment obstacles can help clients stay motivated and remain in treatment. Even though clients may earn a voucher for providing a clean urine sample, the therapist may still need to assist them in the planning process required to attend the clinic and meet the target goal.

Client: Does that mean I can spend my vouchers on anything I want?

Therapist: Well, not anything, but certainly a wide variety of purchases are okay. One of the first things we will do is try to understand what usually happens when you use cocaine. We will identify what activities, people, or places seem to be associated with your cocaine use. Then we will try and come up with activities that you can get involved in that could compete with or replace your cocaine-using activities. It's these alternative activities, in particular, for which voucher spending is most appropriate. So, as I mentioned earlier, maybe you will choose to use vouchers to join a gym, take a class, or go to dinner, a sports event, or the movies. The main purpose of the vouchers is to reward you for the progress you make in treatment with cocaine abstinence. Maybe you would decide to reward yourself with a massage, a haircut, or tickets to a play. You can also use vouchers for more practical items, like buying some new clothes for job interviews or buying materials for an educational or recreational class that interests you.

Many clients hear what they want. When you explain how the voucher program works, some clients will simply hear that they can earn money and spend it on whatever. When this occurs, you want to respond by emphasizing the variety of items that clients can purchase rather than spend much time on those that are not allowed. Remember, at this early stage of treatment you are trying to hook them into the treatment process and keep them motivated for abstinence. The principle to guide your discussion is that whatever helps the client stay clean is worth serious consideration. Moreover, what works for one client may not for another. Stay flexible and keep an open mind. Later in the chapter, we provide an example of how to work a compromise with a client who wants to spend vouchers on an activity that may not seem treatment goal oriented.

▦ INTEGRATING VOUCHER PROGRAMS WITH BEHAVIORAL COUNSELING

As a therapist in a treatment program that uses a CM intervention, you can maximize its benefits by skillfully integrating the CM procedures with your behavioral counseling. Below, we provide examples of how to use a urine-monitoring program most effectively during the therapy process and how to use your counseling skills to enhance the effects of an incentive program.

Urine-Monitoring Program

When clients attend the clinic on a scheduled counseling day, a staff member collects the urine sample *before* meeting with their therapist. This procedure ensures that the voucher intervention is implemented and provides the therapist with objective information on the client's progress with drug abstinence. If the therapist doesn't have this information and the client reports drug abstinence despite having used, the therapist will mistakenly offer social praise for drug abstinence and the session will not focus on the problems that led to the drug use.

Urinalysis Collection and Testing

In our incentive programs for cocaine and marijuana dependence, clients provide a urinalysis specimen to the staff member and then remain in the testing area with the staff member while the urinalysis test is performed. This offers several minutes to engage in pleasant conversation. Then, following each cocaine-negative sample, the staff offers social praise to the client ("Way to go, Mark. You're clean again. That's 6 straight weeks. Keep up the great work."). Social praise serves as an additional way to provide positive reinforcement for drug abstinence. The staff then hands the client a voucher indicating the total amount earned for that day's sample as well as the total earned throughout treatment, followed by an immediate call to the client's therapist to inform him or her of the urinalysis results.

If the urine sample tests positive for cocaine use, the client receives immediate feedback of test results from the staff member in an empathic, nonjudgmental manner. He or she is then asked when the cocaine use occurred and the amount. The staff member reminds the client that by providing five consecutive cocaine-negative samples, the value of the vouchers will return to their value before the slip. The staff member then terminates the conversation, facilitates contact between the client and his or her therapist, and calls the therapist to provide the urinalysis results.

A few comments on the actual testing procedures used are warranted. Much of the early work by us and others on the use of CM to reinforce drug abstinence has involved laboratory-based screening procedures like the Enzyme Multiplied Immunoassay Technique (EMIT, Syva Corp., San Jose, CA). Such lab-based procedures can be conveniently housed at the clinic site, but they require a dedicated wet-lab area and a trained technician. More recently, alternative screening procedures, sometimes referred to as "handheld tests," have become available, such as the Abuscreen ONTRAK (Roache Diagnostic Systems, Montclair, NJ). These procedures do not require a dedicated wet-lab site, can be used out in the field, and require less technical expertise. Hence, they are becoming more common in CM interventions (e.g., Silverman et al., 1996). We recently compared Abuscreen ONTRAK to the Syva lab-based EMIT in the context of a CM intervention to promote marijuana abstinence among individuals with serious mental illness (Sigmon, Steingard, Badger, Anthony, & Higgins, 2000). A total of 618 urine specimens collected from 18 individuals were screened for cannabinoids using the two methods and a 100 ng/ml cutoff. Overall agreement between the two methods was excellent (97%), suggesting that the newer handheld devices are as effective as the more established lab-based screening systems for implementing CM interventions.

Reviewing Urinalysis Results

At the beginning of each session, the therapist reviews with the client an updated graph showing his or her cumulative number of drug-negative test results plotted as a function of consecutive tests conducted to date in treatment (see Box 9.3 for a sample urinalysis graph). This enables both you and your client to begin the session focused on drug abstinence, as well as help to identify any recent problems in the area of drug abstinence. If the client has remained abstinent, this review serves as a prompt for you to socially reinforce abstinence and perhaps ask the client to reiterate how he or she has managed to stay clean. This will help build self-efficacy and confidence that the client can effectively take action to address his or her drug use problems.

If drug use occurred (positive urinalysis), you can help your client analyze the events surrounding the drug use to determine how to avoid using in similar situations in the future. For example, in our clinic, we often encounter clients who use cocaine in particular patterns (e.g., on Friday and Saturday evenings, prompted by receiving a paycheck). Reviewing urinalysis results using the graph may make patterns of drug use easier to identify and can facilitate plans for change.

One problem that arises with some frequency when using urinalysis monitoring to guide counseling is the client's denial of recent drug use in face of a positive urinalysis test. In most cases, we choose not to directly confront the client or challenge the accuracy of their self-report. Rather, we simply reiterate that the program's use of urinalysis results is a means for assessing progress in treatment and that today's result suggests

BOX 9.3 Sample urinalysis graph. This graph shows a client's urinalysis results throughout a 12-week period during which urinalysis was conducted three times per week (36 tests). This client had positive urinalysis test results on Samples 6, 7, and 23.

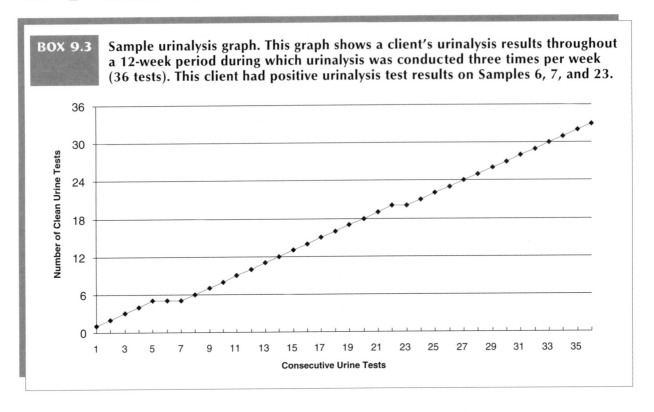

that the client may be experiencing some difficulties in the area of drug abstinence. You may respond to this situation by prompting a review of the previous day's activities, with the goal of identifying any high-risk contacts or situations that the client encountered. Even if the client continues to deny drug use, this discussion may highlight particular areas worth reexamining. Below, we offer an example of how you might handle this type of situation. Before the interaction described below, cocaine urinalysis results showed that this client had abstained from cocaine for 5 consecutive weeks.

Therapist: Hi, Tim. The lab just called me with your urinalysis results. You're positive for cocaine.

Client: That can't be right. I haven't used cocaine. I didn't do anything this weekend.

Therapist: That's how the machine read the sample. Let's talk about what you did over the weekend, and perhaps that will give some insight into what might be going on.

Client: I just closed down the store around midnight, went home, and went to bed on Friday night. Then I worked Saturday morning. After I got off work, I just hung out with some friends for a while.

Therapist: You didn't get to the gym like you planned?

Client: Nope. I should've, but I just got sidetracked by running into some buddies that I hadn't seen in a long time.

Therapist: Do any of those guys use cocaine?

Client: One does, but he knows I'm in treatment. I've used cocaine with him, but now he won't do any cocaine around me anymore.

Therapist: So what exactly did you guys do?

Client: Just hung out at his house, watched a movie, and smoked a little pot. Wow, I wonder if the bowl we used had some cocaine resins in it. Maybe that's what did it.

Therapist: Maybe. What seems pretty clear is that by getting off track of what you had planned for the weekend, you increased your chance for problems.

Client: Yeah, maybe you're right. I'm not sure why I did that. I've been doing really well with sticking to my weekend plans even when I run into old friends. I guess I just happened to run into these guys, started shooting the breeze, and then I decided to skip the gym. I guess I blew it.

Therapist: Well, you certainly have been doing very well staying away from cocaine during the past 5 weeks. I think you identified an important behavior this week that may help you continue to make progress—that is, this week you didn't stick to your plans like you did in past weeks. Sticking with your plans for alternative activities rather than just hanging out has really been working for you. We find that planning and following through with alternative activities increases most people's chances of staying clean. One other thing to keep in mind is that if you weren't still smoking marijuana, you wouldn't have had any need to use a pipe. I know that we've discussed this before, but perhaps we should reopen our discussion concerning marijuana use. The most important thing to do here is to learn from this situation and move on. What do you think you need to do to be sure you'll be cocaine negative on Wednesday?

Client: Well, I guess just keep doing what I've been doing, sticking to my plans: work, visit Mom, and I do have a date tomorrow night. I'm scheduled to go to the gym tonight and I'm definitely sticking with that. Being clean next time won't be a problem.

Therapist: Great. As you know, we have to go by the urinalysis results. So you won't earn a voucher today, and their value gets reset back to the original low value because of today's positive. However, if you can get back on track, providing five consecutive negatives resets the value of the vouchers back to where they were before today's positive.

Client: That's fair enough.

Our experience is that there is little need to quibble over a single instance of denied cocaine use such as the one in this example. If the client has resumed regular drug use, a pattern of positive urinalysis results will soon emerge. Instead, you might try to identify the continued people, places, or things that increase your client's risk of further drug use. The client in this vignette recognized how he deviated from his plan that previously worked for him, and the therapist reinforced his analysis of the situation. The therapist did not need to pursue the matter of denying cocaine use any further. You also will notice that the therapist used this opportunity to praise the client for the progress made with cocaine abstinence to date. Finally, this interaction indicates that the client's treatment plan might focus more on increasing social contact with new, non-drug-using people and perhaps revisiting his previous decision to continue his marijuana use.

Spending Vouchers

You can maximize the utility of the voucher program by guiding clients to spend their voucher earnings on items or activities that are in concert with their treatment goals related to increasing drug-free prosocial activities. Often, appropriate voucher spending is based on knowledge of the client's drug use patterns and triggers. For example, a client's cocaine use may typically occur on Friday nights following a long work week. When you and your client conduct a functional analysis of his or her cocaine use, you might determine that the function of such use is to unwind from the long work week. You might then try to encourage the client to use vouchers to purchase a massage or a gym membership, with the goal of helping him or her learn to relax or reduce stress without using cocaine. Something like a gym membership may serve an additional function of increasing opportunities to meet "safe" non-drug-using individuals.

Although using vouchers to directly enhance particular treatment goals is ideal, you must also give consideration to whatever the client identifies as rewarding. For example, a client may want to use vouchers to pay off fines in order to get a revoked driver's license reinstated. This use of vouchers may not seem appropriate at first, but achieving this goal (obtaining a license) might facilitate transportation necessary to obtain full-time employment or increase contact with safe family or friends. If your client appears motivated to stay clean to obtain vouchers for something like paying off a fine, you may suggest a compromise. Depleting the client's entire voucher earnings on these fines may not be as helpful as saving half of the vouchers for the gym membership or for dinners out with someone that the client previously said interested him or her. Hence, if your client earned $190 in vouchers and wants to spend the entire sum on the fines, you may suggest that he or she split the spending on the fine and the alternative activities. To facilitate such a compromise, you may need to provide skills training focused on budgeting and money management. These skills will help your client save money to put toward the fines, while retaining some vouchers to access other types of prosocial reinforcers.

Below is a short example of how you might negotiate a compromise with a client who wants to use her vouchers for something that is only partially related to a treatment goal.

> *Client:* I've come up with something that I'd really like to spend my vouchers on. I love going tanning and would also enjoy getting a new style cut for my hair.
>
> *Therapist:* I'm glad you're excited, but how do those things relate to your treatment goals?
>
> *Client:* Well, they both make me feel good about myself, and when I feel good I don't feel like using cocaine.
>
> *Therapist:* I was wondering what happened to your idea of joining the gym or taking that office management class at the Adult Education Program.
>
> *Client:* I was thinking that I wasn't quite ready for that class yet, and I probably would never get to the gym. It would be a waste.
>
> *Therapist:* I tell you what, tanning and hairstyles aren't items that we typically consider an appropriate use of vouchers. But you've been doing real well staying clean. How does this sound? You have $105 saved in vouchers. What if you

take $65 of those vouchers and sign up for the office management course. That fits right into your long-term goal of establishing yourself in a job that you can feel proud of. Attending the classes two times a week will also help meet your short-term goal of engaging in regularly scheduled nondrug activities. You could then spend $50 in vouchers on a month-long tanning membership, and if you provide three more negative samples next week, you will have enough to go get your new haircut. We could think of those activities as meeting your goal of rewarding yourself regularly for staying clean.

Client: I guess that would be okay. I do need a push to do things like that class. I always feel nervous going to something new like that. Maybe I could get my old high school friend who doesn't use cocaine to sign up with me. She might also be interested in tanning.

Therapist: That's a great idea. I'm glad you're willing to try it. Perhaps we can spend some time discussing what the class would be like before the first class starts. That might reduce your anxiety a little.

Although this use of vouchers didn't directly relate to a treatment goal, the therapist in this example found a way not to say "no" to the voucher request. The client was doing well in treatment and identified these activities as something she found rewarding. Saying no outright would have created a confrontational environment and most likely would not have been productive to the overall treatment. The therapist found a way to weave the voucher request into the existing treatment plan but, more important, used the request to gain compliance with a potentially more important therapeutic goal (attending the class).

In general, you should keep in mind that the goal of this CM procedure is to use vouchers as a reward for drug abstinence as well as a means of increasing clients' involvement in drug-free prosocial activities. If the voucher spending is not rewarding to the client, it will have little effect. You should remember that an activity or item that is reinforcing to one client may not be so for another, and activities that you think would be reinforcing may not be for them. The therapist and client must decide *together* on voucher spending. Such collaboration will increase the probability of accomplishing the long-term goal of this program, which is regular participation in activities that are incompatible with, or that compete with, the reinforcing effects of drug use.

Slips

You can use the voucher program to address drug use (slips) during treatment in at least two ways. First, if your client's motivation has waned, a review of potential future voucher earnings can contribute to a therapeutic discussion of this important issue. That is, you can remind the client that five drug-negative samples in a row will return their voucher earnings to their value before the drug use. You can make a hypothetical graph showing progress toward the fifth negative sample and the amount of vouchers that the client can still earn if he or she gets back on track with drug abstinence. In addition, you may revisit the list of items that your client had previously identified as desirable purchases to make with voucher earnings. Here, you might encourage the client to choose one that he or she would like to work toward, and again you could graph the progress toward that particular voucher-spending goal.

BOX 9.4 **Integrating Vouchers With Behavioral Therapy**

- Begin each session with a review of urinalysis results.

- Socially reinforce abstinence or functionally analyze drug use.

- If your client denies drug use following a positive urinalysis test, do not engage in confrontation; rather, seek to understand and review treatment progress.

- Review voucher earnings to date and earnings potential for the remainder of the program.

- Discuss voucher spending as it relates to progress toward treatment goals.

- Collaborate with your client on decisions about voucher spending.

- Remember, if the voucher spending is not rewarding to the client, it will have little effect.

- When drug use occurs, discuss how voucher spending might support an abstinence plan.

You can also use the vouchers to facilitate plans that follow from a functional analysis of the slip. For example, if your client had a series of slips throughout treatment that were reflected by drug-positive urinalysis tests on Wednesdays, you may initiate the following conversation:

Therapist: Mike, you've been doing relatively well with cocaine abstinence, although I see a few "slips" during the past month. Can you identify specifically what was going in your life or certain situations that arose that put you at risk for using cocaine during this time?

Client: Not really. I just ran into some old friends, I guess.

Therapist: Well, let's take a closer look at your urinalysis graph. When I compare it with this month's calendar, it looks like these positive samples were all on Wednesdays. Is there anything particular that's going on Monday or Tuesdays that might be associated with these positives on Wednesdays?

Client: Well, now that you mention it, I did join a pool league last month. On Monday nights, we meet at our favorite bar, have a few beers, and play pool all night. I guess I have kind of gotten caught up in hanging out with those guys a few times and ended up partying with them like we used to do. It's not that I plan it, but just that once we all start hanging out and drinking and shooting pool, it's hard to leave. I guess that could be a problem. I had noticed that since I'd been doing well with staying away from cocaine I hadn't spent much time in the bars like I used to.

On the basis of this information, you and your client can discuss a goal to minimize time spent in bars, paying particular attention to helping the client make plans for Monday nights. For example, your client could ask his significant other to dinner, make the reservation at the restaurant, and make a voucher spending request for a gift certificate for the dinner. This plan would reflect a commitment to engaging in a safer activity on Monday night and would place him at lower risk for using cocaine.

If you or your client identify a needed change in the treatment plan that may prevent a future relapse to cocaine use (i.e., increasing activities on weekends or increased contact with safe friends), vouchers can be used effectively to support these changes. Many times, your client's financial situation makes it difficult to engage in alternative plans that cost money. Also, many times clients may use the cost of an activity as an excuse for not being able to do it. Vouchers can remedy this situation. You will find vouchers very useful in expanding the range of alternative prosocial activities that can replace drug-using activities. Both clients and therapists find voucher programs quite appealing for just this reason.

THE FUTURE OF CM ⊞

The use of voucher programs to motivate drug abstinence and support lifestyle change appears logical and obviously can facilitate the therapist's task of engaging clients in therapy and the client's task of finding alternative, nondrug sources of reinforcement. Other types of CM programs, particularly those used in the methadone clinic, also show great promise in motivating behavioral change in some of the most difficult substance abuse patients. Nonetheless, CM interventions have yet to pervade our community clinics.

Both philosophical and practical factors contribute to this situation. As you can imagine, the logistics of initiating CM programs in a typical community clinic can appear daunting. The costs of additional staff, incentives, and regular urine testing may seem beyond reasonable expectations, particularly given today's tight market in health care spending. Moreover, most therapists in the substance abuse treatment field have no training in CM procedures or principles, and their models for treating substance abuse originate from a very different conceptual basis for understanding drug and alcohol dependence. We think that most substance abuse professionals, regardless of their theoretical background, would agree that more effective interventions are needed to better help our clients with serious drug abuse problems. The CM approach offers one method for enhancing outcomes in those who enter substance abuse treatment programs. Hence, we encourage you not to dismiss its potential utility even if you do not share its conceptual basis.

The dissemination of CM will involve many tasks. First, we need to convince program developers, treatment professionals, and policymakers of the value of this approach to substance abuse treatment. Second, innovative methods for funding CM programs will be necessary, as our current health care system does not have clear methods for paying for such services. Some examples of creative ways to fund CM programs already appear in the literature. One group solicited donations from community businesses to use as incentives (Kirby, Amass, & McLellan, 1999). Another program has developed a method to self-sustain a CM program by implementing an abstinence-based work program where patients gain access to work (and salary) by providing drug-free urine specimens (Silverman, Svikis, Robles, Stitzer, & Bigelow, 2001). Moreover, in the methadone clinic, low-cost CM strategies that make access to existing clinic privileges contingent on abstinence or other therapeutic behavior can enhance therapeutic outcomes (Kidorf & Stitzer, 1999). With careful thought and creativity, treatment providers can find ways to bring CM interventions to the community clinics. Finally, educating and training treatment providers in both the theory and practice of CM must occur if we expect these professionals to accept and adopt a model of substance dependence and treatment that may not be congruent with their current belief system and practices.

Given the high cost of problems associated with substance dependence and its seemingly refractory course, it is crucial that we seek alternative strategies for intervening with this difficult treatment population. CM strategies certainly do not provide "the answer" that will eradicate this societal problem. They do, however, offer an alternative approach with great promise to reach and effectively treat more people suffering from serious substance use disorders.

▦ ADDITIONAL INFORMATION AND TRAINING

If you are interested in more details regarding the recent use of CM with various substance dependence disorders, we strongly suggest that you read *Motivating Behavior Change Among Illicit-Drug Abusers: Research on Contingency-Management Interventions* (Higgins & Silverman, 1999). This edited text provides an overview of the empirical and conceptual background that justifies the creation and use of CM programs in the substance abuse treatment field. The majority of the text is devoted to descriptions and discussions of recent treatment research that has applied innovative CM interventions with various substance abuse populations.

You can obtain more information on the background and application of our voucher-based treatments and how to integrate them with behavior therapy in the National Institute on Drug Abuse's treatment manual, *A Community Reinforcement Plus Vouchers Approach: Treating Cocaine Addiction* (Budney & Higgins, 1998).

▦ REFERENCES

Bickel, W. K., Amass, L., Higgins, S. T., Badger, G. J., & Esch, R. A. (1997). Effects of adding a behavioral treatment to opioid detoxification with buprenorphine. *Journal of Consulting and Clinical Psychology, 65*, 803-810.

Budney, A. J., & Higgins, S. T. (1998). *A community reinforcement plus vouchers approach: Treating cocaine addiction.* Rockville, MD: U.S. Department of Health and Human Services.

Budney, A. J., Higgins, S. T., Delaney, D. D., Kent, L., & Bickel, W. K. (1991). Contingent reinforcement of abstinence with individuals abusing cocaine and marijuana. *Journal of Applied Behavior Analysis, 24*, 657-665.

Budney, A. J., Higgins, S. T., Radonovich, K. J., & Novy, P. L. (2000). Adding voucher-based incentives to coping-skills and motivational enhancement improves outcomes during treatment for marijuana dependence. *Journal of Consulting and Clinical Psychology, 68*, 1051-1061.

Downey, K. K., Helmus, T. C., & Schuster, C. R. (2000). Treatment of heroin-dependent poly-drug abusers with contingency management and buprenorphine maintenance. *Experimental and Clinical Psychopharmacology, 8*, 176-184.

Elk, R. (1999). Pregnant women and tuberculosis-exposed drug abusers: Reducing drug use and increasing treatment compliance. In S. T. Higgins & K. Silverman (Eds.), *Motivating behavior change among illicit drug abusers* (pp. 123-144). Washington, DC: American Psychological Association.

Griffiths, R. R., Bigelow, G. E., & Henningfield, J. E. (1980). Similarities in animal and human drug-taking behavior. In N. K. Mello (Ed.), *Advances in substance abuse: Behavioral and biological research* (pp. 1-90). Greenwich, CT: JAI.

Higgins, S. T. (1997). The influence of alternative reinforcers on cocaine use and abuse: A brief review. *Pharmacology, Biochemistry, and Behavior, 57*, 419-427.

Higgins, S. T., Badger, G. J., & Budney, A. J. (2000). Predictors of abstinence and relapse in behavioral treatments for cocaine dependence. *Experimental and Clinical Psychopharmacology, 8*, 377-386.

Higgins, S. T., & Budney, A. J. (1997). From the initial clinic contract to aftercare: A brief review of effective strategies for retaining cocaine abusers in treatment. In L. S. Onken, J. D. Blaine, & J. J. Boren (Eds.), *Beyond the therapeutic alliance: Keeping drug-dependent individuals in treatment* (NIDA Monograph Series No. 165, pp. 25-43). Rockville, MD: National Institutes of Health.

Higgins, S. T., Budney, A. J., Bickel, W. K., Foerg, F., Donham, R., & Badger, G. (1994). Incentives improve outcome in outpatient behavioral treatment of cocaine dependence. *Archives of General Psychiatry, 54*, 568-576.

Higgins, S. T., Budney, A. J., Bickel, W. K., Hughes, J. R., Foerg, F., & Badger, G. (1993). Achieving cocaine abstinence with a behavioral approach. *American Journal of Psychiatry, 150*, 763-769.

Higgins, S. T., & Katz, J. L. (1998). *Cocaine abuse: Behavior, pharmacology, and clinical applications*. San Diego, CA: Academic Press.

Higgins, S. T., & Silverman, K. (1999). *Motivating behavior change among illicit-drug abusers: Research on contingency-management interventions*. Washington, DC: American Psychological Association.

Higgins, S. T., Wong, C. J., Badger, G. J., Ogden, D. H., & Dantona, R. (2000). Contingent reinforcement increases cocaine abstinence during outpatient treatment and 1 year of follow up. *Journal of Consulting and Clinical Psychology, 68*, 64-72.

Iguchi, M. Y., Belding, M. A., Morral, A. R., Lamb, R. J., & Husband, S. D. (1997). Reinforcement operants other than abstinence in drug abuse treatment: An effective alternative for reducing drug use. *Journal of Consulting and Clinical Psychology, 65*, 421-428.

Kidorf, M., & Stitzer, M. L. (1999). Contingent access to clinic privileges reduces drug abuse in methadone maintenance patients. In S. T. Higgins & K. Silverman (Eds.), *Motivating behavior change among illicit drug abusers* (pp. 221-241). Washington, DC: American Psychological Association.

Kirby, K. C., Amass, L., & McLellan, A. T. (1999). Disseminating contingency management research to drug abuse treatment practitioners. In S. T. Higgins & K. Silverman (Eds.), *Motivating behavior change among illicit drug abusers* (pp. 327-344). Washington, DC: American Psychological Association.

Kirby, K. C., Marlowe, D. B., Festinger, D. S., Lamb, R. J., & Platt, J. J. (1998). Schedule of voucher delivery influences initiation of cocaine abstinence. *Journal of Consulting and Clinical Psychology, 66*, 761-767.

Milby, J. B., Schumacher, J. E., McNamara, C., Wallace, D., Usdan, S., McGill, T., & Michael, M. (2000). Initiating abstinence in cocaine abusing dually diagnosed homeless persons. *Drug and Alcohol Dependence, 60*, 55-68.

Miller, L. K. (1984). *Behavior analysis for everyday life*. Pacific Grove, CA: Brooks/Cole.

Petry, N. M. (2000). A comprehensive guide to the application of contingency management procedures in clinical settings. *Drug and Alcohol Dependence, 58*, 9-25.

Petry, N. M., Martin, B., Cooney, J. L., & Kranzler, H. R. (2000). Give them prizes, and they will come: Contingency management for treatment of alcohol dependence. *Journal of Consulting and Clinical Psychology, 68*, 250-257.

Piotrowski, N. A., Tusel, D. J., Sees, K. L., Reilly, P. M., Banys, P., Meek, P., & Hall, S. M. (1999). Contingency contracting with monetary reinforcers for abstinence from multiple drugs in a methadone program. *Experimental and Clinical Psychopharmacology, 7*, 399-411.

Shoptaw, S., Rotheram, E., Frosch, D., Nahom, D., Jarvik, M. E., Rawson, R. A., & Ling, W. (Submitted for publication). *Smoking cessation in methadone maintenance treatment: evaluation of nicotine replacement and behavioral therapies.* Los Angeles: Friends Research Institute and the University of California at Los Angeles.

Sigmon, S. C., Steingard, S., Badger, G. J., Anthony, S. L., & Higgins, S. T. (2000). Contingent reinforcement of marijuana abstinence among individuals with serious mental illness: A feasibility study. *Experimental and Clinical Psychopharmacology, 8*, 508-517.

Silverman, K. S., Higgins, S. T., Brooner, R. K., Montoya, I. D., Cone, E. J., Schuster, C. R., & Preston, K. L. (1996). Sustained cocaine abstinence in methadone maintenance patients through voucher-based reinforcement. *Archives of General Psychiatry, 53*, 409-415.

Silverman, K., Svikis, D., Robles, E., Stitzer, M. L., & Bigelow, G. E. (2001). A reinforcement-based therapeutic workplace for the treatment of drug abuse: Six-month abstinence outcomes. *Experimental and Clinical Psychopharmacology, 9*, 14-23.

Silverman, K., Wong, C. J., Umbricht-Schneiter, A., Montoya, I. D., Schuster, C. R., & Preston, K. L. (1998). Broad beneficial effects of reinforcement for cocaine abstinence in methadone patients. *Journal of Consulting and Clinical Psychology, 60*, 927-934.

Stitzer, M., & Bigelow, G. (1978). Contingency management in a methadone maintenance program: Availability of reinforcers. *International Journal of the Addictions, 13*, 737-746.

Stitzer, M. L., & Higgins, S. T. (1995). Behavioral treatment of drug and alcohol abuse. In F. E. Bloom & D. J. Kupfer (Eds.), *Psychopharmacology: The fourth generation of progress* (pp. 1807-1819). New York: Raven.

Sulzer-Azaroff, B., & Meyer, G. R. (1991). *Behavior analysis for lasting change.* Fort Worth, TX: Holt, Rinehart & Winston.

APPENDIX 9.1
ABSTINENCE CONTRACT

This is an agreement between _____ (the patient) and _____ (the therapist) to help the patient maintain abstinence from cocaine. By this agreement, I direct my counselor to establish a schedule for collecting urine specimens from me for 24 weeks. I will provide urine samples three times per week on a Monday, Wednesday, and Friday during the first 12 weeks of treatment. During the second 12 weeks of treatment (Weeks 13-24), urine samples will be collected two times each week on a Monday and Thursday schedule. A clinical staff member of my same gender will observe the urination. Half of each urine sample will be submitted for immediate analysis, and half will be saved at the treatment agency. Samples will be assayed for a variety of drugs of abuse, including cocaine, amphetamines, opioid drugs, marijuana, and sedatives.

Each specimen collection requires 3 ounces of urine. If the quantity is insufficient for analysis, that will be considered a failure to provide a scheduled sample.

If I travel out of town because of an emergency, I will inform my counselor in advance of leaving. My counselor is authorized to verify such absences with _____. If I require hospitalization, my counselor will arrange to collect urine in the hospital. If I am sick and do not require hospitalization, I will still arrange to produce scheduled urine specimens. If I have difficulty with transportation, or inclement weather makes it difficult to travel, I will work out (with the assistance of the clinical staff) a way to get to the treatment agency. On certain major holidays the agency will be closed. My counselor and I will mutually agree to altered urine schedules on those occasions.

If, for appropriate medical reasons, a prescription is written for a medicine that is sometimes abused, I will supply my counselor with copies of that prescription. The appearance of that drug in the urine will not be counted as a relapse to drug use. I hereby direct my counselor to communicate by mail or telephone with the prescribing physician or dentist when my counselor deems that action to be appropriate.

COCAINE-FREE URINES

For each cocaine-negative urine sample collected during Weeks 1-12 of treatment, points will be earned. Points are worth the monetary equivalent of $0.25, although they are not exchanged directly for cash. A voucher stating the earned point value will be presented to me following the collection of a cocaine-negative sample. This voucher will specify the number of points I earned for that day, as well as the cumulative points earned to date and their monetary equivalent.

During the first 12 weeks of treatment, the first cocaine-free urine sample will earn 10 points. Each consecutive cocaine-free sample collected thereafter will earn another 5 points above the amount earned before. For example, if 10 points are received on Wednesday for a cocaine-free urine sample, Friday's cocaine-free sample will earn 15 points, Monday's will earn 20, and so on. As an added incentive to remain abstinent from cocaine, a $10 bonus will be earned for each week of three consecutive cocaine-negative urine samples collected at the agency. Assuming there are no cocaine-positive urine samples collected, the monetary equivalent of $997.50 can be earned during the first 12 weeks of treatment.

Because a major emphasis in the program is on lifestyle changes, primarily increasing activities that effectively compete with drug use, the money earned on this incentive system must be used toward social or recreational goods and activities agreed upon by myself and my counselor. A list of acceptable uses of vouchers has been developed for this purpose and will be given to me. During the second 12 weeks of treatment, the incentive program will be changed. Rather than earning vouchers for cocaine-negative samples, I will be earning lottery tickets for clean samples.

For the entire 24 weeks of treatment, immediately after the urinalysis test results indicate that the urine sample is cocaine negative, the vouchers (Weeks 1-12) or the lottery tickets (Weeks 13-24) will be delivered. Following the presentation of each voucher, I will be asked if I would like to purchase any goods or services. Vouchers may be used at any time during the program. Earned vouchers cannot be taken away from me under any circumstance.

⊞ COCAINE-POSITIVE URINES

All urine samples will be screened for drug use. A record will be kept of all drugs screened positive, although this contract will be in effect for cocaine only. For each cocaine-positive urine sample collected, I will not receive a voucher. In addition, the voucher earned for the next cocaine-free urine sample will be reset to 10. To reset the voucher value to where it was before the cocaine use, I must provide 5 cocaine-free samples in a row. The fifth clean sample will then earn me the same monetary equivalent as that earned for the sample preceding the cocaine-positive one, and the system outlined above will continue to be in effect (i.e., each clean sample will earn 5 points more than the previous one).

⊞ FAILURE TO PROVIDE A URINE SAMPLE

The failure to provide a urine sample on the designated date (without prior approval of my counselor) will be treated as a cocaine-positive sample, and the procedures noted above will be in effect. Although the clinic may attempt to obtain the sample by coming to my home (with my permission), cocaine-negative urine samples collected in this manner will not earn voucher points, nor will they reset my voucher value to 10. In effect, cocaine-negative samples collected outside the treatment program (except in the case of hospitalization) are neutral. If a sample is obtained from me outside of the program, and the sample is cocaine positive, it will be treated in the manner outlined above for cocaine-positive urine samples.

My signature below acknowledges that I agree to the urinalysis monitoring system outlined above. This system has been carefully explained to me, and I understand the outcome of providing both cocaine-negative and cocaine-positive urine samples while I am a patient at the clinic.

_____
Patient

_____
Therapist

10

Cue Exposure Treatment

New Thoughts About an Old Therapy

Cynthia A. Conklin
Stephen T. Tiffany

CUE EXPOSURE TREATMENT FOR ADDICTION

Addiction researchers have long recognized that drug use and relapse are often tied to specific cues and contexts that addicts associate with past drug administration (e.g., Drummond, Tiffany, Glautier, & Remington, 1995). When an addict confronts cues previously paired with drug ingestion, those cues trigger responses that presumably motivate drug use. This phenomenon has led researchers and clinicians alike to consider the therapeutic benefit of reducing, or extinguishing, addicts' learned responses to drug-related cues as a means of reducing the chances of relapse: that is, cue exposure addiction treatment. This chapter offers a basic understanding of the rationale behind cue exposure treatment, explains how it is typically done, explores potential threats to its effectiveness, and outlines a treatment program designed to make it maximally effective in treating substance-abusing clients.

Consider the case of Andy, a hypothetical heroin drug addict.

Andy is at the end of a month-long inpatient treatment program for heroin addiction. He reports experiencing few urges to use heroin, and he says that he can easily deal with his mild cravings by reminding himself that heroin has only messed up his life. He is confident that this time treatment has been successful and he will not relapse. Upon discharge, Andy returns home and quickly realizes that the mild urges he experienced in the hospital now seem overwhelming. Everywhere he turns, he is reminded of his past drug use. He experiences strong urges during which his hands sweat, he feels shaky, and his mouth goes dry. He starts thinking about finding drugs. When an old drug buddy shows up with some heroin, Andy finds his urge to use unbearable, and he shoots up. Within a week, he is back to his old habit.

Andy's return to drug use following what he considered successful treatment is not uncommon. Regardless of his diminished urge to use and his resolve to remain abstinent, Andy was ill prepared to abstain in the face of cues that reminded him of drug use. The associations he learned during his years of heroin use remained intact, so confrontation with those cues following treatment continued to bring on learned responses that led to or set the stage for Andy's return to heroin use.

To understand this pathway to relapse, consider Andy's addiction from a learning perspective. Over the course of his drug habit, Andy self-administered heroin across a variety of contexts and conditions. Prominent features of his drug administration ritual (e.g., drug paraphernalia, the drug itself) and the contexts in which it occurred (e.g., specific rooms, environmental cues, individuals present) were paired with his heroin use. Over time, those features alone triggered strong responses. Just as Pavlov's dogs came to salivate at a bell paired with food, Andy responded to cues paired with heroin use.

In Andy's case, heroin was the unconditioned stimulus (US), and the effects of heroin were the unconditioned response (UR). The stimuli present when Andy used heroin become conditioned stimuli (CSs) that brought about conditioned responses (CRs). For example, when Andy injected heroin, he experienced the direct effects of the drug, including euphoria and decreases in heart rate and blood pressure (Goodman & Gilman, 1996). Andy might also experience subjective effects from heroin, including changes in his mental state. Over the course of his drug use, objects or situations present when Andy used heroin, through repeated pairing with the drug itself (US), acquired the properties of the CS so that those things alone brought on the responses Andy experienced with the drug. So now, when Andy confronts a cue paired with his past heroin use, he responds to it in ways that mimic his past experience with the drug. He may experience emotional, physiological, and/or behavioral reactions that push him to seek and once again use heroin. The goal of cue exposure treatment is to extinguish conditioned responses so that confrontation with drug cues no longer evokes responses that motivate a return to drug use. This can be accomplished through basic extinction procedures.

▦ THE BASIS OF EXTINCTION

Extinction is the process of eliminating a conditioned response through unreinforced exposure to a conditioned stimulus. To extinguish learned responses to drug cues, addicts must be repeatedly confronted with nonreinforced exposure to drug cues. Clinicians expose addicts to personally relevant drug cues that evoke conditioned responding without allowing them to experience the effects of the drug. This method comes from animal extinction research, showing that conditioned responses to drug cues can be eliminated when the conditioned cue is repeatedly presented without the original unconditioned stimulus (e.g., Pavlov, 1927/1960). The extinction of responses to drug-related stimuli following nonreinforced exposure to drug cues is also demonstrated in human research in which addicts were presented with relevant drug cues (e.g., a syringe) but were not allowed to use drugs (e.g., O'Brien, Childress, McLellan, & Ehrman, 1990). When first presented with these cues, the addicts showed increases in their heart rate and blood pressure and reported intense craving. Over time, presentation of those cues no longer evoked these responses. Their heart rate and blood pressure no longer rose, and they no longer reported significant craving. Their learned responses were extinguished.

CUE EXPOSURE TREATMENT ▦

Cue exposure treatments have been developed for several drugs of abuse, including opiates, alcohol, nicotine, and cocaine (e.g., Drummond & Glautier, 1994; Powell, Gray, & Bradley, 1993; Raw & Russell, 1980). Typically, addicts are repeatedly exposed to personally relevant drug cues in the absence of drug ingestion. Several types of cues are used across cue exposure treatments. In vivo cues, or cues presented "in real life," include such things as handling drug paraphernalia, watching someone smoke a cigarette, or sniffing from a bottle of the alcoholic's favorite alcoholic beverage. Imaginal cues typically involve vividly imagining situations related to past drug use. Presentation of audio, video, and photo cues might include having an addict listen to an audiotaped description of a heroin user shooting up or watch a videotape and view pictures of the same procedure.

Consider the following example of a typical cue exposure treatment session. Following his return to heroin use, Andy decides to try treatment again. This time, he goes to a clinician who offers cue exposure drug treatment. During his sessions, Andy sits at a table and handles a drug syringe. While he does this, the clinician asks him to rate his craving for heroin and describe his mood and physiological reactions. Andy continues to handle the syringe until his responses decrease significantly. The clinician then has Andy close his eyes and imagine being in his apartment talking to his old drug buddy. Again, Andy describes his responses to this cue and continues to imagine the situation until his responsivity decreases. He continues with treatment until the cues no longer evoke conditioned responses.

WHY HASN'T CUE EXPOSURE ▦ TREATMENT BEEN SUCCESSFUL?

We recently conducted a meta-analytic review of cue exposure addiction treatment outcome studies and found that, overall, this treatment is not particularly effective (Conklin & Tiffany, in press). Cue exposure treatments can certainly reduce addicts' responses to cues presented during treatment sessions; however, there is no clear evidence that these treatments increase the probability that addicts will remain abstinent when treatment is completed. We concluded that the relatively weak impact of this treatment is due to the failure of current treatments to protect addicts against phenomena that weaken extinction training. A wealth of information from animal research identifies several processes that can threaten the likelihood of learned responses being fully extinguished or remaining extinguished after treatment. We will describe these threats to extinction and offer examples of how they relate to our heroin addict, Andy. Our goal here is to give you a clear idea of the phenomena that may sabotage your cue exposure treatment so that you can guard against these threats and design a maximally effective treatment program.

WHAT'S REALLY GOING ON WHEN WE ▦ EXTINGUISH LEARNED RESPONDING?

For several years, extinction training was believed to weaken the link between the conditioned stimulus (CS) and the unconditioned, or original stimulus (US) (e.g., Rescorla-Wagner, 1972). Taking Andy as an example, this view suggests that when Andy handles a drug syringe during treatment without actually using heroin, the connection between the syringe and heroin effects breaks down so that he no longer associates the two. From this perspective, extinction is a process of unlearning. However, the recent view of extinction is that repeated unreinforced exposure to the CS does not break the learned association. Rather, the CS-US learning remains intact, but new associations to the CS develop. From this view, extinction is a process of new learning, not unlearning (Bouton, 2000). Andy still knows the association between the syringe and heroin use, but during treatment he is learning a new association, namely that the syringe is also associated with not using heroin. The goal of cue exposure treatment is to increase the probability that, when Andy is faced with a syringe following treatment, he will behave according to the new learning and not use heroin rather than behave according to the original associations and return to drug use. Threats to extinction are processes that reduce the chances that Andy will respond to a syringe in accordance with the new learning he acquired during treatment. The effectiveness of cue exposure treatment will increase when those threats are minimized.

⊞ THREATS TO EXTINCTION

The most prominent threats to effective and long-lasting extinction are the renewal effect, spontaneous recovery, reinstatement, and failure to extinguish the most salient conditioned drug cues. The following explains each of these phenomena, conceptualizes them with regard to addiction, and offers ways to guard against them in designing cue exposure addiction treatment. Threats to extinction and guards against extinction threats are summarized in Box 10.1.

Renewal Effect

Animal research demonstrates that contexts play a major role in determining how an animal responds to an extinguished cue (Bouton, 1994). Following extinction training, a context that recalls a memory of extinction will lead an animal to behave according to what was learned during extinction, whereas one that evokes a memory of conditioning will lead an animal to behave according to original learning. Consider Andy, who learned to associate a syringe with heroin use at home (Context A), went through cue exposure treatment at his therapist's office (Context B), then returned home (Context A) and realized that the syringe once again evoked strong responses from him. This is the renewal effect: A return to the original conditioning context following extinction training leads to renewed conditioned responding.

It is tempting to conclude that cue exposure treatment is effective only if extinction occurs in the original context where learning took place. Indeed, animal research suggests that the renewal effect is reduced when extinction training occurs in the original learning context. However, when an animal is exposed to a new context (e.g., Context C), it often responds with its original learning, not extinction training. This suggests that original learning generalizes easily to new contexts, whereas extinction does not (Bouton, 1994).

However, animal research reveals ways to improve the generalizability of extinction training. Studies demonstrate that increasing the number of contexts in which extinction occurs significantly enhances the probability that an animal will respond to cues in ways indicative of extinction training in both novel contexts and the context of original

---

BOX 10.1	**Threats to Extinction and Guards Against Extinction Threats**

Specific Threats	*Guards Against Extinction Threats*
Renewal Effect: A switch in context from the one in which cue exposure treatment was conducted renews responding.	Conduct extinction training in multiple contexts. Pair an extinction reminder with cue exposures.
Spontaneous Recovery: The passage of time between extinction and re-exposure to an extinguished cue leads to recovery of responding.	Allow ample time between extinction training and re-exposure to a cue to allow for recovery of responding. Provide multiple exposures to each cue. Allow ample time between treatment sessions to allow for recovery of responding.
Reinstatement: Re-exposure to an abused drug during or following cue exposure treatment reinstates responding.	Stress the importance of maintaining complete abstinence both during and after treatment. Encourage clients to be their own therapists during and after treatment. Prepare clients for reinstatement of extinguished responses if they slip up, and encourage them to immediately resume abstinence.
Failure to Extinguish the Drug Administration Ritual: Addicts must be exposed to the act of drug administration without experiencing drug effects so they can learn to associate drug use with the absence of drug effects.	Have clients engage in their actual drug use routine using either drug antagonists or placebo.

---

learning (e.g., Chelonis, Calton, Hart, & Schachtman, 1999). This finding is of considerable importance to addiction therapists conducting cue exposure treatment. To protect Andy against a return to original responding when he returns home, or to any other context, the *extinction contexts must be varied over the course of his treatment.*

You should consider one more thing about the renewal effect. If renewal is due to failure to recall a memory of extinction rather than original learning, then finding a way to trigger memories of extinction should increase the probability that the addict will respond to cues in ways learned during extinction treatment. In fact, animal research has produced this effect (Bouton & Brooks, 1993). A novel cue can be added to the extinction trials so that the cue becomes paired with extinction. When the rat is presented with that cue during re-exposure to conditioned stimuli in the original context, it will be reminded of extinction learning and will not respond to the conditioned stimuli. When Andy attends cue exposure treatment sessions, each extinction trial can be paired with a novel cue. That cue can later serve as a reminder of extinction in various contexts that he will encounter posttreatment.

Spontaneous Recovery

Whereas the renewal effect is controlled by contexts, the threat of spontaneous recovery lies in the passage of time. Animal research shows that extinguished responses to a cue can re-emerge when the cue is again presented after some time has passed between extinction and re-exposure (e.g., Rescorla, 1997). For example, after you extinguished Andy's response to the syringe and think you're done with it, a week later he finds an old syringe and responds to it again. Why? Perhaps for several reasons. First, the passage of time may cause the memory of extinction training to fade, such that the more ingrained original learning wins out when the cue is encountered again in the future. Second, one stint of cue exposure does not cue extinction make. We know from animal research that extinction occurs only after multiple unreinforced exposures to a cue. However, cue exposure treatments often fail to revisit the same cue once it has been extinguished, creating the potential for responding to re-emerge. Third, when a cue is revisited following the passage of time, responding re-emerges but to a lesser degree, suggesting that it was not fully extinguished to begin with. Taken together, these possibilities suggest that *to fully extinguish learned responding to drug cues, addicts must be exposed to those cues several times, with ample time in between exposures to allow for re-emergence of responding.* At that point, additional extinction is needed. Therefore, spacing exposure to drug cues is important in the strength of extinction training and the effectiveness of cue exposure treatment.

Reinstatement

Reinstatement occurs when response to an extinguished cue re-emerges as a consequence of exposure to the original US (e.g., drugs). Suppose Andy undergoes cue exposure treatment; he no longer responds to drug cues when he encounters them, and he successfully remains abstinent. One day, Andy gets into a car accident and sustains painful injuries, for which he is given morphine. He continues to take the morphine to combat pain following his hospital stay and quickly realizes that all of the cues that were extinguished during cue exposure treatment once again bring about conditioned responding. Re-exposure to the drug reinstates learned responding.

This scenario may seem improbable; it is not all that common that addicts will get into accidents and need painkillers. But consider the more likely scenario of addicts who tell themselves that they can handle one drink, one smoke, or one hit and not return to regular substance use. Reinstatement tells us that a return to drug use following cue exposure treatment, no matter what the reason, poses a serious threat to retaining what was learned during extinction training.

Obviously, the most effective way to combat reinstatement is to completely avoid lapses in abstinence. Warn clients of the dangers of slip-ups and the likely consequences if they ingest even a small amount of the abused substance following treatment. But lapses may occur. If they do, prepare addicts for what to do in case of a slip: If you fall off the wagon, immediately get back on and resume abstinence.

Failure to Extinguish the Drug Administration Ritual

Earlier we described the types of cues typically used in cue exposure treatment for addiction. Although all of those cues can bring about considerable craving and responsivity from addicts, there is one cue rarely used in cue exposure treatment that may be most important, namely the actual drug administration ritual. Think about it this way. You place a rat in a cage surrounded by a variety of cues. One is a lever that, when pushed, leads to a dose of morphine. Your rat, now addicted to the drug, continually pushes the lever to receive it. You decide to put your rat through cue exposure treatment. You keep him in that cage, take out the lever so he cannot get his drug, and expose him to all the cues that he has come to associate with drug use. Over time, he stops responding to the cues in the cage, and you proclaim him cured. Now you put him back in the cage and reinstall the lever. You put the mode of drug administration right in front of him. And what does your rat do? He immediately runs to the lever and starts pressing it.

What happened? You thought your rat was over his drug problem, and here he is frantically trying to administer drugs. Now, you may say, "Well, he's a rat, he has no desire to remain abstinent, he has no sense that drugs are bad for his health or that they are messing up his life." And we would agree, but your addicted rat demonstrated something at the heart of drug addiction. Drug effects are so powerfully reinforcing that, regardless of whether addicts want to quit or know full well all the negative consequences that come as a result of addiction, they still know that using their drug of abuse will give them the desired drug effects. Therefore, part of cue exposure treatment needs to be instilling a new association between actual drug administration and the absence of drug effects. Your rat needs to be exposed to that lever during treatment and press it all he likes without experiencing positive effects until he learns that lever pressing does not lead to drug effects.

You have a few choices for teaching that important new association. First, you can use drug antagonists (see Chapter 5). These are agents that pharmacologically block or counteract drug effects. For instance, naltrexone, an opiate antagonist, blocks the euphoric effects of heroin, morphine, and other opiate derivatives. Think back to Andy; if you give Andy naltrexone before heroin use, he quickly learns that heroin use does not produce the positive drug effects to which he has become accustomed. Unfortunately, drug antagonists do not exist for all drugs of abuse. Naltrexone and naloxone are opiate antagonists, mecamylamine is a nicotine antagonist, and although opiate antagonists have been used in clinical trials with alcohol, no specific alcohol or cocaine antagonists have been developed.

If you choose to use drug antagonists, keep in mind one critical drawback to this technique. Drug antagonists can themselves have detectable physiological effects. Although those effects are not positively reinforcing, addicts can tell when they are on antagonist drugs. Therefore, when treatment ends and addicts are no longer taking antagonists, they may find themselves in a state similar to that experienced before treatment, a state reminiscent of original learning, not extinction training.

Another way to expose addicts to unreinforced drug administration is to have addicts self-administer a placebo, a substance that is presented as the drug itself but has no actual drug in it. For example, you can have heroin addicts cook up and inject saline solutions, have smokers inhale denicotinized cigarettes, or have alcoholics drink alcohol-free beer. Although this approach has considerable promise, it has not been widely studied because of the considerable frustration that addicts report when they self-administer a placebo. Some researchers note that this technique is aversive to addicts, which may lead to low treatment compliance (O'Brien, Greenstein, Ternes, & McLellan, 1979). This is not surprising, as drug ingestion is highly rewarding and it is extremely frustrating to not experience expected drug effects. But rather than dismiss this technique as too aversive, focus on preparing addicts for the discomfort this procedure will bring about. *Offer addicts a sound treatment rationale for this technique, and clearly prepare them to endure discomfort.*

⊞ PULLING IT ALL TOGETHER

Now that we've introduced the basic premise of cue exposure treatment and described specific threats to the success of this treatment, it's time to pull it all together and talk about specific ways to translate these ideas into an integrated treatment protocol.

Step 1: The Initial Intake

In your initial intake, focus on four things: (a) offer a clear explanation and rationale for cue exposure treatment, (b) prepare your client for the potential discomfort some techniques might bring about, (c) stress the importance of remaining abstinent, and (d) obtain a personal drug use history from your client.

Rationale for Cue Exposure Treatment and Procedures

It is important that you explain to your clients the rationale behind cue exposure treatment and how it will work to help them remain abstinent. Here's how we would present a treatment explanation and rationale to Andy:

> I've told you that this is a cue exposure treatment; now I want to make sure you understand what the treatment will be like and explain what I mean when I say "cue exposure." When I talk about cue exposure, I'm talking about presenting you with cues, or triggers, that are related to your heroin use. I'm sure you can think of situations, places, or objects that are strongly linked in your mind to using heroin. For example, the sight of your cooking-up equipment might be a strong cue for you. If it is, then when you encounter that cue, you experience certain reactions, like strong craving for heroin, changes in your body like getting sweaty or feeling your heart beat faster, and possibly emotional changes like feeling anxious. When you experience those responses, it may be very difficult for you to refrain from using heroin. That happens because during the time you were using heroin you came to link certain things with your drug use. Those things become cues that remind you of drug use when you encounter them again. Some cues you'll be able to identify right away, but some we'll have to work together to discover. We'll do that in a little while. Now, during treatment, I'll present you with those cues and not let you use drugs so that you develop a new association with those cues, specifically that they are not linked to drug use. The way we'll do that is by exposing you to the cues—that is, presenting them to you—without letting you use heroin, until you no longer experience the reactions to the cues that you normally would, and you learn that those cues are not linked to heroin use.

In addition to offering a clear explanation of treatment, you also want to convey the idea that cue exposure is an ongoing process. Explain to clients that whenever they are confronted with cues and do not use, they are doing their own cue exposure outside of therapy. The more exposure they have to cues without using, the more they strengthen the new association between cues and abstinence.

Preparing Your Client for Discomfort

As we described earlier, extinguishing the actual drug administration ritual is a process that may lead to frustration and discomfort for your clients. Clients need to be prepared for this. Here's how we might explain it to Andy:

Some of the cues we'll expose you to are going to be hard to handle. Specifically, we're going to have you go through with your heroin ritual but not let you actually inject the drug; instead you'll inject a placebo. Now, most heroin users report that this procedure can be very uncomfortable emotionally. You may experience considerable frustration or anger. That's a normal reaction, and we'll work through it together. But this is an important part of the treatment. The reason why is that the link between the act of using the drug and the reactions you get from it is probably the strongest connection you've learned. Now you need to learn that the actual act of using is not linked to heroin effects.

Again, this is merely an example, and you should be creative in how you talk about this issue with your client. It might be helpful for you to draw an analogy between addiction treatment and medical treatment. For example, in the medical field, patients regularly undergo aversive procedures, most often electively, in hopes of a desirable or life-saving outcome. Although a drug habit may be no less life threatening than any medical condition, we may be somewhat hesitant to accept discomfort as part of the addiction treatment process. Because addiction is a tough nut to crack—no one knows that better than drug counselors and the addicts who seek treatment—it is unrealistic to expect the road to recovery to be devoid of pain or discomfort.

Stressing the Importance of Abstinence

As we explained earlier, lapses in abstinence can lead to reinstatement of learned responding to cues previously extinguished. If addicts keep from returning to drug use following a lapse, the benefits of cue exposure should remain intact. The best way for an addict to maintain the gains made in therapy is to avoid slip-ups at all costs. Clients need to understand that having just one cigarette, one drink, or one hit can easily lead to readdiction, and you need to explain to them why that happens within the framework of cue exposure treatment. Here's how we might explain it to Andy:

Now that you understand how cue exposure works, I need to stress to you the importance of not returning to drug use, even just slipping up a little, once you begin therapy. This is important because treatment is based on teaching you new associations between the cues that you used to link with drug use and the way you respond to them. Our goal is for you to learn that those cues are not linked to drug use, so that when you see those cues after therapy, you don't respond to them in ways that lead you to use heroin. We know that if you do use heroin, even just a little, the ways that you responded to cues before treatment might quickly return. This is because the cues that you stopped linking with heroin will again be linked to it, and the prior responding eliminated in therapy will return. Slip-ups might happen, and we'll talk about how to handle them, but you need to know that they will seriously challenge your ability to remain abstinent.

The best way to deal with lapses is for your clients to immediately recommit themselves to abstinence. Clients need to recognize when their prior way of responding to cues has returned. Help them understand that repeated exposure to those cues without using drugs will eventually diminish their responses to them.

Personal Drug Use History

A detailed drug use history will provide the information you need to select the cues to present throughout treatment. This information will also be used to determine multiple treatment contexts. Consider your goals. You want to find out specifically when, where, how, and under what conditions your clients used drugs in the past. One way to do this is to simply ask open-ended questions regarding past drug use, an approach that will probably offer you a wealth of information. We recommend this, but be aware that most clients will not know many of their drug cues or triggers and may describe things that are actually coincidental to their use rather than the actual cues.

If clients can't identify cues, at the very least they can identify responses that are likely to be linked to actual cues. Use those response descriptions to backtrack to the actual cues. For example, you might ask clients about times when they found themselves seeking out drugs, or times when they experienced very strong craving or a desire to use. From there, determine where they were and what was present or going on around them at times when they experienced such responding. To separate more coincidental cues from drug-specific cues, probe clients about the cues they identify by asking such questions as "Are there times when you are in that situation or confronted with that cue and you don't use?" If your client answers yes, you have probably identified a cue that may be only occasionally associated with drug use. A client might say, "When I'm talking on the phone, I smoke." However, your client might report that she does not smoke on the phone at work. Talking on the phone may serve as a cue only when she is at home or only when she is talking to friends who smoke. The trick is to pinpoint the actual cue. Perhaps the cue for this client is just talking to people who are smoking, whether on the phone or in person. In that case, you know that the cue you need to focus on is exposure to other smokers.

Here is how we might work with Andy to determine his strongest drug cues:

Counselor (C):   You've told me that some obvious cues for you are the equipment you use to take heroin, seeing the drug itself, seeing others use heroin, and being in a bad mood. I want to ask you more about being in a bad mood. You see, some things like negative mood are present when you use drugs, but they're not really cues. So think about this: Are there times when you are in a bad mood and don't use heroin?

Andy (A):   Well, I can't always use. So yeah, sometimes I'm feeling bad and I don't have any heroin.

C: Describe that to me.

A: Well, like something makes me mad and I start thinking about using, but I don't have any.

C: What makes you mad?

A: I start thinking about how much I've messed up my life, or my girlfriend gets pissed and we start fighting.

C: What else puts you in a bad mood and makes you want to use heroin?

A: Those are the big ones, thinking about how I've messed things up or fighting with Jessica.

C: How have you messed things up?

A: I can't keep a job. I get fired, or I have a crappy day at work when I am working. Or I think about how I can't pay the bills and I lie to Jessica so I can still use.

C: So it sounds like being in a bad mood is a reaction to thinking about having messed things up or arguing with your girlfriend, and those things are really the cues that lead you to want to use heroin.

Andy is easily able to identify some cues, such as his equipment and the sight of heroin itself or others using it. We would probe Andy further on those cues and find out what specific equipment he uses, where he is when he uses, or what his heroin looks like. Andy also identified negative mood as a cue, which a lot of addicts will do, but negative mood is a reaction, not a cue itself. Therefore, we continued to question Andy about negative mood to identify the underlying cues that make him think about using.

In addition to pinpointing specific cues, you also want to obtain information about mediating cues that Andy may associate with past drug use. This will guide your creation of multiple cue exposure contexts. One way to accomplish this is to have Andy close his eyes, imagine being in situations where his identified cues are present, and ask him to describe the scenario to you. Ask him questions such as "Where are you? What does it look like, feel like, or smell like in the place where you are? Who, if anyone, is with you? What do you hear? Describe to me exactly what's going on around you."

Step 2: Tracking Responses

Now you have gathered the information that you will need to determine the specific cues you will use in treatment. We will explain in the next section how to select cues and decide on various modes of presenting them, but first we need to talk about tracking your clients' responses to exposure cues.

There are several reasons to track a client's responses over the course of therapy. First, tracking allows you to determine the cues to which your client reacts most strongly. That enables you to decide on the most salient cues to focus on during treatment. Second, tracking responses during exposure to a cue lets you know when to end an exposure to one cue and move on to another cue within a given session. Third, we described earlier the importance of fully extinguishing cues through multiple exposures to that cue. When you extinguish a cue in one session and present it again in another, you will see recovery of responding if the cue has not been completely extinguished. Tracking allows you determine when a cue no longer evokes responses from your client, so you can stop presenting it in subsequent sessions.

The easiest way to track your client's responses to drug cues is through self-report measures. During exposure to a cue, periodically ask your client to rate craving, negative mood, and physiological responses on a scale of 1 to 10. The second method of tracking involves physiological responding. When addicts are exposed to drug cues, they have physiological responses such as changes in heart rate, blood pressure, body temperature, and skin conductance (Carter & Tiffany, 1999). You can track these responses by attaching physiological monitors to clients during exposures. Adding physiological measurement to your tracking procedures gives you the advantage of measuring responding across more than one domain of behavior. Thus, you have a more complete picture of a client's cue reactivity. In addition, you may be able to detect the presence of significant bodily reactions to cues even when clients report no responding. However, physiological recording may hinder your ability to conduct exposures in more than one setting unless you use telemetric equipment. Also, the presence of monitors may increase the likelihood of renewal occurring post session because extinction training may come to be associated with physiological attachments that will not be present after treatment. Therefore, you may want to use physiological monitoring as a means of tracking extinction only a few times across the therapy process. For example, you could assess reactions to cues near the beginning, middle, and end of treatment.

Regardless of the procedures you use—self-report, physiological, or a combination of both—it is imperative that you track responses to cues throughout the course of treatment. Tracking gives you the information you need to determine the cues you will use, how often and how long you need to present various cues, and when treatment can be terminated.

Step 3: Cue Selection

To select the cues you will use during treatment, first make a list of those cues you elicited from your client during the initial interview. Next, rank-order cues on the basis of the strength of your client's reactions to them. You have a limited amount of time to conduct therapy with your client, so you want to attack the most potent cues first. One way to determine rankings is to simply ask clients to rate their reactivity to each identified cue. Because clients are sometimes uncertain of how they will respond to cues, or they respond differently than they anticipate, we recommend an initial assessment period during which you actually present the cues and measure your client's responses via self-report and/or physiological measures.

Because it is highly unlikely that you will be able to extinguish all of the salient cues that your clients associate with drug use, choose the most potent cues, and remind clients that when they confront cues outside of session and do not use, they are conducting their own extinction trials.

Step 4: Presenting Cues

Earlier we described the various cue presentation modes used in treatment. No one mode of presentation has been identified as superior, so we recommend that you use a variety and see how your client responds to each. For example, some people may have difficulty imagining. Therefore, imaginal cues may not serve to elicit strong reactions from your client. So your best approach is to present several cues in a variety of different ways and learn which modes bring about the strongest responding from your client.

In our work with Andy, we identified these cues: the sight of drug equipment, the drug itself, seeing others use heroin, arguing with his partner, and general stress at the thought of things going wrong in his life. These cues might be presented to Andy in several different ways, such as having Andy do the following: (a) handle his drug equipment, watch someone prepare a drug syringe in front of him, and have him cook up and inject saline (in vivo cues); (b) watch a tape of someone using heroin (video cue); (d) look at pictures of heroin-related equipment and scenes (photo cues); (d) listen to an audiotape of another addict describing heroin use (audio cue); and (e) vividly imagine an argument with his partner, or instruct him to engage in the type of thinking that leads him to experience negative mood (imaginal cues). These triggers might also be combined, such as having Andy cook up and inject saline while listening to the audiotape or engaging in negative thinking. Many cues can be presented in a variety of ways. Explore the possibilities, keeping in mind that some modes of presentation will work better than others for your client. (See Box 10.2 for a list of possible cues to use in treatment.)

BOX 10.2	Possible Cues for Treatment

Cue Presentation Modes	Specific Examples
In Vivo	
Observing the drug use ritual	Someone smoking a cigarette, shooting up or smoking heroin, drinking a favorite alcoholic beverage
Handling drug use equipment	Syringes, matches, lighters, ashtrays, alcohol glasses or bottles, packs of cigarettes, mirrors, drug vials, pipes
Handling the drug itself	Holding a lit cigarette, sniffing favorite alcoholic beverage, cutting lines of cocaine
Drug administration	Cooking up and injecting saline (or actual drug while taking antagonist), smoking denicotinized cigarettes, drinking alcohol placebo
Imaginal	
Vividly imagining episode of past drug use	Smoking in one's apartment, or at work, drinking at home or at a favorite bar, interacting with individuals with whom one used drugs
Vividly imagining mood states associated with past drug use	Having a bad day at work, fighting with a friend, receiving bad news, feeling anxious about an upcoming event
Video	
Watching scenes associated with drug use	An individual cooking up and injecting heroin, a smoker lighting and inhaling a cigarette, an alcoholic drinking at a bar, an addict purchasing drugs
Audio	
Listening to descriptions of drug-related behaviors	An individual explaining a drug use routine in vivid detail, an alcoholic talking about a strong desire to drink, a smoker describing lighting and inhaling a cigarette, an individual describing the positive drug sensations
Photo	
Viewing drug-related pictures	Drug equipment, smokers lighting cigarettes, individuals sipping a drink, the inside of an alcoholic's favorite bar

Step 5: Choosing an Extinction Reminder

As we described earlier, an extinction reminder can give your clients a portable memory of extinction to increase the likelihood of their responding to cues outside of treatment based on what they learned while they were in treatment. Observe these guidelines for implementing this technique. First, the extinction cue should be compact, allowing for easy mobility and access. Second, it should be novel so that it brings about only a memory of extinction. Third, over the course of treatment, it should be presented to the client only during extinction training. Fourth, following treatment, it should be used only when the addict needs a reminder of extinction, so as to avoid degradation of its effectiveness due to familiarity. Finally, the addict should be trained to deploy the extinction reminder in immediate anticipation of a high-risk situation.

Consider Andy's use of an extinction reminder. At the beginning of treatment, Andy was given a container of lime-scented lip ointment. During cue exposure, Andy was instructed to sniff the container in order to pair the smell with extinction. Following treatment, Andy carried the ointment with him and sniffed from it whenever he found himself tempted to use heroin.

Step 6: Creating Multiple Contexts

During your initial intake interview, you will have obtained information from your clients not only about specific cues but about features of the surrounding environment or circumstances associated with their drug use. Use these mediating cues to guide your creation of multiple treatment contexts in which to conduct exposure sessions. Multiple contexts increase the generalizability of extinction training. Certainly, every therapist will be faced with different challenges in trying to use multiple exposure contexts, and the ease with which novel contexts can be created or used will vary greatly as a function of your treatment setting. Keep in mind that you want to conduct treatment in an environment that maximizes the number of attributes your client has come to associate with drug use. Consider offering treatment in different locales, such as outdoors or in the client's home, or alter the treatment setting with regard to smells, lighting, sounds, and furniture. Allow the various cues that your clients have come to associate with drug use to be a part of the treatment setting. If your client smokes while drinking coffee, reading the newspaper, taking a walk outside, or watching a certain program on television, present cues in environments that incorporate as many of those salient features as possible. If possible, take an alcoholic client to his favorite bar and present cues there. Allow clients who associate smoking with eating to simultaneously eat and confront cues in session.

Step 7: Spacing Cue Exposures and Treatment Sessions

To ensure that drug cue responses have been completely extinguished, *expose your client to each cue multiple times, track the progress of your client's responses, and allow ample time in between exposures for spontaneous recovery to occur.* This requires decisions about spacing both within and between sessions. Considering within-session spacing, multiple exposures to any one cue must be separated by sufficient time to permit some recovery of responding. It is more efficient for you to extinguish two or three cues within one session, alternating between them so that recovery of responding to each can occur before additional exposure. Present cues in random order. You want to avoid having your client learn that certain cues will always be presented before or after one another, as confrontation with those cues outside of treatment will not be so predictable. For an example of cue spacing within session, consider a portion of Andy's treatment protocol presented in Box 10.3.

Between-session spacing should also be long enough to allow for recovery of responding. After clients have been exposed to a cue multiple times in one session, responding to that cue will likely return, albeit with less strength, in subsequent sessions. Continue to incorporate cues in treatment until clients no longer respond to them following

---

BOX 10.3   **Presentation of Cues: Within- and Between-Session Spacing**

Sample Cues

A:	Handle syringe, tie-off, and matches.
B:	Cook up and inject saline.
C:	Watch video of individual using heroin.
D:	Imagine fighting with partner.
E:	View pictures related to heroin use.
F:	Listen to audiotape of an addict describing positive drug sensations while shooting up.

Sample Sessions

Session 1—Monday:	A, B, C, B, A, C, A, C, B
Session 2—Wednesday:	D, E, A, E, D, A, D, A, E
Session 3—Friday:	C, B, F, C, F, B, C, B, F

---

the passage of time. As shown in Box 10.3, Andy attends treatment session three times a week. By the end of three treatment sessions, Andy has been exposed to three cues six times each and three cues three times each. One important point to remember: If a cue fails to bring on responses from your client following exposure, take it out of the rotation and wait until a later session to re-expose your client to it. Some cues will extinguish more quickly than others. However, do not forget to revisit an extinguished cue, as responding may re-emerge at a later time.

One last recommendation with regard to spacing treatment sessions: Avoid weekly sessions. Conducting sessions only once a week will increase the probability of relapse between sessions and slow the progress of treatment.

Step 8: Ending Therapy

Cue exposure treatment can be terminated when the cues you selected for treatment no longer evoke conditioned responses from your client. You probably set at least two specific therapy goals with your clients, namely remaining abstinent and extinguishing responses to the cues you decided upon at the beginning of treatment. Once you and your client agree that the goals of therapy have been met, prepare your client for termination.

An important part of terminating cue exposure treatment is to impress upon clients the need to continue the process of extinction and be their own therapist after treatment. Depending on the treatment setting, clients will vary with regard to the amount of practice they have had in abstaining from drug use in the face of salient cues. However, both inpatient and outpatient clients will have been exposed to potent drug cues outside of session (e.g., talking to other addicts about past use, engaging in a routine that one would normally associate with using). Frame those experiences to clients as personal cue exposures. Encourage clients to recognize when they are reacting to cues and to tell themselves, "I am reacting to triggers right now, and I have to keep myself from using. The more I do this, the quicker the association between this cue and drug use will go away, and I won't experience these responses anymore." Such preparation increases the probability that clients will understand their reactions to cues after treatment and know what they need to do to reduce them.

⊞ CONCLUSION

This chapter offers you a basic understanding of cue exposure treatment, explains how to do it, explores potential threats to its effectiveness, and presents guidelines for designing a solid treatment program. Obviously, we have given you only a general overview. The topics we covered here are considered in much greater detail in a recent paper (Conklin & Tiffany, in press) that describes how information from animal studies of extinction can enhance cue exposure therapy with humans to promote long-term abstinence. Mark Bouton's (2000) work on animal learning inspired many of the ideas presented in this chapter. Bouton (2000) has written an excellent, very readable review of how learning concepts studied in the animal laboratory might be used to produce long-lasting maintenance of behavior learned in treatment.

Finally, if you are interested in reading more about the theory and practice of cue exposure therapy, a book edited by Drummond et al. (1995) provides a comprehensive review of cue exposure therapy. We encourage you to explore this work. The chapters in this book are a rich source of information on a wide range of theoretical and practical issues. Cue exposure is a dynamic area of research. New findings can directly guide your efforts to design an effective treatment program and offer you exciting ideas for developing techniques aimed at extinguishing addictive behavior.

⊞ REFERENCES

Bouton, M. E. (1994). Conditioning, remembering, and forgetting. *Journal of Experimental Psychology: Animal Behavior Processes, 20*, 219-231.

Bouton, M. E. (2000). A learning-theory perspective on lapse, relapse, and the maintenance of behavior change. *Health Psychology, 19*, 57-63.

Bouton, M. E., & Brooks, D. C. (1993). Time and context effects on performance in Pavlovian discrimination reversal. *Journal of Experimental Psychology: Animal Behavior Processes, 19*, 165-179.

Carter, B. L., & Tiffany, S. T. (1999). Meta-analysis of cue-reactivity in addiction research. *Addiction, 94*, 327-340.

Chelonis, J. J., Calton, J. L., Hart, J. A., & Schachtman, T. R. (1999). Attenuation of renewal effect by extinction in multiple contexts. *Learning and Motivation, 30*, 1-14.

Conklin, C. A., & Tiffany, S. T. (In press). Applying extinction research and theory to cue-exposure addiction treatment. *Addiction.*

Drummond, D. C., & Glautier, S. (1994). A controlled trial of cue exposure treatment in alcohol dependence. *Journal of Consulting and Clinical Psychology, 41*, 809-817.

Drummond, D. C., Tiffany, S. T., Glautier, S., & Remington, B. (1995). Cue exposure in understanding and treating addictive behaviour. In D. C. Drummond, S. T. Tiffany, S. Glautier, & B. Remington (Eds.), *Addictive behaviors: Cue exposure theory and practice* (pp. 1-17). New York: John Wiley.

Goodman, L. S., & Gilman, A. (1996). *Goodman and Gilman's pharmacological basis of therapeutics* (9th ed.). New York: McGraw-Hill.

O'Brien, C. P., Childress, A. R., McLellan, T., & Ehrman, R. (1990). Integrating systematic cue exposure with standard treatment in recovering drug dependent patients. *Addictive Behaviors, 15*, 355-365.

O'Brien, C. P., Greenstein, R., Ternes, J. W., & McLellan, A. T. (1979). Unreinforced self-injections: Effects on rituals and outcome in heroin addicts. *Problems of Drug Dependence 1979* (NIDA Research Monograph). Washington, DC: Government Printing Office.

Pavlov, I. P. (1960). *Conditioned reflexes.* New York: Dover. (Original work published 1927)

Powell, J., Gray, J., & Bradley, B. P. (1993). Subjective craving for opiates: Evaluation of a cue exposure protocol for use with detoxified opiate addicts. *British Journal of Clinical Psychology, 32,* 39-53.

Raw, M., & Russell, M. A. H. (1980). Rapid smoking, cue-exposure, and support in the modification of smoking. *Behaviour Research and Therapy, 18,* 363-372.

Rescorla, R. A. (1997). Spontaneous recovery after Pavlovian conditioning with multiple outcomes. *Animal Learning & Behavior, 25,* 99-107.

Rescorla, R. A., & Wagner, A. R. (1972). A theory of Pavlovian conditioning: variations in the effectiveness of reinforcement and nonreinforcement. In A. H. Black & W. F. Prokasy (Eds.), *Classical conditioning II: Current theory and research* (pp. 64-99). New York: Appleton-Century-Crofts.

11

Affect-Regulation Coping-Skills Training

Managing Mood Without Drugs

Raymond L. Scott
Marc F. Kern
Robert H. Coombs

---

sk any addicted client why he drinks or uses nonprescription drugs, and his initial answer will usually reflect a version of "I like the way it makes me feel." Addicts tend to be compulsive and ritualistic, relying on alcohol and other psychoactive drugs to help manipulate their mood, energy, or arousal levels. Like lay chemists, they attempt to chemically self-regulate their emotions and energies. Whether using single or multiple substances, either sequentially or concurrently, their goal is to control how they feel.

From an addict's perspective, substance use is typically purposeful, rational, and pleasurable. Although ambivalent or in denial about the consequences of their addictive behaviors and unaware of the interacting forces that encourage their drinking and drug use, few, if any, are unaware that they use substances to feel good or manage their feelings. "I smoked marijuana every single day for 23 years," said one addict. "I viewed it as a wonder drug because it took away my fears and anxieties about socializing. I had always been timid and afraid in a crowd and couldn't connect with people, especially women. It was hard for me to go to dances, all the things that normal kids do. But with marijuana, I suddenly felt relaxed and sociable, a way to be happy."

Our therapeutic strategy reduces clients' resistance by engaging them with their own words—their perceived motives for using drugs—and helps them find more healthy,

---

AUTHORS' NOTE: Marc Kern developed the clinical model described in this chapter.

less self-destructive ways to regulate their feelings and behaviors. Because this simple approach—to feel good without using drugs—makes intuitive sense to addicts, they are more motivated to change, to learn and adopt better methods to feel good about themselves and their ability to deal with life's challenges. Most important, the treatment goal matches the client's desire: to feel good and to enjoy life.

⊞ WHAT IS COPING?

Coping has a variety of meanings often used interchangeably with such concepts as mastery, defense, and adaptation (Frydenberg & Lewis, 1991). We use this working definition: "efforts, both action oriented and intra-psychic, to manage (i.e., master, tolerate, reduce, minimize) environmental and internal demands and conflicts" (Lazarus & Launier, 1978, p. 311). Alternate terms—*affect, emotion, feeling, mood,* and their derivatives—are used interchangeably.

Unlike more traditional methods of coping-skills training in addiction treatment (Monti, Abrams, Kadden, & Cooney, 1989) such as assertiveness training, drink refusal, problem solving, and time management, we deal with coping exclusively in terms of affect management. Although we readily acknowledge that increased assertiveness, for example, will eventually lead to more comfortable feelings in social situations, we focus on affect regulation from the outset.

⊞ BASIC ASSUMPTIONS

As all clinicians learn, the therapeutic treatment of addictive disorders is extremely complex and often frustrating. Regardless of your theoretical approach, each session is challenging, with unexpected situations and problems.

Affect-regulation training seeks to help addicts develop an internal rather than external (e.g., alcohol) locus of self-control—facilitating acceptance of personal responsibility for change so they can reap the emotional benefits of their efforts. In this way, they move toward ever increasing competency and empowerment and ultimately trust themselves, feeling confident that they can handle life's problems without mood-altering substances. By developing an internal locus of control, they can build lifelong skills that promote healthy self-regulation of emotions.

Keep in mind these principles:

- Your client's use of substances reflects both a biological propensity and a learned method of coping with feelings—whether due to earlier trauma, unconscious conflicts, existential dilemmas, or simply a desire to have fun or alleviate boredom.
- Each therapeutic session is geared toward greater recognition, articulation, and tolerance of unpleasant feelings.
- Each clinical intervention and homework assignment is designed to systematically weaken the client's unhealthy emotional associations and encourage positive associations with healthy behaviors and thinking.
- Do not assume that just because your client cannot identify or articulate a feeling, it doesn't exist.

- Some clients have developed a "phobia" about certain feelings, and this may extend to extreme fearfulness about feelings in general.

- Help clients understand that only by exposing themselves to their uncomfortable feelings will they make any progress. Help them learn how feelings are manifested in their body and mind, what their thoughts are when such feelings occur, how their bodies respond, and how they act when they feel that way. They must become expert about how they feel at any given moment (Kern & Lenon, 1994).

- The treatment goal is to extinguish maladaptive methods (both internal and external) used to deal with their feelings and to replace them with healthy ones.

- Developing an internal locus of control—realizing that motivations and feelings come from "inside" oneself—helps clients realize that externals like alcohol or other drugs do not control them without their permission.

- Only by having an internal locus of control can clients confidently move toward greater independence, competency, empowerment, and the ability to trust themselves to handle life's problems without psychoactive substances.

- Treatment is directed toward enabling clients to cope with the entire spectrum of life's problems without resorting to psychoactive drugs—exchanging a brittle defense against uncomfortable feelings for a flexible and compensatory set of psychological skills that helps them embrace and flow with their feelings that result from life's inevitable ups and downs.

- Shaming, blaming, and creating guilt are never appropriate; clients usually find themselves in their unhealthy situation because of naïveté or because they have been emotionally traumatized, not because they are bad, stupid, or incompetent people.

- A proactive educational approach, rather than a reactive one that focuses on the pathological past, encourages clients to feel optimistic about the future as they develop new skills.

- A stable recovery is only possible when the new way of living becomes more emotionally rewarding than the old, chemically dependent life.

Clients need to feel that you understand their reasons for using drugs and are on their side. Adopt the role of a "coach" (rather than a forceful, critical authority) who teaches them the "skills" that will bring success to their lives. And teach them the principles behind each skill. You may, for example, explain classical conditioning by using the story of Pavlov's dog or Little Arthur and his fear of bunny rabbits, or you may explain operant conditioning by using pigeons or rats as examples. Instruct and train clients so they can function successfully without drugs once your coaching ends.

Reinforce progress by praising and complimenting efforts and achievements: "Good job." "You're growing." "Keep it up." "This is the way out." Acknowledge and empathize with the "bravery" and "courage" it takes to face their fears. By building hope and confidence as they learn new coping skills useful in all life's arenas, clients can extricate themselves from their self-defeating lifestyles and pathological dilemmas.

THE F-A-N MODEL ⊞

Because many addicted clients have difficulty discussing their emotions, we find it beneficial to convey ideas through images—at the root of thinking and learning—using analo-

---

BOX 11.1   **The F-A-N Model**

F + A	= N
Feelings + Actions	= New Feelings
Tense + Alcohol	= Relaxed
Lonely + Socializing	= Not Lonely
Depressed + Walking	= Elevated Mood
Angry + Eating Celery	= Still Angry
Angry + Marijuana	= Calmer

Any A that brings about a positive N will tend to be repeated. Early stages of substance use tend to be more reflective of a desire for a positive N, whereas later stages of drug use tend to reflect more of an avoidance or escape from a negative F.

---

gies, metaphors, and anecdotes. We use the F-A-N diagram (see Box 11.1), for example, in each clinical session, particularly the initial ones, to help our addicted clients understand how they modulate their emotions and behavior. "F + A = N," represents "F [feelings] + A [actions] = N [new feelings]." Actions (e.g., adaptive coping or mood-altering drugs) that bring about a desired new feeling (e.g., relief from uncomfortable feelings) are likely to be repeated, whereas those that result in undesirable feelings are not likely to become habitual. The therapeutic challenge is to help clients find healthy ways to promote new feelings and deal with old ones.

We assume that all behavior is the result of anticipating, either consciously or unconsciously, a "payoff": a projected feeling or state that will make clients feel better than they did before. If a good feeling leads them to do something that brings a new good feeling, they are likely to repeat ("habituate") the action. If, on the other hand, they do something that results in discomforting feelings (e.g., sad, unhappy), they are not likely to repeat it. Instead, they will probably take action to make that feeling go away and replace it with a good feeling. In other words, motivation to act arises from the desire to move toward a good feeling or away from a bad feeling. And we tend to repeat (i.e., make a habit of) actions that we predict bring about positive payoffs.

Show your client that self-confidence grows only by facing the discomforts of life without using alcohol or drugs to mask them. "Doctor, I think I could stop drinking if only I were more self-confident," say many clients. "You have it backward," we respond. "You will only become more self-confident if you do it without the alcohol." The point is, clients must learn to do that which they have been avoiding; otherwise, the bad habit will continue, and they will go on feeling bad about themselves. They must come to realize that there are no shortcuts.

Every time the client avoids a difficult task, self-esteem and self-confidence diminish, making the next time around that much harder. Sometimes this process is so ingrained and self-perpetuating that clients withdraw to the point that even the smallest tasks seem overwhelming. Encourage them to stretch their behavioral limits, to push themselves to do uncomfortable things. They not only will find themselves accomplishing more than they thought but will be laying the foundation for future self-confidence.

Break down difficult tasks into incremental and easily attainable steps. Clients who set up small steps for themselves will slowly, over time, build the confidence needed to attain even more difficult goals.

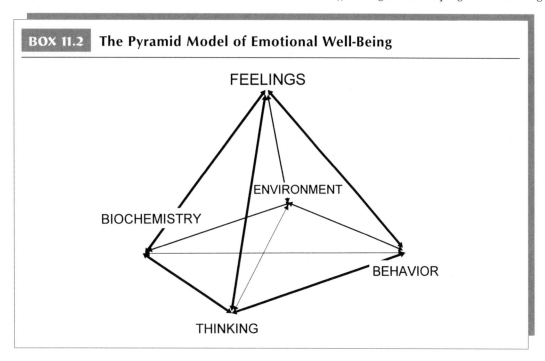

BOX 11.2 **The Pyramid Model of Emotional Well-Being**

Just as intellectual prowess comes through struggling with mental problems, and physical endurance through aerobic exercise, emotional "muscle" develops by wrestling with emotional difficulties. There is no mental, physical, or emotional growth without effort. When mood-altering drugs are used to suppress feelings or bypass stressful circumstances, emotional development not only stops but atrophies. "The first day I used marijuana to cope was the day I stopped growing emotionally," said a client. "I've had to learn all over again how to socialize and live life like regular people. And I'm still learning."

THE PYRAMID MODEL OF EMOTIONAL WELL-BEING ▦

Help your clients understand that when they think of drinking or drugging, they are usually feeling uncomfortable about some things and want to feel differently. When they feel this way, their brain provides a ready solution, one that is most familiar. This is the way they have learned to cope, to feel in control of their feelings: Their mind conjures up a proven solution (an urge to use alcohol or some other psychoactive substance) that has brought relief. Acting on this urge, as clients know all too well, will help them quickly change their distressing feelings and thoughts, and will do so without much effort.

Draw a pyramid to help clients conceptualize how affect consists of four interdependent components. Feelings, at the apex of the triangle, are influenced by each of interdependent foundations at the four corners of its base: thinking, behavior, biochemistry, and social environment. The pyramid figure helps clients understand that drug use is coping gone awry and that they can change their moods by altering any of the four components (Box 11.2).

To emphasize the interdependent nature of these four, ask your clients to conceptualize addiction as a Swiss watch with interlocking gears twisting and turning in different directions, each connected to the other. Imagine that the central gear, their addiction, is moved by each of the smaller interdependent gears. Although the central gear can be temporarily stopped, it won't be for long if the smaller gears are in a state of tension; eventually they will force the central one to move again. In other words, it does little good to discontinue drug use without changing many "little" aspects of life in thinking, behavior, biochemistry, and social environment that drive the addiction. Only when clients address the interdependent aspects of their lives that bring uncomfortable feelings, feelings habitually relieved by mood-altering chemicals, can they make the changes necessary to escape their addictions.

Thinking, as cognitive therapists remind us, affects feelings, behavior, biochemistry, and change of social environment. When I obsess about a challenging event, a forthcoming course exam, for example, I feel anxious (a feeling), take no-doze medications (behavior), begin sweating (biochemistry), and spend more time in the library (social environment).

Your clients will come to understand that they can change their moods by altering any one of the four corners of the pyramid and that changing one alters them all. When you suggest change in any of these four foundations, identify which corner of the pyramid you are addressing. For example, if a client reports drinking to overcome insomnia, you may suggest

- *Biochemical changes*: taking an herbal sleep remedy such as Melatonin, drinking warm milk, getting acupuncture, or avoiding caffeine drinks in the evenings
- *Behavioral changes*: exercising, biofeedback, a hot bath, progressive relaxation
- *Feeling changes*: reflecting on pleasant memories, experiencing a good movie or book, reviewing a list of activities coming up (vacations, holidays, etc.), meditating, self-hypnosis, affirmations, counting sheep, praying
- *Social environment changes*: lying in a quiet room, turning off the TV, darkening the room

Changing any one of these foundations will help the client feel relaxed enough to let go and fall asleep.

Of all the lifestyle changes that clients can make, perhaps the most valuable one is an exercise program. Because physical activity alters biochemistry and boosts energy, it is likely to change the way clients think about themselves and thereby affect their feelings. Not only does exercise benefit the heart and lungs, it improves the immune system, speeds up metabolism, strengthens bone and muscle, and fights depression. And these make clients feel good.

Your clients could try something easy at first, such as a short daily walk. The important thing is to find something they like to do, an enjoyable activity that they will stick with. Instead of signing up for a 2-year stint at a gym, for example, develop a short-term plan, something new like ballroom dancing, golf or tennis lessons, jazzercise, aerobics using home videos, or nature hikes. There are many options; keep trying until clients find something they like. Once an exercise routine is established, clients will feel better and come to see the benefits of a healthy habit.

Encourage your clients to have a physical exam that includes a test for hypoglycemia. This disorder, at the root of many problems, may explain sugar cravings in the form of food or alcohol, and why clients may experience mood swings, depression, and fatigue. Fortunately, this condition can be corrected through dietary changes (see Chapter 17). Consult a nutritionist if your clients test positive for hyperglycemia, and, for alcoholic clients, be sure to get a liver function test.

Changing diet, though simple in the short run, may be the hardest habit to change permanently. Help clients remember that the very first time they cried as infants, their mother fed them to comfort them. At that moment, they came to learn on a primal level the connections between food intake (behavior), biochemical changes, and feelings. Altering one's diet is one of the easiest and most direct way to change feelings.

Although many clients already know that too much caffeine and sugar are not good for them, few connect their use of these substances to their addictions. These quick-fix substances are a way to "press buttons" when they are not comfortable with their feelings and energy level. But when clients load up on coffee or sweets to soothe their mood, they are setting themselves up to continue the bad habits. The quick, temporary emotional lifts that these substances produce typically leave them feeling even lower than before.

The importance of changing social environments cannot be overemphasized. Help your clients visualize their lives as strengthened by social support structures—pillars—that maintain emotional stability. These include rewarding relationships in family networks, friendship groups, schools, religious organizations, recreational groups, and the like. If these structures are to function as adequate supports, attentive effort must be regularly given to each. When clients are addicted to mood-altering chemicals, neglect, rather than caring attention, gradually erodes these supportive structures. When this occurs, addicts are inadvertently left with only one source of feeling good, their psychoactive drugs. "Cocaine blocks out everything, but you don't care," an addict explained. "I look back now and see how cocaine, little by little, took precedence over everything in my life, including food. Unlike other drugs, the cocaine high is so strong that everything else is of little importance, and you are obsessed with that euphoric pleasure that you felt the first time."

Your clients' task is to build new social support structures, replacing the unhealthy ones with those that produce social and psychological rewards that enhance health and wellness. Instead of stopping off at a bar to meet friends after work, for example, encourage clients to go somewhere else, such as meeting nondrinking friends to play racquetball. Any new activity that is inconsistent with drug use (e.g., swimming) is preferable to those that encourage drinking and old unhealthy habits.

Encourage your clients, especially at first, to plan a schedule, charting in advance each day's activities on a calendar. Encourage a balanced lifestyle consisting of a variety of rewarding activities, such as recreational, professional, spiritual, and volunteer activities. And constantly monitor them so they stay on track. Although it may be easy to chart new activities when clients are motivated, once motivation wanes, they may gradually drift back to old ways. But if practiced long enough, and constantly monitored and praised by you, these new routines will eventually become intrinsically rewarding, valued for their own sake.

THERAPEUTIC PROCEDURES ⊞

Assessment

During the initial weeks, organize your sessions to identify and evaluate your clients' thoughts, feelings, and circumstances associated with their drug of choice. Structured clinical interviews as well as paper-and-pencil instruments can provide a wealth of information about clients' family, medical history, psychological status, and social circumstances. It will also allow you to learn whether they seek low- or high-arousal states and their optimal arousal level. It is important to respect clients' desired arousal level and to consistently recommend alternative ways of satisfying this preference without resorting to mood-altering substances.

Arousal, clients' state of "animation," is primarily a phenomenon of the central nervous system. Some clients desire a high-arousal state and others a low one. Picture it as a continuum from a high point of exhilaration or mania to a low point of great calmness. The goal is to help clients who desire low arousal tolerate higher arousal (and vice versa) without turning to drugs and to suggest appropriate activities as alternatives.

Recognize that clients have probably tried many substances and chosen a particular one because of its ability to produce certain feelings. Asking clients if alcohol, for example, is stimulating or relaxing provides an important clue as to whether they prefer high- or low-arousal activities. Knowing clients' drug of choice or their experiences with other drugs will help you formulate an effective treatment plan. With this information, obtained early in your assessment, you can suggest alternative ways of coping compatible with clients' preferred arousal state.

There are generally three types of clients: high-arousal seekers, low-arousal seekers, and those who prefer the "feel of the up/down." This last type prefers moods changes rather than either high or low arousal. Thrill-seeking clients, like those with attention deficit hyperactivity disorder or antisocial personality, usually seek affect relief through a manic style of avoidance of uncomfortable thoughts and feeling. These individuals tend to prefer alternative activities like skydiving or competitive sports versus relaxing in a hot tub (which they would consider dull and boring). By contrast, low-arousal-seeking individuals view high-arousal activities as anxiety provoking and as something to be avoided.

Be attuned to clients' energy level, and pace your sessions accordingly. If a client prefers high arousal, sit forward in your seat and be animated. But if a client prefers a low-arousal state, try to keep him or her relaxed by appearing calm. Most important, help your clients identify and replace their mood-altering drug with an alternative activity that meets their personality needs.

Over the course of your clients' therapy, continually refine your understanding of what affective state they are trying to achieve; help them refine their internal definition of what they are looking for. Providing constant feedback and reflective questions (such as "So you want to feel this or that?") helps clients push through "the fog," their lack of clarity about the motives that drive their behavior.

Again, there are two keys to helping addicted clients. The first teaches them that painful feelings will not kill them and will, with time, diminish in intensity. The second helps them replace the affect created by mood-altering drugs with a healthy, nonaddictive alternative method. This involves helping clients understand their preferred energy arousal levels, ranging from exhilaration to numbness.

Commitments

Ask your clients to make two commitments from the start: (a) to refrain from using all mood-altering drugs and (b) to try not to retreat from uncomfortable feelings. If they are unwilling to refrain cold turkey from all mood-altering drugs (or at least the ones they are having trouble with), ask if they are willing to cut down (warm turkey) their substances. Although some may initially refuse, most will eventually agree to one or the other and in so doing will begin to understand the logic of the F-A-N model.

Typically, permanent abstinence from mood-altering drugs rarely occurs unless forced upon users. So get a verbal commitment to abstain (or at least cut back) from all psychoactive substances for 30, 60, or 90 days. This will bring clients face to face with their disturbing emotions. Then, in each session, process these feelings and associated thoughts that drugs have suppressed. If clients refuse to commit, don't argue. Simply suggest that this alternative is available when they're ready but that until then their progress will be substantially slowed.

To help clients understand the importance of these commitments, we emphasize that for personal growth to occur, they must remain with their unpleasant feelings, not run from them by using drugs. By staying with their feelings and learning how to process them, they will develop the "emotional muscle" necessary to cope with life's problems.

To illustrate how emotions change, we give clients simple examples, such as that of sudden immersion in a cold swimming pool. When I jump into an unheated pool, I am immediately uncomfortable—the water's too cold. But as I stay in, not fleeing from the discomfort, I get used to it; although the water remains cold, my discomfort diminishes. That is what happens when I stay with my feelings, no matter how initially unpleasant.

Another homely, yet effective example: Ask your client, "What's the first thing you notice when you walk into a gym locker room?" The smell, of course—it stinks. But the longer you stay in there (rather than running to a space that smells better), the less you notice the smell.

Emphasize small steps, rather than huge leaps, and praise your clients for staying with their unpleasant feelings, not moving away or trying to change them, if only for 2 seconds longer than yesterday. It may take several months, but they will eventually see how critical it is to their growth to learn to tolerate discomforting feelings.

Keep in mind that addicts are very inexperienced in processing feelings and that this will be a difficult time for them. If their discomforts become too great, they may slip or go into a full relapse, retreating once again to their drugs for emotional security. To avoid this, we sometimes ask clients to take disulfiram (Antabuse) or naltrexone (Revia) for 30, 60, or 90 days as a means of gradually building an "emotional backbone." That is, these antagonists provide addicts time to ease into facing their painful emotions and lifestyle problems. Then, when they feel strong enough, they can begin to practice their emotional skills by dealing with the obstacles and unpleasant problems of life.

Essentially, "sitting with the uncomfortable affect" extinguishes the association between substance use and mood alteration. Depending on the clients' interest and cognitive skills, we explain how classical conditioning works, how associations are built, and how extinction occurs. If the clients can understand, we explain these psychological principles in as much detail as possible but never give them more information than they can process. We also explain the principles of cue exposure (see Chapter 10) so that they will understand why it is important to remove themselves from social environments that trigger drug-related cravings. And, we encourage clients to develop networks of supportive friends to help them remain drug-free.

Many of the techniques we use are similar to the *vajrayana* teachings of Zen Buddhism, in which fears and the other unpleasant feelings are compared to jagged edges. The goal is not to move away from these jagged edges but to lean into them, get to know them and find out how you typically respond when you encounter them. As you come to know the emotions, you develop the ability to tolerate them more and change your responses.

Every time your clients experience a feeling or emotion they do not like and don't seek a "shortcut" with mood-altering drugs, they learn to take control a little more. The more times they do this, the stronger they become and the more "emotional muscle" they develop to cope with life's problems.

Identifying Feelings

Because most chemically dependent individuals cannot identify their feelings and consequently do not know how to express them effectively, we help them understand the difference between thinking and feeling. Tell them that all feelings can be expressed in one word (*sad, joyful, angry,* etc.) and that statements containing more than one word are thoughts. Then identify specific feelings and discuss how each has various intensities. Anger, for example, ranges from mild irritation to rage.

Wurmser (1974, as cited in Thombs, 1999) called the inability to identify and express feelings *concretization*—a condition, he suggested, that often goes hand in hand with compulsive drug use. Regarding drug abusers, he stated that "it is as if they have no language for their emotions of inner life" and that they "are unable to find pleasure in everyday life . . . because they lack the inner resources to create pleasure" (pp. 98-99).

Depending on the client, we spend an entire session on each of the following emotions: anger (ranging from annoyance to frustration to rage), happiness (from peaceful and calm to ecstatic), fear, depression, anxiety, and shame. We help clients identify feeling through their description of (a) which part of their body feels the emotion, (b) which thoughts accompany the feeling, (c) what energy level accompanies the feeling, and (d) what behaviors accompany the feeling.

"In my recovery I've learned how to deal with stress," said one client. "I've learned how to identify my feelings. Before, I never spoke out about how I felt. I never spoke to my family because I didn't want my parents hurt. I remember thinking, 'Oh no, this is hurting them.' Somehow I got that message, and it was a terrible burden to carry as a kid. Now that I'm clean, I've learned to talk about my feelings and to gradually work them out through daily life experiences."

Perkinson (1997) identified eight primary feelings: anger, acceptance, anticipation, joy, disgust, sadness, surprise, and fear. "More complicated emotions are combinations of the basic eight. Jealousy, for example, is feeling sad, angry, and fearful, all at the same time" (p. 125). Assisting your clients to recognize how each feeling consists of smaller units helps them better identify and understand each feeling and figure out how to deal with it.

We ask clients to monitor their feelings by using a handout of a clock. At each hour on the clock, they ask themselves, "How am I feeling?" They could also put a dot on their watch (or some other obvious place) so that whenever they notice the dot, they ask themselves, "How am I feeling now?" The goal is to become consciously aware of internal states, how their feelings change throughout the day, and how their feelings are related to other aspects of their lives.

After they begin to recognize feelings, we teach clients the ABC's of Rational Emotive Behavior Therapy (REBT) as developed by Albert Ellis. You will recall that, in this model, "A" stands for *Activating event,* "B" for *Beliefs,* and "C" for *Consequences.* Most clients think that their undesirable feelings (C) are caused by events (A). We teach them, however, that their beliefs (B) about activating events (A) actually trigger their the consequent feelings or actions (C). If, for example, a client blames his depressed feelings (C) on being rejected by a potential dating partner (A), we help him realize that it is his beliefs (B) about this event (e.g., "I'm unattractive and unlovable, a loser who has no future with women") that activate his depressed mood.

REBT also includes a "D" and an "E." We help clients *dispute* (D) their beliefs that are irrational, illogical, distorted, false, exaggerated, melodramatic, overgeneralized, or overcritical of self (e.g., by stating, "I'm being too hard on myself") and replace these unhealthy beliefs with positive, reality-based affirmations (e.g., "I'm basically a good person; other girls have liked me; I'll learn from this and grow") that will bring a new *effect* (E), a more healthy consequence.

To help clients understand and apply these principles in their lives, encourage them to read books on cognitive-behavioral therapy. Several titles that may be useful include Lynn Clark's *SOS Help for Emotions: Managing Anxiety, Anger, and Depression* (1997); Michael Edelstein and David R. Steele's *Three Minute Therapy: Change Your Thinking, Change Your Life* (1997); Albert Ellis's *How to Make Yourself Happy and Remarkably Less Disturbable* (1999); Paul A. Hauck's *Overcoming Depression* (1973), *Overcoming Frustration and Anger* (1974), and *Overcoming Worry and Fear* (1977); and Gerald Kranzler's *You Can Change How You Feel: A Rational-Emotive Approach* (1974). These sources comfort clients and reinforce a sense of control over their emotions during this transition. It is rewarding to see clients light up when they learn they can change their emotional and behavioral response by identifying and challenging their unhealthy beliefs.

Homework Assignments

Clients rarely master new emotionally laden skills by merely hearing about them, reading about them, or watching others. So provide regular homework assignments—and follow up in your sessions. Help your clients understand why practicing a skill at home (e.g., identifying and differentiating their feelings) will promote healthy coping skills. Expect small, steady steps, not giant leaps or perfection. Clients grow by trying new skills, making mistakes, identifying those mistakes, and trying again.

We use these guidelines to promote completion of homework assignments:

- Ask clients to practice a specific skill outside of sessions and assess whether they think it will be helpful to do so.
- Ask clients why it is difficult to complete this task; failure to complete homework assignments may have a variety of meanings.
- Leave enough time in each session to explain the homework assignment expected for the next session, and then review progress in detail at the beginning of each session thereafter.
- Following up will improve compliance and help assess the effectiveness of each task.
- Ask clients to elaborate what they have learned from the homework assignment.
- For clients who are not fully compliant with homework exercises, use shaping techniques to gradually achieve greater levels of compliance.

Ask your clients to keep a daily journal of thoughts and feelings, at least for the first 2 months. We give each client a DayTimer to track their time and daily activities. Help them plan by Monday what they will be doing on Friday night so that when the weekend arrives they do not wonder, "What am I going to do?" If no plan is in place, they are likely to revert to familiar activities that involve using drugs, not necessarily because they desire them but because they didn't know what else to do with their time. Clients who complete the weekly planning exercises gradually learn how to plan activities for even longer periods.

If a client initially refuses to do this, don't make it a control issue. Constantly monitor client readiness. If clients ask for homework or recommendations on reading materials, give them as much as they can handle. Each person is unique; each has his or her own developmental timetable.

Setting Goals and Measuring Progress

Regard goals as guideposts, something to focus on but not an end in themselves. Although we use a basic formula, every client is different; what works with one may not with another. Therapy must be dynamic and constantly adaptive. What is important is that your client desires the outcome that will occur from the changes in unhealthy behaviors and feels good about his or her process.

We assess progress with these questions:

- Is the harm (legal, economical, social, physical, and emotional health) from the drug habit being reduced?
- Does the client feel that he or she is making progress?
- Is the client acting in his or her own long-term best interest rather than on what feels best at the moment?
- Is the client being more tolerant toward and less avoiding of uncomfortable feelings and activities?
- Is the client becoming more proactive in stretching into a new lifestyle and developing more healthy ways to meet his or her needs and feelings?
- Do the therapeutic tools fit the client's needs?
- How likely is it that the client will continue with these tools after treatment?

Most important, clients must learn how to tolerate acutely uncomfortable feelings without turning to alcohol or drugs and fully understand that if they avoid falling back into their addictive habit long enough, their unhealthy habit will diminish.

It is important to point out that the addictive behavior is never forgotten by the body. Like the old saying "You never forget how to ride a bike," unhealthy ways of dealing with feelings are imprinted on the nervous system. Memory never forgets what it "feels" like to take mood-altering drugs.

Clients are like onions with multiple levels of protective behaviors that must be gently peeled off. Some move more quickly than others in uncovering these levels. Be careful not to move too fast, unraveling too much affect too quickly, or the frightened client may disengage. Constantly gauge his or her pace by asking, "How does that feel?"

Do not expect that clients will move from point A to point Z. Each client goes through multiple starts and stops; the vast array of issues involved in any person's addiction exceeds any one treatment attempt. Immense lifestyle changes usually take years and are never fully completed. Although total stability without slips or relapse cannot be assured, you can accomplish something important with each client.

Stable, enjoyable, and healthy lifestyles *can* replace unhealthy ones that are self-defeating. Remember that after unhealthy habits are broken and healthy behaviors developed, a person never becomes perfectly "cured." But new neurological pathways gradually form and, over time, can dominate unhealthy ones. Change is possible.

Always end your relationship with your clients on a positive note by supporting what they have accomplished to date, and leave the door open for their return or other treatment options.

REFERENCES ▦

Clark, L. (1997). *SOS help for emotions: Managing anxiety, anger and depression.* Bowling Green, KY: Parents Press.

Edelstein, M. R., & Steele, D. R. (1997). *Three minute therapy: Change your thinking, change your life.* Lakewood, CO: Glenbridge.

Ellis, A. (1999). *How to make yourself happy and remarkably less disturbable.* Atascadero, CA: Impact.

Frydenberg, E., & Lewis, R. (1991). Adolescent coping styles and strategies: Is there functional and dysfunctional coping? *Australian Journal of Guidance and Counseling, 1,* 1-8.

Hauck, P. A. (1973). *Overcoming depression.* Philadelphia: Westminster.

Hauck, P. A. (1974). *Overcoming frustration and anger.* Philadelphia: Westminster.

Hauck, P. A. (1977). *Overcoming worry and fear.* Philadelphia: Westminster.

Kern, M., & Lenon, L. (1994). *Take control now!* Available from Life Management Skills, Inc., 9139 W. 24th Street, Los Angeles, CA 90034.

Kranzler, G. (1974). *You can change how you feel: A rational-emotive approach.* New York: Author.

Lazarus, R., & Launier, R. (1978). Stress related transactions between person and environment. In A. Pervin & M. Lewis (Eds.), *Perspectives in international psychology* (pp. 284-327). New York: Plenum.

Monti, P. M., Abrams, D. B., Kadden, R. M., & Cooney, H. L. (1989). *Treating alcohol dependence: A coping skills training guide.* New York: Guilford.

Perkinson, R. R. (1997). *Chemical dependency counseling: A practical guide.* Thousand Oaks, CA: Sage.

Thombs, D. L. (1999). *Introduction to addictive behaviors* (2nd ed.). New York: Guilford.

PART
IV

PSYCHOSOCIAL TOOLS

12

Lifestyle Planning and Monitoring

Readiness, Guidance, and Growth

Fred Zackon

NEWS FLASH: NO MIRACLE CURE IN SIGHT ⊞

Let's start by sharpening our sense of why lifestyle matters so much to addiction recovery. Consider this newspaper headline (something similar catches my eye a few times a year): "Findings Give Hope for Addiction Cure." Reading down, I learn once more that neuro-research has drawn a new bead on craving or withdrawal or foresees around the corner how we might reduce an addicted nervous system's vulnerability to relapse. Hmm, I think, that would be good. But then, how good would or could it be? To be of much value it would have to be a heck of a potion, some extraordinary high-tech fix. Among other things, it would have to greatly reduce conditioned drug craving—not withdrawal symptoms associated with dependence but the deep itches to get high aroused by countless environmental and internal cues. These include the copping sites, old friends, situations, events, smells, music, and memories associated with all of them. Whether any foreseeable neuro-intervention could pinpoint craving responses without affecting other vital brain functions is open to debate. Still, if such a treatment breakthrough occurred, most addicts I've known would try to shake off this "cure" in a hurry—and I mean the ones who really want to get clean. Why? If recently "cured," imagine what you would *still* be up against:

- *The people problem.* Granted, most of the old crowd counted for little except high times, but they were *your* crowd. You knew their ways and even liked a lot of them. You suffered and laughed together; a few suffered for you. Can you, need you, give them up just because you don't get high? If you decide you must make new friends, how will you do it? What would you talk about? Your past is such a shameful mess and so different from theirs, what would you talk about? What will you do together?

- *The work problem.* You need a job or have to get back to your job—or go to school. How will you cope with tedium and summon self-discipline? How will you live according to regular schedules? You've got to manage all the chores of daily life plus pay the bills, not to mention the backlog of issues you've put off for years. These very practical needs must be met whether you are ready or not.

- *The pleasure problem.* If not from drugs, what? You lived for superhighs and high excitement. Even nondrug things that you liked—sports, sex, movies, music—those activities you only did when you were buzzed. Now they all seem dull or uncomfortable. Most straight people get their kicks from their skills and friendships and work achievements and hobbies and families, but as you struggle to get back on your feet, the daily grind doesn't serve up much fun. Besides, nothing you know about or imagine compares with the euphoria you used to live for. One more thing: You're not getting the same peer approval and esteem that helps sustain newly clean and sober people. They get encouragement for building new lives on guts and determination, whereas you are depending on better chemistry.

Each of those big problems goes to core issues of how your clients live and what they live for. Each problem area is likely to be highly stressful. Sobriety alone would resolve none of them. Nor would an absence of the old craving help them to better tolerate stress and deprivation—or protect them from relapse. When the stress and emptiness of it all get too great, just the memory of that old reliable relief sends most former users back to their bottle, cooker, or pipe.

All these problems are lifestyle related or, more exactly, problems of changing one's lifestyle. Because addicts, especially the "hard core," already have a deeply entrenched way to live, they're not starting from zero. Their recovery depends on wrenching changes in relearning how to get by and make sense of each day. They are the people I've worked with the most and whose issues I address here. How can you help?

⊞ FUNDAMENTALS OF A RECOVERING LIFESTYLE

"Awesome," says client Joe Jones. "This program saved me. For real. I can't thank you enough. I got a new life. It's like day and night. No, it's like life and death."

If you are good in your work and lucky in your clients, occasionally a Joe devotedly consumes and as deeply commends your service.

> I got so much from this program. I got clean and sober. And I got my group and a sponsor. And most of all my Higher Power. And I got those relapse skills down, too. I won't forget them. I got my job and a few bucks in the bank. Even my thinking's different. Got new friends. Got my family back. I mean, wow. Of course I know it's a day at a time and I know you'll be here for me if I need you. So thanks for everything. I never thought I'd have all this . . . damn.

Sounds like Joe's got a strong start. But it's only that. The real work of addiction recovery is not in shedding the old life or even acquiring key elements of a new one—it's certainly not in the crash course called treatment—it's in the living of a new life and facing the slapdash slam-bang of the everyday. For this, Joe must build a healthy lifestyle, one that survives these daily assaults.

As a rule, we might say that a healthy lifestyle fits productively within a larger society that we feel a part of and that it gives us a balance of work and pleasure, love and learning. It is a sharing of oneself with family, friends, and community. Some of it is mental, some of it is physical, some of it expresses our spiritual dimension. It gives joy and the energy for new joys, as well as the strength to cope with pain and loss.

Except in the most rigid environments, a recovering lifestyle is personal and unique. If treatment often imposes a standardized regimen with strict schedules, clear rules, and specific skills and precepts, a recovering lifestyle must be very much one's own. But what makes for a recovering lifestyle? Let us assert this: *A recovering lifestyle is no more or less than a healthy lifestyle with particular features that help secure continuing abstinence as a necessary condition for all the other healthy features.*

Beyond abstinence, then, a lifestyle of recovery seems to possess these elements:

- Participation in a community that supports abstinence and nourishes moral or spiritual values
- Productive work (or appropriate training or education) that yields sustenance and social approval
- Social activities with friends who offer drug-free recreation and support
- A home setting that is comforting and relatively free of strong "triggers" (incitements to use)
- Personal growth activities in any or all of the above
- Standard practices for avoiding high-risk (trigger-laden) situations
- Standard practices for coping with unavoidable high-risk situations
- Regularity in one's personal routines and schedules

This inventory comes from 25 years of observing long-term stable recoveries. More than a template generated by only certain kinds of recovery, it comes instead from trying to see what is common to the lifestyles of people with successful recoveries who otherwise have little in common. For I've been privileged to learn from maturely recovering people of different social histories and ethnicities, whose addictions comprise virtually every drug of abuse, who've been through treatment modalities at least as varied, and who in the end constructed healthy lifestyles within countless social environments and many nations. Among graduates of therapeutic communities or medical therapies or skills training or pure self-help, whether they are believers or agnostics, male or female, and among most age groups too, there appear common features marking sustained sobriety and the wellness it allows.

You will find that each client is unique; with this one you must put more emphasis on spirituality, with that one on coping skills, with a third on friends and recreation. Neighborhoods that provide a safe home base for some are dangerous copping grounds for others. Everything depends on one's own history and needs. Helping your client make these judgments is part of your job.

QUESTIONS OF READINESS ⊞

Our program graduate, Joe, typifies someone who has made more progress than most. Consider these other clients:

Carla: I finished detox and I went to all the classes. The meetings helped too. I could find a good meeting in my neighborhood once I started looking. I mean, I feel strong, and I know I have to be strong to overcome addiction. I'm just going to have to change a lot of stuff. That's just it. I can't go back to the same things. Even my boyfriend. It's all up to me.

Jerome: The truth is I'm too old to go through this again. I've had enough, I'm done. Too many of my friends are dead or in jail, and I don't even have the energy to go out and get the stuff anymore. So I'll just move on to the next thing life has to offer. Or I'll just watch it go by. But that old high life and me, we're not partners anymore.

Raymond: I won't lie to you—I don't know what I'll do. Nobody even knows if they'll get hit by a truck tomorrow, so unless you're a millionaire or something, you gotta play the hand you're dealt. I definitely don't want to just keep getting high, then again I can't see exactly how it would go if I just stopped either. It's like there are two of me, and we'll just have to see who wins out.

You've probably known each of these attitudes in countless variations. The personalities are composites drawn from real-life clients I have worked with over the years. I use them here as models for our discussion. Let's assume each has just completed at least a few weeks of intensive inpatient treatment and is speaking honestly. Although they all show a little insight at least, clearly none are Joe. We could usefully encourage Joe to strengthen key friendships and help him handle job stresses that could affect recovery. We could coach him in the real-world use of his relapse prevention skills and help identify how old thinking styles and behaviors might still be intruding. We could help him keep his personal goals and interests consistent with sobriety. These issues are all part of lifestyle counseling, and Joe is ripe for them. But we would probably waste precious time to go after similar issues with Carla or Jerome or Raymond. They are not ready. They each have yet to take charge of their recoveries.

Following contemporary "stages of change" theory (see p. 387), we might say that Joe is fully engaged in the "action" phase. He's maturing toward a "maintenance" phase, and lifestyle issues are becoming paramount. That same model might classify Jerome and Raymond as being in stages of "contemplation" or even "precontemplation." It is not about honesty, or even the sincerity of the desire for change. *There is no use in addressing an addict's life "style" until he or she embraces an essential life "sense." This is nothing short of a whole-hearted commitment to redirecting the course of one's life.* Carla too is shy of "action." Not insight, action. What's missing in her case and the others' is evidence of committed steps outside the treatment environment to make life work differently. *One of the most costly mistakes made by counselors and their programs is offering lifestyle counseling, often called aftercare, to clients who aren't ready. All kinds of waste and frustration result from this common and classic error.* With a renewed vision of recovery, you can avoid it.

⊞ AN ACTION MODEL OF DEVELOPMENTAL RECOVERY

Although recovery sometimes seems to turn on a decisive moment, most therapists understand it as a broad process of growth with many entwined strands. Whether we address the cognitive, the behavioral, or the spiritual, or go after the psychosocial or

---

BOX 12.1 A Recovery Checklist

Enter a P, an N, or an F next to each item:

    P = Past; I had to deal with this, but I am done with it.
    N = Now; I am dealing with this now.
    F = Future; I may deal with this in the future, but I haven't yet.

Bottoming Out

— Until now, the person lives only for the moment and does not face reality
— Experiences collapse of support from others
— Experiences great pressure to change
— Is sick and tired of the hassles, cannot continue this way
— Is despairing and confused about where to turn
— Asks honestly for help (perhaps several times)
— Begins to share personal feelings with a positive supportive person

Ambivalence

— Resists the need to change lifestyle and is uncertain about what needs to be done
— Acknowledges that drug-free lifestyle would be better but doubts personal strength and cannot imagine self as a drug-free person
— Distrusts nonaddicted world
— Experiences great stress
— Has very high craving whenever drugs are available
— Fantasizes about ability to use drugs in future; cannot conceive of never getting high again
— Has few positive activities and friends and is uncomfortable with clean recovering people; tends to be idle and alone a lot
— Feels guilt and shame about the past
— Wants to think of self as recovering but is afraid
— Hides the past from others who are clean
— Has changeable moods, feelings, and opinions
— Becomes absorbed with new values and ideals and is increasingly enthusiastic about being clean

Commitment

— Cuts off relationships with user friends for good
— Begins to get rid of symbols and paraphernalia of drug use
— Begins to set clear practical future goals
— Carefully develops new relationships
— Begins regular learning or a work schedule (school or a job)
— Develops new means of coping with stress and physical pain
— Develops techniques to deal with craving (which is declining) and quickly uses support in case of a relapse
— Helps others as a form of self-help
— Reveals personal past carefully to certain people and is very conscious of being a recovering addict
— May be working very hard and may have intense close relationships
— Begins to look forward to clean social recreation and to enjoy drug-free pleasures

Integration

— Resolves guilt and can reveal past as a personal fact without shame or fear
— Without forgetting the past, feels like a drug-free person and a part of the recovering community
— Applies personal rules that prevent drug use nearly effortlessly
— Helping others becomes an essential part of life
— Openness to growth and self-improvement become second nature
— Lives each day accepting the challenges, responsibilities, and satisfactions of work, love, and respect for others
— Is no longer stimulated by old places, events, or people associated with prior drug use
— Social network is ever widening

SOURCE: Adapted from Zackon, McAuliffe, and Chi'en (1993, p. 82).

---

neurochemical, we see that recovery is organic: The new grows out of the old. And to assist the process, we have to somehow track it. That's where "developmental recovery models" come in.

BOX 12.2   Release Preparation Activity Checklist (RePAC)

This planning guide (RePAC for short) is an important part of the program. You will be expected to give it serious and detailed attention. Not all categories of the RePAC may fully apply to you—for example, you may not have any family to return to, or you may not have been able to line up a job before your release. But for each category you are expected to prepare as much as possible, and if for some reason certain issues do not apply to you or cannot be completely planned out, be sure to identify what plans you have made that relate to the issue. What is important in making good use of RePAC is *hard information, detailed planning, and demonstrated ability*. Just being able to talk about the issues is not good enough. RePAC is meant to bring together many of the ideas and skills you have learned in our program and put them to work for you in the community.

If possible, your plans should be fully written out, giving all the facts, names, numbers, dates, and so on. And to show that you have really thought carefully about what you write down, you should be able to state the important facts from memory.

Living Arrangements
Where will you live and with whom?
How long do you plan to live there? (If you do not expect to live there for more than 3 months following your release, then answer the following for both that place and wherever you think you might go.)
What will it cost?
Describe the neighborhood.
What were your sources of information?

Employment
Describe the work you will do, including specific responsibilities.
What hours will you work?
How will you be trained?
How will you be supervised?
What will your salary be, and what benefits will be included?
Describe the working environment.
How far from home will you be working, and how will you get to work?
Is the position temporary, seasonal, or permanent? Is it in a new or stable business?
What opportunities will you have for advancement?
What were your sources of information?
If you do not yet have a job lined up, what have you done so far to find one? What else will you do to get one? Give all the sources of information and assistance you plan to use.

Recreation
What specific activities will you participate in as recreation?
How often will you do them, and how much time will you devote to each?
Where will you participate in these activities?
Who will join you in these activities?
What materials or extra resources will you need, where will you get them, and how much will they cost?
Why did you choose these activities?
What were your sources of information?

Family
Who will you regard as part of your family and expect to keep relationships with? (Include living partners.)
What specific responsibilities will you have toward these people? (Include financial arrangements.)
What plans and agreements do you have for improving relationships and preventing problems with these people?
Who in your family will be a "recovery partner"?

Friends
Who are the people or specific groups you most need to avoid?
Which old friends would it be good for you to keep and strengthen relationships with?
Who among your current friends could be a recovery partner?
Who are you currently building positive friendships with?
How do you plan to build new friendships?

The most useful recovery models identify markers along the recovery journey that are not peculiar to any one treatment vehicle. For example, only addicts who participate

Community Involvement

What specific community activities and specific organizations will you be involved in?

Where and when will you participate, and what specifically do you expect to do?

What were your sources of information and who are the contact people for these activities or organizations?

Recovery Support

What recovery meetings, organizations, or groups do you plan to participate in? Where are they held? How often will you attend? How will you get to them?

What other recovery support will you have? (Include specific sponsors, counselors, recovery partners, clergy, and so on.) How often will you spend time with each?

What were your sources of information?

Health Care

What specific medical issues or problems do you have that will need continuing treatment?

What kinds of health care services or health care insurance will be available to you?

What will you do to make certain you have adequate health care resources?

What were your sources of information?

Continuing Education

What are your most pressing educational needs, and what are your specific educational goals?

What services or programs will be available to help you meet those needs and goals, and how do you plan to use them? (Include expenses, travel, and so on.)

What were your sources of information, and who are the contact people for these services or programs?

Financial Plan

Define a weekly budget that will carry you through the first month following release, and also define a weekly budget that could carry you through your first full year in the free world. Be certain that the budget can support the activities you have identified in all the above sections of RePAC.

Who will help monitor the budget and how?

What bank or banking services will you use, and how will you handle your savings?

Crisis Plans

To reduce risks of relapse and recidivism, describe specifically each of the following:

Dangerous situations you most need to avoid and your plans for avoiding each one

Dangerous situations that you will not be able to avoid and how you will cope with them

The biggest problems or upsets that you can foresee and how you will cope with them

Who you will go to and anything else you will do if you feel you need emergency support to safeguard your recovery

Goals

Define your most important specific goals for

The next 3 months

The next year

The next 5 years

Be certain that you can achieve each goal or at least make progress toward achieving it by doing what you have said you would do in the other sections of RePAC.

Activity Schedule

Define a weekly (7-day) schedule for your first 90 days in the community. Be certain that it includes all major activities that you have described in all the above sections of RePAC.

SOURCE: Reprinted with permission of CiviGenics, Inc. Copyright © 1994. Further use of this material requires the express permission of CiviGenics.

in 12-step fellowships or equivalents could reach the milestone of "90 meetings in 90 days." It would be great to know a comparable benchmark for participants in other

---

BOX 12.3 **The "How Are You Doing?" Checklist**

If you are making progress in two or more areas in each of the following five categories, you are making real progress in your recovery. And the point is progress, not perfection. Strive for a life that gets an honest "yes" to every item. You can probably come very close. Really. And that would mean you're doing great.

Social Relationships
— I have positive friends in all major aspects of life.
— I feel understood and respected by positive people.
— I have made lifetime bonds with family or other positive people.
— I have no secret relations that can bring harm.
— I am a contributing member of a strong and positive community.
— I am steadily strengthening and building positive relations.

Managing Destructive Urges
— I can keep my attention and energies focused on important tasks
— I am not bothered by desires to get high in everyday life.
— I am not overpowered or weakened by anger or violent impulses.
— I am steadily gaining more self-control.

Routine Activities
— I meet basic responsibilities day in and day out.
— I balance work and pleasure, body and mind.
— I regularly pursue education or practical skill development.
— I maintain a consistent schedule.
— I adapt schedules as needed to changing needs.
— I am steadily becoming more skilled and productive.

Values and Perspective
— I see various options for most problems.
— I can be self-critical and see others' points of view.
— I can make practical plans for future needs.
— I have higher goals to strive for.
— I am steadily improving my problem-solving ability.
— I am steadily honoring personal values more fully.

Guidance and Authority
— I am comfortable in making good use of competent guidance.
— I have positive senior role models in several areas of life.
— I accept constructive criticism thoughtfully.
— I am steadily identifying more with my own personal positive authority.

SOURCE: Reprinted with permission of CiviGenics, Inc. Copyright © 1994. Further use of this material requires the express permission of CiviGenics.

---

kinds of programs. It must be a benchmark that signifies genuine recovery progress and not mere program compliance.

When we look at various types of long-term recoveries among people with different addiction and recovery histories—those who for years live clean and productively satisfying lives—it is apparent that no matter what their particular experiences are, the overwhelming majority have certain kinds of growth events in common. Very likely they have all gone through a period early in their final and successful attempt at sobriety of furious involvement in some organization that excluded substance abuse and was dedicated to new activities and values. Voluntary participants, they began to personally identify with the mission and conduct norms of that group. Whether it was a therapeutic community (TC), a church congregation, or even a school or civic group, they "joined a community" that supported their recovery. This common achievement or "growth event" is typical of those who experience the journey of recovery.

Other growth events also stand out. Here are the basic ones I nominate for treatment goals. I think that treatment programs, especially inpatient programs, that don't make these achievements explicit may miss the mark. They are so important in my experience that I see them as preconditions for working on lifestyle planning.

- Acknowledge one's addiction and the need for major personal change.
- Become drug-free or largely drug-free (i.e., not physically dependent and sufficiently sober to keep appointments and make sense of new information).
- Accept a guide for the journey ahead.
- Join a pro-recovery community.

Addicts achieve these goals in different ways and in different sequences. No single meaning of *major personal change* applies to everyone. A "guide" can be a counselor, sponsor, spiritual teacher, family member, or trusted peer. As noted, one's chosen community can vary too. And there are many ways to get drug-free, from self-imposed cold turkey to medically managed detox. But one truth stands out in all cases: Except for that first step of acknowledging one's addiction and the need for change, these are all *action* steps. Although they imply new attitudes and beliefs, they can be realized only in observable behavior. Even accepting a guide means spending time with the person and acting upon his or her advice. So we are beyond cognitive models and entering the territory where one goes even before the knowing. It's the land of blind faith, of "fake it till you make it," and of simply putting the body where it needs to be so the mind will follow.

Even early on, action matters most. And it is action precisely that defines lifestyle. But we often confuse a readiness for action with strong feelings, such as desperation. That brings to mind another voice I have heard often. I will call her Dawn:

> I can't go on like this, it hurts too, too much. I'm so ashamed of myself and I'm such a wreck that I can't bear to look at myself most mornings. I'll do anything to stop using and to get back my children and be a good mother. My heart is breaking every day and I'm doing it to myself. I can't stand it anymore. Please let me in the program.

You can't know Dawn's readiness for lifestyle change by gauging her honesty; she may mean everything she says. She probably *is* in real pain and gripped by mortal fears. To ease the pain, she may get into a program where she will find some relief and the promise of a better life. But seeking relief is what any suffering organism does. Whether Dawn can actually take identifiable steps toward *recovery* is another matter. Once she's feeling better, will she accept a guide and join a community while doing whatever she must to sustain abstinence? Neither her words nor her tone can tell you. The same for Carla, Jerome, and Raymond. As they act, so shall we know their readiness.

Dawn's ability to take real steps may depend on both her own readiness and the resources available to her, which means everything that touches her life. But as a clinician, the only resource you can really control is you. Here are some tools and suggestions for empowering your role and responsibility when she in fact can use them.

⊞ THE TOOLS: ACTION CHECKLISTS

If you use generic treatment goals of the sort listed above, you already use a checklist. Developmental goals track the progress of each client along a planned path of achievement.

We can do this without fear of committing "cookie cutter" maltreatment, the mistake of assuming that one size fits all. For although each client does have a unique life, both addiction and recovery have remarkable consistencies from one person to another. (After all, it is that consistency that allows for any programming standardization.) It's not that everyone achieves the same goals in the same way in the same sequence; it's that every one of those large goals represents something vital that every recovery must somehow address. As a new lifestyle takes shape outside the clinical environment, and even as individual differences begin to matter more, certain general goals matter no less. These are reflected in several checklists that I helped design.

The Recovery Checklist (Box 12.1), used as a road map, has proven useful to a general population of recovering people. The four phases—bottoming out, ambivalence, commitment, integration—describe a developmental progression. But instead of cognitive stages, the sequence is more about behavioral events that mark the expansion of a recovering person's focus from the core struggle to sustained abstinence toward ever-growing involvement in the social mainstream.

The Release Preparation Activity Checklist (RePAC; Box 12.2) isn't a map but a prejourney checklist. Our correctional programs have used the RePAC with offenders who must demonstrate and document their readiness for community release. It calls on what's been learned so far and directs attention to what lies ahead. Simpler versions might have comparable utility for other institutional clients who want to do more than "feel" ready to build a new outside lifestyle.

The "How Are You Doing?" Checklist (Box 12.3) probes your clients' progress in the big issues of their everyday lives. It is meant to remind them that recovery is not about how you feel on a given day but what you do day by day. And it points to how much more they can do and how much more satisfaction they can have in continuing in recovery.

Each tool can be used in a group or individually, as an accompaniment to a treatment plan or as a template for a plan. Even if you avoid structured, goal-directed counseling, try and use a checklist. Make it a prominent concern that you share with clients as a kind of map for the journey ahead. Just as the 12 steps find their way onto so many walls, so too do many programs put other kinds of behavioral steps on banners or posters, often with graphic flair. (In a Southeast Asian treatment center, I once saw a stunning mural that showed the "recovery journey" complete with dragons, castles, and more: Talk about a thousand words worth of graphics.) However you do it, keep your clients sensitive to the growth events that are so basic to a sound recovery.

▦ SOME COUNSELING GUIDELINES

Without focusing this chapter on detailed clinical techniques, I do want to promote specific approaches beyond essentials like being respectful, clear, and congruent with a client's sensibilities. In the domain of lifestyle counseling, my experience strongly commends the following strategies.

Be a Guide, Not a Gardener

If you've been schooled in client-centered or psychodynamic therapy, you might think your job is mainly to shine a gentle light on an unlit psyche and with steadfast support nurture the emergence of your client's latent strength and innate wisdom.

Well, we've learned that this style doesn't cut it with most addicts. Support, yes, but early on, rules must be imposed, unwelcome confrontations may be in order, and precepts must be inculcated. Even after all that, few clients will know the way. They will need, and if their commitment is real, they will want, sound, practical guidance. You don't have to be *the* guide (as in "Accept a guide for the journey ahead") but you should be an *effective* guide.

This central responsibility means you must teach clients a host of skills: skills like identifying the craving triggers and stressors that are embedded in their home environments, using the cognitive and behavioral practices of avoiding or coping with them, and applying key competencies to help open and ease one's way through the social mainstream. You must learn those skills and how to teach them because you can't just point and expect someone to climb the mountain. Being an effective recovery guide means teaching climbing skills and climbing readiness. You need to alert clients to the slippery slopes and the false summits. Teach them to pace themselves, to summon help before a crisis, and to draw fully on their own resources when they must. For most clients who have already come to grips with the reality of their addictions, this is the real gut work of treatment. To help them with that, you must become adept at modeling, coaching, and supervising behavioral skills practice. These are vital clinical activities.

At every session, group or individual, Joe and his peers engage in role-play skills rehearsal for all kinds of upcoming and recent experiences. We explore individual thinking styles (we call this interior monologue counterpart to role play "sole play") and mutually critique how to realistically envision and manage situations. We spend at least half our time on this kind of skills training. Our checklists help remind us of vital lifestyle areas that need attention or preparation.

Judge by Action

One of the terrific things about "90 meetings in 90 days" is that it is clear, measurable behavior. Maybe it doesn't have to be 90, and how well one participates isn't the issue either, for it's not just about one's state of mind but about showing up. In the end, that's what lifestyle is: what you do with yourself.

Carla comes to mind again. She said, "I could find a good meeting in my neighborhood once I started looking." But she's already in the community. And it sounds like her old boyfriend is still her boyfriend. She says she needs to make changes. What changes? When?

So although you agree with her insight, the real approval comes when she throws out the old pipe and old phone numbers. And when she shows you a local meeting list she got herself and reports on going to one with a friend, you tell her that's a genuine sign of strength. Now it's time to help her get ready to say goodbye to that boyfriend.

Reinforce the Clockwork of Life

Regular schedules help create healthy grooves in the behaviors of everyday life. Sustainable lifestyles, almost by definition, consist of routines—when one goes to bed or goes to work. Even those 90 meetings work better when they are taken one a day rather than "three yesterday and the weekend off." Without regular schedules, moods and impulses can more easily reassert themselves. The dysfunction of addiction, in fact, is very much due to being out of step with the rhythms of everyday social life. Family and friends are also reassured to know the person's regular activity schedule, even as their expectations about where the person will be and when create a benign pressure for him or her to be there.

Joe wants to meet with you on an "as needed" basis. You tell him you will be in favor of that once he shows he is handling everything else with regularity. "But I'm just so busy. . . ." That's good, Joe, and it would be best to make sure you're not taking on too much and that you keep yourself on a healthy pace. Let's meet less often if you want, but let's keep our meetings on a regular schedule for a few months.

Nurture Social Connectedness

New activities and the satisfactions that sustain them grow out of social support and a sense of community. Indeed, real joy is a shared experience. (I'll wager that science finds that the neural pathways of most pleasures streak through brain matter most involved with social skills and social development.) *Especially for recreation, your clients will do better when they join others in the experience.* Solitary activities, even productive ones like reading, need to be balanced with a flesh-and-blood community (the jury is still out on chat rooms) that expands one's range of pleasure and opportunity and limits the dangers that old demons will rise again. Reinforce this truism: It's often who we know, not what we know. Thus, more healthy social contacts make it more likely we will get a better job or a better date, or learn to enjoy a new sport, or indeed a new book. That's just how people are, all of us.

Blair is a loud know-it-all. Tina is a loner. Lee is self-consciously inarticulate. Karen is notably obese. Your clients may also have problems that challenge their social development and hence recovery—just as these same characteristics may have contributed to their addictions. Do what you can to address these issues. Group therapy and cognitive therapies can be especially helpful. But even as you give special clinical attention to these matters, continue to urge your clients to join where they can, casually or otherwise, the healthy groups of all sizes and styles that compose life in the mainstream. The strongest recoveries are built on the smiles, compliments, hugs, handshakes, and back-pats that only come when you belong. I will return to this vital issue.

⬚ FOUR LIFESTYLE DODGES

Consciously or not, most of us resist change even when we know we must change. Here are four classic dodges against lifestyle change to watch out for.

Dangerous Liaisons

We all know this one. Your client says, or more likely hints, that there is an old friend, hangout, lover, or recreation that still has a place, an innocent place, in his new lifestyle. But you know his history, so you know the risk. He says, "It's a ritual after the game—everyone goes out for beers, and I just sit with them and have a cola." You would be arrogant and possibly wrong to simply disapprove. But you would be dead wrong to ignore.

You want to ask, What does your client think about more, the game or the drinks after? The crowd he's with or the temptation? And does he use appropriate coping skills? How else has he demonstrated that he is ready to sit around the table where everyone else is drinking? What has he told his friends about his recovery? How do they support him?

Some risks are worth taking because your clients must learn to accommodate inescapable temptations inherent in life. But it is your job to gauge their readiness and then to teach self-awareness and to make the questions normal and natural for your clients to ask themselves. And you must model standing up for recovery when it is clearly threatened.

The Toxic Environment

"In my world, everyone gets high. Dope is everywhere—straight up." Your streetwise client is explaining how hard sobriety will be, and he may mean it. But his analysis is probably wrong—because even the most drug-saturated streets run along the church basements and meeting halls of sober community-minded people and self-help groups —not to mention sober households. You know the saying: Wherever you go, there you are. Here's another: Where you don't go, you don't know. The point is, when addicts live for dope, it is all around them; they don't notice the sober world right nearby. True, sometimes you may need to help a client adapt to a new neighborhood. But often enough, it's in the old one.

A recent visit to a self-help group in a high-security prison provides a telling example. During follow-up discussion, a staff member said, "Of course, real recovery happens out there when you get back on the street and have to make it all work." This generally sensible reminder roused Mike, a lifer, to respond: "Hey man, I'm just speaking for me, but my real recovery is in here. I can't think about out there. I gotta make it work behind the wall." Mike, a convicted murderer, was at pains to make us understand that he was talking about recovery and not enforced abstinence. That is, in addition to sobriety (which he, like most inmates, could break out of if he wanted), he was committing himself to a set of daily practices consistent with drug-free, prosocial values. His point is sound and important: A recovering lifestyle can take shape almost anywhere, even in the twisted culture of prison.

"That's Not Me"

This is a variation on the toxic environment dodge. As an exercise in stretching self-concept and practicing skills for broadening social experience, we have asked addicts to imagine what they would do if they found themselves in new situations—say, at a suburban yard sale in an unfamiliar neighborhood. Often, we get nervous laughter and dismissal: "I'd never be at a yard sale." That can be a stopper, when clients won't even imagine themselves in a new setting. "That's just not me. Nah. I'm not even into that."

To which you may find it helpful to say something like "I know it's not the Tom you *have* been. It's the Tom you *can* be. That Tom is as real as you have the courage to make him, he's as real as your recovery. Practice being *that* Tom̀you may need him." And don't ask your clients to imagine four or five steps ahead; two or three will do fine.

A Career in Recovery

A final dodge may hardly seem like one. It's making "recovering" one's essential identity and hence clinging to groups and the margins of the old life in the guise of helper and role model. It can be a way to avoid life in the mainstream. I've seen it in therapeutic communities, counseling programs, and self-help groups.

Of course, helping others as a true calling can be the most wonderful lifestyle. The trouble is, too many clients hear the call before hearing much else, and well before they have accomplished enough to be worthy role models and guides for the people they want to help. Maybe they heard the call out of admiration for you. Or maybe they heard it when they had their first big disappointment in some other effort. In any case, when your client announces that she wants to be a drug counselor, find a good time to explore what kind of choice it is or whether it even feels like a choice.

A client who says, "Meetings are my life because I'm all about recovery" may really mean "That's where I belong because it's all I know." Again, before smiling your approval, think—and feel. Twelve-step fellowships can be warm, welcoming, lifesaving, and life-enhancing venues. But if they serve too long as sanctuaries, someone's life is not going well. Don't be afraid to push—gently—and to encourage your clients to see where else they might also safely and joyfully belong. Help them get there, a day at a time.

⊞ FINALLY, DON'T FORGET THE MIRACLE CURE

My opening should actually have read "No *New* Miracle Cure in Sight" because there *is* a miracle cure, though it's not quick or borne of science. It's growth: Life itself is the miracle. Everything I have offered here is about helping your clients experience more growth, fuller life. That platitude has some practical implications that, in conclusion, I want to emphasize.

Addiction is more like a memory than an infection. It lives in the body and soul as a compulsive hunger to re-experience a peculiar physical and mental state. You can kill off germs, but you can't kill a memory. Drug seeking and drug effects become deeply etched into the nervous system, and no foreseeable therapy seems likely to remove that imprint. What we can do, as I've been discussing, is speed the growth of new behaviors and pleasures that can create imprints that become more dominant. As for relapse, it's not so much a recurrence of bad germs as it is the reassertion of the old memory.

For me, all this means that a recovering lifestyle should not be experienced as a barricade against reinfection. Of course, Joe must avoid setups and the multitriggered relapse traps that characterized his old lifestyle. He therefore needs strong relapse prevention skills and keen awareness to avoid the dangers he can and to cope with those he must. But neither he nor you can "sanitize" life; instead, he needs to keep going after the good things. That's how people overcome a memory that may never die but can be made to fade away: They build new satisfying routines with as much social support as possible and etch new grooves in their body and minds.

So we want Joe to keep learning and keep deepening and expanding his friendships. We hope he finds more to enjoy in music, is able to improve his jump shot, can spend more quality time with loved ones. In all this, we will urge him to go easy on himself, for we especially want him to keep enlarging his own space of serenity. The thing is, when life is about new possibilities and personal growth, old memories have less power. In my experience, the people who seem to have the greatest eagerness for self-improvement and growth generally have the strongest, most resilient recoveries. Mike the lifer will probably have to spend a lot of time in the prison library and classrooms and write a lot of letters. Joe has the whole "free world" to explore. Out there, though, his current enthusiasm will fade with the novelty of being straight. He's got to go right at the three problem areas I mentioned at the start: people, work, and pleasure. You'll need to lead and urge him on.

I've been privileged to work with and learn from hundreds of solidly recovering people. The most mature and accomplished often don't even think of themselves as "recovering." If you got to know their lifestyles well, you would probably just call them "growing." What more could any of us want for our own?

REFERENCE ⊞

Zackon, F., McAuliffe, W., & Chi'en, J. (1993). *Recovery training and self-help.* Rockville, MD: National Institute on Drug Abuse.

13

Individual Therapy

Accomplishing the Tasks of Recovery

Joan E. Zweben

T he individual therapist has a variety of roles in the treatment of alcohol and other drug (AOD) problems. Although many addiction programs rely heavily if not exclusively on group activities, the therapist who can work with the client in individual sessions has the leisure to examine issues in more depth. It is important for you to have a clear picture of the advantages and pitfalls of individual work and the ability to collaborate with others involved in the treatment process. It is rare for the person with AOD problems not to be having difficulty with physical health, family, employers, or the social services or criminal justice system, and teamwork with others providing care or some form of monitoring is essential.

The term *therapist* in this chapter is intended to refer to a psychologist, social worker, marriage and family therapist, or physician with general training in conducting psychotherapy. "Counselors" may have received extensive training in addiction, especially in some of the more demanding credentialing programs, but they do not generally call themselves therapists. The term *therapist* implies a more rigorous training in basic clinical skills, although it frequently also entails limited understanding of the addiction and recovery process. To be effective, you must be able to select appropriately from the many tools available, and to do that you must have a good understanding of addictive disorders and the recovery process. This chapter provides an overview of the modality of individual therapy to help you select appropriately from the available tools. Although harm reduction approaches certainly have a place (to be discussed later), the chapter is written from the perspective that abstinence from alcohol and other drugs offers the widest margin of safety and maximizes the potential for other growth.

Your role as therapist will vary according to the setting in which you work. Private practitioners are particularly well positioned to do early intervention. By recognizing clients at risk, you can employ motivational enhancement strategies to encourage a commitment to changing behavior before quality of life becomes significantly impaired. Because most addiction professionals in specialty settings do not see clients until their problems have become severe, they may have little perspective on the power of early intervention. Empirical studies have not sought to measure this phenomenon, but therapists report considerable experience with clients who need little more than an arena for self-examination to acknowledge their risk and begin to change their behavior. A worrisome family heritage, a lover who leaves protesting chronic marijuana or alcohol use, or the onset of health problems can provide the catalyst for the client to reexamine his or her attachment to alcohol and other drugs and begin to consider abstinence.

Therapists can play a major role in enhancing the quality of recovery. Once a client is stable in abstinence, other levels of development become possible. As Brown (1985) has so beautifully described, recovery is more than a behavior change; it is an identity transformation with many dimensions. Psychotherapy offered in the community can guide the client's work on unresolved developmental issues that have increased vulnerability to AOD problems, repair and improve significant relationships, and promote healthy interaction with other aspects of the environment.

It is essential that you have an understanding of the recovery process that includes awareness of relapse warning signs. Relapse can occur at any point in the recovery process, but the alert therapist may be able to intervene effectively if he or she recognizes signals and makes this a priority in the treatment. It is particularly easy for therapists to miss relapse warning signs in high-functioning, highly verbal clients. Drifting away from self-help or other recovery support systems, carelessness with health practices such as diet, sleep, and exercise, and poor stress management are all harbingers of relapse that need to be addressed promptly. Clients who place a premium on performing or functioning under duress may underestimate or underreport the level of stress that they are experiencing. The therapist's ability and willingness to shift attention to behavior at this point is essential. Vulnerability to relapse may also be heightened when the client is addressing painful and anxiety-provoking issues. It is important for the therapist not to misjudge the chronicity of addictive disorders and to make sure that the client has adequate supports in place to weather emotional turbulence.

It is difficult to produce good outcomes through individual psychotherapy alone. The client benefits greatly from a connection to a subculture that supports recovery, whether that is a self-help group like the 12-step system or another commitment that is incompatible with AOD use, such as a meditation discipline or sports activity. It is particularly easy for therapists to underestimate the challenges for high-functioning clients who have good insight into their addictive behavior. Many therapists, especially those who are psychodynamically oriented, hold high expectations for the power of insight and may become disappointed, frustrated, and angry when they encounter the relapsing pattern that is characteristic of addiction. It is particularly difficult for the less seasoned to appreciate how a client who has been stable and doing well can drift into an "altered state" in which painful memories of negative consequences appear to have been erased and there is a seemingly inexorable drift into a relapse state of mind.

Ralph, for example, was a highly paid lawyer in a specialty practice whose methamphetamine use accelerated gradually over 7 years until he lost his lucrative job. After a stay in inpatient treatment, he began individual therapy, participated in an ongoing recovery group, and attended NA sporadically. He stabilized, became solidly abstinent from alcohol and other drugs, and began to focus on repairing the damage in his marriage. It was difficult for him to tolerate the 4 months' unemployment that followed his last drug episode, and he was relieved when he obtained another job.

He rose rapidly in his new firm, and in a little over a year was promoted to a responsible and highly paid position. He continued to attend his treatment activities, but his attitude began to shift. He grew testy when challenged about resuming alcohol use, which he argued was "merely social," though his wife disagreed. Members of his recovery group, who by now knew him well, attempted in vain to remind him of the risks he was taking. His individual therapist vigorously promoted examination of the elements of his new choices, which he did with some insight but little enthusiasm. Within a few months, he had relapsed to methamphetamine use and was soon after fired from his job.

This high-functioning client had discontinued some of his recovery-related activities and was part of a subculture that valued social drinking. Despite his apparent success in his first year of recovery, he remained vulnerable to relapse.

ADDICTION: A BIOPSYCHOSOCIAL DISORDER ⊞

Addiction specialists typically view the disorder as biopsychosocial in nature. This means that there are biological, psychological, and social factors involved in the initiation, maintenance, and progression of addictive patterns and that these vary in each individual. For example, social factors heavily influence the initiation into AOD use, but genetic factors affect the transition from experimental use to more serious problems. Co-existing mental disorders heighten vulnerability in a variety of ways. Therapists outside the addiction field may have great difficulty detaching from their primary therapeutic orientation and thinking simultaneously on all three levels. To be effective, it is essential that you do so.

A biopsychosocial model also underlines the importance of an eclectic intervention repertoire. In a recovery-oriented model, the therapist must shift gears according to the task of recovery at hand. For the client who seeks treatment for other problems, you may need to focus on connecting the presenting complaints to the effects of alcohol and other drugs and to engage the client in addressing this behavior. A focus on motivational issues, without premature emphasis on action, is important at this point. Once the client becomes willing to change the behavior, cognitive-behavioral strategies are typically employed to facilitate the transition to an alcohol- and drug-free state. Simultaneously, there may need to be collaboration with medical professionals to manage the detoxification phase. Insight-oriented work should be focused on navigating through the obstacles to the recovery task, not on open-ended exploration. As the process unfolds, you can shift to broader quality-of-life issues, selecting from the toolbox according to the priority at that time. To summarize, the stages of a recovery-oriented model can be seen as

1. Engaging the client who is actively drinking/using

2. Negotiating an abstinence contract

3. Helping the client stop drinking/using

4. Consolidating abstinence; changing lifestyles

5. Addressing developmental/interpersonal issues

⊞ EARLY INTERVENTION

AOD use is so common today that you need to rule it out rather than wait until signs appear that it is a problem. It is also not necessary to wait until the client meets criteria for substance dependence to suggest that such use be eliminated, at least for a trial period. It is easy for therapists to underestimate the influence of alcohol and other drugs, particularly when the client functions relatively well. When the client has another mental disorder, such as depression or posttraumatic stress disorder, alcohol and other drugs may well be exacerbating symptoms, distorting the therapeutic process or slowing therapeutic progress or contributing to premature dropout. Even seasoned addiction specialists cannot always determine the effect of AOD use, so the period of trial abstinence is instructive for both you and the client.

For example, one client, Joyce, was in psychotherapy and was also taking depakote for mood lability. She had been abstinent from prescription drugs for a significant period of time and was exploring difficult issues in her life. She began occasional and then regular alcohol consumption, insisting that it had never been her drug of choice and that she didn't like it enough to get in trouble with it. Over a 6-month period, her consumption increased to several glasses of wine in the late afternoon and early evening. Her mood lability also increased, and upon inquiry she revealed that she was now less likely to take her medication as prescribed. It was difficult to determine the extent to which her mood instability was produced by the addition of alcohol or by poor medication compliance.

After disputing the importance of eliminating alcohol, she agreed to stop drinking for a month. She was surprised at how difficult this turned out to be and how many feelings were stirred up about drinking. However, her moods became more stable, and she found that her improved stress tolerance permitted her to endure her children's homework period more attentively and calmly than before. She was also able to examine her family's history of drinking problems more forthrightly.

Thus, the client may benefit in ways that are unexpected. Abstinence may also improve the quality of the therapeutic process in a variety of ways. For example, many therapists outside addiction treatment settings are more permissive about marijuana use, viewing it as the most benign of all the drugs. It is also the illicit drug most likely to be used by therapists. Because the negative consequences of marijuana use become apparent most clearly after it is discontinued, it is often difficult to convince clients that abstinence might be worthwhile. Recent research on marijuana use is elucidating the pharmacology and other features of marijuana use (Gold, 1998; Grinspoon & Bakalar, 1997), but the effect on individuals appears to be quite variable. Clinicians have observed an apparent increase in depression, passivity or lack of motivation, or a "blanket" on feelings in some but not all clients.

Marijuana's effect on attention and concentration can have other consequences for the therapeutic process. Roger, for example, was working with a therapist who used visualizations as part of an intensive structured process for exploring and reworking painful childhood experiences that shaped negative coping patterns in adult life. The therapist noted that he was unable to sustain his attention for the 15 to 20 minutes required for most of the visualizations and began to question his regular marijuana use. Although initially surprised, Roger acknowledged that he had had passing concerns that 20 years of marijuana smoking was not good for his lungs, particularly because he had more frequent respiratory infections each winter. He agreed to put aside his marijuana for the 2 to 3 months that it could take to make a distinct improvement in his concentration. The specialized therapy was put on hold, and when he returned he had much less trouble sustaining his attention during the visualization exercises.

You should avoid insisting that a particular drug is the source of a problem. Instead, take the more realistic stance that it is likely to be an influencing factor in ways that cannot be understood until the client gets some distance from the drug. The more the therapist knows about drugs, the more easily he or she can make the case for the relationship between particular symptoms or discomforts and particular drugs. However, the experiment with abstinence focuses the client on making detailed observations and rests on engaging curiosity and commitment to self-examination rather than relying on persuasion.

Treatment Readiness

When clients enter treatment and the therapist suspects or believes that AOD use is an important factor, it is tempting to refer the client to specialty treatment as a condition of accepting him or her for future therapy. Many clients disappear at that point or do so after they investigate addiction treatment and reject the prospect. It is preferable for therapists to become proficient to address mild to moderate levels of AOD use or to work with the client to become "treatment ready" for a specialty setting. These settings are designed for people who understand that they need to give up their use, however ambivalent they may be. When people seek help for "other problems" or enter a system such as social services or an employee assistance program at work, they may lack a full appreciation of the relationship between their AOD use and their other difficulties. It is your task to raise their awareness and increase their commitment to change their behavior. When the therapist already has a relationship with the client, it is often preferable to use the existing therapeutic alliance to address the AOD use.

Enhancing Motivation

Motivational enhancement strategies have been under investigation for some time (Miller, 1999; Miller & Rollnick, 1991; Prochaska, DiClemente, & Norcross, 1992) and are discussed in detail elsewhere in this volume. Briefly, individuals move through stages in deciding to change their behavior, and the therapist with some knowledge of these stages is better prepared to select interventions that will move the client forward. Many come to treatment in the precontemplation stage about their AOD use. They are unaware or minimally aware that it is a problem. Once rapport is established, you can move them forward by exploring the pros and cons of substance use, examining the discrepancies between the client's behavior and the perspectives of others on the consequences of that behavior, providing information about alcohol and other drugs and possible negative consequences, and giving forthright feedback. Clients in the contemplation stage are aware that there is a problem but are ambivalent and uncertain about making changes. The therapist in this situation provides an arena for the exploration of ambivalence and works to strengthen the positive, internal motivation for change rather than punishing resistance or ambivalence. The client in the preparation stage is more committed to making a change in the near future but has not arrived at a clear course of action. You can offer clarification of goals and strategies and provide options for discussion. You can then assist the client to formulate a treatment plan or strategy that draws on past successes from the client's own experiences or observations of others. In the action stage, the client is actively taking steps to change but has not consolidated his or her gains. You can help the client identify high-risk situations, develop appropriate coping strategies for them, and overcome obstacles encountered in the process of change. In the maintenance stage, the client has achieved initial goals and is now working to ensure that the achievements will be stable. Lifestyle changes are the focus at this point. If there is a recurrence or relapse, help the client learn from the experience and find improved coping strategies.

Reasons for Resistance to the Abstinence Commitment

Clients have a variety of reasons to resist an abstinence commitment, and a focused exploration intended to remove motivational barriers (in contrast with a goal to resolve issues) can accomplish a great deal. Common reasons for resistance are

- *Fear of failure*: The client has tried to stop previously and has been unable to succeed. This heightens anxiety that the problem is bigger than the client wished to believe. Refusal to commit to abstinence protects the client from additional experiences of failure.

- *Addiction pattern in the family of origin*: Clients vary in their articulateness on this issue but often understand they will no longer "belong" if they turn away from substances that play a powerful role in their family dynamics. They may have few models for how to live clean and sober and may be deeply apprehensive about moving into such uncharted territory.

- *Significant other who uses*: It is difficult but not impossible to become abstinent when in a relationship with a user; however, there is a strong pull to continue a pattern of using. Clients usually understand on some level that if they choose to give up their substances, they may have to give up their intimate relationship as well.

- *Self-medication*: Clients are often quite convinced that their AOD use represents self-medication and thus that they cannot succeed in giving it up until their other problems are resolved. This conviction is often based on a misunderstanding between short- and longer term effects of AOD use. People are most powerfully influenced by the initial drug effect, and negative consequences that unfold over time are less salient to them. For example, most people report that alcohol makes them feel better (euphoric) and more relaxed, even though they may know it is a central nervous system depressant. You need to help the client extend his or her time frame in order to appreciate that alcohol will inevitably exacerbate depression and frequently will produce a substance-induced mood disorder that is confused with an independent depressive disorder. Most self-medication strategies appear to work in the short run but reveal problems when examined more closely.

- *Trauma history*: Most clients without such a history will experience benefits from abstinence fairly early in the process, though plenty of discomforts will be evident. Clients with a history of traumatic experiences may feel considerably worse. The client must be helped to see that abstinence provides the safety that is necessary to do meaningful trauma resolution (Sullivan & Evans, 1994), though it may initially entail a worsening of symptoms.

- *Hopelessness, fear of the unknown*: Those with long histories are particularly discouraged and have no picture of positive prospects for themselves. It is important for you to provide reassurance and realistic forms of hope.
- *Survivor guilt*: Clients who have left many family members and significant others behind as they made their accomplishments may engage in AOD use as a form of self-sabotage or as a way of maintaining a foot in the old neighborhood.

In exploring these issues, you should keep in mind that the relationship between etiology and intervention in substance abuse is usually more tenuous than assumed by psychodynamically trained therapists. People need to know relatively little about why they use drugs in order to stop; they mainly need to know *how* to stop. In exploring emotional obstacles, you should avoid suggesting that these issues must be resolved for progress to occur. Instead, exploring these factors can help clients understand why they resist changing their behavior even after coming to realize the negative consequences of their AOD use. At this point, clients are often prepared to move on.

The Psychoeducational Component of Motivating Clients

The therapist should seek to become sufficiently knowledgeable about the addiction and recovery process to serve as "coach" at various points in the process. This including knowing some specifics about the intoxication, withdrawal, and protracted abstinence effects of various drugs in order to educate the client and build motivation. There are many common misunderstandings about alcohol, even among highly educated clients. These may be based on the strong human propensity to associate the immediate effect with the main drug effect and to not recognize negative consequences that occur later in time. For example, most people associate alcohol with the euphoria and relaxation that occurs quickly after the first drink. Although they usually know that alcohol is a central nervous system depressant, they do not connect it with their worsening depression. They come to therapy stating that alcohol helps them cope with their difficult life when in fact it is more likely to be exacerbating their depression. They believe alcohol is helping them cope with stress when in fact it is more likely to be undermining their stress tolerance. It is also quite common for clients to believe that if they don't feel intoxicated, or if they can consume considerable alcohol without apparent impairment in functioning, they don't have an alcohol problem. Educating clients that a high inborn tolerance for alcohol is actually a marker for serious problems (Schuckit & Smith, 1996) and is undesirable because it means they lack a warning system allows the therapist to challenge the client's belief system in a way that is more impersonal. Sharing bits of information (not long lectures) often stimulates clients to look at their experience in new ways. The psychoeducational stance allows you to test the waters in a mode of dialogue that allows the client to shift positions without a great loss of face.

ESTABLISHING ABSTINENCE ▦

Both abstinence-oriented treatment and harm reduction approaches may recommend an experiment with abstinence as a place to begin. At this stage, the therapist functions as a teacher and coach to assist the client in breaking the cycle of drug use. Education on drug effects and what to expect in withdrawal is important. The focus is on medical safety, identifying triggers and stressors, exploring what behavior changes will be important initially, and learning new coping patterns.

Therapists in private practice do well to identify an addiction medicine physician to assess and manage the medical aspects of addiction. These can be located through the American Society of Addiction Medicine (www.ASAM.org), based in Rockville, Maryland, or through state chapters affiliated with the national organization. Alcohol, benzodiazepines, and barbiturates can present serious withdrawal hazards, and it is important to have a physician make the determination of whether a managed withdrawal is necessary.

Securing an Abstinence Commitment

The therapist does not need to convince the client that he or she actually has a problem, or is in fact an addict or alcoholic, to suggest the experiment with abstinence to observe what changes when alcohol and other drugs are subtracted out. This approach has also been referred to as "sobriety sampling" (Miller & Page, 1991). It is difficult to convince one's therapist that one is not addicted but that one should not be asked to abstain for a circumscribed period of time. This therapist suggestion quickly confronts the client with his or her level of attachment to drinking and/or using, and the issue can be discussed in those terms. The word *attachment* is less stigmatized than *addiction* or *alcoholism*, and the client may accept the task of examining AOD attachments far more readily than that of abstaining because he or she is possibly addicted or alcoholic. It is also useful to introduce the idea that the client does not need to be alcoholic to benefit from not drinking.

Alcohol affects mood in obvious and subtle ways, and the client with a coexisting mood disorder may be defeating other efforts by continuing to drink. Such clients may be more sensitive to small amounts of alcohol, particularly if they are women. In addition, alcohol may make it difficult to evaluate the effects of antidepressants or contribute to the belief that they are not helpful to the client. When clients with depressive episodes report that they tried antidepressants and they didn't work, it is important for you to inquire if he or she was drinking at the time. In addition to promoting poorer adherence to medication regimens, alcohol may reduce the effect of the medication. It is quite remarkable how frequently physicians prescribe antidepressants without addressing the issue of alcohol. If they inquire at all, they may readily accept their patient's minimized report of consumption. In collaboration with the prescribing physician, such a client can be asked to engage in the experiment with abstinence as a way to conduct a better medication trial.

The framework of complete abstinence allows for much better clarification because it removes the issue of how much of a drug is needed to produce an effect. Clients can be told that because effects can be quite variable, total abstinence allows the issues to come into focus more clearly. They may be prepared for the fact that many people find this more difficult than they imagined it would be, and these difficulties are grist for the therapeutic mill. Goals short of complete abstinence introduce the influence of the client's "accounting system" (Brown, 1985), in which deviations from the agreed-on plan become plausible and the client retains a stake in minimizing negative consequences. Abstinence offers the widest margin of safety, in which the client can be assured that progression of the disorder will be arrested.

Discussions of harm reduction and abstinence often frame the issues as more mutually exclusive than they are. Abstinence-oriented treatment can be seen as an end point on a continuum of activities that reduce the harm of AOD use. Although few individuals achieve long-term, unbroken abstinence, this treatment orientation has repeatedly been shown to produce reduction of AOD use and associated criminal activity and improvement in health status (including psychiatric status), family functioning, and educational and vocational achievements (Gerstein, 1994; Gerstein & Harwood, 1990; McLellan et al., 1996; Simpson & Curry, 1997). Harm reduction approaches have been documented to be effective in the arena of HIV and alcohol use (MacCoun, 1998; Marlatt, 1998; Sorensen et al., 1991). However, there is currently no study that compares similar clients randomly assigned to abstinence-oriented treatment or treatment that accepts other goals to determine if harm reduction therapy produces equivalent or better gains.

Pitfalls of harm reduction include the tendency to have lower expectations for more impaired clients, such that the therapist discourages the desire or attempt to become completely abstinent. It is also common for therapists to underestimate the severity of the addiction problem when the client is high functioning. Therapists outside the addiction field are usually less able to detect warning signs of more serious problems unreported by the client. They may lack the knowledge and confidence to suggest to a particular client that abstinence goals are appropriate for his or her situation. This can prolong risk for the client and create exposure to liability for the therapist. Finally, therapists are no more likely than other educated professionals to recognize these problems in themselves, and this can influence their willingness to ask another to abstain.

The Psychoeducational Component of Quitting

The therapist's role as coach is particularly important as the client works to break the cycle of use and encounters obstacles. For example, it is common for stimulant users to encounter a protracted period of anhedonia (known as "the wall") during which they exhibit at least low-level signs of depression and a conviction that life will never again hold excitement or pleasure. Although antidepressants may be needed at this stage, clients also improve when they introduce regular aerobic exercise and are attentive to other aspects of their health practices and stress management. Explaining the role of dopamine depletion from the stimulant use in producing negative feeling states can reassure the client and give him or her behavioral remedies and a time frame within which feelings of despair are likely to abate. Breaking down the tasks into manageable units (e.g., "Note observations in your journal for the next 30 days as you implement your plan for regular exercise") can help sustain motivation to continue the recovery process.

Because alcohol and other drugs produce altered states that can even mimic many disorders, you need to avoid generalizing from strong feelings that emerge in early abstinence. It is common for clients to focus on painful experiences in their lives as they move through the disordered mood states characteristic of early recovery. Though the issues are real, it is easy to overestimate the severity of the client's problems and underestimate his or her ability to cope if solid abstinence can be established. You should make only tentative judgments based on the intense discomforts that the client often describes during this period.

Coexisting Disorders

It is important for you to be familiar with the range of substance-induced disorders as described in *Diagnostic and Statistical Manual of Mental Disorders* (*DSM-IV*; American Psychiatric Association, 1994) to avoid misdiagnosis. Newly abstinent clients experience a wide range of distress, some of which is related to physical factors and some to beginning to see clearly the negative consequences of their AOD use. In general, most withdrawal symptoms subside after 2 to 3 weeks, though careful inquiry is still needed to distinguish between understandable misery and psychiatric symptoms. A client who has had extended periods of sobriety (longer than 6 months) can be asked to recall in some detail what life was like during that state, giving the therapist a window to check out diagnostic hypotheses. Diagnoses need to remain provisional, however, as a serious recovery process brings many changes. For example, it is common for clients with a misdiagnosis of borderline personality disorder to look quite different a year into recovery, as their presenting characteristics are heavily influenced by their AOD use.

When two or more independent mental disorders exist, it is important to integrate the treatment so that both are addressed simultaneously. The individual therapist needs to make sure that it is clear who coordinates the treatment if services are obtained from different systems. Otherwise, the client is faced with contradictory and conflicting demands at a time when he or she is ill equipped to prioritize appropriately. Principles for integrating treatment emphasize first safety, then stabilization, then consolidation and maintenance of gains. For example, in the early stages, you focus on medical issues, domestic violence, homelessness, or other factors that affect the client's safety. Once crisis issues have been handled, you can focus on assisting the client to obtain stability of situation, symptoms, or other difficulties. A recovery focus requires that abstinence remain a priority to make long-term gains possible, but this does not exclude discussion of any topic the client wishes to raise. In early recovery, however, you are focused on helping the client express or contain difficult feelings without using again. Once stability is established, other issues can be more productively explored in depth.

Treatment Planning and Implementation

The treatment contract should include the time frame, frequency of contacts, and involvement of significant others. Clients should be clear that immediate cessation of all intoxicants is the desired goal and that the therapist's job is to assist with the obstacles. Consequences of relapse, such as increasing the intensity of treatment, should be specified. For example, many resist self-help participation. The therapist can agree that the client can do it his or her own way first but that if this doesn't work within a specified time frame, other activities need to be included. Schedules for urinalysis or breath testing should be clarified. You should recognize that not even seasoned experts can accurately detect AOD use with accuracy sufficient for most clinical purposes, so some form of objective monitoring is desirable. It is simplest if this is built in from the beginning rather than introduced once the therapist has reasons to mistrust the client's account. It can be normalized by stating that it is a routine part of addressing AOD use and that it allows both parties to know where they stand.

A variety of behavioral strategies are invaluable at this point in helping the client break the cycle. These are described elsewhere in this volume and can also be found in the Treatment Improvement Protocol published by the Center for Substance Abuse Treatment and available at no charge (Rawson, 1999). Basically, they involve identifying triggers and stressors and making a plan to cope with hazardous situations. Client worksheets in the Treatment Improvement Protocol help the client approach the tasks systematically and are an aid to therapists without much training in this type of approach. In the early abstinence stage, it is desirable for the client to avoid hazardous situations when this is possible and to make a plan for reducing risks when it is not. For example, later in recovery, clients may be comfortable in situations where alcohol is served, but there is no virtue in remaining in that situation when trying to become abstinent. If a particular event is unavoidable, the client should identify specific ways to reduce the risk. Possibilities include making sure there will be alternative beverages, making an agreement with a partner to leave if the situation becomes too difficult, and/or requesting that the hosts cooperate in reducing peer pressure to drink.

When clients do not establish abstinence after months of trying, it is important to identify where the process has bogged down. It is common for ambivalence to reassert itself about the abstinence commitment, and that is a productive place to begin exploration. Therapists frequently focus on the behavioral strategies, continuing to produce suggestions for improvement when the client does not follow through. A return to the issue of ambivalence is often more productive and reduces the chance that the therapist will get frustrated and angry about the client's lack of progress. It is common for client motivation to wax and wane, particularly when a reduction in use produces improvement. Once motivation is strengthened, behavioral interventions are more likely to be effective.

EARLY RECOVERY ISSUES ⊞

The work of early recovery consists of developing a new identity to match and consolidate changes in behavior. Although for some the identity of addict/alcoholic involves self-disparagement, a healthy integration allows the client to be matter-of-fact and comfortable with the adaptations needed to sustain an abstinent lifestyle. The emotion around this declaration shifts from shame and dismay to an acceptance of a different self-image and accompanying behaviors. This often means disengaging from social networks in which drinking or drug use is glamorized.

For example, Mike and his wife were wealthy due to the success of his widely used invention. He came to treatment after several near-lethal drinking episodes that had required lengthy hospitalizations and had resulted in some liver damage. Although determined to stay sober, he was proud of his fine wine collection and did not want to disengage from his social network of high-status heavy drinkers. He was indignant that this might be necessary. His therapist weathered his scoffing and barbed remarks and persisted in asking him to examine the many ways in which his sense of himself was bound up in associations to alcohol.

Fortunately, he made a good connection with AA and gradually became bored with the antics of his drinking buddies. Over time, he transferred his flamboyant leadership activities from his drinking social events to his AA groups, where he was an energetic participant. After about a year of sobriety, he began volunteering at the hospital where he had been detoxified and took great pleasure in being a good role model in that setting.

Structure is important in early recovery, particularly during times that are high risk for drinking or using. Consistent attendance at treatment activities, self-help groups, exercise sessions, and other events are a marker for progress in building a good foundation. A clear structure provides a container for feelings and impulses and allows the client to gain confidence in his or her ability to create a new lifestyle. It is important at this stage to maintain a focus on AOD use and any hazards that emerge. Therapists often assume that the worst is over once the client has been abstinent for a few months and shows some improvement. You should inquire regularly about whether the client has used *any* substance or is daydreaming about doing so. It may also be useful to review any episode in which the client was offered a drug, how this was handled, and how it felt. Frequently, the client is able to reject the offer, only to find him- or herself vulnerable for the next few days or weeks. Once associations are awakened, cravings often intensify. Those who are firm about their commitment to abstinence make it clear to their friends they are not to be offered any alcohol or other drugs. If necessary, they disengage from that friendship circle. Thus, continuing social pressure is a sign that the client has not closed the door unambivalently.

There are many possible vulnerabilities in the client's recovery program. Resisting a regular focus on abstinence may reflect a desire to see the issue as "the problem I used to have." At the other end of the continuum, a narrow focus on these issues is also detrimental. The client needs to examine the many functions served by AOD use and to discuss how best to meet those needs. This typically involves better attention to stress management, developing new coping strategies, managing feelings differently, and restructuring relationships. At this stage, it is useful for you to be able to readily shift gears between these various levels.

Reciprocal relapse patterns are important to detect early. It is common for male stimulant users to have a strong stimulant-sex connection that is not adequately addressed in treatment. For example, Sam's methamphetamine runs usually included extensive activities with highly paid sex workers. He downplayed the importance of the sexual component of his addiction. After 10 months of abstinence, he decided to celebrate a promotion by treating himself to a call girl. This resulted in a prolonged episode of using methamphetamine.

Thus, a relapse in one area is accompanied by a relapse in another. Perhaps the most common occurrence is a relapse involving another mental disorder. A psychotic client whose symptoms are well controlled is likely to return to using drugs if his voices reemerge. The client with posttraumatic stress disorder is likely to resume using if intrusion symptoms are heightened. The depressed client who discontinues medication because she is upset by her weight gain is at great risk for resuming drinking within a matter of weeks. The therapist needs to keep in mind that any loss of stability in one area is likely to have a domino effect and that it is necessary to move quickly if a serious relapse is to be avoided.

Facilitating the Use of Self-Help Groups

The self-help system is considered a key element in the recovery process by many addiction treatment providers, yet it is perhaps the least well understood by therapists. To remedy this problem, it is useful for you to assign yourself a "field trip" in which you attend appropriate (open) meetings to gain understanding of what actually happens there. You can particularly note your own feelings about attending, observe the rituals and practices, and think about the benefits and limitations of this particular group process. In this manner, you can become more effective at facilitating the use of this system.

The self-help system provides a subculture that supports the recovery effort and a process for personal development with no financial barriers. Clients who resist involvement can be asked to describe how they will accomplish those things. Many resist initially, only to conclude after repeated relapses that the self-help system has much to offer. There are many ways to facilitate a connection discussed in detail elsewhere (Zweben, 1995). Initial objections are often based on stranger anxiety and on unwillingness to admit, "I am an alcoholic/addict." You can keep the issue of attendance on the table without getting into a power struggle with no winners. Feelings about participation in this system mirror ambivalence about the recovery process and provide a reliable catalyst for eliciting issues.

At the other end of the continuum is the therapist who insists that self-help group participation is a condition of treatment. Addressing AOD use may be an appropriate condition of treatment, but launching a struggle over the method at the outset is unwise. Many clients have to work on their ambivalence over considering AOD use as a problem before self-help group attendance is acceptable for them. Although this ambivalence has a way of emerging unexpectedly at any stage of treatment, thorough discussion early in treatment usually has enduring payoffs.

The 12-step system, the largest self-help system in the world, has an immense variety of groups meeting at virtually all times of day and evening in most urban areas. As such, it is important that the client give it a fair try (see Chapter 10). Frequently, stereotypes evaporate and clients become enthusiastic when connected to meetings where they find people like themselves, hear their story, and otherwise feel at home. In addition to the many variations on AA, alternative self-help groups also exist in most large communities. LifeRing (formerly Secular Organization for Sobriety), SMART Recovery, and Women for Sobriety are examples of groups with enthusiastic supporters. More information about these can be located in the telephone book or on the Internet. Chat rooms are increasingly available for those who cannot attend in person.

It is also important for the therapist not to view self-help group participation as adequate in itself to address the addiction. In some cases it may be, but it is unfortunately common for therapists who are relatively unskilled in this area to make such a referral and hope for the best. Your consistent attention to the tasks of early recovery is enormously beneficial, and the skills needed are well within the reach of therapists willing to invest some time into acquiring training.

ONGOING RECOVERY ISSUES ▦

The later stages of recovery work involve issues with which most therapists are familiar and comfortable. Experiencing, expressing, and managing feelings are ongoing issues, as is getting beyond all-or-none thinking and developing ambiguity tolerance. In addition, the therapist should attend to the continuing identify shifts and lifestyle changes that foster the consolidation of abstinence into a life that is comfortable and satisfying without the use of psychoactive substances. Recovery is not about deprivation, and the therapist should keep the client focused on addressing the difficulties and deficits that emerge.

Dreams of drinking and using are common at all stages of recovery (Flowers & Zweben, 1996, 1998), but in later stages they often signal important unfinished business that may have little to do with addiction. Nonetheless, clients may be very upset by them, particularly if they awaken unsure of whether they have actually used or not. After first inquiring about whether the client may be at renewed risk, you can explore what issues feel so overwhelming that the client is dreaming of a coping mechanism characteristic of an earlier time. The basic principle is to examine the possibility that the client is a renewed relapse risk before proceeding to an examination of the many other possibilities.

Awareness of harbingers of relapse is important no matter how many years of abstinence the client has achieved. Poor stress management or inattention to other forms of self-care, disconnecting from recovery supports, and "experimenting" with intoxicants are all warning signals that should be heeded immediately. Clients with long periods of sobriety followed by relapse should be encouraged to examine those episodes in detail, with an eye to identifying specific relapse warning signs and making a plan to address them. Alertness and willingness to focus on AOD issues quickly, rather than viewing this issue as resistance, is the mark of a recovery-sensitive therapist who promotes continuing growth for the client.

⊞ CONCLUSION

The treatment of addiction requires a collaborative stance in which the therapist remains attentive to the client's need to participate in a variety of activities to promote recovery. The therapist with a clear understanding of recovery tasks and the ability to select interventions to address those tasks will maximize the client's success at dealing with these issues. Although specialized knowledge is most important in the early stages of engaging the client in addressing AOD use and successfully modifying behavior, sensitivity to recovery issues is important throughout psychotherapy. Hopefully, more thorough cross-training will allow therapists in all settings to effectively address AOD use in their clients at both early and later stages of problems.

⊞ REFERENCES

American Psychiatric Association. (1994). *Diagnostic and statistical manual of mental disorders* (4th ed.). Washington, DC: Author.

Brown, S. (1985). *Treating the alcoholic: A developmental model of recovery.* New York: John Wiley.

Flowers, L. K., & Zweben, J. E. (1996). The dream interview method in recovery oriented psychotherapy. *Journal of Substance Abuse Treatment, 13,* 99-105.

Flowers, L. K., & Zweben, J. E. (1998). The changing role of "using dreams" in addiction recovery. *Journal of Substance Abuse Treatment, 15,* 193-200.

Gerstein, D. R. (1994). Outcome research: Drug abuse. In M. Galanter & H. D. Kleber (Eds.), *Textbook of substance abuse treatment* (pp. 45-64). Washington, DC: American Psychiatric Press.

Gerstein, D. R., & Harwood, H. J. (1990). *Treating drug problems* (Vol. 1). Washington, DC: National Academy Press.

Gold, M. S. (1998). The pharmacology of marijuana. In A. W. Graham, T. K. Schultz, & B. B. Wilford (Eds.), *Principles of addiction medicine* (2nd ed., pp. 147-152). Chevy Chase, MD: American Society of Addiction Medicine.

Grinspoon, L., & Bakalar, J. B. (1997). Marijuana. In J. H. Lowinson, P. Ruiz, R. B. Millman, & J. G. Langrod (Eds.), *Substance abuse: A comprehensive textbook* (pp. 199-206). Baltimore: Williams & Wilkins.

MacCoun, R. J. (1998). Toward a psychology of harm reduction. *American Psychologist, 53,* 1199-1208.

Marlatt, A. G. (1998). *Harm reduction: Pragmatic strategies for managing high risk behavior.* New York: Guilford.

McLellan, A. T., Woody, G. E., Metzger, D., McKay, J., Durrell, J., Alterman, A. I., & O'Brien, C. P. (1996). Evaluating the effectiveness of addiction treatments: Reasonable expectations, appropriate comparisons. *Milbank Quarterly, 74*(1), 51-85.

Miller, W. R. (1999). *Enhancing motivation for change in substance abuse treatment.* Rockville, MD: U.S. Department of Health and Human Services.

Miller, W. R., & Page, A. C. (1991). Warm turkey: Other routes to abstinence. *Journal of Substance Abuse Treatment, 8*, 227-232.

Miller, W. R., & Rollnick, S. (1991). *Motivational interviewing: Preparing people to change addictive behavior.* New York: Guilford.

Prochaska, J. O., DiClemente, C. C., & Norcross, J. C. (1992). In search of how people change: Applications to addictive behaviors. *American Psychologist, 47*, 1102-1114.

Rawson, R. A. (1999). *Treatment for stimulant use disorders.* Rockville, MD: U.S. Department of Health and Human Services.

Schuckit, M. A., & Smith, T. L. (1996). An 8-year follow-up of 450 sons of alcoholic and control subjects. *Archives of General Psychiatry, 53*, 202-210.

Simpson, D. D., & Curry, S. J. (Eds.). (1997). *Drug Abuse Treatment Outcome Study (DATOS)* (Vol. 11). Washington, DC: Educational Publishing Foundation.

Sorensen, J. L., Wermuth, L. A., Gibson, D. R., Choi, K.-H., Guydish, J. R., & Batki, S. L. (1991). *Preventing AIDS in drug users and their sexual partners.* New York: Guilford.

Sullivan, J. M., & Evans, K. (1994). Integrated treatment for the survivor of childhood trauma who is chemically dependent. *Journal of Psychoactive Drugs, 26*, 369-378.

Zweben, J. E. (1995). Integrating psychotherapy and 12-step approaches. In A. Washton (Ed.), *Psychotherapy and substance abuse: A practitioner's handbook* (pp. 124-140). New York: Guilford.

14

Group Therapy

A Clinician's Guide to Doing What Works

Arnold M. Washton

This chapter describes some of the nuts and bolts of using group therapy as a tool for treating chemical dependency. The techniques described here are part of an integrative approach I have developed, used, and continuously revamped during nearly 25 years of professional experience as an addiction treatment program director in various clinical settings and as an addiction psychologist in private practice. The approach is integrative in the sense of being an amalgam of many different treatment approaches (Washton, in preparation). It does not require or even recommend adherence to one method of doing treatment. It is neither cognitive, behavioral, psychodynamic, interpersonal, 12-step, nor client centered, but rather all of these to some extent (Washton, 1995). Experience has taught me to avoid dogmatic approaches claiming to be the single best method for treating addiction. The guiding principle used here is very simple: Do what works. Do it carefully, do it well, and be open-minded and flexible enough to change what you are doing if it is not producing the desired results. Above all, do no harm.

Maintain unfailing respect for the client, for his or her autonomy, sensitivities, defenses, and personal strengths. Exercise with great caution the awesome power of the therapeutic alliance. It is the one and only source of therapeutic leverage we have to positively influence our clients' behavior. The following are some essential ideas to keep in mind. Start where your patients are, not where you want them to be. Give patients permission to resist. The first and foremost goal of treatment is not abstinence but simply to encourage the patient to come back for the next visit. Establishing and maintaining a solid therapeutic working alliance with your patients takes precedence over everything else except their safety.

The bottom line is that if group members like you, respect you, trust your judgment, think that you have something worthwhile to offer them, and sense that you have a genuine commitment to working in their best interest instead of following some preconceived cookbook approach, then chances are they will let you help them. Otherwise, it will be a frustrating exercise in futility. Take the suggestions I offer here lightly, not as instructions or rigid guidelines. Modify and adapt them to fit your own therapeutic style and especially the patient populations you work with. My clinical experience is extensive, but like yours inevitably limited by what I have been privileged to see and what I am capable of seeing. Use what you can in these pages and leave the rest. Good luck.

:: WHY GROUP THERAPY?

The Nature of Addictive Disorders

A uniquely effective treatment for addicts, group therapy incorporates an unparalleled mixture of therapeutic forces especially well suited for addressing some of the most fundamental aspects of addictive disorders. Addiction is a complex disorder consisting of maladaptive attitudes, thoughts, and feelings, coupled with compulsive use of psychoactive substances, especially in response to emotional stress or discomfort. When faced with problems, the addict responds with malignant denial of inner distress and a misdirected focus on manipulating external circumstances. Elder (1990) described the addicted person as someone who has great "outsight" but very poor insight. Addicts use drugs as "self-medication" in an attempt to cope with distressing feelings and avoid having to deal with them (Khantzian, Halliday, & McAuliffe, 1990). It is a form of acting-out behavior in which the person impulsively seeks immediate relief from inner distress while ignoring the real-life problems that are causing the distress in the first place. An addicted person lacks the ability to recognize internal feelings and use them as signals to mobilize adaptive problem-solving behavior. Without benefit of this emotional "radar," the addicted person flies blindly through life unavoidably colliding with one obstacle after another.

The problem most vehemently denied and obliterated from the addict's consciousness is the addiction problem itself. It is the addict's massive wall of denial that serves as the primary defense against coming to grips with the problem, with the shame and humiliation of being so out of control of oneself, and with the accumulating consequences of this destructive behavior. In addition to this massive denial are the powerful defenses of projection, displacement, and rationalization that the addicted person uses unconsciously to push everything away from him- or herself and to disown problems by attributing them to someone or something else.

Clinical Benefits of Group Therapy

A powerful combination of peer support, encouragement, feedback, and confrontation all delivered under guidance of a trained clinician, group therapy provides an almost ideal forum for addressing core features of the addictive disorder: the person's inability to see and accept the reality that is plain to others, the lack of internal "radar" needed to motivate and guide adaptive responses to the environment, the tendency to disown personal responsibility and focus instead on external solutions, and the overwhelming feelings of failure, guilt, and toxic shame that perpetuate the addictive cycle. Much of the unique therapeutic power of an addiction recovery group derives from the simple fact that the group consists entirely of members who have a common problem. All members know how addicted people think, feel, and behave. They know the defenses, manipulations, schemes, diversions, and obfuscations that are used to protect and rationalize chronic substance use and engage in other maladaptive behaviors. They know the pain and humiliation of suffering with active addiction and how fragile newcomers feel when they first enter the group. This almost automatically creates a common bond between them, stemming from a sense of belonging and an expectation of being intuitively understood. This is critically important in counteracting the intense feelings of isolation, shame, and guilt experienced by people struggling with addiction. Furthermore, the social stigma of addiction and the humiliation of having lost control over one's behavior makes rapid acceptance into a peer group all the more important. The group instills hope by giving the newcomer a chance to make contact with others who are getting better and by instantly supplying him or her with a support network committed to the pursuit of healthy goals.

Groups provide invaluable opportunities for experiential learning and role modeling through watching and interacting with other group members as they grapple with a wide variety of problems and situations. Group members have a unique opportunity to correct distorted self-concepts and resulting maladaptive behaviors through honest, consistent feedback from others. Groups reinforce honest self-disclosure, active involvement in group discussion, compliance with group norms (e.g., abstinence, punctuality, active participation, altruism), cooperation among group members, and, perhaps most important, an emphasis on confronting rather than avoiding problems. In a small therapy group, it is difficult for reluctant members to "hide out," as they might sometimes do in large self-help meetings. Premature dropout is a major problem in addiction treatment, and the strong peer bonding that takes place in a group can be very effective in fostering retention, especially when the going gets rough.

GROUP THERAPY VERSUS SELF-HELP SUPPORT GROUPS ⊞

Group therapy and self-help support groups such as Alcoholics Anonymous (AA) are not good substitutes for one another. Each provides a unique form of help, and ideally they should work synergistically rather than competitively or redundantly (Spitz & Rosecan, 1987; Vannicelli, 1992). Self-help groups are invaluable, but the in-depth attention given to psychological and personal issues that takes place in a small therapy group led by a trained professional cannot and should not be expected to occur in a leaderless self-help meeting. This is not a criticism of self-help, which contains its own unique blend of therapeutic forces, but an important distinction between these two very different forms of help (Spitz & Rosecan, 1987).

GROUPS FOR DIFFERENT STAGES OF RECOVERY ⊞

I prefer to have separate groups for patients in the early versus later stages of recovery (Washton, in press; Washton & Stone-Washton, 1990). New patients typically start off in an early abstinence group and then graduate to a relapse prevention (advanced recovery) group. Although a patient's participation in each group is time limited, the group itself goes on indefinitely because graduations, dropouts, and new admissions are ongoing.

Participation in each stage of group treatment may range from several weeks to several months, depending on how the program is structured. The frequency of group sessions is usually greater in the beginning stage of treatment and then tapers off or steps down to less frequent meetings in subsequent stages. In an intensive outpatient program, for example, patients may attend an early recovery group three to five times per week for the first several weeks (typically some of these groups are topic-oriented education groups and others are open-agenda counseling groups) and then move on to a relapse prevention group that meets only once or twice per week.

Another type of group used to meet the often-overlooked needs of a special subpopulation of substance-using clients is the self-evaluation group (SEG). The rationale and protocol for the SEG are described at length elsewhere (Washton, in press) and due to space limitations are mentioned only in passing here. The SEG is designed specifically for patients in the pretreatment or prerecovery stage who are not ready to enter an early recovery group. It is a motivation enhancement group designed to help participants examine the nature of their involvement with psychoactive substances and to increase their readiness for change. In the stages-of-change model described by Prochaska and DiClemente (1986), these individuals are in the contemplation or decision stage, still wavering about whether they truly have a problem and still trying to decide what, if anything, they may want to do about it. Putting such clients into an early recovery group, where all other members at least acknowledge that they have a problem and are actively working toward a goal of total abstinence, is a prescription for disaster. Typically, the ambivalent newcomer's "denial" is attacked, and in the process other group members become frustrated and demoralized. The SEG is a brief intervention (2-4 weeks) that incorporates many of the motivational interviewing techniques described by Miller and Rollnick (1991).

The Early Recovery Group

The major goals of the early recovery group are to help members establish initial abstinence; stabilize their overall functioning; acknowledge and accept their addiction problem; work through their initial ambivalence and reluctance about giving up alcohol/drug use; establish a recovery support network; become bonded to other members and integrated into the group; overcome early slips and other setbacks without dropping out; deal effectively with consequences of their addiction; learn and use relapse prevention strategies, including identification and management of relapse warning signs as well as behavioral coping and affect-management skills, as alternatives to "self-medication" with mood-altering substances; and begin to identify and change some of the dysfunctional self-defeating cognitions, emotions, and behaviors that perpetuate the addictive cycle (Washton, in press). This is an ideal wish list, and not all members will achieve all of these goals during their tenure in the group. In the absence of strict economic constraints, length of stay in the group varies according to how quickly patients progress toward achieving their goals, but generally participation lasts anywhere from several months to as much as a year, if circumstances (including insurance benefits) permit.

Because outpatient group therapy can be effective only if patients actually show up, integrating newcomers into the group as quickly as possible is absolutely critical.

Asking one or more established group members to maintain daily contact with the newcomer outside the group, including escorting him or her to local self-help meetings, facilitates this process. When patients miss a group session, it is critical that group members and the group leader call to express concern and communicate that his or her presence definitely was missed. One such phone call may go a long way toward preventing precipitous dropout in a relapsed patient who is ashamed to face the group and who assumes, incorrectly, that "no one really cares."

Newcomers just starting out in the group derive immediate benefit from contact with more experienced members, who are often eager to take a neophyte "under their wing." Not only is the newcomer's learning and induction into the group accelerated, but the more experienced members have a chance to experience a greater sense of purpose and a yardstick for becoming more aware of their own progress. Newcomers provide members who are further along with vivid reminders of themselves at an earlier stage of recovery. Listening to newcomers helps to keep their memory "green," an important reminder of just how unmanageable their lives had become during their own active addiction. This can counteract problems of overconfidence, selective forgetting, and secretly harbored fantasies about being able to return someday to controlled use. Additionally, the temporary shake-up of group dynamics caused by arrival of new members often has a decidedly positive impact on the overall character of the group. New members add new points of view, new problems, new ideas, and new sets of life experiences, all of which add "grist to the mill" of the ongoing group process.

In early recovery groups, much time is spent on basic issues of how to maintain abstinence in the face of cravings, urges, and potential triggers of alcohol/drug use. Avoiding people, places, and situations formerly associated with substance use, cutting off contact with dealers and users, and staying away from parties, bars, and other "hangouts" where the temptation to use alcohol and drugs is ever-present are major issues that must be addressed with newcomers and other group members having problems staying clean and sober. Often, obstacles in early recovery stem from difficulty accepting that controlled use is no longer possible and that one's personal determination and willpower are not good defenses against relapse. Established group members are likely to respond by assaulting the newcomer's defenses with aggressive statements about the person's denial and other self-defeating attitudes. You must intervene so as not to allow such discussions to get out of hand. Resistance is to be expected, and prematurely or excessively confronting it may do more harm than good by raising rather than lowering the patient's defenses and by actually driving him or her out of treatment. Furthermore, you should not allow these types of discussions to dominate the group's attention in a way that prevents other important issues from being addressed. When the group repeatedly focuses on one or two chronically problematic members, others may at first welcome having the focus taken off themselves, but eventually they will become resentful and lose interest in the group as their needs remain consistently unmet.

Keep in mind that working through initial resistance to change is a process, not an instantaneous event. It requires time, patience, sustained commitment, and a willingness to tolerate temporary setbacks. The tone of an early abstinence group must unfailingly convey caring, concern, nonjudgmental acceptance, and flexibility within a clearly defined structure. When working with resistant patients in the early phases, you must be careful not to act out your own control fantasies, frustrations, and other negative countertransference reactions that are destructive to the therapeutic work of the group.

Getting locked into combative power struggles with poorly motivated group members will surely drive these patients out of treatment and confirm the dangerous self-fulfilling prophecy that every addict must "hit bottom" and suffer severe consequences before getting serious about recovery. This is a failure to "start where the patient is." When you take a hard-line stance on relapse, patients become very reluctant to share their relapse fantasies with the group and are all the more likely to act out rather than talk out their secret impulses to use. A patient's inability or unwillingness to accept the reality of having an addiction problem may not necessarily be intractable denial but rather a sign that he or she is in a very early stage of change and will require a good deal of respectful coaxing to move forward in the therapeutic process (Miller & Rollnick, 1991).

The Relapse Prevention Group

The relapse prevention or advanced recovery group presumes that members have achieved the initial goals outlined above and are now ready to work on issues such as self-esteem, interpersonal relationships, sexuality, mood/affect management, self-defeating behaviors, and virtually any aspect of an individual's personality or behavior that diminishes the quality of his or her life and leaves him or her prone to self-medication with alcohol/drugs. Relapses that occur after solid abstinence has been firmly established are usually caused not so much by environmental triggers (which is more typical during early abstinence) as by failure of the patient to adequately manage problems that arise in the course of daily living, especially in the face of stress and negative emotions. Recovering addicts often find it difficult to identify and deal with even mildly unpleasant feelings that arise after the chemical blanket of chronic drug use has been removed. Frequently, it is this impaired ability to cope with unpleasant feelings in combination with the resurfacing of important unresolved problems (sexual, relationship, self-esteem, psychological, financial, etc.) that precipitates relapse.

In addition, the delayed consequences of substance use often catch up with people before they have acquired the adaptive coping skills to deal with these consequences. Among the many topics that must be addressed are how to identify negative feelings, how to manage anger, how to avoid impulsive decision making, how to relax and have fun without drugs, how to give and receive constructive criticism, how to be assertive without being aggressive, and how to deal with the give-and-take of interpersonal relationships (Marlatt & Gordon, 1985; Washton, 1989).

This stage of group therapy also addresses psychological issues that go beyond the basic cognitive and behavioral factors that promote relapse. It explores in detail the inner emotional life of each group member and his or her relationship patterns that reliably give rise to the compulsive desire to "self-medicate" with mood-altering chemicals (Khantzian et al., 1990). The ultimate goal here is not merely the acquisition of self-knowledge and insight but fundamental change in the individual's characteristically maladaptive patterns of thinking, feeling, behaving, and interacting. At an appropriate point, the group should help members address long-standing, deep-seated problems such as those stemming, for example, from parental alcoholism, physical/sexual abuse, or other developmental and life traumas. Whenever such sensitive, highly charged issues are being discussed, and even when discussion appears to be well tolerated by the patient, you must be especially mindful of the person's increased potential for relapse and encourage him or her to be especially alert to the possibility of relapse as an attempt to avoid painful material. A good sense of timing on the part of the group leader is critical throughout this stage of treatment—knowing when to press harder on certain issues versus backing off, knowing when to be confrontational versus being supportive, and so on.

Special Groups for Special Populations and Problems

Special groups can be very effective in dealing with special problems and/or patient populations. Sometimes a specialized group offers the only forum in which certain types of issues can be adequately addressed. Perhaps the largest of these subgroups consists of dual-diagnosis patients who suffer from coexisting substance abuse and serious psychiatric disorders. Another large subpopulation consists of female patients who are unwilling to discuss, or highly resistant toward discussing, sensitive personal issues (e.g., sexuality, relationships, incest, domestic violence) in a coed group but are often much more open to doing so in an all-female group led by a female therapist. Similar considerations may arise with gay and lesbian patients. Another subpopulation often in need of a specialized group is those with coexisting chemical and sexual addictions (Washton, 1989).

LEADERSHIP ROLES AND RESPONSIBILITIES ⊞

Your role as group leader includes a variety of essential functions: (a) to establish and enforce group rules in a caring, consistent, nonpunitive manner to protect the group's integrity and progress; (b) to screen, prepare, and orient potential group members to ensure suitability and proper placement in the group; (c) to keep group discussions focused on important issues and to do so in a way that maximizes the therapeutic benefit of these discussions to all members; (d) to emphasize, promote, and maintain group cohesiveness and reduce feelings of personal alienation wherever possible; (e) to create and maintain a caring, nonjudgmental, therapeutic climate in the group that both counteracts self-defeating attitudes and promotes self-awareness, expression of feelings, honest self-disclosure, adaptive alternatives to drug use, and patterns of drug-free living; (f) to handle problem members who are disruptive to the group in a timely and consistent manner to protect the membership and integrity of the group; and (g), where appropriate, to educate patients about selected aspects of drug use, addiction, and recovery.

It is not your role to direct the group per se but rather to facilitate a process whereby members learn how to interact with one another in an increasingly open, honest, compassionate way that promotes positive changes in attitude and behavior (Edelwich & Brodsky, 1992). Ideally, group members should come to feel that just about anything can be openly discussed in the group without fear of reprisal or recrimination.

Topics for group discussion should be largely patient driven so that members' problems, crises, and recovery issues can be dealt with as they arise in the course of daily life. Your main responsibilities are to help keep the group focused on relevant issues, encourage participation of all members, and ensure that members provide helpful therapeutic feedback to one another and refrain from lecturing, advice giving, hostile confrontation, and other negative behaviors that do more harm than good. In an early recovery group, you can suggest from time to time that the group address certain topics or issues based on themes that may have emerged over the course of one or more sessions.

Where appropriate, you might take a portion of the session to review group rules or guidelines such as those regarding how group members can give good feedback to one another (see below), especially when there is an influx of new members. You must be careful, however, not to fall into a didactic teaching role lest you promote passivity among members and stall the functioning of the group. You must be careful not to train the group to expect that you will supply the agenda and content for group sessions or that the primary responsibility for what goes on in any session is up to you. Although early recovery groups will require you to be substantially more active than later-stage groups, you should try to stay out of the group discussion and refrain from intervening as long it is moving along productively.

When the group is working properly, the leader functions as a group manager, staying in the background while the group takes full responsibility for the therapeutic work. When the group is not working properly and therefore not growing, the leader is doing a lot of talking and/or spending a lot of time encouraging group members to participate in the discussion. This requires deliberate and persistent intervention on your part to return maximum responsibility to the group, practicing the psychotherapeutic principle of analyzing resistance before dealing with content (Elder, 1990). It is much more important for you to help group members recognize their passivity than it is to try to drag them into doing the therapeutic work. As compared to early recovery groups, you should help later-stage groups focus increasingly on group process and become reliably self-correcting when the discussion strays off track or becomes unproductive.

⊞ CONSIDERATIONS IN SETTING UP A GROUP

Size and Duration of Group Sessions

Optimal group size is 8 to 10 members, and optimal duration is 90 to 120 minutes. When groups meet longer than 2 hours and/or exceed 10 members, it becomes increasingly very difficult to maintain a focused discussion and keep everyone sufficiently involved. In a large group, the more vocal members will inevitably dominate the discussion while the more passive members quietly sit back as spectators, content that the action is not focusing on them or feeling too shy to "jump in."

Member Selection

Most addicted patients can benefit from group therapy, and many prefer it to other forms of treatment. Some patients, however, are simply not good candidates for group therapy, such as those whose mental status is fragile and unstable, those with debilitating social phobias, and those who are paranoid and/or highly volatile.

Groups function best when there is sufficient diversity among members in terms of age, gender, race, education level, socioeconomic status, drug of choice, stage of recovery, and the nature/severity of addiction and other mental health problems. Membership diversity provides a broader array of personal perspectives and life experiences. It expands possibilities for mutual identification between members and enhances recognition that addiction is truly an "equal opportunity" disease that knows no demographic boundaries. Although diversity can enhance the richness of the group experience, keep certain important limitations in mind to promote rapid identification/bonding between group members and prevent early dropout by newcomers who are truly different from all other members in some important or obvious way and therefore likely to feel out of place from the moment they enter the group. First, wherever possible, avoid placing newcomers in groups where they will be "outliers" (Vannicelli, 1992), differing from all other members in terms of demographics and/or other important dimensions. For example, try to avoid placing one woman in a group of all men, one alcoholic in a group of all intravenous drug users, one gay person in a group of all heterosexuals, one person with debilitating psychiatric illness in a group of all high-functioning professionals, and so on. In cases where practical considerations prevent you from adhering to this guideline, you can pave the way for admitting an "outlier" by preparing both the newcomer and the group for his or her arrival in a way that maximizes the chances that this person will be welcomed and accepted by the group. Take this opportunity to help all concerned focus on similarities rather than differences between one another and see the therapeutic benefits of doing so.

In addition to differing demographics, there should be diversity in the group with regard to members' substances of choice. Group membership should not be based on the patients' primary drug of choice because it is the addictive disorder, not the drug, that is the focus of treatment. Although patients with different types of chemical dependencies can all be treated effectively in the same group, it is essential not to overlook the unique problems commonly associated with each drug class and to make a concerted effort to ensure that they are adequately identified and addressed. For example, drug-related hypersexuality often requires specific clinical attention in male cocaine addicts (Washton, 1989); protracted withdrawal symptoms of depression, apathy, sexual dysfunction, and social withdrawal are commonly seen in recently detoxified opioid addicts; and temporary cognitive impairment may inhibit information processing and therapeutic progress in newly sober alcoholics (Zweben, 1989).

GROUP MANAGEMENT CONSIDERATIONS ▦

Preparing Newcomers for Group Entry

Meet individually with every prospective newcomer for at least one or two sessions before granting entry into the group. The purpose is to describe how the group works and to give newcomers an opportunity to address any questions and concerns they may have about group therapy. Use this opportunity to educate all newcomers about the purpose, goals, expectations, rules, composition, content, and format of the group as well as to give a general orientation on how the group works. It is especially important to teach newcomers how to give good feedback in the group and how to differentiate between helpful versus unhelpful group behaviors. During the pregroup sessions, I provide prospective group members with the handouts "Helpful and Unhelpful Group Behaviors," "Group Ground Rules," and "Giving Good Feedback" (Boxes 14.1 through 14.3), each of which serves as the basis for a more detailed preparatory discussion. You should keep in mind that not all problems that arise in a group are due to denial or other forms of resistance. Most patients simply do not know yet how to make good use of group therapy, and one of your primary tasks as group leader is to teach them these skills through proper orientation, guidance, and role modeling (Vannicelli, 1992).

All newcomers must agree in writing to adhere to the group ground rules as a prerequisite to group membership. I also require all prospective new members to achieve at

---

BOX 14.1   Helpful and Unhelpful Group Behaviors

Helpful Group Behaviors

>   Participate as fully as possible in every session.
>   Give feedback that "holds up a mirror" to the presenter.
>   Use "I" rather than "you" statements when giving feedback.
>   Focus on feelings, not facts.
>   Be a good listener; give the presenter a chance to finish talking.
>   Give feedback in a caring, empathetic manner.
>   Help the discussion stay on track.

Unhelpful Group Behaviors

>   Don't sit silently as an observer.
>   Don't criticize, judge, or "put down" others.
>   Don't give advice, lectures, or long-winded monologues.
>   Don't play therapist or try to explain/analyze anyone else's behavior.
>   Don't give terse or superficial answers.
>   Don't give hostile or aggressive feedback.
>   Don't be overly polite, don't be passive, and don't avoid necessary confrontation.

---

least 1 full week and in some cases 2 weeks of total abstinence (verified by urine testing) immediately before attending a first group meeting. This not only gives prospective members time to recover from the acute aftereffects of any recent alcohol/drug use but also concretizes their motivation to establish initial abstinence and screens out those who are unwilling and/or unable to do so. It also helps to protect the integrity and morale of the group, which can be negatively affected by admission of newcomers who do not agree with the fundamental group goal of abstinence.

When a newcomer arrives to the group for the first time, I ask all existing members to give a brief synopsis of how and why they came into the group, including a brief overview of their addiction/treatment history, what issues they are currently working on in the group, and something about their experiences in the group thus far (both positive and negative). I then ask the newcomer to provide similar types of information, including what he or she expects to get out of being a member of the group. Group members are encouraged to ask questions of the newcomer, offer feedback, and, where possible, identify with selected aspects of the newcomer's past or present experience, all in the service of welcoming the newcomer into the group and creating a sense of kinship (bonding) with existing members.

Requiring a Commitment to Total Abstinence

It is essential for all members of an early recovery or relapse prevention group to be committed to the goal of maintaining abstinence from *all* psychoactive substances, regardless of their drug(s) of choice and even if their use of certain substances was never a problem for them in the past. Failure to do so will inevitably destroy the integrity and therapeutic power of the group or prevent it from ever developing in the first place. Mixing patients with conflicting goals regarding the fundamentally important and overriding issue of abstinence simply does not work in abstinence-oriented group ther-

---

BOX 14.2   Group Ground Rules

---

1. You are expected to come to group sessions completely "straight," not under the influence of or hungover/crashing from any mood-altering chemicals whatsoever.

2. You are expected to abstain from the use of alcohol and all other mood-altering chemicals during your participation in the group, including substances that you may have considered not to be a problem for you in the past. In the event that you do use any substances while a member of the group, you must notify the group leader of this fact before attending your next group session, and you must bring up this issue for discussion at the beginning of that next session. "Slips" will be handled therapeutically (nonpunitively), but you will not be able to continue in the group if you are consistently unable to maintain abstinence. If you are removed from the group due to repeated substance use, you will be given the option, where appropriate, of receiving individual therapy to help you establish a period of uninterrupted abstinence as a prerequisite to possibly returning to the group.

3. You agree to attend all scheduled group sessions and to arrive on time without fail. This may require you to rearrange other obligations and perhaps even postpone vacations and out-of-town trips while participating in the group.

4. You agree to preserve the anonymity and confidentiality of all group members. You must not divulge the identity of any group member or the content of any group discussions to persons outside the group. What goes on in the group stays in the group, without exception.

5. You agree to remain in the group until you have completed the agreed-upon course of treatment. If you have an impulse or desire to leave the group prematurely, you will raise this issue for discussion in no fewer than three group sessions before making any final decision.

6. You agree that throughout your participation in the program you will not become involved romantically, sexually, or financially with other group members. Group members are strictly prohibited from loaning or gifting money to one another, from entering into any employer-employer relationships, and from entering into any formal or informal business partnerships and/or investment transactions with one another.

7. You acknowledge that you will be immediately terminated from treatment if you offer alcohol/ drugs to any group member or use together with another group member.

8. You agree to have your telephone number(s) added to the contact list distributed to all group members.

9. You agree to urine and/or Breathalyzer testing at every group session and whenever the group leader may request it.

10. You agree to raise for discussion in the group any issue that threatens your own or another member's recovery. You will not keep secrets regarding another member's substance use or other destructive behavior.

---

apy. Patients who are not ready to work toward a goal of abstinence may be better suited for a motivation enhancement or goal clarification group, such as the SEG mentioned earlier. It is impossible for an abstinence-oriented group to simultaneously endorse total abstinence in some members and accept "controlled" or occasional "nonproblematic" use in others. This does not mean that every group member must demonstrate an unambiguous ironclad commitment to lifelong abstinence, but all group members must agree to work sincerely toward maintaining abstinence from all mood-altering substances throughout their tenure in the group.

Recovery is not a straight path, and slipping temporarily back to substance use should be dealt with therapeutically by the group wherever possible. But the presence of a member who is actually trying to use mood-altering substances in a controlled fashion (the secret wish of every member) is likely to arouse anger and anxiety in other group members. This often leads to unproductive lecturing aimed at convincing the wayward group member to see the error of his or her ways and "get with the program." It is also likely to provoke cravings, urges, and fantasies about using again and to increase the likelihood of relapse.

| BOX 14.3 | Giving Good Feedback |

What Good Feedback Is

1. Feedback is a group member's honest reaction to a presenter based not only on the content but also on the way in which something is said.
2. Feedback is defined as giving a presenter potentially helpful information about his/her behavior as you see and experience it. It is a process by which you attempt to "hold up a mirror" to let the presenter know how he/she is coming across and what thoughts and feelings his/her presentation stimulates in you.
3. Feedback is most likely to be heard and have a positive impact when spoken with empathy, concern, and caring in a respectful tone of voice.
4. Feedback is descriptive of what is happening and what you have actually observed (not your interpretations), giving current or very recent examples of the behavior in question as it has occurred in the group.
5. Feedback includes a statement of your concern about any self-defeating aspects of the person's behavior and, if possible, an example of similar self-defeating behavior in your own history.
6. Feedback should be delivered directly to the presenter (recipient) and not to the group or the group leader. Look directly at the recipient and maintain eye contact with him/her while delivering feedback.
7. Feedback should be delivered using "I" statements wherever possible. The purpose of "I statements" is to ensure that members delivering the feedback take personal responsibility for what they say and that it reflects their own personal response to what the presenter says rather than an absolute truth. Examples may include: "I have a problem with what you just said, Andy. I think that maybe you are being defensive, and I want to know if that's actually how you are feeling right now. Can you tell me if I'm reading you correctly?"
8. Feedback should seek to identify rather than compare. It is much more helpful for group members to relate to the experience of the presenter than to compare or contrast in ways that set themselves apart from the presenter.
9. Feedback should be requested or welcomed and not imposed on the presenter. If the presenter is being defensive and/or flatly rejecting the feedback, the group should not take a stance that says, "We know you don't want our feedback, but we're going to give it to you anyway." It is much better to say something like "You seem to be backing away—do you want feedback from the group? Is there something going on that's making you uncomfortable with the feedback that's being offered to you?"

What Good Feedback Is Not

1. Feedback is not an opportunity to assassinate a member's character, humiliate him/her into submission, or set him/her straight.
2. Feedback does not include guesses, explanations, interpretations, advice, moralisms, judgments, and criticisms of any kind about the person's behavior.
3. Feedback is not advice giving or proposing solutions to specific problems but rather helping the presenter acquire an understanding of him/herself that could serve as a tool for solving similar types of problems in the future. This is illustrated by the saying: "Give a man a fish and he eats for a day. Teach him how to fish and he eats for a lifetime."
4. Feedback is not an attempt to rescue the presenter from feeling upset or uncomfortable as long as it is being properly delivered.

Drug and Alcohol Testing of Group Members

I require all group members to be tested on site for alcohol/drugs just before the start of every group session. The purpose of the drug testing is not to catch the patient in a lie but to provide a safety net, to give an objective marker of progress, and to instill greater confidence in the treatment (Washton, 1989, in preparation). Addicted patients usually appreciate mandatory testing because it helps them counteract their impulses to use and to hide their use. Not being able to hoodwink the therapist or the group can also keep a patient from devaluing and sabotaging the treatment.

Immediate drug test results are obtained using disposable on-site urine-testing devices that yield accurate readings within only a few minutes after the sample is collected. There are many such devices currently on the market, ranging in price from $5 to $25 per test kit depending on how many different drugs the device tests for. Most kits contain a temperature strip inside the collection vial, obviating the need to directly observe voiding of the sample. Also, most kits are automatic and self-contained so that there is no need for the therapist requesting the sample to come in contact with urine. A recent breakthrough is the availability of saliva drug tests, which have the distinct advantages of allowing direct observation of sample collection and of being experienced by many patients as less intrusive than urine tests. Alcohol is not reliably detected in urine, but saliva test kits and disposable breath-testing devices are readily available for this purpose. Perhaps the easiest way to locate vendors of on-site alcohol and drug-testing devices is by doing an Internet search for "drug tests" or "alcohol tests."

Managing Peer Confrontation and Feedback

Peer confrontation and feedback by fellow group members can be extremely effective in helping patients achieve a more realistic assessment of their maladaptive attitudes and behaviors. But heavy-handed, excessive, and poorly timed feedback can be countertherapeutic and even damaging. Many patients enter groups with the mistaken idea that humiliation and aggressive confrontation are the best ways to force resistant members to face reality. Sometimes harsh confrontations are rationalized as attempts to be "truly honest" with members who are having trouble maintaining abstinence or violating group expectations and norms. Likely targets for attack are members who relapse repeatedly; those who remain defiant, superficial, or insincere; and those who minimize their problems and fail to bond with other members. As group leader you must never allow unpopular, frustrating, resistant, or severely troubled group members to be scapegoated and bludgeoned by their peers, even when the content of what is being said is entirely accurate. Harsh or excessive confrontation must not be used to push unwanted members out of the group and to discourage them from coming back.

Responding to "Slips"

When a group member reports that he or she has used drugs since the last session, the group must give priority to addressing this issue and as the group leader you must maintain a leadership style that models clear, consistent, and nonpunitive behavior. Group members usually have strong feelings in response to another member's use of drugs that must be expressed and put into proper perspective. You task is to help the group use the slip or relapse of one of its members as a therapeutic opportunity to learn something useful.

Suggested guidelines for dealing with group members who have slipped (Washton, 1990) are as follows:

1. Ask the presenter to give the group a detailed account of the sequence of feelings, events, and circumstances that led up to the slip.

2. Invite others to ask the presenter about early warning signs, self-sabotage, and other factors that may have preceded the actual drug use.

3. Ask the presenter to summarize the relapse chain that appears to have led up to the drug use.

4. Ask others to share any suggestions or feedback they can offer to the presenter about his or her slip and how to prevent it from happening again. Also ask them to share their feelings about the slip, reminding them to avoid any tendency they may have to scapegoat the drug-using member or to act out feelings of anger and frustration on him or her.

5. With the participation of the drug-using member, ask the group to develop a list of suggested strategies and behavioral changes to guard against the possibility of further drug use.

6. Ask presenters to share their thoughts and feelings about what impact the slip has had on them and to describe their willingness to take action to reduce the chances of using again.

Although most group members respond supportively to a fellow member's slip, there is an unspecified limit as to how often repeatedly slipping members can expect this type of supportive response. When a group member who is having trouble remaining abstinent shows little evidence of using previous suggestions about how to prevent further slips, others start to become intolerant and feel that the person may be jeopardizing the safety of the group. This can happen after two slips, three slips, four slips, or more, depending on the overall attitude and behavior of the drug-using member and the nature of his or her relationships with other members. Peer confrontation can become very intense, and you must guard against the group's tendency to scapegoat or ostracize the member who has slipped. Help the group deal with slips as avoidable mistakes rather than as willful noncompliance. Reframe slips as a clear signs that the person is still ambivalent about giving up alcohol/drugs and perhaps not yet convinced that he or she really does need to do so.

Managing Common Obstacles

Every patient comes to group with ambivalence about change, whether he or she is consciously aware of this ambivalence or not. There is a conflict between the forces that bring the person to the group wishing for change and the forces of resistance that oppose it. Our task is to recognize patient resistances as they emerge in group therapy and to help the group provide therapeutic feedback to members when they act out resistances, as will inevitably occur even in those who are perceived by others as highly motivated. Resistance takes many forms in group therapy, ranging from failure to adhere to certain group ground rules, to lack of participation in the group's therapeutic work, to disruptive behaviors that obstruct the group's therapeutic work.

Due to space limitations, only several of the most common obstacles are discussed here. More in-depth discussions can be found elsewhere (Edelwich & Brodsky, 1992; Elder, 1990; Spitz & Rosecan, 1987; Vannicelli, 1992; Washton, 1989). Whenever problems arise in group therapy sessions, the goal of your interventions should be to return primary responsibility for handling the problem to the group. If, instead, you always rescue the group and take responsibility for solving problems, you encourage passivity and teach group members that if they fail to intervene you will do it for them. However, it is important to remember that not all problems that arise in group therapy are due to resistance. Often, our patients have no prior experience with group therapy and/or have no idea how to use it appropriately without first going through the process of learning how to do so. Framing nearly everything that goes wrong in group as "resistance" or "denial" will alienate patients and create a negative climate that encourages dropout.

Lateness and Absenteeism

Members must attend group sessions without fail, but you must recognize that sometimes there are truly unavoidable or extenuating circumstances that legitimately prevent patients from showing up. An atmosphere of consistency and predictability is essential to successful group treatment. Because most patients have histories of irresponsible behavior during active addiction, when this type of behavior occurs in the group it must not be allowed to go by unnoticed or unaddressed. Chronic lateness and/or absenteeism adversely affect group morale/cohesion and are a form of treatment resistance that should be therapeutically addressed by the group.

Intoxicated Patients

Patients who arrive actively intoxicated or "crashing" from drugs (a very rare occurrence because being in a group session is probably the last place someone in either state would want to be) can cause havoc in the group. On all such occasions, ask the intoxicated patient to leave the session immediately and to call you the next day when he or she is sober enough to engage in a meaningful conversation.

Hostility and Chronic Complaining

Some group members are occasionally or even chronically antagonistic, argumentative, volatile, and sarcastic. They may take every opportunity to devalue the group, complain about how poorly it is run, point out even the most minor inconsistencies, and categorically reject advice or suggestions. Sometimes the content of what patients say in group is less important than the way they say it. The leader must attend continuously to patients' affect, body language, voice intonation, and overall communication style and help group members do the same. Do not allow sarcastic and aggressive statements to go by unnoticed and unaddressed. An appropriate intervention might be "I wonder if anyone else is experiencing Jim's remarks as hostile and devaluing? Can someone give Jim feedback about how he's coming across and how it is affecting the atmosphere in the group?" Carefully guide the ensuing discussion to make sure that group members do not use this as an opportunity to assault and demean the problem group member for "bad" behavior but rather help him to see the self-defeating nature of his actions as well as the negative impact of his behavior on the entire group.

Silence and Lack of Participation

Some group members sit quietly on the sidelines as observers, glad to have the focus of attention not be on them. Silent members may secretly harbor intense feelings of ambivalence, resentment, and annoyance about being in treatment and doubting whether being in the group is of any use to them. They may feel bored, indifferent, insecure, out of place, or perhaps even superior. Some members are just shy and need gentle coaxing and encouragement from the group to open up. One possible intervention for addressing a silent member is to say: "I've noticed that Dorothy has not participated at all during the past two or three group sessions. Maybe the group can try to find out what's holding her back and perhaps encourage or make it easier for her to join in the discussion."

Terse and Superficial Presentations

Similarly, terse or superficial presentations that reveal little or nothing about the presenter or what's on his or her mind is another form of resistance to participating in the group's therapeutic work. Without your intervention, the group may not see this behavior as resistance or "hiding out" because the presenter does in fact participate at some level, even though he or she fails to bring up issues that are self-revealing or meaningful. In these situations, it might help for you to say something like "I've noticed that when Jeremy talks about himself his statements are very brief and lacking in detail. I'm wondering if others see this as a problem that deserves attention from the group?"

Factual Reporting and Focusing on Externals

Some group members present lengthy factual reports recounting external events and circumstances, devoid of feelings or emotional content. This is often indicative of a member who is just going through the motions of being in treatment to satisfy a spouse, employer, or mandate. Consistent with the group's therapeutic mission to help members acquire skills to deal with internals rather than externals, you must address this type of problem whenever it arises and in the process role-model how the group should best respond on these occasions. You might intervene by saying

> Annie, you've just given the group a very detailed account of what happened to you last week, but we've not yet heard very much regarding how you felt about it or what all this means to you. [Turning to the group] Are you all getting the type of information from Annie that you need in order to give her any helpful feedback? I notice that some of you look bored and uninterested. How are you feeling right now?

Proselytizing and Hiding Behind AA

This is a one of the thorniest and most difficult problems to address in group therapy with addicts (Vannicelli, 1992). In every group, there are likely to be at least some members very solidly linked into AA or other 12-step programs who rigidly insist that AA is the one and only pathway to successful recovery. They are intolerant of group members who do not embrace the 12-step program and are inclined to see them as negative influences in the group. They may see it as their mission to proselytize the benefits of AA and predict failure or even death for those who do not follow the AA program. When difficult problems are being discussed in the group, these clients will often cite AA slogans and passages from the AA "Big Book" instead of engaging more meaningfully in the discussion. They may also complain that there is not enough "recovery talk" in the group and that the format of group sessions does not sufficiently mimic that of an AA meeting. Clients' rigid attachment to AA and refusal to consider that anything short of strict adherence to the AA program will work is often indicative of extreme anxiety about the precariousness of their own recovery and how important it is for them to believe that the only way to avoid relapse is to do exactly what they are doing. It is simply too threatening to allow themselves to think that there are other methods that may be useful to others. These clients will often polarize the group into opposing factions: those who embrace AA and those who do not. This polarization, if left unaddressed, will destroy group cohesion, create a negative climate, divert valuable attention from other important issues, and stall the group's therapeutic work. It is important for you to say outright that although you see AA as extremely useful and hope that everyone in need will be able to benefit from it, you also realize that it is not the one and only pathway to recovery for everyone and that each person must be allowed to find what works for him or her. Nonetheless, having clarified your own stance on the matter, you must then prevent yourself and the group as a whole from getting into a debate about the pros and cons of AA because this will only escalate the polarization of the group and resolve nothing. As with all forms of resistance, the best course of therapeutic action is to focus on the process rather than the content of what is going on in the group. In this case, a potentially helpful intervention may include something like this:

> Well, group, we could probably debate this issue for many sessions and still reach no agreement among everyone in the room. I think it would be more useful to talk about how group members feel that there is a serious split among you on this issue and what it is doing to the atmosphere in this room. How is it affecting your own personal feelings about the group and other members? Is this really helpful? Why are your feelings on this issue so strong?

Playing Co-Therapist

Some patients assume the role of therapist's helper in the group, a role that serves (unconsciously) as a diversion or smokescreen for dealing with their own issues. They often model certain of the group leader's behaviors, such as keeping the group discussion on track, confronting other members on inappropriate behaviors, and reinforcing group norms. Because their input is often very helpful to the group's functioning, it is easy for other members and the group leader as well to overlook the fact that the self-appointed "co-therapist" spends so much time being a helper that he or she fails to address his or her own issues. An appropriate intervention might include a statement like this:

> Jerry, you've been extremely helpful to several people in this room, and it's very apparent that everyone here values your input, but I'm wondering if the group can take some time to get to know you a little better and try to help you identify what you want to work on in this group.

FINAL COMMENT ⊞

This chapter has described some of the nuts and bolts of how to use group therapy as a clinical tool for treating addiction. A cost-effective and clinically effective tool, group therapy continues to be the treatment of choice for many but not all addicted patients. When skillfully orchestrated by a well-trained, self-observing, nondogmatic clinician, group therapy has the power to produce strikingly positive and rapid results. The power of groups—or of any type of therapy, for that matter—depends importantly on the therapist's ability to convey nonjudgmental acceptance, positive regard, and respectful feedback within an atmosphere of safety, support, and compassionate understanding. The group therapy approach described here is not represented as superior to other approaches. Quite simply, it is an approach that has worked reasonably well with my patients. They are the final judge and jury of my intended therapeutic actions.

▦ REFERENCES

Edelwich, J., & Brodsky, A. (1992). *Group counseling for the resistant client: A practical guide to group process.* New York: Lexington.

Elder, I. R. (1990). *Conducting group therapy with addicts.* Brandenton, FL: Human Services Institute. (Also published by Blue Ridge Summit, PA: Tab Books)

Khantzian, E. J., Halliday, K. S., & McAuliffe, W. E. (1990). *Addiction and the vulnerable self: Modified dynamic group therapy for substance abusers.* New York: Guilford.

Marlatt, G. A., & Gordon, J. (1985). *Relapse prevention.* New York: Guilford.

Miller, W. R., & Rollnick, S. (Eds.). (1991). *Motivational interviewing: Preparing people to change addictive behaviors.* New York: Guilford.

Prochaska, J. O., & DiClemente, C. C. (1986). Toward a comprehensive model of change. In W. R. Miller & N. Heather (Eds.), *Treating addictive behaviors* (pp. 3-27). New York: Plenum.

Spitz, H. I., & Rosecan, J. S. (1987). *Cocaine abuse: New directions in treatment and research.* New York: Brunner/Mazel.

Vannicelli, M. (1992). *Removing the roadblocks: Group psychotherapy with substance abusers and family members.* New York: Guilford.

Washton, A. M. (1989). *Cocaine addiction: Treatment, recovery, and relapse prevention.* New York: Norton.

Washton, A. M. (1990). *Cocaine recovery workbooks.* Center City, MN: Hazelden.

Washton, A. M. (Ed.). (1995). *Psychotherapy and substance abuse: A practitioner's handbook.* New York: Guilford.

Washton, A. M. (In press). Outpatient group therapy at different stages of substance abuse treatment. In D. W. Brook & H. I. Spitz (Eds.), *The group psychotherapy of substance abuse.* Washington, DC: American Psychiatric Press.

Washton, A. M. (In preparation). *Substance abuse therapy in office practice: A clinician's guide to doing what works.* New York: Guilford.

Washton, A. M., & Stone-Washton, N. S. (1990). Abstinence and relapse in outpatient cocaine addicts. *Journal of Psychoactive Drugs, 22,* 135-148.

Zweben, J. E. (1989). Recovery-oriented psychotherapy: Patient resistance and therapist dilemmas. *Journal of Substance Abuse Treatment, 6,* 123-132.

15

Peer Support

Key to Maintaining Recovery

Linda Farris Kurtz

Treatment is the first step in recovery from addiction. Recovery after treatment requires finding a whole new peer support system, learning to socialize without the help of a drug, and finding new ways to cope with uncertainty, frustration, and loss. Self-help/mutual aid/support groups provide an essential, supportive, peer-helping community. These communities are typically 12-step groups, affiliated with the worldwide fellowships of Alcoholics Anonymous (AA), Narcotics Anonymous (NA), and other groups derived from the AA model.

Although other peer support groups exist, such as Women for Sobriety, Moderation Management (MM), Smart Recovery, and Secular Organizations for Sobriety (SOS), 12-step fellowships are the most numerous and available groups. MM, founded in 1993, has only 50 face-to-face groups in the United States and several active online discussion groups. Its main goal is to moderate one's drinking and is not for everyone (the others promote total abstinence). MM holds face-to-face meetings, has a published guidebook, and sponsors online groups and a chat room. Links to information about all of these can be found on their Web pages. Women for Sobriety reports only 200 groups worldwide (Women for Sobriety, personal communication, July 24, 2000). SOS is an international association with 750 groups. Smart Recovery is international with 100 groups (see "Online Resources" at the end of this chapter).

For a mutual aid association to function effectively as a recovering community, there must be many groups, frequent meetings, and diverse activities. Only 12-step fellowships have achieved the critical mass of groups and members that make a recovering community possible. There are 100 more AA meetings in Toledo, Ohio, in 1 week, for example, than there are Women for Sobriety groups worldwide.

BOX 15.1 **The 12 Steps of Alcoholics Anonymous**

1. We admitted we were powerless over alcohol—that our lives had become unmanageable.
2. Came to believe that a power greater than ourselves could restore us to sanity.
3. Made a decision to turn our will and lives over to the care of God *as we understood Him.*
4. Made a searching and fearless moral inventory of ourselves.
5. Admitted to God, to ourselves and to another human being the exact nature of our wrongs.
6. Were entirely ready to have God remove all these defects of character.
7. Humbly asked Him to remove our shortcomings.
8. Made a list of all persons we had harmed, and became willing to make amends to them all.
9. Made direct amends to such people wherever possible, except when to do so would injure them or others.
10. Continued to take personal inventory and when we were wrong promptly admitted it.
11. Sought through prayer and meditation to improve our conscious contact with God *as we understood Him,* praying only for knowledge of His will for us and the power to carry that out.
12. Having had a spiritual awakening as the result of these steps, we tried to carry this message to alcoholics, and to practice these principles in all our affairs.

SOURCE: Alcoholics Anonymous (1976, pp. 59-60).

⊞ WHAT IS PEER SUPPORT?

Peer support develops through social encounters with fellow recovering addicts in premeeting chats and discussions and after-meeting talks at the local coffeehouse. It is also found in working with a sponsor, calling fellow members, and sharing stories at the local Alano Club (private clubs run by and for recovering people). Nowadays, you can also access AA or NA Web sites and participate in live chat or asynchronous discussion forums.

⊞ TWELVE-STEP GROUPS

Twelve-step groups follow the 12 steps and traditions. The 12 steps are shown in Box 15.1. The first step is one of acceptance. The addict finally admits that he or she is not in control and cannot continue without help. Critics of the 12-Step method complain that the first step leads one to acceptance of inherent powerlessness and is therefore disempowering. Experience demonstrates that, on the contrary, it is this step that leads to empowerment (Bateson, 1972). By following the steps, seeking fellowship, and turning things one cannot control over to the care of a higher power, the addict regains appropriate control of his or her life and gives up the illusion of controlling what cannot be controlled.

Newcomers to AA or NA do not immediately understand the steps. However, through repetition, discussion, and sharing recovery stories, participants gradually realize how working these steps can improve their lives.

⊞ HOW AND WHY 12-STEP GROUPS WORK

Meetings

Meetings are either open to outsiders or strictly for addicts. Many are speaker meetings, where one or two people tell their recovery story and how they used the steps. Others are discussion meetings where participants take turns sharing insights, solutions, progress, and problems. Still other meetings focus on portions of the AA "Big Book" (formally titled *Alcoholics Anonymous: The Story of How Many Thousands of Men and Women Have Recovered From Alcoholism*, third edition; AA, 1976), the NA basic text *Narcotics Anonymous* (NA, 1987), or other literature.

Newcomers or visitors are often very nervous about their first meeting. Know something about the particular group and, if possible, individual members. Then you can let your clients know what to expect. Some meetings are quite large and impersonal, others small and more intimate. A common anxiety is concern about having to speak up and talk about personal problems. Let clients know that only first names are shared and that very seldom are newcomers asked to say more than what they are comfortable with. Reassure your clients and do your best to allay their fears.

Here is how one recovering drug addict describes the way members reach out to newcomers:

> What I'm saying is that naturally, from a support group standpoint, "We learn to live life on life's terms." That's why, when a newcomer first comes in and he's worried about how he's going to stay clean for 24 hours, we share our war stories for the first 5 minutes—to let newcomers know they are in the right place. We know that you are trying to rinse out your mind—wash it and rinse it and think about something besides drugs. We let you know that any addict can stop using drugs. Any addict can learn how to lose desire and find a new way of living. To me recovery is not a goal. Spiritual and emotional growth is the goal. Total recovery is impossible to have because as long as you are human you will have character defects. Only God has recovered. How can you have a goal of something that's impossible to obtain? I'm not perfect, but I strive for spiritual and emotional growth.

These words describe a common occurrence in meetings: A newcomer shows up unexpectedly, and the topic of the meeting immediately shifts to "how it was in my first meeting and what to expect from us as you continue your recovery." Of course, this may not occur in a large group where there are more newcomers. Larger groups may socialize newcomers by having separate tables for various discussion topics, with a newcomers' table designated as a "First Step table."

Recovery doesn't just happen at meetings. Involvement in a recovering community means participating in additional service and outside activities as well.

Service Work

Service is another way that recovering people become part of the 12-step community. In the 12-step tradition, this means many things, from the very small and mundane (fixing coffee) to the very responsible (representing one's group in a larger forum). As described in the words of one recovering drug addict,

> First of all, I learned how to set up tables and I made the coffee. I picked up the literature and I put the literature out on the table. For me that was a humbling experience without question. It taught me how to give and look for the opportunity to give as opposed to always taking. I came to a full understanding of what it is to give. I found out that putting out the literature was the most important position—to make sure that when you came you would find something there waiting for you. I didn't get that at home, I got that in the meeting. I didn't get that at church because I hadn't been to church. I didn't get it on a job because I never had a

job. It encouraged me to see other individuals do service work. They didn't just make sugges-tions—they demonstrated what they suggested. I saw somebody else do it—somebody said, "Have you ever thought about doing that?" Without those suggestions, I probably wouldn't have found the courage to give.

Studies of participation in AA indicate that *involvement in service work correlates with positive outcome* (i.e., lengthy sobriety and other signs of healthy recovery). En-courage your client to do service work by helping set up meetings; visiting jails, prisons, and treatment centers; sharing stories of recovery in meetings or other forums; or becom-ing a sponsor and/or group secretary or representative. Reinforce this type of activity from the very start.

Working the Steps

The most important part of peer support in AA/NA, however, is working the steps. This happens in meetings but should also become routine throughout the day as the cli-ent engages in the cognitive and behavioral aspects of the recovery program. Perkinson (1997) stated that the "Twelve Steps are the core of treatment for chemical dependency" (p. 101). Whether you see treatment this way or not, the steps *are* the core of peer sup-port in a 12-step fellowship. To understand working the 12 steps in AA, turn to the well-known "Big Book" (AA, 1976, pp. 58-103) and *Twelve Steps and Twelve Traditions* (AA, 1981). The 12 steps of NA are in *Narcotics Anonymous* (NA, 1987, pp. 13-49). These books are in most libraries, are available at meetings, and can be obtained from AA or NA directly (see addresses at the end of this chapter). Another excellent source for professionals wanting to understand and explain the steps to their clients is Nowinski and Baker's (1992) *Twelve-Step Facilitation Handbook*.

As I have mentioned, the first step involves accepting the need for help. Nowinski and Baker (1992) pointed out that no one wants to accept limitation and loss. Denial, a psychological defense, keeps the addict from taking this first step, so "Step 1 can be thought of as the process by which patients come to terms with the limitations and losses imposed on them with alcoholism and addiction" (p. 55). The addicted person must *accept these limitations and grieve these losses.* Support your client's struggle to overcome his or her denial of powerlessness over their use of alcohol and/or drugs. Keep in mind that denial is not conscious deceit but rather a protective device that prevents psychic pain and anxiety.

Steps 2 and 3 are the *surrender* steps. Surrendering to a higher power is a freeing ex-perience. Once addicts turn something over to this higher power, they are not in charge of it any more. There is nothing else they can do to prevent, cause, or otherwise affect the outcome. For example, if you're anxious when flying, turning the plane's safety over to a higher power relieves your anxiety. You don't have to grip the seat with sweaty palms. You relax, knowing that the trip's outcome is simply out of your control.

Steps 4 and 5 involve taking a moral inventory and sharing it with another human being and one's higher power. Encourage your client to take his or her moral inventory in consultation with an AA/NA sponsor and to share that inventory with someone in the 12-step fellowship rather than with you. In my community, a treatment center has changed its practices from taking over the tasks of sponsorship (coaching through the surrender steps, helping with inventories, and listening to "fifth steps") to assisting the client to do these steps within the AA/NA group. This helps the patient form a solid bond with the recovering community where recovery will be maintained.

Steps 6 and 7, "the very heart of the Twelve Step program" (Kurtz, 1996), involve being entirely ready to have God remove defects of character and humbly asking him to remove shortcomings. The member is not seeking to change him- or herself but is open to being changed and willing to pray for change opportunities. This stance fits well with the participant's surrender in Step 3—turning one's life over to the care of a higher power. This approach to change, however, differs from that of many current therapeutic techniques and may introduce some conflict between what you are doing with your client and what he or she is hearing in AA. If this is the case, consider ways of reconciling the two approaches. For example, your work can be regarded as an opportunity for change.

Making a list of all you have harmed and making amends to them are the essence of Steps 8 and 9. Step 9 requires concrete and never-ending action because one realizes slowly how and why a prior act harmed someone else. Amends are not just apologies; they include everyday activities, such as routine attentiveness to someone whom you may have treated badly. For example, making amends for some may mean reaching out to the entire community through drug prevention efforts in the schools for having peddled drugs in the past. It is important that you understand the nuances of Steps 8 and 9 to facilitate this.

The last three steps are based on the personal transformation that occurs through working the first nine steps. The recovering person maintains this transformation by continuing to take personal inventory and when wrong, promptly admitting it; using prayer and meditation in conscious contact with God, and carrying the message to the addict who still suffers (12th-step work). Twelfth-step work is a result of "spiritual awakening." The personal transformation that occurs with a recovering person is not simply living dry but is the change that comes with true sobriety, otherwise known as spiritual growth. Twelfth-step work is not just altruism; it is one of the ways that the recovering person maintains his or her own sobriety. Its primary purpose is not to keep others sober but to keep your client sober. It is also important to recognize that *AA and NA fellowships are not treatment.* Spiritual growth goes on as long as one lives and becomes a part of all that an individual does in life. It is not necessary for a recovering person to attend AA or NA for the rest of his or her life, but it is also not wrong to do so. Lifelong participation in a recovering community is not an addiction; it is a way of life, a way of giving back and perpetuating a recovering community for those who come later.

Sponsorship

Having a sponsor and being a sponsor correlates with better success in developing a sober lifestyle (Sheeren, 1988). Newcomers who successfully avoid relapse truly invest themselves in a meaningful sponsor relationship. Being a sponsor also reinforces the continued sobriety of the recovering addict. A comment in the NA basic text illustrates this: "Nothing has been so rewarding as working with other addicts. No matter what is happening in my life, I know I can get out of my self-centered trip by simply becoming interested in the welfare and recovery of a newcomer or an oldtimer in pain" (NA, 1987, p. 241).

Encourage your client to obtain a sponsor, even if at first it is just a temporary person. There is a 12-step slogan that says, "Stick with the winners." This emphasizes the importance of having a sponsor who has some sobriety, who understands the program well, and who has had success with it. Help your client select a sponsor, and then make use of this resource. Do not do for your client what the sponsor can do better (e.g., hear a fifth step, be too available for crisis work). Reinforce the use of a sponsor at every opportunity. Recognize that the AA/NA sponsor has a kind of knowledge that you do not have—what Borkman (1999) called "experiential knowledge."

Effectiveness

Some dispute AA's effectiveness, yet most practitioners in the field of chemical dependency refer their clients to AA. Recent studies by reputable researchers support 12-step effectiveness. One study, a multisite, large-sample, prospective research design, randomly selected and assigned clients to one of three treatment conditions (Project MATCH Research Group, 1997) and found all three treatments effective. Those who received 12-step facilitation were as successful in reaching treatment goals as those who received the two professional treatments (cognitive-behavioral therapy and motivational interviewing), and they were more likely to be abstinent at follow-up.

A recent study of self-help involvement compared individuals treated in a 12-step-oriented program with patients treated in inpatient units that placed little emphasis on 12-step principles (Humphreys & Moos, 2001). They found that the former had higher rates of abstinence and lower (64%) professional health care costs. "In the current health care climate," the authors stated, "a clinical strategy that reduces substance abuse patients ongoing health care costs by 64% while also promoting good outcome deserves serious attention" (p. 716).

Experiential Social Learning

Experiential knowledge comes from living and coping with a problem, whereas professional knowledge comes from professional training; lay knowledge comes from secondhand information on a nonprofessional level. Borkman (1999) proposed a cycle of experiential-social peer learning that takes place for people involved in a mutual help group. First, they identify with members present; new ideas and insights related to the self begin to form. Second, in group encounters, they reflect on what has been said and decide if these ideas can be applied personally. For example, I remember an individual who was anxious over the possibility that funding for her job would be cut. She was thinking of resigning from the job just to eliminate the anxiety. One day in an AA meeting, someone spoke about a situation quite different from hers. She recognized its similarity, however, because his fear of what might happen almost led him to take premature action that would have ensured the feared outcome (Phase 1). He spoke about how he had dealt with his impulses by turning the situation over to a higher power and recognizing that there was nothing he could do to control the outcome. So, reflecting on his experience (Phase 2) and realizing that her situation resonated with his, the woman decided to turn concern for her job and its continued funding over to a higher power (Phase 3). From that moment on, the anxiety left her, and she calmly waited for the outcome. As it happened, the funds were cut, but her employer found other, more secure funding to support her position. Assessing the consequences (Phase 4) helped her to recognize the value of the process of turning things over to a higher

---

BOX 15.2   **Cycle of Experiential-Social Peer Learning**

1. Gains new ideas and insights.
2. Reflects on whether ideas are applicable to self.
3. Tries out new ideas in daily life.
4. Assesses use of new idea's consequences.

SOURCE: Borkman (1999).

---

power. She could see that the way she had worried over the outcome had been leading her to take inappropriate, premature action that would have resulted in the very outcome she most dreaded. "Turning it over" made a happy ending.

Level of Involvement in a 12-Step Program

In the beginning, newcomers to the fellowships become oriented to them. Attending 90 meetings in 90 days is recommended by many treatment programs and by participants in AA/NA as a way of thoroughly socializing newcomers to the steps, traditions, and practices of the program. This routine also keeps the new member away from old drinking friends and quickly replaces some of the losses a newly recovering person experiences. At the end of 90 meetings, new members have been exposed to groups of all kinds, have gotten to know a group that they can call a "home group," and, hopefully, have found a sponsor.

There are three basic levels of involvement in a peer-helping fellowship: intermittent, regular, and a more intense level that I call "way of life." *Intermittent* participation happens when people are either unsure about whether they want to be involved or, after a period of intense involvement, feel they can cut back on meetings and do something else with their time. Rarely does intermittent involvement result in successful sobriety, but it is also common for people to go through a period of intermittent involvement before they go on to the next level.

Regular participation is when a member attends one or two groups regularly. According to AA's own surveys, North American members attend an average of two meetings per week (AA, 1999). This is one example of how differently 12-step groups function from self-help or support groups that meet only once a week or once a month. It is unlikely that someone wanting to kick an addiction would be successful with less than this norm.

Making the AA or NA fellowship *a way of life* is a step beyond just a few meetings per week. Charlie B., in this account by an anonymous friend of his, exemplifies the "way of life" member:

Charlie was a journalist until his craving for alcohol defeated his desire to work. And then one day Charlie found Alcoholics Anonymous. Although he got dry and even claims that he got somewhat sober, he experienced no great "conversion." During his first 7 years in Alcoholics Anonymous, Charlie immersed himself in a new vocation: buyer and seller of used books. He was so busy that he "never got around to really joining" an AA group. In fact during those years, Charlie never even read through AA's Big Book, the Bible of its fellowship that sets forth its program.

But Charlie did try to work AA's 12 steps. After about 7 years, he began to realize that his "defects of character" were "really coming out and beginning to gang up on me. I realized I needed to join an AA group, and I chose a Big Book study group."

As Charlie described what happened next,

> After a while, I attended an intergroup meeting, mainly out of curiosity, because it was there. I had never been involved in AA service, and I still wasn't interested in it, but suddenly I heard it announced that "Charlie B. is our new State Archivist." Well, I looked around, wondering who else had my name. You can guess what had happened. They tell you, "Never say 'No' to AA," so I couldn't, and so I became archivist and started chasing down the history of Alcoholics Anonymous in our state.
>
> You ask how I got into all the sponsoring I do. All I can say is that the pigeons just started showing up and they kept on coming. I probably have about 70 today, not because I want to, but mainly because you "never say 'no' to AA."

Charlie now is recovering from surgery that had removed over 40% of one lung. He is unmarried, not unusual for an alcoholic his age, and his two siblings live over 1,000 miles away. But during his diagnosis and hospitalization and the subsequent radiation therapy, Charlie's needs were always attended and he was rarely alone. When he couldn't drive, there were always people to drive him. His home, he lived alone, had rarely been empty during the 20-plus years I had known him. The coffee pot was always on, and some struggling drunks would be sitting around, asking about his "experience, strength, and hope" in some matter. Charlie is the least materialistic, most humane person I have ever met. He is not perfect, and he has many rough edges. But I know that Charlie is one of the few people I have met, in or out of Alcoholics Anonymous, "who has what I want"—the ability to make it the center of his life to selflessly and unself-consciously help his fellow creatures.

After 7 years of intermittent and regular attendance, Charlie had an experience that moved him to become more active, to take on an important service role, and gradually to acquire 70 sponsorees. This full-time involvement became his way of life.

Is this kind of involvement an addiction to the fellowship itself? Although for some people intense involvement may represent a compulsive activity, to see the "way-of-life member" as an addict is to misunderstand the nature of the peer support network. Intense participation in AA is no more an addiction than is a fervid attachment to a hobby, running a successful business, or rehabilitating after a serious physical injury.

For solid and sustained recovery, such intense involvement may be necessary. Solid recovery takes a long time, and for most it takes *constant repetition of program principles and practices.* In addition, members who make the fellowship a way of life keep it going for the benefit of others. What would have happened to this growing movement if Bill W. (AA's founder and author of the "Big Book") had become an intermittent user of the program?

▦ MATCHING CLIENTS TO AA/NA

What individual characteristics lead one person to benefit from a 12-step group and another not? Emrick, Tonnigan, Montgomery, and Little's (1993) study found that individuals who have an overinvolvement with alcohol, are anxious about their drinking, are experienced in looking for support outside themselves, and have a proclivity to engage in spiritual activities are more likely to affiliate with AA. I summarize factors that I think are particularly important for success in 12-step support.

Readiness to Change

The words of this recovering drug addict illustrate the importance of peer support at a time when an addict is ready to make a change:

> You know, I was involved in gang violence and being a gang leader for a number of years and a substance abuser for almost 25 years. I had various encounters with law enforcement. I saw a lot of violence. It got to where I was tired of using and tired of violence, but I didn't know any other way: I thought that was the only way. A friend of mine, who was already involved in NA, encouraged me to attend closed meetings. I trusted him enough to go. When I got there I saw individuals that I thought were either dead or in prison, but they weren't. They were doing good—had jobs, back with their families. They were looking real good to me. With their support and their encouragement it helped me to see that recovery was a possibility. They encouraged me to do those 12 steps. Without that type of fellowship, people with those types of backgrounds who understood me better than my own family did, I couldn't be here today. I needed that support. I needed someone to say, "You can make it in spite of what you've done in the past and in spite of what somebody may think about you now."

This addict clearly wanted to change but did not know any other way to live. After prison, he began NA meetings, stayed clean, and got a job as a program director in a social agency. The importance of identification is evident here. When he entered his first meeting, he recognized people he knew, people who had done in the past what he was doing in the present, and it gave him hope.

Cultural Differences

AA exists all over the world and has been adapted to a wide variety of cultures (Makela, 1996). People will go to a meeting most readily *where they fit in and are accepted.* This is most likely in a place where they find others from their culture who look and dress alike and speak their language. If you cannot find a meeting for your clients where they will find this degree of similarity, find at least one person with similar characteristics who can act as a temporary sponsor for them until they become comfortable.

Class Differences

The most recent AA member survey in North America (AA, 1999) shows that members range from higher-paid professional/technical workers (13%) and administrators (10%) to laborers (8%) and the unemployed (6%). In a sociological study with questionable ethics, Lofland and Lejeune (1960) placed research assistants claiming to be alcoholic at newcomer meetings dressed as either higher- or lower-class persons. Interested in whether higher- or lower-class appearance would have an effect on how the subjects were received, they found that regardless of appearance, these pseudoalcoholics were equally met with courtesy and offers of help. Nevertheless, if your clients are acutely uncomfortable in settings where others' social class is at variance with their own, try to find them a meeting in which they will feel most like fitting in.

Racial Differences

AA's most recent surveys of its North American membership show that it remains primarily a white fellowship (88%). Five percent of members are black, 4% are Hispanic, 2% are Native American, and 1% are Asian or "other." Researchers have found that African American members are most comfortable in groups where there are a high percentage of their race and that European American individuals similarly prefer not to be in the minority. The same thing applies with race as with class, culture, or gender; if at all possible, link your client to a peer support person of the same race even if a group dominated by that person's race is not available. Most people find that once they feel accepted by a group, their individual differences become insignificant.

⊞ HELPING PEOPLE GET INVOLVED WITH PEER SUPPORT

Temporary Sponsors and Getting Active

We have already covered the importance of *temporary sponsors* as linking agents. This is especially important when the client is shy about walking into a room of strangers, as most of us are, or is of a different race, gender, social class, or culture than the group available. A temporary sponsor can escort the client to initial meetings, provide education about the fellowship, listen to concerns about staying dry, and introduce the newcomer to less formal activities provided by the fellowship. You can be most helpful to your client by having a list of temporary sponsors you can call. These may be people who want to volunteer for this role as part of their own service work. I recommend you and your clients read *Things My Sponsor Taught Me* by Paul H. (1987).

Encouraging service work cannot be overemphasized. Nowinski and Baker (1992) referred to this as "getting active." Discuss with your client the importance of speaking in meetings, talking informally with members before and after meetings, and socializing with members in other ways. In most groups, there are announcements about AA/NA/Al-Anon activities—picnics, parties, statewide get-togethers, and workshops they can attend.

Lifestyle Changes

Recovery from addiction requires changing a lifestyle. Former peers (friends, family, coworkers) may also be using. Peer support is extremely important during a time when an individual's major coping tool is the drug but existing peer relationships support drug use. Assist the recovering person to break away. Nowinski and Baker (1996) described the importance of helping addicts see how their peers may have been enabling their drug use. The recovering person must change relationships, frequent different places, and establish new routines. You may use a "lifestyle contract" to make such changes (pp. 116-117). In the lifestyle contract, clients make an inventory of the enabling people in their life and identify people who will replace them. The same is done with places, rituals, and routines: Whereas before they would drop in at the neighbor-hood tavern after work, now they go to the AA clubhouse.

Counselor Characteristics

Consult the 12-step facilitation guidelines for suggestions if you act as a facilitator in linking your client to the 12-step community. Use active, conversational, empathic, and nonjudgmental confrontation "as opposed to being merely reflective, detached, and interpretative" (Nowinski & Baker, 1992, p. 20). Balance genuine caring and healthy detachment, and *do not become the client's "total recovery program"* (p. 22):

> It is the AA/NA fellowship, not the individual facilitator, that is the major agent of change. Involvement in AA or NA—including regularly attending a variety of meetings and social ac-tivities, using the telephone to connect with AA/NA friends on a regular basis, and develop-ing a relationship with a sponsor—is preferable to relying on the facilitator. (p. 23)

Your main task is keeping track of the client's activity in the 12-step community. Your client should be attending meetings, reading literature, participating actively in the fel-lowship, and getting a sponsor. Monitor these activities, and process them with your cli-ents. If they did not like a particular group, ask, Why not? What happened in that meet-ing that was upsetting? What did they think about the literature they read that week?

Length of Professional Contact

Continuing your professional contact with the recovering person will vary depend-ing on whether the client has the money to pay you, the policies of your treatment cen-ter/social agency, and the desires of your client. Project MATCH's 12-step facilitation continued weekly for 12 weeks, with follow-up assessments over the year following treatment. During the posttreatment year, subjects kept careful records of their use of alcohol and completed instruments that measured outcomes (Project MATCH, 1997). Ideally, the length of your contacts should be determined by how well your client is do-ing. Individuals with dual problems, such as a mental illness, pathological gambling, or marital conflict, may need longer treatment. As discussed below, make successful bonding with the fellowship one of your treatment goals, and do not require perfect re-covery because your client will never reach it. Relapses are the norm in recovery from chemical dependencies and problems; 12-step fellowships and other support groups understand and accept this.

AVOIDING PITFALLS AND PROBLEMS ▦

Taking Over the Peer Helper Role

One of the pitfalls mentioned earlier is substituting your treatment program for the recovering community. Just as it is important not to do for clients what they can do for themselves, it is also important not to do for clients what the community can do. Assist your clients to find peers who can help with a fourth-step inventory and someone to hear a fifth step instead of doing this yourself. Think of your role as linking your clients to a life of continuing growth, not merely as being a treatment provider who will produce a finished product at the end of your treatment plan.

Overidentification With Resistance

Overidentifying with your clients' resistance to attending meetings can impede their progress. Meetings often happen at night when clients may like to relax after work. The recovering person cannot afford this luxury. Be firm about the need for lifestyle change: finding new friends, leaving a job where alcohol is prevalent, even leaving an alcoholic spouse if need be. If AA/NA is not working for your clients, help them to find replacements for the social network they have lost, such as one of the other self-help organizations for alcoholics/addicts, church, or other nondrinking environment. AA/NA may be necessary as a temporary bridge until other peer associations can be developed.

Problems With Religion

One common objection to AA/NA affiliation is to the spiritual emphasis in 12-step groups. Be knowledgeable about the differences between *spirituality* and *religion,* and read the chapter in the "Big Book" titled "We Agnostics" (AA, 1976). In that chapter, the writers reveal that at least half of all members experienced initial difficulty with the spiritual basis of the AA program. It stresses that the important thing is to find a power greater than the self and that *God* means "your own conception of God" (p. 47). Similarly, the NA basic text says, "Our concept of God comes not from dogma, but from what we believe and what works for us. Many of us understand God to be simply whatever force keeps us clean. The right to a God of your understanding is total and without any catches" (NA, 1987, pp. 24-25).

Some groups are more openly religious-sounding than others. Nevertheless, the spirituality of the 12-step movement really is at its heart. Many if not most scholars in the field view this as its unique contribution to the 20th-century history of ideas (Kurtz, 1996). AA's beginnings are rooted in evangelical Protestantism; still, its teachings are compatible with Catholicism, Judaism, and Islam. For example, there is an organization called JACS (Jewish Alcoholics, Chemically Dependent Persons and Significant Others), headquartered in New York City, that helps Jewish addicts understand the 12-step program as compatible with Judaism. They can be contacted at JACS, 850 Seventh Avenue, New York, NY 10019, phone (212) 397-4197.

Gender Issues

Women often express discomfort about male-dominated AA/NA groups. The most recent survey indicated that one third of members are women (AA, 1999). One way to help your female client adjust to AA is to link her to an all-women's group or to a group with a large number of women in attendance. It is also appropriate to help her deal with male prejudice and sexist comments. An NA member writes of her dealings with men in the NA program in an article titled "How I Learned to Overcome My Fear and Love the Male Chauvinist Pigs in NA" (B.G., 1998). She pointed out that anyone who uses drugs or alcohol is welcome in NA, not just those without prejudice, so it is necessary to forgive and develop tolerance for those in the 12-step groups who may express themselves in ways that make women uncomfortable. As a counselor, you can help your female clients to sort out how much of their resistance to AA/NA may be to the sexism they encounter and how much is actually hesitation about getting active to overcome their own addiction.

Discomfort in Groups

Many treatment outcome studies show that people with high affiliation and group dependency needs do well with peer support groups. Others who prefer to be more socially isolated may need a different kind of intervention. The essence of successful sobriety in a 12-step fellowship seems to rest on one's ability to accept powerlessness, accept a higher power, and depend on the fellowship for making lifestyle changes necessary for sobriety. Therefore, what happens to those who are uncomfortable in groups?

Smith (1993) explored this question in the early 1990s and found that people with high affiliation needs do indeed bond quickly with AA groups, whereas those with low affiliation needs do not. "I just wasn't into all that hugging and such," one loner said. "It was more comfortable at home by myself. Of course, that kept getting me back to drinking" (p. 694). For such people, integration into the AA social world was difficult. With continued attendance, the less extroverted members eventually became involved with the "social world" of AA and developed a sense of belonging. Smith concluded that for some people *a dyadic relationship is often required* before they are able to be involved in an AA group.

Lack of Transportation and Other Logistical Barriers

Help your client find ways to get to meetings. One of the reasons I think AA or NA is the only viable form of peer support is their broad availability throughout the day and evening. In places where there are Alano Clubs, the clubhouse can serve as a drop-in center for people between meetings.

One definition of an AA meeting is simply "one drunk talking to another." Anywhere you can find one other person who has a story to tell, you can consider it a meeting. Thus, your clients might find someone whom they can talk to in person or by telephone at times when a regular meeting is not available. Other 12-step participants will drive by your client's home and take him or her to a meeting (this is a form of 12-step service). Your client may resist this use of peer support, but get past these excuses. The real reason may be that your client wants to continue using or may simply be unwilling to overcome his or her shyness in groups.

Working at Cross Purposes With AA/NA

One of the biggest pitfalls and problems that you'll have in linking your client to a peer support groups is when his or her progress is being undermined by others. This happens most often with issues of medication for psychiatric disorders. Some addicts need prescribed medications for various reasons. An AA pamphlet states,

It becomes clear that just as it is wrong to enable or support any alcoholic to become re-addicted to any drug, it's equally wrong to deprive an alcoholic of medication which can alleviate or control other disabling physical and/or emotional problems. (AA, 1984a, p. 13)

Despite this warning, some are instructed by well-meaning peers to stop their medications. You can do two things to remedy this. First, obtain the AA brochure cited above and share it with your client. Second, recommend that he or she not discuss medications in groups or informal conversations.

⊞ 12-STEP AIDS TO FACILITATE PEER SUPPORT

Inform yourself about Alcoholics Anonymous World Services books, pamphlets, videos, periodicals, and workbooks. These books include the "Big Book" (AA, 1976), *Twelve Steps and Twelve Traditions* (AA, 1981), a biography of Dr. Bob, AA's cofounder (AA, 1980), two books on AA history (AA, 1953, 1984b), and a book of Bill W.'s writings, entitled *As Bill Sees It* (1967). There are also booklets on various topics, numerous pamphlets, and directories. In addition, there are workbooks for cooperating with the professional community and for working in correctional facilities. Much of the literature is published in foreign languages; the "Big Book" is published in 35 different languages, in Braille, and in large print for the visually impaired.

Two videos show how AA works in general. In addition, there are two videos related to correctional facilities, two for young people, two on AA history, one of Bill W. telling his story, and another of him discussing the 12 traditions. (Some of these videos are for members only.) There are also videos in American Sign Language. All of these works are published anonymously and conform to the standard of "conference approved," which means that the AA Service Conference has seen them before publication and approved them. In some places, only conference-approved literature is allowed in AA meeting rooms.

Periodicals include a newsletter titled *Box 459* (news and notes from the General Service Office of AA), *About AA: A Newsletter for Professionals*, and *AA Grapevine* ("our meeting in print"). The first provides news related to the AA organization, such as numbers of members and groups, contributions from groups, a calendar of events, decisions made in conferences, committee reports, and the like. *About AA* contains information about the fellowship that would be of interest to professionals, such as results of member surveys, information about AA's history, available literature, and other products. *AA Grapevine* is composed of writings by members that reveal aspects of their spiritual journeys in recovery. AA's General Service Office can be reached by mail at Alcoholics Anonymous World Services, P.O. Box 459, Grand Central Station, New York, NY 10163, phone (212) 870-3312. Web sites listed in "Online Resources" at the end of this chapter include those for AA and NA and for other self-help organizations in this field. In addition, other informative Web sites are listed.

Narcotics Anonymous World Services is headquartered in Van Nuys, California. It also publishes literature: books, booklets, pamphlets, handbooks and guides, directories, audiocassettes, and one video, *Just for Today*. The video explains NA through the eyes of recovering members, showing their addiction and their recovery. The video has been produced especially for treatment staff training and presentation to clients and to community meetings. NA also publishes *The NA Way Magazine: The International Journal of Narcotics Anonymous*. The magazine's mission is to provide service information and recovery-related entertainment related to current issues and events relevant to and written by members. You can order from NA at their address: Narcotics Anonymous, P.O. Box 9999, Van Nuys, CA 91409, phone (818) 773-9999.

The www.alcoholism.about.com, www.alcoholismhelp.com, and www.recovery.com sites contain information and chat rooms for recovering people. Any search engine, such as google.com, will provide additional sites on the Internet that contain information, online groups, and chat rooms. These are useful alternatives to live face-to-face groups when those are not available.

REFERENCES ▦

Alcoholics Anonymous. (1967). *As Bill sees it.* New York: Author.

Alcoholics Anonymous. (1976). *Alcoholics Anonymous: The story of how many thousands of men and women have recovered from alcoholism* (3rd ed.). New York: Author.

Alcoholics Anonymous. (1980). *Dr. Bob and the good oldtimers.* New York: Author.

Alcoholics Anonymous. (1981). *Twelve Steps and twelve traditions.* New York: Alcoholics Anonymous World Services.

Alcoholics Anonymous. (1984a). *The AA member: Medications and other drugs.* New York: Author.

Alcoholics Anonymous. (1984b). *Pass it on: The story of Bill Wilson and how the A.A. message reached the world.* New York: Author.

Alcoholics Anonymous. (1999). *Alcoholics Anonymous 1998 membership survey.* New York: Author.

Bateson, G. (1972). *Steps to an ecology of the mind.* San Francisco: Chandler.

Borkman, T. J. (1999). *Understanding self-help/mutual aid: Experiential learning in the commons.* New Brunswick, NJ: Rutgers University Press.

Emrick, C., Tonigan, J. S, Montgomery, H., & Little, L. (1993). Alcoholics Anonymous: What is currently known? In B. S. McCrady & W. R. Miller (Eds.), *Research on Alcoholics Anonymous: Opportunities and alternatives* (pp. 41-78). New Brunswick, NJ: Rutgers Center of Alcohol Studies.

G, B. (1998). How I learned to overcome my fear and love the male chauvinist pigs in NA. *NA Way Magazine, 15*(3), 7-8.

H, P. (1987). *Things my sponsor taught me.* Center City, MN: Hazelden.

Humphreys, K., & Moos, R. (2001). Can encouraging substance abuse patients to participate in self help groups reduce demand for health care? A quasi-experimental study. *Alcoholism: Clinical and Experimental Research, 24*(5), 711-716.

Kurtz, E. (1996). Twelve step programs. In P. H. Van Ness (Ed.), *Spirituality and the secular quest.* New York: Crossroad.

Lofland, J. F., & Lejeune, R.A. (1960). Initial interaction of newcomers in Alcoholics Anonymous: A field experiment in class symbols and socialization. *Social Problems, 8,* 102-111.

Makela, K. (1996). *Alcoholics Anonymous as a mutual-help movement: A study in eight societies.* Madison: University of Wisconsin Press.

Narcotics Anonymous World Service Office. (1987). *Narcotics Anonymous* (4th ed.). Van Nuys, CA: Author.

Nowinski, J., & Baker, S. (1992). *The twelve-step facilitation handbook: A systematic approach to early recovery from alcoholism and addiction.* New York: Lexington.

Perkinson, R. R. (1997). *Chemical dependency counseling: A practical guide.* Thousand Oaks, CA: Sage.

Project MATCH Research Group. (1997). Matching alcoholism treatments to client heterogeneity: Project MATCH post-treatment drinking outcomes. *Journal of Studies on Alcohol, 59,* 113-522.

Sheeren, M. (1988). The relationship between relapse and involvement in Alcoholics Anonymous. *Journal of Studies on Alcohol, 49,* 104-106.

Smith, A. R. (1993). The social construction of group dependency in Alcoholics Anonymous. *Journal of Drug Issues, 23,* 689-704.

⊞ ADDITIONAL SUGGESTED READINGS

Kurtz, E. (1979). *Not-God: A history of Alcoholics Anonymous.* Center City, MN: Hazelden.

Kurtz, L. F. (1997). *Self-help and support groups: A handbook for practitioners.* Thousand Oaks, CA: Sage.

⊞ ONLINE RESOURCES

Al-Anon/Alateen: www.al-anon.alateen.org

Alcoholics Anonymous: www.alcoholics-anonymous.org

Alcoholism Home Page (a guide to over 700 sites, including those of alternative, non-12-step recovery support organizations: www.alcoholism.about.com

Another Empty Bottle (informational site that includes links to recovery peer support organizations): www.alcoholismhelp.com

Moderation Management: http://moderation.org

Narcotics Anonymous: www.na.org

Secular Organizations for Sobriety: www.cfiwest.org/sos/

Smart Recovery: www.smartrecovery.org

Women for Sobriety: www.womenforsobriety.org

Online AA Recovery Resources: www.recovery.org/aa

16

Family Treatment

Stage-Appropriate Psychotherapy for the Addicted Family

Joyce Schmid
Stephanie Brown

WHAT IS THE PROBLEM?

Jim is seeing you for the first time today. He comes in for help with his nightmares, anxiety, and depression. He feels he is failing as a husband, father, and professional. He tells you he is overwhelmed with responsibility and is increasingly unable to maintain his composure. He says he yells at the kids, withdraws for hours on end, berates Sandra, his wife, and demands that everyone shape up. He feels like a drill sergeant issuing orders, but he can't get anyone to follow them. He believes he should be able to create the kind of order he craves. They live in chaos, and Jim thinks it is all his fault. So does his family.

What is the problem here? What do you think about Jim and what he is telling us? Maybe you wonder what internal conflicts generate his need for control. Perhaps you listen for past and present circumstances in family history that may be contributing to his problems. These questions and others would certainly be on any therapist's mind. This chapter, however, focuses on a different set of questions: Is there an addict in Jim's life? Could his problems be understood, wholly or in part, as the "normal" coping efforts of someone who is in a relationship with a practicing addict? This point of view is not an alternative to psychodynamic, behavioral, systems, or other ways of understanding human experience. These approaches are integral parts of the treatment model presented here. But whatever else may be going on with a client, whatever theory of psychotherapy you may use, it is crucial to recognize this: Coping with a relationship to an active alcoholic or addict can take a profound psychological and emotional toll.

Clients like Jim often seek therapy with the goal of fixing themselves so a loved one won't use drugs. Others, who do recognize the addiction of their loved one, will seek your help to get the partner to stop using. Either way, clients are likely to invite you to join the pathology by agreeing to define the problem the same way they do. They may very well pressure you to overlook what is in plain view—the addiction—and to explain away the substance use as they do. In other words, they will pressure you to give up your own separate observing self.

Many members of addicted families do not have a separate sense of self. Either they never had one, or they lost it as they learned both to deny the addiction and to adapt to it in order to maintain their connection with the addict. *Adaptation to addiction has been called coalchoholism* or *codependence*. This adaptation, which involves a sacrifice of self, is the pathology of members of an addict's family.

In working with these people, don't agree to fix them (you can't). Also, do not agree to help them get the addict to stop using substances (you can't do that either). Do help them focus on themselves and the reality of addiction in their lives. Stage-appropriate psychotherapy, based on Brown's developmental model of addiction, is a tool to help you accomplish this.

▦ WHAT IS THE DEVELOPMENTAL MODEL OF ADDICTION?

The developmental model describes the experiences of addicts and their families (the *coalcoholics* or *coaddicts*) and defines the tasks of treatment for each stage of addiction/recovery. In this model, addiction is viewed as a "central organizing principle" governing individual, couple, and family dynamics and development in addicted families. Addiction and recovery are regarded as long-term processes consisting of four stages: active addiction, transition, early recovery, and ongoing recovery. The developmental model helps us determine what treatment modality or combination of modalities—behavioral, cognitive, or psychodynamic—to use at any particular time. As you read about our tool of stage-appropriate therapy, you will also be learning the developmental model. This model is explained more fully in books listed at the end of this chapter.

▦ ASSESSMENT

Before providing treatment, you will of course first need to identify or rule out the presence of addiction in the family. Addiction is not only a family member's use of substances but also the pattern of thinking and other defenses in family members. (Keep in mind the potential that the family members may have serious medical or psychiatric illness at the same time that they are affected by the addiction of another person.)

To illustrate assessment for familial addiction, let's return to Jim. Up to now, you have not heard about anybody using drugs or alcohol, so you will need to find out about current and past use of substances by all family members, including himself. Most briefly, you could ask the questions included in the "Family CAGE" questionnaire (see Box 16.1). Or you might prefer to ask directly questions such as these: Do you use alcohol? Does anyone else in the family drink? When? How much? How about other drugs? What happens when someone drinks or uses drugs?

BOX 16.1 **Family CAGE (Revised)**

The following questions help us understand the way you and your family use alcohol (including beer, wine, and wine coolers). Please check the answer that best describes you and your family.

1. Have you ever felt that you or anyone in your family should cut down on your/their drinking?

   You? ____1. Never ____2. Occasionally ____3. Often

   Family? ____1. Never ____2. Occasionally ____3. Often

2. Have you or anyone in your family ever felt annoyed by complaints about drinking?

   You? ____1. Never ____2. Occasionally ____3. Often

   Family? ____1. Never ____2. Occasionally ____3. Often

3. Have you or anyone in your family ever felt bad or guilty about your/their drinking?

   You? ____1. Never ____2. Occasionally ____3. Often

   Family? ____1. Never ____2. Occasionally ____3. Often

4. Have you or anyone in your family ever had a drink first thing in the morning to steady nerves or get rid of a hangover?

   You? ____1. Never ____2. Occasionally ____3. Often

   Family? ____1. Never ____2. Occasionally ____3. Often

SOURCE: Frank, Graham, Zyzanski, and White (1992).
NOTE: CAGE is an acronym: *C*ut down on drinking; *A*nnoyed by complaints about drinking; *G*uilty about drinking; had an *E*ye-opener first thing in the morning.

These kinds of questions can feel uncomfortable for the therapist, especially if the client is defensive, so listen for openings. For example, if Jim spontaneously mentions drinking or drug use, ask for more detail. Or if he mentions typical drinking or drug-using situations, like going to parties, relaxing at home after work, or fighting with Sandra, ask about drinking or drug use related to those occasions. Also, any mention of illness, pain, or doctor visits can be a lead-in to ask about prescription drugs, which, in turn, can be a lead-in to discuss alcohol. If there's no obvious window of opportunity, you may simply say that you have some routine questions about drug and alcohol use. Generally, people don't mind being asked about substance use unless they have some specific reason to be defensive. This, in itself, may suggest a problem.

Returning to Jim, he says that he and his wife enjoy a nightly "glass of wine" that helps him relax and allows them to feel "connected." What does "a glass" mean to him? Literally "a" glass? Or more than one? And how big is that glass? Do they use anything else with it, like marijuana? Jim says that he has one glass, while Sandra finishes the bottle and then continues to drink through the evening. She falls asleep, and Jim takes over putting the children to bed and preparing for the next day. Does he think she has a problem with alcohol? "No," he says, a little angrily. He insists that she works hard all day and needs relief.

When asked about drug use, Jim says matter-of-factly that Sandra takes tranquilizers for her anxiety. Jim explains that she has been stressed for a long time. He wishes he could help more, get things "under control" so she wouldn't need to take anything. He repeats that it's all his fault. He spends long hours at work and lets things get "out of hand" at home.

As you ask Jim about alcohol and drug use in the family, listen for answers to the following questions:

1. *To what extent have alcohol and drugs taken on a central organizing role in the family?* The more this has happened, the more likely it is that addiction is present, and the harder it will be for clients like Jim to see the problem and to change.

2. *To what extent does the client use cognitive distortion, rationalization, and denial about the family member's substance use?* Jim distorts his wife's alcohol consumption: He says she has a "nightly glass of wine." He rationalizes her drug use: She needs tranquilizers because of stress. And he denies the possibility that she has a problem with alcohol. These defenses are signs of the active addiction stage and are key elements of Jim's distorted thinking. In treatment, target your comments to help him unscramble his thinking. For example, wonder with him whether drinking and drugs may add to the family's stress rather than relieving it.

3. *What behaviors contribute to maintaining alcohol and drug use?* If you know this, you will be able to help Jim work on eliminating these behaviors or explore his resistance to change. For example, Jim's and Sandra's social life involves heavy drinking. Try pointing this out, and ask Jim if he has considered withdrawing from activities that involve drinking and substituting others.

"I couldn't do that," Jim insists. "The only fun that Sandra and I really have together is being with our friends in our dinner club." Part of your work in therapy will be to try to understand with him why it would be so hard to leave the club and, perhaps, to help him do so. Although Jim really does want help, and he does want to "fix" the problem, he is afraid to challenge or change anything himself.

4. *What functions are served by the substance use?* Jim says that drinking helps him and Sandra relax and helps them feel close to one another. This could make it hard for Jim to give up the dinner club: He experiences it as an integral part of his attachment to his wife. Do alcohol and drugs serve other functions besides attachment for this couple? Do they also help Jim and Sandra take time away from responsibilities, fight, make love, or, conversely, achieve distance from one another? Once you know this, you can begin to talk about alternative ways to fill the needs now filled by drugs, while continuing to assess Jim's readiness to change, or his resistance.

5. *What are the family members' thoughts, perceptions, feelings, and behaviors about the addict's drinking and using drugs?* In the active addiction stage, family members often use defenses to such an extent that their own thoughts, perceptions, and feelings are not available to them. So if you ask Jim directly about these, he may not be able to tell you. But he can describe his behavior, and you and he can work on changing that. In later stages, you can help Jim address his thoughts, perceptions, and feelings as they emerge.

Jim gives you information that strongly suggests that his wife is an alcoholic and addict. But he himself denies, while at the same time rationalizing, the addiction that he shows you. The addiction seems to serve important functions for him. All of this indicates that he's in the stage of active addiction. Now let's take a closer look at that stage.

STAGE I: ACTIVE ADDICTION ⊞

Living with an actively addicted person is difficult. Active addiction can make addicts undependable, unreasonable, inconsistent, abusive, and physically ill. Addicts lose their jobs, get into automobile accidents, lose their driving licenses, get in trouble with the law. Even more maddening, addicts insist (a) that none of this is happening; (b) that it is not their fault; (c) that it is all the fault of other people, such as family members; and (d) that it certainly has nothing to do with their drinking or using drugs, which (e) they deny doing. Who would want to live with a person like this?

But when the addict is a parent, a spouse, or a relative, there are strong bonds of love and attachment. To stay in relationship with a beloved addict, family members join in denying the addiction or at least in denying its central organizing function. Family members learn not to see and know what they really do see and know. They invent alternative explanations for the realities that cannot be named. The family develops a "story" that denies the addiction and explains it in a way that allows it to be maintained. This often requires someone else to be the "problem." Jim fulfills this needed role.

Such thinking and behavior form a "system" that allows the family to adapt to the addiction, to compensate for the addiction, and to deny it, all at the same time. This system allows the family to stay together and to perform the basic functions of living. The active addiction of family members who do not use alcohol or drugs themselves is their participation in this system.

Participating in an addicted system takes a heavy toll on family members. They are often overwhelmed with emotion or out of control themselves. They may have temper outbursts, suicidal feelings, eating disorders, affairs, or obsessions and compulsions. Physical illness is common among family members of addicts. So it is easy for family members to say, "The problem is me."

Treatment

Family members in active addiction may need several different treatments at once if other pathological conditions exist in addition to familial addiction (the "dual-diagnosis" client). In such cases, provide or refer people to appropriate treatment for the coexisting conditions. Family members may need medical or psychiatric evaluation, evaluation for a substance addiction of their own, hospitalization, or shelter care before or while they address issues of familial addiction.

Treatment for familial addiction itself at this stage is largely educational and cognitive. Family members are often ignorant about what addiction actually is. If they do know, they insist that the criteria for addiction do not fit their family, and they are prepared to explain why. Cognitively, they are steeped in the delusion that there is no addiction in the family. From a behavioral perspective, they are unaware of behaviors of their own that maintain the addictive system. And from a psychodynamic point of view, they may be locked into their behaviors and cognitions by emotional issues.

Education

To educate your clients about addiction and coaddiction, first educate yourself by ongoing reading (see the end of the chapter for suggestions) and related course work. At times, you may recommend readings or films for the family members or simply tell them relevant points directly.

One outstanding educational resource is Al-Anon, a nonprofessional structured support group for families of alcoholics. It is called a "12-step program" because, in addition to group meetings, it provides an outline of suggested steps to take individually with the guidance of another Al-Anon member who functions as a mentor or "sponsor." During the active addiction phase, people are often reluctant to attend Al-Anon meetings because attendance means acknowledging that their loved one is an addict. But it's important to return to the issue, gently and respectfully, because Al-Anon can be enormously helpful. You may want to keep Al-Anon checklists and pamphlets on hand so you can give them to your clients. It's a good idea to attend some meetings yourself to become familiar with Al-Anon procedures and materials and also to experience personally some of the feelings that can arise regarding meeting attendance. There are other programs specifically for families of addicts using drugs other than alcohol, like Nar-Anon for families of narcotics addicts. Al-Anon is the most widespread and generally the most available program.

Cognitive Focus

Challenge defenses and distorted thinking directly. For example, in Jim's case, challenge his denial by helping him acknowledge how much his wife is actually drinking. Help him link her behavior and their interactions to her state of intoxication or withdrawal. Ask about daily life in his family, and help him see that much of what happens is organized around alcohol: social activities, fights, patterns of doing chores. Describe how he is sacrificing his own separate sense of self to join in an addictive system that allows him to maintain his attachment to Sandra by normalizing pathology. Try to help him understand how this system both serves him and harms him at the same time.

Behavioral Awareness

Try to help your clients become aware of the things they do that aid and abet the addiction of their loved one and that sacrifice themselves. For example, help Jim highlight his drinking with Sandra, pouring her drinks, doing her household tasks when she passes out, and losing his temper with her so that his loss of control becomes the designated problem. People at this stage resist efforts to look at their behavior and almost universally reject any suggestion that they might consider changing it. Before tactfully suggesting any change, work on understanding why your clients feel they must behave as they do. Family members, often blamed by the addict for the troubles in the family and drenched in self-blame as well, are likely to feel blamed when we target their behavior.

Psychodynamic Work

Turn to psychodynamic techniques when emotional issues stand in the way of clients' ability to alter their beliefs and behaviors. But there is a caveat in using psychodynamic methods at this stage. If you focus exclusively on feelings related to past times and events, or on transference/countertransference dynamics, you risk colluding with the clients' denial that their pain results from participating in an addictive family system right now. In fact, calling up strong feelings from the past can result in clients' clinging even more tightly to the familiar, if painful, addictive system. Use limited psychodynamic interventions mostly to target emotional issues that make recovery difficult.

For example, as Jim continues to deny the reality of his wife's addiction, and his role in maintaining it, ask him, "What would it mean to you if you thought you were living with an addict? Jim answers, "If my wife were an addict, what would that say about me? What kind of man am I if my own wife is out of control and I can't do anything about it?"

He later comes to realize that he has become just like his father, who berated his mother for her ideas and opinions about the world. Sandra's drinking functions to give Jim the same family patterns he had grown up with, even though his mother was not an alcoholic. He feels identified with his father by being disappointed in his wife the same way his father was disappointed with his mother.

As Jim learns about addiction and untangles the cognitive distortions that have blinded him to the addictive reality around him, he enters the next stage: transition.

STAGE II: TRANSITION ⊞

Transition is the beginning of movement into recovery. It includes two subphases: the addicted mode and the recovery mode.

Addicted Mode

Transition begins as family members start to understand that there is an addict in the family. At first, family members do not realize that they are powerless to control the addict. Instead, they may intensify their own efforts both to control him or her and to fix themselves—to be less demanding and more loving—so that the addict won't "have to" use chemicals. Typically, they also feel angry, guilty, frightened, and ashamed. As they come to recognize that their loved one is addicted and that there is nothing they can do to stop the drug use and its consequences, they often experience despair. Understandably, they may slip back into the delusion that nothing is really wrong with the addict and start again and again trying to fix things.

In the transition stage, a family member's life is often more chaotic than it was during the active addiction stage. The addict's behaviors and the consequences of those behaviors are becoming more traumatic as the disease of addiction progresses. Family members are also more out of control as they try to stop the inevitable decline of the family.

When a family member starts to see the addiction for what it is, to call it by its name, and to seek help and behave in new ways, things become even more chaotic. The family member may stop covering and compensating for the addict or may even ask the addict to leave. The addict fights back, trying to protect his or her addiction. The entire family is reeling, as basic tasks of life are no longer performed. Family members now can see the addiction and their own powerlessness, which causes extreme emotional pain. The old addictive system is starting to collapse, and with it the client's familiar way of life.

When family members reach this point, be ready: Things can get worse. Some of them will eventually give up on recovery and sink back into active addiction.

Treatment

When the family members are in the addicted mode of the transition stage, treatment is the same as it was in active addiction. Challenge thinking and behavior. Help family members see the addiction in the family, and point out and suggest changing behaviors that maintain it. Continue to focus on education and on clearing away psychological roadblocks to change.

For example: Kirsti is a family member in the addicted mode of the transition stage. She has been in therapy for 3 months, emphatically denying that her husband Tommy's drug use is a problem. Now she can see that his many nights and weekends away from home, his critical attitude toward her, the hang-ups on the telephone, and the family's financial problems are related to his addictions to cocaine and alcohol. She realizes she has closed her eyes to seeing this and is overwhelmed with shame, fear, and guilt. We sense that she realizes that things have to change and is desperate enough to risk new behaviors. So we shift our focus to behaviors. We give her Al-Anon pamphlets and meeting lists and talk with her about what it would be like to attend a meeting. She finally does attend one.

At her next session, she tells us that she was "turned off by all the whining" at the meeting. She told herself that she is not a whiner: She gets things done. So after the meeting she went home and scolded Tommy for using so much cocaine and alcohol. He told her that she was just trying to control him because she's such a controlling person. He called her uptight and judgmental. He told her that he has not used cocaine or alcohol for months and invited her out for drinks and dinner. Kirsti comes to her next therapy session saying how controlling, prudish, and intolerant she is. She has the problem, not Tommy. Why can't she be a better wife? No wonder Tommy drinks.

Kirsti has entered the transition stage, but her need to be close to Tommy keeps her in the addicted mode. At this point, she needs continued help to link his behavior with his drug use and also to explore her fears of trusting her own perceptions and facing life on her own. Then, when she finds evidence that he is having an affair, and gives up hope of being connected with him, she is ready to see his addiction again, with all of its devastating consequences for her. She enters the recovery mode of the transition stage.

Recovery Mode

When their attempts at control don't work, family members "hit bottom," just like the addict, acknowledging, in despair, that they are powerless over their loved one's addiction. Support them to tolerate this despair, and don't try to alleviate it, because this recognition and the despair it brings can propel them into recovery. When family members are able to acknowledge that they can't control the addiction of another, they begin to shift the focus of their attention to themselves and their own need to change.

Treatment

In working with family members in the recovery mode of the transition, emphasize a behavioral focus while maintaining a supportive, educational, and cognitive stance. Our clients now see clearly that they have an addict in the family. They can see that addiction is at the root of the addict's out-of-control behavior. They can see that they can't control the addict's drinking or drug use, or his or her behavior when under the influence. They are beginning to see that they contribute to the addictive system. This cognitive work has been done, but the new recovery is fragile. Maintaining it means resisting the temptation to rejoin the addicted relationships and the addictive family system. Most people can't tolerate this separateness without constant support and reinforcement.

Family members know very well how to survive in an addicted family system. But what do they do outside of one? Now they need help in knowing what to do—behavioral help.

Another reason to focus on behavior is that an addicted family system operates on impulse. In active addiction, it is hard to think ahead, to plan, to contain and tolerate feelings. The addict impulsively and compulsively uses alcohol and drugs, and the family members react impulsively and compulsively. They yell, scold, go numb, hide out, overeat, or starve themselves. Because of the dominance of impulse at this stage, we need to help family members establish behavioral alternatives to impulsive action so that they learn to substitute healthy behaviors for problematic ones.

First, *recommend that family members look outside the family for new influences and learning.* Why? Let's remember that the rules of the addicted family system are the only code of behavior known to the addict and the family. So if left to themselves, they do what they know: They act according to the addicted dynamics that prevented recovery in the first place. To avoid this natural return to pathology, family members need outside influence and help. Coming for psychotherapy is a step in this direction.

An important aid for expanding this process is participation in the Al-Anon program. Suggest that your clients substitute new behaviors—meeting attendance, phone calls to Al-Anon friends and sponsors, and Al-Anon readings—for old impulsive behaviors.

Most often, family members are still resistant to Al-Anon, even though they now recognize the addiction. It is difficult for them to see that *they* need help. And it may be very hard for them to see that they become out of control too—that they helped create the addicted family system. A good approach at this point in treatment is a combination of behavioral, cognitive, and focused psychodynamic interventions to help clients resolve resistance to everything recovery represents. Again, as in the addicted mode, use psychodynamic exploration only when there is an emotional issue blocking recovery. An attempt to elicit feelings for their own sake at this stage may increase impulsive behaviors, the outlet for strong feelings up to now.

To illustrate stage-appropriate psychotherapy in the recovery mode of the transition stage, meet John and Liz.

John and Liz sought help in parenting their 18-year-old son Johnny. He cut class, ignored homework assignments, and was failing his senior year. He had stolen from them, broken furniture in a rage, and struck his brother and Liz. After much struggle and soul searching, John and Liz realized that Johnny was addicted to alcohol and marijuana, and probably to cocaine and hallucinogens as well. They tried to "get him" clean and sober in every way they could think of, and nothing helped. They offered him treatment for drug addiction. He scornfully refused, insisting that he had no drug or alcohol problem. They now see that they cannot fix his problem. With sorrow and anxiety, they tell him that they are no longer willing to give him financial support except for alcohol and drug recovery treatment and that they cannot allow him to live in their home. They would like to salvage their own lives. Support them in this, and encourage them to attend Al-Anon for additional help and support.

Liz says that she and John did go to a meeting once but that she was horrified to find that no one responded when a woman at the meeting expressed her terrible emotional pain. Here, you might take an educational stance, explaining that Al-Anon has a "No Talk Rule": Members are asked not to respond to people who talk during the meeting in order to make sure that no one is met with a response that may feel critical or judgmental. However, members do respond personally to one another before and after meetings.

John has a different reaction to that meeting. He says that he couldn't stand having everyone in the room know that his son was such a "loser." Here too you might respond with education, validating and normalizing the feelings he has about Al-Anon. Acknowledge that he felt shame, a common feeling where there is an addict in the family. Everyone at the meeting has felt it too. Al-Anon can help people deal with that shame.

This is paradoxical: Acknowledge what they don't like. Validate their feelings, including the shame that they see in Al-Anon and feel themselves. Do not deny their experience or try to convince them to like Al-Anon, yet do encourage them to go.

When psychodynamic issues interfere with Al-Anon attendance, focus on those issues. People may need to open up the past in an individual or couples format before they can tolerate Al-Anon meetings. For example, to John, Al-Anon feels like the humiliating weekly "family meetings" he was subjected to in childhood, where he and his five siblings were made to confess their "sins" in front of their parents and one another. If you miss underlying meanings, experiences, and feelings, you may push too fast for action when reflection and understanding are called for. You can easily derail fragile, new recoveries by becoming invested in people's changing instead of paying attention to the reasons why they cannot yet change.

In the transition stage, people may go back and forth many times. They may "forget" that they can't control the addict and may revert to the "addicted mode" themselves as they slip back into their old thinking and behavior. It is painful to watch people lose their insight and go back to banging their heads against the same stone wall. But it is your job to tolerate your pain at seeing them revert to denial repeatedly. Remind yourself that you can't control or protect them any more than they can do this for the addict. Your wish to get family members to follow your recommendations may lead to control battles between you and your client, battles that you will lose. When you can be aware of such wishes, approach them as you do other "countertransference." Try to let your feelings teach you something about what your clients are dealing with, and seek consultation if you become too caught up or invested in outcome. Attending Al-Anon meetings yourself can also help you learn to maintain detachment with your clients and to respect their autonomy.

▦ STAGE III: EARLY RECOVERY

Early recovery is a time of stabilization of new behaviors and new knowledge, with the radical changes of the transition stage in place. What are the signs that family members have entered this stage?

The defining difference is that in this stage, family members are no longer driven by impulse. Instead of needing to engage in an immediate behavioral response, like yelling, overeating, berating themselves, or trying to control others, people now have other solid options. They have learned in the recovery mode of the transition stage to substitute the behaviors of abstinence for impulsive, out-of-control actions against themselves or others. Now they may call their sponsor or another recovering person automatically. They may read Al-Anon literature or take a walk. They may use a 12-step program slogan to help them contain their feelings. They try to remember that the impulse could be a reaction to some recent event and attempt to understand why they feel as they do. The difference from previous stages is that now they can think instead of having to act impulsively. Clients are feeling safer, quieter, and more reflective. They have settled into recovery rhythms, patterns, and ideas. Individuals can more easily maintain a focus on themselves, resisting pulls to return to addictive relationship dynamics. They now allow themselves to know that they love an addicted person. Their participation in the old dynamics of the addicted relationship or family system is much less, although they do not necessarily stop participating in the relationship or the family.

Treatment

In therapy, continue to help with solidification of new behavior and new learning. Remember that in active addiction and the addicted mode of the transition stage, the main thrust of treatment was cognitive: You challenged the family members to see the world differently. If that work was successful, they have experienced a radical change in paradigm: Their loved one is an addict, and they are coaddicts. In early recovery, as in transitional recovery, continue to focus on new behavior and cognitions. Maintaining and expanding new knowledge and behavior remain primary. Now, as in the recovery mode of the transition stage, help family members behave differently on the basis of their new knowledge. Behavioral, cognitive, and psychodynamic work may all be useful.

Behavioral

In early recovery, the therapist functions as a coach and monitor, offering support and listening for gaps in recovery development. Are there threats to new behavior and thinking? Are people adequately supported in their new worldview? Perhaps family members need to make structural changes in their lives so that they have the time and energy to focus on themselves. They may need to look at the responsibilities they are carrying and either get more help or give things up. Perhaps they need more Al-Anon meetings. Perhaps it is time for them to get a sponsor. Perhaps they need to widen their net of people to call in times of difficulty.

Cognitive

Family members need education about recovery itself: Where have they come from and where are they going? *The Family Recovery Guide* (Brown & Lewis, 2000) can be helpful here. It is a research-based handbook of information and exercises designed to help families understand and normalize the recovery process. Understanding the normal, predictable difficulties and seeing that others have found light at the end of the tunnel can help families tolerate the pain of recovery. *The Family Recovery Guide* can be used as the basis of a class or as a source of information for clients. For example, a handout like "What Parents Can Do" (Box 16.2) gives some ideas about how recovering parents can help their children. Another idea is the "mentor family." This is a recover-

---

BOX 16.2 **What Parents Can Do**

---

1. *Education:* Explain what alcoholism is in age-appropriate language. Explain that the children are not responsible for their parent's drinking or recovery. Explain what recovery means to you (the parents). Explain the importance of 12-step programs.

2. *Structure:* Provide organization in family life. Children need consistent routines and rules. Develop a family schedule for everyone to see.

3. *Tasks:* Assign and clarify tasks in the family. Discuss who does what and when. Make sure tasks are age appropriate. Keep in mind that the child may have felt special and powerful in the family as a result of the previous role, and avoid "demotions."

4. *Authority:* Clarify that the parents are in charge of the family. (Authority may be expressed in different styles, from relaxed to authoritarian.) Parents assume primary responsibility for family finances, structure, and guidelines of living together. Ask for input from older children.

5. *Humor, Fun, and Play:* Express joy and have fun. Look for humor in the recovery process. Celebrate important events, such as a 6-month anniversary of family recovery.

6. *Support:* Help your children find safe people for support. A safe person is someone who respects and listens to your children. Get to know your children's friends, and make them feel welcome.

7. *Resources:* Help teach children self-care.

   Physical: Discuss and post a list of emergency phone numbers and behaviors. Many children from alcoholic homes can already do basic tasks such as cooking and cleaning. Their main challenge is learning to ask for help. Parents who themselves ask for help from AA or Al-Anon provide a strong new model.

   Emotional: Listen if children need to talk, or make sure they have someone else to talk to. Teach them feeling words. Teach them to cope with difficult feelings by calling a friend, exercising, reading, drawing, etc.

SOURCE: Adapted from Brown and Lewis (1990); Brown and Lewis with Liotta (2000).

---

ing family who make themselves available to help and advise a family that is newer in recovery. Finding a mentor family can be a way to obtain crucial information, support, and inspiration through the recovery process. Treatment centers may be helpful in locating potential mentor families.

Psychodynamic

In early recovery, as in previous stages, use limited psychodynamic work to clear away roadblocks to recovery. If clients are stuck, or are tempted to return to their old thoughts and behaviors, look for emotional issues. As family members become less focused on the addict and are able to think more about themselves, unresolved and perhaps unconscious feelings and issues from the past may emerge. These may be expressed in anxiety, depression, or other symptoms of conflict and pain. Current situations often trigger past trauma, which may be addressed in a psychodynamic frame.

Or current issues may be problems in their own right. For example, one partner may be well rooted in recovery while the other has not made any changes. The gulf between them grows as each feels abandoned and betrayed by the other. They fear the end of their relationship if nothing changes. When issues like these come up, acknowledge the legitimacy of their fear. It is true that a partner in recovery and a partner who does not change may find themselves in different worlds and may eventually break up, whether the recovering person is an addict or a nonaddicted partner. In such a situation, psychodynamic methods may be helpful. For recovering partners, explore difficulties in being emotionally separate as you support them in holding onto their new behaviors and views. For nonrecovering partners, try to resolve resistances to entering recovery, while exploring why the recovering person's new behaviors feel threatening.

In early recovery, the foundations for new emotional development are solid, and the new structures of self are progressing. Family members maintain a focus on themselves, and psychotherapy helps them resist impulses to lose themselves in another. In the following example, both Carl and his alcoholic wife have 3 years of recovery. Carl describes how their recovering relationship system is now different from the addictive system:

> During the drinking, and in the first year or so of recovery, we could not discuss anything without spiraling into a fight. We were so tightly bound to each other that we couldn't get ourselves out of a messy fight once we were in it. But we could know, intellectually, that it wasn't good for us to be in it. We needed others to pull us apart, like giving us a hand out of quicksand. Back then, we were like puzzle pieces—separate completely, or tightly locked. Now we don't fall into those fights. We can both see them coming, so we call a time out and get help from others. We are like loose planets now, connected in a bigger space we share— our recovery programs—but not bound.

If Carl and his wife continue in this way, they will grow out of the early recovery stage into ongoing recovery.

STAGE IV: ONGOING RECOVERY ▦

Family members in ongoing recovery have internalized the cognitive and behavioral changes of previous stages. An addictive system involves sacrifice of self to maintain the pathology of the system. By ongoing recovery, the opposite has happened: The pathological system has been given up, and the self has been allowed to develop. Family members at this stage are no longer dedicating large amounts of psychic energy to denial and to defensive support of that denial. They are learning to give up both allowing others to control them and blaming others for the problems in their lives. They try to take responsibility for their own behavior and its consequences. They generally know that they neither cannot nor should not control others, and if an impulse to do so arises, they are able to think through the impulse rather than acting on it. In many cases, they are able to create for themselves an environment that is more stable and less traumatic than the one they were willing to tolerate in earlier stages, regardless of whether the addict is in recovery. As the self is allowed to develop, and impulsiveness gives way to an ability to think things through, suppressed and repressed emotions about past and present become available for psychodynamic work that can deepen the experience of self and also allow intimacy with others. An openness to factors and values beyond the self often develops, an experience that some call "spirituality."

Treatment

At this stage in the process, recovering family members face difficult tasks. They need to discover and tolerate their feelings, to recover from the trauma they have experienced, and to resolve difficulties in intimacy with others. Turn to psychodynamic methods to address these issues. Use educational, cognitive, and behavioral approaches as needed when internal or external events threaten the client with relapse to old thoughts and behaviors. But for the most part, work with the family members' feelings and the memories that go with them.

Often, people who have been in close relationships with addicts are afraid of their feelings. Their experience has been that feelings—their own or others'—have meant terrifying out-of-control behavior. Recognize these fears, and also encourage clients to express emotions to learn that they can be tolerated safely and will pass. Feelings related to the traumatic experiences of addicted relationships are particularly frightening to clients. Encourage them to tell you their traumatic experiences as they become ready to do so and to have the feelings that go with them. Often, Al-Anon can function as part of a complete trauma treatment plan by providing another safe, validating place to tell the traumatic stories.

Psychodynamic techniques are useful in ongoing recovery to help family members resolve blocks to trust and closeness with others, blocks created as protection in an addictive system. Help family members see the ways that they keep you and others in their lives at a distance. At this stage, you may refer your clients to couples, family, or group therapies as supplements if needed to help them achieve interpersonal intimacy. Groups for adult children of alcoholics can be particularly useful.

In ongoing recovery, David looks back on where he was and where he is now:

I can see that I'm no longer trying to get Mom to stop drinking and using Valium. I'm not telling Ginger and Bessie [his sisters] what they oughta do about Mom. I just know that I don't visit her or talk on the phone [with her] when she's drinking. Now we can have Christmas and Thanksgiving just for the kids and Evie and me. I don't let Mom step all over me, and you know what? When mom's sober, I can even enjoy her. I used to be totally shocked and devastated when she started drinking again. I still feel bad when that happens, but now I know it's part of her disease. And Evie and I are getting closer. I'm beginning to see what she means about me getting angry with her when she needs my support. I'm realizing in my therapy that when Evie needs me, I start feeling the way I did as a kid when mom was screaming at me to clean up the dishes she broke, or yelling at me that I couldn't go to baseball practice because she was too sick to mind the girls.

⌗ CONCLUSION

The stages of recovery involve self-reclamation and development as family members of addicts progressively disengage themselves from the addictive family system. Using stage-appropriate psychotherapy, employ largely cognitive and educational methods in the active addiction stage and the addicted mode of the transition stage. This helps family members dissolve barriers to believing the evidence of their own senses and allows them to see the addiction in the family, as well as their own behavior that maintains it. Suggest alternate behaviors and use psychodynamic methods in a targeted fashion. In the recovery mode of the transition stage and in early recovery, behavioral methods take center stage, with continuing cognitive reinforcement, as family members learn and practice new recovery-oriented behaviors. In these stages, psychodynamic methods play a supporting role when the individual cannot maintain recovery. Finally, in ongoing recovery, psychodynamic work becomes the focus to help people recognize and express their feelings, recover from trauma, and resolve blocks to closeness and intimacy with others. We expect that at the end of this process, we will see family members who have emerged with a new, separate self, no longer dominated by someone else's addiction.

REFERENCES ▓

Brown, S., & Lewis, V. (1990). *Maintaining abstinence programs (MAPS).* Unpublished curriculum, Family Recovery Research Project, Mental Research Institute, Palo Alto, CA.

Brown, S., Lewis, V., & Liotta, A. (2000). *The family recovery guide: A map for healthy growth.* Oakland, CA: New Harbinger.

Frank, S. H., Graham, A. V., Zyzanski, S. J., & White, S. (1992). Use of the Family CAGE in screening for alcohol problems in primary care. *Archives of Family Medicine, 1,* 209-216.

ADDITIONAL SUGGESTED READINGS ▓

Brown, S. (1992). *Safe passage.* New York: John Wiley.

> Presents the experiences of adult children of alcoholics from a developmental point of view in vivid, simple, and clear language. Useful for adult children of alcoholics to read.

Brown, S., & Lewis, V. (1995). The alcoholic family: A developmental model of recovery. In S. Brown (Ed.), *Treating alcoholism* (chap. 8). San Francisco: Jossey-Bass.

Brown, S., & Lewis, V. (1999). *The alcoholic family in recovery: A developmental model.* New York: Guilford.

> Based on the Family Recovery Project research study conducted by Brown and Lewis. Applies Brown's developmental model of recovery to the whole family. Describes in detail stages of family recovery, with examples from recovering families.

Brown, S., & Schmid, J. (1999). Adult children of alcoholics. In P. J. Ott, R. E. Tarter, & R. T. Ammerman (Eds.), *Sourcebook on substance abuse* (pp. 416-429). Boston: Allyn & Bacon.

> Updates research, assessment, and treatment concepts for adult children of alcoholics.

Herman, J. (1992). *Trauma and recovery.* New York: Basic Books.

> Principles of recovery from trauma, applicable to working with traumatized members of addicted families.

Lawson, G., & Lawson, A. (1989). *Alcoholism and substance abuse in special populations.* Gaithersburg, MD: Aspen.

> Contains material on addiction in different cultures, ethnicities, and sexual orientations.

Schmid, J. (1995). Alcoholism and the family. In S. Brown (Ed.), *Treating alcoholism* (chap. 10). San Francisco: Jossey-Bass.

Steinglass, P., et al. (1987). *The alcoholic family.* New York: Basic Books.

> Based on research with families; looks at normal stages of family development in alcoholic context.

VanBree, G. (1995). Treating the alcoholic couple. In S. Brown (Ed.), *Treating alcoholism* (chap. 9). San Francisco: Jossey-Bass.

▦ FILMS

Desert Bloom. Columbia Pictures. (1986). Commercial film: view of life with an alcoholic, war-traumatized stepfather through the eyes of teenage girl. Demonstrates emotional traumas and addicted family system.

Once Were Warriors. Fine Line Features and Communicado in association with the New Zealand Film Commission. (1995). Commercial film: tragic story of violent ethnic alcoholic family in New Zealand and their dearly bought emergence from addiction to recovery. Example of highly traumatizing and neglectful alcoholic family.

Treating Alcoholism With Stephanie Brown, PhD: Vol. 2. The Developmental Model in Theory: A Live Workshop. (1997). Directed by George Spies, produced by Victor Yalom. Available from Jaylen Productions, 4625 California Street, San Francisco, CA 94118. Lecture, question-and-answer presentation of the developmental model as it applies to the alcoholic. Aids understanding of the developmental model and of the alcoholic's experience during addiction/recovery.

When a Man Loves a Woman. Touchstone Pictures. Commercial film that accurately presents the progress of a family from addiction through early recovery.

HOLISTIC TOOLS

17

Nutritional Counseling

How to Get the Big High

Joseph D. Beasley

n the last 20 years, I have treated directly or supervised the diagnosis, treatment, and care of over 15,000 chemically dependent patients. I have also continually studied and researched these complex biobehavioral diseases. Restoring the nutritional and biochemical equilibrium and health of the body is absolutely essential to achieving and maintaining high recovery rates in the treatment of addiction.

As clinicians, we are all pressed for time, and modern insurance and managed care keep forcing us, if we are to survive economically, to spend less and less time in patient education, diagnosis, and treatment. However, if you educate yourself and use the proper teaching guides/aids, you can add the important nutritional modality to your individual and professional capacity. The benefits of high recovery rates to your practices are well worth the effort.

The hard fact for those of us who treat alcoholism and drug abuse without using nutritional principles is that most recovery programs don't work. When you limit your practice to the usual and standard treatment protocols in your specialties, omitting nutritional counseling, you will find yourself with high treatment failure rates. Consider the following:

- Up to 70% of individuals who start treatment programs drop out before the end of the first year (Gordis, Dorth, Sepe, & Smith, 1981).
- One study of a hospital-based program found that 45% of the patients dropped out of contact within the first month (Emrick, 1975).
- Almost 25 years ago, a review of 384 recovery rate studies of patients who participated in alcoholism treatment programs compared with a sample of alcoholics who received no treatment found that alcoholics who received absolutely no treatment were just as likely to stop drinking for 6 months (or more) as those who received treatment (Emrick, 1975; Gordis et al., 1981).

- In 1985, a study published in the *New England Journal of Medicine* detailed the status of 400 patients with alcoholism who had received standard treatment 3 years before. The findings were very depressing to those of us in the field. Only 15% of the patients had maintained their sobriety; 85% of those treated had not been able to stay in recovery (Helzer et al., 1985).

- Another study published in 1985 reported that 60 out of 100 alcoholic patients in our society would never receive treatment for their disease. This same study predicted that only 5 of the 40 who did get treatment would achieve "measurable sobriety" (Williams, 1985).

Although these results come from early studies, studies published since 1985, with few exceptions, are no more encouraging. In fact, the number of patients with alcoholism cross-addicted with other drugs has increased dramatically. The National Household Survey on Drug Abuse shows that overall teenage drug use increased by 78% from 1994 to 1998 (Substance Abuse and Mental Health Services Administration [SAMHSA], 2000). The recovery rate of patients who are dually addicted to alcohol and other drugs and who are treated by current conventional methods is even lower than that for patients treated for alcoholism addiction alone. These results are discouraging, but let's take a look at the exciting future for both patients and those of us who are attempting to treat addictive disease.

▦ ADDICTION PREVENTION AND TREATMENT

Addiction is one facet of a vast number of conditions that are giving the United States the highest levels of chronic human disease in history. We are literally experiencing a pandemic of chronic physical and mental illness.

The causes of our epidemic, and especially the epidemiology of the superimposed, rising levels of alcohol/drug abuse/addiction, are complex, but they involve at least the following:

1. *Genetics*: Inherited differences in metabolism, nutritional needs, neurochemistry, and the like can render us more susceptible to the toxic and addictive effects of many substances (including foods).

2. *Allergy*: Unique susceptibilities to various pollens, foods, and other substances contribute to overall ill health and many cravings.

3. *Toxicity*: Heavy metals and hundreds of toxic chemicals (such as lead, cadmium, PCBs, and insecticides) contaminate our water, air, and food supplies.

4. *Malnutrition*: This is the result of eating a "typical American diet," as full of saturated fat, sugars, and chemical additives as it is deficient in the most important nutrients.

5. *Cultural pressures*: Our society promotes alcohol and many other legal drugs (such as caffeine and cigarettes) as the way to success, popularity, and happiness; often glamorizes illegal drug use as part of chic "alternative lifestyles"; and worships at the altar of leanness even as more than 40% of the population is overweight.

6. *Psychological distress/mental illness*: This can exacerbate (and be exacerbated by) the above factors and sometimes serves as the immediate trigger for using potentially addictive substances and starting compulsive patterns of behavior.

The data indicate that most of the U.S. population—children, teenagers, and adults—are operating physically and mentally at a suboptimum level. As reported in a special joint briefing by the American Medical Association and the American Diabetes Association, "The rise in childhood Type 2 (adult onset) diabetes has reached epidemic levels" (American Diabetes Association, 2001; see also Burke et al., 1999). The high rate of Type 2 diabetes is associated with the severe diet and lifestyle factors associated with the over 50% obesity rate among adolescents and the increasing rates of hypertension and atherosclerosis also now commonly seen in the adolescent population. This disease trend, according to Henry Ginsberg, MD, Professor of Medicine at Columbia University, raises "fear of heart attacks at age 30" (American Diabetes Association, 2001). The higher rates of chronic diseases in the United States are now affecting younger and younger age groups. What could we be if we were not all chronically ill from the way we feed ourselves and conduct our lifestyle? It now appears necessary to address as many of the above lifestyle factors as possible as an integral component of addiction treatment.

IMPROVING RECOVERY RATES BY ADDING ▦ NUTRITIONAL IMPROVEMENTS AND BIOCHEMICAL STABILIZATION TO TREATMENT PROTOCOLS

In the 1940s and 1950s, researchers under the direction of the late Roger Williams, director of the Clayton Foundation for Biochemical Research at the University of Texas, conducted some remarkable research concerning the prevention of alcohol toxicity and alcohol consumption in cell cultures and laboratory animals. Williams and his colleagues found that bacterial cultures show retarded growth when they are exposed to relatively small concentrations of alcohol. If one increases the levels of alcohol in these cultures, it causes the death of the cultures, but when the level of amino acids and other nutrients in the cultures is increased, the cultures are protected against the severe toxic effects of alcohol (Ravel, Felsing, Lansford, Trubey, & Shive, 1955).

Williams and colleagues also investigated the impact of diet on alcohol consumption in animals. When given a free choice between alcohol and water, nutritionally deficient animals chose alcohol far more often than their well-nourished controls. "When the animals were given well-fortified diets supplemented with vitamins, they all developed wisdom of the body and turned away from alcohol consumption" (Rogers, Pelton, & Williams, 1955, p. 241; see also Rogers, Pelton, & Williams, 1956).

This classical scientific work in the early 1980s—first cellular research, then research with experimental animals—formed the basis for clinical research with human subjects. One of the first studies to demonstrate the power of nutritional treatment in humans was conducted in the early 1980s by Guenther (1983). From her extensive review of the scientific literature, she knew that most alcoholics were malnourished and that the majority of them return to drinking even after treatment. What would happen, she wondered, if nutritional therapy were added to a standard alcoholism treatment program? Could humans regain their "wisdom of the body" in the same way experimental animals had nearly three decades before?

To investigate this possibility, Guenther undertook a study at an alcoholism treatment unit in a local Veterans Administration medical center. The control group consisted of patients in a 28-day inpatient treatment program that included detoxification, alcohol education, AA meetings, AA-oriented group counseling, and work incentive, followed by outpatient follow-up care. The study groups went through the same program and were given in addition nutrition education, dietary supplements, and an enhanced nutritional program, delineated below. Both groups were in treatment for 28 days with the same physicians, social workers, nurses, educational program, and counseling. The nutrition treatment was the only difference between the two groups.

The nutrition program consisted of dietary change, vitamin and mineral supplements, and nutrition education. The normal hospital diet was adjusted to include wheat germ and bran with each meal, whole-grain bread, decaffeinated beverages, sugar substitutes, and unsweetened canned, frozen, or fresh fruits for dessert instead of pies, cakes, puddings, or sweetened fruits. Nuts, cheese, and whole-grain bread and peanut butter were available for snacks.

Individual and family education included weekly classes on the basics of nutrition, menu planning, shopping and food preparation, and how to read labels to recognize hidden sugars, alcohol, and preservatives. Patients were taught about the effects of alcoholism on their health and nutritional state and the importance of maintaining a healthy diet and lifestyle after their discharge. Most important, they were given specific, useful information on how they could actively improve their health and well-being in recovery and were encouraged to maintain this regimen after leaving the hospital. From Day 1 through their discharge, patients were encouraged to regard the nutritional principles as their lifelong plan.

Six months after their discharge from the hospital, 81% of the study group were not drinking, compared with only 38% of the control group. Because all the patients were randomly selected and assigned to either the study group or a control group, the only difference between the two groups was the element of nutritional therapy. Although some members of the study group admitted to slacking off on their diet and supplements, the difference in recovery rates cannot have been mere chance (in fact, statistical analysis showed that the odds of these results occurring by chance were less than 2 in 1,000). As one patient said, "Something has helped, because I don't crave alcohol anymore." Another explained it as "I not only lost my cravings, but I lost my jitters and troubles sleeping. You get your health—you get more resistance."

Several years later, I led a research team at Brunswick Hospital Center and at Comprehensive Medical Care in New York in conjunction with statistical experts at the State University of New York Medical Center at Stony Brook (Beasley et al., 1991). We used a similar program with 111 patients who had severe and chronic alcoholism. All had long and difficult histories of alcohol and drug abuse, with many failed treatment attempts (one had been through 20 detoxifications). All their diets were deficient; 80% were overtly clinically malnourished, almost two thirds had liver disease, and almost half were also addicted to other drugs. On the whole, they were a difficult group with little apparent chance of achieving long-term sobriety. Would a combined program of nutritional restoration and psychological measures succeed where other primarily psychological measures had not?

The patients spent 28 days in the hospital in a treatment program similar to that designed by Guenther and her colleagues. In addition to nutrition education, supplements, and a monitored diet, each patient underwent blood testing to identify potential food allergens. During inpatient treatment, each patient's diet was individualized to limit exposure to these foods.

At the end of the 28 days, the patients began a 12-month program of medical follow-up. In addition to aftercare and AA meetings, patients came in at least once a month for medical evaluations and workups, nutrition counseling and supplements, and random urine screens and blood work.

At the end of 1 year, 91 of the original 111 patients were still in the program. Of these, 74% were sober and stable (confirmed by lab work and at least one significant other). The research and treatment teams were pleased. After years of reading about failure rates hovering around 85%, we were finally seeing successful outcomes. And if these results could be achieved by patients with such severe dual addictions and discouraging histories, the prospects for individuals in the early stage of addiction are truly bright, provided that they receive the right kind of care. Indeed, it should be possible to turn those 85% failure rates into 85% success.

These studies and many others show that your chemically dependent clients will benefit significantly from the nutritional and biochemical tools I describe in this chapter. I venture to say that no matter what other recovery tools you use to help your clients, your program will be incomplete without proper attention to nutritional principles. In my view, neglecting nutritional and biochemical tools is negligent patient care, regardless of whether the treatment occurs in an inpatient or outpatient setting.

HELPING YOUR PATIENT ⊞
PRACTICE OPTIMAL NUTRITION

How do we help the patient practice optimal nutrition? Susan Knightly, a master chef, and I wrote *Food for Recovery, The Complete Nutritional Companion for Recovering From Alcoholism, Drug Addiction, and Eating Disorders* (1994). If your patients can read and comprehend at a seventh-grade level, this book will provide all the information they need to know.

Nutritional science has only emerged during the last 100 years. For most of recorded history, people have thought that anything they could get to eat that didn't eat them, or poison them, was good nutrition. Millions of sailors died horrible deaths from scurvy (a chronic vitamin C deficiency) before the importance of providing fruits (particularly limes) on long voyages was recognized and acted upon. Because the British Navy was the first to use this practice, English sailors were nicknamed "limeys."

The human body is designed so that if it has the proper nutritional building blocks (about 50 at last count), it can build the miraculous number of biochemical compounds it must have to conduct the thousands of complex biochemical processes that maintain life. Each of us has biochemically individual and unique engines. Optimal nutrition involves fitting the types of fuel to our individually designed bodies so that they can function optimally.

The 50 essential nutrients, along with their sources, their functions, and the foods they are contained in, are outlined in Box 17.1.

WHERE, WHEN, AND WITH WHOM DOES ⊞
THE THERAPY TOOL OF NUTRITIONAL
COUNSELING WORK BEST/LEAST WELL?

Nutritional counseling is such a fundamental requirement of recovery that you must find a way to educate and motivate each and all of your patients. This tool works best for

BOX 17.1 **Essential Nutrients and Their Functions**

I. The Essential Macronutrients

The macronutrients are

Water

Carbohydrates

Fats

Protein

Fiber

The carbohydrates, fats, and protein provide essential calories.

A. Protein

Protein contains essential amino acids:

1. Arginine(for children)
2. Histidine (for children)
3. Leucine
4. Isoleucine
5. Lysine
6. Methionine
7. Phenylalanine
8. Thereonine
9. Tryptophan
10. Valine

Sources: Fish, chicken, beef, pork, beans, peas, and other vegetables/grains.

Functions: To provide essential nutrients and the essential amino acids, which are the building blocks of protein.

Signs of Deficiency: Muscle wasting, weight loss, malnutrition, and disease.

B. Carbohydrates

Sources: Fruits, vegetables, grains, and legumes.

Functions: To provide vitamins, minerals, essential nutrients, fiber, and energy.

Signs of Deficiency: Muscle wasting, weight loss, malnutrition, and disease.

C. Fats

Fats contain essential fatty acids:

1. Linoleic acid
2. Linolenic acid
3. Arachidonic acid

Sources: Animal fats, dairy products, and vegetable oils. The fish oils and the nonhydrogenated vegetable oils are the main sources of the essential fatty acids. They are contained in the following types of fat:

— *Saturated fat*: Chicken fat, lard, beef tallow, palm oil, butter, cocoa butter, palm kernel/oil coconut meat/oil.

— *Monounsaturated fat*: Olive oil, canola oil, peanut oil, sunflower oil.

— *Polyunsaturated fat*: Safflower oil, corn oil, soybean oil, cottonseed oil, sesame oil, sunflower oil, fish oils.

Functions: To provide the essential fatty acids, calories, and energy.

Signs of Deficiency: Same symptoms as those for the fat-soluble vitamins listed in the micronutrients.

D. Fiber

Sources: Vegetables, fruits, grains, and legumes.

Functions: Bulk for proper digestion.

Signs of Deficiency: Constipation, indigestion.

II. The Essential Micronutrients

A. Vitamins

1. Vitamin A

Sources: fish, fish oils, eggs, green and yellow vegetables, dairy products.

Functions: maintains health of skin and photoreceptors in the retina.

Signs of Deficiency: night blindness, rough skin, dry eyes, corneal softening and clouding.

Signs of Toxicity: headaches, peeling skin, enlarged spleen.

2. Vitamin B1

Sources: whole grains, meats, nuts, legumes, potatoes.

Functions: carbohydrate metabolism nerve function, heart function.

Signs of Deficiency: nerve damage (Wernicke-Korsakoff syndrome).

3. Vitamin B2

Sources: fish, liver, meats, whole grains, legumes.

Functions: energy and protein metabolism, maintains integrity of mucous membranes.

Signs of Deficiency: dryness, scaling, and splitting of lips and mouth, corneal changes, dry and inflamed skin.

4. Vitamin B5 (Pantothenic Acid): This nutrient is so widely distributed in the major macronutrients that it is unusual to have recognizable signs of a deficiency.

5. **Vitamin B6**

   Sources: fish, liver, meats, whole grains, legumes.

   Functions: crucial to metabolism, linoleic acid helps convert tryptophan to niacin; important in formation of blood cells and blood clotting.

   Signs of Deficiency: anemias, skin neuropathy convulsions (in infants); contributes to development of dependency syndromes.

6. **Vitamin B12**

   Sources: liver, meats, eggs, milk and milk products.

   Functions: maturation of red blood cells, nerve function, DNA synthesis, folate and methionine metabolism.

   Signs of Deficiency: anemias, psychological disorders, loss of visual acuity; contributes to development of dependency syndromes.

7. **Biotin**

   Sources: liver, kidney, yeast, egg yolk, cauliflower, nuts, legumes.

   Functions: amino acid and fatty acid metabolism.

   Signs of Deficiency: inflammation of the skin and tongue; contributes to development of dependency syndromes.

8. **Niacin**

   Sources: dried yeast, liver, meat, fish, legumes, enriched whole-grain products.

   Functions: carbohydrate metabolism, oxidation-reduction reactions.

   Signs of Deficiency: inflamed, peeling skin and tongue, gastrointestinal disorders (including severe diarrhea), central nervous system dysfunction (dementia).

9. **Folic Acid**

   Sources: fresh green leafy vegetables, fruit, organ meats, liver, dried yeast.

   Functions: maturation of red blood cells, synthesis of components of DNA.

   Signs of Deficiency: anemias, red blood cell abnormalities, neural tube defects (infants of folic acid-deficient mothers).

10. **Vitamin C**

    Sources: green peppers, citrus fruits, tomatoes, potatoes, cabbage.

    Functions: bone formation, vascular function, tissue respiration and repair.

    Signs of Deficiency: inflammation of the gums and mouth, tooth loss, hemorrhaging.

11. **Vitamin D**

    Sources: sunlight, fish liver oils, egg yolk, liver, fortified dairy products.

    Functions: absorption and utilization of calcium and phosphorous bone formation.

    Signs of Deficiency: rickets.

    Signs of Toxicity: anorexia, kidney failure, calcification of soft tissues.

12. **Vitamin E**

    Sources: vegetable oils, wheat germ, green leafy vegetables, egg yolk, legumes.

    Functions: stability of cellular membranes, antioxidant.

    Signs of Deficiency: loss of hemoglobin from red blood cells, muscle damage.

13. **Vitamin K**

    Sources: cabbage, cauliflower, spinach, and other green leafy vegetables, cereals, soybeans, and other vegetables. Vitamin K is also made by the bacteria lining the gastrointestinal tract.

    Functions and Signs of Deficiency: Vitamin K is known as the clotting vitamin because without it blood would not clot. Some studies indicate that it helps in maintaining strong bones in the elderly.

B. **Minerals**

1. **Sodium**

   Sources: most processed foods; naturally in seafood, sea vegetables, and cheeses.

   Functions: fluid balance, nerve transmission, muscle contractility.

   Signs of Deficiency: dehydration.

   Signs of Toxicity: mental confusion, coma.

2. **Potassium**

   Sources: bananas, prunes, raisins, milk.

   Functions: nerve transmission, muscle activity, and fluid retention.

   Signs of Deficiency: cardiac disturbances, paralysis.

   Signs of Toxicity: same as deficiency.

3. **Calcium**

   Sources: milk and milk products, meat, fish, eggs, whole grains, beans, fruits, vegetables.

   Functions: bone and tooth formation, blood clotting, cardiac function, muscle function.

   Signs of Deficiency: neuromuscular hyperexcitability.

   Signs of Toxicity: diarrhea, renal failure, psychosis.

BOX 17.1   Continued

4. **Phosphorus**

Sources: milk and milk products, meat, poultry, fish, whole grains, nuts, legumes.
Functions: bone and tooth formation, part of DNA, energy production.
Signs of Deficiency: irritability, weakness, blood cell disorders, gastrointestinal and renal problems.
Signs of Toxicity: kidney failure.

5. **Magnesium**

Sources: green leaves, nuts, whole grains, seafoods.
Functions: bone and tooth formation, nerve conduction, enzyme activation, muscle contraction.
Signs of Deficiency: neuromuscular irritability, respiratory failure, cardiac disturbances.
Signs of Toxicity: low blood pressure.

6. **Iron**

Sources: widely distributed in most foods other than dairy products, but less than 20% is absorbed by the body.
Functions: blood formation, enzyme function.
Signs of Deficiency: anemia.
Signs of Toxicity: liver damage, skin pigment changes, diabetes; may contribute to the development of heart disease.

7. **Iodine**

Sources: seafoods, sea vegetables, dairy products.
Functions: thyroid function, energy control mechanisms.
Signs of Deficiency: goiter, brain damage (in infants).
Signs of Toxicity: skin changes, swollen lips and nose.

8. **Fluorine**

Sources: widely distributed.
Functions: bone and tooth formation.
Signs of Deficiency: tooth decay, osteoporosis.
Signs of Toxicity: pitted teeth, spinal spurs.

9. **Zinc**

Sources: widely distributed in vegetables but not well absorbed.
Functions: wound healing, growth, enzyme and insulin formation.
Signs of Deficiency: growth retardation, gastrointestinal problems, skin disorders, liver damage.

10. **Copper**

Sources: organ meats, oysters, nuts, legumes, whole grains.
Functions: component of enzymes.
Signs of Deficiency: anemia, Menke's kinky hair syndrome.
Signs of Toxicity: liver damage.

11. **Cobalt**

Sources: green leafy vegetables.
Functions: part of B12 molecule.
Signs of Deficiency: anemia.
Signs of Toxicity: cardiomyopathy.

12. **Chromium**

Sources: brewer's yeast; widely distributed in most foods.
Functions: glucose metabolism.
Signs of Deficiency: impaired glucose tolerance in malnourished children and diabetics.

The other essential minerals are

13. Manganese
14. Tin
15. Nickel
16. Silicon
17. Molybdenum
18. Selenium
19. Vanadium
20. Arsenic
21. Chlorine

These are so widely distributed and combined with other minerals that there is rarely a deficiency or sign of deficiency except in overt starvation or bizarre diets.

individuals who are intelligent and have strong family support and least well for those who are mentally impaired and without the support/knowledge of significant others. One of the important challenges to you, the therapist, is to find ways to help each patient to develop and maintain optimum nutrition and a toxic-free state to the fullest extent possible.

POTENTIAL DIFFICULTIES TO ⊞ ANTICIPATE AND MINIMIZE

I have faced several difficulties in adding nutritional therapy to the treatment protocols for chemical addiction. First, almost all our patients and an unfortunately high percentage of professionals are monumentally ignorant about the principles of sound nutrition (Pierce, 1976; Rudell, 1979).

Second, during the past century, several factors drastically changed the diet and nutritional intake/habits of the U.S. population (Agricultural Research Service, 1975). Whereas once 90% of the population lived in rural areas and either grew their own food or were very near to where food was produced, now the situation is reversed: As of 1990, 90% of the population were living in metropolitan areas far removed from their food supply (U.S. Bureau of the Census, 1995), so that the food supply had to be processed or manufactured to avoid spoilage. This necessity has given rise to the largest industry in the United States—the food-processing industry.

Further, whereas in the past many women had homemaking as a primary role and took on the tasks of food shopping, meal planning, preparation, and cleanup as a part of that role, today a large percentage of women are working outside the home and are less and less inclined to devote much time to these activities. Often, men have little time or inclination for food preparation either. Also, many people have few skills in food preparation. Thus, they rely increasingly on less nutritious preprepared and processed foods. Finally, TV, radio, billboards, and print constantly present advertisements from the food-processing industry enticing us to consume non-nutritional food.

Because of these and many other large changes in our way of life, it is no wonder that we are a malnourished, chronically ill nation and that almost half of men, women, and children are overweight. Add to this the toxic and malnourishing effects of chemical addiction and we begin to get an idea of the scope of the problem. Only when we consider the emotional, cultural, traditional, ethnic, and economic aspects of nutritional practice can we glimpse the difficulty of changing nutritional patterns and individual behavior in contemporary society.

The treatment tools and resources noted in this chapter are designed to help therapists become more knowledgeable and better able to educate their patients and clients. By recognizing and applying the tools outlined in Boxes 17.2 and 17.3, the treatment team can better deal with and overcome the obstacles discussed above.

BOX 17.2 Do's and Don'ts of Nutritional Counseling

As a Practitioner, Do Not:	As a Practitioner, Do:	Promotes Recovery Because:
Think nutritional and biochemical stabilization is unimportant for patients.	Learn the essentials of nutritional science so that you are comfortable and effective in giving your patients nutritional counseling.	Data indicate that adding the regimens recommended in this chapter increases recovery rates over matched controls.
Let yourself be discouraged by ignorant practitioners who minimize the importance of nutrition to recovery.	Get armed with good science; go forward, and encourage others to follow suit.	Patients become both knowledgeable and confident about the importance of nutrition to recovery.
Allow your patients to continue with a high refined sugar and refined carbohydrate diet (e.g., white bread) (refined sugars and carbohydrates now constitute 40% of the average U.S. diet; see Bill W.'s story, Williams, 1968, of the improvements in his own sobriety when he improved his nutritional practices).	Teach your patients to shop for and prepare meals with natural sugars from fruits and some vegetables and to eat whole-grain cereals, bread, and pasta.	This stabilizes the insulin, adrenaline, and blood sugar levels, an effect that in turn helps to stabilize the serotonin-dopamine neurotransmitters and greatly decreases anxiety, depression, mood swings, fatigue, and cravings.
Allow your patients to continue in their addiction and consume high doses of caffeine and refined sugar in soft drinks, tea, coffee, and other beverages.	Encourage your patients to eliminate caffeine entirely or limit it to that contained in two cups of coffee, tea, or cola beverages per 24-hour period. Substitute with fruit juices, herbal teas, or decaffeinated teas and coffees.	Caffeine is a strong and very addictive stimulant. It has direct stimulating effects on the nerve cells, but it also has a significant effect on the entire body. Caffeine gives the nervous system the message that it is in danger and prepares the individual for a "fight or flight" reaction. Those who consume it are initially more alert and energetic, but over time, if caffeine raises the energy levels by a factor of two, it raises the rebound fatigue levels by a factor of three. Biochemically, caffeine has a similar effect to refined sugar and refined carbohydrates. The more caffeine consumed, the more intense the fight/flight message. This contributes to fatigue, depression, and cravings for addictive substances.
Let patients consume the 9 to 10 pounds of chemical food additives, pesticides, hormones, and antibiotics that the average citizen eats and drinks in a year if he or she eats the U.S. diet as advertised on TV, etc.	Encourage your patients to eat more fresh fruits, vegetables, and antibiotic/hormone-free beef, pork, chicken, turkey, and seafood.	This dietary change decreases the load of foreign chemical and free radicals the body has to deal with. Also, some people have adverse reactions to specific chemicals (such as MSG).
Allow your patients to go long periods of time without eating.	Encourage your patients to eat more frequent, smaller meals with some protein at every meal; to eat breakfast, lunch, and dinner; and to have whole-food snacks in between and at bedtime.	Starvation can cause imbalance in insulin, glucose, adrenalin, serotonin, and dopamine levels and trigger biochemical fight/flight messages. Frequent meals stabilize levels of these substances and consequently stabilize mood as well; they also reduce fatigue and cravings.

Allow your patients to ignore nutritional aspects of their recovery.	Teach your patients to shop for and prepare whole foods as chemically free as possible. Show them how to set a pleasant table and enjoy foods in a leisurely manner, and remind them that breakfast is the most important meal of the day.	Good nutrition is not only essential to regaining health and sobriety but pleasant and enjoyable. Eating with family and friends promotes bonding, communication, and good digestion.
Be misled by physicians or other health professionals and lay people who claim you do not need nutritional supplements.	Teach your patients to take nutritional supplements that contain the optimum nutrients listed in Table 17.3. Show your patients that nutrition and lifestyle change can dramatically increase their recovery.	The level of intake that I recommend is optimal for the first 3 months of recovery. Then it can be reduced by one third. Supplements may be purchased at any health food store or pharmacy or in simple-to-take packages at www.addictionend.com, a nonprofit organization organized to promote research and education in chemical dependency (see box).
Neglect to advise your patients to start exercising and not be couch potatoes.	Under supervision of a physician or other health care professional, have your patients start exercising gradually, building tolerance, capability, and enjoyment.	Exercise stimulates and promotes internal nutrition, raises the body's metabolic rate to provide more energy, and encourages weight maintenance or loss. It also helps to stabilize the dopamine/serotonin neurotransmitters and increases the production of endorphins. The patient's own endorphins are the most powerful painkillers and pleasure givers that science has discovered.
Allow patients to isolate and have little contact with family and friends.	Encourage your patients to seek out and spend time with family and friends. Work out, with your patients, the most appropriate counseling and support modalities.	Anxiety shared is anxiety lessened. Sharing in a safe environment is healing and helps patients deal with unresolved problems. Help your patients learn how to confide and share.
Advise patients to try to quit smoking without help.	Realize that nicotine addiction is a serious medical problem. It causes more sickness and death than any other addiction. Offer a patient who wants to stop smoking all the support available. This includes Nicorette gum, Nicorette patches, and behavior modification techniques.	The cessation of nicotine addiction greatly improves patients' health, social desirability, financial situation, and sense of well-being.
Minimize patients' complaints of asthma, hay fever, adverse food or chemical reactions, or other problems involved with the immune system.	Find and work with a physician trained in allergies who can test your patient for respiratory allergies and adverse food reactions (Bjamason, Ward, & Peters, 1984; Sugarman, Southern, & Curran, 1982). Also, make sure that the physician you refer to understands adverse chemical reactions.	Patients in recovery from alcoholism have a higher rate of allergic antibodies than control groups without alcoholism.
Neglect to ensure that your patients have an unspoiled water and air supply.	Add questions about your patients' physical environment to their intake evaluation. Teach your patients how to obtain and maintain an environment as toxin-free as possible.	Improves the quality of patients' physical environment.
Allow patients to continue to feel lousy.	Continue to encourage your patients to practice these steps as part of an overall program.	Your patients can, by practicing the principles delineated here, obtain the biggest high they ever had—the *natural high their bodies can produce.*

BOX 17.3 **Recommended Supplement Intake (I through VI)**[a]

I. Vitamin/Mineral Supplement (2 Tablets 3 Times Each Day after Meals)

  A. Vitamin Components

Vitamin A	15,000 iu
Vitamin D	400 iu
Vitamin E	400 iu
Vitamin K (menedione)	2 mg
Ascorbic acid	2,500 mg
Vitamin B1	20 mg
Vitamin B2	20 mg
Vitamin B6	30 mg
Vitamin B12	90 mg
Niacinamide	200 mg
Pantothenic acid	150 mg
Biotin	3 mg
Folic acid	4 mg
Choline	500 mg
Inositol	500 mg
P-aminobenzoic acid	30 mg
Rutin	200 mg

  B. Mineral Components

Phosphate	750 mg
Iron	30 mg
Zinc	30 mg
Copper	2 mg
Iodine	0.3 mg
Manganese	10 mg
Molybdenum	0.2 mg
Chromium	2 mg
Selenium	0.1 mg
Cobalt	0.2 mg

II. Omega-3 Fatty Acid Marine Lipid Concentrate
(1 Capsule 3 Times Each Day after Meals)

Each soft gel	1,000 mg
EPA (elcosapentaenoic acid)	300 mg
DHA (docosahexaenoic acid)	200 mg
Total omega-3 fatty acid	500 mg
Natural vitamin E (d-alpha tocopherol) antioxidant	50 iu

III. Omega-6 Fatty Acids (1 Capsule 3 Times Each Day after Meals)

Black currant seed in soft gel oil	295 mg
Gamma linolenic acid	50 mg
Linoleic acid	110 mg
Vitamin E (d-alpha tocopherol)	10 iu

IV. Calcium Complex with Magnesium (1 Capsule 3 Times Each Day after Meals)

Calcium from oyster shell	600 mg
Calcium from egg shell	338 mg
Calcium from calcium citrate	115 mg
Total calcium per tablet	1,053 mg
Magnesium (from magnesium oxide) each tablet	310 mg

V. Flax Seed Oil Capsule (1 Capsule 3 Times Each Day after Meals)

VI. L-Glutamineb (1 Capsule 3 Times Each Day after Meals)

L-glutamine	500 mg

SOURCES: Beasley et al. (1991), Guenther (1983), Rogers et al. (1956), Trulson, Fleming, and Stare (1954).
NOTE: For more detailed information, consult www.addictionend.com.

NOTE FROM THE AUTHOR: I see this as an ongoing process with you, the reader. I have donated the rights to the books listed in the suggested readings to the nonprofit 501(c)(3) Mother and Child Corporation so that they may be available on a nonprofit basis. Also, this source **www.addictionend.com** will provide teaching, slides, nutrient sources, personal consultation to professionals, and educational tools as they are developed. Please contact us at

motherchildcorp@aol.com if we may be of any assistance.

REFERENCES ◫

Agricultural Research Service. (1975). *Homemakers' food and nutrition knowledge, practices, and opinions* (Home Economics Research Report No. 39). Washington, DC: U.S. Department of Agriculture.

American Diabetes Association. (2001, January). The American Diabetes Association teams up with the American Medical Association to brief the media on "Advances in Research and Care." org/ada/nycmedia.asp.

Beasley, J. D. (1987). *Wrong diagnosis—wrong treatment: The plight of the alcoholic in America.* Dallas, TX: Essential Medical Information Systems.

> Based on monthly columns in the *International Medical Tribune* for 7 years. It traces an executive, Cooper, through the development of the alcoholism and cross-addiction with benzodiazepines. The complications in family, job, and medical condition caused by Cooper's addiction are described and related to the malnutrition and toxicity caused by Cooper's addiction.

Beasley, J. D. (1990). *How to defeat alcoholism.* New York: Times Books-Random House.

> This work traces alcoholism and details the scientific basis for the nutritional tools described in this chapter.

Beasley, J. D. (1991). *The betrayal of health.* New York: Times Books-Random House.

> Traces the underlying cause and epidemiology of the current chronic disease epidemic in America. An important resource for the counselor to understand the chronic disease pattern upon which alcoholism and chemical dependency are superimposed.

Beasley, J. D. (1995). *Diagnosing and managing chemical dependency* (3rd ed.). Dallas, TX: Essential Medical Information Systems.

> The fourth edition has a July 2001 publication date. This book was used by American Medical Television of the American Medical Association as the basis for training programs for professionals in addiction medicine during the 1990s. The fourth edition will soon be available in Spanish, French, Mandarin, and Russian.

Beasley, J. D., Grimson, R. C., Bicker, A. A., Closson, W. J., Heusel, C. A., & Faust, F. I. (1991). Follow-up of a cohort of alcoholic patients through 12 months of comprehensive biobehavioral treatment. *Journal of Substance Abuse Treatment, 8,* 133-142.

Beasley, J. D., & Knightly, S. (1994). *Food for recovery: The complete nutrition companion for recovering from alcoholism, drug addiction, and eating disorders.* New York: Crown.

Bjamason, I., Ward, K., & Peters, T. J. (1984). The "leaky gut" of alcoholism: Possible route of entry for toxic compounds. *Lancet, 1*(8370), 179-182.

Burke, J. P., Williams, K., Gaskill, S. P., Hazuda, H. P., Haffner, S. M., & Stern M. P. (1999). Rapid rise in the incidence of Type 2 diabetes from 1987 to 1996: Results from the San Antonio Heart Study. *Archives of Internal Medicine, 159,* 1450-1456.

Emrick, C. D. (1975). A review of psychologically oriented treatment of alcoholism: II. The relative effectiveness of different treatment approaches and the effectiveness of treatment versus no treatment. *Quarterly Journal of Studies on Alcohol, 36*(1), 88-108.

Gordis, E., Dorth, D., Sepe, V., & Smith, H. (1981). Outcome of alcoholism treatment among 5,578 patients in an urban comprehensive hospital based program: Application of a computerized data system. *Alcoholism: Clinical and Experimental Research, 5,* 509-522.

Guenther, R. M. (1983). The role of nutritional therapy in alcoholism treatment. *International Journal of Biosocial Research, 4*(1), 5-18.

Helzer, J. E., Robins, L. N., Taylor, J. R., Carey, K., Miller, R. H., Combs d'Orme, T., & Farmer, A. (1985). The extent of long-term moderate drinking among alcoholics discharged from medical and psychiatric treatment facilities. *New England Journal of Medicine, 312,* 1678-1682.

Pierce, J. (1976, June). Nutrition beliefs: More fashion than fact. *FDA Consumer,* pp. 25-27.

Ravel, J. M., Felsing, B., Lansford, E. M., Jr., Trubey, R. H., & Shive, W. (1955). Reversal of alcohol toxicity by glutamine. *Journal of Biological Chemistry, 214,* 497.

Rogers, L. L., Pelton, R. B., & Williams, R. J. (1955). Dietary deficiencies in animals in relation to voluntary alcohol and sugar consumption. *Quarterly Journal of Studies on Alcohol, 16,* 234-244.

Rogers, L. L., Pelton, R. B., & Williams, R. J. (1956). Amino acid supplementation and voluntary alcohol consumption by rats. *Journal of Biological Chemistry, 220,* 221-223.

Rudell, F. (1979). *Consumer food selection and nutrition information.* New York: Prager.

Sugerman, A. A., Southern, D. L., & Curran, J. F. (1982). A study of antibody levels in alcoholic, depressive, and schizophrenic patients. *Annals in Allergy, 48,* 166-171.

Substance Abuse and Mental Health Services Administration. (2000). *1998 National Household Survey on Drug Abuse.* Washington, DC: Government Printing Office.

Trulson, M. F., Fleming, R., & Stare, S. J. (1954). Vitamin medication in alcoholism. *Journal of the American Medical Association, 155,* 114-119.

U.S. Bureau of the Census. (1995). *1990 census of population and housing.* Washington, DC: Government Printing Office.

Williams, R. H. (1985, December). Treatment of alcoholism. *Consumer Research, 19,* 16-19.

ADDITIONAL SUGGESTED READINGS ▦

Beasley, J. D. (1981). *The impact of nutrition on the health of Americans: A report to the Ford Foundation.* Annandale-on-Hudson, NY: Bard Center.

| Report on nutrition and malnutrition in America.

Beasley, J. D., & Swift, J. (1989). *The impact of nutrition, the environment, and lifestyle on the health of Americans: A report to the Kellogg Foundation.* Annandale-on-Hudson, NY: Bard Center.

| An extensive review of the epidemiology of chronic disease in the United States.

Coombs, R. H. (1997). *Chemical dependency counseling: A practical guide.* Thousand Oaks, CA: Sage.

Mendelson, J. H., Miller, K. D., Mello, N. K., Pratt, H., & Schmitz, R.(1980). Hospital treatment of alcoholism: A profile of middle-income Americans. *Alcoholism: Clinical and Experimental Research, 6,* 277-383.

Milam, J. R., & Ketcham, K. (1983). *Under the influence: A guide to the myths and realities of alcoholism.* New York: Bantam.

Pettinati, H. A., Sugerman, A., DiDonato, N., & Maurer, H. S. (1982). The natural history of alcoholism over four years after treatment. *Journal of Studies on Alcohol, 43,* 201-215.

Schuckit, M. A. (2000). *Drug and alcohol abuse: A clinical guide to diagnosis and treatment.* New York: Kluwer Academic Publishers.

| An excellent quick summary of the genetic, biochemical and neurotransmitter aspects of alcoholism and chemical dependency.

Williams, B. (Bill W.). (1968, February). *The Vitamin B-3 therapy: A second communication to AA physicians.* Unpublished manuscript, circulated privately in AA. Available upon request from Dr. Joseph Beasley, e-mail motherchildcorp@aol.com.

Williams, R. J. (1981). *The prevention of alcoholism through nutrition: New hope in the battle against alcoholism. Dr. Williams' revolutionary seven-step program.* New York: Bantam.

Williams, R. J. (1998). *Biochemical individuality: The key to understanding what shapes your health.* New Canaan, CT: Keats.

18

Meditation

The Path to Recovery Through Inner Wisdom

Carol A. Snarr
Patricia A. Norris
Steven L. Fahrion

What is meditation? Although many definitions exist, together with many different meditative techniques, we use the term to describe a specific state of attending to a particular focus while withdrawing one's attention from the outside world. Meditation has been demonstrated to result in characteristic patterns of neural activity and cerebral blood flow different from those of the resting state of normal consciousness (Lou et al., 1999). It results in a state of quieting the body, the mind, and active thoughts and an openness and receptivity to intuitive processes. It is contemplative and reflective, a means of inner focus, a way of tapping into the inner wisdom inherent in us all.

BOX 18.1	The Rational Mind

My understanding of the fundamental laws of the universe did not come out of my rational mind.

—Albert Einstein

USES OF MEDITATION WITH ADDICTION

Literature concerning the application of meditation and imagery techniques in addiction shows their usefulness. Meditation strengthens motivation toward rehabilitation by those misusing substances and is a quick, effective, and cost-efficient method of detoxification (Lohman, 1999). Using meditation in drug and alcohol treatment is vital to the client's success not only in remaining abstinent but also in leading a productive, satisfying life.

Meditation, the core of our program, is a powerful means of retrieving information about one's past, understanding one's current situation, and creating ideas to help with future growth. It has the potential to open clients to problem solving, insights, and balance. It enables them to develop self-awareness and self-regulation skills that reduce stress and enhance well-being.

Psychophysiology, or the mind-body connection, is the guiding principle in our work. As stated by Green and Green (1975),

> Every change in the physiological state is accompanied by an appropriate change in the mental-emotional state, conscious or unconscious; and conversely every change in the mental-emotional state, conscious or unconscious, is accompanied by an appropriate change in the physiological state. (pp. 33-34)

How does this relate to meditation? As the client learns how to quiet the body with meditation, quieting the fight-flight response to challenge, a reduction of sympathetic nervous system activity occurs. Because mind and body are connected, the emotional-mental state then begins to quiet as well. Likewise, as the emotional state improves, it has a positive effect on the functioning of the body. A cycle of physical and emotional well-being, initiated by the meditation techniques, results.

There are two major forms of meditation: concentration and mindfulness. Concentration meditation seeks to block out ordinary thinking by focusing on one object, such as the flame of a candle, a single sound, or the rising and falling of the breath. Mindfulness meditation takes the mind itself as the object of meditation, admitting all thoughts, sensations, and emotions equally in an open focus. We use both methods in our addictive treatment program.

Although learning to meditate is a simple process, it takes patience and practice. To facilitate the learning process for our clients, we at Life Sciences Institute of Mind-Body Health developed a unique, integrated substance abuse program that includes various meditative techniques: (a) diaphragmatic breathing; (b) several biofeedback modalities (such as hand warming to aid in lowering states of autonomic arousal and neurofeedback to engender the deeper states of consciousness associated with slowed brain rhythms); (c) visualization and imagery; and (d) psychosynthesis. We combined these techniques to facilitate developing awareness and volition of physiological states and the understanding of and ability to modify states of consciousness, as well as to gain awareness and volition over personality, psychological, and psychodynamic aspects of self. Our unique treatment approach is based on our philosophy that every individual has the capacity to enhance natural processes of healing. Mind, body, emotions, and spirit are interacting parts of the whole person, with the goal of treatment being to help the client achieve psychological, physical, social, and spiritual well-being. There is, of course, much more to an individual than his or her abuse, crimes, and addictions. We relate primarily to that "much more" part, the Self of the individual, and help the client to do the same, expanding his or her potential.

⊞ BREATHING AS A MEDITATION TECHNIQUE

Almost every Eastern and Western meditation technique focuses on breathing either as a part of meditation or as part of readiness to meditate. In our drug and alcohol addiction program, we use breathing exercises to assist clients to learn how to meditate. A primary tool in learning to develop a meditative state is diaphragmatic breathing. Breath is life. Breathing, a natural function, is usually accomplished without our conscious attention, but it can also be consciously controlled, so it can be used as a bridge between conscious and unconscious processes.

BOX 18.2   **Breath**

Life is in the breath. He who half breathes, half lives.
—Ancient Proverb

In our practice, we observe that the majority of the population has reverted to a shallow thoracic breathing pattern that over time sustains the body in a fight-or-flight mode. Physical illness often results, and in the case of the addicted individual it can be the onset of relapse. Mastering diaphragmatic breathing is vital to attain and maintain optimal health. It is also central to reaching a deep meditative state by quieting all physiological processes, increasing endorphin production that enhances psychological well-being, and affording a focus of attention that eliminates mind chatter.

We teach diaphragmatic breathing by having the client lie in a supine position in a recliner chair or on the floor. We instruct the client to put one hand on the abdomen, exhale completely, and then inhale while raising the abdomen. The upper chest should remain quiet. It helps to watch the hand rising on inhalation and falling on exhalation. A small book or a tissue box on the abdomen works well also. At first we concentrate on helping the client learn to breathe using the diaphragm. It can take several weeks or more of daily practice to change a breathing pattern of thoracic breathing to diaphragmatic breathing.

The next step is to make the breath cycle even, and the third step is to gradually increase the length of each breath. For example, if breathing 2 seconds in and 2 seconds out is comfortable, we recommend increasing to 3 seconds in and 3 seconds out. Practice this two to three times a day until that becomes comfortable, then increase to 4 seconds in and 4 seconds out, practice that until comfortable, and so on. It may take a week or more to be comfortable at any one level. A reasonable goal is to reach 10 seconds in and 10 seconds out. If one practices long enough, it is possible to breathe one cycle in 60 seconds during deep meditation.

Two times we recommend to practice that are easy to incorporate into the client's schedule are while lying on one's back first thing in the morning before getting up and the last thing at night before going to sleep. If one spends 5 or 10 minutes several times a day practicing, breathing diaphragmatically becomes more automatic; the individual interacts with daily life events in a calmer frame of mind and is able to get into a meditative state more easily.

HAND TEMPERATURE TRAINING ⊞ AS A MEDITATIVE TECHNIQUE

Thermal biofeedback or hand warming, another useful tool to enhance the meditative experience, quiets the autonomic nervous system and helps the client move from an external focus to a self-reflective state. We have used biofeedback for 30-plus years as a means of helping clients develop self-awareness and self-regulation skills. The term *biofeedback* simply means feeding back biological information to an individual about some body process. Feedback of any kind accelerates learning; using biofeedback, clients learn control of physiologic functions and are able to master self-awareness and self-regulation skills.

An increase in sympathetic arousal results in decreased blood flow to the hands, and the hands get cooler. Because peripheral blood flow is regulated by the sympathetic nervous system, using a thermal biofeedback instrument taped to a finger enables a client to learn to increase blood flow to their hands, and their hands become warmer, an indication of sympathetic quieting. Learning to regulate the autonomic nervous system is powerful. It gives your client a direct experiential knowing of self-regulation, of the capacity for choice, for self-control. Knowing that the body, the psychophysiologic reactions, can be controlled by the mind, by intention, is very empowering for individuals who have felt out of control and very much the victims of their own emotions and circumstances. This is especially true for those caught in an addiction cycle.

The autonomic nervous system affects every organ and gland in the body. The continuous hyperarousal state so prevalent in drug addicts and alcoholics leads to physical and/or emotional distress, the direct path to relapse. Practicing hand warming daily as a meditative technique resets the thermostat of the body, promotes autonomic nervous system balance, and returns all physiological and psychological functioning to a more normal state.

Although there are inexpensive thermometers available to use for thermal biofeedback, it is possible to learn to warm hands by direct internal feedback. We recommend that you sit in a physically comfortable position. Recline to some degree, but don't lie down, as it is likely to induce sleep and thereby interrupt your meditation. Now turn your hands palms up, gently curling your fingers up; then turn one hand over and lay it on top of the other hand. The fingers are now easily curled together. Close your eyes, and let your attention rest on your hands and fingers. Can you be aware of any warmth, pulsating, tingling, flushing, sense of touch, or fullness in your fingers? Can you be aware of a warm pocket created between your fingers? Can you be aware of the palms of your hands? The palms are very vascular, and you often can experience a tingling or pulsating feeling in them. Imagine that whatever sensation you are experiencing is increasing in intensity. If your mind wanders, bring your attention gently back to your hands. As you feel your hands getting warmer, know that the only way blood flow can increase to the periphery is to turn down your sympathetic activation. Stop reading at this point and try this exercise yourself. Become aware of all thoughts, emotions, physical sensations, and spontaneous dreamlike experiences that occur during the relaxation exercise. We recommend writing your observations down after each practice session. Writing in a journal following each meditation experience provides an opportunity to increase self-awareness and to ponder the meaning of any images that occurred.

We recommend at least a 20- to 30-minute practice session daily. As with any skill one wants to learn, practice makes perfect. The more you practice, the easier it becomes, and the better you get. Once you have mastered warming your hands, any time you are in a stressful situation, you can bring your hands together, and you will immediately notice a calming effect. Some of the more common reported effects of doing daily meditation are "I'm feeling less stressed," "I'm sleeping better," "Things don't bother me as much," "I can make better decisions," "I feel better about myself," "I can control my anger," and "Physically I feel healthier."

⠿ REVERIE

The core of our addiction program is 30 sessions of deep reverie during which clients become still and turn within. Reverie, the state of consciousness that occurs just before sleep, is a totally internally focused state of consciousness where one can access "the higher self . . . the inner source of wisdom and guidance which becomes more available as the person develops deeper levels of self-awareness" (Schaub & Schaub, 1997, p. 147). We give simple instructions for meditation that include the diaphragmatic breathing and hand warming described earlier. We discuss with the client both concentration meditation and the mindfulness method of attending to whatever thoughts arise.

We use neurofeedback or alpha/theta brain wave biofeedback to help clients achieve this state of consciousness; it is a tool that assists clients in getting to the heart of the matter of their lives. It also gives us an objective measure of increases in amplitude and duration of alpha and theta brain waves that accompany meditative states. Neurofeedback equipment can be expensive, and we recommend

---

> **BOX 18.3** **The Subconscious Mind**
>
> *Just as the conscious mind is the source of thought, so the subconscious is the source of power.*
>
> —Claude M. Bristol, *The Magic of Believing*

---

at least a month of training and 30 sessions of brain wave training for the therapist before beginning to work with clients. Although one can learn to get into a deep meditative state without brain wave biofeedback, merely by using the techniques of breathing and increasing hand temperature, neurofeedback training enables our clients to learn to reach the state of reverie much more quickly.

To find that source of inner wisdom, it is imperative to implement regular daily practice. Any of the techniques described, used on a persistent and consistent basis, afford you the ability to recognize and to move freely from one state of consciousness to another. As you begin to relax, attention is withdrawn from the external environment, and you move from a beta brain wave state to a daydreamlike thoughtful state characterized by an increase in alpha waves. With eyes closed, you then can move into a deeper more internally focused state, characterized by slower alpha brain waves, where thoughts flow more freely. Moving toward sleep, you encounter a state of reverie characterized by predominantly theta brain waves, with enough alpha brain waves to recall inner experiences. This desired state of consciousness gives access to your creative processes, problem-solving ideas, and insights for future growth.

Reverie is the state of consciousness where meaningful images arise from the unconscious, and visualizations have the greatest impact on the unconscious. Helping clients create their own visualizations related specifically to rejecting the addictive substance and to being abstinent adds another powerful dimension to the meditation. Used at the beginning of each meditation session, these visualizations have a self-fulfilling effect.

VISUALIZATION AND IMAGERY IN MEDITATION ▣

Throughout the world in ancient and modern times, both visualization and imagery have been used in a number of healing applications. Only recently have these techniques for self-change been applied to substance abuse programs, although in a sense some of the 12 steps involve aspects of both visualization and imagery. As one searches oneself and one's past, one employs intentionality or will to make change.

An important part of self-regulation is each person's development of his or her own individual visualizations, using symbols and images that have deep meaning for him or her and that fit his or her own deepest desires and intentions. There is no uniform terminology, but we distinguish between imagery and visualization as two different processes, and/or two different aspects of the same process. Together, they form an internal dialogue, an intrapsychic communication between mind and body using the language of visualization and imagery.

Visualization is the consciously chosen, intentional instruction to the self, a communication *to* the unconscious. It involves *will*, a will to wellness, to change. Visualization precedes action and leads to internal actions as well as external actions. We reserve the word *imagery* to refer to *spontaneously arising communications from the unconscious*, arising suddenly and unbidden into consciousness. The imagery can represent wishes, needs and fears, and a whole array of unconscious ideas and beliefs. The relaxation and meditation process encourages hypnagogic-like images to arise, which are usually quite meaningful. The images are messages from the unconscious to consciousness, much like dreams. The images that arise are generally related to what is uppermost in the person's life. The images that clients become aware of during addiction treatment are related to issues of use, sobriety, past understandings, and future possibilities.

Gradually, through the use of visualization and imagery, a bridge is built between the conscious and the unconscious; this includes cortical and subcortical processes, the conscious and "unconscious" portions of the brain. A whole new science is emerging on the neurobiology of addictions, with much evidence for the neurohumoral, biochemical mechanisms that underlie the effectiveness of meditation, visualization, and imagery in effecting change.

Effective Visualization

In forming effective visualizations, a number of important characteristics need to be taken into consideration. One of the most important is that the visualization be idiosyncratic. Canned visualizations, or other people's visualizations, lack power for the individual. Also of great importance is that the visualizations be ego-syntonic, that they represent the person's true values and intentions. Visualizations must be stated in a positive way, they must represent what the person *wants* to have happen, not what he or she *doesn't* want. The *unconscious* operating in primary process receives only mental *pictures*. It does not accept negatives, does not hear the word "no," and will embrace only the picture that is being sent. For example, the mental picture in the sentence "I will not open the door," is very different from the mental picture of "I will leave the door shut." The first phrase is received by the unconscious as a picture of an open door, whereas the latter states exactly what the client wants to happen. These and other characteristics of effective visualization will be discussed as the individual visualizations are described.

Each session begins with suggestions for centering, letting go of worries and cares, and beginning to relax. We say, "Now take several deep, cleansing breaths, bringing in energy and letting yourself relax as much as possible with each exhalation. Allow your muscles to relax, letting any tensions flow away. Begin to increase warmth to your hands as you relax more and more deeply," or words to that effect. After a couple of minutes of relaxation, we give the following visualizations. The first three are standard, having to do with the physiologic process.

1. "I can visualize *and experience* the center of my brain where alpha and theta rhythms originate." The use of the word *can* gives a sense of permissiveness rather than authority and is more likely to engender a desire to comply. The words *and experience* are emphasized; participants have been instructed to *feel* the center of the brain and imagine the space and that they are in it as much as

they can. A kinesthetic and/or somatosensory component to visualizations is very important. We believe that this felt sense is important; without feedback, the visualization could be modified to "the center of my brain, where deep relaxation originates."

2. "I can visualize *and experience* the relaxation increasing in depth and duration." We continue to emphasize attention to the feelings associated with a meditative state.

3. "I can visualize *and experience* all my neurohormones, neurotransmitters, and neurochemicals becoming normalized and functioning optimally." This phrase evokes a feeling, a somatosensory awareness of the sensations of sobriety, and evokes images of brain healing. During the introductory week of our addiction program, participants are informed of the research demonstrating the biochemistry of addiction and recovery. Recently there has been great growth in these fields. *The brain shows itself to have incredible plasticity and healing ability* and great versatility of function. Meditation, visualization, and neurofeedback play a vital role in recovery.

These three visualizations provide practice for a felt sense of healing, clearness, sobriety, and well-being. We encourage participants to practice briefly but frequently at other times, such as just before going to sleep and when feeling tension, craving, or other stress.

Substance Rejection and Abstinence

The two most important visualizations are the substance rejection scene and the abstinence scene. Several hours are often needed and devoted to perfecting these visualizations and to helping each participant create strong effective visualizations.

Rejection Scene

Rejection scenes are central to the meditation and visualization procedure. A rejection scene must first and foremost be truly what the individual wants for him- or herself. We tell clients to have the visualization be for their true heart's desire; if they have reservations about stopping use (and some do, especially in the case of marijuana), then pick something else, such as anger, gambling, or violent responses. We cannot lie to ourselves, and to do so subverts the whole process. Most of the participants sincerely long to be free of the alcohol or drug to which they are addicted, and the rejection scene simply needs to address their triggers or their fears.

A few of the inmates in our prison programs want to stay off marijuana only until they are off parole. They feel that this drug should be legalized, and for them smoking is very ego-syntonic (i.e., in conformance with their values and ideals). We do our best to convince them of other disadvantages of smoking marijuana, in addition to the fact that it is illegal and constitutes risky behavior. Chief among these is the will-sapping effect of marijuana: Often, once it is smoked, the best of intentions go out the window. We also talk about the gradual reductions in both short- and long-term memory that accompany consistent use and the considerable functional damage to the brain as shown by SPECT scans. A real and lasting change occurs within the self from new knowledge and experience, not from coercion, pressure, or the desire to gain approval or to "pass" to complete the program. Therefore, if clients still feel that they do not wish to stop their use, we honor that and recognize it is a personal choice. Most participants will at least gladly create a rejection scene for the duration of parole, and this may have more lasting positive consequences.

One of our participants created a visualization of turning away from all use of marijuana; as friends approached him with some, he asked them to leave his house, or get out of his car, informing them he would abstain while on parole. He avoided going places where it would be used and left at once if it appeared. For his abstinence scene, he pictured himself doing things with his family, saying they were happy because "they like me so much better when I'm not smoking." Perhaps this visualization carried out over 30 sessions, plus abstinence while on parole, will be enough to end his use. We can't emphasize enough that it is essential to meet people where they are. We make clear that we expect honesty and integrity, not responses that the client comes up with because he or she thinks that is what we expect or want to hear. Many of our clients report that in most drug programs they have attended, they are expected to say that they are addicts, or that they intend not to use, regardless of what they believe to be true.

Another example is a prisoner who said his problem was not really addiction but repeatedly getting in trouble for burglaries. He wanted to stop but kept doing it anyway and experienced it as extremely compelling, just like any other addiction. The rejection scene he developed was

> When I see a place that I could burglarize, I start to think how I could get inside, and what I might find, and the money I could have (his triggers). I say NO, I do not do this anymore. I think of the consequences of burglary, and then I think of my desire to stay with my family and out of trouble, and that this is what I want for me. I feel strong and positive about my choice.

Abstinence Scene

The abstinence scene can involve any activity that the participant enjoys, such as camping or fishing, barbecuing with the family, or playing with his or her children. In the scene, clients picture themselves doing the activity free of substances and feeling clear-headed, healthy, in control of themselves, and in full enjoyment. These scenes are valuable because so many addicts find it easier to imagine staying sober than to imagine enjoying themselves without their drug of choice. A usual difficulty of abstinence is "white-knuckle sobriety," and the belief that "I may be able to stay sober, but I will never feel comfortable or happy again." As people begin to experience the joys of sobriety in imagery, they begin to believe in a life after use.

Unconditional Positive Self-Regard

The last visualization connects with unconditional positive self-regard. A goal of the program is to increase individual experiences of self-worth and self-esteem, often either never acquired or demolished over the years. The phrase might be "I love and accept myself exactly as I am, including all my hopes and dreams, all my failures and successes, and all the things I am working to become." Sometimes the question comes up, "How can I love and respect myself with all the mistakes and wrong things I have done?" This love and acceptance is the most essential ingredient for change. A concept, just as important as the idea of a higher self, is the idea and experience of an inner self, the one who dreams and hopes and intends. Psychosynthesis is directed toward *experiential* understanding of this inner self, the true self, the center of consciousness and will. Understanding of disidentification helps the client realize that we can love the actor but not the action.

Psychosynthesis and Meditation

Psychosynthesis was born about the same time as psychoanalysis and Jungian analysis, starting around the beginning of the last century. Its founder, Roberto Assagioli, was a contemporary of Freud and Jung and part of the Vienna group that became excited about the possibilities for change brought about by a growing understanding of the human unconscious. In creating psychosynthesis, Assagioli brought together psychoanalytic and psycho-spiritual concepts, with a strong focus on human potential for self-direction and change. He formed an integral psychology that examines our past associations and experiences, explores how they molded what we have become, and provides a number of ways to consciously direct our future being and becoming. Assagioli saw the basic construct of the human personality as a center of consciousness and will, capable of observing, directing, and synthesizing all the psychological processes and the physical body. Psychosynthesis is broad and comprehensive in scope; it provides a theoretical model of the nature and structure of the personality and a comprehensive, dynamic psychotherapy, and it facilitates, partly through a series of exercises, a proactive, conscious participation in the growth of the self (Assagioli, 1971).

Our entire theoretical framework and philosophy of treatment is based on the psychosynthesis model. In our addiction treatment program, we use a small set of five or six meditative procedures widely used in psychosynthesis. Psychosynthesis partners and harmonizes with meditation, relaxation, and self-regulation of psychophysiology. In psychosynthesis, *consciousness* and *will* are the essence of the person around which all the psychological processes and the physical body can be harmonized and integrated. In the case of psychophysiologic self-regulation, acquisition of skills depends upon *awareness* and *volition*. All our actions except the purely reflexive ones—all deliberate actions—proceed on the basis of awareness and volition, of consciousness and will.

The first self-exploration exercise has three parts. The first part is an open free association to the question "Who am I?" These words are written at the top of a sheet of paper, and the only instructions are to make a list of only single or possibly two words. Participants write down everything that comes to mind, without judging or making decisions, being open and looking deeply inside. Lists can vary greatly in length, but we try to get at least 20 words.

The second part of this exercise is to place each of the words from that list into one, and only one, of the major divisions of the self: body, emotions, mind, and spirit. We provide a sheet of paper with these four column headings. Especially in our multicultural environment, it is necessary to make some clarifying remarks about spirit. The model of the self put forward by Assagioli recognizes spirituality as an innate aspect of human nature, existing *beyond* any specific beliefs, religions, dogmas, or theologies. Being in touch with that aspect of self is essential to the healing process, to transformation, and, we believe, to continuing recovery. It is the basis for self-acceptance, leading eventually to recognition of "the one within," the organizing principle, the center of consciousness and will that can observe, direct, and integrate mind, emotions, and all the psychological processes.

It is greatly interesting to us and to our clients to see how they initially define themselves as they examine and share their lists. The relative length of the lists is informative, and we return to it again as we go deeper into the self-exploration. Some people have nothing or only one or two things from their list on body, for example, and almost all of their self-ascribed qualities, roles, and activities fall under just one of the other categories—emotions, mind, or spirit.

After this initial division, clients draw a line right under each list, denoting the first self-definitions, and then add to the list. For example, for clients who have only one or two items on their body list, ask what else they can say about their bodies.

The last part of this exercise is to dialogue with each aspect of self. This is usually the first introduction to inner dialogue in our substance abuse program. Ask participants, "What would you like to tell your body right now? What would your body like to say to you, what does it want to tell you?" "What would you like to say to your mind right now? What does your mind want you to know?" Almost everyone gets into this part of the work with ease, and it serves as a gentle introduction to a disidentification process as they sequentially observe, and dialogue with, their body, their emotions, their mind, and their spirit. They can recognize these inner voices and their particular needs and strengths. Who is the *I* that dialogues? This question will be asked later; at this time, the experience suffices.

The initial list can be divided up in a number of other ways. How many of the items are self-evaluations: a good person, no good, honest? Roles: a father (mother), husband, student? Characteristics or qualities: cheerful, intelligent, playful? Conditions: sad, afraid, an addict? Is "addict" a condition, a characteristic, a role? Is it all of these? In group sharing, the participant begins to get a glimmer of how they define themselves, how others define themselves, and how many ways there are to look at things. The possibilities for discussion and insight are endless; you could spend a week just on this exercise. In fact, you could spend a whole year on the "Who Am I?" exercise, and there would still be more to learn.

Another way to explore self-images is the ideal model technique. Explain that the images are like partial models of the personality and that they are present in us, consciously and unconsciously, in great diversity. Often, they are in conflict with each other. Explore and bring to awareness some of the models and begin to formulate an ideal model, a visualization of some particular aspect of what the client wants to be, to develop or nurture. Explore the steps in some depth. Ask the client to think and write about the following points: (a) how I underevaluate myself; (b) how I overevaluate myself; (c) a secret, daydream model (Superman, omnipotent fantasy); (d) how I wish to appear to others; (e) how I believe I *do* appear to others; and (f) how I believe others want or expect me to be or would change me if they could. The last three can be explored in a number of specific relationships: How do I wish to appear to my husband, wife, my children, supervisor or boss, colleagues, peers? The differences can be remarkable and enlightening. The final step in this exercise is to create an image of one quality or pattern of behavior of an ideal model that the client would like to embody (e.g., patience, assertiveness, spending more time with family). The client then visualizes having made that change, noticing how he or she would look—face, eyes, expression, posture—and visualizing everyday situations in which he or she possesses or acts out the qualities and attitudes of that image (Assagioli, 1971). This visualization added to the daily meditation can become a self-fulfilling prophecy.

A guided meditation from psychosynthesis includes climbing a mountain in search of one's own personal cup and sword. Tell your client that these symbols appear constantly in all the world's religions, legends, and mythology. The Christian Bible, as well as Jewish, Islamic, Buddhist, and Hindu literature, among others, has numerous references to cups and swords, with many symbolic meanings. In legend, these two powerful symbols are central to King Arthur's court. The cup, the Holy Grail, represents femininity, and the sword, Excalibur, represents masculinity. On the level of personality, the cup represents the emotions, and the sword represents the mind; and on the level of the high self, the sword represents the will, and the cup represents *agape*, unconditional love—for humanity and for the earth. This exercise can help clients recognize and accept more aspects of their nature.

One of the most important and useful tasks of psychosynthesis is the task of disidentification and self-identification. The central concept is that we are dominated by everything with which our self is identified but that we can control, influence, and make choices about every aspect of self from which we are disidentified. Realizing this fundamental concept affects every aspect of life and creates an expansive freedom, a freedom from being the victim of our self-identifications. If people are identified (ego-identified) with their possessions, then the possessions are the master and they the slave. Some people are identified primarily with their bodies: They act and live as if they *were* their bodies, and emotions, mind, and other parts are more superficial. Others live primarily in their emotions, and how they *feel* is of primary importance. Some identify mostly with their minds, ascribing little importance or attention to their bodies and emotions; and still others identify primarily with their roles, particularly the ones that are providing the greatest attraction or satisfaction. Each partial identification carries its own risks.

Basically, the technique is summarized by the affirmation that

> I have a body, but I am not my body; I have emotions, but I am not my emotions; I have a mind, but I am not my mind. I have desires, but I am not my desires; I have many roles in life, but I am not the roles, I am more than the roles. I am self-directed, and not only the actor, but the *director* of the acting. I am a center of consciousness and will, and from this center I can learn to observe, direct, and gradually integrate all of my psychological processes and my physical body. (Assagioli, 1971, p. 119)

As understanding and experience of these concepts grow, increased empowerment and freedom occur, and victim consciousness diminishes and disappears. This can be applied to many other parts of life: I have a job, but I am not my job; I have an illness (e.g., diabetes) but I am not the illness. We cease to experience ourselves as a victim of our emotions, our body and its condition, our thoughts, or any separate aspect of ourselves.

One other short but highly useful mindfulness meditation that we also teach is to instruct clients to gaze at a single object, focusing sequentially on everything they can see without moving their eyes; then on everything they see and hear; and then on everything they see, hear, and feel. In a noisy, raucous environment, allowing all the sounds to be present like a symphony without trying to block out the sounds or single any out is very restful and is an excellent stress-relieving technique. Other techniques and strategies for self-exploration that we employ, such as guided imageries, can be found in the psychosynthesis literature (Brown, 1993; Weiser & Yeomans, 1988). They involve experiencing some of the archetypal symbols for healing, forgiveness, and integration and are useful for synthesizing various parts of the self that may be disharmonious.

▦ THE MEDITATION SESSION

Our addiction treatment program, 7 weeks in length, 2 to 3 hours per day, meets on Monday through Friday. During the first, introductory week, participants in the treatment program learn about the brain and some basic psychophysiology. They learn hand-warming techniques and diaphragmatic breathing to lower arousal. Both of these have profound effects on the autonomic nervous system. Another important task during the first week is to help participants develop their own visualizations for substance rejection and for abstinence, described in detail previously.

Each day of treatment includes 30 minutes of meditation followed by discussion and processing of the experience. Meditation can be practiced in a group setting or on an individual basis. Groups work well. Postmeditation discussion augments each individual's experience with new insights gleaned from the experience of others in the group. In preparation for a meditation session, we provide a quiet room with recliner chairs, dim lighting, light blankets if necessary, and an atmosphere of unconditional acceptance. We begin each session guiding the client(s) through a brief 3- to 5-minute visualization exercise. Focusing on the breath, we say,

> Take three or four deep diaphragmatic breaths as cleansing breaths. Imagine that you are breathing away any muscle tension, any emotions, or any thoughts that may interfere with moving into a relaxed state (pause). Now allow your breathing to fall into a slow, deep, equalized breathing pattern. Focus your attention only on your breath. If your mind wanders to anything else, bring your attention gently back to the breath, becoming aware of your abdomen rising and falling as you inhale and exhale (pause for 1-2 minutes).

At this point, we guide the client through the specific visualizations that have been created. We begin with the three visualizations (described earlier) dealing with increasing amplitude of alpha and theta brain waves and the normalization of all neurochemistry. A pause after reading each visualization gives the client time to internalize it. Then we continue by saying,

> Now visualize and imagine your alcohol and/or drug rejection scene. As clearly and vividly as possible, imagine yourself in your scene, and imagine the feelings of confidence in your rejection decision (pause). Now visualize and imagine your abstinence scene. As clearly and vividly as possible imagine yourself in your scene. Use as many senses as possible, including the feelings of pleasure, safety, self-confidence, and the power of choice (pause). Now imagine planting all of those visualizations in the unconscious part of your brain where mind over matter resides, and let them go. Allow yourself to be physically still, emotionally calm, and mentally quiet. Become an observer of internal events that may present themselves. Just let go.

After finishing this guided visualization, the counselor remains quiet for 25 to 30 minutes while the client continues the meditation session.

At the end of the meditation time, the counselor quietly suggests that clients gently bring awareness back into the room. Allow clients plenty of time to write about the experience before any discussion begins. Experiences that occur in reverie are very fragile and are easily forgotten if too much cognitive activity takes place before journal writing.

The spontaneous experiences that present themselves during meditation are rich in meaning. They are highly personal and have specific relevance to the client's past, present situation, or anticipated future. In early meditation sessions, images often but not always are related to the past. Memories and perceptions of past events that need to be revisited present themselves. They can be related to happier times and sometimes are related to trauma or sad times. These "memory" images often indicate to clients potential for the future or something they need to let go of in order to grow. After the client has practiced meditation for a while, many of the images that arise have a very spiritual or transpersonal meaning and/or effect on the client's life.

Because images occur in a highly symbolic format, we developed a method of processing them to enable clients to determine what significance this particular experience has for their life. This method minimizes analyzing at a cortical level and maximizes understanding at a deeper level. It discourages interpretation by the counselor.

We begin by breaking the image into components or separate words and have the client free-associate to determine in a symbolic way what each component represents. For example for an image of a door ajar with a bright light shining through, we ask the client, "What is door? . . . What is ajar? . . . What is bright? . . . What is light? . . . Avoid the phrase "What does it mean?" This pulls the client into a more cortical mode rather than a contemplative one. Then we bundle all of the components and their interpretation together, read them back to the client, and ask him or her how this applies to the past, present, or future. Most of the time, clients have an insight into what the experience means on a very personal level. If they do not, we recommend being open to any ideas or thoughts that may occur in relation to the image at a later time.

Here are a few examples of images and the meaning arrived at by the client. We have included some additional questions that are important for the counselor to ask.

- *Image*: A brief image of a door ajar with a bright light shining on the other side.

- *Insight*: the door to the future is ajar, not wide open, but enough to let me know the way, and gives me hope of being able to move forward through it. The light is showing me the way. It also could be my spiritual self, letting me know that it is there to guide me. [How do you feel about that?] I feel confident and safe. [Why do you think this presented itself now?] I am at a place in my life where I need to make some major changes. I want to move forward and stop making the same mistakes that result in my returning to prison.

- *Image*: Loose salt and pepper lying on a table. I am trying to clean it up.

- *Insight*: The salt and pepper represents common spices, relating to the everyday "stuff of life." The black and white of them represents the polarities of life—that things are not always black or white but a combination of the two. The table represents a family gathering place; the family's "stuff" is on the table. In the past, I have taken all the responsibility for looking after everyone's "stuff." [How do you feel about that?] I'm worn out. I'm tired of them always looking to me to be there. I guess I need to let everyone take responsibility for his or her own actions.

- *Image*: I was standing at the mouth of a cave. I wanted to go in but felt very frightened. The image ended.

- *Insight*: I guess the cave is me, and it contains all the past trauma in my life. It is frightening to look at it. [Why do you suppose this presented now?] I think it is time for me to face all of the pain of the abuse I was subjected to. It will be hard, but I think I am ready to look at it and then let it go. I need to explore the cave in order to grow.

The insights clients have about their images are a vehicle for increased self-awareness and offer opportunities for setting goals and putting plans into place to meet those goals. We believe that this method of processing is a powerful tool for understanding the significance of spontaneous images that occur during meditation. The processing dovetails beautifully with the psychosynthesis exercises to empower clients by providing them with a wealth of information that opens the way for personal growth.

▦ CONCLUSION

We described a number of meditation techniques that we employ in our drug and alcohol treatment program. We use diaphragmatic breathing, hand warming, neurofeedback, visualization, and psychosynthesis to ensure that clients get every opportunity to learn to reach a deep meditative state. Although the reverie state is central in meditation, it is important for clients to have an understanding of, and be able to move freely between, states of consciousness. The range extends from an alert external focus (beta state) through a relaxed, daydreamlike thoughtful alpha state, to a theta reverie meditative state, and on to sleep, delta, at the appropriate times. Every state of consciousness is necessary; being stuck in any one of them results in a host of difficulties for an individual.

BOX 18.4   **Looking Inward**

Dwelling in stillness and looking inward for some part of each day, we touch what is most real and reliable in ourselves.

—Jon Kabat-Zinn, *Wherever You Go There You Are*

Multitudes of benefits are reported from daily meditation. It provides a means to manage stress in everyday life. Most clients report that stress is the main factor that puts them on the road to relapse. Self-awareness developed through meditation helps clients recognize changes in behavior, changes in emotions, physiologic changes, and changes in thought processes. The earlier they recognize these stress signals, the easier it is for them to intervene. The confidence gained from learning self-regulation techniques makes it possible to take control of situations and to make healthier, more intelligent decisions. Clients tend to approach life situations in a calmer, more confident manner. Meditation promotes stability in the physical realm as well as the emotional and mental realm. One can relax arousal anytime, anywhere, in the crunch. It creates a clear mind, which leads to action and spontaneity to life events rather than reaction and rigidity. Regular practice of meditation reduces anxiety both by decreasing hypervigilance and by increasing a sense of well-being. When the brain rhythms are slow, the brain produces mind-altering and brain-healing substances, such as neuropeptides, enkephalins, and endogenous opiates, that have been shown to ameliorate craving and promote abstinence (Blum & Payne, 1991). For this reason, it is a powerful aid in relapse prevention.

Meditation practice builds a bridge between conscious and unconscious processes. One attains a direct, experiential knowing of self-regulation, of the capacity for choice, self-control, and a deeper understanding of "who I am" and "where I am going." The mind is quiet, and the body is prepared to receive communication from the unconscious, often from the High Self. The potential for seeing new possibilities is enhanced. One can tap into a deeper source of wisdom, "wisdom [that] provides us with a perspective that alleviates our personal fears" (Schaub, & Schaub, 1997, p. 148). One can let go of old, limiting identifications, thoughts, and attitudes that stand in the way of growth and healing. One can move away from victim consciousness, feelings of helplessness and hopelessness, and the idea that one is isolated and unlovable. "The self-reflection we sometimes practice when confronted with difficulty can be deepened by means of sustained meditation" (Murphy, 1992, p. 543).

Meditation provides a personal path to transformation. One often discovers a sense of meaning and purpose to life. Increased ability to observe thoughts, emotions, and sensations enhances the sense of trust in one's inner strength. One can begin to identify with a higher power that resides within and that can be contacted quite easily.

We have observed a dramatic change in clients after 30 meditation sessions. They attain higher consciousness, which manifests qualities of acceptance, love, contentment, harmony, peacefulness, and serenity. All of these qualities have a profound effect on the physical well-being. Emotions and attitudes have biological consequences in terms of biochemistry and in terms of energy patterns in our bodies. Higher-consciousness awareness developed through meditation gives one a sense of eternality, continuity, and feelings of empowerment and meaningfulness.

REFERENCES ⊞

Assagioli, R. (1971). *Psychosynthesis.* New York: Hobbs, Dorman.

Blum, K., & Payne, J. (1991). *Alcohol and the addictive brain.* New York: Free Press.

Brown, M. (1993). *Growing whole.* New York: HarperCollins.

Green, E. E., & Green, A. (1975). *Beyond biofeedback.* New York: Delacourt.

Lohman, R. (1999). Yoga techniques applicable within drug and alcohol rehabilitation programmes. *Therapeutic Communities: International Journal for Therapeutic and Supportive Organizations, 20*(1), 61-72.

Lou, H. C., Kjaer, T. W., Friberg, L., Wildschiodtz, G., Holm, S., & Nowak, M. A. (1999). A 15O-H2O PET study of meditation and the resting state of normal consciousness. *Human Brain Mapping, 7*(2), 98-105.

Murphy, M. (1992). *The future of the body.* Los Angeles: Tarcher.

Schaub, B., & Schaub, R. (1997). *Healing addiction.* New York: Delmar.

Weiser, J., & Yeomans, T. (1988). *Readings in psychosynthesis: Theory, process, and practice.* Toronto: Canadian Department of Applied Psychology, Ontario Institute for Studies in Education.

ADDITIONAL SUGGESTED READINGS ⊞

Fried, R. (1990). *The breath connection.* New York: Plenum.

Loehr, J., & Migdow, J. (1986). *Take a deep breath.* New York: Villard.

19

Spirituality Enhancement

From Distilled Spirits to Instilled Spirit

Robert J. Kus

Long ago and far away, there was a young man who became a monk to "find spirituality." Every day, the young monk sat outside the monastery with his hands clasped in prayer. He looked very pious and chanted prayers all day long. Day after day, he intoned these words, believing that he was becoming more "spiritual."

The wise old abbot observed the young man from his window for many days. Finally, the abbot came outside the monastery, sat down near the young monk and began rubbing a piece of brick against a stone. Day after day, week after week, the abbot rubbed one against the other. Finally, the young man could no longer contain his curiosity. He blurted out, "Father, what are you doing?"

"I'm making a mirror," said the abbot.

"But that's impossible," replied the young monk. "You can't make a mirror out of a brick."

"True," replied the abbot. "But it is just as impossible for you to attempt to become spiritual by doing nothing except chanting all day long" (Cavanaugh, 1996, p. 29).

The young man was right in trying to increase his spirituality but very wrong in his approach. He assumed that spirituality came from doing out-of-the-ordinary kinds of things such as sitting and chanting from sunrise to sundown.

But spirituality, as we will see, is something we all possess. It is lived and increased by living the ordinariness of life in extraordinary ways. It is not achieved by removing ourselves from work and play and leisure and others. On the contrary, our spirituality can only be enhanced when we realize it is part of every bit of our lives. It is a lens

---

AUTHOR'S NOTE: In this chapter, I often use *we* when referring to recovering persons because I myself am a person in my 20th year of recovery.

through which we see the entirety of our lives and the world around us. Through such a lens, we come to realize that "all is spiritual."

⊞ PURPOSE

The purpose of this chapter is to explore the concept of spirituality. In particular, we will distinguish spirituality from religion, examine some of the traditional sources of nurturing spirituality that people have found through the centuries, and examine what healthy versus unhealthy spirituality looks like. We will look at how our spirituality affects all our life realms and view one type of spirituality known as 12-step spirituality. Finally, we will assess how helping professionals can assist their addicted clients in coping with the concept of spirituality.

But before we delve into this topic, it is wise to answer this question: Why is spirituality important for the treatment of addiction? The answer is simple: Because it works. For centuries, alcoholism and other forms of addiction were treated with a variety of sources that did not work. Among these sources were religion, jails and prisons, banishment, shunning, divorce, beatings, drug therapy, hospital confinement, and the like. These did not work.

Then one day, a new approach—spirituality—was tried. It worked for two alcoholic men, Bill Wilson and Bob Smith. Their approach, 12-step spirituality, formed the basis of their movement, Alcoholics Anonymous (AA). From their meeting, millions of people have discovered that spirituality can indeed lead to sobriety from alcohol.

But do spiritual programs such as AA always work? My answer is, "Yes, AA always works, but not everyone always works AA."

⊞ DEFINING SPIRITUALITY

Everyone has spirituality, but not everyone has religion. Religion is concerned with such things as doctrines and rituals and hierarchies and rules and formal organization. Spirituality, on the other hand, has to do with that related to "the spirit" or the transcendent aspects of our lives. Included in the concept of spirituality are such things as our basic values, the behaviors that reflect our value system, and our notions of good and evil, right and wrong. Often, our spirituality incorporates notions of God, the meaning of life, and the afterlife.

Just because we all have a spirituality does not mean each spirituality is identical. Our spirituality is formed and demonstrated by our individual gifts and our calling in life and how we live that out in our day-to-day existence. For example, a mother's spirituality is demonstrated by how she cares for her children. This spirituality is different from that of someone like the late Mother Theresa, whose spirituality was demonstrated by caring for the poorest of the poor.

Our spirituality is to be judged on how we live out our adult social roles and responsibilities in the best way we can. Thus, a woman called to be a preacher should be the best preacher she can be, whereas a man called to be a nurse should be the best nurse he can be. This will become clearer as we explore how spirituality affects our various life realms later in this chapter. First, however, let us look at traditional sources of spirituality.

TRADITIONAL SOURCES OF SPIRITUALITY ▦

When people think of "spirituality," they often think of traditional sources that they learned about from childhood onward. For example, most people think about prayer and meditation. Others think about attending church or synagogue. Others think of reading spiritual books or engaging in solitude. Each of these traditional sources of spirituality is valid.

In this section, we review some traditional sources of spirituality. Later in the chapter, we will see how the clinician can help clients use these sources and come to see spirituality in every aspect of life.

Prayer

Prayer may be defined as a person talking with God. Prayers may be formal, such as the Lord's Prayer or "Our Father," or they may be informal. A simple morning prayer upon awakening may be "Good morning, God." Quick prayers include "Help" and "Thanks." Needless to say, everyone has time to pray.

Some spiritual writers have divided prayers into four types. These types may be remembered by using the acronym ACTS: Adoration, Contrition, Thanksgiving, and Supplication. *Adoration prayers* are worship prayers, acknowledging that God is almighty. "I adore you, Lord" is such a prayer. *Prayers of contrition* ask God for forgiveness for doing something wrong or failing to something good. For example, "Forgive me, God, for I am a sinner" is such a prayer. In *thanksgiving prayers,* we thank God for the blessings we have received. In general, the more time people have in recovery, the more likely it is that their prayers will be prayers of thanksgiving. After all, sobriety brings a treasure trove of blessings. In *prayers of supplication,* individuals ask God for individual favors. In the 12-step way of life, people are encouraged to ask for "knowledge of God's will and the power to carry that out." Finally, there is such a thing as cursing God. Because it is a human-to-God communication, some might call it a prayer. In this scenario, the individual vents his or her anger at God. Such "prayer" is typically seen when a person loses a loved one or is in the depths of addiction.

Meditation

If we say that prayer is "me talking with God," meditation is "God talking to me." Though there are different forms of meditation, all have as their goal to achieve new insights and serenity.

Active meditation involves reflecting on a particular Scripture passage or AA slogan or sacred picture. "What does this mean to me?" the individual asks. Needless to say, this works best in solitude. Passive meditation, which has been popularized by such movements as transcendental meditation, encourages individuals to clear their minds of all thoughts. In this method, individuals come in silence and focus on their breathing. Some use a mantra, a word or phrase said over and over again. For example, a person might say, "Jesus" or "Omar," the first syllable on inspiration, and the second on exhalation.

Not only does meditation produce serenity, but this serenity often has profound mental and physical effects such as lowering blood pressure, renewing energy, and helping people cope with the stresses of everyday life more readily.

Solitude

Spiritual masters throughout the ages have recognized the power of solitude in nurturing the human spirit. Today, many of us have lifestyles that are so hectic that we become numbed by the stimuli around us. Many Americans, in fact, cannot stand to be in silence. When they travel in their cars or go on walks, they surround themselves with music. When they are at home, television fills the void.

Solitude, however, is healing. It allows God (or nature) time to work within us. If we are bombarding ourselves with continual noise and "busyness," we have less chance of hearing the "voice of God" in our lives. Many people find that combining solitude with spending time in nature is quite refreshing.

I have found that when I walk on the beach or in the woods, I get new insights into my life or new ideas for articles to write. I never find solitude to be a waste of time.

Spiritual Reading

In the early 1500s, there lived a young man in Spain who was filled with romantic notions of chivalry. Inspired by tales of adventure, valor, and glory, he decided to become a knight. Unfortunately, this young knight was shot in the leg in battle and ended up in a castle to heal. To avoid boredom, the young knight asked for some romance novels. The castle, however, had nothing to offer him except a life of Christ and a book about saints. From his reading, a profound change came over his heart, and he decided to become a "knight of God," a priest instead of warrior-knight. This man, Ignatius of Loyola, went on to found a group of like-minded men who wanted to turn their lives over to God. The group, called the Society of Jesus, is now more commonly known as the Jesuits.

Not everyone who engages in spiritual reading has such profound life changes as St. Ignatius. Nevertheless, spiritual reading has touched the lives of millions of people throughout the ages. The Bible is perhaps the most influential of spiritual reading books, but there are many more. In fact, books in spirituality are one of the most popular forms of writing in the early 21st century.

Churchgoing

Many people grew up attending church (or synagogue or some other form of worship space). For some it was a good experience, whereas others found it not so good. Some stick with their church all through life, whereas others take time off. Addicts, in particular, may take time off.

In recovery, many people long to go back to their church roots. Via such 12-step programs as AA, they often find themselves back in "church." Others choose new places of worship. During major holy days, such as Christmas, Easter, or Passover, many people find that they are called to more formal ways of celebrating the day. Although one does not need to be religious to be spiritual, many, if not most, Americans find religious participation to be an important aspect of their spirituality.

BOX 19.1 **Portrait of a Healthy Spirituality**

- Joy
- Sense of humor
- Sensitivity toward others
- Sound value system
- Behavior in harmony with values and beliefs
- Openness to new ideas
- High self-esteem
- Honesty
- Acceptance of those different from self
- Gentleness
- Kindness
- Forgiveness of self and others
- Generosity of time, talents, and treasure
- Closeness to a power greater than oneself
- Gratitude for blessings
- Responsibility in meeting adult social roles

Having looked at some traditional sources of spirituality, let us now explore the concepts of "healthy" versus "unhealthy" spirituality.

"HEALTHY" VERSUS "UNHEALTHY" SPIRITUALITY ▦

Because of my nursing background, I like using words like *healthy* and *unhealthy* to describe various states of spirituality. Others might prefer using *good* and *evil* or *high* or *low*. The advantage of health words is that they imply the ability to change: Sickness can become health, and health can become sickness. Further, there is no such thing as a totally sick person, just as there is no such thing as a totally well person. We are all on a continuum. Thus, the ideas of a "healthy spirituality" or "unhealthy spirituality" are ideal concepts. Further, when we use the notions of "healthy" or "unhealthy" in relation to spirituality, we realize that we are making value judgments. My view of a "healthy spirituality" may radically differ from that of a fundamentalist-type of person.

Portrait of a Healthy Spirituality

Spiritually healthy people are joyful people, people who have a deep-seated appreciation for being part of the universe. They value themselves appropriately and love their neighbors. They tend to be sensitive and compassionate toward others and are generous with their time, talent, and treasure.

If they believe in God, they pray and worship. They have grateful hearts. Such people tend to be open to new ideas and are tolerant and accepting of those who are not like

---

BOX 19.2 **Portrait of an Unhealthy Spirituality**

- Self-pity
- Selfishness
- Self-loathing
- Envy and jealousy
- Greed
- Feelings of despair
- Secretiveness
- Judgmental attitude
- Constant fear and anxiety
- Lack of direction in life
- Lack of joy
- Resentments
- "Me-orientation"
- Failure to meet adult social roles responsibly
- Intolerance of self and others
- Rigid thinking
- Lack of acceptance of those different from self

---

them; they respect others with different views. They decry sexism (both anti-male and anti-female varieties), homophobia, racism, ageism, and the like.

Spiritually healthy persons consistently meet their adult social roles in a responsible way. They realize the importance of humor and are the first to laugh at themselves and their mistakes. Not surprisingly, persons with a vibrant spirituality are people that others love to be around. They uplift the spirits of others just by their presence and presentation of self.

They strive to be good citizens, family members, spouses, parents, friends, and co-workers. In short, they strive to be always better. Needless to say, a healthy spirituality is richly reflected in other virtues such as hope, faith, courage, prudence, and fortitude.

Portrait of an Unhealthy Spirituality

It would be simple to say that an unhealthy spirituality is just the opposite of a healthy spirituality. Although this is true, an unhealthy spirituality is most vividly portrayed by those who are descending into the hell of addiction. This section focuses on such persons.

"Being a good person" is an ideal that most people adopt in early childhood. (Does any child want to grow up to be a "bad person?") Alcoholics and other addicts are no exception.

But to be "good persons" means that our behavior must match our beliefs and values. As addiction becomes more severe, addicts' behaviors often vary from their beliefs and values. For example, we all believe it is good to be fine parents, workers, and citizens. But for many addicts, the drug becomes the primary focus; parenting, working, and being a productive citizens are left by the wayside.

Another hallmark of addiction is a lack of joy. Joy is a spiritual virtue that is present in prosperous and nonprosperous times. Happiness and sadness are transitory states that we all experience. Persons with joy, however, weather the storms of life because they have a deep abiding sense of gladness at being part of the universe. Addicts, however, often find themselves in the darkness of depression, the experience of being in a black tunnel with no light at the end. As the addiction progresses, suicidal ideation, suicide gestures, and suicide attempts are not uncommon.

For Bill Wilson and many in the 12-step way of life, resentments are a clear signal that all is not well in one's spiritual life. If a person continues to harbor resentments, he or she is probably headed for a fall. This is seen in the following story.

In the Bay of Naples, there is a jellyfish, called the medusa, that sometimes eats small snails. Because of its shell, however, the snail cannot be digested. When swallowed, it attaches itself to the inside of the jellyfish and slowly begins to eat the jellyfish. When the snail is full grown, it has eaten the entire jellyfish.

Resentments, like snails, destroy from the inside. Likewise, we can be destroyed by such "snails" as envy, greed, pride, anger, rage, and hostility. There are many such "snails" ready and willing to "eat us alive" if we let them.

As addiction progresses, alcoholics and other addicts often turn away from God. Because they believe that God has abandoned them, they angrily blame God for making their lives a series of crises, never realizing that it is the addiction that is causing the crises. Needless to say, cursing God often replaces prayers of thanksgiving, which decline as addiction progresses.

Selfishness and self-centeredness, common characteristics of the addicted person, become dominant. Addicts' suffering, needs, and wants take priority. Because all their energy goes into managing one crisis after another, it is difficult for them to be other-directed and generous with time, talent, and treasure.

Persons with an unhealthy spirituality, often intolerant and nonaccepting of persons different from themselves, are often rigid thinkers who see the world in stark black-and-white terms rather than shades of gray. Pessimism is their middle name.

Other characteristics of an unhealthy spirituality include self-pity, self-loathing, secretiveness, feelings of hopelessness, lack of faith in God or others, and a lack of charity toward self or others.

SPIRITUALITY IN EVERYDAY LIFE: ⊞
A LIFE-REALM APPROACH

Many who have a very vibrant spiritual life, oblivious to that fact, mistakenly believe that traditional religiosity is the only manifestation of "spirituality." As a result, they fail to identify how the essence of life is spiritual. Take Juan Carlos, for example.

Juan Carlos is a 35-year-old member of AA who works as a financial consultant for a major national bank. He is the devoted husband of Maria and father of two sons, ages 10 and 12.

A good worker who always gives an honest day's work for an honest day's pay, Juan Carlos is kind to fellow employees and customers alike. He follows the Golden Rule in his daily life toward all people, treating others as he would have them treat him. Everybody who knows Juan Carlos has something good to say about him. He is known as a very upbeat person with a sunny outlook and kind disposition.

Juan Carlos attends the local Catholic church each Sunday and always gives to the collection. Likewise, he gives of his time and energy to his sons' various activities, and he keeps up to date on the world around him. He votes and has many friends.

In AA, he can always be counted on to help out. He sponsors two men and is his home group's district representative. When interviewed about his life in AA, he said, "I love AA. It saved my life. It really did. I don't get the 'spiritual angle' very much, though. I guess I'm just not a very spiritual person."

From all appearances, Juan Carlos has an excellent spirituality. Yet he confuses spirituality with some form of "heavy-duty" religiosity.

Let us look at how spirituality, especially in recovery, shows itself in the various realms of life.

Mental Health

Addiction always negatively affects mental health to various degrees. Common symptoms include self-loathing, self-pity, guilt, low self-esteem, anger, and resentfulness.

Long and frequent periods of depression are common in addiction. If addiction is not arrested, the addict can experience feelings of helplessness, hopelessness, and despair. Suicide *gestures,* common with intoxication, are calls for help from persons who do not actually want to kill themselves. Suicide *attempts,* however, are actual efforts to end one's life. Because it is difficult to tell the difference between the two, both gestures and attempts should be treated seriously.

In recovery, the wounded spirit is renewed. Individuals now learn to love instead of hate themselves. Guilt and unforgiving attitudes are seen as obstacles for good mental health.

Individuals in recovery are able to meet the two main criteria for positive adult mental health: (a) They meet their adult social roles (which psychotic persons generally do not), and (b) they experience an abiding joy, a feeling of being glad to be part of the universe (which depressed persons rarely, if ever, feel). Persons in recovery who do not experience an end to their depression over time should seek competent medical treatment.

Physical Health

Most people, I believe, see their bodies as gifts from God or nature. While using drugs, however, addicts abuse this gift. Alcoholism, for example, can cause a multitude of physical health problems, such as diseases of the liver, kidney, heart and circulatory system, and brain and nervous system. Broken bones from accidents and infectious diseases from uninhibited and unsafe sex are not uncommon. Death, the logical end result of many forms of chemical abuse, comes from suicide, homicide, or a drug-related disease such as cirrhosis of the liver.

In recovery, most come to realize that they should take better care of their bodies. This has spiritual value. We begin to do things such as getting more exercise, eating more balanced meals, getting plenty of rest and relaxation, and having annual physical checkups. This new regime usually pays off in experiencing more energy and feeling better.

Leisure

Leisure, well spent, is essential for a vibrant spiritual life, for without it, we can become drones.

When drinking or using, people often define leisure time in terms of drugs. Many alcoholics, for example, would no more consider going to a Perkins Pancake House for a dinner than they would consider flying to the moon; Perkins does not serve alcohol. They would rather find restaurants with at least a beer and wine license. Likewise, many addicts define their vacations, weekends, and hobbies as drug related. For the alcoholic fisherman, for example, fishing may merely be an excuse to sit on a boat all day with a friend getting drunk.

In recovery, however, we learn to enjoy leisure without alcohol and other mind-altering drugs. Faced with more leisure time, plus a clear head to enjoy it, many in recovery find new hobbies and interests. The workaholic learns to take time to "smell the roses."

Celebration Rituals

Some of you may think that "celebration rituals" as a life realm is a rather strange concept. But for addicted people, celebration rituals can be very important. Adult children of alcoholics, for example, tell stories of how holidays were ruined by the drunk parent. Christmas and other holidays are recalled as sad and sometimes scary times. Those were the days when mom or dad got really smashed, knocked over the Christmas tree, and sometimes got violent. And New Year's Eve, well, that was something else again.

Very sad indeed, for holidays, birthdays, and other special occasions put sparkle in our lives. Each holiday is rich in meaning and takes us away from the ordinariness of our daily lives. Rituals help us make these days special.

In recovery, we appreciate such days for their true meaning, not as days to get stoned but as days to be cherished. Christmas, for example, can be appreciated as the birth of Christ, Hanukkah as a festival of lights, and the Fourth of July as the birth of a nation. And the list goes on.

In recovery, we develop new celebration rituals and revive the old ones that mean so much. We treat ourselves and loved ones specially on these days, perhaps by sending cards or gifts or by decorating our homes. Maybe we invite a lonely person to celebrate with us, or we call relatives and friends to wish them a good day.

Finances and Spending Habits

I will never forget "Philip," a man in his late 20s whom I met in a chemical dependency center where I was teaching. Philip, a cocaine addict, like many cocaine addicts I know, experienced a very rapid descent into financial ruin. His addiction led him to sell his car, house, and most of his possessions and even to lose his wife and kids. Despite his devastating circumstances, he asked, in full seriousness, "Do you think I might have a problem with cocaine?"

Although cocaine addiction may result more quickly in financial calamity than other forms of drug addiction, any mind-altering drugs can lead to shaky finances and inappropriate spending habits. Lowered inhibitions caused by the drug, for example, may cause one to buy "rounds for the house." Impulse spending is another problem.

Financial problems can also result from actions caused by intoxicated states (such as car accidents) or from long-term effects of the addiction (such as divorce, alimony, child-support payments, loss of job, or illness treatments). Finally, some drugs themselves are so expensive that addicts go into debt quickly.

In recovery, people develop better spending habits. Yet some say that this is one life realm whose mastery still eludes them. One recovering addict from Chicago said about his spending habits in recovery, "Well, I still spend as much. But now I have something to show for my money. I buy things I can keep and look at and enjoy rather than blowing it in bars."

Recovering persons may ask themselves such questions as: Do I attempt to have a sound budget? Do I save regularly? Do I pay off bills on time? Do I use credit cards appropriately, or do I use them impulsively? Do I have adequate insurance so I am not a burden to others? Am I grateful for my finances, or do I constantly wish for more without ever being satisfied?

Managing finances successfully can bring simple joys that nonaddicts take for granted. "I love to pay bills now," said one recovering addict. "It is great to actually have money to pay bills."

Stewardship

Stewardship refers to how we use our time, talent, and treasure. It also refers to how we care for our possessions and the world around us. Addicts are often notorious for their lack of care for their possessions. I remember one alcoholic counselor who observed, "I can almost always tell a car owned by an alcoholic by its dents and general state of disrepair."

Because addicts are often so focused on their addiction, they become selfish with their time, talent, and treasure. For example, full-blown alcoholics in their drinking days do not have the time or inclination to give of themselves for others. They often have no money to give to worthy causes such as their synagogue, church, or charity.

Recovery tends to be a wake-up call. We are responsible for the world around us, for using our gifts wisely and generously. Do I use my time, talent, and treasure for the betterment of society? Do I care for my home in such a way that I am proud to have company over? Do I care for my car and lawn and other possessions? Am I the type of person who feels responsible for doing his or her part to make the environment beautiful for future generations? In sobriety, individuals come to see being a good steward as an integral part of their spiritual life.

Sexuality

From a spiritual perspective, sexuality is a gift with several components such as libido (or desire) and sexual orientation. Addicts sometimes do not use their gift wisely. All people, under the influence of their drug of choice, can have sex outside of their committed relationships that they would never have when clean or sober. When addicts' inhibitions fly out the window during periods of intoxication, they often do things they would never do when sober. I have found that engaging in "unsafe sex," for example, is more often a matter of being "horny" and having few inhibitions than a result of deficient knowledge. Or the intoxicated person may go home with a stranger or have sex in dangerous places that could lead to a legal citation. One man told me about his one-night stands during his drinking days: "I used to wake up in the morning and look at the person next to me and say, 'Oh, my God.' I didn't know I had a problem with alcohol, however, until one day the person next to me woke up and looked at me and said, 'Oh, my God.'"

Gay and lesbian addicts often see their sexual orientation as a curse rather than as a blessing. Unfortunately, such folks incorporate the homophobic culture around them —internalized homophobia—and come to see their sexuality as bad.

So what does a healthy sexuality look like through a spiritual lens? First, sex is fun. It's a gift to be treasured and enjoyed. It is something to celebrate. It is not something dirty and shameful. Do I use my sexuality to celebrate life? Second, it is something that can grow. Do I try to add new and fresh techniques to make sex more exciting for me and my partner? Third, healthy sex is responsible sex. In the Age of AIDS, it is wise to practice "safer sex" when possible. For cosexual couples trying to have a baby, this is often not possible, as there must be an exchange of body fluids. Fourth, one's sexual activity should be in harmony with one's sexual orientation. Gay and lesbian persons should not be "passing as straight" by having sex with the opposite sex; to do so is violating their nature. Fifth, gay men and lesbians can fight their internalized homophobia by getting to know other positive gay or lesbian persons, by prayer for acceptance, and by reading positive gay or lesbian literature (Kus, 1988). In short, they can come to see their sexual orientation as a gift no less precious than that of heterosexuality. Sixth, we should teach children that sex is something good, a wonderful gift for which to be grateful. Ideas of sex as shameful or dirty should be discarded.

In early sobriety, people often report feeling very self-conscious about having sex with others. They report that they have been using alcohol or other mind-altering drugs to anesthetize the feelings of shame or guilt that they have about sex. Now that the anesthesia is gone, it is difficult to enjoy sex. The good news is, however, that sex generally becomes more enjoyable as sobriety lengthens.

Lover/Spouse Relations

Addiction affects one's loved ones negatively. Spouses and lovers can become codependants devoted to rescuing the addict. In the process, spouses or lovers often lose their own identity and self-esteem, and they enter the downward spiral of depression, becoming filled with resentment, fear, and anger. In short, they develop an unhealthy spiritual life just like the addict.

People live a healthy spirituality in their love relationships when they see their significant other as their best friend. They are faithful to their vows or promises to each other. They are devoted to helping the other grow as a person and are not jealous of the growth. They rejoice at the successes of the other.

Many people find that praying and worshiping creates tight bonds between couples and that these bonds see the couple through tough times. Spiritually healthy couples know the value of humor and are able to laugh at themselves and not take themselves too seriously. They have a balanced view of each other and are able to accept each other's faults.

Citizenship

When persons are in active addiction, they often remove themselves from the world around them. They are out of sync with world and community events. They are so much "into themselves" that they have little energy for outside concerns. Thus, they often neglect their citizenship responsibilities.

We show our spirituality in the citizenship realm when we acknowledge our duties as citizens and act accordingly. Spiritually healthy persons keep up to date on current issues in the world and in their community. They know the candidates and what they stand for. They realize they are part of a larger world in which they are obligated to participate. They are concerned about such things as world hunger and destruction of the rain forests and violence in neighborhood schools.

Because of their concerns, they vote and give of their time, talents, and treasure to causes they believe in. They may find themselves volunteering at local hospitals or schools or parks.

Family Relations

We often hear about alcoholism and other addicts as being "family diseases." How alcoholism and other addictions affect children and other family members is well documented. The literature in this field could fill a library. Yet often family members refuse to recognize their loved one's addiction. The addiction becomes like the proverbial elephant in the living room that everyone pretends is not there.

Spiritually healthy persons are able to treat their families in a different way than active addicts. They spend quality time with their children. Unlike active addicts, who are nice one day and moody and distant the next, they are consistent in how they react to them. Children and spouses can count on their stability.

Spiritually healthy people value their families and put their families before other concerns. They respect their parents and can be counted on to help when help is needed. Spiritually healthy families rejoice in each other's successes and do everything possible to help one another grow and thrive.

Work and School

Active addicts often have trouble in the work and school realms.

Their work suffers when they are stoned, hung over, or drunk. From a spiritual perspective, one is cheating—stealing—the employer out of an honest day's work for an honest day's pay. In some cases, addicts lose their jobs as their addiction progresses. Those who do not lose their jobs cheat themselves by not being able to advance as they should. They find themselves in a rut, on a road to Nowheresville.

We demonstrate healthy spirituality in the workforce when we do an honest day's work for our pay, are on time for work, and do consistently excellent work. We bring our values into the workplace. We do not steal from our employer by using computers for personal entertainment having nothing to do with the job, by making personal phone calls, or by taking office supplies home.

In the school realm, spiritually healthy persons put their all into their learning. This is impossible when our addiction prohibits us from giving full attention to our work. Giving ourselves to our schoolwork shows love for ourselves in that we are striving to make the most of our lives, and it shows love for others in preparing ourselves for service. Needless to say, when we're in the depths of addiction, we are unable to "do school" well, thus cheating ourselves and those whom we will serve in the future and who are counting on us to be qualified.

Friendships

An interesting thing often happens with addicts as their disease worsens: They begin to change their friendship circles. Many alcoholics, for example, say that "I don't drink nearly as much as those around me." And often this is true, for as their addiction progresses, they begin to associate only with those who drink as much as themselves. When they sober up, they are surprised to learn that most of the so-called "friends" were actually only "drinking buddies."

Addicted persons often are unable to keep their promises they made to their friends —if they even remember making promises. Untrustworthy, they cannot be counted on to show up for meetings that they said they would attend. Drugs come before friendships.

We exercise healthy spirituality when we are value our friends and help them grow. We open ourselves up to our friends, share ourselves, rejoice with their accomplishments, and offer support when needed. We can be counted on through thick and thin; we are dependable.

Legal Status

We exercise our spirituality when we obey the law, at least laws that are just. Alcoholics and other addicts often find themselves in legal difficulty. Getting a "driving while intoxicated" (DWI) or "driving under the influence" (DUI) citation can cause tremendous problems for the addict in many life realms, including mental health, finances, family relationships, citizenship, work, and school.

Those addicted to illegal substances violate the law. Although many cocaine addicts, for example, violate laws about purchasing and possession cocaine to support their habit, when asked if they regard themselves as criminal, they say, "No. I'm a good person, not a criminal." Yet their behavior does not match the spiritual value of "being a good person."

Summary

Spirituality is not an isolated part of life. It permeates every life realm. When addicted, we find that we are living life in less-than-ideal ways. In fact, we often find out our life is unmanageable in many life realms.

The good news about recovery is that our spirituality can shine through all life realms and be put into practice while we are being parents or workers or lovers or whatever.

"WORKING THE PROGRAM:" ⊞
DOING 12-STEP SPIRITUALITY

No discussion of spirituality and recovery would be complete without discussing what has become known as 12-step spirituality. Millions of people throughout the world have used this form of spirituality to achieve and maintain sobriety and other forms of recovery regardless of their religion or complete lack of religion.

When persons in AA or other 12-step fellowships talk about their recovery program, they often talk about "working the program." To learn exactly what this entails, I conducted an in-depth sociological study in the 1980s with gay American men who were all AA members (Kus, 1988). I found that "working the program" was composed of seven large clusters of activities. Taken together, I refer to them as "12-step spirituality." (This term applies as well, of course, to other 12-step fellowships such as Narcotics Anonymous [NA] and Cocaine Anonymous.) The clusters are (a) working the 12 steps of AA (see p. 258); (b) attending and participating in AA meetings; (c) reading literature; (d) recalling and applying common AA slogans to everyday life; (e) sharing self with others; (f) doing non-AA activities that arise from living the 12-step way of life; and (g) doing everyday tasks as well as one can.

Working the 12 Steps

Imagine a dirty house. Recovery is recognizing that the house is a mess, cleaning the house from stem to stern, and then taking steps to keep it clean. Steps 1 to 3, which are often called the "surrender" steps, help persons admit that their "house" is out of control and needs a thorough cleaning. Because they cannot do this themselves, they ask for help. In AA terminology, this help is from God as we understand Him. Steps 4 through 9, often called the "working" steps, are designed to clean the house. Finally, after the house is nice and clean, we have the "maintenance" steps, 10 through 12, which are designed to keep the house clean through time. The beauty of these 12 steps is their simplicity. Anyone can work them.

Attending AA Meetings

Attending AA meetings, although not part of the 12 steps, is usually crucial for recovery. This is especially important in the early days of recovery. In meetings, individuals learn that they are not unique; their stories are shared by thousands of others. They learn about AA and its literature and wisdom and history. They learn to listen, and they learn to share. Meetings present opportunities for helping others by doing such things as making coffee, giving rides to others, or taking down folding chairs.

Reading Literature

All persons in my study reported that reading literature—bibliotherapy—was an integral part of their recovery program. The most popular book was *Alcoholics Anonymous* (third edition; AA, 1976), more commonly known as the "Big Book." Almost all of the men also read daily meditation guides. Other types of literature used were books on alcoholism and AA, spirituality, self-help books, and the like.

Recalling and Applying AA Slogans

All men reported that recalling and applying common AA slogans in their everyday lives was an integral part of "working the program" for them. Some common AA slogans are "Easy does it," "Live and let live," "One day at a time," "But for the grace of God

..., " "First things first," "Keep it simple," and "H.A.L.T.," (i.e., don't let yourself get too hungry, angry, lonely, or tired).

Sharing Self

In 12-step circles, one often hears the idea that "a problem shared is a problem halved, while a problem kept secret is a problem doubled." In a similar vein, we hear, "You are as sick as your secrets." Three of the steps specifically ask individuals to share themselves with other human beings: Steps 5, 9, and 12. Many AA members report, however, that they also feel that sharing themselves with a sponsor and other AA members is critical to quality sobriety.

Doing Non-AA Activities

In one small Iowa town with which I am familiar, the local AA group met in the town hall that was attached to the fire trucks of the volunteer fire department. It would be common for several members to have to leave the meetings when a fire call came in, as they were volunteer firefighters. These volunteers explained that, in their drinking days, they had given nothing to their community. Now, in recovery, they realized that they needed to "pay back" what they had not given in the past. Thus, many people in recovery find themselves volunteering in their communities in addition to helping out their AA group.

Doing Everyday Tasks Well

In Step 12, individuals are asked to "practice these principles" in all their affairs. Yet when one looks at the 12 steps themselves, there are not too many actual "principles" listed. So the men in my study interpreted this to mean doing everyday tasks as well as they could. This is sometimes known as the "little way"—doing even the little things of life as well as one possibly can. The person most associated with this "little way" is St. Theresa, the "Little Flower."

HOW HELPING PROFESSIONALS CAN HELP ⊞

Just as a teacher must start at the level of the learner, the helping professional must start at the client's level. The first thing I would advise you, the addiction specialist, to do is to learn how clients see spirituality. Are they confusing it with religion? Do they see it as an isolated part of life? Or do they see it as I do, something that permeates all life realms? If clients confuse spirituality with religion, help them distinguish between the two.

Explore with your clients traditional sources of spirituality. How do they pray? Do they meditate? Do they take time for solitude and communing with nature? Do they get nourished in a faith community? Share how you use spirituality. Share your own spiritual journey if you are comfortable. One does not need to proselytize here. Rather, keep it simple.

Encourage your addicted clients to explore the 12-step way of life, whether AA, NA, Cocaine Anonymous, or some other group. Encourage them to attend "90 meetings in 90 days." Try to help them see that the 12-step way of life always works if one "works it," just as a ball will roll if we put the effort into pushing it. By thoroughly living a 12-step way of life, your clients will learn how to pray, meditate, and see their lives as spiritual.

Emphasize that 12-step spirituality, like recovery, is a 24-hour-a-day endeavor. It is a way of life, not a series of meetings or a group one simply "joins."

Encourage your clients to find a helper on their journey. Those in the 12-step way of life often have a "sponsor"; others may utilize a counselor or other trusted friend.

Encourage your clients to open up and share themselves. Keeping things bottled up is harmful not only to one's spiritual growth but to one's mental health as well.

Know your community resources in addiction recovery. Keep lists of recovery group meetings in your offices, and know clergy and other spiritual advisors who are especially tuned into recovery issues.

Keep up to date on current readings in 12-step spirituality and related areas (see my collection of scholarly essays titled *Spirituality and Chemical Dependency*; Kus, 1995). I would recommend, of course, that persons in 12-step programs definitely read the "Big Book" or official manual of their fellowship (e.g., AA, 1976; NA, 1987). Another book that I have found very helpful is Pittman's *The 12 Step Prayer Book: A Collection of Favorite 12 Step Prayers and Inspirational Writings* (1990). I also encourage readers to get on the mailing list for Hazelden, which has a large collection of up-to-date books on spirituality and recovery (phone 1-800-328-9000), and to use Internet bookstores such as Amazon.com and BarnesandNoble.com.

Most important, praise your clients for their efforts in their spiritual journeys. An ounce of praise is far more potent than a pound of scorn.

▦ REFERENCES

Alcoholics Anonymous World Services. (1976). *Alcoholics Anonymous: The story of how many thousands of men and women have recovered from alcoholism* (3rd ed.). New York: Author.

Alcoholics Anonymous. (1981). *Twelve Steps and twelve traditions.* New York: Author.

Cavanaugh, B. (1996). *Sower's seeds aplenty: Fourth planting.* Mahway, NJ: Paulist Press.

Kus, R. J. (1988). "Working the program": The Alcoholics Anonymous experience and gay American men. *Holistic Nursing Practice, 2*(4), 62-74.

Kus, R. J. (Ed.). (1995). *Spirituality and chemical dependency.* New York: Harrington Park.

Narcotics Anonymous World Service Office. (1987). *Narcotics Anonymous* (4th ed.). Van Nuys, CA: Author.

Pittman, B. (1990). *The 12 step prayer book: A collection of favorite 12 step prayers and inspirational writings.* Seattle, WA: Glen Abbey.

20

Acupuncture
A Venerable Nonverbal Therapy

Michael O. Smith
Kathryn P. White

cupuncture is currently used in the treatment of addictions by approximately 1,000 addiction treatment programs. Clinical evidence supports that it is effective in ameliorating withdrawal and craving symptoms associated with alcohol, opiate, and cocaine dependence, as well as symptoms associated with most other addictions. Acupuncture for cocaine dependence has been particularly recognized as an important innovation, since there are presently no established pharmaceutical treatments for cocaine dependence. Acupuncture is used by programs as a foundation for later psychosocial recovery. It is a nonverbal, nonthreatening, "first step" intervention that has an immediate calming effect on patients. Initial participation with acupuncture has been found to improve patients' overall treatment retention and to facilitate their subsequent involvement. In most programs, patients receive 4-5 ear acupuncture points while seated together in a large group room so that a substantial number of patients can be treated conveniently. This safe and cost-efficient procedure has gained increasing acceptance from agencies responsible for overseeing addiction treatment. This chapter describes the practical use and research findings relating to acupuncture for addiction. We also cover mechanisms of action that involve physiology and psychosocial process.

Acupuncture is a major component of the ancient tradition of Chinese medicine. The principles and goals of this form of treatment have remained constant through time. The textbook that is most often used today, the *Nei Jing*, was written 2,000 years ago. Acupuncture was used by numerous 19th century U.S. practitioners, including Sir William Osler. In the early 1970s, American interest was renewed when relations with China were opened. In the U.S., most states have acupuncture licensing laws. Acupuncture is recognized by established medical organizations in virtually every part of the world. Veterinary medical journals cite many examples of objective clinical success, including treatment of potentially lethal arthritis in horses and congenital hip dysplasia in dogs. Effective treatment of animals is usually cited as proof that acupuncture is not merely a placebo procedure.

⊞ CHARACTERISTICS OF POINTS

Acupuncture consists of the stimulation of specified locations on the surface of the body that alters and improves bodily function. The Chinese term for a treatment location is *xue*, which means opening. The traditional Chinese names for these locations often refer to flow on the surface of the earth such as valley, marsh, crevice, or stream. In the West, the term *point* is used. Acupuncture points are physiologically distinct from the immediate environment; they have less electrical resistance and, therefore, greater electrical conductivity. The points are warmer than the surrounding area by 0.1-0.2 of a degree. The difference in warmth and electrical activity can be detected by the human hand as well as by instruments. A painful response to pressure may also be used as a point indicator. The precise location of these phenomena varies within a small area that corresponds to the acupuncture point as denoted on an acupuncture chart. Descriptions of the location and functions of these points have remained constant through the centuries.

Acupuncture points can be stimulated by various means: touch, movement, heat, electricity, as well as needling. Health-related procedures such as acupressure, shiatsu, reiki, and tai ji chuan work on the same principles as acupuncture even though no needles are used. Needling is the most convenient and efficient means of stimulating acupuncture points.

Acupuncture needles are stainless steel shafts of varying length and thickness. The handle of the needle usually has an additional spiral winding made of copper. Most needles are silver coated. The needles may be cleaned, sterilized, and reused as is the case with surgical equipment. Most Western facilities use the needles once and discard them. Acupuncture needles are provided in convenient sterile packages. Needles are inserted with a brief but steady movement. Ear needles penetrate one eighth inch, contacting the cartilage if it is present in that location. Needles are twirled 180 degrees for smoother insertion. The patient may feel a momentary sensation like a pinch. Occasionally there is a brief, sharper sensation that may cause the patient to complain. The procedure is nearly painless and causes the rapid onset of a gratifying sense of relaxation. On first exposure, most patients express fear of the pain of needle insertion and are confused by the idea that little needles can cope with their big problems. This fear is easily solved by letting prospective patients observe other patients undergoing the actual process of treatment. It is a mistake to rely on leaflets and verbal explanations.

⊞ PATIENTS' EXPERIENCE

Patients may notice local paresthesia effects, such as warmth and tingling. There may be sensations of warmth, electrical movement, or heaviness in other parts of the body, although these reactions are more typical of body acupuncture rather than ear acupuncture. Patients may feel quite sleepy after each of the first several treatments. This reaction is part of the acute recovery process and passes readily. A few patients develop a headache at the end of a treatment session. Shortening the length of the session or reducing the number of needles resolves this problem. Rarely, a needling reaction occurs in which the patient feels dizzy, light-headed, and may actually faint. This reaction (postural hypotension) occurs in many medical and dental settings. When it occurs, remove the needles and help the patient lie on a flat surface. The syncope will resolve within a few minutes, and the patient will exhibit relaxed behavior as though the full treatment had been given. Needling reactions occur more often in persons with a relatively labile autonomic nervous system. Fortunately these reactions are quite rare in the treatment of addiction. Patients should be told to eat before coming for treatment in order to reduce the possibility of a needling reaction.

The insertion of acupuncture needles never causes bleeding. Hence there is no need for special blood contact precautions during application of treatment. Based on our experience, treatment sites in the ear bleed about 1% of time after the needles are removed. Thus 10-20% of patients will have such a reaction. There are several methods that are being used to cope with this problem in terms of appropriate risk management precautions. Commonly, the patients are asked to remove their own needles and place them directly in a sharps container. Staff may remove needles by only touching the handle and giving the patient a cotton pad to use if bleeding is noted. A small hematoma may also occur. Staff may press each location with a Q-tip as necessary. Most gloves do not provide dexterity in grasping small needles. It should be noted that ear needles are inserted so shallowly that about 10% fall out during the period of treatment. Therefore many needles must be retrieved which have fallen on the patient's clothing. Even wearing gloves will not protect staff who might try to search for such needles. Hence the patients must be instructed to locate any fallen needles and discard them properly. Often programs use a needle count procedure. Patients place needles in a paper cup or bowl so that staff can verify that all needles are present before they are discarded in the sharps container. This procedure is particularly appropriate if acupuncture is conducted in a room that is used for other purposes.

PHYSIOLOGICAL MECHANISMS OF ACTION ⊞

There have been many efforts to determine the underlying physiological mechanisms of acupuncture. Some of the efforts were based on the misleading assumption that acupuncture is primarily a treatment for pain relief. Many acupuncture functions, such as autonomic and gastrointestinal effects, are independent of any aspect that relates to pain. In other cases, such as the treatment of frozen shoulder, pain is actually temporarily increased after successful acupuncture needling. More accurately, acupuncture is frequently an effective treatment for the circulatory, neurological, or inflammatory causes of pain.

Acupuncture charts have a superficial resemblance to Western neuroanatomical charts. The functions of the meridian channels on acupuncture charts differ substantially, however, from those of nearby peripheral nerve trunks. Ear acupuncture is a particularly clear example in this regard. The acupuncture chart of the external ear identifies more than a hundred separate acupuncture points. These points relate primarily to different body locations and to various organic functions. One can easily verify some of these correlations by noting that the shoulder point on the ear shows abnormally low electrical resistance in patients with shoulder injuries, as does the ureter point in patients who are passing a kidney stone. The simple innervation pattern of the external ear cannot be used to explain these effects.

Researchers have noted the following variety of specific physiological effects associated with acupuncture as cited in Brewington (1994). It has been reported that acupuncture at traditional points produced dramatic effects in EEG, GSR, blood flow, and breathing rate, while stimulation by needle placement in placebo points produced no appreciable effects. Various studies have linked acupuncture to the production of endogenous opiate peptides, such as beta-endorphin and metenkephalins, and this has been speculated as a physiological mechanism behind the treatment's effects on withdrawal discomfort. Acupuncture has also been related to changes regarding other neurotransmitters, including ACTH and cortisol levels, serotonin and norepinephrine and 5-HT. A review of research linking endogenous opiate peptide (EOP) production to optimal immune system functioning concluded that acupuncture appears to have beneficial effects on the immune system. A substantial literature thus exists supporting that acupuncture has a variety of neurochemical and other physiological effects.

It should be noted that certain medications—namely, methadone, corticosteroids, and benzodiazepines—seem to suppress part of the acupuncture effect. Patients taking these medications in substantial quantity have clearly less relaxation effect during treatment and may have a slower response to treatment. Nevertheless, acupuncture is an effective treatment for secondary addiction in high dose methadone patients. Acupuncture is also widely used to treat adrenal suppressed patients who need to be weaned off corticosteroid medication. This may suggest that part of the initial relaxation response is endorphin- and steroid-dependent but that the more important mechanisms relate to a different type of process.

Acupuncture effects have been documented in a wide range of organisms. Needling the stem of a plant at a low resistance point will correlate with a rapid increase in the temperature of the tips of the leaves as measured by thermography. Needling a point of normal resistance will produce no such effect (Eory, 1995).

It is too restrictive to define acupuncture mechanisms in terms of highly evolved structures such as the human brain and the endocrine system. Rather, it seems clear that acupuncture involves the primitive and pervasive functions that are common to all life. Such functions include circulation on a microscopic level, homeostasis, wound healing, immune function, and microneurological functioning. Acupuncture has an obvious impact on the autonomic nervous system that is an example of a relatively primitive and homeostatic system in human beings. Acupuncture seems to enhance the integrity of these basic life functions. Pharmaceutic medicine, at best, can only suppress one or more parts of these systems. The Society for Acupuncture Research (SAR) meets yearly to discuss these issues of mechanism and research. Acupuncture research may provide a window of opportunity for us to enhance our understanding of basic and pervasive vital processes.

⊞ LINCOLN HOSPITAL PROTOCOL

Acupuncture treatment for drug and alcohol problems was primarily developed at Lincoln Hospital, a New York City owned facility in the impoverished South Bronx. The Lincoln Recovery Center is a state-licensed treatment program that has provided more than 500,000 acupuncture treatments in the past 20 years. Dr. Yoshiaki Omura was the consultant who began the program (Omura, 1975).

Initially, in 1974, Lincoln used Dr. H. L. Wen's method, applying electrical stimulation to the lung point in the ear (Wen, 1973). Lincoln was a methadone detoxification program at that time; therefore, acupuncture was used as an adjunctive treatment for prolonged withdrawal symptoms after the 10-day detoxification cycle. Patients reported less malaise and better relaxation in symptom surveys.

Subsequently, twice daily acupuncture was used concurrently with tapering methadone doses. Reduction in opiate withdrawal symptoms and prolonged program retention were noted.

It was accidentally discovered that electrical stimulation was not necessary to produce symptomatic relief. Simple manual needling produced a more prolonged effect. Patients were able to use acupuncture only one time a day and still experience a suppression of their withdrawal symptoms. A reduction in craving for alcohol and heroin was described for the first time. This observation corresponds to the general rule in acupuncture that strong stimulation has primarily a symptom-suppression or sedation effect and that more gentle stimulation has more of a long term, preventive or tonification effect.

Gradually the acupuncture protocol was expanded by adding the shen men (spirit gate), a point known for producing relaxation. Other ear points were tried on the basis of lower resistance, pain sensitivity, and clinical indication during a several year developmental process. The author added the sympathetic, kidney, and liver points to create a basic five point formula.

Numerous other point formulas using body acupuncture points were tried on an individual basis without any significant improvement. Some programs omit the sympathetic point in pregnant patients. There is no basis in acupuncture texts for this precaution.

A standard acupuncture textbook (Bensky, 1986) describes the functions of each of the five points in the basic formula as follows:

- **Sympathetic**: used for numerous diseases related to disruption in both sympathetic and parasympathetic nervous systems. It has a strong analgesic and relaxant effect upon internal organs. It dilates blood vessels.
- **Shen men**: regulates excitation and inhibition of the cerebral cortex. Sedative and antiallergy effects. Used for many neuropsychiatric disorders.
- **Lung**: used for analgesia, sweating, and various respiratory conditions.
- **Liver**: used for hepatitis, anemia, neuralgia, muscle spasms, and eye diseases.
- **Kidney**: strengthening point for the cerebrum, hematopoietic system, and kidneys. Used for neurasthenia, lassitude, headache, and urogenital problems.

Traditional Chinese theory associates the lung with the grieving process, the liver with resolving aggression, and the kidney with will power, coping with fear, and new growth.

VALUE OF STANDARD POINTS ⊞

The value of using one standard group of acupuncture points became increasingly clear. The standard formula seemed to be equally effective for different drugs of abuse and at different stages of treatment. Patients responded better when acupuncture treatment was administered quickly without a self-conscious, diagnostic prelude. Because acu-

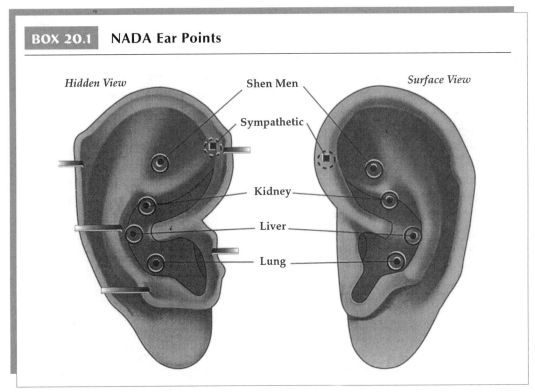

BOX 20.1 **NADA Ear Points**

Hidden View   Shen Men   *Surface View*

Sympathetic

Kidney

Liver

Lung

SOURCE: From Auriculotherapy Handbook, copyright © Terrance Oleson. Used with permission

puncture produces a homeostatic response, it was not necessary to adjust the formula for mood swings, agitation, or anergy.

From the point of view of Chinese theory, using a single basic formula for such generally depleted patients is appropriate. In traditional Chinese medicine, the lack of a calm inner tone in a person is described as a condition of empty fire (xu huo), because the heat of aggressiveness burns out of control when the calm inner tone is lost. It is easy to be confused by the empty fire that many addicts exhibit and to conclude that the main goal should be the sedation of excess fire. Addicts themselves take this approach in the extreme by using sedative drugs. The empty fire condition represents the illusion of power, an illusion that leads to more desperate use of chemicals and to senseless violence. Acupuncture helps patients with this condition to restore their inner control.

A group setting enhances the acupuncture effect. A group size of less than six members seems to diminish symptoms relief and retention significantly. Patients receiving acupuncture in an individual setting are often self-conscious and easily distracted. These problems are more evident in the management of new patients. In general, acupuncture treatment sessions need to last 20-25 minutes. Because chemical dependency patients are more resistant and dysfunctional, they should be instructed to remain in the acupuncture group setting for 40-45 minutes so that a full effect is obtained. The atmosphere of the treatment room should be adjusted to fit varying clinical circumstances. Programs with a significant number of new intakes and/or socially isolated patients should use a well-lighted room and allow a moderate amount of conversation in order to minimize alienation and encourage social bonding. On the other hand, programs with relatively fixed clientele who relate to each other frequently in other group settings should dim the lights and not allow any conversation in order to minimize distracting cross talk. Background music is often used in the latter circumstance.

The location of ear points and the technique of insertion can be taught effectively in a 70-hour apprenticeship-based program. Most acupuncture components can be staffed by a wide range of addiction clinicians such as counselors, social workers, nurses, medical doctors, and psychologists. Training must include a clinical apprenticeship because coping with the individual distractions and group process is more important and more difficult to learn than the technical skill of repetitive needle insertion. Each clinician can provide about 15 treatments per hour in a group setting. General supervision should be provided by licensed or certified acupuncturists. This arrangement allows for acupuncture to be integrated with existing services in a flexible and cost-effective manner. Lincoln Hospital has trained more than 3,000 clinicians, usually referred to as Acu Detox Specialists (ADS), in the past seven years. The National Acupuncture Detoxification Association (NADA) was established in 1985 to increase the use of the Lincoln model and to maintain quality and responsibility in the field.

ROLE OF HERBAL FORMULA

The first author developed an herbal formula known as sleep mix that is used in most acupuncture for addiction settings and many other health care settings as well. The formula includes camomile, peppermint, yarrow, scullcap, hops, and catnip. These are inexpensive herbs, traditionally used in Europe, which are reputed to calm and soothe the nervous system and tend to stimulate circulation and the elimination of waste products. The herb formula is taken as a tea on a nightly basis or frequently during the day as symptoms indicate. Sleep mix can be used for the treatment of conventional stress and insomnia as well as providing an adjunctive support in addiction treatment settings. Sleep mix is particularly appropriate for the management of alcohol withdrawal symptoms. Patients receiving conventional benzodiazepine treatment will often voluntarily refuse this medication if sleep mix is available.

The Lincoln Hospital model can be summarized and defined as follows:

1. Clinicians use 3-5 ear acupuncture points including sympathetic, shen men, lung, kidney, and liver.

2. Treatment is provided in a group setting for a duration of 40-45 minutes.

3. Acupuncture treatment is integrated with conventional elements of psychosocial rehabilitation.

4. Several components of the Lincoln program are frequently combined with acupuncture in other treatment facilities. These items include a supportive, nonconfrontational approach to individual counseling; an emphasis on Narcotics Anonymous and other 12-Step activities early in the treatment process; an absence of screening for appropriate patients; the use of herbal sleep mix; the use of frequent toxicologies; a willingness to work with court-related agencies; and a tolerant, informal, family-like atmosphere.

CONTROLLED RESEARCH

H. L. Wen, MD, of Hong Kong was the first physician to report successful use of acupuncture treatment of addiction withdrawal symptoms (Wen, 1973). He observed that opium addicts receiving electro acupuncture as postsurgical analgesia experienced relief of withdrawal symptoms. The lung ear point was used. Subsequently, Wen conducted several basic clinical pilot studies that formed the basis of subsequent research.

Results from available placebo-design studies support the conclusion that acupuncture's effectiveness in facilitating abstinence with alcohol, opiate, and cocaine abusers is not due to a simple placebo effect (Brewington, 1994). Seven published studies involving animal subjects (i.e., mice or rats) indicate that electro acupuncture (EA) reduces opiate withdrawal symptoms with morphine-addicted subjects. In these studies, experimental and control animals show behavioral differences regarding rodent opiate withdrawal symptoms, such as hyperactivity, wet dog shakes, and teeth chattering. Each of these studies notes significantly less withdrawal symptoms with subjects receiving EA relative to controls. Significantly different hormonal and beta endorphin levels post-EA are noted between experimental and control subjects in several of these studies.

A number of controlled studies have been conducted on human subjects using various modified versions of the Lincoln Hospital ear point formula. Washburn (1993) reported that opiate-addicted individuals receiving correct site acupuncture showed significantly better program attendance relative to subjects receiving acupuncture on placebo sites. Two placebo-design studies provide strong support regarding acupuncture's use as a treatment for alcoholics. Bullock (1987) studied 54 chronic alcoholics randomly assigned to receive acupuncture either at points related to addiction or at nearby point locations not specifically related to addiction. Subjects were treated in an inpatient setting but were free to leave the program each day.

Throughout the study, experimental subjects showed significantly better outcomes regarding attendance and their self-reported need for alcohol. Significant differences favoring the experimental group were also found regarding (a) the number self-reported drinking episodes, (b) self reports concerning the effectiveness of acupuncture in affecting the desire to drink, and (c) the number of subjects admitted to a local detoxification unit for alcohol-related treatment. Bullock (1989) replicated Bullock (1987) using a larger ($n = 80$) sample over a longer (6 months) follow-up period. Twenty-one of 40 patients in the treatment group completed the 8-week treatment period as compared with 1 of 40 controls. Significant differences favoring the experimental group were again noted. Placebo subjects self-reported over twice the number of drinking episode reported by experimentals. Placebo subjects were also readmitted to the local hospital alcohol detoxification unit at over twice the rate as experimental subjects during the follow-up period. Worner (1992) examined outpatient treatment outcomes for a sample ($n = 56$) of alcoholic subjects assigned to one of three conditions; acupuncture ($n = 19$), sham transdermal stimulation ($n = 21$), and control/standard care ($n = 16$). Acupuncture involved both ear and body points, provided only 3 times weekly over a 3-month period. Subjects exposed to sham transdermal stimulation had electrocardiogram pads attached to their arms and legs and were told that the procedure was a needleless form of acupuncture. No significant between-group differences were noted on outcome measures (e.g., retention, AA attendance, alcohol relapse). It was concluded that acupuncture's purported effectiveness in treating alcohol withdrawal may be a placebo effect, and that their results were at variance with Bullock (1987). While statistically significant effects were not observed, it should be noted that the acupuncture group showed the best outcomes on seven of eight measures reported. Given this trend, it seems probable that results may have reached statistical significance if a larger sample were used.

Lipton (1994) conducted a placebo design experiment regarding the effectiveness of acupuncture treatment for chronic cocaine/crack abuse. Subjects ($n = 150$) were randomly assigned to receive either auricular acupuncture at correct sites or acupuncture at nearby ear points not related to detoxification. Self-report measures and urinalysis profiles showed a significant tendency with both groups toward decreased cocaine consumption. Pretreatment cocaine/crack usage averaged about 20 days per month with all subjects. Self-reported use was reduced to an average of 5 days per month with both groups. Urinalysis profiles indicated superior outcomes with the experimental group during treatment. Over the course of treatment, experimental subjects showed a significant tendency toward greater day-to-day decreases in cocaine metabolite levels. This result was particularly pronounced after 2 weeks of treatment. Placebo subjects who remained in treatment over 2 weeks showed cocaine metabolite levels that were on average slightly higher than that shown at baseline (i.e., on treatment day number 1). Experimental subjects consistently showed lower than baseline metabolite levels throughout treatment.

"PLACEBO" POINTS MAY BE "ACTIVE" ▦

Konefal (1995) examined the efficacy of different acupuncture point protocol with patients with various alcohol and other drug problems. Subjects (*n* = 321) were randomly assigned to one of three groups: a one-needle auricular treatment protocol using the shen men point, the five-needle Lincoln protocol, or the five-needle Lincoln protocol plus selected body points for self-reported symptoms. All groups showed an increase in the proportion of drug-free urine tests over the course of treatment. Subjects with the single-needle protocol, however, showed significantly less improvement compared to the other two groups.

During the trial and error search conducted at Lincoln Hospital for a more effective ear acupuncture formula for addiction treatment, it was clear that a large number of points had some effect on acute withdrawal symptoms. Ear acupuncture charts indicate that all areas on the anterior surface of the ear are identified as active treatment locations. Using a placebo or sham acupuncture technique is actually an effort to use relatively ineffective points in contrast to the conventional use of totally ineffective sugar pills in pharmaceutical trials. Sham points are usually located on the external helix or rim of the ear, although there is no consensus about the level of effectiveness of this procedure. Bullock's alcoholism studies used highly failure-prone subjects and hence may have revealed the difference between active and sham points more effectively.

CLINICAL APPLICATIONS ▦

Acupuncture is being used in numerous diverse treatment settings. Outcome reports have been published only to a limited degree because of the journals' emphasis on placebo controlled studies. Unless otherwise noted, these outcomes are based on clinical experiences at Lincoln Hospital or personal observation of other programs made by the first author.

Opiate addiction was first treated by Dr. Wen in Hong Kong and has been treated at Lincoln Hospital since 1974. Acupuncture provides nearly complete relief of acute observable opiate withdrawal symptoms in 5 to 30 minutes. This effect lasts for 8 to 24 hours. The duration of this effect increases with the number of serial treatments provided. Patients often sleep during the first session and may feel hungry afterward. Patients who are acutely intoxicated at the time acupuncture is administered will behave in a much less intoxicated manner after the session. Surprisingly, these patients are gratified by this result, in contrast to patient reports of discomfort after Narcan administration.

Acupuncture for opiate addiction is typically administered 2 to 3 times daily in acute detoxification settings. Alternatively, it may be administered only once a day with clonidine or methadone on an outpatient basis. Many patients do well on once-daily acupuncture because they taper their illicit opiate usage over a 3- to 4-day period. Heroin addicts usually seek detox to reduce the size of their habit, so this arrangement fits their immediate goals. The addition of an acupuncture component to an opiate detoxification program typically leads to a 50% increase in retention for completion of the recommend length of stay.

ALCOHOL ADDICTION

Directors of the acupuncture social setting detox program conducted by the Tulalip Tribe at Marysville, Washington have estimated a yearly saving of $148,000 due to less frequent referrals to hospital programs. Inpatient alcohol detoxification units typically combine acupuncture and herbal "sleep mix" with a tapering benzodiazepine protocol. Patients report few symptoms and better sleep. Their vital signs indicate stability and hence, there is much less use of benzodiazepines. One residential program in Connecticut noted a 90% decrease in Valium use when only herbal "sleep mix" was added to their protocol.

Retention of alcohol detox patients generally increases by 50% when an acupuncture component is added to conventional settings. Some alcoholics who receive acupuncture actually report an aversion to alcohol. Woodhull Hospital in Brooklyn reported that 94% of the patients in the acupuncture supplement group remained abstinent as compared to 43% of the control group who only received conventional outpatient services. The widely quoted controlled study by Bullock (1989) showed a 52% retention of alcoholism patients as compared to a two percent sham acupuncture retention rate.

COCAINE ADDICTION

Cocaine addiction has provided the most important challenge for acupuncture treatment because there are no significant pharmaceutical agents for this condition. Acupuncture patients report more calmness and reduced craving for cocaine even after the first treatment. The acute psychological indications of cocaine toxicity are visibly reduced during the treatment session. This improvement is sustained for a variable length of time after the first acupuncture treatment. After 3 to 7 sequential treatments, the anticraving effect is more or less continuous as long as acupuncture is received on a regular basis.

Researchers from the substance abuse treatment unit at Yale University describe 32 cocaine-dependent methadone-maintained patients who received an 8-week course of auricular acupuncture for the treatment of cocaine dependence. Fifty percent completed treatment, with 88% of study completers attained abstinence, defined as providing cocaine-free urine samples for the last 2 weeks of the study, yielding an overall abstinence rate of 44%. Abstainers reported decreased depression, a shift in self-definition, decreased craving, and increased aversion to cocaine-related cues. Post-hoc comparisons to pharmacotherapy with desipramine (DMI), amantadine (AMA), and placebo revealed a higher abstinence rate for acupuncture (44%) than for AMA (15%) or placebo (13%), but not significantly higher than for DMI (26%)(Margolin, 1993).

Urinalysis outcomes were examined for Lincoln Hospital patients using cocaine or crack who had more than 20 treatment visits and were active during the 1-week study period in March 1991. At Lincoln, patients typically provide urine samples for testing during each visit. Of the entire study group of 226 patients, 149 had more than 80% negative tests during their entire treatment involvement. Of the remaining patients, 39 had at least 80% negative tests during the two weeks prior to data collection.

Urinalysis Results	*Number*	*%*
More than 80% negative	149	65
Recent 80% negative	39	17
Recent relapse	26	12

Methamphetamine using patients experience similar dramatic increases in treatment retention. Hooper Foundation, the public detoxification center in Portland, Oregon, reported five percent retention of methamphetamine users prior to the use of acupuncture and 90% retention after adding acupuncture to their protocol. Increased psychological stability and decreased craving were cited.

METHADONE ⊞

Methadone maintenance patients receive acupuncture in a number of different settings. Patients report a decrease in secondary symptoms of methadone use such as constipation, sweating, and sleep problems. Typically there is a substantial drop in requests for symptomatic medication. Treatment staff usually notice decreased hostility and increased compliance in methadone-acupuncture patients. The most important impact of acupuncture in maintenance programs is reduction of secondary substance abuse, primarily involving cocaine, even in patients with minimal motivation (Margolin, 1993). Reductions in secondary alcohol use are also frequently described. Acupuncture is effective with patients in any dosage level of methadone.

Lincoln Hospital used methadone and acupuncture together from 1974 to 1978. Several hundred methadone maintenance patients were detoxified during that period using tapered doses of methadone and acupuncture. Based on our previous nonacupuncture experience, we observed that patients were much more comfortable and confident when they received acupuncture. Even though patients regularly complained about withdrawal symptoms, there were very few requests for dosage increase. The large majority of patients completed the entire detoxification process and provided at least one negative toxicology after the cessation of methadone.

Methadone dosages were decreased 5 to 10 mg per week with a slower schedule during the final 10 mg. Starting levels of methadone ranged from 20 mg to 90 mg with a median of 60 mg. Acupuncture was provided 6 days per week and continued up to 2 months after the last methadone dose. Although many of these patients had been referred for administrative or mandatory detoxification due to secondary drug use, toxicologies were usually drug-free after the first 2 to 3 weeks of treatment.

Methadone withdrawal is notable for unpredictable variations in symptoms and significant postwithdrawal malaise. Symptoms such as depression, anergy, and atypical insomnia are quite difficult to manage without acupuncture. Patients are usually fearful and have considerable difficulty participating in psychosocial therapy during the detoxification period. Acupuncture is particularly valuable in the methadone-to-abstinence (MTA) setting, because the patients' future well being depends on their ability to utilize psychosocial support during the detoxification period.

⊞ MARIJUANA

At Lincoln, the first author has had a significant number of primary marijuana users seeking care. These patients usually report a rapid reduction in craving and improved mental well being. Secondary marijuana use is usually eliminated along with the detoxification of the primary drug (e.g., cocaine).

⊞ EFFECTS ON PATIENT RETENTION AND RECIDIVISM

The beneficial effects of acupuncture in cocaine treatment often lead to dramatic increases in retention of cocaine patients. Women in Need, a program located near Times Square in New York, reported the following outcome figures in their treatment for pregnant crack using women:

1. Patients with conventional outpatient treatment averaged 3 visits a year.

2. Patients who took acupuncture in addition to conventional treatment averaged 27 visits a year.

3. Patients who participated in an educational component in addition to acupuncture and conventional treatment averaged 67 visits a year.

Patients averaging 3 visits per year would be unlikely to participate in an educational component. Therefore, it seems likely that the increased retention correlated with acupuncture set a foundation for successful participation in the educational component.

Acupuncture detoxification programs report substantial reduction in their recidivism rates. Hooper Foundation cited a decrease from 25% to 6% in comparison to the previous nonacupuncture year. Kent-Sussex Detoxification Center (in Delaware) reported a decrease in recidivism from 87% to 18%.

Substance Abuse Recovery (Flint, Michigan) noted that 83% of a group of 100 General Motors employees were drug- and alcohol-free productive workers a year after entering acupuncture-based treatment. Most of these patients had repeated prior attempts at treatment and frequent relapse. All of the 17% failure group had less than 5 program visits. Seventy-four percent of the success group continued to attend AA and NA meetings after completing the treatment program. Programs specifically designed for adolescents, such as the Alcohol Treatment Center in Chicago and a Job Corps related program in Brooklyn, have shown retention rates comparable to adult programs.

FREQUENCY, DURATION OF TREATMENT ⊞

Acupuncture treatment is generally made available to patients 5 to 6 days per week. Lincoln offers treatment during an 8-hour period, but many smaller programs offer acupuncture during 1- to 2-hour time periods each day. Morning treatment hours seem to be more beneficial. Active patients will receive treatment 3 to 6 times per week. Initially acupuncture should be defined as an expected part of the program. If one describes acupuncture as a voluntary or optional part of the program, this description is not useful to a crisis-ridden addicted person. Such a person cannot handle choice and ambivalence effectively. Initially, patients need direction and clarity. They should be asked to sit in the treatment room without needles if they are unsure about receiving acupuncture. New patients will learn about acupuncture from other more experienced patients and they will observe the process of treatment on a first hand basis. Sometimes a patient will be willing to try just one or two needles at first. Eventually a high percentage of patients will be active participants.

The duration of acupuncture treatment depends on many factors. Inpatient programs will want to stress acupuncture in the beginning for detoxification and stabilization and prior to discharge for separation anxiety. Outpatients in a drug-free setting typically receive acupuncture for 1 to 3 months on an active basis. About 10% of these outpatients will choose to take acupuncture for more than 1 year if possible. Such patients usually have significant difficulties bonding on a psychosocial basis.

Lincoln Hospital used to provide acupuncture 7 days a week for the benefit of patients in crisis. Eventually it became clear that full weekend coverage did not appreciably improve clinical results. Patients who began the treatment program on Friday have essentially the same outcomes as patients who begin the program on Monday. Acupuncture is not primarily a dose-related phenomenon as is pharmaceutical treatment. Acupuncture more appropriately represents a qualitative service comparable to a school room class or psychotherapy session.

Patients who are using acupuncture appropriately should be allowed to choose how often they receive acupuncture treatment. Duration of the effect of each individual treatment increases as the patient becomes more stable. Because this treatment is a private, personal process, it should come under the patient's control as soon as possible. Some patients will discontinue acupuncture too quickly, but they should be able to learn from the resultant loss of well being in order to make better decisions in the future. Participation in acupuncture is a different kind of decision than participation in group or individual psychotherapy.

EFFECT ON THE WHOLE TREATMENT PROCESS ⊞

Relapsing patients are often able to continue to be involved in acupuncture even though they are no longer constructive participants in psychotherapy. Acupuncture patients do not tend to burn their bridges as quickly; hence, retention and eventual success are increased in the acupuncture based program.

A wide range of patients can be accepted for the initial stage of treatment because there is no verbal motivational requirement. Also, acupuncture is effective for most drugs and a wide range of psychological states. A low threshold, easily staffed program can be established for new patients. Ambivalent streetwise patients find the acupuncture setting almost impossible to manipulate. The setting is so soothing and self-protective that even extremely antisocial people are able to fit in. Problems relating to language and cultural differences are diminished. For new patients, frequent acupuncture treatment permits the gradual completion of assessment on a more accurate basis. Patients can be evaluated and triaged according to their daily response to treatment and testing rather than merely on the basis of the initial interview.

The tolerant, nonverbal aspect of acupuncture facilitates retention during periods when the patient would otherwise be ambivalent, fearful, or resentful within a more intense verbal interpersonal setting. Ear acupuncture makes it easy to provide outpatient treatment on demand, without appointments, while the patients are being acclimated to the interpersonal treatment setting. Patients are often willing to be tested even when they know that their toxicology results are positive, thereby showing respect for the value system of the overall treatment process. Those same patients may be unable or unwilling to share their crises and failures verbally until they have time to reach more solid ground. In the acupuncture setting, time is on our side.

Acupuncture has many characteristics in common with 12-step programs such as AA and NA. It uses group process in a tolerant, supportive, and present-time oriented manner. Participation is independent of diagnosis and level of recovery. Both approaches are simple, reinforcing, nurturing and conveniently available. The emphasis on self-responsibility is common to both systems. In practice, acupuncture provides an excellent foundation for 12-Step recovery. Patients seem less fearful and more receptive when they first enter the meetings. The traditional advice: listen to learn and learn to listen fits this model well. Acupuncture reduces white knuckle sobriety considerably. There is less guarding and greater ability to support each other warmly. The increased ability to use 12-Step meetings provides more stable support for continuing treatment on an outpatient basis.

⊞ AIDS-RELATED TREATMENT

Easy access and better retention encourage the outpatient management of difficult patients with less need for additional drugs or services. One can select times for hospitalization more appropriately. An outpatient continuum also facilitates primary health care management for AIDS, tuberculosis, and STDs. Acupuncture is used in a large proportion of AIDS prevention and outreach programs in New York and London, as well as other cities. These facilities include needle exchange and harm reduction programs; recovery readiness and pre-treatment programs, as well as health service providers for HIV-positive and AIDS patients. In relationship to addiction treatment, each of these programs faces similar dilemmas. Their clients are likely to have ever increasing addiction related problems, however, these clients minimize their need for help. Furthermore, the clients are often overwhelmed by problems relating to immune deficiency. Acupuncture is uniquely appropriate entry-level treatment because it is convenient, relaxing, and not dependent on any mutually agreed upon diagnosis or treatment plan. Acupuncture also provides treatment for emotions such as fear and depression. Many of these clients may be ashamed and confused, not knowing how to describe their ever-changing feelings in a conventional therapeutic context.

⊞ MATERNAL TREATMENT

The use of acupuncture has led to a considerable expansion of treatment services for cocaine and crack-using women. Lincoln Hospital has been treating more than a 100 pregnant cocaine users per year since 1987. Lincoln patients have regular visits with a nurse-midwife and receive specific education and counseling relative to pregnancy and child care. The Lincoln program was cited in 1991 by the American Hospital Association as a model innovative program for prenatal care.

The average birth weight for babies at Lincoln with more than 10 maternal visits is 6 pounds, 10 ounces. The average birth weight for less than 10 visits is 4 pounds, 8 ounces, which is typical of high-risk cocaine mothers. There is a high correlation between clean toxicologies, retention in the clinic program, and higher birth weights. Seventy-six percent of Lincoln's pregnant intakes are retained in longterm treatment and give birth to nontoxic infants.

Premature birth is a serious health risk. The Hospital of St. Raphael in New Haven has been using the Lincoln acupuncture model for 8 years. The director of obstetrics, Dr. Requero, reports a drop in perinatal death rate from 18.5 to 7.1 from 1990 to 1992, following the use of acupuncture and other innovative outreach techniques. Special acupuncture based components have also been developed for women with children in longterm foster care in the Drug Strategies Institute program in Baltimore.

Female patients are often trapped in destructive and exploitative relationships and therefore have special difficulty with any therapeutic relationship. A consistently tolerant and nonconfrontational approach prepares the way to establish a trauma survivor support service for patients at an early sobriety stage of recovery. The supportive atmosphere makes it relatively easy for patients to keep children with them during treatment activities. The acupuncture point formula used for addictions is also specific for the kind of emotional and muscular guarding associated with early sexual trauma. These patients will suffer intermittent crises and experience profound challenges to their physical and spiritual identity. All of their relationships will be strained and transformed. Acupuncture is a very appropriate adjunct to trauma survivors' support work.

CRIMINAL JUSTICE RELATED SERVICES ⊞

Patients referred by court-related agencies often enter treatment in total denial or with a basic conflict with the referring agency. The nonverbal aspect of acupuncture allows the intake staff to get beyond these protests and offer acupuncture for stress relief, instead of forcing the issue. Using acupuncture, we are able to wait until the patients feel more comfortable and less threatened so they can admit their addiction and ask for help.

Addicts have trouble with discipline. They need order in their lives but cannot develop internal structure. Addicts have trouble liking themselves. They are depressed and depersonalized and cannot accept good things. The result is self-destruction and adherence to a masochistic lifestyle. The ability to like oneself builds the foundation for internal discipline. Acupuncture provides significant advantage in meeting the paradoxical requirement of tough love. Verbal interpersonal intensity is reduced. Patients feel that their immediate needs and their urges toward independence have been satisfied. A tolerant, flexible atmosphere exists. Acupuncture delivered in a consistent and caring manner provides the basis for the love side of the equation. The foundation for the development of more effective discipline has been set.

Frequent urine testing provides an objective, nonpersonalized measure of success that can be accepted equally by all parties. In this system, the counselor is the good cop and urine machine is the bad cop. The counseling process can be totally separated from the process of judgment and evaluation. Discipline is separated from the difficulties of interpersonal relationships. Within this context, discipline or leniency by the judicial authority leads to constructive—not escapist—behavior. Positive toxicology results are primarily used to require a more prolonged or intense commitment to treatment.

The well-known Drug Court program in Miami uses the acupuncture-based model we have described. This program diverts thousands of felony drug possession arrestees into treatment each year. More than 50% of these patients eventually graduate the program on the basis of providing 90 consecutive negative toxicologies over the period of a year or more. Drug Court diversion and treatment programs have been established in several hundred settings nationwide. This expansion represents a valuable increased commitment to addiction treatment throughout the U.S. The majority of the largest and oldest Drug Court programs use acupuncture as a primary component of their protocol. Acupuncture is also being used in more than 70 jails and prisons in the U.S. and abroad. A follow-up study in Santa Barbara, California, for example, showed that women who received acupuncture were 50% less likely to be rearrested after being released from the county jail.

Sex offenders in a maximum security prison in Oak Park Heights, Minnesota, received acupuncture on a regular basis. There was a significant reduction in anger and violent intrusive sexual fantasies as compared to a control population (Culliton, 1996).

⊞ COEXISTING MENTAL HEALTH PROBLEMS

There is very little substantive published literature on the use of acupuncture in the treatment of primary psychiatric problems. During the past 20 years at Lincoln Hospital, the numerous effects of acupuncture on patients with coexisting addiction and psychiatric conditions have been noted. Agitated patients routinely fall asleep while receiving acupuncture. Chronic paranoid patients have a higher than average retention rate. We have seen many examples in which grossly paranoid addicted persons have made special efforts to access acupuncture treatment, not projecting paranoid ideation on the treatment, even though they may be floridly psychotic otherwise. These patients experience a gradual reduction in psychiatric symptoms as well as a typical response in terms of craving and withdrawal symptoms. Psychotropic medication does not interact with acupuncture. Patients should remain on psychotropic medicines while using acupuncture, since the improved level of compliance that correlates with acupuncture often makes the process of medication more reliable and effective.

A recent pilot program used acupuncture according to the Lincoln model in the public mental health system in Waco, Texas with a goal of the reduction in the rate of rehospitalization. Highly disturbed, noncompliant, chronic, dual-diagnosed patients were deliberately selected for this trial. Rates of hospitalization dropped from 50% to 6% in the group of 15 patients. Harbor House, a residential program or mentally ill chemical abusers (MICA) in the Bronx, reported a 50% reduction in psychiatric hospitalization in the first year of acupuncture utilization. Their dropout rate during the first month of treatment decreased 85%.

Acupuncture has an obvious advantage in the treatment of MICA patients because it can be used for wide variety of substance use and psychiatric problems. MICA patients have particular difficulty with bonding and verbal relationships. Acupuncture facilitates the required lenient supportive process, but, at the same time, it provides an acute anticraving treatment that is also necessary. The use of acupuncture can resolve the contradictory needs of MICA patients. More work needs to be done to evaluate and understand this anecdotal data.

INTERNATIONAL SPREAD ⊞

More than 500 programs outside of the U.S. have implemented the Lincoln model of acupuncture addiction treatment. Most of this expansion has occurred in public institutions such as hospitals, correctional facilities, and street outreach components. These programs represent a broad range of cultural settings including Saudi Arabia, Nepal, and Trinidad, in addition to most Western and Eastern European countries. Independent NADA training and certification programs have been established in ten countries during the past three years.

PSYCHOSOCIAL MECHANISMS OF ACTION ⊞

It is essential to understand acupuncture's psychological and social mechanisms of action to use this modality effectively. Acupuncture has an impact on the patients' thoughts and feelings that is different from conventional pharmaceutical treatments. Subsequently, we discuss how the use of acupuncture has a valuable and profound impact on the dynamics of the treatment processes as a whole. We should emphasize that acupuncture for addictions is provided in a group setting. The new acupuncture patient is immediately introduced to a calm and supportive group process. Patients describe acupuncture as a unique kind of balancing experience. "I was relaxed but alert. I was able to relax without losing control." Patients who are depressed or tired say that they feel more energetic. This encouraging and balancing group experience becomes a critically important basis for the entire treatment process.

The perception that a person can be both relaxed and alert is rather unusual in Western culture. We are used to associating relaxation with somewhat lazy or spacey behavior and alertness with a certain degree of anxiety. The relaxed and alert state is basic to the concept of health in all Asian culture. Acupuncture encourages a centering, focusing process that is typical of meditation and yoga. Therapists report that patients are able to listen and remember what we tell them. Restless impulsive behavior is greatly reduced. On the other hand, discouragement and apathy are reduced as well. It is a balancing, centering process.

One of the striking characteristics of the acupuncture treatment setting is that patients seem comfortable in their own spaces and in their own thinking processes. One patient explained, "I sat and thought about things in a slow way like I did when I was ten years old." Acupuncture treatment causes the perception of various relaxing bodily processes. Patients gradually gain confidence that their minds and bodies can function in a more balanced and autonomous manner. A hopeful process is developed on a private and personal basis, laying a foundation for the development of increasing self-awareness and self-responsibility.

Addiction is about trading present experience for past and future realities. Patients hang onto the present, because the past and future seem to offer nothing but pain. Unfortunately, conventional treatment efforts tend to focus on assessment of past activities and planning for the future. Patients are obsessed by present sensations and problems. They often feel alienated and resentful that we cannot focus on their immediate needs. Acupuncture is one of the only ways that treatment staff can respond to a patients' immediate needs without using addictive drugs. We can meet patients in the present time reality, validating their needs and providing substantial relief. Once a comfortable day-to-day reality support is established, we can approach past and future issues with a better alliance with the patient.

The nature of recovery from addiction is that patients often have quickly changing needs for crisis relief and wellness treatment. Many persons in recovery have relatively high levels of wellness functioning. Even so, a crisis of craving or past association may reappear at any time. Conventional treatment settings have trouble coping with such intense and confusing behavioral swings. Often merely the fear of a possible crisis can sabotage clinical progress. Acupuncture provides either crisis or wellness treatment using the same ear point formula. The nonverbal, present time aspects of the treatment make it easy to respond to a patient in whatever stage of crisis or denial that may exist.

▦ THE EASING OF INTERNAL CHANGE

Patients readily accept that it is possible to improve their acute addictive status. They seek external help to provide hospitalization and medication for withdrawal symptoms. The challenge develops when they encounter the necessity for internal change. Addicts perceive themselves as being unable to change from within. Their whole lives revolve around powerful external change agents. Addicts remember countless examples of weakness, poor choices, and overwhelming circumstance that lead to the conclusion that they cannot help themselves become drug-free. Indeed, many influential members of society agree that once an addict, always an addict.

Many of the complicating factors in our patients' lives echo this challenge of past internal failure. Persons leaving prison are confronted with a bleak, uncaring world. Their own feelings of inadequacy frequently become so overwhelming that a return to prior drug and alcohol use may occur within hours of release. When a person learns they are HIV positive, their self-esteem drops precipitously. A drug abusing seropositive person typically feels punished for past weaknesses by their HIV status. How can such a person have the confidence to seek out internal personal strength in the future?

Victims of incest and childhood abuse are well known to have been robbed of an internal sense of value. Their innermost physical and emotional responses have become sources of betrayal. It is not surprising, therefore, that a large majority of female addicts have been injured in this way.

All of us pass through a period of fearful internal inadequacy during the process of adolescence. Powerful trends of self-doubt and internal vulnerability are manifested at that time. No amount of external support will eliminate the need to confront internal fears on a private, personal basis. Hopefully, adolescents gradually learn to accept and appreciate themselves. They may also learn to rely on internal resources in their efforts to improve their circumstances. This archetypal challenge of adolescence is echoed in the struggle to become drug-free, as well as countless other efforts to become more internally resourceful and resilient in daily life. The question "does treatment work?" is comparable to asking whether internal self discovery and redefinition are possible.

Acupuncture provides uniquely valuable assistance in coping with this challenge of internal redefinition. Patients often begin acupuncture treatment seeking external escape and sedation as they do when they use drugs. When there is a rapid calming effect, they often assume there was some sort of chemical agent in the acupuncture needle. After a few treatments they come to the astonishing conclusion that acupuncture works by revealing and employing their internal capability rather than by inserting an external chemical. Patients begin to realize that their minds are capable of calm focused thoughts on a regular basis. There seems to be no indication of permanent damage to their thinking and consciousness. On the contrary, their ability to listen, think, and learn seems to be growing steadily each day.

Inevitably, a critical point will be reached. The newly drug-free patient will enter treatment one day with the feeling that "I don't deserve to be relaxed today because of all the bad things that I have done in the past." Such feelings frequently sabotage early treatment achievements. In an acupuncture program, however, patients realize that their minds can become calm and clear even in the face of such overwhelming feelings of inadequacy. This lesson demonstrates that change based on internal resources is possible. In other words, successful treatment is possible. Regular participation in acupuncture helps a patient use and revalue their internal resources much faster than conventional treatment processes. This effect contributes to the calm cooperative atmosphere in most acupuncture settings. It reduces dropouts based on fears of failure and low self-esteem that typify the early stage of treatment.

FOUNDATION FOR AUTONOMY ⊞

The use of acupuncture sets a foundation so that patients can have more autonomy in developing their own plan of treatment. A more calm, less resentful atmosphere is created. The tolerant, self-validating process helps patients find their level and type of involvement in a productive manner. Patients must choose to talk sincerely with their counselor just as they must choose to avoid temptation and return to the program each day. These choices may fluctuate widely and be mistaken at times, but such independence is the only path toward growing up. When a program properly encourages structure but ignores the patient's own independence efforts, these actions undermine future success. Acupuncture creates a better atmosphere so that treatment staff can spend their energies helping patients make choices rather than being fatigued by trying to impose authority on a resistant clientele.

We describe acupuncture as a foundation for psychosocial rehabilitation. In the beginning of treatment, building a proper foundation is very important. If we are building on a weak "sandy" personality, work on the foundation may take many months or years before it is strong enough to support any significant psychosocial treatment efforts. However, once a foundation is established, the focus of treatment should shift away from acupuncture toward building a house of psychosocial recovery on that foundation. When one of our patients testified at city council hearings, she described how important it was to attend daily NA meetings and barely mentioned acupuncture. For a patient with 3 months sobriety, this emphasis was appropriate. Of course, during her first two weeks in our program, she was quite angry and ambivalent and was able to relate only to the acupuncture component of the program.

A NONVERBAL THERAPY ⊞

Acupuncture is a nonverbal type of therapy. Words and verbal relationships are not necessary components of this treatment. We do not mean that the therapist should not talk with the patient. Verbal interaction can be quite flexible so that a patient who does not feel like talking can be accommodated easily and naturally. Acupuncture will be just as effective even when the patient lies to us.

The most difficult paradox in this field is the common reality that addicted persons usually deny their need for help. Such patients do not say anything helpful to the treatment process. Nevertheless, resistant patients often find themselves in a treatment setting due to referral or other pressures. Using acupuncture can bypass much of the verbal denial and resistance that otherwise limit retention of new and relapsed patients. Addicts are frequently ambivalent. Acupuncture helps us reach the needy part of their psyche that wants help. Acupuncture can reduce stress and craving so that patients gradually become more ready to participate in the treatment process.

Addiction patients often cannot tolerate intense interpersonal relationships. Using a conventional one-to-one approach often creates a brittle therapeutic connection. It is easily broken by events or any stress. Patients have difficulty trusting a counselor's words when they can hardly trust themselves. Even after confiding to a counselor during an intake session, patients may feel frightened and confused about expanding that relationship. Many of their concerns are so complex and troublesome that talking honestly about their lives could be difficult in the best of circumstances. The ambivalence typical of addicts makes it easy to develop misunderstandings. All of these factors support the usefulness of nonverbal technique during early and critical relapse phases of treatment and critical periods of relapse.

A women six months pregnant entered our clinic several years ago. She said, "I can't tell you much about myself because my husband is out in the street with a baseball bat, he'll hit me in my knees if I say too much." We provided an emergency acupuncture treatment and conducted a simplified intake interview. Two weeks later this patient told us, "This is my husband, he doesn't have a drug problem, but he is nervous, can you help him?" Both of them received acupuncture that day. The woman needed nonverbal access to treatment because of real physical danger. Overprotective spouses often forcefully oppose all social contacts outside the marriage. This patient was protected because there was no premature verbal bonding that would have threatened the husband. The whole process was so supportive that the husband was able to trust his wife and seek help himself. Like many fearful people, he was literally unable to make any verbal approach on his own.

One mistake in treatment interaction should be highlighted. We should avoid reverbalizing the acupuncture interaction. Anxiety and depression are common indications for acupuncture. However, it is a mistake to require that the patient admit to anxiety or depression in order to qualify for acupuncture. Addicts who have significant anxiety or depression will usually not admit these feelings. They will avoid anyone who asks such questions. At a later stage of sobriety and recovery, talking about these feelings will be important, but at an early stage of treatment, verbalizing these feelings can lead to drop out. Likewise, it is not productive to ask patients why they have missed a previous acupuncture session. Use the advantage that acupuncture will be effective even if we don't know the issues involved.

Treatment programs without acupuncture are compelled to screen for patients who are able to talk readily with authority figures. Many verbally needy patients become quite dependent on the program and quite involved with numerous staff members. Such patients may be the focus of many conferences, but they are often too needy to remain drug-free outside the hospital. In contrast, acupuncture-assisted intake can retain patients who are relatively more paranoid, independent, assertive, and hostile. Noisy, troublesome patients who are frustrated with the world and with themselves actually may be more likely to sustain a drug-free lifestyle than patients with verbal dependency needs.

Acupuncture helps develop an underlying environment of acceptance, tolerance, and patience. There is ample space for the ambivalence and temporary setbacks that are a necessary part of any transformation. Patients can have a quiet day by attending the program and receiving acupuncture without having to discuss their status with a therapeutic authority figure. Since acupuncture reduces the agitated defensive tone in the whole clinical environment, patients are able to interact with each other on a much more comfortable level. Their increased ability to listen to others and accept internal changes have a profound effect on the quality and depth of communication in group therapy sessions and 12-Step meetings. Being a sympathetic witness to a description of past tragedies can be easier to achieve in a setting that is not charged with defensive self-centered associations. The primary community agenda can focus on the acceptance of each person and a tolerant encouragement of change rather than coping with defensive and antagonistic interactions.

BODY ACUPUNCTURE: ⊞
A MERIDIAN APPROACH TO TREATMENT

One of us (KW) experimented for several years with the use of a classical Chinese medicine meridian approach to body acupuncture for treating common psychological problems in addicted and nonaddicted psychiatric patients. Body acupuncture can be used to effectively address a variety of secondary psychiatric diagnoses in chemically dependent persons.

In classical Chinese medicine, there are six different types of acupuncture meridians or energy pathways, each reflecting different psychological processes and levels of psychological development. Each type of channel is said to carry one or more different expressions of *qi,* the life energy that is responsible for the origin and maintenance of life in humans, plants, and animals. In psychological terms, these different expressions of *qi* reflect

- Our ways of relating to people and events in our exterior world (*wei qi*)
- Our relationship with our internal world, the world of our emotions and thoughts *(ying qi)*
- Our deepest sense of self *(yuan qi)* (Yuen, 1995a)

This paradigm, taught by Taoist priest Jeffrey Yuen, can be used to decide which meridian system to use in treating the psychological issues of patients struggling with addictions.

Acupuncture to Treat Depression

Depression, one of the most common secondary diagnoses among chemically dependent individuals, is often very effectively treated with acupuncture. Some researchers estimate that most persons who enter treatment for addiction to alcohol or other substances suffer from some form of depression, ranging from mild to severe (Dorus, Kennedy, Gibbons, & Raci, 1987; Hesselbrock, Meyer, & Kenner, 1985). Chemical dependency patients may have originally turned to alcohol or drugs in an attempt to "medicate" their own depressive disorders, whether they stem from organic, cognitive, or interpersonal causes. In addition, the use of alcohol and drugs can precipitate or exacerbate depression due to the substance's impact on the central nervous system and various chemicals in the brain known as neurotransmitters. Common depressive symptoms include constant sadness, the inability to experience pleasure in life, difficulty sleeping or sleeping too much, poor or excessive appetite, feelings of exhaustion, difficulty concentrating, and feelings of helplessness, hopelessness, and worthlessness.

Usually, KW uses a set of meridians known as the 12 primary channels to treat depressive disorders. The primary meridians are conduits of the *qi* that has to do with the ways we relate to people and events in our exterior world (*wei qi*) and the *qi* that reflects our relationship with our internal world, the world of our thoughts and emotions (*ying qi*). The primary meridians can be divided into three energetic layers. The first energetic layer deals with issues of survival-breathing, eating, sleeping, and letting go of things we don't need in our lives (Yuen, 1996). KW uses acupuncture points from the four meridians in this layer to treat depressed patients who are experiencing difficulty breathing, eating, defecating, or sleeping. The second energetic layer concerns our social interactions in the world and our searches, quests, and conquests in life (Yuen, 1997b). KW performs acupuncture on points from the four meridians in this layer for patients whose depressions stem from interpersonal difficulties or from giving up on their goals and conquests in life. The third energetic layer involves issues in the process of self-differentiation. One of the meridians in this layer, the pericardium or heart protector, tries to protect our hearts from the onslaught of the world and its inevitable injuries. A person operating out of his or her pericardium meridian does not want to truly deal with his or her pain and suffering but rather wants a sense of comfort and protection (Yuen, 1999)-a common finding in chemically dependent patients. For depressed patients avoiding issues in their lives, KW uses points from the pericardium meridian and other channels in this energetic layer to spur them to look at their pain and suffering and to move through them rather than use substances to avoid them.

Research (Hitt, Allen, & Schnyer, 1995; Luo, Jia, & Zhan, 1985; Yang, Liu, Luo, & Jia, 1994) demonstrates body acupuncture's effectiveness in treating persons with depressive disorders in comparison with depressed patients receiving antidepressant medication or depressed patients on a waiting list to receive acupuncture.

Body Acupuncture to Treat Various Emotions

Anger and resentment, emotions that frequently beset chemically dependent persons, can often be beneficially treated by body acupuncture. *Alcoholics Anonymous* (AA, 1976) states, "Resentment . . . destroys more alcoholics than anything else" (p. 64), prompting many to turn once again to alcohol. Classical Chinese medicine treats anger, resentment, and most other emotions by using a set of meridians known as the *luo*-connecting channels, one of six different types of meridians or energy pathways in Chinese medicine. The *luo* channels can be used to help patients moderate or temper emotions that they are expressing too intensely (e.g., rage reactions) or to uncover emotions that they have been suppressing or repressing (e.g., unacknowledged anger or resentment). In classical Chinese medicine, the *luo* channels are said to carry *ying qi*, which reflects the internal world of our emotions and thoughts. The *luo* channels are said to fill up when we hold, suppress, or repress various emotions and thoughts. Needling the *luo* vessels with a special seven-star needle can help unleash suppressed or repressed emotions (Yuen, 1995b, 1997a).

For example, KW treated a woman with a history of alcohol abuse who was feeling intense resentment and anger at her estranged husband during the process of divorce. Her constant rage-filled thoughts were interfering with her capacity to concentrate at work and her efforts to sort out the possessions that each would take from the marriage.

Using a seven-star needle, KW treated the *luo*-connecting channel that deals with anger and resentment as well as the *luo*-connecting vessels that treat the way she was handling these emotions. The patient experienced an immediate and profound shift in her emotions. She felt that she was much better able to deal with her husband on issues on which she had harbored resentment for many years.

SUMMARY ⊞

Both auriculotherapy and body acupuncture can play key roles in chemical dependency programs by supporting patients' physical and psychological changes and by helping to develop an atmosphere of acceptance, respect, and patience. Acupuncture creates an environment that allows room for patients' ambivalence and temporary setbacks, necessary parts of any process of transformation. It enables patients to have "a quiet day" on some days in the program, participating in acupuncture without having to discuss their progress or setbacks with an authority figure. Acupuncture tends to decrease patients' defensiveness and agitation, enabling them to interact with others more comfortably and to accept their own internal changes. Overall, acupuncture enhances patients' progress in group therapy, individual therapy, and 12-step meetings, enabling more patients to achieve ultimate success in their treatment programs.

REFERENCES ⊞

Alcoholics Anonymous World Services. (1976). *Alcoholics Anonymous* (3rd ed.). New York: Author.

Bensky, D., & O'Connor, G. (1985). *Acupuncture: A comprehensive text.* Seattle: Eastland.

Brewington, V., Smith, M., & Lipton, D. (1994). Acupuncture as a detoxification treatment: An analysis of controlled research. *Journal of Substance Abuse Treatment, 11,* 289-307.

Bullock, M., Culliton, P., & Olander, R. (1989). Controlled trial of acupuncture for severe recidivist alcoholism. *Lancet,* 1435-1439.

Bullock, M., Umen, A., Culliton, P., & Olander, R. (1987). Acupuncture treatment of alcoholic recidivism: A pilot study. *Alcoholism: Clinical and Experimental Research, 11,* 292-295.

Dorus, W., Kennedy, J., Gibbons, R. D., & Raci, S. D. (1987). Symptoms and diagnosis of depression in alcoholics. *Alcoholism, 11,* 150-154.

Eory, A. (1995). Society for Acupuncture Research discussion.

Hesselbrock, M. N., Meyer, R. E., & Kenner, J. J. (1985). Psychopathology in hospitalized alcoholics. *Archives of General Psychiatry, 46,* 3-5.

Hitt, S. K., Allen, J. J. B., & Schnyer, R. N. (1995). Acupuncture as a treatment for major depression in women. *Proceedings of the Symposium of the Society for Acupuncture Research, 3,* 135-149.

Konefal, J., Duncan, R., & Clemence, C. (1995, September). Comparison of three levels of auricular acupuncture in an outpatient substance abuse treatment program. *Alternative Medicine Journal, 2*(5).

Luo, H., Jia, Y., & Zhan, L. (1985). Electro-acupuncture v. amitriptyline in the treatment of depressive states. *Journal of Traditional Chinese Medicine, 5,* 3-8.

Omura, T., Smith, M, Wong, F., Apfel, F., Taft, R., & Mintz, T. (1975). Electro-acupuncture for drug addiction withdrawal. *Acupuncture and Electro-Therapeutic Research International Journal, 1,* 231-233.

Washburn, A. M., Fullilove, R. E., Fullilove, M. T., Keenan, P. A., McGee, B., Morris, K. A., Sorenson, J. L., & Clark, W. W. (1993). Acupuncture heroin detoxification: A single-blind clinical trial. *Journal of Substance Abuse Treatment, 10*, 345-351.

Wen, H. L., & Cheung, S.Y.C. (1973). Treatment of drug addictions by acupuncture and electrical stimulation. *Asian Journal of Medicine, 9*, 139-141.

Worner, T. M., Zeller, B., Schwartz, H., Zwas, F., & Lyon, D. (1992). Acupuncture fails to improve treatment outcomes in alcoholics. *Drug and Alcohol Dependence, 30*, 169-173.

Yang, X., Liu, X., Luo, H., & Jia, Y. (1994). Clinical observation of needling extrachannel points in treating mental depression. *Journal of Traditional Chinese Medicine, 14*, 14-18.

Yuen, J. C. (1995a, May 20-21). *Chronic degenerative disorders.* Continuing education course presented at Emperor's College of Traditional Oriental Medicine, Santa Monica, CA.

Yuen, J. C. (1996, October 19). *Little-known energetics of the primary meridians.* Continuing education course presented under the auspices of Kathryn P. White, Ph.D., Los Angeles.

Yuen, J. C. (1997a, March 1). *Classical Chinese medical treatments of Shen disturbances.* Continuing education course presented under the auspices of Kathryn P. White, PhD, Los Angeles.

Yuen, J. C. (1997b, October 18). *Primary meridian energetics, Part II.* Continuing education course presented under the auspices of Kathryn P. White, PhD, Los Angeles.

Yuen, J. C. (1999, October 2). *The heart protector in lifespan development.* Continuing education course presented under the auspices of Kathryn P. White, PhD, Los Angeles.

⊞ ADDITIONAL SUGGESTED READINGS

Bannerman, R. H., Burton, I., & Chieh, W. (Eds.). (1983). *Traditional medicine and health care coverage.* Geneva, Switzerland: World Health Organization.

Birch, S., & Hammerschlag, R. (1996). *Acupuncture efficacy: A compendium of controlled clinical studies.* Terrytown, NY: National Academy of Acupuncture and Oriental Medicine.

Clement-Jones, V., McLoughlin, L., Lowry, P., Besser, G., Res, L., & Wen, H. (1979). Acupuncture in heroin addicts: Changes in met-enkephalin and beta endorphin in blood and cerebrospinal fluid. *Lancet*, 380-382.

Clevel, F., Benhamou, S., Company-Huertas, A., & Flamant, R. (1985). Helping people to stop smoking: Randomized comparison of groups being treated with acupuncture and nicotine gum with control group. *British Medical Journal, 291*, 1538-1539.

Guizhen, L., Yunjun, Z., Linxiang, G., & Aizhen, L. (1998). Comparative study of acupuncture combined with behavioral desensitization for treatment of anxiety neuroses. *American Journal of Acupuncture, 26*(2/3), 117-120.

Khantzian, E. J., & Treece, C. (1985). *DSM-III* psychiatric diagnosis of narcotics addicts: Recent findings. *Archives of General Psychiatry, 42*, 1067-1071.

Lanza, U. (1986). The contribution of acupuncture to clinical psychotherapy by means of biofeedback training. *International Journal of Acupuncture and Electro-Therapeutics Research, 11*(1), 53-57.

Lipton, D. S., Brewington, V., & Smith, M. (1994). Acupuncture for crack-cocaine detoxification: Experimental evaluation of efficacy. *Journal of Substance Abuse Treatment, 11*, 205-215.

Margolin, A., Avants, S. K., Chang, P., & Kosten, T. R. (1993). Acupuncture for the treatment of cocaine dependence in methadone-maintained patients. *American Journal of Addiction, 2*, 194-201.

Mitchell, B. (2001). *Acupuncture and Oriental medicine laws.* Olala, WA: National Acupuncture Foundation.

Nogier, P. (1972). *Treatise of auriculotherapy.* Moulins-les-Metz, France: Maisonneure.

Oleson, T. (1998). *Auriculotherapy manual: Chinese and Western systems of ear acupuncture* (2nd ed.). Los Angeles: Health Care Alternatives.

Oleson, T., Kroening, R., & Bresler, D. (1980). An experimental evaluation of auricular diagnosis: The somatotopic mapping of musculoskeletal pain at ear acupuncture points. *Pain, 8,* 217-229.

Smith, M. O. (1999). *Acupuncture for addiction treatment.* Vancouver, WA: J&M Reports LLC.

Weiss, R. D., Mirin, S. N., Griffin, M. L., & Michaels, J. K. (1988). Psychopathology in cocaine abusers: Changing trends. *Journal of Nervous and Mental Disorders, 176,* 719-725.

World Health Organization. (1991). *A proposed standard international acupuncture nomenclature: Report of a World Health Organization Scientific Group.* Geneva, Switzerland: Author.

Yuen, J. C. (1995, November 17). *The emotions and Chinese medicine.* Continuing education course presented under the auspices of Emperor's College of Traditional Chinese Medicine, Santa Monica, CA.

INFORMATION RESOURCES ⊞

Auriculotherapy

NADA Clearinghouse, Box 1927, Vancouver, WA 98668, fax (360) 260-8620, e-mail NADAClear @aol.com.
| A wide variety of articles and videotapes are available.

Locating Licensed or Certified Acupuncturists in Your Area

National Certification Commission for Acupuncture and Oriental Medicine, 11 Canal Center Plaza, Suite 300, Alexandria, VA 22314, phone (703) 548-9004, e-mail www.nccaom.org

National Acupuncture and Oriental Medical Alliance, 14637 Starr Road SE, Olalla, WA 98359, phone (253) 851-5896, e-mail www.acuall.org

American Association of Oriental Medicine, 433 Front Street, Catasauqua, PA 18032, phone (610) 266-1433, e-mail www.aaom.org

Education in Acupuncture and Oriental Medicine

Council of Colleges of Acupuncture and Oriental Medicine (CCAOM), 1010 Wayne Avenue, Suite 1270, Silver Spring, MD 20910, phone (301) 608-0175, fax (301) 608-9576.

USING RECOVERY TOOLS IN VARIOUS SETTINGS AND PROGRAMS

21

Harm Reduction Programs

Progress Rather Than Perfection

Arthur W. Blume
Britt K. Anderson
Jonathan S. Fader
G. Alan Marlatt

W e know a lot more about addictive behaviors than we did in the 1930s when Alcoholics Anonymous (AA) began, or even in the 1970s when the Minnesota Model became the standard treatment of choice for people with addictive behaviors. For example, we know that there are many different ways people can reduce the harm involved with using substances, some on their own and some with outside help. Abstinence still may be ideal for many people with addictive behaviors, but it is not the only effective path to health.

Harm reduction strategies provide more options for both client and therapist. Although often misinterpreted as "enabling," harm reduction strategies are scientifically supported as effective to help many people improve their lives. Examples of harm reduction strategies in practice today include needle exchanges to reduce the risk of HIV and hepatitis, methadone programs for reduction of heroin and injected drug use, moderate drinking programs, pharmacotherapy (see Chapter 5) to reduce cravings, and designated drivers or taxi services to reduce drinking and driving fatalities.

Simply put, the goal of harm reduction is to improve your client's quality of life by reducing the potential harm associated with substance use behavior. Harm reduction meets clients *where they are* by listening to and respecting the goals that each client has for his or her own recovery of health. Within this framework, there are no preconceived notions of what is best for the new client that steps through your door. Another important difference from traditional treatment is the emphasis in harm reduction upon a *gradual step-down approach* rather than advocacy of a total leap toward abstinence.

BOX 21.1   **Principles of Harm Reduction**

- Reduce harmful consequences of drug and alcohol use.
- Collaborate with the client on treatment goals and interventions.
- Practice pragmatism: Use what works.

If you believe in the disease or medical models of addiction, look at harm reduction as providing a range of treatment options. Our job as therapists is to help patients make informed choices concerning their treatment, not to make the choices for them. An excellent analogy comes from the treatment of cancer. People are not asked to be in remission from cancer before treatment is provided. Rather, they are treated whether they are in remission or not. Furthermore, cancer is treated by a variety of methods such as chemotherapy, radiation, and surgery. Other people, despite their physician's advice, may choose naturopathic means to treat the disease. More recently, many hospitals and clinics, to meet the needs of the cancer patients and maintain patient contact with people who want to explore "nontraditional" means of treatment, have combined naturopathy and medical treatments.

We believe that addictive behaviors can and should be treated similarly. We have found that people do not necessarily have to be abstinent to improve in therapy, nor do they have to comply with one particular model or pathway of recovery. Cancer patients are not routinely told they must have one type of treatment only, nor are they told that a disease relapse will be grounds for discharge, but that is exactly what has been done with people who abuse substances. We have found greater success in keeping clients involved in the system than in closing the door to them because of their behavior. Harm reduction programs meet the needs of people who would not otherwise darken the doors of treatment. The approach is "user friendly" and strongly appeals to potential consumers of addiction treatment services.

Harm reduction incorporates cognitive-behavioral principles that research has shown to facilitate behavior change: Reinforcement principles are used to reward successive approximations toward the goal of health and the reduction of harmful consequences. In other words, people are praised and supported for progress rather than perfection, and guilt for failing to abstain is exchanged for confidence in being able to improve. We have found that rewarding successful behavior change and learning from lapses into old behavior is a very successful way to create long-term behavior change. Rewarding positive change and punishing the person for experiencing a lapse into old behavior, even inadvertently, may enhance compliance in the short run but often does not give the patient incentive to take personal credit and responsibility for sustained behavior change. This is why the policy of discharging people from treatment for using really makes little sense and actually makes it less likely for the person to seek help again in the future (Miller & Hester, 1986).

Several general strategies developed from cognitive-behavioral principles are effective for behavior change. These cognitive-behavioral strategies are guided by the principle that any movement toward healthiness by the patient or client, no matter how small, should be supported and encouraged by the therapist. The first strategy, *monitoring* substance use (see Chapter 9), is an effective way to help the client understand the scope and relationship of problems and substance use. Asking a client to keep daily

---

BOX 21.2   **Harm Reduction Strategies**

- Monitor drug and alcohol use.
- Utilize assessment as intervention.
- Cut down or use safer alternatives.
- Taper use down (warm turkey vs. cold turkey).
- Make using inconvenient.
- Use only in familiar surroundings.
- Emphasize quality of use over quantity.
- Use pharmacotherapy to reduce withdrawal and psychiatric symptoms.
- Try abstinence for a short time.
- Use urge surfing, distress tolerance, distraction techniques, meditation.
- Use relapse management.

---

diaries of time, type, amount, cues to use substances, and consequences of substance use can be quite helpful. Assessment also allows clients to objectively reflect upon consequences of substance use. Some research has found that assessment alone (without feedback) may contribute to reductions in substance use, presumably by increasing awareness of the desirability for behavior change through exploration of personal concerns about substance use.

Another effective method for reducing substance use is to ask clients to *switch* to a less harmful substance or to *alternate* what they typically use with something less harmful. For example, beer drinkers can be encouraged to switch from high-alcohol-content beer to a less potent beer. Alternating an alcoholic beverage with another nonalcoholic beverage, or eating, can be effective in slowing the rate of alcohol consumption. Switching people from "harder" drugs to marijuana has been used successfully in European countries, suggesting that the so-called "gateway" drug also may be an exit. Tapering is a very important harm reduction strategy: A taper often begins with either alternating or switching to safer alternatives. Slowing consumption can be enhanced by limiting access: We have found it helpful to ask our clients to buy less at a time and have less on hand, rather than stocking up, to make it less convenient to drink, smoke, or use. Furthermore, the quality of the experience is emphasized above the quantity; we have found that emphasizing that tolerance actually diminishes the positive effects of substance use is quite powerful for increasing motivation to moderate drug use (see the discussion later in this chapter about the biphasic response of alcohol).

Pharmacotherapy (see Chapter 5) can be a particularly helpful harm reduction intervention. Some medications seem to reduce cravings, and others address symptoms that clients believe they are "self-medicating," such as depression and anxiety (see Blume, Schmaling, & Marlatt, 2000, for discussion of beliefs about self-medication). Pharmacotherapy can be used to help people in the tapering process by alleviating other uncomfortable symptoms (e.g., anxiety or depression). Furthermore, clients can be taught about improving vitamin (e.g., thiamine) and nutrient intake, as well as avoiding potentially harmful over-the-counter medications (e.g., acetamenophen with heavy drinking can harm the liver).

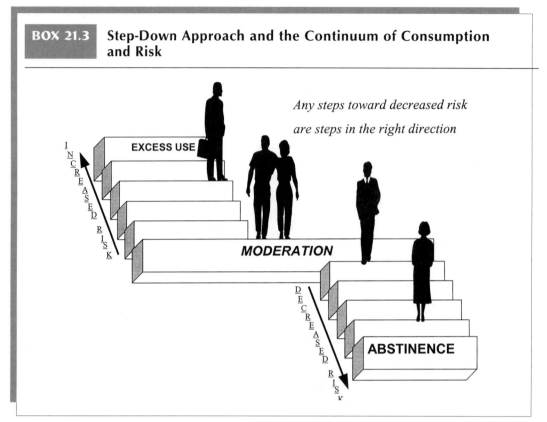

BOX 21.3   Step-Down Approach and the Continuum of Consumption and Risk

Any steps toward decreased risk are steps in the right direction

INCREASED RISK

EXCESS USE

MODERATION

DECREASED RISK

ABSTINENCE

SOURCE: Courtesy of Jessica Cronce.

Time is finite: People who engage in activities incompatible with alcohol or drug use have less time to get high or drunk. Encourage and offer access to exciting, interesting, and challenging *alternative activities* that diminish available "free" time to be using substances. It is important to help clients fill their days with nonusing structured activities. Furthermore, if clients choose to use, teach them where and when to do so more safely. Many research studies show that people are more likely to overdose in unfamiliar surroundings or using unfamiliar substances, especially when they are alone. Harm reduction teaches clients to be smart and safe when using: to use familiar substances in familiar surroundings with familiar people who can provide help in case of emergency (e.g., drug overdose).

Other effective harm reduction strategies include "urge surfing" (see below for details), distress tolerance strategies (see References and Additional Suggested Readings), and meditation (see Chapter 18 and Marlatt & Kristeller, 1998). One of us (AB) has used a distraction technique in which clients were told to hold ice in their hands until cravings passed; clients said later that they forgot about the craving after a few minutes of pain, which is precisely the point. Meditation and "urge surfing" teach that discomfort is transitory. Teach your clients that thoughts are just thoughts and that there is no compelling need for the thoughts to be acted upon. It is not important that thoughts be changed; it is more important to help clients change the way they perceive and accept their thoughts in a nonjudgmental manner. Clients are empowered to break the chain of negative thinking that accelerates the perception of losing behavioral control.

Finally, both abstinence goals and relapse prevention techniques (see below) can be used within the harm reduction model. Asking a client to engage in a "trial period" of abstinence (sometimes called *sobriety sampling*) can be quite useful for a variety of reasons. From the harm reduction perspective, any period of abstinence may allow cognitive abilities to improve, increasing the ability of clients to make better choices. Furthermore, another important aspect of relapse prevention is to recognize that periodic substance use after treatment is the norm rather than the exception. We have found that relapse-related guilt (the "abstinence violation effect") harms people. Normalize lapses and relapse as behavioral lessons, and encourage clients to learn and become more skilled from the experiences, rather than inadvertently punishing the client for "failing" to maintain abstinence by making a big deal out of the relapse.

The following sections describe more specifically how to use harm reduction effectively across different types of substances, among different types of clients, and for a variety of problems clients may face.

HARM REDUCTION AND ALCOHOL USE ▦

Harm reduction when treating alcohol problems acknowledges the drinker's perceived positive aspects of alcohol use and is nonjudgmental, meeting clients "where they are" instead of where the treatment program thinks they "should" be. Many traditional alcohol treatment programs label people as "alcoholic" and define success solely as total abstinence. Though helpful for some individuals, these approaches often represent barriers to seeking and receiving treatment for many others (Miller & Hester, 1986). In contrast, harm reduction does not rely on diagnostic labels and involves collaborative negotiation with the client to determine treatment goals.

Moderate Drinking

When beginning treatment with clients experiencing alcohol problems, we have found it important to discuss desired goals. Although people who are severely dependent on alcohol and who find it difficult to moderate their alcohol use may be most successful with a goal of abstinence, we (and others) have found that many problem drinkers can learn to limit their drinking to moderate levels. Moderate drinking programs (such as Moderation Management) often encourage individuals to attempt 30 days of abstinence as a first step. This experiment decreases tolerance, improves client thought processes, and clarifies how dependent your client is upon alcohol.

If your client decides to try moderation after this experiment, the decrease in tolerance will allow him or her to feel the pleasurable effects of alcohol at lower doses than before, thereby reducing consumption. We have found it important to discuss and establish firm drinking limits before moderate or controlled drinking is attempted, such as limiting oneself to a certain number of drinks per occasion to staying under an established blood alcohol level (a recommended "safe" level is typically .05 to .06). The goal must be realistic and meaningful to your client in order to be effective. Additionally, we have found that the client can predict fairly accurately where, when, and with whom moderation will become difficult to maintain. Addressing and rehearsing strategies to cope with those risky situations can be quite helpful for clients. In addition to self-groups such as Moderation Management, self-help-type books such as *Problem Drinkers: Guided Self-Change Treatment* by Sobell and Sobell (1993) can be quite useful.

Brief Interventions

Although even a single session of "professional advice" to problematic drinkers has been found a powerful tool in changing people's behavior, brief interventions typically involve a period of assessment followed by the provision of feedback to enhance motivation to change. When assessing drinking behavior, it is important to determine the frequency and quantity of use over the past several months, the context and precursors of use (e.g., where clients are and whom they are with when they drink to excess), the alcohol-related negative consequences experienced, whether any other drugs are being used independently or in combination with alcohol, and the degree of alcohol dependency that clients are currently experiencing. There are several paper-and-pencil inventories, such as the Comprehensive Drinker Profile (Marlatt & Miller, 1984), to facilitate the assessment process and provide guidelines for determining the severity of the problem. Following this assessment, the information is provided to clients in a nonjudgmental, motivational manner that allows them to reflect on their behavior and weigh the benefits and costs of changing their pattern of drinking in the future (see Chapters 1 and 2).

Relapse Prevention

From a harm reduction perspective, behavioral change is viewed as cyclical rather than linear. Slips are not failures but opportunities to learn. It is very common to "slip" when establishing new habits, and it is important to prepare your clients for that possibility. Clients should be told that slips provide ways to learn more about what may stand in the way of their reaching their reduction goals. This reframing makes it less likely that clients will perceive themselves as failing and will feel that change is hopeless when a highly likely lapse occurs. *Relapse management*, like harm reduction, works with clients to minimize the harmful effects of active alcohol or drug use while helping them "get back on track."

We have found that identifying potentially high-risk situations for lapses before they happen effectively circumvents or minimizes their occurrence. High-risk situations include any situations or environments that represent a threat to clients' ability to cope effectively with urges or cravings to drink excessively (or to drink at all if the goal is abstinence). Identifying these situations and preparing coping strategies ahead of time is important to minimize the likelihood of relapse.

Teaching clients to use imagery to cope with alcohol cravings also is effective. One effective technique is called *urge surfing* (see Marlatt & Gordon, 1985, for greater detail). Urges or cravings are usually triggered by external cues (as in the case of Pavlov's dog salivating at the sound of a bell) and not by erosion of willpower. When urges or cravings occur, they may feel overwhelming, and it is important to discuss with your client the cyclical nature of these sensations. Like waves in an ocean, urges and cravings increase in intensity until they reach a peak and then naturally, and inevitably, subside. Clients can conceptualize their cravings as waves and gain a sense of mastery as they "ride the wave" with the knowledge that the urges and cravings will pass. Practicing this technique in session (while experiencing imagined or real cravings) will facilitate clients' confidence in managing cravings on their own in future situations.

BOX 21.4   **Identifying High-Risk Situations**

- Have your client describe relapses in great detail to understand triggers and warning signs.
- Have your client write a drinking history or autobiography to provide clues for high-risk drinking situations or experiences.
- Evaluate *why* your client is drinking—what purpose it serves in his or her current lifestyle, relationships, and manner of coping with life's stressors.

HARM REDUCTION AND OTHER SUBSTANCE USE ⊞

The most well-known harm reduction approach used with drug users is methadone replacement therapy for heroin use. However, it is only one of many strategies that a therapist can use with this population. Methadone replacement is an excellent example of switching to a safer substance. Switching interventions encourage clients to use substances that may be safer to obtain, may be less harmful, and may allow a return of some control over substance use. For instance, as mentioned, marijuana sometimes is used to replace other more addictive and harmful substances.

Similarly, altering a person's route of drug administration reduces harm. Encouraging clients to give up the needle for a less intrusive and risky route of administration (e.g., snorting or smoking) can reduce the risk of HIV, hepatitis, and overdose. Furthermore, clients can be educated about dangerous substance interaction or antagonistic effects and can be encouraged to use one substance at a time.

Another very important harm reduction program provides clean needles to drug users. Most new cases of HIV in the United States today occur among injected drug users and their sexual partners. Needle exchanges reduce the spread of HIV and other pathogens by eliminating the need to share needles. Furthermore, teaching injecting drug users how to clean their works if needle exchanges are unavailable saves lives. It is difficult to help injecting drug users already infected with hepatitis or HIV, so prevention is important. Finally, as with alcohol, pharmacotherapy may be used as an adjunct to reduce cravings or control psychiatric symptoms (see Chapter 6).

HARM REDUCTION AND TOBACCO USE ⊞

Unlike alcohol and other substances, tobacco does not noticeably impair an individual's functioning or performance in the short term. In fact, the majority of negative consequences related to tobacco consumption, such as cancer, emphysema, and heart disease, are long-term health risks that may not motivate behavioral changes as effectively as more immediate harmful consequences. Although nicotine is the source of the addictive behavior, harm reduction strategies designed for smokers and users of smokeless tobacco products (e.g., chewing tobacco or snuff) often target reducing tar, carbon monoxide, and other chemicals in the tobacco products that represent the real risk and cause the majority of health problems.

As mentioned, an important element of harm reduction is understanding the function that the substance or addictive behavior serves in an individual's life. Before any changes can be made to a smoker's behavior, it is essential to understand the context in which the smoking occurs. Does the person smoke to relax, to avoid eating excessively, to fit in with a peer group, or to just have some time away from other people? A thorough evaluation of the role that smoking occupies can contribute to more meaningful behavioral goals and a more effective approach to treatment.

Limited Smoking/Controlled Smoking

Setting a goal of reduced use of tobacco products is fairly controversial in that there is no research to report what constitutes a "safe" level of tobacco use. Some evidence suggests that physical dependency may be lower among those smoking fewer than 10 cigarettes a day, but there do not appear to be any substantial long-term health benefits to making this change. However, having controlled smoking as an option may open the door to more smokers seeking help and attempting change.

Switching Brands

One strategy to reducing the harm related to tobacco use is to switch to a brand of cigarettes that contain less tar and/or nicotine. Clients can gradually shift to brands containing progressively less tar/nicotine. If you consider this strategy with a client, discuss the tendency of smokers to "oversmoke" when shifting to low-tar/low-nicotine brands. They may inhale more deeply, take more frequent puffs, or block the filter vents, all of which can increase their overall risks.

Nicotine Replacement

As with other addictive substances, the cessation of tobacco use is associated with unpleasant withdrawal symptoms that can discourage clients from maintaining changes. As an adjunct to treatment, various products provide nicotine without the harmful effects of tar and carbon monoxide. Nicotine gum, transdermal delivery systems ("the patch"), nicotine inhalers, and nasal sprays all supply nicotine in a less harmful manner and allow clients to cease tobacco use at their own pace. Some antidepressants show promise in controlling withdrawal symptoms.

⊞ HARM REDUCTION AND SPECIAL POPULATIONS

Women

Effective harm reduction programs must take into account individual differences and also gender differences. Women face a unique constellation of health risks and consequences associated with their substance abuse. Women typically initiate and use illicit and other drugs during their childbearing years. Beyond the risks of HIV, accidental death, and long-term health problems, women also risk damaging their children if they use during pregnancy. Alcohol and other drug use can lead to fetal alcohol syndrome or

> ## BOX 21.5   Women's Problems Differ From Men's
>
> - Male partners often leave female users.
> - Women often have primary responsibilities for children.
> - Women often have fewer economic resources than men.
> - Abuse rates for substance-using women are high.
> - Power (and powerlessness) are male concepts.
> - Self-help groups are often dominated by men.

effects, miscarriage, an addicted or HIV-infected infant, and a multitude of other damaging effects. Female smokers also are more likely to have difficulties with infertility and ectopic pregnancies.

Although women in general appear to respond better to interventions than men, it is often more difficult for women to gain access to treatment because of the stigma associated with alcohol or drug problems. Treatment programs designed for women have to address special needs, such as providing child care during treatment, information about domestic violence, and concurrent treatment for sexual abuse. Many women do not feel as comfortable as men in traditional 12-step support groups. Support groups are often guided by traditionally male ways of thinking, and many groups are male dominated. Furthermore, women are often discouraged from seeking treatment by their male partners and may fear losing their children if they acknowledge any alcohol or drug abuse. Because of these special considerations for women, an important element of harm reduction programs for women is teaching assertion skills.

Nonmajority Cultures

People of nonmajority ethnic-cultural groups often find traditional therapy intrusive and rude. For many cultural groups in the United States, the traditional medical model is not accepted, and illness, disease, and discomfort are viewed much differently. To ignore ethnic-cultural differences in therapy is to invite disaster.

The harm reduction model meets clients where they are, including culturally. The client's bicultural or multicultural competence and level of acculturation (see box for definitions) are assessed and strongly influence how therapy proceeds (see Marlatt's *Harm Reduction* [1998] for examples). It also is important to recognize and respect that many cultures use certain psychoactive substances religiously.

Cultural considerations are very tricky because individual differences can be huge. When in doubt, ask your client. Appropriate questions include: What are family, clan, and community opinions about substance use? How many generations has the family lived in the United States? Did the person speak English or another language in the home as a child? Furthermore, there are often cultural differences between urban and rural people of color and indigenous people.

Sexual orientation also is very important to consider. Harm reduction programs, often viewed as more tolerant, will attract people who feel oppressed by the majority cul-

> **BOX 21.6** **Cultural Differences**
>
> - Bi- and multicultural competence is defined as how skilled a person of color is at interacting in his or her own culture and the culture of the majority community.
> - Acculturation is the degree to which the person identifies with and functions within the majority culture.
> - Acculturation is often influenced by generation, education, family, and environment.
> - Cultural sensitivity enhances the therapeutic alliance.

ture, such as gay, lesbian, transgendered, and bisexual clients. Harm reduction does not attempt to judge or change the person and often provides a safe place for a person to be him- or herself.

Furthermore, people of nonmajority cultures, like women, often feel out of place in support groups that do not necessarily speak to their needs. Although some specialized support circles have been formed, often the gulf of differences between majority and nonmajority cultural beliefs is too great to bridge. Some basic 12-step principles such as belief in higher powers and powerlessness are not compatible with many nonmajority cultural belief systems. We have found that balance, self-control, and moderation are frequently more congruent with cultural beliefs of many nonmajority clients in the United States.

Youth

Traditional approaches for adolescent alcohol and drug use focus on achieving complete abstinence. However, for youth, abstinence is often an unrealistic goal. To ask teenagers or college students to "just say no" is to lose the attention of up to three quarters of our audience because the vast majority have already said "yes."

Remember, one of the guiding principles in harm reduction is to "meet people where they are." When working with adolescents and college students, consider where they are on a continuum of biopsychosocial development, as well as how motivated they are to change behavior. Adolescence is a time of great change: Youth are experiencing radical changes in peer, family, romantic love, and other social relationships related to the development of independence and emotional maturity. Substance use in this context can be part of a pattern of deviant behavior, a reflection of comorbid psychopathology, or simply experimentation. Harm reduction considers these contextual factors when treating adolescent substance users.

Adolescents can be particularly sensitive to others, such as therapists, exerting control over their lives. Clearly spell out that you are not here to make them do anything and that it will be their choice when, if, and how they want to change. Being candid and modeling tolerance are very important to establish a therapeutic alliance. We have found it helpful to say, "This information may or may not fit your own situation. Take and use what you find to be useful and ignore the rest."

A particularly effective way to talk about choices regarding substance use with adolescents is the "driving analogy." We say that driving a car is a high-risk behavior that the majority of people in our society engage in at least occasionally. Driving has its ben-

---

BOX 21.7 **Being Young Does Have Its Privileges**

- Very rarely do young adults have the long history of negative consequences of substance use that often prompt adults to seek help.

- Because of this, very rarely do youth seek treatment on their own accord.

- Coerced into treatment, youth may appear more hostile and resistant to treatment than adults.

- Experimentation is often not problematic use.

- Many youth naturally mature out of substance abuse in adulthood.

- Youth are often naive about risks and less intimidated by the negative physical consequences of substance use.

---

efits, to be sure, but these benefits do not come free of risk; severe injury or death can occur if one drives recklessly. The same is true for alcohol or using drugs. A lot of people consume alcohol or use drugs occasionally. Although some people find it to be pleasurable, serious injury and death can result from abuse.

One major impasse in discussing drug and alcohol problems among adolescents and college students is the fear of punishment, which is precisely why harm reduction, with its tolerant and pragmatic features, may be most appropriate for young adults. Youth often do not feel free to talk about substance use in hierarchical environments. Many young people have told us that they would not approach a parent, teacher, or youth worker if they or someone they knew had a problem with drug use. This reluctance to talk with adult authority figures impedes the ability to intervene with youth at risk.

We have found that in working with school officials, parents, and youth clients it is important to *develop a contractual agreement* that the primary goal is the well-being of the youth and that full confidentiality will be provided for the adolescent within the restraints of the law. If parents or others object to being deprived of information about their child's use, do your best to persuade them that confidentiality will make progress in therapy more likely, presumably in the best interest of all involved.

After building a rapport with adolescent clients and reviewing their use patterns to understand the context of substance use, ask them *what they think is risky or harmful* about certain substances and how they could minimize those risks. Sometimes it is helpful to ask them what kind of advice they might give a friend who was engaging in the same behavior. These and other techniques are elaborated in *Taking Drugs Seriously: A Manual of Harm Reduction Education on Drugs* (Clements, Cohen, & Kay, 1990).

As youth discuss their perceptions of the costs and benefits of their substance use, find the crucial issue or concern that may be the catalyst for change. This issue, or "hook," for adolescents and college students can be how alcohol and other drugs affect athletic performance, weight gain or exercise, sleep, sex, memory, money, or school performance. When talking about drinking with college women especially, we have described the calories of a beer as "just like eating a hotdog, and would you eat six of those in one night?" which usually makes the point. One adolescent who needed a car discovered in therapy that he would have enough money to buy the car if he reduced smoking cigarettes and marijuana, which gave him incentives to do so.

> ### BOX 21.8 The Basics of the Alcohol Skills Training Program (ASTP)
>
> 1. Review how much alcohol is in a standard drink.
> 2. Discuss the effects of alcohol on the body.
> 3. Have your client monitor alcohol intake and its effects on him or her.
> 4. Provide individual BAL charts for drinkers and teach them how and when to use them.
> 5. Teach the biphasic effects of substance use.
> 6. Examine how substance abuse causes contextual myopia.
> 7. Explore your client's expectancies and provide the facts in nonjudgmental way.
> 8. Assist your client in finding his or her point of diminishing euphoric returns.
> 9. Explore mood-dependent substance use, and offer alternative activities.
> 10. Identify and overcome roadblocks to reaching personal goals.

It also is important to *anticipate periods of developmental risk* for using or drinking excessively. For high school, such times of concern are turning age 16 with driving privileges and graduation; for college-age drinkers, turning 21 years of age is a time of higher risk. Many school-based prevention programs emphasize unreasonable goals, such as insisting upon total abstinence during these rites of passage. Harm reduction strategies focus on alternatives, such as providing safe havens or transportation for youth during these events. For college students, teaching safe celebration and the use of a buddy system to keep an eye on the safety of one another is important. For example, we have presented college students with personalized blood alcohol level (BAL) cards and taught them how to use these cards to plan safe drinking events. Encourage youth to *plan ahead* for drinking and drug-using events and to *rehearse contingency plans* for safety.

Harm reduction drug education involves teaching clients about social reinforcement of intoxication behavior, the role of positive alcohol and drug expectancies in perpetuating substance use mythology, and the biphasic response to substances, especially alcohol. Research has determined that the pleasurable effects of alcohol peak at a BAL of .05 to .06 (as discussed earlier) and that increased negative effects (including tolerance, which can develop with consistent heavy drinking) then begin to diminish the positive effects (thus the term *biphasic*). The Alcohol Skills Training Program (ASTP; described in Dimeff, Baer, Kivlahan, and Marlatt's *Brief Alcohol Screening and Intervention for College Students*, 1999), is a harm reduction prevention program for young adults (see Box 21.8). Furthermore, Web-based technology is being used successfully to provide information and self-assessment for teenagers and college students. Internet resources allow young people to answer questions and concerns confidentially, and the objective feedback provided by the sites may enhance motivation to reduce substance abuse.

Homeless street youth have special needs to be considered. Street youth often engage in a variety of high-risk sexual and substance-related activities and are often at high risk to be victims of violence. Many come from environments where they were abused or neglected, lack trust for adults, and have comorbid mental health issues. Youthful mentors who work the streets are effective in attracting street youth to services. Once contact is made, harm reduction strategies of providing youth with clean needles, condoms, and safe housing can be implemented. Treatment issues are out of the question until basic needs are met and street youth trust the programs. However, word about trustworthy programs with reputations for confidential and nonjudgmental services travels quickly on the street.

Only after basic needs have been met and other risky behaviors have been assessed can reduction of substance use be realistically achieved. Again, as with all youth, therapy involves an honest and long-term negotiation between therapist and client. Mental health issues may be addressed concurrently. But nothing works until they trust you.

People With Health Problems

Harm reduction works well with people who have comorbid substance abuse and physical health problems. For example, victims of trauma often turn to substances to cope or have difficulties, because of brain injuries, in regulating their substance use. *Journaling, diaries, and structured daily and weekly calendars* can be helpful to reduce unstructured time available to use substances.

Sleep disorders can lead to increased substance-related coping, and teaching alternative strategies for sleeping behavior is quite useful. We have discussed with clients how drinking lots of liquids (such as alcohol) before bedtime can cause frequent urination (contributing to insomnia or long sleep-onset periods). Furthermore, teaching about the adverse effects of drinking and substance use upon sleep patterns, such as interference with REM and rebound effects that actually lengthen sleep onset, is helpful.

Pain behavior accounts for a large amount of substance abuse. Behavioral strategies for coping with pain are quite effective. Just as with distressing thoughts, the client can be taught that even chronic pain ebbs and flows and that pain does not necessarily have to control the way a person behaves (encouraging ability rather than disability). Pain medications should *always* be prescribed on a schedule rather than as needed to avoid intermittent negative reinforcement of pain behavior. Tapering or stopping pain medication may lead to a natural increase in pain complaints (an "extinction burst" in behavioral terms), but this normal response will diminish with time as long as the pain complaints are not rewarded with an increase in medicine. Other techniques such as acupuncture may be helpful to manage pain without medication.

People With Co-Occurring Psychiatric Disorders

People with co-occurring mental and substance use disorders are often the highest utilizers of mental health services. Because there is a high prevalence rate of co-occurring psychiatric disorders with substance use, it is important to screen for comorbidity with all clients, especially those prone to relapse or extremely impulsive behavior. People with psychiatric disorders also contend with the effects of psychotropic medications and cognitive impairment. These problems, along with lowered social support and social skills secondary to mental health issues, make abstinence difficult to achieve and maintain. We have found harm reduction to be quite helpful when working with people with comorbid disorders.

Issues of self-medication often muddy the waters with such clients. The evidence as to whether people really self-medicate is inconclusive (e.g., Blume, Schmaling, &

BOX 21.9 **Cognitive Impairment: Phantom Roadblock to Improvement**

- Clients may appear normal in session but act impulsively in the world: if so, they may benefit from neuropsychological assessment.
- Head injuries are possible in all clients.
- Psychiatric disorders often cause cognitive problems.
- Be concrete, patient, and repetitious in therapy, and provide daily structure for clients.
- Memory and impulse control problems may make abstinence an unrealistic goal.

Marlatt, 2000). However, most clients with co-occurring disorders *believe* that they are self-medicating symptoms and that the substances they are using are at least partially effective in reducing psychiatric symptoms. Such *expected* results may be related to intermittent symptom relief or may represent a placebo effect. Assessing self-medication expectancies can help you understand the context for substance use by the client. Because self-medication expectancies are reinforced positively (euphoria) and negatively (intermittent symptom reduction), cognitive distortions that substances always help with symptoms persist.

Furthermore, because psychotropic medications often take quite a while to reach therapeutic dosage, and often come with numerous unpleasant side effects, a client may not want to stick with the medication or may supplement the medication with an illicit substance. Clients have told us that using psychotropic medication seems punishing because of the side effects and the slow relief of symptoms. Therefore, even though self-medication may physically occur at times, cognitive-behavioral interventions provide the greatest hope for reducing use because beliefs perpetuate the cycle of abuse.

Abstinence may not be a reasonable goal for many clients with co-occurring disorders. Instead, we reward small steps toward moderation (successive approximations). Harm reduction suggests that clients taper substance use in a stepwise fashion as their prescribed medications reach therapeutic dosage, rather than demanding abstinence before starting the medications. Furthermore, physicians may unwittingly encourage relapse by frequently readmitting people with co-occurring disorders when they slip. Our experience has been that people with co-occurring disorders may not seek therapy if abstinence is demanded. We have found that compromises often enhance the therapeutic alliance with our clients.

Relapse prevention as harm reduction is especially useful among this population (see Larimer & Marlatt, 1990). One of us (AB) has converted the concept of "urge surfing" (see Marlatt & Gordon, 1985, for greater detail), into "discomfort surfing" to cope with side effects of medication or with the latency periods before medications reach therapeutic strength. Meditation practices and distress tolerance strategies (see above) may help a person "surf" uncomfortable symptoms (Marlatt & Kristeller, 1999). Furthermore, structuring time, assessing cognitive function, and providing memory prompts may promote self-regulation of behavior, as well as help clients to find rewards in everyday life apart from substance use.

CONCLUSIONS

Timing is very important in therapy, especially for harm reduction therapy with substance users, who often bolt from therapy when they feel misunderstood or disrespected. Although abstinence is an appropriate goal for many clients, such a goal may be incomprehensible during the first point of therapeutic contact. Harm reduction buys time to allow abstinence to seem more obtainable and desirable, although reduction alone may be enough to arrest the problems.

Harm reduction relies upon scientifically tested behavioral research to inform strategies to use with different populations. These strategies involve respect for clients' goals for therapy, for cultural and gender differences, and for individual differences: One size definitely does not fit all. Therapy in a harm reduction model is a collaborative venture with the goal of improving the client's health and reducing his or her risk of harm.

Furthermore, harm reduction is a public health model, rather than a moralistic or punitive model. At this writing, almost 2 million Americans are imprisoned, a great many for substance-related crimes, and a majority are people of color or indigenous; more than twice as much money is being spent on prisons for substance users as for treatment. Furthermore, the U.S. government refused to fund needle exchanges despite a recommendation by a blue-ribbon science panel. Our government has declared war on our fellow citizens instead of treating addiction as a complex health problem. Harm reduction, because of its emphasis on using what has been shown to help people, offers hope for many people who would otherwise be lost. Although grassroots harm reduction is being practiced successfully, public policy will have to change if access is to be provided for all the people who would benefit from alternatives to what currently exists. It is up to therapists to advocate for those who are in need but do not have a voice.

REFERENCES

Blume, A. W., Schmaling, K. B., & Marlatt, G. A. (2000). Revisiting the self-medication hypothesis from a behavioral perspective. *Cognitive and Behavioral Practice, 7*, 379-384.

Clements, I., Cohen, J., & Kay, J. (1990). *Taking drugs seriously: A manual of harm reduction education on drugs.* Liverpool: Healthwise Helpline Ltd.

Dimeff, L., Baer, J., Kivlahan, D., & Marlatt, G. A. (1999). *Brief alcohol screening and intervention for college students: A harm reduction approach.* New York: Guilford.

Larimer, M. E., & Marlatt, G. A. (1990). Applications of relapse prevention with moderation goals. *Journal of Psychoactive Drugs, 22*, 189-195.

Marlatt, G. A. (1998). *Harm reduction: Pragmatic strategies for managing high-risk behaviors.* New York: Guilford.

Marlatt, G. A., & Gordon, J. (1985). *Relapse prevention.* New York: Guilford.

Marlatt, G. A., & Kristeller, J. (1999). Mindfulness and meditation. In W. R. Miller (Ed.), *Integrating spirituality into treatment.* Washington, DC: American Psychological Association.

Marlatt, G. A., & Miller, W. R. (1984). *Comprehensive drinker profile.* Odessa, FL: Psychological Assessment Resources, Inc.

Miller, W. R., & Hester, R. K. (1986). The effectiveness of alcoholism treatment methods: What research reveals. In W. R. Miller & N. Heather (Eds.), *Treating addictive behaviors: Processes of change.* New York: Plenum.

Sobell, M., & Sobell, L. (1993). *Problem drinkers: Guided self-change treatment.* New York: Guilford.

◫ ADDITIONAL SUGGESTED READINGS

Daley, D. C., & Marlatt, G. A. (1998). *Managing your drug or alcohol problem.* New York: Academic Press.

Linehan, M. (1993). *Skills training manual for treating borderline personality disorder.* New York: Guilford.

22

Matching Clients With Recovery Tools

Finding the Right Keys to Unlock the Door

Reid Hester
Theresa Moyers

One of your tasks as a clinician is to develop a plan of action for each of your clients that is most likely to result in positive outcomes. Matching clients to different interventions holds promise for improving these outcomes. Decades of outcome research and our own clinical experience tell us that there is no single approach that works best with every client. Rather, there are a number of effective alternatives, many of which are described in the other chapters in this book. Matching clients with specific, effective interventions involves knowing your clients and their needs, the recovery tools available to them both inside and outside your treatment program, and what the research indicates are matching strategies likely to improve outcomes.

EXPERIENCE WITH MATCHING CLIENTS TO TREATMENTS

Our Clinical Experience

Personally, we have a total of 34 years of clinical experience in matching clients to treatments (RH has 22, TM has 12). In our clinical experience, matching is a necessary consideration for every client and in every setting. Just as you need to make a decision about the level of care (intensity, location), you also need to decide which specific interventions are most likely to be helpful for a particular client. Tailor treatment to the individual rather than assuming the Procrustean notion of making the client fit the treatment.

Our clients have taught us many things about how to match them to different interventions. These include

- The importance of working collaboratively with the client in choosing approaches
- Giving priority to what the client wants to work on (e.g., marital concerns)
- Addressing the goal of change in drinking (moderation vs. abstinence), especially with less severely dependent clients
- Having backup plans ready in the event that your initial choice of approach(es) is not as successful as you hoped
- Following up to minimize the chances of relapse

When you are developing a plan of action for a client, involve him or her in the process. Your client will always decide whether to participate fully in a course of treatment anyway. We know that client compliance in treatment predicts outcome, so everything you can do to increase compliance and retention in treatment will be helpful. If you give careful consideration to what the client says he or she wants to address, then the client is more likely to work with the plan rather than resist it.

The same can be said for negotiating the goals of change in drinking with clients. This is less difficult than many people think. We'll address this issue later. Suffice it for now to say that your willingness to discuss moderation versus abstinence in considering your client's goals can affect how honest your client will be with you about them. You can do without covert resistance.

Matching clients to different approaches is an imprecise science. You're going to make mistakes. So if Plan A isn't entirely successful for a particular client, what are your Plans B and C? Plan B might be to continue with Plan A but add an additional tool (e.g., a disulfiram compliance protocol). Also, letting clients know at the beginning that you'll continue working with them on alternatives helps them to feel less like a failure if Plan A isn't entirely successful and leads to a lapse to drinking. You'll be modeling persistence and perseverance, qualities that clients in recovery sometimes lack.

Keep in touch with your clients after the initial phase of recovery. Periodic follow-ups over the course of 12 to 24 months enable you to provide additional assistance when your clients encounter problems that threaten their sobriety. Clients also see follow-up as a continuing resource.

Research About Matching: Specific Content of Treatment

Research suggesting that clients with different characteristics have different outcomes in a given treatment has been around since the 1940s. Many treatment outcome studies that examined the effectiveness of a particular approach or compared two approaches noted matching effects over the years (e.g., Miller & Hester, 1980, 1986). However, much of this early research, although suggestive, was retrospective, and replication was not reported. To address the question of the value of treatment matching, the National Institute on Alcohol Abuse and Alcoholism (NIAAA) funded a multisite trial of patient-treatment matching (Project MATCH) investigating three different treatments supported by empirical evidence. The three treatments (cognitive-behavioral, 12-step facilitation, and motivational enhancement therapy) were designed by experts in the field and were delivered with a high level of integrity.

The surprising results indicated no matching effects for client variables commonly assumed to be important in the selection of treatments. For example, client endorsement of a spiritual focus and measures of client conceptual level yielded no matching effects for 12-step or cognitive-behavioral treatments. All the interventions were equally effective, with some minor advantages for each with some subgroups. The Project MATCH research group concluded that there was no evidence suggesting that any of the treatments were more effective than others. In some respects, this is very good news indeed because therapists proficient in any of these methods can find empirical support for their treatment approach. However, you should be aware that their findings of no differences in the effectiveness of these treatments stands in contrast to a large body of clinical outcome research (Miller, Zweban, DiClemente, & Rychtarik, 1995). What is left for the provider who is genuinely struggling to individualize treatments for alcohol abusers? Several important findings from the empirical literature may be helpful.

A substantial amount of evidence indicates that clients with coexisting antisocial personality disorders will respond more favorably to treatments focused on acquiring specific skills (e.g., refusing requests to drink) as opposed to treatments that stress the enhancement of social relationships (Cooney, Kadden, Litt, & Getter, 1991; Kadden, Cooney, Getter, & Litt, 1989; Longabaugh et al., 1994). This series of studies implies that when you are treating clients with an antisocial personality disorder, you would do well to focus on helping the client acquire alcohol-related coping skills rather than to emphasize the client's social network as a means of avoiding drinking. It is likely that these clients will also be male, have a family history of drinking problems and childhood behavior problems, and have a more severe course for their drinking disorder (Brown, Babor, Litt, & Kranzler, 1994). In general, treatments that enrich a person's social environment and interpersonal relationships are an excellent investment of your time as a therapist, but this group is an exception to that rule.

Another important variable for selecting treatments for your clients is that of psychiatric symptomatology. Clients with psychiatric disorders such as depression and anxiety will respond better to your interventions, and will drink less after treatment, if they receive the proper pharmacotherapy for their psychiatric problems (Cornelius et al., 1993; Kranzler et al., 1995; Mason, Kocsis, Ritvo, & Cutler, 1996). Although it may seem elementary, proper assessment and treatment of affective disorders are critical variables in alcohol treatment outcome with such clients. Clients who continue to be significantly anxious or depressed following a 4-week period of abstinence should receive an evaluation for pharmacological treatment. Clients with affective disorders that *precede* substance abuse or those who exhibit suicidal thoughts and impulses should be evaluated without delay to improve the outcomes of substance abuse treatment.

The treatment literature also clearly indicates that alcohol-abusing clients who have viable marriages or long-term partners will have better drinking outcomes if they receive behavioral marital therapy that specifically addresses their alcohol use. This type of therapy might include training family members not to reinforce drinking behavior (Meyers & Smith, 1995; Noel & McCrady, 1993; Sisson & Azrin, 1986), making behavioral contracts for abstinence (O'Farrell, 1995), or increasing the quality of the relationship with communication skills training and increasing recreational activities (McCrady & Epstein, 1999; O'Farrell & Langenbucher, 1987).

Finally, another variable that has received attention in matching clients to treatments is conceptual level (McLachlan, 1974; Project MATCH Research Group, 1997). Clients with a high conceptual level are abstract thinkers, whereas clients with a low conceptual level tend to be more concrete in their thinking and prefer rules and structure in most situations. Although Project MATCH did not find matching effects based on therapist and client conceptual level, a newer study indicates that this variable may influence client compliance with treatment and subsequent improvement in drinking behavior (Nielson & Wrane, 1998). Clients with higher conceptual levels complied better with treatments that were flexible and negotiable, whereas clients with low conceptual levels complied better with highly structured treatments. The Nielson and Wrane study is strong from a scientific standpoint because it was prospective: That is, it set out to look for matching effects rather than discovering them after the fact or retrospectively.

▦ MATCHING: A PROCESS APPROACH

As we discussed earlier, every client has specific needs. Matching treatments to meet these needs is a routine part of our treatment planning. Matching should, at the very least, be done at the beginning of treatment, following the assessment. It can also be done during the active phase of treatment if the client's clinical picture changes (e.g., he loses his driving job because of his DWI). Finally, it is a consideration in planning, aftercare, or follow-up.

Prochaska and DiClemente (1986) developed a model to describe behavior change that can help guide treatment-matching choices. The stages-of-change model is based on the finding that individuals often move through a series of stages as they progress through difficult behavior changes (Box 22.1). The change process begins with little concern about the behavior, progresses to a period of ambivalence characterized by internal conflict about the need for change, and finally moves to a period of decision and action culminating in positive change. Once the behavior change has been made successfully, the person makes a transition to the task of maintaining it. Of course, the process can be interrupted at any time by a relapse.

This model provides an excellent conceptual model for the treatment-matching process, for it prescribes specific therapist tasks for each stage of the change process. For example, when clients are struggling through the ambivalence of the contemplation stage of change, you would be wise to avoid advice and persuasion because it is likely to elicit resistance at this point. Instead, you might implement strategies specifically for raising awareness or resolving ambivalence, such as motivational interviewing. For clients who have decided to make a change but are not sure how, you may want to consider presenting a menu of options and weighing the pros and cons of each. For clients fully committed to action, you may want to implement one or more of the empirically supported tools mentioned in other parts of this book. For those who are maintaining the change, relapse prevention is an obvious choice, as well as other interventions to support balance in the client's activities and interests (Marlatt & Gordon, 1985). Thus, treatment matching involves selecting interventions appropriate to the treatment process, rather than content (Prochaska, DiClemente, & Norcross, 1998).

BOX 22.1 **Movement Through the Stages of Making a Behavioral Change**

Stages of Change

Let's see how this might look, using a case example. Bob P. is referred to you because he has recently been convicted of DWI and must receive some alcohol-related counseling as part of his sentence. He knows he has an alcohol problem but doesn't believe he is an alcoholic. He's worried but angry. Bob is in the contemplation stage of change, so your approach with him is nonconfrontational and empathic rather than confrontational (see Chapter 2). Because you have used a stage-appropriate intervention, Bob makes a shift in readiness and is now considering what options he might have for change. What do you do now?

Because Bob is in the preparation stage of change, and not yet ready to commit, you present him with many options, including weekly sessions, involving his wife in treatment, taking disulfiram, and undergoing behavioral self-control training. Because he does not want further trouble from the legal system, Bob decides to try a period of abstinence and to bring his wife into treatment with him in the hopes of improving their relationship. This type of treatment is covered in Chapter 16.

Once Bob starts seeing you on a weekly basis and makes a change in his drinking, he encounters predictable difficulties. For example, he has trouble refusing drinks at company parties, and he feels unpredictable urges to drink and worries he will slip. Now Bob is in the action stage of change, so you are able to choose among treatment strategies that seem most useful to him and that are supported by research and clinical common sense.

Notice that you have chosen different interventions depending on Bob's readiness to change. You might even have measured this readiness to change with a paper-and-pencil test called the Stages of Change and Treatment Eagerness Scale (SOCRATES; Miller & Tonigan, 1996). In any case, you have tailored your treatment to Bob's developmental progress in his difficult decision: In other words, you have done treatment matching.

Evidence indicates that your clients will do better if you do not aggressively confront or push them to make a change when they are in the initial stages of change and ambivalent (Miller, Benefield, & Tonigan, 1993). You will be more successful if you use different tools with clients depending on their stages of change than if you use the same treatment regardless of your client's readiness.

⊞ PITFALLS AND PROBLEMS

How Do You Match Clients in the Action Stage to Interventions?

Baseline Information

What follows presumes that you have done a thorough assessment with your client and are aware of where he or she falls on the following continua:

- The need for detoxification
- Severity of alcohol dependence
- Presence of other substance abuse and/or dependence
- Concomitant psychopathology (Axes I and II)
- Social stability and social support for sobriety
- Motivation for change
- Health issues associated with heavy drinking (e.g., elevated liver enzymes)
- Type and severity of drinking-related consequences
- Client's presenting concerns

We also assume that you are aware of resources both within your program and outside your program. These include

- Liaison with a detoxification facility and outpatient detoxification programs
- Liaison with physicians willing to consider prescribing disulfiram or naltrexone
- Liaison with psychiatrists for treating persistent mood disorders that persist into sobriety as well as for treating clients with severe mental illnesses (e.g., bipolar disorder)
- Liaison with psychologists and other therapists for psychological treatment of persisting Axis I and II disorders
- Liaison with psychologists and other therapists who have expertise in recovery tools that you do not have
- Local self-help group meetings, including the dynamics and styles of different groups
- Liaison with self-help group members willing to take your clients to meetings
- Online resources for self-help groups that are not available in your area (e.g., www.smartrecovery.org)
- Online listings of therapists for aftercare referrals outside of your area

With this information and information that we provide you in this section, you'll be able to start making informed choices with your clients about approaches and recovery tools from which they are most likely to benefit.

The Process of Client/Treatment Matching

One of the first decisions you'll need to make regards detoxification. In some instances, this is a simple decision. The client arrives on your door step highly intoxicated, and you walk him down to the detox unit for admission. In other instances, the need for detox is less obvious. The client arrives sober, but you learn that she has a long history of diazepam (Valium) use and that she stopped 3 days ago. Because of the long half-life of benzodiazepines, she could be at risk for serious withdrawal problems for the next 2 weeks.

If your program deals with more severely dependent clients, chances are good that it will have some protocol for referring clients to detox. Use it. When in doubt, ask for a consultation from someone from the detox unit, or call the client's physician and discuss the case with him or her.

On the other hand, if you tend to see less severely dependent clients, then you may rarely need to make referrals for detox. However, you should still have a physician you can call or a liaison with a treatment center with detox facilities when the need arises.

The next decision point in treating clients comes after you've built rapport with them (see Chapter 2 on motivational interviewing), done a thorough assessment of the domains described above, and provided the client with feedback about the results. The feedback session is important because it can enhance the client's motivation for change. It can also be the beginning of negotiating a treatment plan with the client.

In cases of significant alcohol dependence and/or drug abuse, most clients realize that the only realistic way to get rid of their alcohol and drug-related problems is to quit entirely, to abstain. And abstaining is always the safest course. With respect to illegal drugs, it's the only safe course, as any use poses the risk of legal consequences. However, alcohol is another matter. Some clients, typically the less severely dependent, will be interested in discussing a goal of cutting back: that is, moderation.

Goals of Change: Moderation Versus Abstinence

We mentioned earlier that it's important for you to be willing to discuss how the client is going to change his or her drinking. It is ultimately the client's choice. He or she will make this decision with you if you're willing to discuss it in a matter-of-fact manner. Or the client will make it without you if you tell him or her that he or she has no choice but to abstain.

An interesting clinical study illustrates this point. Sanchez-Craig (1980) recruited non-alcohol-dependent heavy drinkers to a program she ran outside of Toronto. After carefully assessing clients, she randomly assigned them either to a moderation group or to an abstinence group, telling each client that this was the best goal for him or her. Both groups received behavioral self-control training. At 12-month follow-up, she found no differences between the two groups in the ratio of those abstaining to moderating to unimproved. What she told them was the most appropriate goal turned out to be irrelevant. The clients decided for themselves what drinking goal to pursue. And your clients will also.

Most heavy drinkers and those with severe alcohol dependence choose to abstain when they decide to change their drinking. This is clearly the safest course and is most likely to enable them to get rid of their alcohol-related problems. Outcome research indicates that the likelihood of success with moderation declines with increasing severity of alcohol dependence (Hester, 1995). At the same time, lifelong abstinence can seem pretty intimidating. To reduce this, consider using a sobriety sampling procedure from the community reinforcement approach (CRA; Meyers & Smith, 1995).

On the other end of the spectrum of severity, those with less severe alcohol problems are much more likely to be successful with a goal of moderation. Also, long-term follow-up 2 to 8 years after moderation training shows that for many, successful moderation is a stepping-stone to abstinence (Miller, Leckman, Delaney, & Tinkham, 1992). Miller et al. described different ways to classify clients at the beginning of treatment that are predictive of long-term success with moderation. To optimize treatment matching (not necessarily for optimal screening of patients), use the Michigan Alcoholism Screening Test (MAST; Selzer, 1971). Higher scores on the MAST at pretreatment are predictive of poorer outcomes with moderation as a goal. We suggest a strong cutoff score of 19. In the Miller et al. study, no one with a score of 20+ was successful at eliminating his or her alcohol-related problems over the long haul by moderating his or her drinking. Clients with lower scores had increasingly better chances of success. The details of these scores and outcomes can be found in a table in the Project MATCH motivational enhancement therapy manual (Project MATCH, 1997).

Know what is meant by moderation, in the event that a client is interested in it. Moderate drinking consists of no more than two to three standard drinks per drinking occasion for men, one to two for women; no more than 12 drinks per week for men and 9 for women. Also, BACs stay under 55 mg%, which precludes guzzling this alcohol over a short period of time. There is no safe drinking limit for pregnant women, and other medical conditions are also contraindications to even moderate drinking (e.g., congestive heart failure). A standard drink is the equivalent of 12 ounces of 5% beer, 5 ounces of 12.5% wine, or 1.5 ounces of 80 proof spirits.

In my (RH's) clinical experience, most severely dependent clients will scoff at this amount of drinking and say something like, "That's not drinking. It'd be easier not to get started in the first place." To which I reply, "You're right." However, I've had a few severely alcohol-dependent clients want to try moderation before being willing to consider abstinence. In those few instances, I've offered them a behavioral contract (see Chapter 8). I'll work with them for 6 to 8 weeks, providing them with a protocol that's been shown to be effective (Hester, 1995) in helping clients moderate their drinking. If the client is successful, then we'll shift into follow-up mode. However, if the client is still struggling after this period of time and overdrinking, then the chances of their succeeding long term are nil, and I'll ask the client to switch to a goal of abstinence. I've yet to have a client refuse this contract. It's a strategy to engage them in treatment from which they otherwise might have dropped out. It's also a low-threshold approach consistent with harm reduction (see Chapter 21). And usually after a couple weeks of attempted moderation, the clients realize it's unrealistic and switch to abstinence.

If a client wishes to pursue moderation and you are not skilled in moderation training, you have several choices. First, you can refer to a therapist with expertise in moderation training. (Our Web site, **www.behaviortherapy.com**, provides a current list.) Second, you can provide them with a moderation self-help manual (e.g., Miller & Munoz, 1992) or moderation training software (our Web site, **www.behaviortherapy.com**, has the software that we developed, Behavioral Self-Control Program for Windows [BSCPWIN]; see also Chapter 3 of this book).

But what about the client who is mandated by the court to enter treatment and be abstinent or face jail? Well, the client still has a choice. He or she can continue drinking and risk going to jail. However, you may feel constrained to offer interventions with a goal of moderation that is in conflict with a court order. In our experience in New Mexico, this is usually not a problem. Court-mandated abstinence typically happens with the multiple DWI offender, who is less likely to be successful with moderation because of the severity of his alcohol dependence. However, in San Juan County, first offenders are mandated to a 28-day inpatient program and 12 months of abstinence, which is monitored by random breath checks. In this program, we advise the counselors to reframe the 12 months of abstinence as a time-out or experiment. During this time, the therapist and client can work to make the client's sober life more rewarding than his or her drinking life, which often happens.

Matching Clients to Specific Recovery Tools or Approaches

The next matching issue is to choose specific interventions or tools that the client can use to achieve and maintain his or her sobriety. Address the change in drinking or drug use behaviors first. If the client anticipates experiencing urges and cravings to drink, consider naltrexone or disulfiram. The former reduces urges cravings to drink and blocks the "high" if the client does drink. Disulfiram, on the other hand, produces a psychological fence because the client knows that nausea and vomiting will follow close on the heels of any drinking. If you're considering disulfiram, we highly recommend a behavioral compliance protocol to ensure its ingestion (Meyers & Smith, 1995). Yet another alternative is teaching psychological strategies for coping with urges and cravings (Horvath, 1998).

Once you have implemented a plan to stop the drinking or drug using, turn your attention to your client's most pressing concerns. Giving priority to the alcohol- or drug-related problems that are of greatest concern to your client will increase the chances that he or she will stay in treatment with you and improve your client's outcomes. For instance, if the client is at risk for losing his job because he's lost his license *and* you have an ignition interlock program available, advocate for getting him into it so he can continue to drive legally. Similarly, if the client's marriage is in a shambles, offer to either provide behavioral marital therapy or to get her to a qualified therapist who can.

Once your clients have achieved some success with sobriety, consider the tools they need to maintain it. Having a balance in their lives between those things they "should" do and "want" to do reduces the chances that clients will get to the point of saying, "To hell with it, I deserve a break" and then relapse to drinking or drug using. This is also a time when clients can benefit from spiritual enhancement, meditation, or other holistic tools. These are all ways to help the client from relapsing.

If your collaborative efforts are not entirely successful and the client relapses, then your task is to help him or her stop the relapse as quickly as possible. Don't become discouraged if the client isn't entirely successful the first time around. You may need to enhance motivation for change again and help the client see the lapse or relapse as a learning experience rather than a failure. What else does the client need to learn that he or she had not learned from the previous treatment?

▦ REFERENCES

Brown, J., Babor, T. F., Litt, M. D., & Kranzler, H. R. (1994, February 28). The Type A, Type B distinction: Subtyping alcoholics according to indicators of vulnerability and severity. *Annals of the New York Academy of Science, 708,* 23-33.

Cooney, N. L., Kadden, R. M., Litt, M. D., & Getter, H. (1991). Matching alcoholics to coping skills or interactional therapies: Two year follow-up results. *Journal of Consulting and Clinical Psychology, 59,* 598-601.

Cornelius, J. R., Salloum, I. M., Cornelius, M. D., Perel, J. M., Thase, M. E., Ehler, J. G., & Mann, J. J. (1993). Fluoxetine trial in suicidal depressed alcoholics. *Psychopharmacology Bulletin, 29,* 195-199.

Hester, R. K. (1995). Behavioral self-control training. In W. R. Miller & R. K. Hester (Eds.), *Handbook of alcoholism treatment approaches: Effective alternatives* (2nd ed., pp. 148-159). Boston: Allyn & Bacon.

Horvath, A. T. (1998). *Sex, drugs, gambling and chocolate: A workbook for overcoming addictions.* San Luis Obispo, CA: Impact.

Kadden, R. M., Cooney, N. L., Getter, H., & Litt, M. D. (1989). Matching alcoholics to coping skills or interactional therapies: Posttreatment results. *Journal of Consulting and Clinical Psychology, 57,* 698-704.

Kranzler, H. R., Burleson, J. A., Korner, P., Del Boca, F. K., Bohn, M. J., Brown, J., & Liebowitz, N. (1995). Placebo-controlled trial of fluoxetine as an adjunct to relapse prevention in alcoholics. *American Journal of Psychiatry, 152,* 391-397.

Longabaugh, R., Rubin, A., Malloy, P., Beattie, M., Clifford, P. R., & Noel, N. (1994). Drinking outcomes of alcohol abusers diagnosed as antisocial personality disorder. *Alcoholism: Clinical and Experimental Research, 18,* 778-785.

Marlatt, G. A., & Gordon, J. R. (1985). *Relapse prevention: Maintenance strategies in the treatment of addictive behaviors.* New York: Guilford.

Mason, B. J., Kocsis, J. H., Ritvo, E. C., & Cutler, R. B. (1996). A double-blind, placebo-controlled trial of desipramine for primary alcohol dependence stratified on the presence or absence of major depression. *Journal of the American Medical Association, 275,* 761-767.

McCrady, B. S., & Epstein, E. E. (Eds.). (1999). *Addictions: A comprehensive guidebook.* New York: Oxford University Press.

McLachlan, J. (1974). Therapy strategies, personality orientation and recovery from alcoholism. *Canadian Psychiatric Association Journal, 19*(1), 25-30.

Meyers, R. J., & Smith, J. E. (1995). *Clinical guide to alcohol treatment: The community reinforcement approach.* New York: Guilford.

Miller, W. R., Benefield, R. G., & Tonigan, J. S. (1993). Enhancing motivation for change in problem drinking: A controlled comparison of two therapist styles. *Journal of Consulting and Clinical Psychology, 61,* 455-461.

Miller, W. R., & Hester, R. K. (1980). Treating the problem drinker: Modern approaches. In W. R. Miller (Ed.), *The addictive behaviors: Treatment of alcoholism, drug abuse, smoking and obesity.* New York: Pergamon.

Miller, W. R., & Hester, R. K. (1986). Matching problem drinkers with optimal treatments. In W. R. Miller & N. Heather (Eds.), *Treating addictive behaviors: Processes of change* (pp. 175-204). New York: Pergamon.

Miller, W. R., Leckman, A. L., Delaney, H. D., & Tinkhom, M. (1992). Long-term follow-up of behavioral self-control training. *Journal of Studies on Alcohol, 53,* 249-261.

Miller, W. R., & Munoz, R. F. (1982). *How to control your drinking* (Rev. ed.). Albuquerque: University of New Mexico Press.

Miller, W. R., & Tonigan, J. S. (1996). Assessing drinker's motivation for change: The Stages of Change Readiness and Treatment Eagerness Scale (SOCRATES). *Psychology of Addictive Behaviors, 10*(2), 81-89.

Miller, W. R., Zweben, A., DiClemente, C. C., & Rychtarik, R. G. (1995). *Motivational enhancement therapy manual: A clinical research guide for therapists treating individuals with alcohol abuse and dependence* (DHHS Pub. No. ADM94-573). Washington, DC: U.S. Department of Health and Human Services.

Nielson, N. B., & Wrane, O. (1998). Patient-treatment matching improves compliance of alcoholics in outpatient treatment. *Journal of Nervous and Mental Diseases, 186,* 752-760.

Noel, N. E., & McCrady, B. S. (1993). Alcohol-focused spouse involvement with behavioral marital therapy. In T. J. O'Farrell (Ed.), *Treating alcohol problems: Marital and family interventions* (pp. 210-235). New York: Guilford.

O'Farrell, T. J. (1995). Marital and family therapy. In R. K. Hester & W. R. Miller (Eds.), *Handbook of alcoholism treatment approaches* (2nd ed., pp. 195-220). Boston: Allyn & Bacon.

O'Farrell, T. J., & Langenbucher, J. (1987). Inpatient treatment of alcoholism: A behavioral approach. *Journal of Substance Abuse Treatment, 4,* 215-231.

Prochaska, J. O., & DiClemente, C. C. (1986). Towards a comprehensive model of change. In W. R. Miller & N. Heather (Eds.), *Treating addictive behaviors: Processes of change* (pp. 3-28). New York: Pergamon.

Prochaska, J. O., DiClemente, C. C., & Norcross, J. C. (1998). Stages of change: Prescriptive guidelines for behavioral medicine and psychotherapy. In G. O. Koocher, J. C. Norcross, & S. S. Hill (Eds.), *Psychologists' desk reference* (pp. 230-240). New York: Oxford University Press.

Project MATCH Research Group. (1997). Project MATCH secondary a priori hypotheses. *Addiction, 92,* 1671-1698.

Sanchez-Craig, M. (1980). Random assignment to abstinence or controlled drinking in a cognitive-behavioral program: Short-term effects on drinking behavior. *Addictive Behaviors, 5,* 35-39.

Selzer, M. L. (1971). The Michigan Alcoholism Screening Test: The quest for a new diagnostic instrument. *American Journal of Psychiatry, 127,* 1653-1658.

Sisson, R. W., & Azrin, N. H. (1986). Family-member involvement to initiate and promote treatment of problem drinkers. *Journal of Behavior Therapy and Experimental Psychiatry, 17,* 15-21.

INDEX

About the Editor

Robert H. Coombs, PhD, Professor of Biobehavioral Sciences at the University of California, Los Angeles (UCLA), School of Medicine, is trained as a sociologist (doctorate), counseling psychologist (postdoctoral master's), family therapist (California licensed), and group psychotherapist (nationally certified). He has authored 14 books and 175 other publications; his latest books include *Handbook on Drug-Abuse Prevention* (with D. Ziedonis, Allyn & Bacon, 1995), *Drug-Impaired Professionals* (Harvard University Press, 1997), *Surviving Medical School* (Sage, 1998) and *Cool Parents, Drug-Free Kids: A Family Survival Guide* (Allyn & Bacon, 2001). The National Science Foundation partially supported his graduate training, and his research has been funded by grants from the National Institute on Mental Health, the National Institute on Drug Abuse, the National Institute of Justice, the U.S. Department of Labor, the National Fund for Medical Education, the California Department of Alcohol and Drug Programs, Father Flanagan's Boys' Foundation, and the UCLA Chancellor's Office. The U.S. Congress cited one of his applied research endeavors as an Exemplary Project. A Fellow of the American Association for the Advancement of Science, the American Psychological Society, and the American Association of Applied and Preventive Psychology, he teaches UCLA courses on addiction, where he received the Award for Excellence in Education from the UCLA School of Medicine and the Distinguished Faculty Educator Award from the UCLA Neuropsychiatric Institute and Hospital.

About the Contributors

Britt K. Anderson, PhC, a doctoral candidate in the clinical psychology program at the University of Washington, received specialized training in the assessment and treatment of addictive behaviors. The focus of her current research involves the development and evaluation of preventive intervention programs for addictive behaviors. Her current applied research involves clinical interaction with college-aged students and adults who are either problem drinkers or alcohol dependent, as well as the promotion of optimal health practices among lighter and moderate drinkers.

Joseph D. Beasley, MD, Director of the Addiction Project at the Mother and Child Corporation in Amityville, New York, is a consulting physician, educator, author, and policy advisor. He served as Professor and Department Head at Harvard and Tulane Universities, as Dean of the School of Public Health and Tropical Medicine at Tulane University, as Chairman of Planned Parenthood Federation of America, and as a member of the National Commission on Population Growth and the American Future. Currently he directs a nonprofit international project to provide the latest scientific information on alcoholism and chemical dependency prevention and treatment. His fourth edition of *Diagnosing and Managing Chemical Dependency* will be published in 2001.

Arthur W. Blume, PhD, a clinical psychology resident at the University of Washington School of Medicine, did his graduate work in the Addictive Behaviors Research Center at the University of Washington. A certified chemical dependency counselor, he formerly worked at Harborview Medical Center in Seattle with clients having co-occurring disorders and traumatic substance-related injuries. As a faculty member of the State of Washington Institute, he trains mental health, corrections, and addiction service professionals to use motivational enhancement therapy in a variety of treatment environments. His research in addictive behaviors focuses primarily upon harm reduction, ethnic-cultural considerations, co-occurring disorders, the transtheoretical model, and neuropsychological aspects of addictive behaviors.

Stephanie Brown, PhD, a clinician, teacher, researcher, consultant, and author in the field of alcoholism, founded the Alcohol Clinic at Stanford University Medical Center in 1977 and served as its director for 8 years. She is a Research Associate and Co-Director of the Family Recovery Project at the Mental Research Institute in Palo Alto, California. She directs the Addictions Institute in Menlo Park, California, and also maintains a private practice as a licensed psychologist. The National Council on Alcoholism recognized her with the Bronze Key Award and the Humanitarian Award. Her latest coauthored books include *Treating Alcoholism, The Alcoholic Family in Recovery: A Developmental Model* and *The Family Recovery Guide: A Map for Healthy Growth.*

Alan J. Budney, PhD, Associate Professor of Psychiatry and Psychology at the University of Vermont, completed his doctoral studies in clinical psychology at Rutgers University and his postdoctoral studies at the University of Vermont, where he assisted in the development and evaluation of the community reinforcement approach (CRA) plus vouchers treatment for cocaine dependence. He directs the Marijuana Treatment Research Center at the University of Vermont and is Clinical Director of the teaching hospital's substance abuse treatment clinic. Funded primarily by the National Institute of Drug Abuse, his current research focuses on behavioral treatments for marijuana dependence and understanding marijuana withdrawal. He has authored numerous scientific articles and book chapters addressing cocaine and marijuana dependence.

Cynthia A. Conklin, PhD, a clinical psychologist trained at Purdue University and the Western Psychiatric Institute & Clinic in Pittsburgh, served as Senior Research Coordinator of the Psychopharmacology Laboratory and the Purdue Smoking Project and conducted psychotherapy with a variety of patient groups, including clients diagnosed with drug abuse disorders, personality disorders, and anxiety disorders. She also worked as a counselor conducting both individual and group therapy at the Center for Drug Free Living in Orlando, Florida and as a therapist in the Nicotine Cessation Program at the Indiana University Cancer Research Center in Indianapolis. She received the 2000 James Linden Award from the Purdue Department of Psychological Sciences in recognition of her outstanding academic and clinical accomplishments in clinical psychology.

Linda R. Crosby, MSN, RN, Director of Business Development at the Talbott Recovery Center in Atlanta, Georgia, formerly worked at the American Dental Association, where she was a pioneer in providing recovery programs for addicted professionals. She has authored or coauthored many professional chemical dependency publications, including *To Care Enough: Intervention With Chemically Dependent Colleagues* and *Peer Assistance for Alcoholism and Drug Abuse Counselors.*

Jonathan S. Fader, a researcher at the University of Washington pursuing a doctorate in clinical psychology, has worked with adults and adolescents in the area of addictions in many arenas, including inpatient, outpatient, and detoxification settings. His current research and clinical work focuses on the prevention of alcohol-related problems in children and adolescents. Actively seeing a wide range of clients who present with a variety of addictive behaviors, he is currently designing a prevention program that seeks to fully utilize the principles of harm reduction in the prevention of addictions problems among young adults.

Steven L. Fahrion, PhD, Research Director at the Life Sciences Institute of Mind-Body Health in Topeka, Kansas, is a clinical psychologist with over 30 years of professional experience in biofeedback and psychophysiologic self-regulation. A former faculty member of the Karl Menninger School of Psychiatry, he served as Adjunct Professor of Psychology at the Union Graduate School and was Director of the Menninger Center for Applied Psychophysiology and Biofeedback. Formerly President of the Biofeedback Society of

America and of the Biofeedback Society of Kansas, he is the current editor of *Subtle Energies.*

Reid Hester, PhD, Director of the Research Division of Behavior Therapy Associates in Albuquerque, New Mexico (www.behaviortherapy.com), is a Fellow in the Addictions Division in the American Psychological Association and senior editor of the *Handbook of Alcoholism Treatment Approaches: Effective Alternatives.* He has published reviews of treatment outcome literature and developed computer-based treatment interventions for drinkers. Recently he developed a program that interactively teaches moderate drinking skills to nonalcoholic problem drinkers. Currently he is developing a computer-based brief motivational intervention for drinkers.

Stephen T. Higgins, PhD, Professor in the Departments of Psychiatry and Psychology at the University of Vermont, earned his PhD from the University of Kansas and was a postdoctoral fellow at the Johns Hopkins University School of Medicine. A recipient of the College on Problems of Drug Dependence's Joseph Cochin Young Investigator Award (1993), he also won the Hazelden Foundation's Dan Anderson Research Award (1996) and the University of Vermont's University Scholar Award (1997). Past President of the Division of Psychopharmacology and Substance Abuse of the American Psychological Association, he is currently Principal and Co-Investigator on five grants from the National Institute on Drug Abuse and has more than 160 publications, including two edited books and a treatment manual on drug dependence.

Marc F. Kern, PhD, Founding Director and Chief Executive Officer of Life Management Skills, Inc., a corporation that houses his private psychological practice and professional training programs called Addiction Alternatives, hosts two national nonprofit self-help networks in Los Angeles and Orange Counties, California: S.M.A.R.T. Recovery and Moderation Management. A licensed clinical psychologist, he is certified by the American Psychological Association as a certified addictions specialist. Author of *Take Control Now! A Do-It-Yourself Blueprint for Breaking Unwanted Habits,* he provides scientifically based treatment alternatives to those facing a broad spectrum of addiction problems.

Jonathan Krejci, PhD, Project Director and Clinical Instructor at the University of Medicine and Dentistry of New Jersey (UMDNJ), Robert Wood Johnson Medical School, earned a major in clinical psychology and a minor in addictive behaviors at the University of New Mexico, where he worked on a grant from the National Institute on Alcohol Abuse and Alcoholism (NIAAA) investigating the community reinforcement approach with homeless alcoholic men. Current research activities include acting as Project Director, both for UMDNJ's role in NIDA's Clinical Trials Network and for a Center for Substance Abuse Treatment grant investigating dual diagnosis treatment approaches. He is a certified motivational interviewing trainer and has been involved in curriculum development and training initiatives at UMDNJ.

Linda Farris Kurtz, DPA, Professor in the Department of Social Work at Eastern Michigan University, teaches courses in chemical dependency and mental health/substance abuse policy. She completed her doctorate in public administration at the University of Georgia, her dissertation focusing on Alcoholics Anonymous and the interorganizational relationships between 12-step groups and mental health professionals. She previously worked as a social worker in the Georgia mental health system giving direct service to substance abusers. Her research focuses on self-help groups, particularly 12-step programs. Author of numerous articles and book chapters dealing with substance abuse, self-help groups, and mental health, she published *Self-Help and Support Groups: A Handbook for Practitioners* (Sage, 1997).

Robert J. Kus, RN, PhD, a Catholic priest since 1998, previously earned a PhD in sociology and postdoctoral master's degrees in psychiatric-mental health nursing and in divinity. He taught at the University of Iowa for 10 years and conducted research in Hungary, Czechoslovakia, and the United States in alcohol studies and gay men's issues. Pastor of St. Catherine of Siena Catholic Church in Wake Forest, North Carolina, he is also an adjunct faculty member in the School of Nursing at the University of North Carolina at Wilmington and a Visiting Lecturer in the Department of Sociology and Anthropology at North Carolina State University in Raleigh. He has edited four books about spirituality and sobriety and is currently working on autobiographical works in nursing and priesthood, including his forthcoming book, *Scattered Marbles: Tales of a Psych Nurse.*

G. Alan Marlatt, PhD, Professor of Psychology and Director of the Addictive Behaviors Research Center at the University of Washington, previously served on the faculties of the University of British Columbia (1968-69) and the University of Wisconsin (1969-72). His basic research focuses on cognitive-behavioral factors in addiction and his applied research on relapse prevention in the treatment of addictive behavior problems. His most recent work investigated the harm reduction approach to reducing alcohol problems in young adults, including high-risk college students. Author of over 150 journal articles and book chapters, a few of his books include *Alcoholism: New Directions in Behavioral Research and Treatment, Relapse Prevention, Assessment of Addictive Behaviors, Addictive Behaviors Across the Lifespan* (Sage, 1993), and *Harm Reduction: Pragmatic Strategies for Managing High Risk Behaviors.* He has served on the editorial boards of 15 professional journals and consulted with a wide variety of national organizations, including the National Institute of Alcohol Abuse and Alcoholism and the Institute of Medicine. In 1996, he was appointed a member of the National Advisory Council on Drug Abuse for the National Institute on Drug Abuse.

Tom Mieczkowski, PhD, Professor of Criminology at the University of South Florida, has published more than 50 scholarly articles, 10 book chapters, and two books on drug policy and drug-testing technology. A member of the International Association of Forensic Toxicology, the British Academy of Forensic Sciences, the European Hair Research Society, and the American Society of Criminology, he is recognized as an authority on the use of human hair for the detection of psychoactive drugs. His research interests include smuggling theories of syndicated criminal organizations, drug distribution organizations and methods, and drug epidemiology, especially drug prevalence estimation using bioassays. His current research includes an assessment of the toxicity of environmental exposure to cocaine, the analysis of patters of drug use in juvenile arrestees by various bioassay methods, the recovery of LSD and nor-LSD from human hair, and the use of ion mobility spectrometry in drug detection in various analytic matrices.

Norman S. Miller, MD, Professor of Psychiatry and Medicine and Director of Addiction Medicine at Michigan State University's College of Human Medicine, is Medical Consultant for the Division of Substance Abuse Services for the State of Michigan. A member of Alpha Omega Alpha at Howard University Medical College, he is certified in Addiction Medicine and is a Diplomate in Psychiatry, Neurology, Addiction Psychiatry, and Forensic Psychiatry with the American Board of Psychiatry and Neurology. Currently a law student at Michigan State University, he is author of 12 books on addiction medicine and 250 other publications. He was a member of the Task Force on Treatment for the Office of National Drug Control Policy (ONDCP), and chair of the Center for Substance Abuse Treatment (CSAT) on Detoxification and Engagement for Treatment Improvement Protocols.

Theresa Moyers, PhD, Assistant Research Professor at the University of New Mexico and the Training Coordinator at the Center for Alcohol, Substance Abuse and Addictions, received her doctorate from the University of New Mexico and worked for 9 years as Clinical Director of the Substance Abuse Treatment Program at the VA Medical Center in Albuquerque. Her research interests focus on therapist characteristics in substance abuse treatment. A founding member of the Motivational Interviewing Network of Trainers (MINT), she has produced a set of instructional videotapes about motivational interviewing.

Patricia A. Norris, PhD, Clinical Director at Life Sciences Institute of Mind-Body Health in Topeka, Kansas, has been a faculty member at the Union Graduate School and the Karl Menninger School of Psychiatry, where she was Clinical Director of the Center for Applied Psychophysiology and Biofeedback. President of the Biofeedback Society of America and also the International Society for the Study of Subtle Energy and Energy Medicine, she has used biofeedback and psychophysiologic psychotherapy in her therapeutic work since 1970. She emphasizes integration of body, emotions, mind, and spirit; psychosynthesis; imagery and visualization; and psychoneuroimmunology.

Christopher P. Rice, PhD, Assistant Professor in the School of Social Work at Florida International University, was coinvestigator with Project MATCH, a national multisite clinical trial of treatment for alcoholics, and MATCH Site Manager at Brown University's Center for Alcohol and Addiction Studies. He has published in the National Institutes of Health-sponsored Project MATCH Monograph Series (1998). His other addiction related work appears in leading academic journals. He won several awards during his graduate training, including the William E. Gordon Research Excellence Award from Washington University.

David B. Rosengren, PhD, a clinical psychologist in Seattle, Washington, divides his time between private practice, research at the University of Washington's Alcohol and Drug Abuse Institute, and community-based motivational interviewing (MI) training. His research focus is on the application of MI in both addiction and nonaddiction settings. The initial Director of the International Association of MI Trainers (MINT), he is former editor of the MINT newsletter.

Joyce Schmid, PhD, a licensed Marriage and Family Therapist in private practice in Menlo Park, California, does psychodynamically oriented individual and couples therapy with addicts and their families. While a staff psychotherapist at the Stanford Alcohol and Drug Treatment Center, she was Coordinator of Psychotherapy Groups for Adult Children of Alcoholics. She has taught classes for psychotherapists on the treatment of addicts and their families at the University of California, Santa Cruz Extension, and at the Santa Clara University Lifelong Learning Center, and is an Associate of the Addictions Institute.

Raymond L. Scott, PhD, Assistant Professor in the Department of Psychiatry at Charles R. Drew University of Medicine and Science in Los Angeles, has worked for 10 years in the field of chemical dependency as a clinician and researcher. He served as the initial research coordinator and interview coordinator for two projects funded by the Center for Substance Abuse Treatment (CSAT). Additionally, he was Principal Investigator for "An Ethnography of the Relationships Between Crack Use, Sexuality, and Engaging in HIV Risk Behaviors Among Persons of African Decent," funded by the City of Los Angeles Office of AIDS.

Richard B. Seymour, MA, Manager of Information and Education at the Haight-Ashbury Free Clinics Office of the President, is also Director of Haight-Ashbury Publications; Managing Editor of the *Journal of Psychoactive Drugs* and the *International Addictions Infoline*. He serves as Executive Editor of AlcoholMD.com, board member and treasurer of the International Society of Addiction Journal Editors. He has authored 10 books and over 40 articles on addiction and other related substance abuse topics.

Stacey C. Sigmon, a predoctoral fellow at the University of Vermont in experimental psychology/behavioral pharmacology, did her master's research focusing on using a contingency management intervention to reduce marijuana use among individuals with schizophrenia and other serious mental illness. For the past several years, she comanaged a treatment research project evaluating voucher-based incentives for the treatment of cocaine dependence.

David E. Smith, MD, Founder, President, and Medical Director of the Haight-Ashbury Free Clinics, is Professor at the University of California Medical School at San Francisco, Medical Director for the State of California Alcohol and Drug Abuse Programs, and Medical Director of the California Collaborative Center for Substance Abuse Policy Research. He is also publisher of the *Journal of Psychoactive Drugs*, Editor-in-Chief of Alcohol-MD.com, member and past president of the American Society on Addiction Medicine. He has authored over a dozen books and hundreds of articles on addiction treatment and recovery.

Michael O. Smith, MD, Director of Lincoln Hospital Substance Abuse Division since 1974, is a psychiatrist, acupuncture addiction specialist, and public health planner. Assistant Professor at Cornell University Medical School, he is certified by the American Society of Addiction Medicine. As Founding Chairperson of the National Acupuncture Detoxification Association (NADA), he provided consultation to city, county, state, federal, and United Nations agencies in more than 100 settings. A principal coinvestigator on research studies conducted by the New York State Department of Health, Columbia University, and private research institutions, he is also known for his expertise in clinical toxicology, herbology, community psychiatry, medical information systems, treatment of multiple sclerosis, Chinese philosophy, and addiction treatment planning. His 5-year study on the use of Chinese medicine in the treatment of AIDS has been published in many countries. He is a recipient of the Samuel and May Rudin Community Service Award by Mayor Dinkins, serves on the Governor's Advisory Council on Substance Abuse, and was named Acupuncturist of the Year by the American Association of Acupuncture and Oriental Medicine.

Carol A. Snarr, RN, BA, Director of Education at Life Sciences Institute of Mind-Body Health in Topeka, Kansas, is past president of the Biofeedback Society of Kansas and was Associate Director of Education of the Menninger Center for Applied Psychophysiology. With over 20 years' experience in psychophysiologic therapy and biofeedback, her treatment focuses on integrating mind, body, emotions, and spirit to achieve optimum health and enhance self-esteem and personal growth.

Edward Storti, BA, an internationally and California-certified alcohol and drug abuse counselor and registered addiction specialist, has choreographed over 3,000 motivational interventions throughout the world and maintains admitting privileges at numerous domestic and international treatment facilities. He did graduate work in the Rehabilitation Program at the University of Southern California and lectures at both the University of California, Los Angeles, Medical Center and School of Dentistry. A member of the National Association of Alcoholism and Drug Abuse Counselors, the California Association of Alcoholism and Drug Abuse Counselors, and the Association of Intervention Specialists, his books include *Crisis Intervention: Acting Against Addiction* and *Heart to Heart, the Honorable Approach to Motivational Intervention.*

G. Douglas Talbott, MD, Founder and Medical Director of the Talbott Recovery Campus, a national Impaired Health Professions Treatment Program in Atlanta, Georgia, has treated more than 5,000 health professionals. Past president of the American Society of Addiction Medicine (ASAM) and vice-president of the International Society of Addiction Medicine, he is Clinical Professor of Family Practice at the Morehouse School of Medicine, Adjunct Professor of Pharmacology at the Mercer University School of Pharmacy, and medical consultant to the Atlanta Braves, the National Football League, and the National Basketball Association. He coauthored *Healing the Healer: The Addicted Physician.*

Stephen T. Tiffany, PhD, Professor in the Department of Psychological Sciences at Purdue University in West Lafayette and a member of the Neuroscience Program at Purdue University directs the Smoking Clinic in the Purdue Psychological Sciences Treatment Research Clinics. He has conducted extensive animal and human research on addictive disorders and has authored over 70 professional publications. His research has been funded by the National Institutes of Health, the American Cancer Society, and the Robert Wood Johnson Foundation. On the editorial board of the *Journal of Studies on Alcohol*, the *Journal of Abnormal Psychology* and *Experimental and Clinical Psychopharmacology*, he received in 1993 the American Psychological Association Distinguished Scientific Award for Early Career Contribution to Psychology and in 1999 was named a Purdue University Faculty Scholar in recognition of outstanding academic achievement.

Christopher C. Wagner, PhD, Assistant Professor of Rehabilitation Counseling, Psychology and Psychiatry at Virginia Commonwealth University, is a clinical psychologist who works with the Mid-Atlantic Addiction Technology Transfer Center (funded by the Center for Substance Abuse Treatment) in providing training and consultation services to community-based agencies. His research has focused primarily on interpersonal elements of psychopathology and psychotherapy. He hosts the motivational interviewing Web site at www.motivationalinterview.org

Arnold M. Washton, PhD, an addiction psychologist in private practice in New York City and Princeton, New Jersey, is an internationally known clinician, researcher, and author, who has specialized in the treatment of alcohol and substance abuse for over 25 years. His publications include over 40 articles in medical/scientific journals and nine books, including *Cocaine Addiction: Treatment, Recovery, and Relapse Prevention; Psychotherapy and Substance Abuse: A Practitioner's Handbook;* and *Substance Abuse Therapy in Office Practice: A Clinician's Guide to Doing What Works.*

Kathryn P. White, PhD, LAc, a licensed psychologist, acupuncturist, board-certified herbologist, and doctor of homeopathic medicine who practices psychology and complementary medicine in West Los Angeles, California, is Assistant Clinical Professor of Medical Psychology at the UCLA Medical School and Professor at the California School of Professional Psychology (Los Angeles). Her PhD in clinical psychology was earned at the University of North Carolina at Chapel Hill. She later interned at Harvard Medical School and completed a National Institute of Mental Health Postdoctoral Fellowship in Clinical Psychology at the University of California, Los Angeles, Neuropsychiatric Institute and Hospital. She earned a Master of Traditional Oriental Medicine degree from Emperor's College of Traditional Chinese Medicine and interned at Shanghai People's Hospital Number Six and Shanghai Mental Health Center. She also completed a Doctor of Homeopathic Medicine degree at Hahnemann College of Homeopathy in the United Kingdom, interned in homeopathic clinics in Bombay, India, and completed courses in Ayurvedic medicine. She has presented at national and international conferences on psychology and complementary and alternative medicine, has authored articles on these subjects, and is currently writing a book.

Fred Zackon, MEd, Senior Program Designer for CiviGenics, Inc., the nation's largest private provider of rehabilitative services to offenders in correctional settings, currently is developing interactive multimedia interventions for incarcerated addicts. He has worked with hard-core addicts for more than two decades, directing both an inner-city therapeutic community and, later, a large methadone program. Under a grant from the National Institute on Drug Abuse to the Harvard School of Public Health, he designed and implemented innovative relapse prevention and aftercare curricula. With the United Nations, he served as a principal program consultant and trainer in addiction rehabilitation to developing nations.

Douglas Ziedonis, MD, Director of the Division of Addiction Psychiatry and Associate Professor at University of Medicine and Dentistry of New Jersey (UMDNJ), Robert Wood Johnson Medical School, is also Director of the UMDNJ-University Behavioral HealthCare's Addiction Services. On the faculty at Rutgers University's Center for Alcohol Studies and the Princeton Theological Seminary, he has worked in the field of addiction psychiatry for over 15 years and is an expert on co-occurring disorders and both therapy and medication development. Certified as a Diplomate in both General Psychiatry and Addiction Psychiatry, he serves on the American Psychiatric Association's (APA's) Addiction Council and helped develop the APA's Treatment Guidelines for Individuals with Nicotine Dependence. A principal investigator or coinvestigator on numerous National Institute on Drug Abuse, National Institute on Alcohol Abuse and Alcoholism, National Institute of Mental Health, Center for Substance Abuse Prevention, and other funded research grants, he has published extensively in the area of addiction and dual diagnosis and consulted with numerous community recovery-oriented addiction treatment programs.

Joan E. Zweben, PhD, Founder and Executive Director of the East Bay Community Recovery Project and the 14th Street Clinic and Medical Group in Oakland, California, developed the medical and psychological services of both affiliated organizations. A clinical psychologist with over 30 years' experience in treating addiction and training treatment practitioners (peer counselors, social workers, marriage and family counselors, psychologists, probation officers, nurses and physicians), she is a Clinical Professor of Psychiatry at the University of California San Francisco School of Medicine. Author of two books and over 40 articles or book chapters, she is the editor of 12 monographs on treating addiction.